THE SOUTH CHINA SEA ARBITRATION

THE SOUTH CHINA SEA ARBITRATION

UNDERSTANDING THE AWARDS AND DEBATING WITH CHINA

ALFREDO C. ROBLES, JR.

De La Salle University · Manila

sussex
ACADEMIC
PRESS
Brighton • Chicago • Toronto

2 4 6 8 10 9 7 5 3 1

Published and distributed in the Philippines under ISBN 978-971-555-661-3 *by*
De La Salle University Publishing House
2401 Taft Avenue, 0922 Manila, Philippines

This edition published and distributed under ISBN 978-1-84519-962-3 *in Great Britain in 2019 by* SUSSEX ACADEMIC PRESS
PO Box 139, Eastbourne BN24 9BP

and in North America by SUSSEX ACADEMIC PRESS
Independent Publishers Group
814 N. Franklin Street
Chicago, IL 60610

Cover Photograph: Photograph from Jurisdictional Hearing—July 2015—Hearing in Session. Permanent Court of Arbitration, https//pcacases.com/web/sendAttach/1494
Cover Concept: Alfredo C. Robles, Jr.
Cover Design: John David Roasa

British Library Cataloguing in Publication Data
A CIP catalogue record for this book is available from the British Library.

Library of Congress Cataloging-in-Publication Data
Robles, Alfredo C., Jr.
The South China Sea arbitration : understanding the awards
and debating with China / Alfredo C. Robles, Jr.—Manila, Philippines
De La Salle University Publishing House/Sussex Academic Press, 2019.
360 pages ; 15 cm.
ISBN 978-971-555-661-3 (pbk)

MIX
Paper | Supporting responsible forestry
FSC www.fsc.org FSC® C013604

Typeset & designed by De La Salle University Publishing House.
Printed and bound by CPI Group (UK) Ltd, Croydon, CR0 4YY

Contents

Acknowledgments	vii
Series Editor's Preface *Mina Roces*	ix
Preface	xi
Maps	xiii
Abbreviations	xix
Introduction	xxi

Part I Understanding the Award on Jurisdiction and Admissibility and Debating with China

1	Summary of the Award on Jurisdiction and Admissibility of 29 October 2015	3
2	Victory in Round 1, but Not Really a Knockout	46
3	China's Informal Participation in the Arbitration in Contravention of International Law	51
4	The Arbitral Tribunal: 200 Years of Combined Personal Professional Experience	55
5	The Lawyers of the Philippines: A Brilliant Track Record	73
6	China Should Emulate Africa in the Area of Peaceful Dispute Settlement	94
7	The South China Sea Disputes: A View from Togo (West Africa)	101

Part II Understanding the Award of 12 July 2016 and Debating with China

8	Summary of the Award of 12 July 2016	107
9	Reading the Award of 12 July 2016	218
10	Are You Going to Scarborough Shoal?	222
11	Territorial and Maritime Claims in Multilateral Forums: The Example of China	228
12	Memo to Taiwan: Beijing Is (Almost Always) to Blame	235
13	The Binding Force of the Award of 12 July 2016	242
14	Unraveling China's Conspiracy Theory of International Arbitration	253

Annexes

Table 1	Maritime Features That Are the Object of Submissions No. 3 to 7	268
Table 2	South China Sea Maritime Features Referred to in Chapter VI.C of the Award of 12 July 2016	269

Table 3	Overview of China's Construction Activities in the Spratly Islands	270
Table 4	Comparison of the Assessment of the Environmental Impact of China's Construction Activities in the Spratly Islands by China's SOA and by the Tribunal's Experts	272

References 273
Index 299

Acknowledgments

In the course of writing this book, much of which was done between July and October 2016, I have accumulated a number of debts that I am happy to acknowledge.

My sister-in-law Raissa Robles invariably responded favorably to my inquiries whether this or that topic would be of interest to Filipino readers and herself suggested some topics. She formatted the articles—no mean task in view of the number of references attached to each—and posted earlier versions of several of the chapters on her blog, www.raissarobles.com. Publication on her blog made it possible to reach a vast audience here and abroad (including China, the US, and Latin America).

Thaemar Tana helped me obtain materials that were unavailable in the Philippines.

Benjamin Lelis read the summary of the Award on Jurisdiction and Admissibility and identified inconsistencies and omissions that would have been very serious if they had remained uncorrected.

Antonio Gabriel Antonio, Cheryl Arcibal, Dr. Lowell Bautista (University of Wollongong), Dr. Aileen San Pablo-Baviera (University of the Philippines), John Harvey Gamas (Ateneo de Davao University), Richard Ip Chun Yin, Kurt Molina, John Michael Nicholas, Kevin Punzalan, Dr. Carmelita Quebengco (De La Salle University), Dr. Dinah Roma (De La Salle University), Daryll Saclag, Edwin Santiago (De La Salle University), and Dr. Charmaine Misalucha-Willoughby (De La Salle University) gave me feedback on one or more of the blog posts or chapters and thus indirectly encouraged me to persevere in my undertaking. One of them also helped me get in touch with a Filipino journalist who plagiarized the contents of one of the blog posts. Another wrote a letter to the editor of the publication in which the plagiarized article appeared, to no avail (no thanks are due to the plagiarist and the editor). It is saddening to note that this journalist thought nothing of committing plagiarism, whereas Chinese journalists always cite their authorities.

Two anonymous readers gave valuable comments that served as the basis for improvements, some of them substantial, in the manuscript.

Last, but not least, Dr. David Jonathan Bayot and the staff of the De La Salle University Publishing House deserve a special word of thanks. Dr. Bayot, whose inspired ideas have given new impetus to the activity of the Publishing House, was supportive of the project from the very moment that I broached the idea to him sometime in 2015. He expertly steered the manuscript through the review, revision, and publication process. This is the first time that I have had the opportunity to work with a Filipino publisher, my first three books having all been published in the United Kingdom. The decision to entrust the publication of this book to the DLSU Publishing House has proven to be a sound one.

The usual caveats apply.

Series Editor's Preface

The *Sussex Library of Asian Studies* series publishes original scholarly work in various disciplines (including interdisciplinary and transnational approaches) under the rubric of Asian studies—particularly Economics, Education, Religion, History, Politics, Gender, Comparative Studies with the West, and Regional Studies in Asia. The Series is keen to publish in emerging topics that demand attention in the Asian context—from the politics of dress to the heteronormative in India and Indonesia for example. Seminal works and approaches will find a home here. The Series also welcomes single-country studies or anthologies that explore one important theme across a number of Asian contexts. We expect the Series to contribute to scholarly debates on topical issues, highlighting the importance of the region.

Alfredo C. Robles, Jr.'s *The South China Sea Arbitration: Understanding the Awards and Debating with China* is arguably one of the the first serious books written to assist readers in understanding the two judgements made in 2015 and 2016 by the Arbitral Tribunal in the landmark case the *Republic of the Philippines v. People's Republic of China.* Robles's detailed and nuanced study summarises the legal arguments presented by both parties, explains the rationale of the Philippine strategy (which included hiring foreign lawyers), and analyses and rebuts the Chinese responses. The author provides a comprehensive account of the arguments presented, including the way debates have been framed to argue for traditional fishing rights in the area. In addition, short biographies of the judges and lawyers involved highlight the international dimension of the arbitration process.

While the book discusses both the Filipino and Chinese positions, it is an interpretation from the Philippine perspective, including the way in which China from May 2012 onwards "had unlawfully prevented fishermen from the Philippines from engaging in traditional fishing at Scarborough Shoal." This important and timely contribution to the fields of International Law and International Relations will be widely read by the many Filipinos interested in and concerned about the contemporary conflict in the South China Sea, but will also be a prime resource for foreign embassy personnel and government agencies engaged in Southeast Asia. For Asian studies scholars, this book is an excellent case study in which to dissect, analyse and understand the dynamics of legal debates in the international arbitration process; its territorial focus has implications for ongoing and potential area disputes in their area of interest.

Professor Mina Roces
School of Humanities and Languages
The University of New South Wales

Preface

When I embarked in mid-2015 on research relating to the *South China Sea Arbitration*, I could not but ask myself whether there was room for another title on the subject. Several circumstances led me to conclude that scholarly commentary addressed to a general audience would be a worthwhile endeavor.

From its initiation in 2013, the arbitration received extensive coverage in the Philippine press, but many writers repeated each other, and few titles were scholarly in nature. The few scholarly works that appeared at this time were mostly written by non-Filipinos and published in foreign scholarly journals that would have been difficult to access for the ordinary reader. The first of my commentaries, posted on my sister-in-law's blog, presented the preliminary results of my research. For example, the post on China's attempts to lobby the Arbitral Tribunal (Chapter 3 of this book) was based on a close reading of the Award on Jurisdiction and Admissibility. The post on the judges (Chapter 4 of this book) explained the duties of the President of the International Tribunal for the Law of the Sea (ITLOS). The post on the lawyers (Chapter 5 of this book) presented the difficulties encountered by developing countries that are parties to disputes before international tribunals in preparing their written and oral pleadings. The responses to the blog posts, some of which were shared by thousands of readers, indicated that there could be a wide audience for commentary informed by scholarly research.

Following the issuance in July 2016 of an Award on the merits, public interest in and press coverage of an award that was largely favorable to Philippine theses understandably started to diminish, even before the details of the Tribunal's decisions had been properly understood. At the same time, the volte-face in the Philippine position operated by the administration of President Duterte, who had been elected in May 2016, inhibited it from responding to the disinformation and vilification campaign launched by China against the Award and the Tribunal. It seemed essential to present to a wider audience the contents of the two Awards at greater length than press accounts had done, as well as to respond to China's propaganda campaign.

I am convinced that regardless of the twists and turns of Philippine foreign policy, Filipinos must familiarize themselves with the issues decided in the *South China Sea Arbitration*. I hope that this book will stimulate interest in the *Arbitration* and spur readers to explore these and other related issues for themselves. For these purposes, an effort has been made to make the reader aware of the wealth of scholarly resources available on the Internet, including publications in languages other than English. In addition, the URLs of the documents on the websites of the International Court of Justice (ICJ) and the Permanent Court of Arbitration (PCA), which had been redesigned by the time this book was being prepared for publication, have been updated.

If my efforts contribute to a greater appreciation of the significance of the *South China Sea Arbitration* for the Philippines and for the law of the sea, I will consider myself amply rewarded.

MAP 1

The South China Sea

Source: Award on Jurisdiction and Admissibility, p. 3. Permanent Court of Arbitration, https://pcacases.com/web/sendAttach/1506, accessed 30 March 2018. (see p. 6)

MAP 2

Map attached to China's Notes Verbales to the United Nations Secretary General, Nos. CML/17/2009 & CML/18/2009 (showing so-called "Nine-Dash Line")

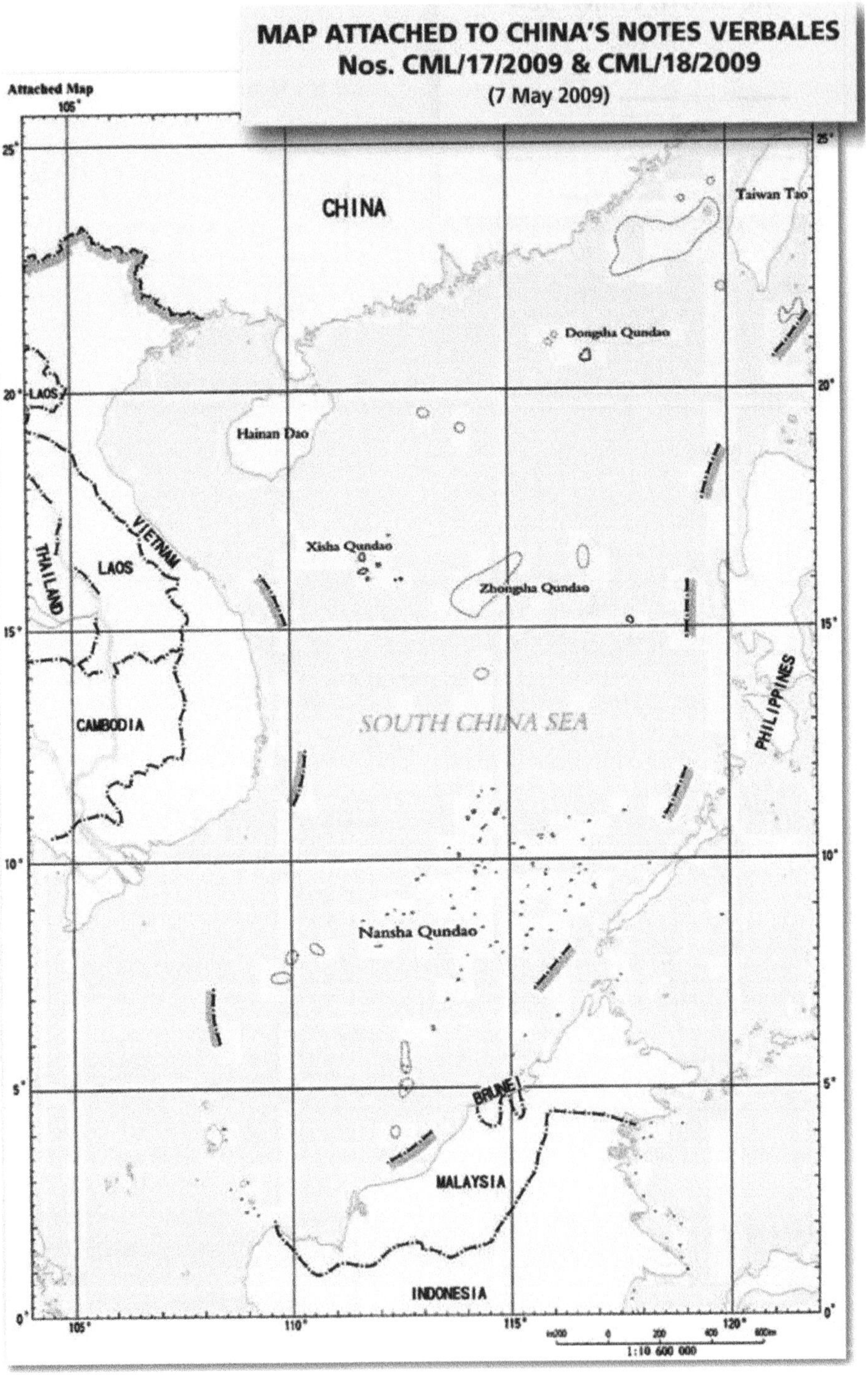

Source: Award on Jurisdiction and Admissibility, p. 5. Permanent Court of Arbitration, https://pcacases.com/web/sendAttach/1506, accessed 30 March 2018. (see p. 6)

MAP 3

China's Maximum Potential Entitlements under UNCLOS Compared to its Nine-Dash Line Claim in the Southern Sector

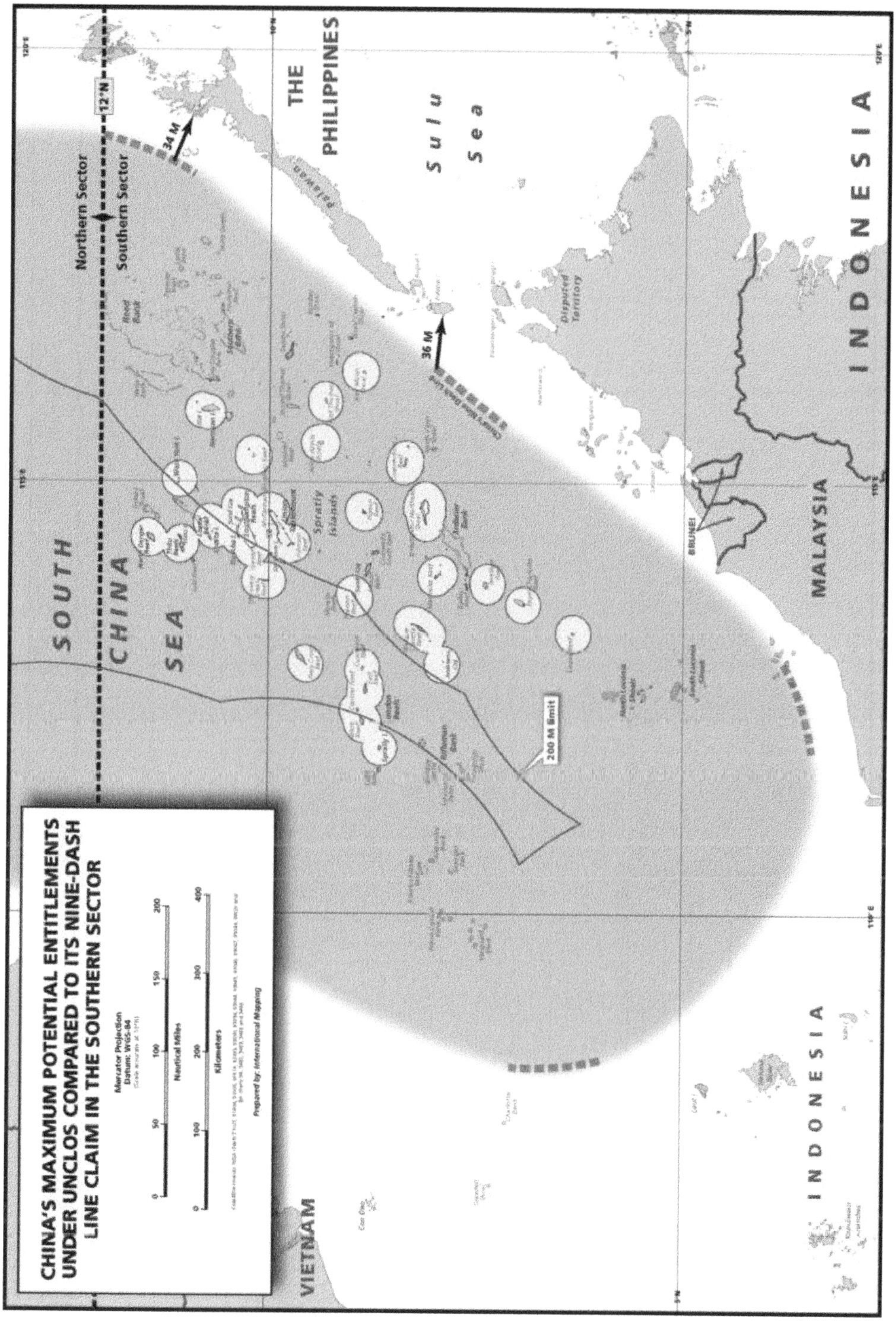

Source: Award on Jurisdiction and Admissibility, p. 51. Permanent Court of Arbitration, https://pcacases.com/web/sendAttach/1506, accessed 30 March 2018. (see p. 18)

MAP 4

Northern Sector of the South China Sea
(including Scarborough Shoal)

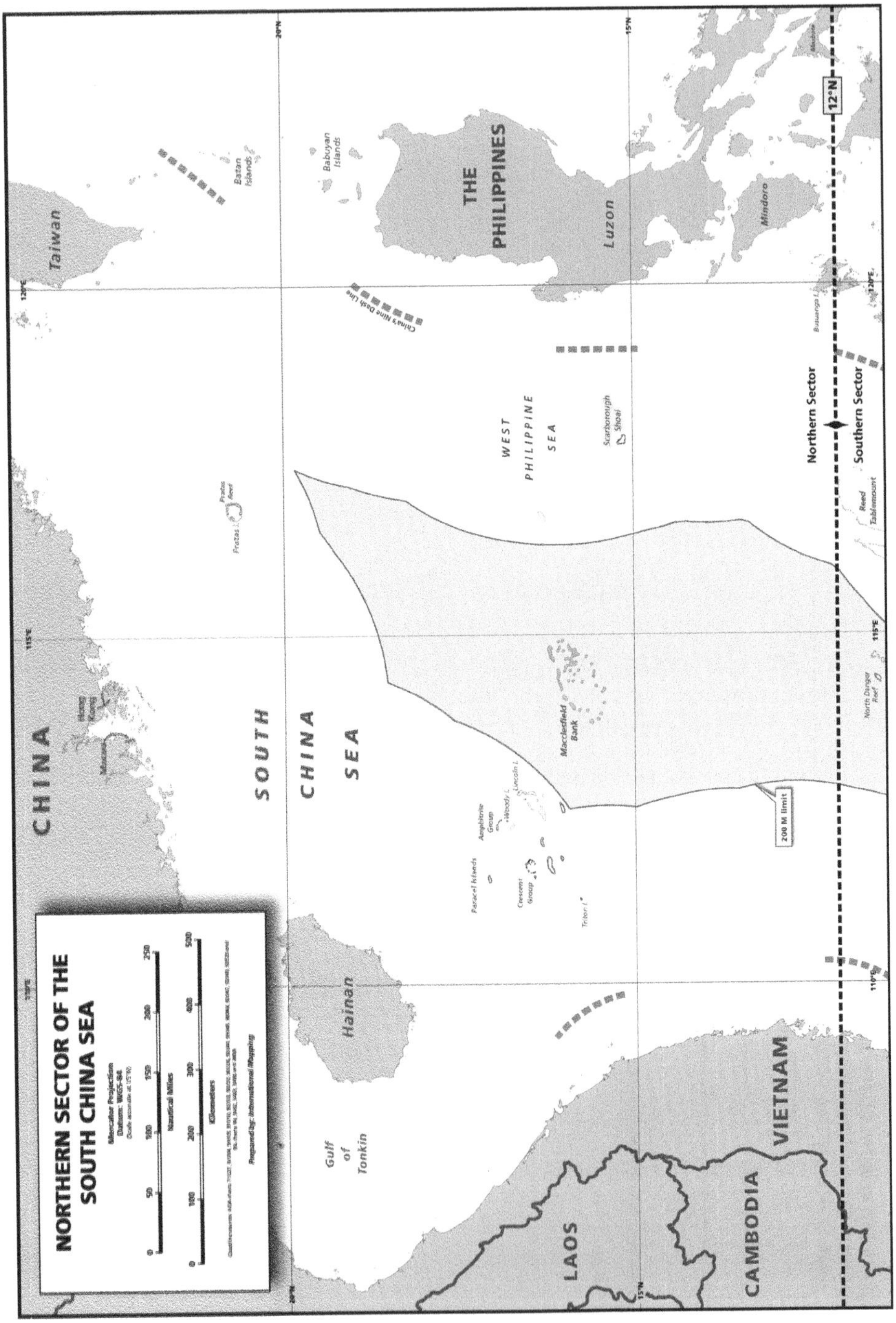

Source: Award on Jurisdiction and Admissibility, p. 7. Permanent Court of Arbitration, https://pcacases.com/web/sendAttach/1506, accessed 30 March 2018. (see p. 137)

MAP 5

Southern Sector of the South China Sea
(including Scarborough Shoal)

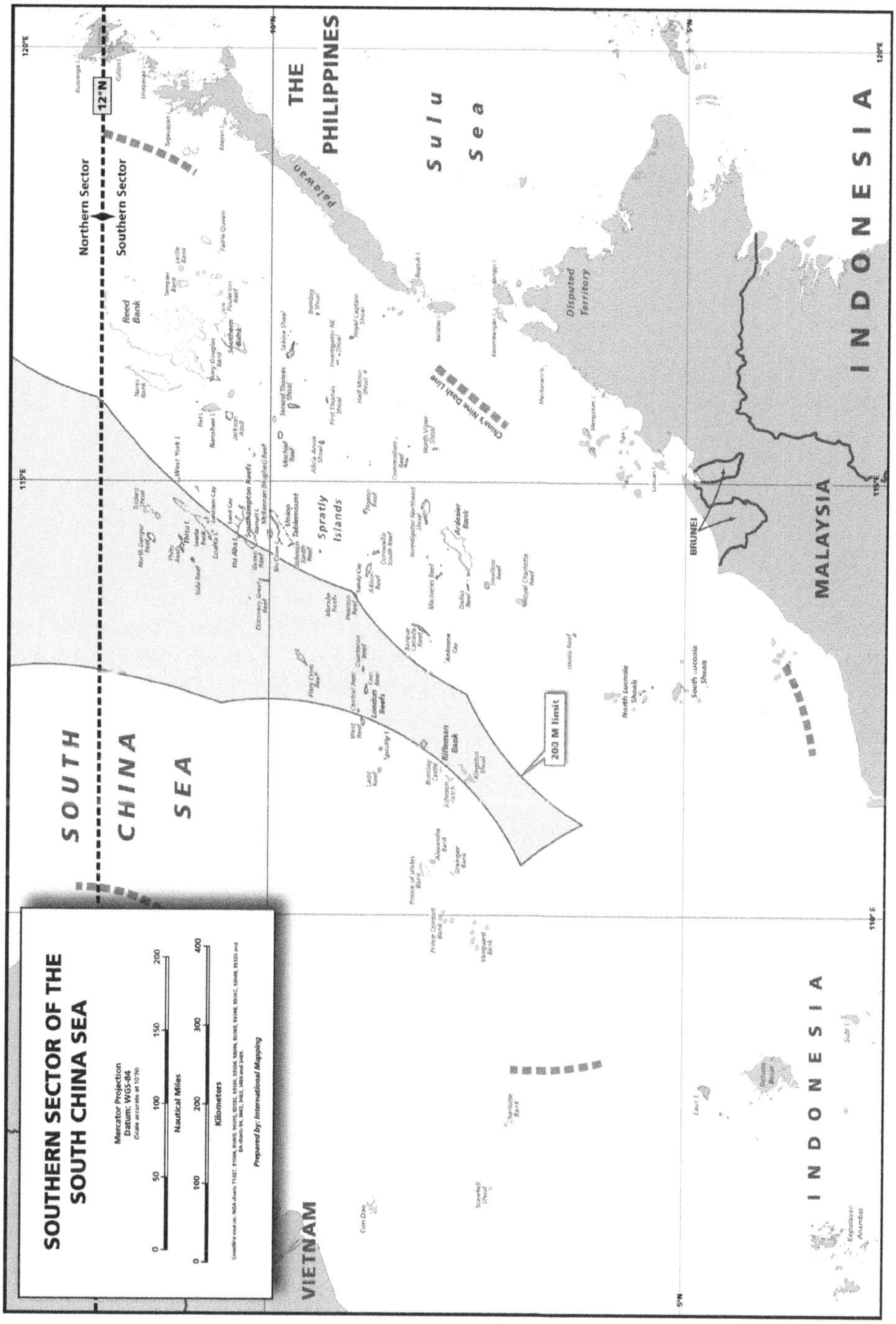

Source: Award on Jurisdiction and Admissibility, p. 9. Permanent Court of Arbitration, https://pcacases.com/web/sendAttach/1506, accessed 30 March 2018. (see p. 137)

Abbreviations

AFDI	*Annuaire Français de Droit International*
AFP	Armed Forces of the Philippines
AJIL	*American Journal of International Law*
ASEAN	Association of Southeast Asian Nations
BFAR	Bureau of Fisheries and Aquatic Resources (Philippines)
BRP	*Barko ng Republika ng Pilipinas* (Ship of the Republic of the Philippines)
CBD	Convention on Biological Diversity (adopted 5 June 1992)
CCG	China Coast Guard
CITES	Convention on the International Trade in Endangered Species of Wild Fauna and Flora (adopted 3 March 1973)
CLCS	Commission on the Limits of the Continental Shelf
CMS	China Marine Surveillance
COLREGS	Convention on the International Regulations for Preventing Collisions at Sea (adopted 20 October 1972)
Convention	United Nations Convention on the Law of the Sea (adopted 10 December 1982)
DFA	Department of Foreign Affairs (Philippines)
DOC	The China–ASEAN Declaration on the Conduct of Parties in the South China Sea (adopted 4 November 2002)
EEZ	Exclusive Economic Zone
EIA	Environmental Impact Assessment
EU	European Union
FLEC	Fisheries Law Enforcement Command of China
ICJ	International Court of Justice
IHO	International Hydrographic Organization
ITLOS	International Tribunal for the Law of the Sea
MOFA	Ministry of Foreign Affairs (Republic of China)
PCA	Permanent Court of Arbitration
PCIJ	Permanent Court of International Justice
PDI	*Philippine Daily Inquirer*
PLA	People's Liberation Army (China)
RIAA	*Reports of International Arbitral Awards*
ROC	Republic of China (Taiwan)
SOA	State Oceanic Administration (China)

TAC	Treaty of Amity and Cooperation in Southeast Asia (adopted 24 February 1976)
WTO	World Trade Organization
UNCLOS	United Nations Convention on the Law of the Sea (adopted 10 December 1982)
ZaöRV	*Zeitschrift für ausländisches öffentliches Recht und Völkerrecht*

Introduction

The *South China Sea Arbitration (Republic of the Philippines v. People's Republic of China)* is undoubtedly a landmark case for the two Parties and for the law of the sea. For each Party, it is the first international dispute of any type that has been submitted to compulsory settlement. For the Philippines in particular, the Tribunal's decisions are important because they have made clear that China's encroachment on its maritime zones, embodied in the so-called nine-dash line, is illegal; reiterated the exclusive right of the Philippines to explore and exploit the living and non-living resources of its exclusive economic zone (EEZ) and continental shelf; refuted China's claims of excessive maritime entitlements for Scarborough Shoal and the Spratly Islands; vindicated Philippine claims that China's construction activities and its toleration of fishing of endangered species by its nationals have inflicted irreparable harm on the marine environment in the South China Sea; and confirmed that the behavior of China's vessels that deliberately sought to provoke collision with Philippine vessels is illegal. For the law of the sea, the final decisions are important because they have tackled head-on a number of substantive issues, such as the relationship between the 1982 UN Convention on the Law of the Sea and so-called historic rights or the differences between "islands" and "rocks that cannot sustain human habitation or economic life of their own," that other international tribunals have hitherto managed to avoid. If only for these reasons, it is imperative that Filipinos understand the details of the decisions of the Arbitral Tribunal, notwithstanding Chinese rejection of the decisions and Philippine vacillation, followed by a volte-face, in responding to the Chinese rejection.

This book is intended to assist students and interested laypersons who wish to understand the decisions in the arbitration and to respond to China's propaganda campaign during the proceedings and following the issuance of the Award of 12 July 2016. It will not discuss the implications of the two Awards for Philippine foreign policy, for Chinese foreign policy, or for Philippine–China relations. Making sense of the Awards already poses sufficient challenges to the commentator and the reader. Attempting to anticipate the vagaries of each country's foreign policy and of bilateral relations, not to mention the implications for other States in and outside the region, would make the task unmanageable for a single author.

In the two parts of the book, the chapters that seek to facilitate understanding of the Arbitral Tribunal's decisions start with summaries of the two Awards themselves: the Award on Jurisdiction and Admissibility of 29 October 2015 and the Award of 12 July 2016 (Chapter 1 and Chapter 8, respectively). Unlike the summaries that secondary school students are taught to prepare, each summary uses, as far as possible, the actual words and phrases of the original text, in the hope that this will make it easier for readers to find the corresponding sections of the original text. For convenience, several tables are supplied in the Annexes. The tables do not appear in the 2016 Award itself, a circumstance that is indicated by a note attached to each table. The summaries may serve as aide-mémoire for the reader who has read the text beforehand.

They may also serve as an introduction for the reader who is intimidated by either the legal language or the length of the texts or both and who reads the summary as a guide to reading the original text.[1] Obviously the summaries are not intended to replace the original decisions. The summaries, which represent approximately between one-third and one-fourth of the originals, are much longer than the summaries prepared by the Permanent Court of Arbitration (PCA), the Registry in the case.[2] Lengthy summaries—an oxymoron if ever there was one—are justified by the need to explain the respective positions of the two Parties and the reasoning of the Tribunal. Such detailed knowledge is indispensable not only to comprehend the conclusions of the Tribunal but also to rebut criticisms of the decisions that are based on hasty, superficial reading, and, occasionally, deliberate obfuscation, of the Awards. A basic knowledge of public international law is desirable, but it is the author's hope that even without such a background, the interested reader will still be able to follow the summary. When reading the summaries, the reader should consult online the treaties and other legal instruments that are cited.

The other chapters that aim to promote understanding of the awards discuss aspects that are of interest to Filipinos and that have been rarely dealt with in most of commentaries published since the initiation of the arbitration in January 2013. In Part I, Chapter 2 explains the implications of the fact that the Tribunal, while declaring that it had jurisdiction over half of the Philippines' submissions, decided to reserve consideration of its jurisdiction over the other half for the merits phase of the proceedings. Chapters 4 and 5 respond to two questions in the mind of many Filipinos: why was an African appointed president of the Arbitral Tribunal? Why were no Filipino lawyers hired by the Philippine government?

In Part II, Chapter 9 provides some guidance on the way to read the Award of 12 July 2016 to readers who might otherwise feel overwhelmed by the length and/or language of the Award. Chapter 10 examines in greater detail one issue —traditional fishing in the waters surrounding Scarborough Shoal—that was of great practical interest to Filipinos at the time of the issuance of the Award. Chapter 12 highlights the failure of the current Philippine administration to reassert its territorial and maritime claims in multilateral forums and China's resort to multilateral forums to object to Japan's claims to an extended continental shelf.

A second set of texts responds to arguments raised by the Chinese government or authors associated with it when the proceedings were ongoing and after the issuance of the Award of 12 July 2016. These texts, to the extent that they involve basic principles of international law and depict China's cavalier attitude to international law, should also be of interest to readers in other countries, particularly in those that have territorial disputes with China.

In Part I, Chapter 3 highlights the contradiction between China's position that its refusal to participate in the arbitration was "solidly grounded" in international law and the reality of its behind-the-scene maneuvers to undermine and perhaps to end the proceedings. Chapters 6 and 7 were prompted by China's campaign to shore up its position with the support of African

---

1 As he was completing the manuscript, the author met a government official who asked him if it was true that the Tribunal had awarded the Philippines sovereignty over five maritime features. As the author had a copy of the Award of 12 July 2016 at the time with him, he drew the official's attention to the dispositif and explained that such an outcome was impossible, as the Tribunal did not have jurisdiction over territorial sovereignty questions. The incident confirmed the author's intuition that it was essential to provide a guide to the Awards to a Filipino audience that might a priori be overwhelmed by their complexity and length.

2 See the summary of the Award on Jurisdiction and Admissibility prepared by the Permanent Court of Arbitration (PCA), the registry in the case, in *Arbitration Between the Republic of the Philippines and the People's Republic of China. The Tribunal Renders Award on Jurisdiction and Admissibility; Will Hold Further Hearings*, Seventh Press Release, 29 October 2015, https://pcacases.com/web/sendAttach/1503, accessed 30 March 2018; for the summary of the Award of 12 July 2016, see *The South China Sea Arbitration (The Republic of the Philippines v. The People's Republic of China. The Tribunal Renders Its Award*, Eleventh Press Release, 12 July 2016, https://pcacases.com/web/sendAttach/1801, accessed 30 March 2018.

countries. Chapter 6 argues that China, rather than seeking the support of African countries for its non-participation in the proceedings, should emulate the example of a growing number of African countries that have shown their willingness to submit their disputes to compulsory settlement by the International Court of Justice. Chapter 7 identifies a skeptical reaction from anonymous observers in one West African country, Togo, which should be of concern to a country that is as intolerant of criticism as China.

In Part II, Chapter 12 refutes arguments put forward by the Republic of China (Taiwan) to justify its claim that the Award of 12 July 2016 was invalid. Chapters 13 and 14 examine China's strategy, composed of equal parts of disinformation and conspiracy theory, in the propaganda campaign aimed at distracting attention from the Tribunal's rejection of most of China's theses. The disinformation component exploits the public's lack of understanding of the nature of international arbitral tribunals. Chapter 13 seeks to refute China's claim that the Award of 12 July 2016 is not binding because the PCA is neither permanent nor a court, the Arbitral Tribunal is not part of a system of permanent international courts, and the Award was issued despite China's refusal to participate in the proceedings. Chapter 14 aims to provide factual and logical reasons for refuting China's conspiracy theory of international arbitration, based on charges of manipulation of the Tribunal's composition, the lack of knowledge of Asia on the part of the Tribunal members, their lack of fairness and integrity, and the manipulation of the date of issuance of the Award by the US.

One might wonder whether it is necessary to respond with rational arguments to a government that oversteps all normal bounds in its effort to justify its position before domestic and international audiences. One might also ask whether it is not better to simply wait for the implausible arguments to collapse under their own weight. The answer to the first question is yes: one should respond to a government that exceeds the limits of rational discourse. Many readers, particularly those in the Philippines, will probably suspect from the virulent tone of China's discourse that its arguments are implausible, but they might well be hard-pressed to oppose them with rational arguments. Other readers might not even be aware that China has gone beyond the limits of rational discourse and for this reason might be receptive to China's arguments. A factually and logically based refutation will be equally valuable for these readers. The answer to the second question is no: one cannot wait for the implausible arguments to collapse on their own. If unsuspecting readers and captive audiences are not aware—and have no way of knowing—that China's arguments are implausible, ignoring them will not prevent them from penetrating insidiously and unconsciously into their minds. It is all the more necessary to rebut the Chinese arguments because of the failure of the current Philippine administration to respond to them.

Despite the vicissitudes of domestic politics or bilateral relations, it will be essential in the long run for Filipinos to have a sound understanding of the two Awards. Only such an understanding can provide proper guidance for policy towards China and more broadly a sound basis for a Filipino foreign policy that, in the words of the 1987 Constitution (Article II, Section 2), "adopts the generally accepted principles of international law as part of the law of the land and adheres to the policy of peace, equality, justice, freedom, cooperation and amity with all nations."

PART I

Understanding the Award on Jurisdiction and Admissibility and Debating with China

I

Summary of the Award on Jurisdiction and Admissibility of 29 October 2015

TABLE OF CONTENTS[1]

I.	INTRODUCTION		6	1
II.	PROCEDURAL HISTORY		7	15
	A.	Initiation of the Arbitration	7	15
	B.	Constitution of the Tribunal	8	16
	C.	Administrative Directive No. 1, Procedural Order No. 1, and Rules of Procedure	8	16
	D.	Written Arguments	8	18
	E.	Bifurcation of Proceedings	9	23
	F.	Pre-Hearing Procedures and Requests from Other States	10	25
	G.	Hearing on Jurisdiction and Admissibility	10	28
	H.	Post-Hearing Proceedings	11	31
	I.	Deposits for Costs of the Arbitration	11	32
III.	RELIEF REQUESTED AND SUBMISSIONS		11	33
IV.	PRELIMINARY MATTERS		15	37
	A.	The Status of the Philippines and China as Parties to the Convention	15	37
	B.	The Legal and Practical Consequences of China's Non-Participation	16	39
	C.	Whether the Arbitration Constitutes an Abuse of Legal Process	16	42

[1] The Table of Contents reproduces that of the Award on Jurisdiction and Admissibility. The first set of numbers refers to the pages in the Summary; the second set, to the pages in the Award itself. All headings and enumerations that are not included in this Table of Contents and that have been supplied by the author are indicated by footnotes.

V. **IDENTIFICATION AND CHARACTERISATION OF THE DISPUTE.. 17** **45**

A. **The Parties' Positions 17** **45**

1. China's Position 17 45

2. The Philippines' Position 18 48

B. **The Tribunal's Decision 19** **57**

VI. **WHETHER ANY THIRD PARTIES ARE INDISPENSABLE TO THE PROCEEDINGS 22** **71**

VII. **PRECONDITIONS TO THE TRIBUNAL'S JURISDICTION 22** **75**

A. **Article 281 (Procedure Where no Settlement Has Been Reached by the Parties).......... 22** **76**

1. Application of Article 281 to the DOC 23 77

(a) China's Position 23 78

(b) The Philippines' Position 23 79

(c) The Tribunal's Decision 24 82

2. Application of Article 281 to Other Bilateral Statements 26 89

(a) China's Position 26 91

(b) The Philippines' Position 26 92

(c) The Tribunal's Decision 26 93

3. Application of Article 281 to the Treaty of Amity 27 97

(a) Possible Objections 28 98

(b) The Philippines' Position 28 99

(c) The Tribunal's Decision 28 100

4. Application of Article 281 to the CBD 28 101

(a) Possible Objections 28 102

(b) The Philippines' Position 29 102

(c) The Tribunal's Decision 29 103

B. **Article 282 (Obligations Under General, Regional or Bilateral Agreements).......... 30** **106**

1. Application of Article 282 to the DOC and Other Bilateral Statements.......... 30 106

(a) Possible Objections 30 106

(b) The Philippines' Position 30 106

(c) The Tribunal's Decision 30 107

2. Application of Article 282 to the Treaty of Amity 31 108

(a) Possible Objections 31 108

(b) The Philippines' Position 31 108

(c) The Tribunal's Decision 31 109

3. Application of Article 282 to the CBD 31 109

(a) Possible Objections 31 109

(b) The Philippines' Position 32 110

(c) The Tribunal's Decision 32 110

	C.	**Article 283 (Exchange of Views) and Obligation to Negotiate**	**32**	**112**
		1. China's Position	32	112
		2. The Philippines' Position	33	113
		3. The Tribunal's Decision	33	115
VIII.	**LIMITATIONS AND EXCEPTIONS TO THE TRIBUNAL'S JURISDICTION**		**34**	**125**
	A.	**Article 297 and Automatic Limitations to the Tribunal's Jurisdiction**	**35**	**125**
		1. Possible Objections	35	126
		2. The Philippines' Position	35	128
	B.	**Article 298 and Optional Exceptions to the Tribunal's Jurisdiction**	**36**	**129**
		1. China's Position and Possible Further Objections	36	130
		2. The Philippines' Position	37	132
	C.	**The Application of Articles 297 and 298 and the Tribunal's Findings on the Scope of its Jurisdiction**	**38**	**134**
		1. Whether Issues of Jurisdiction Possess an "Exclusively Preliminary Character"	38	135
		(a) The Applicable Legal Standard	38	135
		(b) The Parties' Positions on the Link between Jurisdiction and the Merits	39	137
		(c) The Tribunal's Decision	39	138
		2. The Tribunal's Conclusions on its Jurisdiction	40	140
IX.	**DECISION**		**44**	**149**

I. INTRODUCTION[2]

The Parties to the arbitration are the Philippines, which ratified the UN Convention on the Law of the Sea ("the Convention") on 8 May 1984, and China, which ratified it on 7 June 1996.[3] The Convention establishes a comprehensive legal order for the world's seas and oceans; an integral part of the Convention is a system for dispute settlement set out in its Part XV (Settlement of disputes), pursuant to which the Philippines initiated this arbitration.

The South China Sea is a semi-enclosed sea in the Western Pacific, spanning almost 3.5 million square kilometers and including thousands of geographical features (see Map 1). It is a crucial shipping lane and a rich fishing ground and believed to hold substantial oil and gas reserves. It abuts seven States, five of which have competing claims to its waters.

The Philippines requests that the Tribunal

1. declare that the rights and obligations of China and the Philippines under the Convention in regard to the waters, seabed, and maritime features of the South China Sea are governed by the Convention and that China's claims based on "historic rights" encompassed within the "nine-dash line" are inconsistent with the Convention, and therefore invalid (see Map 2);
2. determine whether eight maritime features claimed by both China and the Philippines are properly characterized as islands (which could generate a territorial sea, contiguous zone, exclusive economic zone, and continental shelf), rocks (which generate only a territorial sea), or low-tide elevations (which are incapable of generating entitlements); and
3. declare that China has violated the Convention by interfering with the exercise of Philippine sovereign rights and freedoms under the Convention and through construction and fishing activities that have harmed the marine environment.[4]

The Philippines is conscious that (1) the Convention is not concerned with territorial disputes and has thus stated that it is not asking the Tribunal to rule on the territorial sovereignty aspect of its disputes with China and (2) that China made a declaration in 2006 to exclude maritime boundary delimitation from its acceptance of compulsory dispute settlement procedures; the Philippines is therefore not asking the Tribunal to delimit any maritime boundaries.[5]

The Philippines, referring to a long history of the Parties' attempts to resolve their dispute by negotiations, considered that these efforts had failed or become futile, hence its resort to arbitration under Annex VII (Arbitration) of the Convention.[6] China has consistently rejected the Philippine recourse to arbitration and adhered to the position, expressed in a Position Paper (7 December 2014), two letters to the Tribunal, and other statements of neither accepting nor participating in the proceedings.

Pursuant to Article 9 of Annex VII of the Convention, on "Default of appearance", China's non-participation does not bar the Tribunal from proceeding with the arbitration. China is

2 Award on Jurisdiction and Admissibility, pp. 1–14, paras. 1–25, https://pcacases.com/web/sendAttach/1506, accessed 30 March 2018. All notes to this Summary have been prepared by the author. All footnotes in the original text have been eliminated.

3 United Nations Convention on the Law of the Sea, adopted 10 December 1982, https://treaties.un.org/doc/Publication/UNTS/Volume%201833/v1833.pdf, accessed 16 July 2016.

4 The preceding enumeration has been prepared by the author and does not appear in this form in the original text.

5 The preceding enumeration has been prepared by the author and does not appear in this form in the original text.

6 Annex VII, http://www.un.org/depts/los/convention_agreements/texts/unclos/annex7.htm, accessed 12 September 2016.

still a party to the arbitration and will be bound by any Award that it issues. However, China's non-participation imposes a special responsibility on the Tribunal, which does not simply adopt Philippine claims. There can be no default judgment; under Article 9 of Annex VII, the Tribunal must satisfy itself not only that it has jurisdiction but also that the claim is well founded in fact and in law.

The Philippines attempted to anticipate and address possible objections by China to the Tribunal's jurisdiction and suggested that the Tribunal take into account statements by China's officials and the academic literature. The Tribunal actively sought to satisfy itself that it has jurisdiction, in particular by asking the Philippines, following China's non-submission of its Counter-Memorial, to provide further written arguments and by posing questions to the Philippines. The publication of China's Position Paper facilitated the Tribunal's task by expounding three main objections to the Tribunal's jurisdiction.[7]

1. The essence of the arbitration's subject matter is territorial sovereignty over maritime features in the South China Sea, which is beyond the scope of the Convention.
2. China and the Philippines have agreed, through bilateral instruments and the Declaration on the Conduct of Parties in the South China Sea, to settle their disputes through negotiation.
3. The subject matter of the dispute constitutes an integral part of maritime delimitation, which China excluded from compulsory dispute settlement through its 2006 Declaration.

The Tribunal decided to treat China's Position Paper as a plea concerning jurisdiction and to conduct a hearing on jurisdiction and admissibility, held at The Hague from 7 to 13 July 2015. The Tribunal did not limit the Hearing to China's three objections and asked the Philippines to address other possible jurisdictional objections. China did not attend the Hearings but received the daily transcripts and all documents submitted during the hearing. In addition to a large delegation from the Philippines, observers from Malaysia, Indonesia, Viet Nam, Thailand, and Japan attended the Hearing.

The present Award only addresses questions of jurisdiction and admissibility. If the Tribunal finds that it has no jurisdiction, the matter ends here. If it finds it has jurisdiction over any Philippine claims, it will hold hearings on the merits of the claims. If it finds that any of the issues are so closely intertwined with the merits that they cannot be decided as preliminary questions, the Tribunal will defer them for decision after hearing the arguments on the merits.

II. PROCEDURAL HISTORY[8]

A. INITIATION OF THE ARBITRATION

On 22 January 2013, the Philippines initiated the arbitration through a Notification and Statement of Claim pursuant to Articles 286 and 297 and in accordance with Article 6 of Annex VII of the Convention. On 19 February 2013, China rejected and returned the Notification.

---

[7] The following enumeration has been prepared by the author and does not appear in this form in the original text.

[8] Award on Jurisdiction and Admissibility, pp. 15–32, paras. 26–98, supra note 2.

B. CONSTITUTION OF THE TRIBUNAL

In its Notification, the Philippines appointed Rüdiger Wolfrum, a national of Germany, as a member of the Tribunal. Following China's failure to appoint its arbitrator within 30 days and a Philippine request on 22 February made pursuant to Articles 3(c) and Article 3(e) of Annex VII of the Convention, the President of the International Tribunal for the Law of the Sea (ITLOS) appointed Stanisław Pawlak (a national of Poland) on 23 March. Following another Philippine request, the ITLOS President appointed Jean-Pierre Cot (a national of France) and Alfred H.A. Soons (a national of the Netherlands) as arbitrators and M.C.W. Pinto (a national of Sri Lanka) as arbitrator and President of the Tribunal on 24 April. Pinto withdrew from the Tribunal on 21 May and was replaced on 21 June by Thomas A. Mensah (a national of Ghana), who was also appointed the President of the Tribunal.

C. ADMINISTRATIVE DIRECTIVE NO. 1, PROCEDURAL ORDER NO. 1, AND RULES OF PROCEDURE

Following inquiries with the Permanent Court of Arbitration (PCA) and the PCA's agreement to serve as Registry, the Tribunal sought the views of the Philippines and China on the designation of The Hague as the seat of the arbitration and of the PCA as Registry. Only the Philippines responded. On 11 July, the Tribunal, at its first meeting, adopted Administrative Directive No. 1, in which it formalized the appointment of the PCA as Registry, made arrangements for a deposit to cover fees and expenses, and sought the Parties' comments on the draft Rules of Procedure and the Declaration of Independence and Impartiality signed by each arbitrator. On 29 July, China reiterated its rejection of the arbitration and returned the Tribunal's letter and accompanying documents. On 27 August, the Tribunal's Procedural Order No. 1 adopted the Rules of Procedure and set 30 March 2014 as the date for the Philippines to submit its memorial.

On 14 November, following a request from China's ambassador to the UK for a meeting with the Tribunal's President, the Tribunal reminded the parties to refrain from ex parte communications with Tribunal members and reminded them that all statements made by Parties would be made available to all Tribunal members, the Registry, and the other Party. It encouraged the parties to direct procedural questions to the PCA. China's Embassy in the Netherlands had already on two occasions discussed procedural questions with the PCA.

D. WRITTEN ARGUMENTS

On 28 February 2014, the Philippines applied for leave to amend its Statement of Claims by adding a request to determine the status of Second Thomas Shoal. Having sought comments and receiving none from China, the Tribunal granted the request on 11 March. On 18 March and 7 April, the Philippines wrote to the Tribunal that China's actions to prevent rotation and resupply of Philippine personnel stationed at Second Thomas Shoal seriously aggravated and extended the dispute and reserved its rights to apply for an indication of provisional measures.

On 30 March, the Philippines submitted its Memorial and Annexes, copies of which were sent to China's Embassy in the Netherlands. On 7 April, the Philippines wrote to the Tribunal regarding China's recent actions in and around Second Thomas Shoal and expressed concern about its ability to resupply its personnel there. On 12 April, Viet Nam requested copies of all pleadings and documents, since its legal rights and interests could be affected by the arbitration. The Philippines did not consider that Viet Nam's legal rights and interests could be affected but consented to Viet Nam's request. On 24 April, the Tribunal agreed to Viet Nam's request.

At a meeting held on 14–15 May, the Tribunal proposed a timetable and noted that it remained open to China to participate in the proceedings. On 2 June, the Tribunal set 15 December 2014 as the deadline for China's Counter-Memorial. On 30 July, the Philippines drew the Tribunal's attention to China's activities in the South China Sea, particularly land reclamation at McKennan Reef, Johnson Reef, Gaven Reef, and Cuarteron Reef, and expressed concern regarding their effects on maritime entitlements, on the environment, and on the status quo.

On 5 December, Viet Nam sent a statement to the Tribunal, requesting that it give due regard to Viet Nam's position and preserve Viet Nam's legal rights and interests. Viet Nam had no doubt that the Tribunal had jurisdiction in the proceedings; resolutely protested against and rejected any Chinese claim based on the "nine-dash line"; supported the Tribunal's competence to interpret and apply Articles 60, 80, 194(5), 206, 293(1), and 300 of the Convention; and reserved the right to intervene in the proceedings.

On 7 December, China published a Position Paper. On 16 December, the Tribunal, in accordance with Article 25(2) of the Rules of Procedure, requested through Procedural Order No. 3 that the Philippines submit further written arguments by 16 March 2015. China was given until 6 June 2015 to respond to the Philippine submission. The Tribunal requested the Parties' views on the possible bifurcation of the proceedings, the appointment of an expert hydrographer, a site visit, the procedure with regard to amicus curiae, and the scheduling of a hearing in July 2015.[9]

On 22 December, Viet Nam requested a copy of Procedural Order No. 3 and any other communications. On 26 January 2015, the Philippines, noting that it valued the principle of openness and transparency, agreed that Viet Nam should be allowed access to the documents. The Philippines recognized that the Tribunal's broad discretion on procedural matters encompassed the power to permit intervention, to accept Viet Nam's statement into the record, and to take any appropriate steps to request information from Viet Nam.

Writing on the same day, the Philippines opposed bifurcation. On 6 February, China wrote to the Tribunal's members to express its "omnibus objection to all procedural applications or steps that would require some kind of response from China." In particular, it expressed firm opposition to intervention by other States, amicus curiae submissions and site visits. On 17 February, the Tribunal agreed to provide Viet Nam with copies of the requested documents and declared that it would address the permissibility of intervention only in the event that Viet Nam made a formal application for intervention. On 16 March, the Philippines submitted its Supplemental Written Submissions.

E. BIFURCATION OF PROCEEDINGS

On 21 April, the Tribunal noted in Procedural Order No. 4 the practice of international courts and tribunals of taking note of public statements or informal communications made by non-appearing Parties; treating these statements and communications as equivalent to or as constituting preliminary objections; and bifurcating proceedings to address objections to jurisdiction. It decided that it was appropriate to bifurcate the proceedings and convene a hearing to consider jurisdiction and admissibility.

---

9 *Amicus curiae* (lit. "friend of the court"). "A person with a strong interest in or views on the subject of an action may petition the court for permission to file a brief, ostensibly on behalf of a party but actually to suggest a rationale consistent with its own views. Such *amicus curiae* briefs are commonly filed in appeals concerning matters of a broad public interest; e.g., civil rights cases." Henry Campbell Black, *Black's Law Dictionary*, 5th ed. (St. Paul, MN: West Publishing Co., 1979), p. 75.

The Hearing would not be limited to questions raised in China's Position Paper. The Tribunal would circulate its own questions on 22 June. The Philippines would not be limited to addressing those questions, while individual Tribunal members could raise questions during the hearing. The Tribunal, conscious of its duty to avoid unnecessary delay and expense and the Philippines' concern about delay and disruption, would endeavor to issue its decision as soon as possible after the Hearing. The Hearing would not be open to the public, but the Tribunal would consider the possibility of allowing observer States to attend the hearing and of making the verbatim record of the Hearings available to the public. The Tribunal sought the Parties' views on whether it should reserve the next 12–15 months for a hearing on the merits and it should ascertain the availability of technical experts.

F. PRE-HEARING PROCEDURES AND REQUESTS FROM OTHER STATES

On 11 May, the Philippines, declaring its strong interest in transparency and public access to information, proposed that the verbatim records of the Hearing be published and urged the Tribunal to consider opening the Hearing to the public. On 21 May, the Tribunal received a letter from the Philippines dated 27 April, informing the Tribunal of China's massive land reclamation at various features in the South China Sea, which violated Philippine rights and disregarded China's duty not to cause serious harm to the marine environment. On 2 June, the Tribunal confirmed the date of the hearing, which would not be open to the public. States who so requested could attend as observers, and the corrected transcripts of the hearing would be published shortly after the Hearing.

On 11 June, Malaysia, as one of the littoral States in the South China Sea, considered that its interests might be affected and requested copies of the pleadings and other documents, as well as permission to attend the hearing. On 21 June, the Philippines replied that it had no objection to both requests, which were granted by the Tribunal on 25 June. On 23 June, the Tribunal wrote to the Parties in preparation for the Hearing and set out a list of issues that the Philippines might wish to address during the Hearing.

Requests for permission to attend the Hearing as observers were received from Japan (26 June), Viet Nam and Indonesia (29 June), and Thailand (30 June). The Philippines raised no objection to these requests. These were granted by the Tribunal on 3 July, which reminded the observer States that their role was to watch and listen, not to make statements. On 7 July, Brunei Darussalam requested copies of the Hearing transcripts and other information.

On 1 July, China, in another letter to the Tribunal, recalled its consistent policy and practice of settling territorial and maritime disputes through negotiation and consultation with the States directly concerned, noted China's "legitimate right under the Convention" not to accept any imposed solution or any unilateral resort to third-party settlement, and the concern that the Philippines unilateral resort to arbitration would "erode the confidence shared by China and ASEAN Member States in jointly safeguarding peace and stability in the South China Sea."

G. HEARING ON JURISDICTION AND ADMISSIBILITY

The Hearing took place in two rounds, the first on 7 and 8 July and the second on 13 July. The Registry delivered to the Chinese Embassy in the Netherlands daily transcripts of the Hearing and other materials submitted by the Philippines. On 10 July, the Tribunal provided the parties with "Questions for the Philippines to Address in the Second Round," to which the Philippines responded on 13 July. On 12 July, the Philippines submitted several items, including a Note Verbale from China's Embassy in the Philippines of 6 July 2015, a list of data about satellite photos and navigational charts and a list of new annexes referred to in the proceedings. On 13 July, the Philippines responded to the Tribunal's written questions and to oral questions from individual arbitrators. At the hearing's conclusion, the Philippines was invited to submit by 23 July written responses to questions posed during the second round. China was given until 17 August to comment on any matter raised during the hearing.

H. POST-HEARING PROCEEDINGS

On 23 July, the Philippines filed Written Responses to the Tribunal's questions. On 24 July, the Tribunal granted the observers and Brunei access to certain documents. China did not submit any comments, although the Ministry of Foreign Affairs spokesperson made remarks on 24 August, upon the release of the transcripts of the hearing. On 27 September, the Tribunal requested further information from the Philippines about certain annexes, to which the Philippines responded on 7 October.

I. DEPOSITS FOR COSTS OF THE ARBITRATION

In accordance with Article 33 of the Rules of Procedure, the Tribunal may from time to time request the Parties to deposit equal amounts as advances for the costs. If either Party fails to make a deposit within 45 days, the Tribunal may inform the Parties in order that one may make the payment. The Parties have been requested to make payments on two occasions. The Philippines paid its share of the deposit within the time limit, but China did not. The Philippines then paid China's share of the deposit.

III. RELIEF REQUESTED AND SUBMISSIONS[10]

99. In its Amended Statement of Claim, the Philippines requested, under the heading "Relief Sought," that the Tribunal issue an Award that:

- Declares that China's rights in regard to maritime areas in the South China Sea, like the rights of the Philippines, are those that are established by UNCLOS, and consist of its rights to a Territorial Sea and Contiguous Zone under Part II of the Convention, to an Exclusive Economic Zone under Part V, and to a Continental Shelf under Part VI;

- Declares that China's maritime claims in the South China Sea based on its so-called 'nine-dash line' are contrary to UNCLOS and invalid;

- Requires China to bring its domestic legislation into conformity with its obligations under UNCLOS;

- Declares that Mischief Reef, McKennan Reef, and Second Thomas Shoal are submerged features that form part of the Continental Shelf of the Philippines under Part VI of the Convention, and that China's occupation of and construction activities on Mischief Reef and McKennan Reefs, and its exclusion of Philippine vessels from Second Thomas Shoal, violate the sovereign rights of the Philippines;

[10] This Chapter reproduces Chapter III of the Award on Jurisdiction and Admissibility.

- Requires that China end its occupation of and activities on Mischief Reef and McKennan Reef and at Second Thomas Shoal;
- Declares that Gaven Reef and Subi Reef are submerged features in the South China Sea that are not above sea level at high tide, are not islands under the Convention, and are not located on China's Continental Shelf, and that China's occupation of and construction activities on these features are unlawful;
- Requires China to terminate its occupation of and activities on Gaven Reef and Subi Reef;
- Declares that Scarborough Shoal, Johnson Reef, Cuarteron Reef, and Fiery Cross Reef are submerged features that are below sea level at high tide, except that each has small protrusions that remain above water at high tide, which are "rocks" under Article 121(3) of the Convention and which therefore generate entitlements only to a Territorial Sea no broader than 12 M,[11] and that China has unlawfully claimed maritime entitlements beyond 12 M from these features;
- Requires that China refrain from preventing Philippine vessels from exploiting in a sustainable manner the living resources in the waters adjacent to Scarborough Shoal and Johnson Reef, and from undertaking other activities inconsistent with the Convention at or in the vicinity of these features;
- Declares that the Philippines is entitled under UNCLOS to a 12 M Territorial Sea, a 200 M Exclusive Economic Zone, and a Continental Shelf under Parts II, V and VI of UNCLOS, measured from its archipelagic baselines;
- Declares that China has unlawfully claimed, and has unlawfully exploited the living and non-living resources in the Philippines' Exclusive Economic Zone and Continental Shelf, and has unlawfully prevented the Philippines from exploiting living and non-living resources within its Exclusive Economic Zone and Continental Shelf;
- Declares that China has unlawfully interfered with the exercise by the Philippines of its rights to navigation and other rights under the Convention in areas within and beyond 200 M of the Philippines' archipelagic baselines; and
- Requires that China desist from these unlawful activities.

100. With respect specifically to jurisdiction, the Philippines submitted in its Memorial "that the Tribunal has jurisdiction in regard to all of the claims raised by the Philippines in its Amended Statement of Claim and in [the] Memorial" because:

    1. All aspects of the disputes raised in the Philippines' Amended Statement of Claim concern the interpretation and application of UNCLOS;

[11] "Mile" in this context refers to a nautical mile, which is not defined in the Convention. It is equivalent to 1852 meters or 6076.115 feet; one degree of latitude corresponds to 60 nautical miles. George K. Walker, *Definitions for the Law of the Sea: Terms Not Defined by the Convention* (Leiden: Martinus Nijhoff Publishers, 2012), p. 52.

2. China's decision not to appear has no effect on the Tribunal's jurisdiction;

3. The 2002 ASEAN Declaration on the Conduct of the Parties in the South China Sea does not bar the exercise of jurisdiction by this Tribunal;

4. The Philippines fulfilled the requirement to engage in an exchange of views with China;

5. The limitations to jurisdiction provided in Article 297 are inapplicable to the claims of the Philippines in this case; and

6. The optional exceptions to jurisdiction provided in Article 298 also do not apply to the claims of the Philippines.

101. The Philippines' final submissions as set out at pages 271 and 272 of its Memorial (the "**Submissions**") are as follows:

> On the basis of the facts and law set forth in this Memorial, the Philippines respectfully requests the Tribunal to adjudge and declare that:
>
> 1) China's maritime entitlements in the South China Sea, like those of the Philippines, may not extend beyond those permitted by the United Nations Convention on the Law of the Sea ("UNCLOS" or the "Convention");
>
> 2) China's claims to sovereign rights and jurisdiction, and to "historic rights", with respect to the maritime areas of the South China Sea encompassed by the so-called "nine-dash line" are contrary to the Convention and without lawful effect to the extent that they exceed the geographic and substantive limits of China's maritime entitlements under UNCLOS;
>
> 3) Scarborough Shoal generates no entitlement to an exclusive economic zone or continental shelf;
>
> 4) Mischief Reef, Second Thomas Shoal, and Subi Reef are low-tide elevations that do not generate entitlement to a territorial sea, exclusive economic zone or continental shelf, and are not features that are capable of appropriation by occupation or otherwise;
>
> 5) Mischief Reef and Second Thomas Shoal are part of the exclusive economic zone and continental shelf of the Philippines;
>
> 6) Gaven Reef and McKennan Reef (including Hughes Reef) are low-tide elevations that do not generate entitlement to a territorial sea, exclusive economic zone or continental shelf, but their low-water line may be used to determine the baseline from which the breadth of the territorial sea of Namyit and Sin Cowe, respectively, is measured;

7) Johnson Reef, Cuarteron Reef, and Fiery Cross Reef generate no entitlement to an exclusive economic zone or continental shelf;

8) China has unlawfully interfered with the enjoyment and exercise of the sovereign rights of the Philippines with respect to the living and non-living resources of its exclusive economic zone and continental shelf;

9) China has unlawfully failed to prevent its nationals and vessels from exploiting the living resources in the exclusive economic zone of the Philippines;

10) China has unlawfully prevented Philippine fishermen from pursuing their livelihoods by interfering with traditional fishing activities at Scarborough Shoal;

11) China has violated its obligations under the Convention to protect and preserve the marine environment at Scarborough Shoal and Second Thomas Shoal;

12) China's occupation and construction activities on Mischief Reef:

    (a) violate the provisions of the Convention concerning artificial islands, Installations, and structures;

    (b) violate China's duties to protect and preserve the marine environment under the Convention; and

    (c) constitute unlawful acts of attempted appropriation in violation of the Convention;

13) China has breached its obligations under the Convention by operating its law enforcement vessels in a dangerous manner causing serious risk of collision to Philippine vessels navigating in the vicinity of Scarborough Shoal;

14) Since the commencement of this arbitration in January 2013, China has unlawfully aggravated and extended the dispute by, among other things:

    (a) interfering with the Philippines' rights of navigation in the waters at, and adjacent to, Second Thomas Shoal;

    (b) preventing the rotation and resupply of Philippine personnel stationed at Second Thomas Shoal; and

    (c) endangering the health and well-being of Philippine personnel stationed at Second Thomas Shoal; and

15) China shall desist from further unlawful claims and activities.

102. At the close of the Hearing on Jurisdiction, the Philippines presented its final submissions as follows:

The Philippines respectfully asks the Tribunal to adjudge and declare that the claims brought by the Philippines, as reflected in its submission recorded at pages 271 and 272 of our Memorial, are entirely within its jurisdiction and are fully admissible.

103. While China does not accept and is not participating in this arbitration, it has stated its position that the Tribunal "does not have jurisdiction over this case."

104. As set out in Procedural Order No. 4 of 21 April 2015, the Tribunal considered China's "statements and communications as equivalent to or as constituting preliminary objections" and decided that they "effectively constitute a plea concerning this Tribunal's jurisdiction."

105. China points out that its Position Paper "does not express any position on the substantive issues related to the subject-matter of the arbitration initiated by the Philippines."

IV. PRELIMINARY MATTERS[12]

A. THE STATUS OF THE PHILIPPINES AND CHINA AS PARTIES TO THE CONVENTION

As Parties to the Convention, the Philippines and China are both bound by the dispute settlement procedures provided for in the Convention's Part XV for any dispute between them concerning the interpretation and application of the Convention.

These procedures were heavily negotiated and reflect a compromise. While according State parties to the Convention the flexibility to resolve disputes in the manner of their choosing, the Convention provides for compulsory dispute settlement procedures that are subject only to very specific exceptions spelled out in the Convention itself. China's Declaration, made on 25 August 2006, is an example of a declaration intended to activate certain exceptions to compulsory dispute settlement set out in Article 298 (Optional exceptions to applicability of section 2). Beyond these specific exceptions, "no reservations or exceptions may be made" to the Convention unless expressly permitted (Article 309, Reservations and Exceptions). States parties are not free to pick and choose the portions of the Convention that they wish to accept.

Part XV is structured in 3 sections. Section 1's general provisions aim at reaching agreement through negotiation and other peaceful means. Section 2 provides for compulsory procedures entailing binding decisions if no settlement is reached by recourse to Section 1. However, recourse to Section 2 is subject to the specific exceptions and limitations set out in Section 3. Article 287 (Choice of procedure) accords States parties the choice of dispute settlement procedures, but since neither the Philippines nor China has chosen one of the means of dispute settlement listed in paragraph 1 of Article 287, they are deemed under Article 287, paragraph 3 to have accepted arbitration in accordance with Annex VII of the Convention. The present dispute has therefore correctly been submitted to arbitration before a tribunal constituted under Annex VII.

The arbitral tribunal's jurisdiction (Article 288, Jurisdiction) depends on a finding that the Parties actually have a dispute and that the dispute concerns the interpretation or application of the Convention. Further, the Tribunal must be satisfied that (1) no settlement has been reached by other peaceful means (Section 1 of Part XV) and (2) none of the specific limitations and exceptions set out in Section 3 applies. In case of dispute over the tribunal's jurisdiction, the matter will be settled by a decision of the tribunal (Article 288(4)).[13]

---

12 Award on Jurisdiction and Admissibility, pp. 37–45, paras. 106–29, *supra* note 2.

13 The preceding enumeration has been prepared by the author and does not appear in this form in the original text.

B. THE LEGAL AND PRACTICAL CONSEQUENCES OF CHINA'S NON-PARTICIPATION

China has not participated in the arbitration at any stage. Throughout the proceedings, China has rejected and returned correspondence sent by the Tribunal.

In case of non-participation of a State party to a dispute in arbitration proceedings, Article 9 (Default of appearance) of Annex VII applies. To avoid any doubt, the Philippines expressly requested in its Memorial that the proceedings continue, and the Tribunal has continued the proceedings. Despite its non-appearance, China remains a Party to the proceedings; it will be bound by any decision of the tribunal (Article 296(1), Finality and binding force of decisions; Article 11 of Annex VII, Finality of award).

Article 9 of Annex VII seeks to balance the risks of prejudice that could be suffered by either the participating or non-participating Party. It protects the first by ensuring that the proceedings will not be frustrated as a result of non-participation. It protects the second by ensuring that the Tribunal does not simply accept by default the participating Party's claims. The Tribunal has conducted the proceedings in such a way as to avoid prejudice to either Party that could arise as a result of China's non-participation.

To safeguard China's procedural rights, the Tribunal has ensured that all communications and materials as well as transcripts and documents of hearings have been delivered to China's Embassy in the Netherlands; granted China adequate and equal time to respond to Philippine pleadings; invited China's comments on all procedural steps, on anything said during the hearing, and on post-hearing submissions; provided China with adequate notice of the hearing; made the PCA staff available to China's Embassy for any administrative or procedural questions; and reiterated that it remains open to China to participate in the proceedings at any stage.

To safeguard the Philippines' procedural rights, the Tribunal has been responsive to the Parties' views on scheduling and logistics. The Tribunal introduced a procedure in Article 25(2) (Failure to appear or to make submissions) of the Rules of Procedure that took into account two Philippine concerns: the Philippines would "have to guess" what China's arguments might be and formulate arguments for both States; and the Philippines would not have the opportunity to address specific issues that in the Tribunal's view might have been inadequately canvassed (or not at all) by the Philippines. The Tribunal implemented this procedure by issuing a request on 16 December 2014 for further written argument from the Philippines, containing 26 questions. The Tribunal issued further questions on 23 June and on 10 July 2015.

As recounted in the Procedural History, the Tribunal decided to bifurcate the proceedings. The Tribunal would not confine itself to the issues raised in China's Position Paper and would consider other issues that might pose an obstacle to the continuation of the proceedings.

C. WHETHER THE ARBITRATION CONSTITUTES AN ABUSE OF LEGAL PROCESS

In the Position Paper, China repeatedly claims that the Tribunal "manifestly" lacks jurisdiction and that the Philippines' initiation of arbitration is an abuse of the Convention's compulsory dispute settlement procedure. These statements call to mind Article 300 (Good faith and abuse of rights) and Article 294 (Preliminary proceedings) of the Convention.

However, China has not specifically tied its allegations of abuse to Article 300 and has not requested a declaration that the Philippines has breached Article 300. The mere act of unilaterally initiating arbitration under Part XV in itself cannot constitute an abuse of right.

China has not made an application to the Tribunal pursuant to Article 294; the Tribunal is therefore under no obligation to follow the procedure under Article 294(2), which would involve notifying the Philippines of any application and fixing a time limit for a decision. While the Tribunal is entitled to determine *proprio motu*[14] whether a claim constitutes an abuse or is prima facie unfounded, it declines to do so, given the serious consequences of a finding of abuse. Such a finding would mean that the Tribunal would take no further action on the Philippine claims. The procedure in Article 294 is appropriate only for the most blatant cases of abuse or harassment; it is a safeguard against harassment arising from frivolous or unfounded claims. China's concerns about potential obstacles to the Tribunal's jurisdiction are more appropriately dealt with as preliminary objections.

V. IDENTIFICATION AND CHARACTERISATION OF THE DISPUTE[15]

Article 288 of the Convention limits the Tribunal's jurisdiction to "disputes concerning the interpretation and application of the Convention." Hence, the Tribunal must determine, first, whether there is a dispute between the Parties and, second, whether the dispute concerns the interpretation and application of the Convention.

A. THE PARTIES' POSITIONS

1. China's Position

China presented two alternative characterizations of the disputes with the Philippines.[16]

a. The essence of the subject matter of the arbitration is territorial sovereignty over maritime features in the South China Sea, which is beyond the Convention's scope and does not concern the interpretation or application of the Convention.

To decide on the Philippines' claims, the Tribunal would have to determine sovereignty over these maritime features. The Philippine Submissions are concerned with China's historic rights, the status of certain maritime features and China's exercise of rights in the South China Sea.

1) Submissions No. 1 and 2 (on China's nine-dash line) concern the extent of China's historic rights and reflect a dispute about sovereignty.

It is only after the extent of China's territorial sovereignty in the South China Sea is determined that a decision can be made whether China's maritime claims have exceeded the extent allowed by the Convention. China recalls the general principle that sovereignty over land territory is the basis for the determination of maritime rights.

2) Submissions No. 3 to 7 (status of maritime features) also constitute sovereignty disputes because without determining sovereignty over a maritime feature, it is impossible to determine whether the maritime claims based on that feature are consistent with the Convention.

---

14 On its own initiative.

15 Award on Jurisdiction and Admissibility, pp. 45–70, paras. 130–78, supra note 2.

16 The following enumeration has been prepared by the author and does not appear in this form in the original text.

When not subject to State sovereignty, a maritime feature possesses no maritime entitlements. If sovereignty is undecided, there can be no concrete and real dispute for arbitration. Whether a low-tide elevation can be appropriated is also a question of territorial sovereignty. By focusing on only a few features, the Philippines is attempting to gainsay Chinese sovereignty over the whole of the Spratly Islands and to distort the nature of the dispute.

3) The remaining Submissions (relating to Chinese activities in the South China Sea) reflect a dispute over sovereignty, because the legality of Chinese actions in the waters of the Spratly Islands and Scarborough Shoal rests on Chinese sovereignty over the features.

The Philippine submissions are based on the premise that the spatial extent of Philippine maritime jurisdiction is defined and undisputable and that Chinese actions have encroached on these areas.

b. Second, even if the Parties' dispute was concerned with the Convention, the legal issues presented by the Philippines, including the legal nature of maritime features, the extent of maritime rights, and law enforcement activities, would constitute an integral part of maritime delimitation, thus falling within the scope of the 2006 Chinese Declaration. Certain Philippine Submissions (e.g., No. 5 and 8) amount to a request for maritime delimitation in disguise.

2. The Philippines' Position

None of its Submissions requires a priori determination of sovereignty.[17]

a. First, a dispute regarding sovereignty over maritime features in the South China Sea does exist, but Philippine disputes with China have more than one layer.

That a dispute may have different elements does not preclude some elements from falling within a tribunal's jurisdiction. None of the Philippine submissions requires the Tribunal to express any view on the extent of Chinese sovereignty over land territory. Several arbitral awards support the conclusion that sovereignty claims over maritime features raise no impediments to the determination of their maritime entitlements.

1) The Convention includes provisions on the maximum extent of maritime entitlements.

These entitlements emanate exclusively from maritime features. Even assuming that China is sovereign over all of the insular features in the South China Sea that it claims, its claim to historic rights within the "nine-dash line" exceeds the limits of its potential entitlement under the Convention (see Map 3).

2) To determine the existence of a maritime entitlement, one must necessarily and logically determine the nature and character of a feature.

---

17 The following enumeration has been prepared by the author and does not appear in this form in the original text.

This does not require prior determination of which State has sovereignty over the feature because entitlement is a matter for objective determination. The same feature could not be a rock if it pertains to one State but an island if it belongs to another. The choice of features in the Submissions is pragmatic, given the large number of features in the Spratly Islands. If the largest of the Spratly features is incapable of generating an entitlement to an EEZ and a continental shelf, then it is unlikely that any of the other 750 features will be able to do so. The status of a feature as a low-tide elevation is to be determined by reference to Article 13, paragraph 1, and hence, it is within the Tribunal's jurisdiction.

3) The Philippines' claims on China's unlawful conduct are premised on China's maximum permissible entitlements under the Convention, even assuming that it has sovereignty over all the disputed features in the South China Sea.

b. Second, China conflates 1) entitlement to maritime areas and 2) delimitation of areas where the areas overlap.

Maritime delimitation issues may require prior resolution of entitlement issues, but this does not mean that entitlement issues are an integral part of maritime delimitation. Each and every one of the Philippines' Submissions is a subject of a legal dispute, as proven by diplomatic exchanges between the two countries since 1995.

B. THE TRIBUNAL'S DECISION

Under international law, a dispute is "a disagreement on a point of law or fact, a conflict of legal views or of interests between two persons." Whether a dispute exists is a matter for objective determination. The mere assertion by one Party that a dispute exists is not sufficient to prove its existence, any more than the denial of its existence proves its non- existence. It is not adequate to show that the interests of the two Parties are in conflict. It must be shown that the claims of one Party are positively opposed by the other and that the dispute exists at the time proceedings are commenced. Where a dispute exists, it is necessary to identify and characterize it, as its nature may determine whether it concerns interpretation or application of the Convention or whether the exclusions from jurisdiction are applicable. It is for an international court to determine on an objective basis the nature of the dispute by examining the application, the final submissions, diplomatic exchanges, public statements, and other pertinent evidence.

1) There is no question that there exists a dispute between the Philippines and China regarding land sovereignty over the maritime features in the South China Sea.[18]

It does not follow that sovereignty is also the appropriate characterization of Philippine claims. It is entirely ordinary and expected that the Philippines and China, which have an extensive and multifaceted relationship, would have disputes on several distinct matters. The Tribunal agrees with the International Court of Justice (ICJ) that there are no grounds to "decline to take cognizance of one aspect of a dispute because that dispute has other aspects."

[18] The following enumeration has been prepared by the author and does not appear in this form in the original text.

The Philippines has not asked the Tribunal to rule on sovereignty and has requested that the Tribunal refrain from so doing. None of the Philippine Submissions requires an implicit determination of sovereignty. In the Tribunal's view, it is entirely possible to approach the Philippine Submissions from the premise—as the Philippines suggests—that China is correct in its assertion of sovereignty over the Spratly Islands and Scarborough Shoal. The Tribunal intends to ensure that its decision neither advances nor detracts from either Party's claims to land sovereignty in the South China Sea. The Tribunal does not see that success on the Philippines' Submissions would have an effect on the Philippines' sovereignty claims and accepts that the Philippines has initiated the proceedings with the entirely proper objective of narrowing the issues in dispute.

The Philippine focus only on maritime features occupied by China does not carry implications for the question of sovereignty. However, this narrow selection may have implications for the merits of Philippine claims. If a claim is premised on the absence of any overlapping entitlements of any Chinese claim to an EEZ or a continental shelf, it will be necessary to consider the maritime zones generated by any feature in the South China Sea claimed by China, whether or not the feature is presently occupied by China.

2) The Tribunal is not convinced by China's objection that the dispute is properly characterized as relating to maritime boundary delimitation.

It agrees with China that maritime delimitation is an integral and systemic process. The concepts of equitable solution, special circumstances relating to the territorial sea, and relevant circumstances regarding the EEZ and the continental shelf may entail consideration of a wide variety of issues. It does not follow that a dispute over issues that may be considered in the course of maritime delimitation constitutes a dispute over maritime delimitation itself. A dispute over the existence of entitlements to maritime zones is distinct from a dispute regarding the delimitation of maritime zones in areas where the Parties' entitlements overlap. A maritime boundary may be delimited only between States with opposite or adjacent coasts and overlapping entitlements. In contrast, a dispute over claimed entitlements may exist even without an overlap, for example, where a State claims a maritime zone in an area understood by other States to form part of the high seas.

The Philippines has not requested the Tribunal to delimit any overlapping entitlement between the two States, nor will the Tribunal effect delimitation of any maritime boundaries. However, Philippine Submissions No. 5, 8, and 9 are based on the premise that certain areas of the South China Sea form part of the Philippine EEZ or continental shelf. The Tribunal will be able to address these claims only if it determines that China could not possess any potentially overlapping entitlements in the area.

3) An issue arises from the fact that China has not elaborated on certain significant aspects of its claimed rights and entitlements in the South China Sea.

The existence of a dispute in international law requires "positive opposition" between the Parties, which will be apparent from the diplomatic correspondence. China has repeatedly claimed that its historic rights are "rights formed in history" but it has not clarified the nature or scope of these rights. It has not clarified its understanding of the meaning of the "nine-dash line" set out in a 2009 map. Similarly, China has not expressed views on the status of particular maritime features in the Spratly Islands, although it has argued generally that the Spratly Islands are fully entitled to a territorial sea, EEZ, and continental shelf. The Tribunal sees nothing improper about this. China is free to set out its public positions as it considers most appropriate.

On the issue whether a dispute can be reasonably said to exist when the Philippines' claims involve matters over which China has not expressed a detailed position, the Tribunal examines the jurisprudence of the ICJ and derives two principles from it. First, the Tribunal is entitled to examine the conduct of the Parties or the fact of silence in a situation in which a response would be expected, and second, the dispute's existence must be evaluated objectively.

Philippine Submissions No. 1 and 2 reflect a dispute over the source of entitlements in the South China Sea and the interaction of China's "historic rights" with the Convention. The existence of the dispute is evident from diplomatic exchanges at the UN between 2009 and 2011. The existence of a dispute is not diminished by the fact that China has not clarified the meaning of the "nine-dash line" or elaborated its claims on historic rights. This is not a dispute about the existence of specific historic rights, but rather a dispute about historic rights in the framework of the Convention. A dispute concerning the interaction of the Convention with another instrument or body of law is unequivocally a dispute concerning the interpretation and application of the Convention. Philippine Submissions No. 3, 4, 6, and 7 reflect a dispute over the status of maritime features and the source of maritime entitlements in the South China Sea. Although the two Parties have only rarely exchanged views on the status of specific individual features, a dispute exists, viewed objectively. A dispute is not negated by the absence of granular exchanges on every feature. International law does not require a State to expound its legal arguments before a dispute can arise. Philippine Submission No. 5 merely presents another aspect of the same general dispute concerning the source of entitlements in the South China Sea. However, by requesting the Tribunal to declare that Mischief Reef and Second Thomas Shoal are part of its EEZ and continental shelf, the Philippines has in fact presented a dispute concerning the status of every maritime feature claimed by China within 200 nautical miles of Scarborough Shoal and Second Thomas Shoal and the capacity of each feature to generate an entitlement to an EEZ and continental shelf. The Tribunal would be able to make the requested declaration only if no overlapping entitlement exists and only if China is not entitled to claim rights in the South China Sea beyond those permitted by the Convention.

Submissions No. 8 to 14 concern disputes relating to Chinese activities in the South China Sea. The incidents giving rise to the Submissions are well documented in the diplomatic correspondence between the two countries. The Tribunal concludes that disputes implicating provisions of the Convention exist between the two countries concerning their respective petroleum and survey activities, fishing, Chinese installations on Mischief Reef, the actions of Chinese law enforcement vessels, and the Philippine military presence on Second Thomas Shoal.

Submissions No. 11 and 12(b) require particular consideration because they refer to the Convention on Biological Diversity (CBD). The Tribunal is satisfied that the incidents alleged by the Philippines could involve violations of obligations under Article 194 and Article 192 of the Convention to take measures to prevent, reduce, and control pollution of the marine environment. It accepts the Philippine assertion that while it considers Chinese actions and failures to be inconsistent with provisions of the CBD, the Philippines has not presented a claim arising under the CBD as such.

Article 293, paragraph 1 of the Convention and Article 31, paragraph 3 of the 1969 Vienna Convention on the Law of Treaties enable the Tribunal to consider provisions of the CBD for the purpose of interpreting the content and standards of Article 192 and Article 194 of the Convention. The Tribunal is accordingly satisfied that disputes between the Parties concerning the interpretation and application of the Convention exist with respect to the matters raised by the Philippines in all of its submissions.

VI. WHETHER ANY THIRD PARTIES ARE INDISPENSABLE TO THE PROCEEDINGS[19]

The Tribunal has been asked to rule on the status of and maritime entitlements generated by a number of features over which sovereignty is claimed not only by the Philippines and China but also by Viet Nam and/or other States.

China has not argued that Viet Nam's absence as a Party is a factor that would bar jurisdiction. Its Position Paper simply pointed out that the South China Sea issue involves a number of States and that it is not an easy task to solve it. It refers to the negotiated boundaries with Viet Nam as an example of successful peaceful negotiations between China and its neighbors. Nevertheless, it is appropriate to dispose of the issue, which has been addressed by the Philippines and was the subject of correspondence between the Tribunal and the Parties.

The determination of the nature of and entitlements generated by maritime features in the South China Sea does not require a decision on territorial sovereignty. Viet Nam's legal rights and obligations therefore do not need to be determined as a prerequisite to the determination of the merits. The situation is different from the few cases in which international courts or tribunals have declined to proceed due to the absence of indispensable third parties. In those cases, the rights of third parties would not only have been affected by the decision but would have formed the very subject matter of the decision. The lawfulness of the activities of third parties was in question. Here, none of the Philippine claims entail allegations of unlawful conduct by Viet Nam or other third States.

The Tribunal's conclusion is supported by the position that Viet Nam has taken (see II. Procedural History). In the circumstances, and in the light of Viet Nam's own stance, the Tribunal finds that Viet Nam is not an indispensable third party. Its absence as a party does not preclude the Tribunal from proceeding with the arbitration.

The absence of other States as parties to the arbitration poses no obstacle. Like Viet Nam, Malaysia and Indonesia have received copies of the pleadings and attended the Hearing on Jurisdiction and Admissibility. Brunei Darussalam has been provided with copies of the documents. No argument has been made by China, the Philippines, or any neighboring States that their participation is indispensable to the Tribunal proceeding with this case.

VII. PRECONDITIONS TO THE TRIBUNAL'S JURISDICTION[20]

Having found that disputes between the Philippines and China concerning the interpretation and application of the Convention exist, the Tribunal examines whether China and the Philippines had an agreement that would preclude recourse to arbitration by virtue of Articles 281 and 282 of the Convention (A). It then addresses whether they have engaged in an "exchange of views" as required by Article 283 (B).

A. ARTICLE 281 (PROCEDURE WHERE NO SETTLEMENT HAS BEEN REACHED BY THE PARTIES)

The Philippines implied that by invoking Article 281, China conceded the existence of a dispute concerning interpretation or application of the Convention. The Tribunal does not accept that China makes that admission.

19 Award on Jurisdiction and Admissibility, pp. 71–74, paras. 179–88, supra note 2.

20 Ibid., pp. 75–123, paras. 189–353.

Under Article 281, if the States parties to a dispute have "agreed to seek settlement of the dispute by a peaceful means of their own choice," they can only resort to compulsory dispute settlement (Section 2 of Part XV) on condition that

i. no settlement has been reached by recourse to the agreed means,
ii. the Parties' agreement does not exclude any further procedure, and
iii. any agreed time limits have expired.

This section examines the instruments that may possibly be viewed as forming such an agreement.

1. Application of Article 281 to the DOC

(a) China's Position[21]

(1) By signing the 2002 Declaration on the Conduct of the Parties in the South China Sea (DOC), the Philippines and China have undertaken an obligation to settle their South China Sea disputes through friendly consultations and negotiations and agreed to seek dispute settlement by means of their own choice.

To constitute a binding agreement, the instrument must evince a "clear intention" to establish rights and obligations between the parties, irrespective of the form or designation of the instrument. The word undertake in DOC, paragraph 4 of the DOC means "to give a formal promise, to bind or engage oneself, to give a promise, to agree, to accept an obligation."

(2) While the DOC does not expressly exclude further procedures, an express exclusion is not necessary.

Third-party settlement is "obviously" excluded by virtue of the DOC's emphasis on negotiations between the sovereign States directly concerned and the Parties' reaffirmation in the DOC and other instruments of negotiations as a means for dispute settlement.

(3) China rejects the Philippine suggestion that China should be prevented from invoking the DOC in light of China's violations of DOC.

It was the Philippines that first resorted to the use of force around Scarborough Shoal in 2012. The Philippines takes a "selective and self-contradictory" approach to the DOC, which violates the principle of good faith. The DOC plays a positive role in building trust and maintaining peace and stability in the South China Sea. Denying its significance could lead to serious retrogression in ASEAN–China relations.

(b) The Philippines' Position[22]

(1) The DOC is not a legally binding agreement; it is merely a non-binding political document that was never intended to create legal rights and obligations.

---

21 This enumeration has been prepared by the author and does not appear in this form in the original text.

22 The following enumeration has been prepared by the author and does not appear in this form in the original text.

This is evident from (i) its content, replete with aspirational and hortatory language, merely confirming existing obligations; (ii) the circumstances of its adoption, which show that it was intended as a political document, reflecting a compromise reached as a "stop-gap" measure to reduce tensions, following years of trying for a legally binding code of conduct; and (iii) the Parties' subsequent conduct (they have characterized the DOC as political, not legal, and they have continued to strive for a binding code of conduct).

(2) Even if it was intended to be legally binding, no settlement has been reached through negotiations.

The Philippines was justified in concluding that continued negotiations would be futile. Article 281 does not require Parties to negotiate indefinitely.

(3) Even if the DOC was intended to be a binding agreement, it does not exclude recourse to Section 2 of Part XV of the Convention.

The terms of an agreement to resolve a dispute by other peaceful means must expressly exclude recourse to dispute settlement under Part XV. The DOC contains no express exclusion of recourse to further procedures and does not imply such an exclusion. In fact, its paragraph 4 refers to the Convention, a reference that necessarily incorporates Part XV as an integral part of the Convention.

(4) Even if the DOC were binding and excluded further procedures, China cannot rely on it to avoid jurisdiction, due to China's flagrant disregard of the DOC, particularly paragraph 5 on self-restraint.

Under paragraph 5, States undertake to exercise self-restraint in the conduct of activities that would complicate and affect the dispute. Yet China has expelled Filipino fishermen from Scarborough Shoal. China's disregard of paragraph 5 deprives it of the benefit of its alleged rights under the DOC.

(c) The Tribunal's Decision[23]

(1) To constitute a binding agreement, the instrument must evince a clear intention to establish rights and obligations between the Parties.

A clear intention is determined by reference to the agreement's actual terms, the circumstances of its adoption and the Parties' subsequent conduct.

Although the DOC is entitled a Declaration rather than a treaty, international agreements may take a number of forms and be given a variety of names. The form of designation of the instrument is not decisive of its status as an agreement establishing legal obligations. The DOC shows some hallmarks of a treaty. It is a formal document with a preamble, it was signed by the ministers of foreign affairs of China and ASEAN members, and the signatory States are described as "Parties."

---

[23] The following enumeration has been prepared by the author and does not appear in this form in the original text.

However, the DOC in many instances (e.g., paragraphs 1, 5, and 10) simply reaffirms existing obligations (such as the commitment to the UN Charter and the Convention). It only uses the word *agree* in paragraph 10: "agree to work towards the eventual attainment of a Code of Conduct." This language is not consistent with the creation of new obligations; it restates existing obligations pending the attainment of a Code of Conduct. The use of the word *undertake* in paragraphs 4 and 5 is suggestive of the existence of an agreement. However, if we give weight to the DOC's object and purpose and its negotiating history, it becomes apparent that it was not intended by its drafters to be a legally binding agreement on dispute resolution. Rather, it was an aspirational political document. In 1999, China described its own draft as reflecting the consensus that it should be a "political document of principle" and as constituting an alternative to a Code of Conduct that was unacceptable to it. In August 2000, China described the document as political, not legal. The ASEAN Secretary General at the time recalled that the DOC was reduced to a political document from the originally envisioned legally binding document.

The Parties' subsequent conduct confirms that the DOC is not a binding agreement. Prior to the arbitration, Chinese officials described the DOC as a political document. Moreover, for over a decade, the parties to DOC attempted to negotiate a legally binding Code of Conduct.

(2) For completeness, the Tribunal examines the remaining elements of Article 281.[24]

(i) Whether a settlement has been reached by recourse to the agreed means—no settlement has been reached; if anything, the disputes have intensified.

Article 281 does not require Parties to a dispute to pursue any agreed means of settlement indefinitely. It only requires that they abide by any time limits set out in their agreement.

(ii) whether the agreement excludes any further procedure—the DOC does not exclude Part XV or the resort to third-party settlement.

The Philippines believes that an express exclusion is required, while China believes that it is unnecessary. In the Tribunal's view, Article 281 requires some clear statement of the exclusion of further procedures. It also requires "opting out" of Part XV procedures; it does not require "opting in," whereby the Parties must positively agree to Part XV procedures. "Opting in" is only required under Article 282, not under Article 281. Requiring an express exclusion for Article 281 is consistent with the overall object and purpose of the Convention as a comprehensive agreement. For the drafters of the Convention, a system for dispute settlement forms an integral part and an essential element of the Convention. It is not possible for States to pick what they like and to disregard what they do not like.

The DOC does not even implicitly exclude recourse to Part XV procedures. Its paragraphs 1 and 3 repeatedly invoke the Convention and the United Nations Charter, without differentiating among the component parts of these instruments. Paragraph 4 embraces the Convention. The Tribunal concludes that the DOC does not, by virtue of Article 281, bar its jurisdiction.

[24] The following enumeration has been prepared by the author and does not appear in this form in the original text.

2. Application of Article 281 to Other Bilateral Statements

(a) China's Position[25]

(1) China pointed to a series of bilateral documents, which predate (1995, 1999, 2000, 2001) or post-date (2004 and 2011) the DOC, to show that China and the Philippines have a long-standing agreement to settle their disputes through negotiations, to the exclusion of other means of settlement.

So long as the instruments intend to create rights and obligations for the parties, these rights and obligations are binding; the designation or the form of the instrument is not decisive. The repeated use of the word *agree* in many instruments evinces a clear obligation to establish obligations between them. The instruments taken together and with the DOC are a "mutually reinforcing" agreement between the Philippines and China for purposes of Article 281.

(2) The absence of an express exclusion of any further dispute settlement procedures is not decisive.

The bilateral statements exclude any means of third-party settlement by virtue of two factors. China always insists on peaceful settlement of disputes by negotiation between the States directly concerned, a position that was well-known and clear to the Philippines during the adoption and drafting of bilateral instruments. The use of the word *eventually* in a 1995 statement emphasizes that negotiations are the only means the parties have chosen for dispute settlement.

(b) The Philippines' Position[26]

(1) None of the bilateral instruments invoked by China, individually or collectively, constitute a legally binding instrument.

Joint statements are commonplace in international practice and do not purport to establish binding legal obligations. States everywhere would be dismayed to learn otherwise.

(2) Nothing in any statement, explicitly or implicitly, excludes recourse to dispute settlement under Part XV.

The 2000 statement refers to negotiations being conducted "in accordance with universally recognized principles of international law," including the Convention. The reference to the Convention reflects an understanding that while negotiations are to be encouraged, the recourse to alternative procedures is entirely appropriate when negotiations have failed or are futile. The two bilateral statements adopted after the DOC merely reaffirm the DOC; their binding force "can extend no further than that of the DOC."

(c) The Tribunal's Decision[27]

To determine if the bilateral instruments are legally binding, the Tribunal applies the standards set out with respect to the DOC.

---

[25] The following enumeration has been prepared by the author and does not appear in this form in the original text.

[26] The following enumeration has been prepared by the author and does not appear in this form in the original text.

[27] The following enumeration has been prepared by the author and does not appear in this form in the original text.

(1) None is designed as an agreement; they are press statements and reports of officials of varying ranks.

(2) The usage of the word *agree* occurs in the context of other terms suggestive of the documents being political and aspirational in nature.

Many statements refer to the aspiration to conclude a Code of Conduct. These statements do not mutually reinforce each other so as to render them legally binding. The repetition of aspirational political statements across multiple documents does not per se transform them into a legally binding agreement. They do not constitute a binding agreement to settle disputes by other peaceful means.

(3) None of the instruments expressly rule out compulsory dispute settlement.

To the contrary, most (e.g., 1995, 1999, 2004) expressly refer to the Convention, of which Part XV is an integral part. The Tribunal will not imply exclusion of that integral part of the Convention from documents that, in the context of dispute settlement, implores adherence to that very instrument.

The Tribunal understands that China has always insisted on negotiation and has made this preference clear and well-known to the Philippines. However, one State's preference for one means of dispute settlement cannot imply that if negotiations fail or become futile, the other Party has relinquished its right to have recourse to other means of dispute settlement set out in Section 2 of Part XV.

Whether treated individually or collectively, the bilateral statements made both before and after the DOC's adoption do not bar jurisdiction under Article 281.

(4) During the Hearing, the Philippines was asked whether Philippine statements and conduct in respect of the DOC estopped the Philippines from seeking recourse to arbitration.

Estoppel is a general principle of law that is designed to protect the legitimate expectations of a State that acts in reliance on the representations of another State. Estoppel may be invoked where (a) a State has made clear and consistent representations by word, conduct or silence; (b) the representations were made through an authorized agent of the State; (c) the State invoking estoppel was induced by the representations to act, to its detriment, to suffer a prejudice, or to convey a benefit to the representing state; and (d) the reliance was legitimate, as the representation was one on which the State was entitled to rely. The Tribunal finds no evidence that the Philippines made clear and consistent representations that it would not resort to compulsory dispute settlement procedures. In fact, the Philippines specifically raised the prospect of recourse to compulsory dispute settlement if it were left with no other choice and negotiations were failing. No estoppel arises.

3. Application of Article 281 to the Treaty on Amity

The Tribunal considers *proprio motu* whether the Treaty on Amity and Cooperation in Southeast Asia (TAC, Chapter IV, Articles 13 to 17) could preclude submission of the dispute to arbitration. The TAC is a multilateral treaty that predates the Convention; the original parties were Indonesia, Malaysia, the Philippines, Singapore, and Thailand. It was concluded on 24 February 1976 and entered into force on 15 July 1976. A number of non-ASEAN Member States, including China, have acceded to the TAC.

(a) Possible Objections

China is silent on this point. On its face, the TAC is an agreement between the Parties that includes a range of choices for peaceful means of dispute settlement. In December 2014 and June 2015, the Tribunal asked the Philippines to address the question whether it was necessary for the Philippines to attempt dispute settlement through the High Council of the TAC as an agreed means of dispute settlement.

(b) The Philippines' Position

Unlike the DOC and other bilateral instruments, the TAC is a legally binding instrument to which both the Philippines and China are parties. It does not constitute an agreement to settle disputes in any particular manner. A High Council may recommend non-adversarial means of dispute settlement, but this provision will not apply unless all Parties to the dispute agree to it (Article 16). TAC cannot apply to the present case because China and the Philippines have never agreed to submit disputes to the High Council. Article 17 does not mandate pre-arbitration negotiations; it merely encourages States to attempt to settle their disputes by negotiation. State practice demonstrates the understanding that the High Council provisions of the TAC are not compulsory. States parties to the TAC have submitted disputes to arbitration under the Convention without any prior resort to the High Council; the respondent States did not raise any objection based on the TAC; and the TAC has never been constituted.

(c) The Tribunal's Decision

The TAC is a legally binding agreement, but it does not prescribe any particular form of dispute settlement, and it certainly does not exclude recourse to compulsory dispute settlement. Read in isolation, Articles 13 to 15 of the TAC appear to impose the obligation on States parties to the TAC to settle their disputes at all times through negotiation and to resort to a High Council in the event direct negotiations fail. However, according to Article 16, these obligations will not apply unless all the parties to the dispute agree to their application to the dispute. Thus, the TAC does not constitute a binding means to resolve disputes by negotiations or other means. There has been no settlement of the dispute between the Philippines and China, and the Philippines is not required to pursue the optional High Council mechanism as a precursor to arbitration. In any event, the TAC does not exclude any further procedures, as it envisages recourse to modes of dispute settlement contained in Article 33(1) of the UN Charter, among which is arbitration.

The Tribunal concludes that the TAC is not a bar to the Tribunal's jurisdiction under Article 281.

4. Application of Article 281 to the CBD

The Tribunal considers *proprio motu* whether the CBD could preclude submission of the dispute to arbitration. The CBD is a multilateral treaty that obliges parties to regulate and manage biological resources important for the conservation of biodiversity. Both China (since 29 December 1993) and the Philippines (since 1 June 1994) are parties to the CBD.

(a) Possible Objections

China is silent on this point. Philippine Submissions No. 11 and 12(b) allege violations of the

CBD as well as Articles 192 and 194 of the Convention. In December 2014 and during the Hearing on Jurisdiction, the Tribunal asked the Philippines to address the question whether the Philippines and China have agreed, in ratifying the CBD, to seek settlement of the dispute through the compulsory conciliation process provided for in Article 27 of the CBD.

(b) The Philippines' Position

The CBD's dispute settlement procedures relate exclusively to disputes over the interpretation and application of the CBD. If Article 27 of the CBD were intended to constitute an agreement between the Philippines and China to settle their disputes regarding the interpretation and application of the Convention, a clear and unambiguous wording would be required to that effect. The intention to entrust dispute settlement with respect to interpretation and application of the Convention to other institutions must be expressed explicitly in the respective agreement. None of the wording in the CBD or its Annexes expressly excludes further proceedings under the Convention.

(c) The Tribunal's Decision

The Philippines has clarified that it does not separately plead a claim for a breach of the CBD. It refers to the CBD only insofar as it informs the normative content of Articles 192 and 194 of the Convention. That the CBD can be used in this way to interpret the Convention is clear from Article 31(3) of the Vienna Convention on the Law of Treaties and Article 293 of the Convention and has been confirmed in recent cases relating to the interpretation and application of the Convention.

There is some overlap in the subject matter of Part XII of the Convention (e.g., Articles 192 and 194) and that of the CBD. The alleged Chinese conduct (toleration of and active support for environmentally harmful practices employed by Chinese nationals at Scarborough Shoal and Second Thomas Shoal) could constitute breaches of the Convention and the CBD. However, the overlap of subject matter is not sufficient to bring the CBD within the meaning of Article 281. The CBD's objective of protecting biodiversity in general potentially overlaps with, but also goes well beyond, the scope of Articles 192 and 194 of the Convention. The scope of the Convention goes well beyond the obligation to protect and preserve the marine environment. The two treaties establish parallel environmental regimes that overlap in discrete areas. The same facts may give rise to violations of both treaties, but the violation of Articles 192 and 194 does not necessarily give rise to violations of CBD, such that Article 27 of the CBD may be invoked to settle disputes relating to interpretation and application of the Convention. The Tribunal agrees with the Philippines that a dispute under the Convention does not become a dispute under the CBD merely because there is some overlap between the two. Parallel regimes remain parallel regimes.

This conclusion is supported by the fact that Article 27 of the CBD does not expressly exclude dispute settlement under Section 2 of Part XV of the Convention. A clear exclusion of Part XV procedures is required in order for Article 281 to present an obstacle for the Tribunal's jurisdiction. Moreover, Article 22, paragraph 1 of the CBD, on the relationship between the CBD and other international conventions, preserves the rights and obligations of the Philippines and China under the Convention, including under Part XV, Section 2. Article 22(2) of the CBD recognizes the substantive overlap between the two parallel Conventions and requires that they be implemented consistently.

The dispute settlement provisions of the CBD cannot, by virtue of Article 281, preclude the Tribunal's jurisdiction over Philippine Submissions No. 11 and 12(b).

B. ARTICLE 282 (OBLIGATIONS UNDER GENERAL, REGIONAL OR BILATERAL AGREEMENTS)

Article 282 would only displace the dispute settlement provisions in Section 2 of Part XV if four requirements are met: (a) the Parties to the dispute must have agreed through "general, regional or bilateral agreements or otherwise" that, (b) at the request of any Party to the dispute, (c) the dispute shall be submitted to a procedure that entails a binding decision, and (d) the Parties have not otherwise agreed to retain access (i.e., to opt back in) to the procedures of Section 2, Part XV.

1. Application of Article 282 to the DOC and Other Bilateral Statements

(a) Possible Objections

China's Position Paper does not mention Article 282. In December 2014, the Tribunal requested that the Philippines elaborate on whether the DOC constitutes an agreement within the meaning of Article 282. In June 2015, the Tribunal asked the Philippines what the applicable standard was for determining whether an agreement provided for a procedure that entails a binding decision and whether the DOC, the TAC, or the CBD constituted such agreements.

(b) The Philippines' Position

The DOC does not fall within the meaning of Article 282. It is not an agreement but a political undertaking; it does not purport to create legally binding obligations. It does not provide for a procedure that entails binding decisions. The applicable standard is that the agreement must make express provision for a procedure that entails binding decisions. Such procedures can never be implied. There is no such procedure in the DOC, which indicates that when negotiations fail, a dispute should be settled in according with the Convention's binding procedures. There is nothing to imply a procedure that was intended to apply in lieu of Section 2 of Part XV.

The other bilateral statements are all political and aspirational in nature and are not legally binding. None even arguably reflects the intent to exclude recourse to compulsory procedures entailing binding decisions.

(c) The Tribunal's Decision

For the reasons expounded in connection with Article 281, the Tribunal does not consider the DOC to constitute a legally binding agreement. In any event, the DOC does not provide expressly for compulsory and binding procedures "in lieu of" Part XV. "Friendly consultations and negotiations" do not entail binding decisions. The DOC specifically contemplates recourse to the Convention.

None of the other joint statements constitute a binding agreement. None can be read as providing for compulsory procedures that entail binding decisions, let alone replacing the dispute settlement provisions in the Convention.

Neither the DOC nor the joint statements are legally binding; they have no impact on the Tribunal's jurisdiction.

2. Application of Article 282 to the Treaty of Amity

(a) Possible Objections

The Position Paper does not mention Article 282 and includes only a passing reference to the TAC. On its face, the TAC is an agreement between the Parties that refers to a compulsory and binding dispute settlement mechanism. In December 2014, the Tribunal requested further arguments from the Philippines on the effect of the TAC on jurisdiction and admissibility in reference to Article 282.

(b) The Philippines' Position

The TAC does not implicate Article 282, because none of its dispute settlement provisions establishes procedures that entail binding decisions. Failing negotiations, the High Council is at most empowered only to make recommendations concerning the appropriate means of settlement and/or to constitute itself as a committee of mediation, inquiry, or conciliation. Even those procedures must be specifically agreed on by all disputing parties. They cannot be initiated at the request of any party to the dispute and thus fall short of the requirements of Article 282.

(c) The Tribunal's Decision

The TAC is a binding agreement, but it does not meet the criteria specified in Article 282 for three reasons: [28]

(1) It does not contain an agreement for a dispute to be submitted "at the request of any party to the dispute." Articles 13–15 of the TAC shall not apply unless all parties agree;
(2) There is no agreement to binding dispute settlement. The mechanisms under Articles 13 to 15 do not entail binding decisions; and
(3) None of the TAC's provisions preclude the dispute settlement modes contained in Article 33(1) of the UN Charter, which include arbitration. It is not possible to imply an agreement to submit to compulsory dispute "in lieu of" the procedures provided for in Section 2 of Part XV.

3. Application of Article 282 to the CBD

(a) Possible Objections

China's Position Paper does not address the CBD or Philippine claims under Articles 192 and 194 of the Convention. It might be arguable that the Philippines and China, in ratifying the CBD, agreed to seek settlement of disputes involving Submissions No. 11 and 12(b) in accordance with Article 27 of the CBD. In June 2015, the Tribunal asked the Philippines whether the CBD constituted an agreement referring to compulsory and binding procedures within the meaning of Article 282.

---

[28] The following enumeration has been prepared by the author and does not appear in this form in the original text.

(b) The Philippines' Position

The Philippines does not allege separate breaches of the CBD. Therefore, the CBD procedures (Article 27) are entirely irrelevant. Submissions No. 11 and 12(a) concern the interpretation and application of the Convention, and not of the CBD. The Philippines refers to the CBD insofar as it informs the normative content of Articles192 and 194. Article 27 of the CBD is not an agreement for the settlement of disputes concerning the interpretation and application of the Convention. Even if it were such an agreement, it is not a compulsory procedure that entails binding decisions.

(c) The Tribunal's Decision

There is no doubt that the CBD is a legally binding agreement to which both the Philippines and China are parties. In order for the CBD to constitute a bar by virtue of Article 282, it must be shown that[29]

(1) Article 27 constitutes an agreement for the settlement of disputes relating to the interpretation and application of the Convention;
(2) there is agreement to submit the disputes to compulsory procedures, in the sense that the procedure is capable of being unilaterally initiated at the request of any party to the dispute; and
(3) the agreed compulsory procedure entails binding decisions.

The Tribunal finds that even if the first requirement were satisfied, the CBD does not meet the second and third criteria. Article 27 of the CBD requires the parties to seek solutions by negotiation and, failing negotiations, good offices or mediation. These procedures are not compulsory and do not entail binding decisions. Parties to the CBD may make a declaration accepting arbitration or the ICJ's jurisdiction for dispute settlement, but neither the Philippines nor China has made such a declaration. States that do not accept arbitration or the ICJ's jurisdiction for dispute settlement can only resort unilaterally to conciliation. This procedure is compulsory, but it does not entail a binding decision. The CBD's dispute settlement provisions cannot preclude jurisdiction over Submissions No. 11 and 12(b).

C. ARTICLE 283 (EXCHANGE OF VIEWS) AND OBLIGATION TO NEGOTIATE

Article 283 sets out an obligation on the Parties to exchange views concerning the settlement of the dispute by negotiation or other peaceful means prior to the commencement of arbitral proceedings.

1. China's Position

The two States have never engaged in negotiations regarding the subject matter of the dispute. General exchanges of views, without having the purpose of settling a given dispute, do not constitute negotiations. Their exchanges of views pertained to incidents at sea, conflict prevention, the reduction of frictions, the maintenance of peace and stability in the region, and the promotion of cooperation. These exchanges were far from constituting negotiations and did not concern the subject matter of the Philippines' claims. The Philippines could not have

[29] The following enumeration has been prepared by the author and does not appear in this form in the original text.

exchanged views with China regarding the interpretation and application of the Convention since it brought its own maritime claims in conformity with the Convention only in 2009.

2. The Philippines' Position

The Philippines addressed the application of Article 283 in its Memorial and during the hearing, but in different terms. In the Memorial, the Philippines argued that it had over many years had extensive exchanges of views with China regarding its claims. At the Hearing, the Philippines argued that Article 283 is not a requirement to negotiate as such. It is only an obligation to exchange views, and the obligation imposes a modest burden on disputing States. The Philippines had exchanged views with China on the means to settle the dispute and on the substance of the dispute. It is not necessary to exchange views on the substance of each and every submission. As long as there has been an exchange of views on the general subject matter of the dispute, broadly construed, Article 283 is satisfied. There is no need for the exchanges to touch on specific articles of the Convention. It is not even necessary that the Convention itself be mentioned.

3. The Tribunal's Decision

The Parties' positions reflect the uncertainty that has sometimes surrounded the meaning of Article 283. Diplomatic communications and exchanges do not divide neatly between procedural and substantive matters. States in the midst of pressing disputes will not separate their communications between the two. Correspondence elaborating views on substantive matters may shed a great deal of light on their respective views on how the dispute may or may not be settled. Proposals on the mode of settlement necessarily involve some discussion of substance. The Convention must be applied with this reality in mind.

The bilateral consultations between 1994 and 2012 included exchanges of views on the means of resolving the dispute between the Parties. The DOC itself and the discussions on the creation of a Code of Conduct represent an exchange of views on the means of settling the dispute.

The various disputes relating to the South China Sea are related. It may occur that parties will comprehensively exchange views on dispute settlement, only to have the dispute develop further, or related disputes arise, prior to the commencement of arbitration.

The Tribunal need not definitively determine the application of Article 283 to the situation, because the record indicates that the Philippines and China continued to exchange views on the means of settling their dispute until shortly before the Philippines initiated the arbitration.

The Parties having exchanged views, in particular in January 2012, and failing to reach an agreement on the approach for resolving the disputes, Article 283 has been satisfied. The extensive record of communications between the Parties establishes that China was aware of the issues over which they disagreed. China cannot have been taken by surprise when the Philippines decided to proceed with arbitration. The Parties explored whether any mutually agreeable mode of settlement could be identified and found none. It is well-established that thereafter, the Philippines was not obliged to continue exchanges of views when it considered that the possibilities of reaching agreement had been exhausted.

The Tribunal examines the question whether the Convention, independently of Article 283, imposes an obligation on State parties to engage in negotiations prior to resorting to compulsory settlement. In any event, neither in the UN Charter nor in international law is a rule to be found that exhaustion of diplomatic negotiations constitutes a precondition for a matter to be referred to international adjudication. Such an obligation may only arise as a result of a particular customary legal regime or a treaty applicable between the parties.

It is unnecessary to determine precisely the full scope of the obligation to seek solutions through recourse to Section 1 of Part XV or any obligation to negotiate arising from the nature of the Parties' rights, because the Tribunal is satisfied that the Philippines did seek to negotiate with China regarding the dispute. Its obligations, under both the Convention and customary law, have been satisfied. The Philippines held regular bilateral discussions with China, addressing a wide range of issues of concern to the two States, including the South China Sea. These meetings were termed consultations, rather than negotiations, but nomenclature is not dispositive.

The discussions between the Parties accomplished one of the principal goals of prior negotiations—to clarify the Parties' respective positions on the issues in dispute. Most importantly, these discussions were meaningful. Both the Philippines and China approached them in good faith and were genuinely interested in seeking an agreed solution. That more sustained negotiations did not occur and no agreement was reached do not reflect a lack of interest or commitment by either, but rather their mutually incompatible views as to how the talks should be conducted. For the Philippines, it was necessary to take a multilateral approach involving other littoral States. China was committed to addressing matters on a bilateral basis. The Parties' frequent discussions and exchanges left them well positioned to assess the likelihood of any mutually agreeable compromise.

A State party is not obliged to pursue procedures under section 1 of Part XV of the Convention when it concludes that the possibilities of settlement have been exhausted. Moreover, even the obligation to negotiate does not imply the obligation to reach an agreement. The States concerned are in the best position to judge as to the political reasons which may prevent the settlement of a dispute by negotiation.

The Parties' many discussions and consultations did not address all of the matters in dispute with the same level of specificity that is now reflected in the Philippine Submissions. This is to be expected and constitutes no bar to the Philippine claims. Even an express obligation to negotiate requires only that the subject matter of the negotiations must relate to the subject matter of the dispute. The Convention does not require the Parties to a dispute to set out the specifics of their legal claims in advance of dispute settlement.

Neither Article 283 nor the obligation to seek solutions through pacific means, including negotiations, poses any bar to the Tribunal's consideration of the Philippine Submissions. None of the provisions in Section 1 of Part XV pose any bar to the Philippine Submissions.

VIII. LIMITATIONS AND EXCEPTIONS TO THE TRIBUNAL'S JURISDICTION[30]

Section 3 of Part XV sets out certain limitations and exceptions to jurisdiction.[31]

1. Article 297 (Limitations on applicability of section 2) sets out limitations that apply automatically to any dispute between States parties to the Convention.
2. Article 298 (Optional exceptions to applicability of section 2) sets out further optional exceptions that a State may activate by declaration.
3. Article 299 (Right of the parties to agree upon a procedure) confirms that in the event a limitation or exception is applicable, a dispute excluded under Article 297 or excepted by a declaration under Article 298 may be submitted to compulsory dispute settlement procedures only by agreement.

30 Award on Jurisdiction and Admissibility, pp. 125–47, paras. 354–412, supra note 2

31 The following enumeration has been prepared by the author and does not appear in this form in the original text.

A. ARTICLE 297 AND AUTOMATIC LIMITATIONS TO THE TRIBUNAL'S JURISDICTION

1. Possible Objections

China's Position Paper did not raise objections on the basis of specific automatic limitations. China has accepted Section 2 of Part XV, but this acceptance does not mean that these procedures apply to disputes already excluded by Article 297. China has never accepted any of the compulsory procedures of Section 2 of Part XV.

The Tribunal has already held that the Convention does not permit a State party to exempt itself generally from the dispute settlement provisions of Part XV. No consequences for the Tribunal's jurisdiction follow from China's decision not to participate in the proceedings.

It is imperative to examine *proprio motu* and in the light of China's general remarks on Article 297 whether limitations to the Tribunal's jurisdiction follow from Article 297. Two issues could potentially impact the Tribunal's jurisdiction. First, Article 297 could be understood as implicitly limiting jurisdiction over disputes concerning sovereign rights and jurisdiction in the EEZ only to the cases specifically identified in Article 297. Second, Article 297(3) could bar the Tribunal's jurisdiction over the Philippines' claim in relation to fisheries, to the extent that the events complained of took place in China's EEZ or in an area of overlapping entitlements.

In December 2014, the Tribunal requested further written arguments from the Philippines on the following issues:

a. the relationship between Article 288, Article 297, and the Tribunal's jurisdiction;
b. the application of Article 297(1)(c) to Philippine claims regarding the preservation of the marine environment; and
c. the application of Article 297(3) to Philippine claims concerning fisheries.

2. The Philippines' Position

The Philippines' interpretation of the first portion of Article 297 has evolved in the course of the proceedings. In the Memorial, the Philippines argued that Article 297(1) excluded from jurisdiction disputes concerning the coastal State's exercise of sovereign rights and jurisdiction, except those listed in Article 297(1)(a) to (c). During the Hearing, the Philippines endorsed the conclusion of a 2015 arbitral award, *The Chagos Marine Protected Area*, which ruled that Article 297(1) confirms and expands jurisdiction over environmental disputes but does not limit it.

The Tribunal has jurisdiction over the dispute concerning the preservation of the marine environment at Scarborough Shoal because the relevant waters constitute the territorial sea, to which Article 297 does not apply. The Tribunal also has jurisdiction over the dispute in and around Second Thomas Shoal because Article 297 applies only to the exercise of sovereign rights and jurisdiction by the coastal State. Because only the Philippines is the coastal State with an entitlement to an EEZ in the area of Second Thomas Shoal, issues regarding Chinese activities cannot involve the exercise of China's sovereign rights and jurisdiction; Article 297 cannot apply. In any event, following *Chagos*, Article 297, paragraph 1 supports the Philippine case on jurisdiction over environmental disputes within the territorial sea and on the continental shelf, even if China were the relevant coastal State.

Nothing in Article 297(3) impairs the Tribunal's jurisdiction to address Submissions No. 8, 9, and 10. Article 297(3) would only limit the Tribunal's jurisdiction if the relevant areas were part of China's EEZ. As the Philippines has demonstrated that none of the insular features claimed by China in the Southern sector of the South China Sea generates an entitlement to an EEZ or continental shelf, Article 297, paragraph 3 can have no application.

Article 297(3) is also inapplicable to traditional fishing activities at Scarborough Shoal because such fishing only ever occurs within the 12-nautical-mile territorial sea surrounding the Shoal.

B. ARTICLE 298 AND OPTIONAL EXCEPTIONS TO THE TRIBUNAL'S JURISDICTION

1. China's Position and Possible Further Objections

China's Position Paper recalls China's 2006 Declaration under Article 298 and argues that the issues presented by the Philippines are fully excluded from compulsory dispute settlement because they constitute an integral part of maritime delimitation. If the Philippines and China disagree whether the dispute is covered by China's 2006 Declaration, the Philippines must first take up the issue with China. The Tribunal has already rejected this characterization of the dispute.

The Position Paper does not raise any further objections on Article 298, although the latter contains a number of other exceptions to jurisdiction. It is imperative to examine *proprio motu* whether any further exception to jurisdiction follows from Article 298.

Although the Tribunal does not agree with China's characterization of the dispute, Article 298's exclusion over disputes relating to sea boundary delimitation may nevertheless constrain the Tribunal's jurisdiction. [32]

a. Jurisdiction over some Philippine Submissions could be barred if a maritime feature claimed by China in the South China Sea were found to be an island within the meaning of Article 121, entitled to an EEZ or continental shelf overlapping those generated by the Philippine archipelago.[33]

The resolution of the merits of certain Philippine claims would not be possible without first delimiting overlapping entitlements, a step that would be outside the scope of the Tribunal's jurisdiction. The question of delimiting overlapping entitlements would not arise if the Tribunal were to find at the merits phase that none of the maritime features claimed are islands that generate their own EEZ or continental shelf.

b. Article 298 excludes disputes "involving historic bays or titles" which could bear on the Philippine Submissions concerning China's claims to historic rights, if such rights were found to be permitted by the Convention and within the scope of the exclusion.

c. Article 298 excludes disputes concerning "military activities" as well as "law enforcement activities" related to marine scientific research or fisheries. This could be a bar to the Tribunal's jurisdiction over the disputes relating to Chinese fisheries enforcement measures, land reclamation and construction at Mischief

[32] The following enumeration has been prepared by the author and does not appear in this form in the original text.

[33] The following enumeration has been prepared by the author and does not appear in this form in the original text.

Reef, the operation of Chinese law enforcement vessels, and the standoff between the Philippines and China at Second Thomas Shoal.

In December 2014, the Tribunal requested that the Philippines elaborate on the following issues:

a. the scope of the exceptions for disputes relating to maritime boundary delimitation and the relationship between Philippine Submissions and maritime delimitation;
b. the relationship between the reference in Article 298 to "historic bays or titles" and any claim by China to historic rights;
c. whether Chinese activities addressed in Submissions No. 8 to 14 constitute "military activities" within the scope of Article 298(1)(b); and
d. whether Chinese activities addressed in Submissions No. 8 to 14 constitute "law enforcement activities" within the scope of Article 298(1)(b).

In connection with the Philippine argument that none of the features in the Spratly Islands is capable of generating an entitlement to an EEZ or a continental shelf, the Tribunal requested that the Philippines provide additional maps, charts, tidal data, satellite images, photographs, and historical, anthropological, geographic, and hydrographic information concerning certain features in the Spratly Islands.

2. The Philippines' Position[34]

a. The Philippines rejects the contention that the disputes constitute an integral part of maritime boundary delimitation. Article 298(1)(1) refers not simply to maritime boundary disputes, but specifically to "disputes concerning the interpretation or application of articles 15, 74, and 83 relating to sea boundary delimitation."

Article 298 has no effect unless the Tribunal is called on to interpret or apply one of the three articles that relate to the actual delimitation of the territorial sea, the EEZ, and the continental shelf.

Article 298 does not exclude the jurisdiction of the Tribunal because questions of maritime delimitation arise only in the context of overlapping entitlements of coastal States. The Philippines has demonstrated that none of the insular features claimed by China in the Southern sector of the South China Sea generates an entitlement to an EEZ or continental shelf. Thus, the waters, seabed, and subsoil within 200 nautical miles of the Philippines, but beyond 12 nautical miles from any high-tide feature, constitute the EEZ and the continental shelf of the Philippines. No situation of overlapping entitlements potentially requiring maritime delimitation occurs in the areas in which the events addressed in the Philippine Submissions took place.

b. Article 298 does not apply because China is not claiming historic titles in the South China Sea.

[34] The following enumeration has been prepared by the author and does not appear in this form in the original text.

The Philippines examined the term for "historic title" in the Chinese text of the Convention and the references to historic rights in China's Exclusive Economic Zone and Continental Shelf Act (1998). It is clear that China claimed "historical rights" as distinguished from "historic title." In any event, the concept of historic title as used in Article 298 has a specific and limited meaning. It pertains only to near-shore areas of the sea that are susceptible to a claim of sovereignty as such. Furthermore, Article 298 was crafted with the delimitation of the Gulf of Fonseca, a historic bay, in mind, and applies only to disputes over the delimitation of historic bays and titles.

Article 298 applies only to disputes over the delimitation of historic bays or titles. No such dispute over delimitation is implicated by Philippine submissions.

c. None of the activities undertaken by Chinese government vessels of which the Philippines complains are properly considered "military activities."

The nature and purpose of the activity determine whether it is to be categorized as "military" or "law enforcement," not the identity of the actor. Absent evidence to the contrary, it can ordinarily be assumed that non-military vessels and aircraft are not engaged in military activities.

China's unlawful activities in the Philippine EEZ, its interference with Philippine exercise of its sovereign rights to exploit the living and non-living resources of the continental shelf, and the interdiction of Philippine vessels at Scarborough Shoal were carried out by law enforcement vessels (China Marine Surveillance, CMS; Fisheries and Law Enforcement Command, FLEC; and/or China Coast Guard, CCG).

Evidence that Mischief Reef is now occupied by Chinese military personnel is not relevant to the question of jurisdiction over China's conduct at the time of its initial occupation and construction activities. At the time, China repeatedly asserted that its activities were for civilian purposes. Even since the expansion of Chinese reclamation activities, China declares that the main purpose of its construction activities is to meet "various civilian demands."

Finally, only certain types of law enforcement activities may be excluded by China's 2006 Declaration. The activities must be related to jurisdictional limitations for marine scientific research and fisheries set out in Article 297. The Philippines makes no claims regarding China's exercise of its rights to regulate marine scientific research or the exercise of sovereign rights with respect to living resources in China's EEZ. Philippine claims only concern areas where China has no entitlement to an EEZ or continental shelf and where neither Article 297 nor Article 298(1)(b) can apply. The law enforcement exception is therefore inapplicable.

C. THE APPLICATION OF ARTICLES 297 AND 298 AND THE TRIBUNAL'S FINDINGS ON THE SCOPE OF ITS JURISDICTION

As an initial step, it is necessary to address the question whether possible issues of jurisdiction are even capable of being decided at this phase of the arbitration or whether they are so interwoven with the merits that they should properly be deferred for decision at a later stage (Rules of Procedure, Article 20(3); Procedural Order No. 4).

1. Whether Issues of Jurisdiction Possess an "Exclusively Preliminary Character"

(a) The Applicable Legal Standard

The "exclusively preliminary character" test is modelled on Article 79(9) of the ICJ's Rules of Court, under which the ICJ may issue a judgment declaring that a preliminary objection does not possess an exclusively preliminary character. In the ICJ's jurisprudence, such a decision will depend on two types of enquiry: (1) whether the Court has had the opportunity to examine all the necessary facts to dispose of the preliminary objection and (2) whether a preliminary objection would entail prejudging a dispute or some of its elements on the merits. Similar tests have been applied in the context of arbitrations.

(b) The Parties' Positions on the Link between Jurisdiction and the Merits

China's Position Paper did not express any views on the timing of the Tribunal's consideration of its jurisdiction, expressly limiting its arguments to issues of jurisdiction and excluding any consideration of the merits of the dispute.

The Philippine position has evolved in the course of the proceedings. Initially, the Philippines opposed any preliminary consideration of matters of jurisdiction. In its view, the jurisdictional issues were interwoven with the merits and did not possess an exclusively preliminary character, making bifurcation inappropriate. At the Hearing, the Philippines argued that there was no need to defer any question of jurisdiction for further consideration with the merits. Notwithstanding some inconsistency, the Tribunal understands the latter to be the Philippine position.

(c) The Tribunal's Decision

The basic principle governing the handling of disputes before international tribunals is that a State should not have to give an account of itself on issues of merits before a Tribunal which lacks jurisdiction in the matter or whose jurisdiction has not been established.

China's objections to jurisdiction set out in the Position Paper concerning the characterization of the dispute and Philippine compliance with Section 1 of Part XV are exclusively preliminary in nature.

It is incumbent on the Tribunal to address any issues of jurisdiction not raised by China and to satisfy itself as to whether it has jurisdiction over the dispute in this preliminary phase to the greatest extent possible. The remaining issues, particularly the limitations and exceptions in Article 297 and 298, are in significant respects interwoven with the merits, for the following reasons.[35]

1) The Tribunal's jurisdiction over Submissions No. 1 and 2 may depend on the nature and validity of any claim by China to historic rights in the South China.

The nature of these rights may determine whether the dispute is covered by the exclusion from jurisdiction of "historic bays or titles" in Article 298 and whether a situation of overlapping entitlements to maritime zones exists in areas in which certain Chinese activities are alleged to have occurred. The possible existence of any overlapping entitlements would in turn potentially impact the application of other imitations and exceptions in Articles 297 and 298. The Philippine request that the Tribunal determine the nature and validity of any Chinese historic rights (Submission No. 2) is a merits determination that the Tribunal cannot make at this stage.

[35] The following enumeration has been prepared by the author and does not appear in this form in the original text.

2) The Tribunal's jurisdiction to decide on the merits of Submissions No. 5, 8, and 9 may depend on the status of maritime features in the South China Sea.

If any maritime feature in the Spratly Islands constitutes an island within the meaning of Article 121, generating an entitlement to an EEZ and a continental shelf, it may be the case that the Philippines and China possess overlapping entitlements to maritime zones. The Tribunal may not be able to reach a decision on the merits without first delimiting their overlapping entitlements, a step that it cannot take in the light of Article 298 and China's 2006 Declaration. The Philippine request that the Tribunal determine the status of a number of maritime features is a merits determination that the Tribunal cannot make at this stage.

3) The Tribunal's jurisdiction to decide on the merits of Submissions No. 8, 9, 10, and 13 may depend on the maritime area in which the alleged Chinese law enforcement activities took place.

The exclusion from jurisdiction in Article 298 may apply to the extent that the activities took place within China's EEZ or in areas in which the Parties possess overlapping entitlements to an EEZ. Whether any maritime feature claimed by China generates entitlements to an EEZ or continental shelf and whether any situation of overlapping entitlements exists as a result is a merits determination that the Tribunal cannot make at this stage.

4) The Tribunal's jurisdiction to decide on the merits of Submissions No. 12 and 14 may depend upon whether certain Chinese activities are military.

If they are, the exclusion from jurisdiction in Article 298 may bar the Tribunal's jurisdiction. The nature of such activities is a merits determination that the Tribunal cannot make at this stage.

2. The Tribunal's Conclusions on its Jurisdiction

Submissions No. 1 and 2 reflect a dispute concerning the source of maritime entitlements in the South China Sea and the Convention's role. This is not a dispute concerning sovereignty or maritime boundary delimitation, nor is it barred from the Tribunal's consideration by any requirement of Section 1 of Part XV. It requires the Tribunal to consider the effect of any historic rights claimed by China to maritime entitlements in the South China Sea and the interaction of such rights with the Convention. The Tribunal's jurisdiction to consider the question would be dependent upon the nature of any such rights and whether they are covered by the exclusion from jurisdiction over "historic bays and titles" in Article 298. The nature and validity of any historic rights is a merits determination. The possible jurisdictional objections with respect to the dispute therefore do not possess an exclusively preliminary character. The Tribunal reserves a decision on its jurisdiction with respect to Submissions No. 1 and 2 for consideration in conjunction with the merits of the Philippine claims.

Submission No. 3 reflects a dispute regarding the status of Scarborough Shoal as an island or a rock within the meaning of Article 121. This is not a dispute concerning sovereignty and is not barred from the Tribunal's consideration by any requirement of Section 1 of Part XV. Nor is this a dispute concerning maritime boundary delimitation. Given that Scarborough Shoal lies over 200 nautical miles from any maritime feature claimed by any State to generate an EEZ or a continental shelf, no delimitation is required before the Tribunal may determine its status. Exceptions or limitations to jurisdiction in Article 297 or 298 are not applicable. The Tribunal concludes that it has jurisdiction to address the matters raised in Submission No. 3.

Submission No. 4 reflects a dispute concerning the status of Mischief Reef, Second Thomas Shoal, and Subi Reef as low-tide elevations within the meaning of Article 13. This is not a dispute concerning sovereignty and is not barred from the Tribunal's consideration by any requirement of Section 1 of Part XV. Nor is this a dispute concerning maritime boundary delimitation. The Tribunal concludes that it has jurisdiction to address the matters raised in Submission No. 4.

Submission No. 5 reflects a dispute concerning the sources of maritime entitlements in the South China Sea and whether a situation of overlapping entitlements to an EEZ or to a continental shelf exists in the area of Mischief Reef and Second Thomas Shoal. This is not a dispute concerning sovereignty and is not barred from the Tribunal's consideration by any requirement of Section 1 of Part XV. Nor is this a dispute concerning maritime boundary delimitation, as the Philippines' premise is that no overlapping entitlements can exist. If, however, another maritime feature claimed by China within 200 nautical miles of Mischief Reef or Second Thomas Shoal were to be an "island" for the purposes of Article 121, capable of generating an entitlement to an EEZ and continental shelf, the resulting overlap and the exclusion of boundary delimitation from the Tribunal's jurisdiction by Article 298 would prevent the Tribunal from addressing this Submission. Whether this is the case depends upon a merits determination on the status of maritime features in the South China Sea. The possible jurisdictional objections with respect to the dispute underlying Submission No.5 do not possess an exclusively preliminary character. The Tribunal reserves a decision on its jurisdiction with respect to Submission No. 5 for consideration in conjunction with the merits of the Philippines' claims.

Submission No. 6 reflects a dispute concerning the status of Gaven Reef and McKennan Reef (including Hughes Reef) as "low-tide elevations" within the meaning of Article 13 of the Convention. This is not a dispute concerning sovereignty and is not barred from the Tribunal's consideration by any requirement of Section 1 of Part XV. Nor is this a dispute concerning maritime boundary delimitation. If, however, China has entitlement to EEZ or to a continental shelf overlapping that of the Philippines in the area of Gaven Reef or McKennan Reef (including Hughes Reef), the existence of overlapping entitlements may have practical considerations for the selection of the vertical datum[36] and tidal model against which the status of the features is to be assessed. This may be particularly true if the Parties' respective data and models indicate differing results. Subject to a caveat with respect to the possible effects of any overlapping entitlements, the Tribunal concludes that it has jurisdiction to address the matters raised in the Philippines' Submission No. 6.

Submission No. 7 reflects a dispute concerning the status of Johnson Reef, Cuarteron Reef, and Fiery Cross Reef as "islands" or "rocks" within the meaning of Article 121 of the Convention. This is not a dispute concerning sovereignty and is not barred from the Tribunal's consideration by any requirement of Section 1 of Part XV. Nor is this a dispute concerning maritime boundary delimitation. Exceptions or limitations to jurisdiction in Article 297 or 298 are not applicable. The Tribunal concludes that it has jurisdiction to address the matters raised in Submission No. 7.

---

36 A vertical datum is the zero surface to which elevations or heights are referred. National Geospatial- Intelligence Agency, *Vertical Datums, Elevations and Heights* (Springfield, VA: NGA, 2011), http://earth-info.nga.mil/GandG/publications/vertdatum.html, accessed 4 September 2016.

Submission No. 8 reflects a dispute concerning China's actions that allegedly interfere with the Philippines' petroleum exploration, seismic surveys, and fishing in what the Philippines claims as its EEZ. This is not a dispute concerning sovereignty and is not barred from the Tribunal's consideration by any requirement of Section 1 of Part XV. Nor is this a dispute concerning maritime boundary delimitation. The premise is that no overlapping entitlements exist because only the Philippines possesses an entitlement to an EEZ in the relevant areas. If, however, another maritime feature claimed by China within 200 nautical miles of these areas were to be an "island" for the purposes of Article 121, capable of generating an entitlement to an EEZ and continental shelf, the resulting overlap and the exclusion of boundary delimitation from the Tribunal's jurisdiction by Article 298 would prevent the Tribunal from addressing this Submission. Whether this is the case depends upon a merits determination on the status of maritime features in the South China Sea. The possible jurisdictional objections with respect to Submission No. 8 therefore do not possess an exclusively preliminary character. The Tribunal reserves a decision on its jurisdiction with respect to Submission No. 8 for consideration in conjunction with the merits of the Philippines' claims.

Submission No. 9 reflects a dispute concerning Chinese fishing activities in what the Philippines claims as its EEZ. This is not a dispute concerning sovereignty or maritime boundary delimitation, nor is it barred from the Tribunal's consideration by any requirement of Section 1 of Part XV. Articles 297 and 298, however, would restrict the Tribunal's jurisdiction over fishing and fisheries-related law enforcement in the event that the relevant areas formed part of China's EEZ. The Philippine premise is that no overlapping entitlements exist because only the Philippines possesses an entitlement to an EEZ in the relevant areas. If, however, another maritime feature claimed by China within 200 nautical miles of these areas were to be an "island" for the purposes of Article 121, capable of generating an entitlement to an EEZ and continental shelf, the resulting overlap and the exclusion of boundary delimitation from the Tribunal's jurisdiction by Article 298 would prevent the Tribunal from addressing this Submission. Whether this is the case depends upon a merits determination on the status of maritime features in the South China Sea. The possible jurisdictional objections with respect to Submission No. 9 therefore do not possess an exclusively preliminary character. The Tribunal reserves a decision on its jurisdiction with respect to Submission No. 9 for consideration in conjunction with the merits of the Philippines' claims

Submission No. 10 reflects a dispute concerning China's actions that allegedly interfere with the traditional fishing activities of Philippine nationals at Scarborough Shoal. This is not a dispute concerning sovereignty or maritime boundary delimitation, nor is it barred from the Tribunal's consideration by any requirement of Section 1 of Part XV. The Philippines has clarified that these activities occur within the 12-nautical-mile territorial sea that would be generated by Scarborough Shoal, whether the latter is considered a rock or an island pursuant to Article 121. The Tribunal notes that traditional fishing rights may exist even within the territorial waters of another State. The Tribunal concludes that it has jurisdiction to address the matters raised in the Philippines' Submission No. 10.

Submission No. 11 reflects a dispute concerning the protection and preservation of the marine environment at Scarborough Shoal and Second Thomas Shoal and the application of Articles 192 and 194 of the Convention. This is not a dispute concerning sovereignty or maritime boundary delimitation, nor is it barred from the Tribunal's consideration by any requirement of Section 1 of Part XV. Depending on the Tribunal's ultimate decision on the status of these features, the basis for its jurisdiction may differ:

(a) To the extent that the alleged harmful activities took place in the territorial sea surrounding Scarborough Shoal, or in any territorial sea generated by Second Thomas Shoal, the environmental provisions of the Convention impose obligations on States Parties including in the territorial sea. The Tribunal's jurisdiction is thus not dependent on a prior determination of the status of Second Thomas Shoal or of sovereignty over either feature, and Articles 297 and 298 of the Convention have no application in the territorial sea.

(b) To the extent that the alleged harmful activities took place in the EEZ of the Philippines, of China, or in an area of overlapping entitlements, Article 297(1)(c) expressly affirms the Tribunal's jurisdiction over disputes concerning the alleged violation of "specified international rules and standards for the protection and preservation of the marine environment" in the EEZ. Under neither circumstance, however, is jurisdiction precluded. The Tribunal's jurisdiction is thus not dependent on a prior determination of the status of any maritime feature, on the existence of an entitlement by China to an EEZ in the area, or on the prior delimitation of any overlapping entitlements. The Tribunal concludes that it has jurisdiction to address the matters raised in Submission No. 11.

Submission No. 12 reflects a dispute concerning China's activities on Mischief Reef and their effects on the marine environment. This is not a dispute concerning sovereignty or maritime boundary delimitation, nor is it barred from the Tribunal's consideration by any requirement of Section 1 of Part XV. However, the Tribunal's jurisdiction to address these questions is dependent on the status of Mischief Reef as an "island," "rock," or "low-tide elevation." If the Tribunal were to find—contrary to the Submission's premise—that Mischief Reef is an "island" or "rock" and thus constitutes land territory, the Tribunal would lack jurisdiction to consider the lawfulness of China's construction activities or the appropriation of the feature. The status of Mischief Reef is a matter for the merits. Additionally, Article 298 excludes disputes concerning military activities from the Tribunal's jurisdiction. The specifics of China's activities on Mischief Reef and whether such activities are military in nature are matters best assessed in conjunction with the merits. The possible jurisdictional objections with respect to Submission No. 12 therefore do not possess an exclusively preliminary character. The Tribunal reserves a decision on its jurisdiction with respect to Submission No. 12 for consideration in conjunction with the merits of the Philippines' claims.

Submission No. 13 reflects a dispute concerning the operation of China's law enforcement activities in the vicinity of Scarborough Shoal and the application of Articles 21, 24, and 94 of the Convention. This is not a dispute concerning sovereignty or maritime boundary delimitation, nor is it barred from the Tribunal's consideration by any requirement of Section 1 of Part XV. This dispute relates principally to events occurring in the territorial sea surrounding Scarborough Shoal. Article 298(1)(b) has no application in the territorial sea. The Convention imposes duties on both the coastal State and on vessels engaged in innocent passage. The Tribunal's jurisdiction is thus not dependent on a prior determination of sovereignty over Scarborough Shoal. The Tribunal concludes that it has jurisdiction to address the matters raised in Submission No. 13.

Submission No. 14 reflects a dispute concerning China's activities in and around Second Thomas Shoal and China's interaction with the Philippine military forces stationed on the Shoal. This is not a dispute concerning sovereignty or maritime boundary delimitation, nor is it barred from the Tribunal's consideration by any requirement of Section 1 of Part XV. However, the Tribunal's jurisdiction to address these questions may depend on the status of Second Thomas Shoal as an "island," "rock," or "low-tide elevation," which is a matter for the merits. Additionally, Article 298 excludes disputes concerning military activities from the Tribunal's jurisdiction. The specifics of China's activities in and around Second Thomas Shoal and whether such activities are military in nature are matters best assessed in conjunction with the merits. The possible jurisdictional objections with respect to Submission No.14 therefore do not possess an exclusively preliminary character. The Tribunal reserves a decision on its jurisdiction with respect to Submission No. 14 for consideration in conjunction with the merits of the Philippines' claims.

The claims and activities to which Submission No. 15 could potentially relate are unclear from the Philippines pleadings. The Tribunal is presently unable to determine whether there exists a dispute between the Parties concerning the interpretation or application of the Convention or to assess the scope of the Tribunal's jurisdiction in this respect. The Tribunal directs the Philippines to clarify the content and narrow the scope of its Submission No. 15. The Tribunal reserves the question of its jurisdiction in relation to Submission No. 15 for consideration in conjunction with the merits of the Philippines' claims.

IX. DECISION[37]

413. For the above reasons, the Tribunal unanimously

A. FINDS that the Tribunal was properly constituted in accordance with Annex VII to the Convention.

B. FINDS that China's non-appearance in these proceedings does not deprive the Tribunal of jurisdiction.

C. FINDS that the Philippines' act of initiating this arbitration did not constitute an abuse of process.

D. FINDS that there is no indispensable third party whose absence deprives the Tribunal of jurisdiction.

E. FINDS that the 2002 China–ASEAN Declaration on Conduct of the Parties in the South China Sea, the joint statements of the Parties referred to in paragraphs 231 to 232 of this Award, the Treaty of Amity and Cooperation in Southeast Asia, and the Convention on Biological Diversity do not preclude, under Articles 281 or 282 of the Convention, recourse to the compulsory dispute settlement procedures available under Section 2 of Part XV of the Convention.

F. FINDS that the Parties have exchanged views as required by Article 283 of the Convention.

37 Award on Jurisdiction and Admissibility, p. 149, para. 413 supra note 2. This Chapter reproduces Chapter IX of the Award.

G. FINDS that the Tribunal has jurisdiction to consider the Philippines' Submissions No. 3, 4, 6, 7, 10, 11, and 13, subject to the conditions noted in paragraphs 400, 401, 403, 404, 407, 408, and 410 of this Award.

H. FINDS that a determination of whether the Tribunal has jurisdiction to consider the Philippines' Submissions No. 1, 2, 5, 8, 9, 12, and 14 would involve consideration of issues that do not possess an exclusively preliminary character, and accordingly RESERVES consideration of its jurisdiction to rule on Submissions No. 1, 2, 5, 8, 9, 12, and 14 to the merits phase.

I. DIRECTS the Philippines to clarify the content and narrow the scope of its Submission 15 and RESERVES consideration of its jurisdiction over Submission No. 15 to the merits phase.

J. RESERVES for further consideration and directions all issues not decided in this Award.

2

Victory in Round 1, but Not Really a Knockout[1]

The Award on Jurisdiction and Admissibility issued on 29 October 2015 by the Arbitral Tribunal[2] created the impression that this was a knockout (as a reporter for the *Philippine Daily Inquirer* put it)[3] for the Philippines. The triumphalist attitude of the Solicitor General, who erroneously declared that China's preliminary objections had been eliminated,[4] was undoubtedly exhibited for the benefit of public opinion, and it could be justified by the Tribunal's unanimous adoption and China's rejection of the Award.[5]

The Award was certainly a triumph for the Philippines, in that China's preliminary objections to the jurisdiction of the Tribunal, which were intended to terminate the proceedings, failed to prevent the Tribunal from proceeding to the next phase, the merits phase. In the latter, the Tribunal, having decided that it has jurisdiction on 6 of the 15 Submissions, would hear the arguments on the substantive issues over Submissions No. 3 (Scarborough Shoal generates no entitlement to an Exclusive Economic Zone, EEZ, or continental shelf), No. 4 (Mischief Reef, Second Thomas Shoal, and Subi Reef are low-tide elevations that do not generate entitlement to a territorial sea, EEZ, or continental shelf), No. 6 (Gaven Reef and McKennan Reef, including Hughes Reef, are low-tide elevations that do not generate entitlement to a territorial sea, EEZ, or continental shelf), No. 7 (Johnson Reef, Cuarteron Reef, and Fiery Cross Reef generate no entitlement to an EEZ or continental shelf), No. 10 (China has prevented Filipino fishermen from fishing at Scarborough Shoal), and No. 13 (China operates law enforcement vessels in a dangerous manner causing risk of collision to Philippine vessels in the vicinity of Scarborough Shoal).

---

1 An earlier version of this Chapter was posted on 4 November 2015 on the blog of the author's sister-in-law, https://www.raissarobles.com/2015/11/04/victory-in-round-1-on-the-south-china-sea-arbitration-but-not-really-a-knockout/.

2 Award on Jurisdiction and Admissibility, 29 October 2015, http://www.pcacases.com/web/sendAttach/1506, accessed 30 October 2015.

3 Matikas Santos, "Key Points of the Arbitral Tribunal's First Ruling in Philippines vs China Case," *Philippine Daily Inquirer (PDI)*, 31 October 2015, http://globalnation.inquirer.net/130215/south-china-sea-arbitration-philippines-china-spratly-islands-west-philippine-sea, accessed 31 October 2015.

4 "'The elimination of preliminary objections to the exercise of the tribunal's jurisdiction opens the way for the presentation of the merits of the Philippines' substantive claims,' Hilbay said in a statement sent via text Friday morning." Tarra Quismundo, "PH Hails Hague Court Ruling to Take Up Arbitration Case vs China," PDI, 30 October 2015, http://globalnation.inquirer.net/130174/ph-hails-hague-court-ruling-to-take-up-arbitration-case-vs-china, accessed 30 October 2015.

5 Matikas Santos, "UN Tribunal Ruling 'Null, Void, Nonbinding'—China," *PDI*, 30 October 2015, http://globalnation.inquirer.net/130235/un-tribunal-ruling-null-and-void-china, accessed 30 October 2015.

Nevertheless, the Award on Jurisdiction and Admissibility did not represent a total victory for the Philippines. In the first place, the Philippines, as the Award made very clear, had opposed the bifurcation—the separation into two phases (jurisdiction/admissibility and merits)—of the proceedings and wished to argue jurisdiction and merits at the same time, in part to save money, as the Solicitor General admitted in April 2014.[6] The holding of the hearings on jurisdiction and admissibility was not part of the Philippine strategy. More importantly, if we read the text of the Award, or even just the summary,[7] we realize that the Tribunal did not decide that it had jurisdiction on 8 of the 15 Submissions by the Philippines, including the Submission on the nine-dash line. Rather, it asked the Philippines to clarify the content and narrow the scope of Submission No. 15 (China shall desist from further unlawful claims and activities) and decided that the preliminary objections to Submissions No. 1, 2, 5, 8, 9, 12, and 14 did not possess an exclusively preliminary character. Consequently, it postponed consideration of jurisdiction to rule on these submissions to the merits phase. This meant that in the merits phase, the Tribunal could still decide that it had no jurisdiction to rule over these submissions and could have ended up not ruling on them after all.

To understand the situation, we have to clarify the nature of preliminary objections. Settlement of international disputes by international courts is based on consent given by States parties to the dispute. A State may give its consent to have certain classes of disputes with other States submitted to an international tribunal before the emergence of a concrete dispute, but when a dispute is actually submitted by a specific State to a tribunal, the first State may nevertheless argue that it has not given its consent for that particular type of dispute with the second State. The first State will then challenge the jurisdiction—the power to hear and decide the case—of the tribunal by filing preliminary objections. The practice of international tribunals, notably the International Court of Justice (ICJ), is to suspend the proceedings on the merits in order to rule on the preliminary objections.

There are three possible outcomes at this stage. The tribunal may decide to uphold the preliminary objections, in which case the proceedings are terminated. It may decide to reject them, in which case it will hear the merits. Finally, the tribunal may decide that the objection to its jurisdiction does not possess an exclusively preliminary character. This third possibility arises when the questions raised by the objections and those arising on the merits are too intimately related and too closely interconnected for a court to be able to rule on the former without prejudging the latter. On the third and last day of the July 2015 hearings, the lawyers for the Philippines explicitly declared that there were no issues of jurisdiction or admissibility that had to be deferred to the merits phase.

The reason for this is understandable if one refers to the *Nicaragua v. US* case *(Military and Paramilitary Activities in and against Nicaragua*, 1984–91), submitted unilaterally by Nicaragua to the ICJ. The Court postponed for consideration in the merits phase a US preliminary objection.[8] During the merits phase, it upheld the preliminary objection.[9] However, the Court

6 Paterno Esmaquel II, "PH Faces Major Hurdle in China Case," *Rappler.com*, 12 March 2014, http://www.rappler.com/nation/52764-philippines-china-arbitral-tribunal-jurisdiction, accessed 26 July 2015.

7 *Arbitration Between the Republic of the Philippines and the People's Republic of China. The Tribunal Renders Award on Jurisdiction and Admissibility; Will Hold Further Hearings*, Seventh Press Release, 29 October 2015, http://www.pcacases.com/web/sendAttach/1503, accessed 30 October 2015.

8 *Military and Paramilitary Activities in and Against Nicaragua (Nicaragua v. United States of America), Jurisdiction and Admissibility, Judgment, I.C.J. Reports 1984*, pp. 424–26, paras. 72–76, http://www.icj-cij.org/files/case-related/70/070-19841126-JUD-01-00-BI.pdf, accessed 16 March 2018.

9 *Military and Paramilitary Activities in and Against Nicaragua (Nicaragua v. United States of America), Merits, Judgment, I.C.J. Reports 1986*, pp. 31–38, paras. 42–56, http://www.icj-cij.org/files/case-related/70/070-19860627-JUD-01-00-BI.pdf, accessed 10 October 2017.

found another legal basis for ruling on the case.[10] Had it not done so, it would not have been able to render a decision on Nicaragua's claims, which had been argued at length and at great expense.

If we now examine the Philippine Submissions that, in the Tribunal's view, did not possess an exclusively preliminary character—Submissions No. 1, 2, 5, 8, 9, 12, and 14—we discover that they were among the most important of the Philippine Submissions. Submissions No. 1 and 2 asked the Tribunal to declare that China's claim to historic rights, as embodied in the "nine-dash line," are invalid. According to the Tribunal, consideration of these two Submissions would depend on the nature of China's historic rights and examination of China's 2006 Declaration excluding jurisdiction over historic bays or titles.[11] Hence, they would have to be examined together with the merits. Submission No. 5 requested the Tribunal to declare that Mischief Reef and Second Thomas Shoal are part of the Philippine EEZ and continental shelf. Mischief Reef is 126 nautical miles and Second Thomas Shoal is 104 nautical miles from the nearest point in Palawan. Since a coastal State has an entitlement to an EEZ and a continental shelf of 200 nautical miles from its baselines, the two are in theory within the Philippine EEZ and continental shelf. However, as the Tribunal pointed out, if it found that there were a Chinese island within 200 nautical miles of either of these two features, then the feature(s) would also be in the Chinese EEZ and continental shelf. The reason for this is that an island, like any other land territory, has an entitlement to a continental shelf and an EEZ. The Philippine and Chinese EEZs and continental shelves would overlap and thus have to be delimited—but maritime delimitation is excluded by the 2006 Chinese Declaration excluding certain types of disputes from compulsory dispute settlement entailing a binding decision. For the same reason, the Tribunal would be prevented from ruling on the eighth and ninth Submissions, which complain about China's interference with Philippine oil exploration, seismic surveys, and fishing in what the Philippines claims to be its continental shelf and EEZ.

In Submission No. 12, the Philippines argued that China violated its duties under the 1982 Convention by occupation, construction of artificial islands, installations and structures and damage to the marine environment on Mischief Reef, which in the Philippine view is a low-tide elevation. The latter is defined by the 1982 United Nations Convention on the Law of the Sea as "a naturally formed area of land which is surrounded by and above water at low tide but submerged at high tide" and does not generate entitlement to a territorial sea, EEZ, or continental shelf.[12] If the Tribunal found that Mischief Reef is a rock or island and thus constitutes land territory, it would not have jurisdiction to consider whether China's activities and appropriation were lawful. The same reasoning would apply to Submission No. 14, which alleged that China aggravated and extended the dispute through its activities in and around Second Thomas Shoal (interfering with Philippine navigation, preventing the rotation and resupply of Philippine personnel, and endangering their health and well-being). In addition, if China's activities in and around Second Thomas Shoal were military activities, they would be excluded from jurisdiction by China's 2006 Declaration.

If we consult the transcripts of the Hearing on Jurisdiction and Admissibility held at The Hague in July 2015, we realize that the Tribunal asked the Philippines questions on these points both before and during the hearings; moreover, it gave the Philippines the opportunity to reply to them in writing after the hearing. For example, as regards Submission 1, Judge

10 *Ibid.*, pp. 91–97, paras. 172–82.

11 United Nations, Division for Ocean Affairs and the Law of the Sea, *Oceans and the Law of the Sea. Declarations and Statements*, 2013, http://www.un.org/Depts/los/convention_agreements/convention_declarations.htm, accessed 30 October 2015.

12 http://www.un.org/depts/los/convention_agreements/texts/unclos/unclos_e.pdf, accessed 15 July 2015.

Rüdiger Wolfrum asked the Philippines whether it would be first necessary to establish China's entitlements under the 1982 Convention before it could be possible to determine that China's claims exceeded those permitted by the Convention. Before the hearings, the Tribunal asked the Philippines with regard to Submissions No. 5, 8, and 9, whether they presupposed a prior determination of sovereignty over any feature in dispute between the Philippines and China, which might have an entitlement to an EEZ that overlapped with the Philippine EEZ. In relation to Submission No. 8, the Tribunal asked the Philippines about the implications, if any, of a continental shelf claim by China for the Tribunal's jurisdiction. If China could claim a continental shelf that overlapped with that of the Philippines, then the two continental shelves would have to be delimited—but maritime delimitation is excluded by China's 2006 Declaration. The Tribunal also asked the Philippines, in relation to Submission No. 12, whether China's activities in Mischief Reef could be covered by China's Declaration, which also excluded military activities. Finally, as regards Submission No. 14, the Tribunal asked whether a military activity would cease to be a military activity if it concurrently served other purposes.

The fact that the Tribunal decided to postpone consideration of its jurisdiction on these Submissions to the merits phase meant that the Philippines, which did not want any issue to be deferred, was not able to convince the Tribunal that it could rule on jurisdiction without examining the merits of these Submissions. In the merits phase, therefore, the Philippines had to attempt to convince the Tribunal that it had jurisdiction over these Submissions. Most, if not all, of the Philippine arguments on the merits had been prepared well in advance of the Hearing on the Merits in November 2015, since the Philippines prepared its Memorial (the first written pleadings) on the assumption that there would be only one phase (jurisdiction and merits). During the Hearing on the Merits and the Remaining Issues of Jurisdiction and Admissibility, the Philippines had to present once more its arguments in favor of the Tribunal's jurisdiction over Submissions No. 1, 2, 8, 9, 12, and 14, suitably modified, where appropriate, in order to take into account the decisions on jurisdiction.

We now know that in its Award of 12 July 2016, the Tribunal decided that it had jurisdiction over Submissions No. 1, 2, 8, 9, 12, and 14(d). It found that the "military activities" exception prevented it from exercising jurisdiction with respect to the dispute arising from the standoff between the two Parties around Second Thomas Shoal (Submission No. 14(a) to (c)).[13] As for the reformulated Submission No. 15, which asked the Tribunal to declare that China should respect the rights and freedoms of the Philippines under the Convention and comply with its (China's) duties under the Convention, the Tribunal decided that a dispute did not exist between the Parties and declined to make any further declaration.[14] The Tribunal's decisions on the merits of the Submissions were overwhelmingly favorable to the Philippines. The only Submission that the Tribunal did not accept was the claim that McKennan Reef and Gaven Reef (North) were low-tide elevations. Instead, the Tribunal found that they were high-tide elevations.[15]

Nevertheless the outcomes were not guaranteed in advance. In a revealing phrase, the then Secretary of Foreign Affairs, Albert P. del Rosario, admitted at the closing of the Hearing on the Merits that the Philippines had not even been certain that the proceedings would reach the

13 Award of 12 July 2016, pp. 453–56, paras. 1150–62, https://pcacases.com/web/sendAttach/2086, accessed 29 March 2018.

14 *Ibid.*, pp. 465–69, paras. 1182–201.

15 *Ibid.*, pp. 148–56, paras. 352–54, pp. 157–65, paras. 359–66. The Tribunal did find that they were "rocks which cannot sustain human habitation or economic life of their own" and not fully entitled islands. As rocks within the meaning of Article 121(3) of the Convention, they were only entitled to a territorial sea, i.e., they were not entitled to an EEZ and a continental shelf.

merits phase.[16] The uncertainty must have been heightened by the fact that even after the Hearing on the Merits had concluded, the Tribunal requested further evidence from the Philippines and from Tribunal-appointed experts.[17] In these circumstances, the actual approach of the Philippines to the merits phase of the proceedings must have departed from the triumphalism demonstrated following the issuance of the Award on Jurisdiction and Admissibility. That attitude was adopted in all likelihood for the benefit of domestic public opinion.

16 In his closing statement delivered on 30 November 2015, Foreign Secretary del Rosario admitted that "[w]hen I first had the privilege of appearing before you in July, it was at the beginning of the hearings on jurisdiction. We did not know then whether or not we would ever reach this point." *South China Sea Arbitration, Hearing on the Merits and Remaining Issues of Jurisdiction and Admissibility, Final Transcript. Day 4, Monday, 30th November 2015*, p. 188, https://pcacases.com/web/sendAttach/1550, accessed 16 February 2016.

17 Award of 12 July 2016, pp. 29–37, paras. 84–105, *supra* note 13.

3

China's Informal Participation in the Arbitration in Contravention of International Law[1]

Upon the release of the transcripts of the Hearing on Jurisdiction and Admissibility, China issued a statement reaffirming its non-acceptance of and non-participation in the arbitration, a position that it claimed was "solidly grounded in international law."[2] The reality is that China, through its letters to the Tribunal and to its individual members, the press briefings given by its officials, and its campaign to mobilize international support for its position, has participated informally in the arbitration.[3] Some of the forms of that participation have contradicted the claim of conformity with international law. The most glaring evidence of this contradiction is an attempt by China to lobby the Tribunal, an attempt that it thought it could keep secret from the Philippines. In this incident, which can only put China in the worst possible light, it is the response of the Tribunal, which China has consistently abused since the issuance of the Award on Jurisdiction and Admissibility,[4] that demonstrates its sense of responsibility and impartiality.

1 An earlier version of this Chapter was posted on 10 July 2016 on the blog of the author's sister-in-law, https://www.raissarobles.com/2016/07/10/exclusive-china-secretly-lobbied-with-arbitral-court-to-scrap-philippine-suit-on-south-china-sea/. The post on China's attempts to lobby the Tribunal was picked up by a newspaper published in the US by Chinese-American Falung Gong practitioners, *The Epoch Times* and its Spanish-language edition, *La gran época*. See Leo Timm, "How China Tried, and Failed, to Influence The Hague on the South China Sea Dispute," *Epoch Times*, 11 July 2016, https://www.theepochtimes.com/how-china-tried-and-failed-to-influence-the-hague-on-the-south-china-sea-dispute_2112535.html, and "Cómo China trató manipular la decisión de La Haya sobre el Mar de China Meridional," *La gran época*, 12 July 2016, https://www.lagranepoca.com/china/regimen-chino/73137-como-china-trato-manipular-la-decision-de-la-haya-sobre-el-mar-de-china-meridional.html, both accessed 30 March 2018.

2 *Foreign Ministry Spokesperson Hua Chunying's Remarks on the Release of the Transcript of the Oral Hearing on Jurisdiction by the South China Sea Arbitral Tribunal Established at the Request of the Philippines, 2015/08/24*, http://www.fmprc.gov.cn/mfa_eng/xwfw_665399/s2510_665401/2535_665405/t1290752.shtml, accessed 2 November 2015.

3 An attack on the PCA website during the first round of the hearing on jurisdiction and admissibility, detected on 9 July 2015, was traced to Chinese APT (Advanced Persistent Threat) actors. The malware would have infected the computers of those visiting the website of the PCA, which shut it down for several days to prevent the spread of the malware. During the shutdown, the author emailed the PCA to call their attention to the fact that the website was inaccessible. As a safety measure, the author had to have his hard disk scanned. Since the hacking could not be definitively traced to the Chinese government, it is not (yet) possible to describe the attack on the PCA website as a form of China's informal, not to say underhanded, participation in the arbitration. See ThreatConnect Intelligence Research Team (TCIRT), *China Hacks the Peace Palace: All Your EEZ's Are Belong [sic] to Us*, 20 July 2015, https://www.threatconnect.com/blog/china-hacks-the-peace-palace-all-your-eezs-are-belong-to-us/, accessed 26 July 2015.

4 Wang Xu, "Diplomat Slams 'Biased' Nansha Arbitration Panel," *China Daily USA*, 18 April 2016, http://usa.chinadaily.com.cn/epaper/2016-04/18/content_24631887.htm, accessed 1 July 2016.

When we read carefully the entire Award on Jurisdiction and Admissibility, we stumble upon interesting facts.[5] On paragraph 40, p. 18, we discover that the Chinese Ambassador to the UK contacted the President of the Tribunal to request a meeting: "On 14 November 2013, after the Chinese Ambassador to the United Kingdom requested a meeting with the President of the Tribunal…."

The Tribunal's response to this request is remarkable in at least three respects. First, it did not publicize, and has not publicized, the Chinese request. The public only learned of China's maneuver upon the issuance of the Award on Jurisdiction and Admissibility. The incident is no longer mentioned in the Procedural History of the Award of 12 July 2016. The letter is not among the documents of the arbitration that have been uploaded on the website of the Permanent Court of Arbitration (PCA), which is acting as the Registry in the arbitration, and it is not likely that it will ever be uploaded.[6] It is possible that the Tribunal consulted the Philippines whether it was appropriate to publish the Chinese communication, but we should recall that the Tribunal has adopted procedural decisions that did not conform to Philippine wishes. We can only speculate on the reasons for the Tribunal's attitude, but it is tempting to assume that the Tribunal wished, and wishes, to avoid humiliating China, inflaming public opinion in China and the Philippines, and thus heightening the tension between the two countries. There can be no doubt, though, that the Philippines was informed of the request.

Second, the Tribunal wrote a letter not just to China but also to the Philippines, to remind them of the procedure: "the Tribunal sent a letter to remind the Parties to refrain from *ex parte* communications with members of the Tribunal." An *ex parte* communication is defined by the *Model Code of Judicial Conduct* of the American Bar Association (ABA) as communication "made to the judge outside the presence of the parties or their lawyers, concerning a pending or impending matter."[7] The Tribunal stated something that China should have known by this time:

> [i]f a Party wishes to express its position on matters in dispute, it should be aware that such statements will be made available to all members of the Tribunal, the Registry and the other Party, in accordance with the Rules of Procedure and the need to ensure that the Parties are treated with equality.

By November 2013 China should have known this, simply because it had been receiving, despite its refusal to participate in the proceedings, copies of all communications sent by the Philippines to the Tribunal and all decisions of the Tribunal, such as the Rules of Procedure and other procedural orders.[8]

The Tribunal then "encouraged the Parties to direct any questions of a procedural nature to the Registry." Why did the Tribunal also write to the Philippines? The reason is that according to the Rules of the Procedure of the arbitration, the Parties have to be "treated with equality."[9] In reality, it was only China that was being courteously "encouraged" to avoid contacting the Tribunal without the other party's knowledge, but since the parties had to be "treated with equality," the Tribunal could not very well single out China, at the risk of humiliating it.

5 Award on Jurisdiction and Admissibility, 29 October 2015, http://www.pcacases.com/web/sendAttach/1506, accessed 30 March 2018.

6 *The Republic of Philippines v. The People's Republic of China*, https://pca-cpa.org/en/cases/7/, accessed 30 March 2018.

7 American Bar Association, *Model Code of Judicial Conduct* (Chicago: American Bar Association, 2011), http://www.americanbar.org/groups/professional_responsibility/publications/model_code_of_judicial_conduct/model_code_of_judicial_conduct_canon_2/rule2_9expartecommunications.html, accessed 5 July 2015.

8 *Rules of Procedure*, 27 August 2013, https://pcacases.com/web/sendAttach/233, accessed 30 March 2018.

9 *Ibid.*, Article 10, para. 1.

Third, the Tribunal did not explain in the Award on Jurisdiction and Admissibility the reason(s) for China's request. Upon reading the paragraph, we cannot help but immediately ask,

- What did China hope to achieve through such contacts? Surely not the termination of the proceedings?
- Did China believe it could sway the President of the Tribunal, after failing to dissuade the Philippines from proceeding with the arbitration?
- In a country of more than 1.3 billion people, is there not—or should there not be—a sufficiently large number of international lawyers who know that this kind of maneuvers is unacceptable, and worse, useless?

We are left hanging in the air by the Award, as it does not inform us of the purpose of the meeting requested by the Ambassador. Again, the Tribunal's silence can most probably be attributed to a desire not to embarrass China.

We should note in passing that even before contacting the Tribunal in November 2013, China had also attempted to contact the PCA. To quote the Award, "The Tribunal recalled that the Registry had on two prior occasions discussed informal questions of a procedural nature with a representative of the Chinese Embassy…." The Embassy in question was the Chinese Embassy to the Netherlands, where the PCA headquarters are located.

Again, only the most stoic can resist the temptation to ask,

- If China refused to participate in the proceedings, why did it have procedural questions?
- Did China find anything vague or disturbing in the Rules of Procedure of the arbitration, adopted on 27 August 2013?
- Did it wish the Rules to be amended?
- If China had procedural questions, would it not have been simpler to participate in the proceedings instead of resorting to "informal questions"?
- Can the subsequent intervention of China's Ambassador to the UK be explained by the failure of China's Embassy in the Netherlands to obtain the information it was seeking?

We can take it for granted that the PCA informed the Tribunal and the Philippines of China's inquiries. Once more, the Tribunal is silent on the nature of China's procedural inquiries and the responses to the inquiries from the PCA and/or the Tribunal. The inquiries are not mentioned again in the Procedural History of the Award of 12 July 2016, and no communication on this matter appears on the website of the PCA.

It is most likely that once again, the Tribunal's silence on these matters is motivated by a desire to avoid embarrassing China, which had again apparently circumvented the Rules of Procedure.

If these two incidents are anything to go by, then we can say that the Tribunal acted in a responsible manner. A fervent supporter of the Philippines would be forgiven for going further and arguing that the Tribunal had not been impartial and should have published any communications on these incidents, regardless of their impact on China's reputation and China's possible reaction. In this scenario, the Tribunal would find itself in the paradoxical position of being accused of bias by both China and the Philippines. If this thought had ever occurred to representatives of the Philippines, then it would perhaps have been a further sign, if any were still necessary, that the Tribunal is impartial, after all.

4

The Arbitral Tribunal: 200 Years of Combined Personal Professional Experience[1]

Between October 2015, when the Award on Jurisdiction and Admissibility was issued, and July 2016, when the Award on the merits was rendered, China insisted on repeating the arguments that it had already put forward in its Position Paper and that the Tribunal had rejected.[2] Whatever the reason for China's unwillingness or inability to engage in the debate, China found no better alternative strategy than to insult the Tribunal. The latter was accused by the Deputy Director-General of the Foreign Ministry's Department of Boundary and Ocean Affairs of being "careless, negligent and irresponsible."[3]

China's abuse of the Tribunal, together with the response of the President of the Arbitral Tribunal to China's request for a meeting with him, underscores the importance of the selection of judges in international arbitration. Arbitration is defined by the 1899 Convention for the Pacific Settlement of International Disputes as "the settlement of disputes between States by Judges of their own choice and on the basis of respect for law."[4] The appointment by the parties to the dispute of their own judges differentiates arbitration from adjudication by a permanent international tribunal. In the latter case, when a dispute is submitted to the tribunal, such as the International Court of Justice (ICJ), or the International Tribunal for the Law of the Sea (ITLOS), the case is heard by the judges that comprise the tribunal at that particular moment, by virtue of having been previously elected to the tribunal by the States parties to the treaty that established the tribunal. The number of members of an arbitral tribunal, which is usually three or five, is set by the parties to the dispute through a treaty. It is Annex VII of the United Nations Convention on the Law of the Sea that provides that the arbitral tribunal shall consist of five members, unless the parties to the dispute otherwise agree.[5]

1 An earlier version of this Chapter was posted on 11 July 2016 on the blog of the author's sister-in-law, https://www.raissarobles.com/2016/07/11/meet-the-five-judges-in-the-south-china-sea-arbitration-court/.

2 In fact, China would reiterate these arguments even after the Award on the merits had already been issued.

3 "China Doesn't Accept or Recognize the South China Sea Arbitration," *chinausfocus.com*, 20 April 2016, http://www.chinausfocus.com/uncategorized/china-doesnt-accept-or-recognize-the-south-china-sea-arbitration/, accessed 8 September 2016.

4 Article 15, 1899 Convention for the Pacific Settlement of International Disputes, https://pca-cpa.org/wp-content/uploads/sites/175/2016/01/1899-Convention-for-the-Pacific-Settlement-of-International-Disputes.pdf, accessed 30 March 2018; see also Article 37 of the 1907 Convention for the Pacific Settlement of International Disputes, https://pca-cpa.org/wp-content/uploads/sites/175/2016/01/1907-Convention-for-the-Pacific-Settlement-of-International-Disputes.pdf, accessed 30 March 2018.

5 The Statute of the International Court of Justice, which is annexed to an international treaty, the UN Charter,

The Philippines, in its Notification and Statement of Claim of 22 January 2013, appointed Judge Rüdiger Wolfrum, a German national.[6] Upon receipt of the Notification, China was supposed to appoint its own judge. However, in view of China's refusal to participate in the arbitration, the Philippines, pursuant to Article 3(3) of Annex VII of the Convention, requested on 22 February 2013 that the President of ITLOS, Shunji Yanai, appoint one in China's place.[7] The President appointed Judge Stanisław Pawlak, a Polish national. The three remaining arbitrators were appointed according to the same procedure by the ITLOS President, following a Philippine request made on 25 March 2013.[8] They were Jean-Pierre Cot of France, Alfred H.A. Soons of the Netherlands, and Moragodage Christopher Walter Pinto of Sri Lanka. Pinto, who was Chairman of the Sri Lankan delegation to the Third UN Conference on the Law of the Sea (1973–82) and Chairman of the Conference's Negotiating Group on the Seabed beyond National Jurisdiction, was also appointed as the Tribunal's President. On 6 May 2013, Pinto resigned as member and president, citing the fact that his wife was a Filipina.[9] To replace him, the ITLOS President appointed Thomas A. Mensah of Ghana in June.[10]

The five judges that comprise the arbitral tribunal have in common several things. They all have advanced degrees (a minimum of a doctorate). They all have academic experience. They all have scholarly publications. And they all have professional experience, averaging 40 years, as national or international civil servants, and as international lawyers and judges.[11]

---

stipulates that the Court comprises 15 members. See Article 3, para. 1 of the Statute of the International Court of Justice, http://legal.un.org/avl/pdf/ha/sicj/icj_statute_e.pdf, accessed 11 September 2016. The Statute of the International Tribunal for the Law of the Sea, which forms Annex VI of the UN Convention on the Law of the Sea, provides that the Tribunal shall consist of 21 members. See Article 2, para. 1 of the Statute of the International Tribunal for the Law of the Sea, https://www.itlos.org/fileadmin/itlos/documents/basic_texts/statute_en.pdf, accessed 16 September 2016.

6 http://www.philippineembassy-usa.org/uploads/pdfs/embassy/2013/2013-0122-Notification%20and%20Statement%20of%20Claim%20on%20West%20Philippine%20Sea.pdf, accessed 7 September 2016. For some reason, the document is no longer available on the website of the Department of Foreign Affairs (DFA).

7 See Article 3 of Annex VII, http://www.un.org/depts/los/convention_agreements/texts/unclos/annex7.htm, accessed 7 September 2016.

8 ITLOS, *Arbitrators Appointed in the Arbitral Proceedings Instituted by the Republic of the Philippines Against the People's Republic of China*, Doc. ITLOS/Press 191 (25 April 2013), https://www.itlos.org/fileadmin/itlos/documents/press_releases_english/PR_191_E.pdf, accessed 12 October 2015.

9 Michaela del Callar, "For Having Pinay Wife, Sri Lankan Judge in PHL Arbitral Proceedings vs China Resigns," *Phillippine Daily Inquirer*, 7 June 2013, http://www.gmanetwork.com/news/story/311870/news/nation/for-having-pinay-wife-sri-lankan-judge-in-phl-arbitral-proceedings-vs-china-resigns, accessed 27 July 2015.

9 ITLOS, *New Arbitrator and President Appointed in the Arbitral Proceedings Instituted by the Republic of the Philippines against the People's Republic of China*, Doc. ITLOS/Press 197, 24 June 2013, https://www.itlos.org/fileadmin/itlos/documents/press_releases_english/PR_197_E.pdf, accessed 8 July 2015.

11 On the PCA website, one may find the following photographs of the Tribunal:

1. Photograph from Jurisdictional Hearing—July 2015—Arbitral Tribunal, https://pcacases.com/web/sendAttach/1498, L to R: Judge Cot, Judge Pawlak, Judge Mensah, Judge Wolfrum, and Professor Soons.

2. Photograph from Jurisdictional Hearing—July 2015—Arbitral Tribunal with PCA Staff Members, https://pcacases.com/web/sendAttach/1495, (seated) Judge Mensah, Judge Pawlak; (standing) PCA Staff Member, Judge Cot, Judge Wolfrum, Professor Soons, and PCA Staff Member.

3. Photograph from Merits Hearing—November 2015—Tribunal in Session, https://pcacases.com/web/sendAttach/1526, L to R: Judge Pawlak, Professor Soons, Judge Mensah, Judge Cot, and Judge Wolfrum (all accessed 30 March 2018).

THE PRESIDENT OF THE TRIBUNAL: JUDGE THOMAS A. MENSAH

Judge Mensah was born in Kumasi, Ghana, on 12 May 1932.[12]

A. Education

He obtained a BA at the University of Ghana in 1956, an LLB at the University of London in 1959, and an LLM (*Legum Magister*, Master of Laws) and a JSD (*Juris Scientiae Doctor*, Doctor of Juridical Science) at Yale University in 1962 and 1964, respectively.

B. Academic Experience

He taught law at the University of Ghana from 1963 to 1968, serving as Dean of the Faculty of Law in 1967–68. He was a Professor at the World Maritime University, Malmö, Sweden (1981–90), a Visiting Professor at the University of Leiden in the Netherlands (1994), and Professor of Law and Director of the Law of the Sea Institute at the William S. Richardson School of Law at the University of Hawaii (1993–95).

C. Publications

Judge Mensah is the author of articles, monographs, and papers in the field of public international law, law of the sea, maritime law, and international environmental law. One of his articles that the author encountered as a graduate student in France was entitled "L'activité réglementaire de l'OMCI (The Regulatory Activity of the IMCO)," co-authored with Christopher H. Zimmerli, presented at an annual meeting of the *Société Française pour le Droit International* (French Society for International Law),[13] and published in the proceedings of the meeting.[14] Judge Mensah's article entitled "Provisional Measures in the International Tribunal for the Law of the Sea (ITLOS)" is available online.[15]

D. Professional Experience

Judge Mensah was Associate Legal Officer at the International Atomic Energy Agency (IAEA) in Vienna (1965–66), before joining the IMCO (International Maritime Consultative Organization, now the IMO, International Organization) as Head of the Organization's Legal Division, in London. He became Director of Legal Affairs and External Relations in 1976 and was appointed Assistant Secretary General in 1981. After 22 years of service, he took early retirement in 1990.

But his career did not end there. He continued his career as an international civil servant, as a Special Advisor on Environmental Law and Institutions of the United Nations Environment Programme (UNEP), which is based in Nairobi, Kenya (1991–92). From 1999 to 2005, he was Chairman of the "F4" (Environmental) Panel of Commissioners of the United Nations Compensation Commission (UNCC) to consider claims submitted by several governments

[12] Unless otherwise indicated, the following information is obtained from "Judge Thomas A. Mensah: Biographical Note," in Tafsir Malick Ndiaye and Rüdiger Wolfrum (eds.), *Law of the Sea, Environmental Law and Settlement of Disputes. Liber Amicorum Judge Thomas A. Mensah* (Leiden: Martinus Nijhoff Publishers, 2007), pp. xiv–xvi.

[13] www.sfdi.org, accessed 7 September 2016.

[14] *L'élaboration du droit international public* (Paris: Éditions A. Pedone, 1975). The proceedings of the SFDI constitute an invaluable resource on the state of the art of the topic chosen for that meeting.

[15] *Zeitschrift für ausländisches Recht und Völkerrecht* (*ZaöRV*), 63 (2002), pp. 43–54, http://www.zaoerv.de/62_2002/62_2002_1_a_43_54.pdf, accessed 14 November 2015.

for compensation for environmental damage resulting from Iraq's invasion and occupation of Kuwait in 1990.

He briefly served his government as the first High Commissioner (the term used for "Ambassador" among members of the British Commonwealth) of Ghana to the Republic of South Africa in 1995, a year after the end of the apartheid regime in the latter.

His "retirement" is characterized by a brilliant career as an international judge. He was elected as a Judge of the newly created International Tribunal for the Law of the Sea (ITLOS) for a nine-year term on 1 August 1996, at the fifth Meeting of States Parties to the Convention, held in New York.[16] In October 1996, he was elected the first President of the Tribunal, for a three-year term. During his term as President, the Tribunal decided its first four cases[17] and adopted its internal judicial practice.[18] After the expiry of his term as President, he continued as a judge until 2005.

We cannot appreciate the significance of Judge Mensah's election to ITLOS and his election as its first President without a brief explanation of ITLOS and the role of its President. ITLOS, which is composed of 21 independent members, is an independent judicial body established by the 1982 Convention to settle disputes arising out of the interpretation and application of the Convention, with its 320 articles and 9 annexes. ITLOS is the main procedural innovation in dispute settlement established by the 1982 Convention.[19]

The functions of the President are crucial in the Tribunal's internal practice. After the two States parties to a dispute have submitted their arguments in written form, the President, on the basis of the written submissions (which may very easily run into thousands of pages) and written notes by the 20 other judges, prepares a working paper in which he/she summarizes the facts and the theses of the parties. He/she also makes proposals to the other judges concerning indications or questions to be put to the parties and evidence or explanations to be requested from them during the oral proceedings.

Before the oral proceedings, he/she presides over a private meeting of the Tribunal. During the oral proceedings, he/she may convene meetings of the Tribunal for exchanges of views. After the oral proceedings, he/she presides over deliberations of the Tribunal and "may seek to establish a majority opinion as it appears then to exist on each issue and on the reasons to be given."

If a majority has not yet emerged at this time, the judges prepare written notes and discuss them in the course of further deliberations. If he/she shares the views of the majority, the President is ex officio a member of the Drafting Committee, which prepares two drafts of the judgment.

The other four members of the Committee are elected upon the President's proposal. The President then presides over two readings of the second draft, after which the judges vote on the judgment. We can thus say that the position of ITLOS President is far from being a sinecure.

After having served as ITLOS Judge and President, Judge Mensah has been appointed judge ad hoc in three disputes submitted to ITLOS:

16 *Report of the Fifth Meeting of States Parties*, Doc. SPLOS/14 (20 September 1996), p. 7, para. 18, https://documents-dds-ny.un.org/doc/UNDOC/GEN/N96/249/47/PDF/N9624947.pdf?OpenElement). His CV was circulated to the States Parties one month before the election. See *Curricula Vitae of Candidates Nominated by States Parties for Election to the International Tribunal for the Law of the Sea. Note by the Secretary-General*, Doc. SPLOS/11 (25 June 1996), https://documents-dds-ny.un.org/doc/UNDOC/GEN/N96/158/21/PDF/N9615821.pdf?OpenElement, accessed 18 July 2016.

17 The list of cases is available on the ITLOS website: https://www.itlos.org/cases/list-of-cases/, accessed 24 November 2015.

18 ITLOS, *Resolution on the Internal Judicial Practice of the Tribunal*, Doc. ITLOS/10 (27 April 2005), https://www.itlos.org/fileadmin/itlos/documents/basic_texts/Itlos.10.E.27.04.05.pdf, accessed 24 November 2015.

19 Raymond Ranjeva, "Le règlement des différends," in René-Jean Dupuy and Daniel Vignes (eds.), *Traité du Nouveau Droit de la Mer* (Paris: Editions Economica, 1985), pp. 1105–68.

- The *Dispute Concerning Delimitation of the Maritime Boundary between Bangladesh and Myanmar in the Bay of Bengal* (Bangladesh/Myanmar) (2009–12, appointed by Bangladesh);[20]
- *The "ARA Libertad" Case (Argentina v. Ghana), Provisional Measures* (2011);[21] and
- *The Dispute Concerning Delimitation of the Maritime Boundary between Ghana and Côte d'Ivoire in the Atlantic Ocean (Ghana/Côte d'Ivoire)* (2014–17).[22]

In the last two cases, he was appointed by his country.

In the last 15 years, Judge Mensah was a member of the Arbitral Tribunal in the *Bay of Bengal Maritime Boundary Arbitration* between Bangladesh and India[23] and was President of several arbitral tribunals constituted under Annex VII of the Convention:

- The *MOX Plant Case*, initiated in 2001 by Ireland against the United Kingdom;[24]
- The *Atlanto-Scandian Herring Arbitration (The Kingdom of Denmark in Respect of the Faroe Islands v. The European Union)* (2013–14);[25] and
- The *Arctic Sunrise Arbitration (Netherlands v. Russia)* (2013–15).[26]

This last case concerned the boarding and detention of the vessel *Arctic Sunrise*, belonging to Greenpeace and registered in the Netherlands, in the exclusive economic zone of Russia and the detention of the persons on board the vessel by the Russian authorities. Initiated in October 2013, nine months after the commencement of the *Philippines v. China* arbitration, the case is interesting because of two procedural similarities with the latter. The respondent State (in this case Russia) also refused to appear before the Tribunal and the procedure was bifurcated. However, it was the applicant state (the Netherlands) that took the initiative to request bifurcation.

Another difference is that the Tribunal decided not to hold a hearing on jurisdiction and admissibility. The Tribunal rendered its Award on Jurisdiction on 26 November 2014, a little over two months after the Netherlands submitted its Memorial and a mere five days after its Procedural Order announcing that it would rule on jurisdiction without holding a hearing.[27] The Award on the merits was issued in August 2015, nine months after the Award on Jurisdiction. Differences in the complexity of the legal issues concerned may explain why the proceedings in this case were concluded in approximately two years.[28]

Finally, Judge Mensah was appointed Judge ad hoc by Nicaragua in the *Territorial and Maritime Dispute (Nicaragua v. Colombia)*.[29] A judge ad hoc is appointed by a party to a case before the ICJ that does not have a judge of its nationality on the Court, but he/she does not have to be a national of the country appointing him/her.[30] The appointment as a judge ad hoc is

20 https://www.itlos.org/cases/list-of-cases/case-no-16/, accessed 20 November 2015.

21 https://www.itlos.org/cases/list-of-cases/case-no-20/, accessed 20 November 2015.

22 https://www.itlos.org/fileadmin/itlos/documents/cases/case_no.23_merits/C23_Judgment_23.09.2017_corr.pdf, accessed 15 March 2018.

23 https://pcacases.com/web/view/18, accessed 30 March 2018.

24 https://pcacases.com/web/view/100, accessed 30 March 2018.

25 https://pcacases.com/web/view/25, accessed 30 March 2018. Judge Wolfrum was also a member of this Tribunal.

26 https://pcacases.com/web/view/21, accessed 30 March 2018.

27 *Arctic Sunrise Arbitration*, Award on Jurisdiction, 26 November 2014, https://pcacases.com/web/sendAttach/1325, accessed 30 March 2018.

28 https://pcacases.com/web/sendAttach/1438, accessed 30 March 2018.

29 http://www.icj-cij.org/en/case/124, accessed 16 March 2018.

30 ICJ, *Judges ad hoc*, http://www.icj-cij.org/en/judges-ad-hoc, accessed 16 March 2018.

thus a recognition of and tribute to the competence of the person concerned. The judge ad hoc only hears the case for which he/she is appointed and ceases to be a member of the Court when a judgment on the case is issued. Interestingly enough, in the said case, Judge Cot was the judge ad hoc appointed by the other party, Colombia.

MEMBER OF THE TRIBUNAL: JUDGE JEAN-PIERRE COT[31]

Judge Cot, a French national, was born on 23 October 1937 in Geneva.[32]

A. Education

He studied for his *licence*,[33] the first degree in French higher education, and his doctorate in law at the University of Paris (1955–65). He passed the agrégation,[34] an extremely competitive national examination for university professors in law, political science, economics, and management, in 1966.[35]

B. Academic Experience

He was a lecturer in law at the University of Paris from 1962 to 1966. After passing the *agrégation*, he became Professor in the Faculty of Law at the Université d'Amiens in 1966. In 1969, he moved to the Université Paris I (Pantheon-Sorbonne), where he was professor of international law and political sociology until 1981, and then from 1982 to 1998. He has been an Associate Research Fellow at the Université Libre de Bruxelles (Free University of Brussels) since 1999.

C. Publications

Judge Cot is the author of numerous books and articles dealing with international law, European law, and political science.[36] From 1960 onwards, he regularly wrote commentaries on ICJ judgments that were published in the *Annuaire Français de Droit International* (French Yearbook of International Law).[37] Judge Cot was very critical of the attitude of the French government in the Nuclear Tests cases.[38]

His PhD dissertation was published as *La conciliation internationale* in 1968.[39] It is one of the few French books on international law that have been translated into English, under

[31] This video gives the correct pronunciation of Judge Cot's last name: https://www.youtube.com/watch?v=pN_QWEGDCT4, accessed 7 September 2016.

[32] Unless otherwise indicated, the following information is obtained from Judge Cot's biography on the ITLOS website, https://www.itlos.org/the-tribunal/members/judge-jean-pierre-cot/, accessed 11 November 2015.

[33] This website gives the correct pronunciation of *licence* in French: http://forvo.com/word/licence/#fr, accessed 7 September 2016.

[34] This website gives the correct pronunciation of *agrégation* in French: https://www.howtopronounce.com/french/agregation/, accessed 7 September 2016.

[35] For a description of this competitive examination, see Ministère de l'Éducation nationale, de l'Enseignement Supérieur et de la Recherche, *Les concours nationaux d'agrégation*, http://www.enseignementsup-recherche.gouv.fr/cid22721/les-concours-nationaux-d-agregation.html, accessed 12 November 2015.

[36] http://www.unesdoc.unesco.org/images/0015/001532/153214eo.pdf, accessed 11 November 2015.

[37] http://www.cnrseditions.fr/droitlegislation/6667-annuaire-francais-de-droit-international-57-joe-verhoeven.html, accessed 11 November 2015.

[38] Jean-Pierre Cot, "Affaire des Essais nucléaires (Australie c. France et Nouvelle-Zélande c. France). Demandes en indication de mesures conservatoires. Ordonnances du 22 juin 1973," *Annuaire Français de Droit International (AFDI)*, 19 (1973), pp. 252–71, http://www.persee.fr/doc/afdi_0066-3085_1973_num_19_1_2213?q=Jean-Pierre%20Cot%20essais%20nucl%C3%A9aires, accessed 11 November 2015.

[39] As a graduate student in Paris, the author used to see it displayed on the window of the publisher Pedone, but at the time the price of the book was beyond his means.

the title *International Conciliation* (1972), a clear indicator of its scholarly value. Judge Cot is also known to the undersigned as the co-author of a two-volume work on political sociology entitled *Pour une sociologie politique*[40] and as the co-editor of the massive two-volume work *La Charte des Nations Unies, commentaire article par article (The UN Charter: Article-by-Article Commentary)*.[41]

D. Professional Experience

Like many French intellectuals and academics, Judge Cot was able to combine his scholarly activities with public office. This is perhaps not so surprising, as he is the son of Pierre Cot, who was a member of Parliament for the Savoie *département* (a subnational administrative division between the region and the commune) and a minister in several cabinets of the Third Republic (1870–1940), notably that of Léon Blum of the Popular Front of the Left in 1936–37.[42]

Like his father, Judge Cot was a member of Parliament for Savoie (1973–81), during which period he was a member of the Foreign Affairs Committee and the Finance Committee of the National Assembly (the lower house of Parliament). He was Junior Minister for Cooperation and Development (1981–82) in the cabinet of Pierre Mauroy, Prime Minister under the Socialist President François Mitterand. As Minister, he chaired the first Conference on the Least Developed Countries, held in Paris in 1981. He was also elected member of the Executive Board of UNESCO (1983–84), which has its headquarters in Paris.

Judge Cot has also had a political career at the European level.[43] He was appointed to the European Parliament (1978–79) and was elected to the Parliament for three successive terms (1984–99). The European Parliament[44] is one of the major institutions of the European Union.[45] At the Parliament, he served as President of the Budget Committee (1984–89); President of the Socialist Group (1989–94), which brings together all the European Socialist parties represented in the European Parliament; and Vice-President of the Parliament (1997–99).

From the 1980s onwards, Judge Cot served as Counsel and Advocate in a number of cases before the ICJ:

- *Frontier Dispute (Burkina Faso/Republic of Mali)* (1983–86, counsel for Burkina Faso);[46]
- *Territorial Dispute (Libyan Arab Jamahiriya/Chad)* (1990–94, counsel for Chad);[47]
- *Kasikili/Sedudu Islands (Botswana/Namibia)* (1996-99, counsel for Namibia);[48]

[40] https://www.amazon.fr/Pour-une-sociologie-politique-1/dp/2020003694/ref=sr_1_6?ie=UTF8&qid=1447232819&sr=8-6&keywords=Jean-Pierre+Cot, accessed 7 September 2016.

[41] https://www.amazon.com/Charte-Nations-Unies-volumes-Commentaire/dp/2717850570/ref=sr_1_2?ie=UTF8&qid=1446994867&sr=8-2&keywords=La+Charte+des+Nations+Unies%2C+commentaire+article+par+article, accessed 7 September 2016. The undersigned was a subscriber to the first edition of the book, i.e., he purchased it before publication, and as a result, the name of the undersigned appears at the end of the book together with the names of the other subscribers.

[42] Centre d'histoire de Sciences Po, *Cot, Pierre* (Paris: Fondation Nationale des Sciences Politiques, n.d.), http://chsp.sciences-po.fr/fond-archive/cot-pierre, accessed 12 November 2015.

[43] See his biography published on the European Parliament website, http://www.europarl.europa.eu/meps/en/1027/JEAN-PIERRE_COT_home.html, accessed 12 November 2015.

[44] http://www.europarl.europa.eu/portal/en, accessed 7 September 2016.

[45] https://europa.eu/european-union/index_en, accessed 7 September 2016.

[46] http://www.icj-cij.org/en/case/69, accessed 16 March 2018.

[47] http://www.icj-cij.org/en/case/83, accessed 16 March 2018.

[48] http://www.icj-cij.org/en/case/98, accessed 16 March 2018.

- *Armed Activities on the Territory of the Congo (Democratic Republic of the Congo* v. *Burundi)* (1993–2001);[49]
- *Land and Maritime Boundary Between Cameroon and Nigeria (Cameroon* v. *Nigeria)* (1994–2002, counsel for Cameroon);[50]
- *Sovereignty over Pulau Ligitan and Pulau Sipadan (Indonesia/Malaysia)* (1998–2002, counsel for Malaysia);[51] and
- *Tax regime governing pensions paid to retired UNESCO officials residing in France* (France/UNESCO) (2003).[52]

Judge Cot was elected to the ITLOS in 2002 and was re-elected in 2011. He served as President of the Chamber for Marine Environment Disputes from 2008 to 2011.

Parallel to the exercise of his functions as ITLOS judge, Judge Cot has been a judge in cases before other international tribunals. He was President of an arbitral tribunal established within the framework of the European Development Fund, a fund supported by voluntary contributions from members of the European Union (EU) in order to finance development cooperation between the European Union and the ACP (African, Caribbean, and Pacific) group.[53] No information is available on this arbitration on the EU website or in the *Reports on International Arbitral Awards/Recueil des sentences arbitrales.* Possibly the parties to the case (whose identities cannot even be verified) preferred to keep the proceedings confidential.[54]

He was appointed judge ad hoc in several cases before the ICJ:

- *Territorial and Maritime Dispute (Nicaragua* v. *Colombia)* (2001–12, appointed by Colombia);[55]
- *Maritime Delimitation in the Black Sea (Romania* v. *Ukraine)* (2004–09, appointed by Romania);[56]
- *Aerial Herbicide Spraying (Ecuador* v. *Colombia)* (2008–13);[57]
- *Temple of Preah Vihear, Interpretation (Cambodia* v. *Thailand)* (2011–13, appointed by Thailand);[58] and
- *Questions Relating to the Seizure and Detention of Certain Documents and Data (Timor-Leste* v. *Australia)* (2013–15, appointed by Timor Leste).[59]

The Temple Case would have been of particular interest to Judge Cot, for he had written in the 1960s two commentaries on the ICJ judgment for which Cambodia sought an interpretation. The first article discussed the Judgment on the preliminary objections,[60] and the second article

49 http://www.icj-cij.org/en/case/115, accessed 16 March 2018.

50 http://www.icj-cij.org/en/case/94, accessed 16 March 2018.

51 http://www.icj-cij.org/en/case/102, accessed 16 March 2018.

52 http://legal.un.org/riaa/cases/vol_XXV/231-266.pdf, accessed 12 November 2015.

53 http://www.acp.int/, accessed 12 November 2015.

54 A "Round-up of Known Claims Under European Development Fund Arbitration Rules," 3 August 2015, by Jarrod Hepburn, is available only to subscribers of *Investment Arbitration Reporter*, https://www.iareporter.com/articles/round-up-of-known-claims-under-european-development-fund-arbitration-rules/, accessed 10 November 2017. The *Reports of International Arbitral Awards* are available at http://www.un.org/law/riaa/, accessed 12 November 2015.

55 *Supra* note 28.

56 http://www.icj-cij.org/en/case/132, accessed 16 March 2018.

57 http://www.icj-cij.org/en/case/138, accessed 16 March 2018.

58 http://www.icj-cij.org/en/case/151, accessed 30 March 2018.

59 http://www.icj-cij.org/en/case/156, accessed 16 March 2018.

60 Jean-Pierre Cot, "L'arrêt de la Cour internationale de Justice dans l'affaire du temple Preah Vihear (Cambodge c/Thaïlande). Exceptions préliminaires," *AFDI*, 7 (1961), pp. 229–51, http://www.persee.fr/web/revues/home/prescript/article/afdi_0066-3085_1961_num_7_1_1087, accessed 12 November 2015. The text of the Judgment is

analyzed the Judgment on the merits.[61]

Prior to his appointment to the Tribunal in the *South China Sea Arbitration*, Judge Cot was member of another arbitral tribunal constituted under Annex VII to the 1982 Convention: the *Bay of Bengal Maritime Boundary Arbitration between Bangladesh and India* (2009–14).[62]

MEMBER OF THE TRIBUNAL: JUDGE STANISŁAW PAWLAK

Prof. Stanisław Pawlak[63] was born in Kalisz, Poland, in 1933.[64]

A. Education

Judge Pawlak graduated from the Faculty of Law and Administration of the University of Warsaw in 1955 with a Master in Law. He subsequently obtained two doctorates: a PhD in Law (1967) and a DLitt (Doctor of Letters) in Political Science (1973), also from the University of Warsaw.

B. Academic Experience

While working in the Polish Ministry of Foreign Affairs, he was successively Associate Professor (1974–2001), Professor (2002–12), and Professor Emeritus (2013) of International Law and International Relations in the Faculty of Journalism and Political Science of the University of Warsaw. He has taught at the Institute of International Relations of the same University since 1975. Since 2005, he has been Professor and Dean of the Faculty of Social Science and Administration, Warsaw Academy of Computer Science and Administration. Between 1967 and 2001, he was Visiting Professor at various universities in the United States, Canada, and Syria.

C. Publications

Judge Pawlak is the author of numerous books and scholarly articles on international law, the law of the sea, the UN, disarmament, international terrorism, and Japanese, Chinese, Canadian, and American foreign policy.[65] Noteworthy is the fact that Judge Pawlak wrote two books that cover nearly 40 years of US–China relations: *The United States Policy towards China 1941–1955* (in Polish), 1973 (also published in Russian in 1974), and *The United States Policy towards China 1956–1978* (in Polish), 1982. He is also author of *Okinawa* (in Polish, 1972)

On the law of the sea, he has written the following titles:

---

available at http://www.icj-cij.org/files/case-related/45/045-19610526-JUD-01-00-BI.pdf, accessed 16 March 2018.

61 Jean-Pierre Cot, "L'arrêt de la Cour internationale de Justice dans l'affaire du temple de Préah Vihéar (Cambodge c. Thaïlande - Fond)," *AFDI*, 8 (1962), pp. 217–47, http://www.persee.fr/web/revues/home/prescript/article/afdi_0066-3085_1962_num_8_1_969, accessed 12 November 2015. The text of the Judgment is available at http://www.icj-cij.org/files/case-related/45/045-19620615-JUD-01-00-BI.pdf, accessed 16 March 2018.

62 *Supra* note 23.

63 This website gives the correct pronunciation of Judge Pawlak's last name: http://forvo.com/user/gabii24/, accessed 12 November 2015.

64 Unless otherwise indicated, the following information is obtained from Judge Pawlak's biography on the ITLOS website, https://www.itlos.org/the-tribunal/members/judge-stanislaw-michal-pawlak/, accessed 12 November 2015.

65 See his biography published on the University of Warsaw website, http://www.en.ism.uw.edu.pl/prof-stanislaw-pawlak/, accessed 9 November 2015.

- "The Jurisdiction of the International Tribunal for the Law of the Sea (in Polish)," Yearbook *Prawo Morskie*, vol. XXV (2009);
- "Some Reflections on Factors Exerting Influence on Maritime Boundary Delimitation," in *Coexistence, Cooperation and Solidarity: Liber Amicorum Rüdiger Wolfrum*, eds. Holger P. Hestermeyer et al. (Leiden: Martinus Nijhoff, 2011);
- "The Baltic Sea Region—An Area of Interdependence of Baltic States," in *Governing Ocean Resources: New Challenges and Emerging Regimes, A Tribute to Judge Choon-Ho Park*, eds. J.M. Van Dyke, S.P. Broder, S. Lee, and J.-H. Paik (Leiden: Martinus Nijhoff, 2013).

His other publications in Polish include

- "Political and Legal Aspects of International Terrorism," *Sprawy Międzynarodowe* (September 1988);
- *Present Value of the Idea of Atomic-Free Zones in the World* (1987);
- *Yalta and Potsdam* (1985);
- "The Legal Aspects of Verification," *The International Law of Arms Control and Disarmament* (1991);
- "Poland's Treaty Policy 1990–1993," *Yearbook of Polish Foreign Policy* (1993–1994);
- *Protection of National Minorities in Europe*, Warsaw, 2001;
- "The United Nations Towards International Terrorism," *Organizacja Narodow Zjednoczonych-Bilans i Peryspektywy* (2006);
- "Multilateral Diplomacy—Its Role and Tasks," *Stosunki Miedzynarodowe w XXI wieku* (2006);
- "The Protection of National Minorities in Eastern Europe," *OSCE and Minorities—Assessment and Prospects* (2007);
- "Poland's Policy Towards the Middle East," in *Directions and Areas of Polish Foreign Policy* (2012); and
- *Publications and Documents From the Years 1962 to 2012* (Selection) (in Polish and English) (2013).

D. Professional Experience

Judge Pawlak's career in the Polish Ministry of Foreign Affairs spanned 50 years (1955–2005). He served for many years in Asia, as

- Legal Adviser and Analytic Officer of the Polish delegation to the Neutral Nations Supervisory Commission in Panmunjom, Korea (1956–58);
- Attaché and Second Secretary at the Polish Embassy in Tokyo (1958–63);
- Deputy Chief of the Polish delegation to the International Control Commission, Saigon, Viet Nam (1965–66); and
- Ambassador to Syria and Jordan (1996–2001).

He was posted in North America as First Secretary at the Polish Embassy to the US (1967–70) and as Ambassador to Canada (1978-83).

Judge Pawlak's experience of multilateral organizations is extensive. He was Polish Representative to the UN General Assembly (1973–78, 1983–91, and 2002–05) and to the Steering Committee for Human Rights (CDDH) of the Council of Europe (1992–95).[66] He was chair of the Polish delegation to the Vienna diplomatic conference that was held under the auspices of the UN and that drew up the draft Convention on the Law of Treaties between States and International Organizations or between International Organizations (1986).[67]

In the Home Office, most of his assignments related to international law and international organizations. He was Director of the Department of International Organizations (1975–78 and again 1986–89) and Director of the Legal and Treaty Department (1983–86). After representing Poland at the United Nations, he became Adviser to the President of the Republic (2001–05).

Judge Pawlak's involvement in law of the sea issues covers a period of over 30 years:

- In the 1980s, he headed the Polish delegation in talks with the German Democratic Republic (East Germany) on the Agreement of 22 May 1989 on delimitation of the maritime boundary between the two countries (1983–88) and with the USSR on the delimitation of the Polish–Soviet sea border (1985).
- In the 1990s, he was Chair of the group of Polish experts that engaged in talks with experts from the Russian Federation and other interested States on the protection and conservation of marine resources of the Sea of Okhotsk (1992–95).
- He chaired the Polish Delegations to the International Conference that drew up the 1994 Convention on Protection of Pollock Resources in the Bering Sea (1993–94)[68] and to the UN Conference for the Agreement for the Implementation of the Provisions of the United Nations Convention on the Law of the Sea of 10 December 1982 relating to the Conservation and Management of Straddling Fish Stocks and Highly Migratory Fish Stocks (1993–95).[69]
- He was Chairman of the Polish delegation to the 13th President, Meeting of States Parties to the 1982 Convention in 2003, when he was elected president of the meeting.
- In 2004, he was again Chair of the Polish delegation to the Meetings of States Parties to the Convention.
- In 2004, he was nominated to the List of Arbitrators under Article 2 of Annexes V and VII to the Convention.
- The following year, he was elected to the ITLOS; he was reelected in 2014.

The *South China Sea Arbitration* seems to be the first time that Judge Pawlak has been appointed a member of an arbitral tribunal constituted under Annex VII of the 1982 Convention. Nevertheless, apart from his expertise in law of the sea issues acquired over more than three decades, he has the inestimable advantage of extensive knowledge of Socialist legal

---

66 *Council of Europe, www.coe.int/en/,* accessed 9 November 2015.

67 For the text of the treaty, see http://legal.un.org/ilc/texts/instruments/english/conventions/1_2_1986.pdf, accessed 9 November 2015.

68 The text of the Convention may be found at http://www.jus.uio.no/english/services/library/treaties/06/6-05/pollock-resources-bering.xml, accessed 12 November 2015.

69 The text of the Convention may be found at http://www.un.org/Depts/los/convention_agreements/convention_overview_fish_stocks.htm, accessed 12 November 2015.

systems as well as of East Asia. It is thus understandable that he was appointed to the Tribunal by the President of ITLOS when China failed to designate its arbitrator.

MEMBER OF THE TRIBUNAL: PROFESSOR ALFRED H.A. SOONS

Professor Alfred H.A. Soons[70] was born in 1948 in the Dutch Colony of Aruba, an island off the coast of Venezuela in the Caribbean.[71]

A. Education

Professor Soons obtained his undergraduate degree in Law at the University of Utrecht (1971) and an LLM in Law and Maritime Affairs at the University of Washington in Seattle (1974). After graduate studies at Cambridge University, he obtained a PhD from Utrecht University in 1982 with a dissertation on the international legal regime of marine scientific research.

B. Academic Experience

Professor Soons was Lecturer in Law at the University of Amsterdam in 1975–76 and Adjunct Professor of Public International Law at Erasmus University Rotterdam (1985–87). He was Professor of International Law at his alma mater from 1987 to 2014, serving as Dean of the Faculty of Law from 1995 to 1998.

He has also lectured on "The Exercise of Enforcement Jurisdiction at Sea" at the Hague Academy of International Law in 1994[72] and has been a visiting lecturer at various institutions, including Universitas Padjadjaran (Bandung), University of Helsinki, University of the Netherlands Antilles, University of Aruba, University of Washington, IMO Maritime Law Institute (Malta), and the Netherlands Defense College.

Currently, he occupies the following academic posts:

- Chair of the Scientific Advisory Council of the Netherlands Defense Academy;
- Member of the Executive Board of the Law of the Sea Institute, University of Hawaii, now at the University of Miami (since 1990); and
- Co-director, Rhodes Academy of Oceans Law and Policy, Rhodes (since 1995).

He has occupied the following posts in scholarly organizations on international law:

- Vice-President (1991–92) and President (1992–97) of the Netherlands Society of International Law;
- Chairman of the ILA (International Law Association) Committee on the Exclusive Economic Zone (1989–92); and
- Chairman of the ILA Committee on Coastal State Jurisdiction Relating to Marine Pollution (1992–97).

Currently, he is a member of the following scholarly organizations:

- International Law Association (ILA) Executive Council;

70 This website gives the correct pronunciation of Professor Soons's last name: https://www.howtopronounce.com/dutch/soons/, accessed 12 November 2015.

71 http://www.marecentre.nl/people_and_the_sea_2/documents/CVSoons.pdf, accessed 12 November 2015.

72 The address of the Academy website is https://www.hagueacademy.nl/, accessed 9 November 2015.

- Chair of the Jury for the Hague Prize for International Law;
- Chair of the Standing Advisory Committee on Public International Law of the Netherlands Ministry of Foreign Affairs;
- Scientific Council and the Commission on Public International Law of the T.M.C. Asser Instituut (since 1986);
- Executive Board of the Law of the Sea Institute, University of Hawaii;
- Chair of the Scientific Advisory Council of the Netherlands Defense Academy; and
- Advisory Body of Experts on the Law of the Sea of the Intergovernmental Oceanographic Commission (IOC/ABE-LOS).

C. Publications

Professor Soons has an impressive publication record.[73] In 1974, the University of Washington School of Law published his paper *Remote Sensing of the Ocean: International Legal Aspects*. Even before completing his doctorate, he had already published *Artificial Islands and Installations in International Law* (1974). The publication of his book *Marine Scientific Research and the Law of the Sea* (The Hague: Kluwer, 1982) was timely, for the UN Convention on the Law of the Sea, whose Part XIII regulates Marine Scientific Research, was adopted in that year. He edited the Proceedings of the 23rd Annual Conference of the Law of the Sea entitled *Implementation of the Law of the Sea Convention Through International Institutions* (1991).

For the years 2000 to 2013 alone, his CV lists four books, ten book chapters, seven articles, seven reports, and three edited books. The list would surely be even longer if it included his publications since the 1980s.

D. Professional Experience

Professor Soons has several decades of professional experience at the national and international levels.

He has a long and distinguished record of public service in both the judicial and executive branches in the Netherlands. He was Deputy-Judge in the District Court of Rotterdam for over a decade (1981–92). Prior to taking up his position as Professor at the University of Utrecht in 1987, he was Head of the Legal Affairs Section, North Sea Directorate (1976–78); Assistant Legal Counsel (international law) (1978–80); Deputy Legal Counsel (1980–85); and Head of the Division of Maritime Waterways and Ports (1985–87), all in the Ministry of Transport, Water Management, and Public Works.

Between 1976 and 1987, he was a member of the Dutch delegation to meetings in the framework of international agreements, such as the 1972 Oslo Dumping Convention (Convention for the Prevention of Marine Pollution by Dumping From Ships and Aircraft),[74] the 1969 Bonn Agreement (Agreement for Cooperation in Dealing With Pollution of the North Sea by Oil),[75] and the 1972 London Dumping Convention (London Convention on the Prevention of Marine Pollution by Dumping of Wastes and Other Matter).[76] He also was a

---

73 The list may be found at the University of Utrecht website: http://www.uu.nl/staff/default.aspx?lng=NL&Profielpagina=AHASoons&t=0, accessed 6 November 2015.

74 The text of the Convention may be found at http://sedac.ciesin.org/entri/texts/marine.pollution.dumping.ships.aircraft.1972.html, accessed 12 November 2015.

75 The text of the Convention may be found at http://www.bonnagreement.org/about/history, accessed 12 November 2015.

76 The text of the Convention may be found at http://www.imo.org/en/OurWork/Environment/LCLP/Pages/default.

member of the Dutch delegation to meetings of the International Maritime Organization,[77] the OECD (the Organisation for Economic Co-operation and Development),[78] and the International Commission for the Protection of the Rhine.[79]

He was a Member and Vice-Chair of the Netherlands delegation for negotiations with Belgium on questions concerning the rivers Meuse and Scheldt (1987–93) and a Member of the North Sea Commission of the National Advisory Council on Water Management and Public Works (1987–92). He was also a Consultant on fisheries and marine pollution legislation to the Governments of the Netherlands Antilles and Aruba (1989–92).

At the international level, Professor Soons has also worked as a consultant for foreign governments and international organizations. He was Consultant on maritime legislation to the Department of Sea Communications, Republic of Indonesia (1983–86), and Project-leader law of the sea (1987–91) Netherlands–Indonesian Legal Cooperation Program. He was a Consultant for the South Pacific Forum Fisheries Agency (1993–94).[80] Since 1998, he has been a member of the Advisory Body of Experts on the Law of the Sea of the Intergovernmental Oceanographic Commission.[81]

Professor Soons has considerable experience both as a lawyer and as a judge. He was counsel to Indonesia in the *Case concerning Sovereignty over Pulau Ligitan and Pulau Sipadan (Indonesia/Malaysia)*, International Court of Justice (1998–2002),[82] and counsel to Suriname in the *Guyana v. Suriname* arbitration under Annex VII of the 1982 Convention (2004–07).[83] He was Chairman of the ICC (International Chamber of Commerce) Arbitral Tribunals in case No. 8351 (1994–1996) and case No. 8311 (1995–1999). The ICC is a private organization with headquarters in Paris, which offers arbitration as "a flexible and efficient dispute resolution procedure leading to binding and final decisions subject to enforcement worldwide."[84] ICC arbitration differs from inter-state arbitration in that non-State actors may be parties to a case. No further information seems to be available on the two cases. It is possible that the parties to both cases wanted the proceedings to be kept confidential.

In addition to his appointment as a member of the tribunal in the *South China Sea Arbitration*, he was a member of the tribunal in the *Arctic Sunrise Arbitration (Netherlands v. Russia)* (2013–15).[85] He is the President of the Arbitral Tribunal in *Duzgit Integrity Arbitration (Malta v. São Tomé and Príncipe)*, which was initiated in 2013 and is still pending.[86]

MEMBER OF THE TRIBUNAL: JUDGE RÜDIGER WOLFRUM

Judge Rüdiger Wolfrum was born in Berlin, Germany, in 1941.[87]

---

aspx, accessed 12 November 2015.

77 www.imo.org, accessed 6 November 2015.

78 http://www.oecd.org, accessed 6 November 2015.

79 http://www.iksr.org/index.php?L=3, accessed 6 November 2015.

80 http://www.ffa.int, accessed 6 November 2015.

81 http://www.ioc-unesco.org, accessed 6 November 2015.

82 *Supra* note 51.

83 https://pca-cpa.org/en/cases/9/, accessed 30 March 2018.

84 http://www.iccwbo.org/products-and-services/arbitration-and-adr/, accessed 6 November 2015.

85 *Supra* note 26.

86 https://pcacases.com/web/view/53, accessed 6 November 2015.

87 The following websites give the correct pronunciation of the first and last names of Judge Wolfrum: https://www.howtopronounce.com/german/rudiger/, accessed 12 November 2015, and http://forvo.com/word/wolfrum/, accessed 7 September 2016. Unless otherwise indicated, the following information is obtained from Judge Wolfrum's biography on the University of Heidelberg website, https://www.rzuser.uni-heidelberg.de/~p00/down/cv_wolfrum_en.pdf, accessed 6 November 2015.

A. Education

He studied Law at the Universities of Bonn and Tübingen, passing his First State Examination (*Staatsexamen*) in 1969 and his Second State Examination in 1973. The State Examination is a final examination in law and certain other fields that is organized by the State and not by universities.[88] He completed his doctorate in laws (Dr. jur.) at the University of Bonn in 1973. He received the *Habilitation, venia legendi* for National Public and International Public Law in 1980. The *Habilitation* is a requirement in Germany and several other European countries for a tenured full professorship and supervision of doctoral research.[89] One can only apply for it when one already has a PhD, after which the candidate must write a substantial piece of research, which in practice is the equivalent of a second doctoral thesis, and then defend it. The *venia legendi* is the teaching license.[90]

B. Academic Experience

Judge Wolfrum started his academic career as Assistant Professor at the Institute of International Law of the University of Bonn (1973–82). While he was an Assistant Professor, he spent a year as a Research Fellow at the Center for Oceans Law and Policy, University of Virginia (1977–78). After receiving the *Habilitation*, he was appointed Professor of National Public and International Public Law at the University of Mainz in 1982.

He then moved to the University of Kiel, where he was also Director of the Institute of International Law (1982–93) and Vice-Rector of the University (1990–93). He was Visiting professor at the University of Minnesota, Minneapolis, Law School in 1987 and 1990.

From 1993 to 2013, he was Professor at the Faculty of Law of the University of Heidelberg as well as Director of the Max Planck Institute for Comparative Public Law and International Law, also in Heidelberg. The Institute, which focuses on basic research in public international law, European Union law, and comparative constitutional and administrative law, had been founded in 1924 in Berlin.[91] It was reestablished in 1949 as the Max Planck Institute for Comparative Public Law and International Law in Heidelberg by the Max Planck Society for the Advancement of Science, an independent, non-profit research organization founded in 1948.[92]

In 1998, Judge Wolfrum lectured at The Hague Academy of International Law on "Means of Ensuring Compliance With and Enforcement of International Law."

Judge Wolfrum has been a member of the following scholarly societies:

- Chairman of the board of the German United Nations Association (1994–97);
- Vice-President of the German Research Foundation (1996–2002);
- Vice-President of the Max Planck Society for the Advancement of Science (since 2002);

88 "Staatsexamen (auch: Staatsprüfung)," *Studisonline*, 21 January 2016, http://www.studis-online.de/StudInfo/studienabschluesse.php#stex, accessed 7 September 2016.

89 "Was genau ist eine Habilitation?," *bild.de*, http://www.bild.de/infos/studium/studium/habilitation-10692372.bild.html, accessed 12 November 2015.

90 European University Institute, *Germany, Academic Career Structure*, 30 July 2015, http://www.eui.eu/ProgrammesAndFellowships/AcademicCareersObservatory/AcademicCareersbyCountry/Germany.aspx, accessed 12 November 2015.

91 Max Planck Institute for Comparative Public Law and International Law, *About Us*, http://www.mpil.de/en/pub/news.cfm, accessed 12 November 2015.

92 Max-Planck-Gesellschaft, *Organisational Structure of the Max Planck Society*, http://www.mpg.de/183267/organisation, accessed 12 November 2015.

- International Law Association (Board, German section, since 1994);
- Executive Board, Law of the Sea Institute, University of Hawaii and University of Miami (since 1994);
- Executive Board of *Zentrum für deutsches Recht am Institut für Staat und Recht der Russischen Akademie der Wissenschaften* (Center for German Law at the Institute of State and Law at the Russian Academy of Sciences) (1994–2003);
- Executive Board of the *Stiftung für marine Geowissenschaften* (Foundation for Marine Geosciences) (GEOMAR) (1995–2003);
- Council of the *Deutsche Gesellschaft für Völkerrecht* (German Society for International Law) (since 1997); and
- Working Group *Biodiversität* ("Biodiversity") at the *Europäischen Akademie zur Erforschung von Folgen wissenschaftlichtechnischer Entwicklungen* (European Academy for the Research into Consequences of Scientific–Technological Developments).

C. Publications

The breadth of Judge Wolfrum's research is impressive. He is the author and editor of numerous books and articles on various issues of public international law, the law of the sea, international environmental law, human rights, the United Nations, and the Antarctic. These include

- *Die Internationalisierung staatsfreier Räume* (The Internationalization of Common Spaces Outside National Jurisdiction: The Development of an International Administration for Antarctica, Outer Space, High Seas and Deep Seabed; in German, 1984);
- *United Nations: Law, Policies, and Practice* (1995);
- *Enforcing Environmental Standards: Economic Mechanisms as Viable Means,* (1996);
- *The Right to a Fair Trial* (together with D. Weissbrodt) (1997);
- "Means of Ensuring Compliance with and Enforcement of International Law," *Recueil des Cours de l'Académie de Droit International de La Haye* (Collected Courses of the Hague Academy of International Law), vol. 272 (1998);
- *International Law*, vol. I/1, I/2, I/3 (in German; together with J. Delbrück), 2002;
- *Conflicts in International Environmental Law* (together with N. Matz, 2003);
- *Equality and Non-Discrimination in the National and International Human Rights Protection* (ed., 2003);
- *Developments of International Law in Treaty Making*, eds. V. Röben and R. Wolfum (2005);
- "The Role of International Dispute Settlement Institutions in the Delimitation of the Outer Continental Shelf," in *Maritime Delimitation*, eds. R. Lagoni and D. Vignes (2006);
- "Freedom of Navigation: New Challenges," in *Freedom of Seas, Passage Rights and the 1982 Law of the Sea Convention*, eds. M.H. Nordquist, T.B. Koh, and J. Norton Moore (Leiden: Martinus Nijhoff Publishers, 2009); and
- "Ad hoc Chambers," in *Governing Ocean Resources: New Challenges and Emerging Regimes, A Tribute to Judge Choon-Ho Park*, eds. J.M. Van Dyke, S.P. Broder, S. Lee, and J.-H. Paik (Leiden: Martinus Nijhoff Publishers, 2013).

Some of his articles in English on the law of the sea and other topics are available online for free:

- the Common Heritage of Mankind;[93]
- the military use of outer space;[94]
- indigenous peoples in international law;[95] and
- land-based tourism in Antarctica (with Silja Vöneky and Jürgen Friedrich).[96]

Judge Wolfrum is co-editor of the massive 11-volume *Max Planck Encyclopedia of Public International Law* (MPEPIL), which started to appear online in 2008 and in print in 2012,[97] and is co-editor of the *Max Planck Yearbook on United Nations Law*.[98]

D. Professional Experience

Judge Wolfrum has occupied the following positions at the national and international levels:

- Judge at the Courts of Appeal for Administrative Matters in Lüneburg and Schleswig (1986–93);
- Member of the German delegation to international meetings relating to the law of the sea and to Antarctica, the Third UN Conference on the Law of the Sea (1980–82), the Preparatory Commission for the International Seabed Authority and for ITLOS (1982), and the 4th Special Consultative Meeting concerning Antarctic mineral resource activities (1983–88);
- Chairman of the Legal Working Group of the Antarctic Treaty Consultative Meetings preparing an Annex to the Protocol on Environmental Protection to the Antarctic Treaty on responsibility for environmental damage (1993–98);
- Member of the UN Committee on the Elimination of Racial Discrimination (1990–2000);
- Member of ITLOS, 1996, re-elected in 1999 and 2008;
- Vice President of the ITLOS (1996–99),
- President of the Chamber for Marine Environment Disputes (1997–99);
- President of the ITLOS (2005–08);
- Member of the Special Chamber formed to deal with the *Case Concerning the Conservation and Sustainable Exploitation of Swordfish Stocks in the South-Eastern Pacific Ocean (Chile/European Union)* (2000–09);[99] and
- Member of the Special Chamber formed to deal with the *Dispute Concerning Delimitation of the Maritime Boundary between Ghana and Côte d'Ivoire in the Atlantic Ocean (Ghana/Côte d'Ivoire)*, initiated in 2014.[100]

---

93 "The Principle of the Common Heritage of Mankind," *ZaöRV*, 43 (1983), 312–37, http://www.zaoerv.de/43_1983/43_1983_2_a_312_337.pdf, accessed 12 November 2015.

94 "The Problems of Limitation and Prohibition of Military Use of Outer Space," *ZaöRV*, 44 (1984), 784–805, http://www.zaoerv.de/44_1984/44_1984_4_a_784_805.pdf, accessed 12 November 2015.

95 "The Protection of Indigenous Peoples in International Law," *ZaöRV*, 59 (1999), 369–82, http://www.zaoerv.de/59_1999/59_1999_2_a_369_382.pdf, accessed 12 November 2015.

96 "The Admissibility of Land-Based Tourism in Antarctica Under International Law," *ZaöRV*, 65 (2005), pp. 735–40, http://www.zaoerv.de/65_2005/65_2005_3_b_735_740.pdf, accessed 12 November 2015.

97 http://www.mpil.de/en/pub/research/areas/public-international-law/max-planck-encyclopedia.cfm, accessed 12 November 2015.

98 http://www.mpil.de/en/pub/publications/periodic-publications/max-planck-yearbook.cfm, accessed 12 November 2015.

99 https://www.itlos.org/cases/list-of-cases/case-no-7/, accessed 12 November 2015.

100 *Supra* note 22.

Prior to his appointment as a member of the Tribunal in the *Philippines v. China arbitration*, Judge Wolfrum was a member of three arbitral tribunals constituted under Annex VII to the 1982 Convention:

- *The Atlanto-Scandian Herring Arbitration (The Kingdom of Denmark in Respect of the Faroe Islands v. The European Union)* (2013–14);[101]
- *Chagos Marine Protected Area Arbitration (Mauritius v. United Kingdom)* (2010–15);[102] and
- President of the *Bay of Bengal Maritime Boundary Arbitration Between Bangladesh and India* (2009–14).[103]

To sum up, the combined personal professional experience in international law and law of the sea of the five members of the Arbitral Tribunal totals around 200 years. Seen in this context, China's insults against the Tribunal can only appear ridiculous, as it is evident that none of the five would have lasted a year—nay, even a day—as academic, civil servant, legal counsel, and judge if he had been "careless, negligent and irresponsible." Anyone who is familiar with the backgrounds of the five judges will realize that China's denigration of the judges reflects the accuser's character more than that of the accused.

[101] *Supra* note 25.
[102] https://www.pcacases.com/web/view/11, accessed 30 March 2018.
[103] *Supra* note 23.

5

The Lawyers of the Philippines: A Brilliant Track Record[1]

The curious Filipino reader who clicks on the PCA website on the images of the Hearing on Jurisdiction and Admissibility and the Hearing on the Merits will have noticed some distinctly unfamiliar faces in the photographs captioned "counsel team for the Philippines," none of whom is Filipino.[2] Despite the fact that the Philippines sent a large delegation to The Hague for each Hearing, only two members of the delegation took the floor.[3] The then Secretary of Foreign Affairs gave the opening remarks at the Hearing on Jurisdiction and Admissibility, followed by the then Solicitor General, who explained the order of the speakers. At the close of the first Hearing, the Solicitor General presented the Philippines' final submissions. At the opening of the Hearing on the Merits, the then Solicitor General explained the order of the oral presentations. At the close of the Hearing, the then Foreign Secretary made concluding remarks, followed by the Solicitor General, who presented the country's final submissions. Otherwise, none of the members of the Philippine delegation took the floor.

The reason for this situation may be found in the Philippine government's answer to a question raised on the eve of the July 2015 Hearing on Jurisdiction and Admissibility whether foreign lawyers could competently defend the Philippines' case.[4] The Presidential spokesman defended them in these terms:

---

1 An earlier version of this Chapter was posted on 11 July 2016 on the blog of the author's sister-in-law, https://www.raissarobles.com/2016/07/12/why-china-has-not-lambasted-the-foreign-lawyers-representing-the-philippines-in-the-south-china-sea-arbitration/.

2 For the photograph during the July 2015 Hearing, see https://pcacases.com/web/sendAttach/1488, accessed 30 March 2018. L to R: Professor Philippe Sands, Professor Bernard H. Oxman, Professor Alan E. Boyle, and Lawrence H. Martin. For the photograph during the November 2015 Hearing, see https://pcacases.com/web/sendAttach/1528, accessed 30 March 2018. In the image are Andrew B. Loewenstein and Professor Bernhard H. Oxman. See the image of the Statement by Paul S. Reichler, https://pcacases.com/web/sendAttach/1489, accessed 30 March 2018.

3 Forty-one representatives from the Philippines are listed in the Award on Jurisdiction and Admissibility, pp. 28–29, para. 86, https://pcacases.com/web/sendAttach/1506, accessed 30 March 2018. The Award of 12 July 2016 lists 36 representatives from the Philippines (pp. 73–74, para. 20), https://pcacases.com/web/sendAttach/2086, accessed 30 March 2018.

4 Andreo Calonzo, "Palace Defends Hiring of Foreign Lawyers for PHL Arbitration Case vs. China," *Philippine Daily Inquirer* (*PDI*), 8 July 2015, http://www.gmanetwork.com/news/story/518286/news/nation/palace-defends-hiring-of-foreign-lawyers-for-phl-arbitration-case-vs-china, accessed 24 September 2015.

> These are lawyers who have international reputation appearing before the tribunal. We can rely on them…We have the knowledge, but in so far as appearing before international tribunal [sic], you get the best persons you can hire for that…It will be foolhardy for us not to hire experts with experience with appearing before this tribunal.

Writing in 2002, Jean-Pierre Cot, one of the five members of the Tribunal in the *South China Sea Arbitration*, explained the requirements for legal counsel appearing before international tribunals:

> Counsel appearing before such tribunals are expected to deliver perfect or near-perfect performances. Their briefs are to be crisp, yet thorough. Their oral presentation must be exciting, but duly restrained. They are expected to be in full command of the latest developments with regard to a large amount of complex and sophisticated information.[5]

The appearance during the oral proceedings represents only the tip of the iceberg. The legal team's role in the drafting of the written pleadings is equally crucial, if not more so.

As explained by French professor Alain Pellet, the legal counsel hired by the State might take charge of the drafting of the pleadings. Alternatively, the State itself might undertake this task, but he believes that this is rarely the case.[6] Given the complexity of the issues raised by the case and the extremely high stakes involved, it is understandable that the Philippines entrusted the drafting of all of the country's written and oral pleadings to Foley Hoag, the law firm of Paul Reichler, notwithstanding the statement by the then Secretary of Foreign Affairs upon the filing of the Memorial in 2014 that the role of the foreign lawyers was limited to "guidance and assistance."[7]

The "happy few" who can draft States' pleadings or assist them in doing so and represent States in the oral proceedings constitute an "invisible" bar, "mainly composed of a handful of eminent professors of international law, teaching at the most prestigious universities, and an occasional and highly specialized barrister, backed by a few major law firms." Their number is estimated by Pellet, himself one of the members of the "invisible bar," to be at most 15.[8] According to a survey by Spanish professor Luis Ignacio Sánchez Rodríguez, they are recruited mostly from France, the UK, Belgium, Switzerland, and, to a much lesser extent, the US. Rarely do developing countries recruit legal counsel from their own countries or from other developing countries.[9]

The reasons for this situation are as numerous as they are obvious. Developing countries

5 Jean-Pierre Cot, "Appearing 'for' or 'on behalf of' a State: The Role of Private Counsel Before International Tribunals," in Nisuke Ando, Edward McWhinney, and Rüdiger Wolfrum (eds.), *Liber Amicorum Judge Shigeru Oda* (The Hague: Kluwer Law International, 2002), II, p. 836.

6 Alain Pellet, "Remarques sur le 'métier' de conseil devant la Cour internationale de Justice," in United Nations Office of Legal Affairs, *Collection of Essays by Legal Advisers of States, Legal Advisers of International Organizations and Practitioners in the Field of International Law* (New York: United Nations, 1999), pp. 451–54, http://legal.un.org/cod/books/CollectionOfEssaysByLegalAdvisers.pdf, accessed 19 November 2015.

7 Confirmation of the author's supposition that the Philippine pleadings were drafted by the foreign lawyers was provided by two separate, highly placed sources, who spoke on condition of anonymity. For the statement of the Foreign Secretary, see *Statement of the Foreign Affairs Secretary: PH Files Memorial Under UNCLOS Against China*, 30 March 2014, http://www.officialgazette.gov.ph/2014/03/30/statement-of-the-secretary-of-foreign-affairs-ph-files-memorial-under-unclos-against-china/, accessed 13 November 2015.

8 Pellet, p. 437, *supra* note 6.

9 Luis Ignacio Sánchez Rodríguez, "Litigation Practice Before the International Court of Justice: Some Specific Problems of Developing and Small Countries," *in Collection of Essays by Legal Advisers*, pp. 459–78, *supra* note 6.

have few civil servants having expertise in international law or in international legal procedures. These isolated individuals have no competent or experienced national legal teams on which they can rely.[10] The lack of human resources is reflected in the fact that few developing countries are able to produce periodical publications in international law. The exceptions that confirm the rule might be several Latin American countries, who are more successful than most developing countries in sustaining such publications. At present, Brazil seems to be the leader in the field among developing countries, with three publications (*Anuário Brasileiro de Direito Internacional* [Brazilian Yearbook of International Law],[11] *Revista Brasileira de Direito Internacional,* [Brazilian Journal of International Law],[12] and *Revista Eletrônica de Direito Internacional* [Electronic Journal of International Law]).[13] The Mexicans publish the *Anuario Mexicano de Derecho Internacional* (Mexican Yearbook of International Law);[14] the Argentines, the *Anuario Argentino de Derecho Internacional* (Argentine Yearbook of International Law);[15] and the Colombians, the *Revista Colombiana de Derecho Internacional* (Colombian Journal of International Law).[16] At least six scholarly journals are published in English in Asia (the *Asian Journal of International Law,*[17] the *Asian Yearbook of International Law,*[18] the *Chinese Journal of International Law,*[19] the *Indian Journal of International Law,*[20] the *Japanese Yearbook of International Law,*[21] and the *Korean Journal of International and Comparative Law*),[22] and two in Africa (the *African Yearbook of International Law*[23] and the *Revue Egyptienne de Droit International* [Egyptian Journal of International Law]. In general, the Latin American journals are of more recent vintage, but they have the priceless advantage of being available online for free. Unfortunately, very few scholars outside Latin America are able to read Spanish and/or Portuguese.

The ability to sustain regular publications implies not just the existence of human resources but also the availability of decent libraries. In most developing countries, the penury of human resources is aggravated by the fact that the few specialists do not have at their disposal libraries specializing in international law, which "demand sophisticated doctrinal and jurisprudential collections, as well as records of judicial practice, all covering distinct judicial circuits for both historical and modem developments," according to Sánchez Rodríguez.[24] Electronic databases, such as Heinonline, Lexis-Nexis, JSTOR, and Ebscohost, have gone a long way towards making up for the deficiencies of library collections in the Philippines in all fields. Nevertheless, the databases still have lacunae. Unless one is lucky enough to stumble across journals that have generously put online most of their archives (the *Annuaire Français de Droit International* [French Yearbook of International Law],[25] the *Revue Belge de Droit International* [Belgian Journal

[10] *Ibid.*, pp. 461–62.
[11] http://centrodireitointernacional.com.br/publicacoes/anuario-brasileiro-de-direito-internacional/, accessed 30 March 2018.
[12] http://revistas.ufpr.br/dint, accessed 30 March 2018.
[13] http://centrodireitointernacional.com.br/publicacoes/revista-eletronica/, accessed 30 March 2018.
[14] https://revistas.juridicas.unam.mx/index.php/derecho-internacional, accessed 30 March 2018.
[15] http://www.aadi.org.ar/index.php?acc=4, accessed 30 March 2018.
[16] http://revistas.javeriana.edu.co/index.php/internationallaw/index, accessed 30 March 2018.
[17] https://www.cambridge.org/core/journals/asian-journal-of-international-law (subscription required), accessed 1 April 2018.
[18] https://brill.com/view/title/34781 (subscription required), accessed 1 April 2018.
[19] https://academic.oup.com/chinesejil/pages/About (subscription required), accessed 1 April 2018.
[20] http://www.isil-aca.org/publication.htm (subscription required), accessed 30 March 2018.
[21] http://www.ilajapan.org/jyil/ (subscription required), accessed 1 April 2018.
[22] https://brill.com/view/journals/kjic/kjic-overview.xml (subscription required), accessed 1 April 2018.
[23] https://brill.com/view/journals/afyo/afyo-overview.xml (subscription required), accessed 1 April 2018.
[24] Sánchez Rodríguez, pp. 461–62, *supra* note 6.
[25] http://www.persee.fr/collection/afdi (five-year embargo), accessed 30 March 2018.

of International Law],[26] and the *Zeitschrift für ausländisches öffentliches Recht und Völkerrecht* [Heidelberg Journal of International Law]),[27] separate or additional subscriptions are required for the outstanding European periodicals, such as the *British Yearbook of International Law*,[28] the *Revue Générale de Droit International Public* (General Journal of Public International Law),[29] the *Journal du Droit International* (Journal of International Law),[30] the *Revista Española de Derecho Internacional* (Spanish Journal of International Law),[31] the *Archiv des* Völkerrechts (Archive of International Law),[32] the *German Yearbook of International Law*,[33] the *Rivista di Diritto Internazionale* (Journal of International Law),[34] the *Netherlands International Law Review*,[35] and the *Netherlands Yearbook of International Law*.[36] And of course, the journal databases do not contain books, which cost considerably more than paperbacks.[37]

Developing countries, as Judge Cot reminds us, are free to choose whoever they wish to represent them: "It is their sovereign right and privilege."[38] There is little doubt that the five members of the Philippine legal team are part of the "invisible bar" or the "invisible college of international lawyers." Like the judges that compose the tribunal, all of them have decades of international experience as practitioners. Unlike the judges, not all of them are academics. Unlike the judges, none of them belongs to French, Belgian, or Swiss circles. Undoubtedly, the reason for this is purely pragmatic. Even if one of the Tribunal's members is French, the language of the arbitration is English. A French member of the legal team would have had to express himself/herself in English, or else interpretation from and into French would have had to be provided, thus increasing substantially the costs of the proceedings. Since Judge Cot agreed to have English as the sole language of the proceedings, there was no need for French-speaking legal counsel.

A confidential admission by Chinese officials to the *South China Morning Post* will give us an idea of the reputation of the members of the Philippine legal team: "[Chinese] Foreign Ministry officials confided privately that Beijing had thought about recruiting a team of top-flight lawyers to beat the Philippines in court, but discovered the best maritime lawyers had already been hired by rival claimants."[39]

The biographies of the members of the legal team are presented below in the order in which they appear on the website of the Permanent Court of Arbitration (PCA), which acts as

26 http://rbdi.bruylant.be/public/index.php?module_id=00000000009&rec_id=00000107432_00000011782, archives 1965–99, accessed 30 March 2018.

27 http://www.zaoerv.de/, archives 1929–2015, accessed 30 March 2018.

28 https://academic.oup.com/bybil (subscription required), accessed 30 March 2018.

29 http://www.rgdip.com (subscription required), accessed 30 March 2018.

30 http://www.lexisnexis.fr/droit-document/numeros/journal-droit-international-clunet-.htm (subscription required), accessed 1 April 2018.

31 http://www.revista-redi.es/ (subscription required), accessed 1 April 2018.

32 https://www.mohr.de/en/journals/archiv-des-voelkerrechts-avr (subscription required), accessed 1 April 2018.

33 http://www.gyil.org/ (subscription required), accessed 1 April 2018.

34 https://www.iusexplorer.it/Rivista/Rivista_di_Diritto_Internazionale?area=riv_internazionale (subscription required), accessed 1 April 2018.

35 https://www.cambridge.org/core/journals/netherlands-international-law-review/all-issues (subscription required), accessed 1 April 2018.

36 http://www.springer.com/series/8913 (subscription required), accessed 1 April 2018.

37 The cost of the two volumes in which Judge Cot's piece (*supra* note 5) appeared is €508 (approximately $600, depending on the exchange rate), an amount that is higher than the average monthly salary of academics in any field in most developing countries. http://www.brill.com/liber-amicorum-judge-shigeru-oda-2-vols, accessed 17 November 2015.

38 Cot, p. 836, *supra* note 5.

39 Shi Jiangtao, "Is Beijing Courting Disaster by Shunning South China Sea Tribunal?," *South China Morning Post*, 19 June, 2016, http://www.scmp.com/news/china/diplomacy-defence/article/1977418/beijing-courting-disaster-shunning-south-china-sea, accessed 21 June 2016.

the Registry for the arbitration.[40] Their biographies will be presented using the same categories as those employed for the judges' biographies: Education, Academic Experience, Publications, and Professional Experience.

PAUL S. REICHLER

A. Education

Reichler is a summa cum laude graduate of Tufts University in Medford, Massachusetts (1969), and a cum laude graduate of Harvard Law School (1973).

B. Professional Experience

In 1979, Reichler was an associate at the Washington-based law firm of Arnold and Porter, when the latter was approached by Nicaragua upon the advice of the Panamanian leader Omar Torrijos.[41] Nicaragua was seeking assistance in recovering some of the assets of the overthrown Nicaraguan dictator, Anastasio Somoza, and in dealing with the US. Reichler was assigned to represent Nicaragua because of his knowledge of Spanish. The election of Ronald Reagan in 1980 and the deterioration of Nicaragua's relations with the US, which was supporting a rebel group seeking to overthrow the government of Nicaragua, caused apprehension in the firm about its representation of Nicaragua. Reichler left the firm for the Atlanta firm of Powell, Goldstein, Frazer, and Murphy, which was opening a Washington office. In 1984, when this firm voted against representing Nicaragua before the ICJ, Reichler established his own firm, Reichler, Appelbaum, and Wippmann.

Reichler explained his attitude to the case in an interview:

> I felt at the time that I had an obligation to my client to pursue the case and a moral obligation not to refuse to help end the war, which I considered to be illegal, immoral and contrary to the interests of my own country….I think for the Reagan Administration to flagrantly violate international law as it is doing in Nicaragua is not only wrong in itself but contrary to the best interests of the U.S. It squanders our moral authority as a world leader, and by weakening the system of international law it encourages other states to flout the law with impunity.[42]

Reichler declared, "'I have come to believe that international law is the best safeguard against war, destruction and chaos.'"

Reichler was part of a team of four that presented the Nicaraguan case before the ICJ, the other three all being international law professors: Ian Brownlie from Oxford,[43] Abram Chayes from Harvard,[44] and Pellet from Paris.[45] In the wake of the *Nicaragua Judgment* on the merits, in

---

40 https://pcacases.com/web/view/7, accessed 30 March 2018.

41 "Washington Talk: Nicaragua Peace Talks; American Sitting Opposite U.S.-Backed Rebels," *New York Times*, 19 February 1988, http://www.nytimes.com/1988/02/19/us/washington-talk-nicaragua-peace-talks-american-sitting-opposite-us-backed-rebels.html?pagewanted=print, accessed 15 November 2015

42 *Ibid.*

43 Philippe Sands, "Sir Ian Brownlie Obituary," *The Guardian*, 11 January 2010, http://www.theguardian.com/theguardian/2010/jan/11/sir-ian-brownlie-obituary, accessed 17 November 2015.

44 David E. Rosenbaum, "Abram Chayes, John Kennedy Aide, Dies at 77," *New York Times*, 18 April 2000, http://www.nytimes.com/2000/04/18/us/abram-chayes-john-kennedy-aide-dies-at-77.html, accessed 17 November 2015.

45 http://www.alainpellet.eu/, accessed 17 November 2015.

which the ICJ declared that the US had violated international law by supporting the Contras,[46] demand for the services of Brownlie, Pellet, and Reichler increased considerably.

At present, Reichler[47] is Senior Partner and Co-Chair of the International Litigation and Arbitration Department of the Boston-based law firm Foley Hoag, which was established in 1943 and has offices in Washington, D.C., and Paris.[48] Reichler himself is based in Washington, D.C. For thirty years now, Reichler has represented a large number of States before US and international tribunals.

In the US, he has represented foreign States before federal and state courts and is one of the leading experts on litigation under the Foreign Sovereign Immunities Act. The Act "define[s] the jurisdiction of United States courts in suits against foreign states, the circumstances in which foreign states are immune from suit and in which execution may not be levied on their property, and for other purposes."[49] His clients have included Bolivia,[50] Chile, Guyana, Kenya, Liberia, Nicaragua, Tanzania, Thailand, and Venezuela.

At the international level, he has been legal counsel for States in two types of disputes: investor-State disputes and inter-State disputes. In investor-State disputes, he has represented States in the International Centre for the Settlement of Investment Disputes (ICSID),[51] the International Chamber of Commerce (ICC),[52] the PCA, and the Stockholm Chamber of Commerce (SCC). His clients have included Bolivia,[53] Ecuador, Guyana, Nicaragua, the Philippines, Uruguay,[54] and Venezuela.

He has been legal counsel for states before permanent tribunals (the ICJ and the ITLOS) as well as ad hoc international tribunals. At the ICJ, he was legal counsel for two more cases involving the use of force: *Armed Activities on the Territory of the Congo (Democratic Republic of the Congo v. Uganda)* (1999–2005, appointed by Uganda)[55] and *Application of the International Convention on the Elimination of All Forms of Racial Discrimination (Georgia v. Russian Federation)* (2008–11, appointed by Georgia).[56]

At the ICJ as well as at the ITLOS and *ad hoc tribunals*, his cases in the last 15 years involve land and maritime disputes and one environmental dispute:

- Guyana against Suriname (ad hoc tribunal under Annex VII of the 1982 UN Convention on the Law of the Sea, 2004–07, counsel for Guyana);[57]
- *Dispute Regarding Navigational and Related Rights (Costa Rica v. Nicaragua)* in the ICJ (2005–09, counsel for Nicaragua);[58]

---

46 http://www.icj-cij.org/files/case-related/70/070-19860627-JUD-01-00-BI.pdf, accessed 29 March 2018.

47 See his biography on the firm's website, http://www.foleyhoag.com/people/reichler-paul, accessed 18 November 2015. Unless otherwise indicated, the following information is obtained from this biography.

48 http://www.foleyhoag.com/our-firm/history, accessed 18 November 2015.

49 http://www.gpo.gov/fdsys/pkg/USCODE-2011-title28/html/USCODE-2011-title28-partIV-chap97.htm, accessed 18 November 2015.

50 Oliver Shykles, "Foley Hoag Wins Key Victory for Government of Bolivia in Investor Dispute," 1 August 2008, http://lists.noticias.nl/pipermail/eti-l/2008-August/000283.html, accessed 18 November 2015.

51 https://icsid.worldbank.org/ICSID/StaticFiles/basicdoc/main-eng.htm, accessed 18 November 2015.

52 http://www.iccwbo.org/, accessed 18 November 2015.

53 "Cleary Gottlieb Takes Over Treaty Case against Bolivia," *Latin Lawyer Online*, 27 July 2009, http://doclink.demarest.com.br/fds/fds.aspx?lib=BIBLIOTECA&doc=63088, accessed 18 November 2015.

54 *Philip Morris Brands SARL, Philip Morris Products S.A. and Abal Hermanos S.A. (The Claimants) and Oriental Republic of Uruguay (The Respondent)* (ICSID Case No. ARB/10/7), Decision on Jurisdiction, 2 July 2013, http://www.italaw.com/sites/default/files/case-documents/italaw1531.pdf, accessed 18 November 2015.

55 http://www.icj-cij.org/en/case/116, accessed 16 March 2018.

56 http://www.icj-cij.org/en/case/140, accessed 16 March 2018.

57 http://legal.un.org/riaa/cases/vol_XXX/1-144.pdf, accessed 1 September 2016.

58 http://www.icj-cij.org/en/case/133, accessed16 March 2018.

- *Pulp Mills on the River Uruguay (Argentina v. Uruguay)* in the ICJ (2006–10, counsel for Uruguay);[59]
- *Territorial and Maritime Dispute (Nicaragua v. Colombia)* in the ICJ, (2007–12, counsel for Nicaragua);[60]
- *Aerial Herbicide Spraying (Ecuador v. Colombia)* in the ICJ (2008–13, counsel for Ecuador, together with Sands);[61]
- *Dispute Concerning Delimitation of the Maritime Boundary between Bangladesh and Myanmar in the Bay of Bengal* in the ITLOS (2009–12, counsel for Bangladesh, together with Martin and Sands);[62]
- *Bay of Bengal Maritime Boundary Arbitration between Bangladesh and India* (ad hoc tribunal under Annex VII of the 1982 UN Convention on the Law of the Sea, 2009–14, counsel for Bangladesh, together with Sands);[63]
- *Chagos Marine Protected Area Arbitration (Mauritius v. United Kingdom)* (ad hoc tribunal under Annex VII of the 1982 UN Convention on the Law of the Sea, 2011–15, counsel for Mauritius, together with Sands);[64]
- *Certain Activities Carried out by Nicaragua in the Border Area (Costa Rica v. Nicaragua)* in the ICJ (2010–15, counsel for Nicaragua);[65]
- *Construction of a Road in Costa Rica Along the San Juan River (Nicaragua v. Costa Rica)* in the ICJ (2011–15, counsel for Nicaragua);[66]
- *Maritime Delimitation in the Caribbean Sea and the Pacific Ocean (Costa Rica v. Nicaragua)* in the ICJ (2014–18);[67]
- *Maritime Delimitation in the Indian Ocean (Somalia v. Kenya)*, in the ICJ (commenced in 2014);[68] and
- *Dispute Concerning Delimitation of the Maritime Boundary between Ghana and Côte d'Ivoire in the Atlantic Ocean (Ghana/Côte d'Ivoire)* in the ITLOS (2014–17).[69]

Finally, Reichler served as Mediator, appointed by the Secretary General of the Organization of American States (OAS), in the land and maritime boundary dispute between Guatemala and Belize (2000–02).

Little wonder that Reichler was evaluated in 2010 by Chambers Guides, specialized in "researching the world's best lawyers," as

> one of the world's most respected and experienced practitioners of Public International Law, specializing for more than 25 years in the representation of Sovereign States in disputes with other States, and in disputes with foreign investors. He belongs to a select group of elite lawyers with extensive experience litigating on behalf of Sovereign States before the International Court of Justice in The Hague, and the International Tribunal on the Law of the Sea in Hamburg.[70]

59 http://www.icj-cij.org/en/case/135, accessed 16 March 2018.
60 http://www.icj-cij.org/en/case/124, accessed 16 March 2018.
61 http://www.icj-cij.org/en/case/138, accessed 16 March 2018.
62 https://www.itlos.org/en/cases/list-of-cases/case-no-16/, accessed 16 November 2015.
63 https://pcacases.com/web/view/18, accessed 30 March 2018.
64 https://pcacases.com/web/view/11, accessed 30 March 2018.
65 http://www.icj-cij.org/en/case/150, accessed 16 March 2018.
66 http://www.icj-cij.org/en/case/152, accessed 16 March 2018.
67 http://www.icj-cij.org/en/case/157, accessed 16 March 2018.
68 http://www.icj-cij.org/en/case/161, accessed 16 March 2018.
69 https://www.itlos.org/en/cases/list-of-cases/case-no-23/, accessed 18 November 2015.
70 *Foley Hoag LLP*, http://www.chambersandpartners.com/15649/96/editorial/2/1, accessed 17 November 2015.

LAWRENCE H. MARTIN

A. Education

Lawrence Martin is a younger colleague of Paul Reichler.[71] He obtained his bachelor's degree, summa cum laude, from Bowdoin College, a small private liberal arts college in Brunswick, Maine, in 1988 and his JD, magna cum laude, from Harvard Law School in 1997. Martin speaks fluent Chinese.

B. Professional Experience

He is at present a partner in Foley Hoag's Washington, D.C. office and a member of its International Litigation and Arbitration Department. According to the Foley Hoag website, Martin has considerable experience in general civil litigation matters before US courts, including insurance industry controversies, copyright disputes, and product liability lawsuits. By 2004, or a mere seven years after finishing law school, he was already named by *Washingtonian* as one of Washington's top lawyers in civil defense.[72] He also represents foreign States, such as Bolivia, in litigation before US courts.

At the international level, he has represented states in investor-State and inter-State disputes. In investor-State disputes, he has been counsel for States, such as Bolivia[73] and Uruguay,[74] before the ICSID.

In inter-State disputes, he has worked with Reichler in a number of disputes involving maritime delimitation and environmental issues submitted to the ICJ, to ITLOS, or to ad hoc arbitral tribunals constituted under Annex VII of the 1982 Convention:

- Guyana Against Suriname (ad hoc tribunal under Annex VII of the 1982 UN Convention on the Law of the Sea, 2004–07, counsel for Guyana);[75]
- *Dispute Regarding Navigational and Related Rights (Costa Rica v. Nicaragua)* in the ICJ (2005–09, counsel for Nicaragua);[76]
- *Pulp Mills on the River Uruguay (Argentina v. Uruguay)* in the ICJ (2006–10, counsel for Uruguay);[77]
- *Dispute Concerning Delimitation of the Maritime Boundary between Bangladesh and Myanmar in the Bay of Bengal (Bangladesh/Myanmar)* in the ITLOS (2009–12, counsel for Bangladesh);[78]
- *Bay of Bengal Maritime Boundary Arbitration between Bangladesh and India* (ad hoc tribunal under Annex VII of the 1982 Convention, 2009–14, counsel for Bangladesh);[79] and
- *Construction of a Road in Costa Rica Along the San Juan River (Nicaragua v. Costa Rica)* in the ICJ (2011–15, counsel for Nicaragua).[80]

71 See his biography on the website of Foley Hoag, http://www.foleyhoag.com/people/martin-lawrence, accessed 25 November 2015. Unless otherwise indicated, the following information is obtained from this biography.

72 "Washington, DC's Best Lawyers: Civil Defense," *Washingtonian*, 4 November 2015, https://www.washingtonian.com/2015/11/04/washington-dcs-best-lawyers-civil-defense/, accessed 8 September 2016.

73 *Supra* note 53.

74 *Supra* note 54.

75 *Supra* note 57.

76 *Supra* note 58.

77 *Supra* note 59.

78 *Supra* note 62.

79 *Supra* note 63.

80 *Supra* note 66.

In 2015, Martin was described by one source quoted in Chambers Global as "exceptional not only in terms of knowledge, expertise of the law, and organizational and managerial skills, but more importantly because of his character, attitude, ethics and advocacy."[81]

ANDREW B. LOEWENSTEIN

Andrew Loewenstein is a partner with the International Litigation and Arbitration Department of Foley Hoag.[82] He is based in Boston, MA. He appeared before the Tribunal in the *South China Sea Arbitration* during the Hearing on the Merits.

A. Education

He graduated with a BA in Political Science, magna cum laude, from Brown University in Providence, Rhode Island, in 1996. Brown is one of the eight Ivy League Schools in the US.[83] In his senior year, he was editor-in-chief of the University's journal specializing in international relations, *Brown Journal of World Affairs*.[84] Immediately after graduating from Brown, he attended the London School of Economics, where he obtained a Master's degree in 1997, although his profile does not specify the field of specialization. On his return to the US, he studied law at Georgetown University, completing his J.D. in 2000. In his third (and last) year of law school, he was the Managing Editor of the *American Criminal Law Review*, a publication of the Georgetown University Law Center.[85]

B. Publications

Despite his professional obligations, Loewenstein has found the time to publish a number of articles, mostly on international criminal law and the US Foreign Sovereign Immunities Act, a list of which may be found in his biography on the Foley Hoag's website.

C. Professional Experience

For a year after graduation, Loewenstein was Law Clerk to Judge William J. Holloway, Jr., US Court of Appeals for the Tenth Circuit (2000–01). Judicial clerkships are widely sought after by fresh law school graduates in the US as a "way to bridge the gap between law school and the practice of law."[86] The reason is that the experience acquired by clerks makes them attractive to employers. Loewenstein was a clerk at an appellate court, which reviews cases for error from the trial court. His primary tasks as an appellate judicial clerk would have consisted of reviewing the record from the trial court, reviewing the parties' briefs to the court, researching the applicable law, and drafting either a memorandum of law or a draft opinion for the judge.[87]

---

81 Chambers and Partners, *Public International Law—Global-Wide*, http://www.chambersandpartners.com/15649/96/editorial/2/1, accessed 25 November 2015.

82 http://foleyhoag.com/people/loewenstein-andrew, accessed 2 September 2016. Unless otherwise indicated, the following information is obtained from this biography.

83 The Ivy League is a group of colleges and universities in the northeastern US, consisting of Yale, Harvard, Princeton, Columbia, Dartmouth, Cornell, the University of Pennsylvania, and Brown, having a reputation for high scholastic achievement and social prestige. http://www.dictionary.com/browse/ivy-league, accessed 2 September 1996.

84 https://www.brown.edu/initiatives/journal-world-affairs/, accessed 2 September 2016.

85 http://www.americancriminallawreview.com/, accessed 2 September 2016.

86 Indiana University, Robert H. McKinney School of Law, *Judicial Clerkship Guide*, http://mckinneylaw.iu.edu/careers/judicial-clerkships-guide.html, accessed 2 September 2016.

87 *Ibid.*

It seems that he had already joined Foley Hoag when he served in 2005 as a member of an Atrocities Documentation Team sent by the US State Department and the US Agency for International Development (AID) to investigate alleged human rights abuses against the black African population in the Darfur region of Sudan.[88] Twenty-four interviewers, primarily attorneys with international experience as well as law enforcement officers, visited both the refugee camps and makeshift shelters in eastern Chad. The study resulted in a US declaration that the violence in Darfur constituted genocide. In this connection, Loewenstein advised a major human rights organization regarding the application of public international law to the situation in Darfur, including with respect to genocide and reparations for violations of international law.

At the domestic level, he specializes in business investigation (estimated to account for 50% of his practice) and criminal defense (20%).[89] His corporate clients are in industries ranging from financial services and health care to energy and construction, and he assists such individual professionals as managers, executives, and engineers. His success in these fields is reflected in his being classified as a "Rising Star" in business litigation, *Super Lawyers' Massachusetts Rising Stars: A Comprehensive Listing of the Best Young Lawyers in Massachusetts*, from 2005 to 2008.[90] He has also represented foreign states, such as Thailand, in litigation in the US.

At the international level, Loewenstein, like Reichler and Martin, represents States, and corporations in disputes with investors and other States. He was legal counsel for Guyana, Ecuador, and Uruguay in arbitrations with foreign investors organized under the auspices of the ICSID. The dispute between Uruguay and Philip Morris (2010–16) recently attracted widespread attention, because the tobacco company challenged two of Uruguay's tobacco control measures: the requirement that graphic warning labels cover 80 percent of the front and back of cigarette packs and the requirement that each brand of cigarettes have only a single presentation (i.e., that there only be one type of Marlboro cigarette on the market, not Marlboro Red, Marlboro Gold, and Marlboro Blue). Philip Morris claimed that the two regulations were arbitrary, constituted an expropriation, and infringed on its trademark rights. Uruguay showed that, as a result of these and other measures, the smoking rate among adults in Uruguay dropped from 35 percent to 22 percent between 2005 and 2014. Among teenagers, the impact was even greater; the smoking rate dropped dramatically to just 8.4 percent. The tribunal rejected the claims of Philip Morris and affirmed that the two measures were reasonable exercises of Uruguay sovereign right and duty to protect public health from the death and disease that smoking causes. In addition to upholding Uruguay's measures, the arbitral tribunal ordered Philip Morris to reimburse Uruguay for its legal fees and other costs incurred in the case, amounting to $7 million.[91] This decision was followed four days later by the announcement of the decision of the Arbitral Tribunal in the *South China Sea Arbitration*.[92]

---

88 Andrew B. Loewenstein, "An Interview With Stephanie Morin and Amanda Nagai. Reflections on Darfur: A Personal and Political Account," *Brown Journal of World Affairs*, 11:2 (Winter/Spring 2005), p. 235; Andrew B. Loewenstein, "Words Fail," *New Republic*, 14 May 2006, https://newrepublic.com/article/62957/words-fail, accessed 2 September 2016.

89 "Andrew B. Loewenstein," *superlawyers*, http://profiles.superlawyers.com/massachusetts/boston/lawyer/andrew-b-loewenstein/7b399d78-0651-41f9-bf3c-b96a2bdd4e5f.html, accessed 2 September 2016.

90 http://www.foleyhoag.com/people/loewenstein-andrew, accessed 2 September 2016. Unless otherwise indicated, the following information is obtained from this biography.

91 "Foley Hoag Helps Uruguay Secure Landmark Victory Over Philip Morris; Arbitral Tribunal Affirms Uruguay's Sovereign Right to Regulate Tobacco," *businesswire.com*, 8 July 2016, http://www.businesswire.com/news/home/20160708005865/en/Foley-Hoag-Helps-Uruguay-Secure-Landmark-Victory, accessed 2 September 2016; *Philip Morris Brand Sàrl (Switzerland), Philip Morris Products S.A. (Switzerland) and Abal Hermanos S.A. (Uruguay) v. Oriental Republic of Uruguay* (ICSID Case No. ARB/10/7), http://www.italaw.com/sites/default/files/case-documents/italaw7417.pdf, accessed 2 September 2016.

92 "Foley Hoag Wins Historic Victory for the Philippines in the South China Sea," 12 July 2016, http://www.fox19.

Loewenstein has appeared before the ICJ as counsel in the following cases:

- *Case Concerning Application of the International Convention on the Elimination of All Forms of Racial Discrimination (Georgia v. Russia)* (2008–11, counsel for Georgia, together with Reichler);[93]
- *Case Concerning Pulp Mills on the River Uruguay (Argentina v. Uruguay)* (2006–10, counsel for Uruguay, together with Reichler and Martin);[94]
- *Case Concerning Aerial Spraying Along the Border (Ecuador v. Columbia)* (2008–13, counsel for Ecuador, together with Reichler);[95] and
- *Case Concerning Certain Activities Carried out by Nicaragua in the Border Area (Costa Rica v. Nicaragua)* (2010–15, counsel for Nicaragua, together with Reichler).[96]

Before joining the Philippine team in the arbitration with China, Loewenstein had already appeared in two arbitrations organized under Annex VII of the Convention. He represented Mauritius (together with Reichler) in the *Chagos Marine Protected Area Arbitration (Mauritius v. UK)* (2010–15)[97] and Guyana (together with Martin) over the delimitation of a disputed international maritime boundary (Guyana v. Suriname) (2004–07).[98]

Finally, he has provided advice to several States in Latin America, Africa, and the Pacific regarding their maritime boundary disputes with neighboring states.

PROFESSOR BERNARD H. OXMAN

A. Education

Professor Bernard H. Oxman earned an AB from Columbia College in 1962 and a JD from Columbia Law School in 1965.[99]

B. Academic Experience

In 1977, Professor Oxman joined the University of Miami Law School. He served as Associate Dean of the Law School from 1987 to 1990; currently, he is the Faculty Chair of the Law School's Master of Laws Program in Ocean and Coastal Law. He has been a member of the University's Faculty Senate since 1996. In 2008, he was appointed to the Richard A. Hausler Chair at the University of Miami; on the occasion of his installation, he gave a lecture entitled "The United States and the Future of International Law."[100]

---

com/story/32423284/foley-hoag-wins-historic-victory-for-the-philippines-in-the-south-china-sea, accessed 2 September 2016.

93 *Supra* note 56.

94 *Supra* note 59.

95 *Supra* note 61.

96 *Supra* note 65.

97 *Supra* note 64.

98 *Supra* note 57.

99 See his biography on the University of Miami website: http://www.law.miami.edu/faculty/bernard-h-oxman, accessed 25 November 2015. Unless otherwise indicated, the following information is obtained from this biography.

100 The text of the lecture is available at http://media.law.miami.edu/faculty-administration/pdf/bernard-oxman/hausler-chair-lecture.pdf, accessed 25 November 2015.

C. Publications

Professor Oxman has published numerous articles and book chapters on the law of the sea and other international law subjects. On the 20th anniversary of the opening for signature of the 1982 Convention, he published an overview of the Convention.[101] The authoritative character of his scholarly views may be deduced from the fact that one of his articles was quoted by a Judge of the ITLOS in a separate opinion in the *ARA Libertad Case (Argentina v. Ghana)*, in 2012.[102]

D. Professional Experience

Professor Oxman was Legal Adviser of the Department of the Navy from 1965 to 1968, then Assistant Legal Adviser for Oceans, Environment, and Scientific Affairs of the US Department of State from 1968 to 1977.

During his years of service with the US government, Professor Oxman was a member from its very first session of the UN Ad Hoc Committee to Study the Peaceful Uses of the Sea-Bed and the Ocean Floor beyond the Limits of National Jurisdiction, established in 1967, and the UN Committee on the Peaceful Uses of the Sea-Bed and the Ocean Floor beyond the Limits of National Jurisdiction, established in 1968.[103] The latter Committee acted as a preparatory body for the Third United Nations Conference on the Law of the Sea (UNCLOS III), which the UN General Assembly convened in 1970 and which, in the course of 11 sessions between 1973 and 1982, drafted the UN Convention on the Law of the Sea. From 1975 to 1982, Professor Oxman was Vice-President of the US Delegation to the Conference and one of the coordinators of the English language group of the Drafting Committee of the Conference. The coordinators of the six language groups (Arabic, Chinese, English, French, Russian, and Spanish) harmonized the views of the language groups and prepared proposals for the Drafting Committee, which was responsible for refining drafts, harmonizing recurring words and expressions, and achieving concordance of the text of the Convention in six languages. The significance of these tasks cannot be underestimated, since the six texts of the Convention are authentic.

Professor Oxman and Ambassador John R. Stevenson published reports of the first three sessions of UNCLOS (1973, 1974, and 1975) in the *American Journal of International Law*, while Professor Oxman was responsible for reports of the fourth to the tenth sessions (1976–82); unsurprisingly, he authored the chapter on UNCLOS III in one of the first major handbooks on the new Law of the Sea, published in French in 1985.[104] Professor Oxman has testified twice (in

---

101 Bernard H. Oxman, "Twenty Years of the United Nations Convention on the Law of the Sea," *International Oceanographic Commission Annual Report 2002*, pp. 16–17, http://unesdoc.unesco.org/images/0013/001351/135127e.pdf, accessed 8 September 2016.

102 Separate Opinion of Judge Chandrasekhara Rao, https://www.itlos.org/fileadmin/itlos/documents/cases/case_no.20/C20_Ord_15_12_2012_SepOp_Ch_Rao_E_.pdf, accessed 25 November 2015.

103 *United Nations Diplomatic Conferences. Third United Nations Conference on the Law of the Sea, 1973–1982*, http://legal.un.org/diplomaticconferences/lawofthesea-1982/lawofthesea-1982.html, accessed 25 November 2015.

104 John R. Stevenson and Bernard H. Oxman, "The Preparations for the Law of the Sea Conference," *American Journal of International Law* (*AJIL*), 68:1 (January 1974), pp. 1–32; Stevenson and Oxman, "The Third United Nations Conference on the Law of the Sea: The 1974 Caracas Session," *AJIL*, 69:1 (January 1975), pp. 1–30; Stevenson and Oxman, "The Third United Nations Conference on the Law of the Sea: The 1975 Geneva Session," *AJIL*, 69:4 (October 1975), pp. 763–97; Oxman, "The Third United Nations Conference on the Law of the Sea: The 1976 New York Sessions," *AJIL*, 71:2 (April 1977), pp. 247–69; Oxman, "The Third United Nations Conference on the Law of the Sea: The 1977 New York Session," *AJIL*, 72:1 (January 1978), pp. 57–83; Oxman, "The Third United Nations Conference on the Law of the Sea: The Seventh Session (1978)," *AJIL*, 73:1 (January 1979), pp. 1–41; Oxman, "The Third United Nations Conference on the Law of the Sea: The Eighth Session (1979)," *AJIL*, 74:1 (January 1980), pp. 1–47; Oxman, "The Third United Nations Conference on the Law of the Sea: The Ninth Session (1980)," *AJIL*, 75:2 (April 1981), pp. 211–56; Oxman, "The Third United Nations Conference on the Law of the Sea: The Tenth Session

2004[105] and 2007[106]) before the US Congress in favor of US ratification of the 1982 Convention. No other member of the legal team, or even of the Arbitral Tribunal itself, has such a long and close association with the history of the 1982 Convention, which the Tribunal in the *South China Sea Arbitration* had to interpret and apply.

Professor Oxman served as legal counsel for Suriname in the *Guyana v. Suriname* arbitration under Annex VII of the 1982 Convention, concerning the delimitation of Guyana's maritime boundary with Suriname.[107] In the same case, Reichler, Martin, and Sands were counsel for Guyana.

Professor Oxman is the only member of the Philippines' legal team who has had experience as a judge ad hoc or member of an arbitral tribunal. He was judge ad hoc of ITLOS in two cases: *Case Concerning Land Reclamation by Singapore In and Around the Straits of Johor (Malaysia v. Singapore), Provisional Measures* (2003, appointed by Singapore),[108] and *Dispute Concerning Delimitation of the Maritime Boundary Between Bangladesh and Myanmar in the Bay of Bengal (Bangladesh/Myanmar)* (2009–12, appointed by Myanmar, with Judge Mensah as the judge ad hoc appointed by Bangladesh).[109]

He was judge ad hoc of the ICJ, appointed by Ukraine, in a maritime delimitation case between Romania and Ukraine (2004–09; the judge ad hoc for Rumania was Judge Cot).[110] As the University of Miami website points out, he is the only American lawyer ever appointed to serve as judge ad hoc before both international tribunals. At the ITLOS, there is no judge of American nationality, for the simple reason that the US has not ratified the 1982 Convention, is not a party to the Convention, and thus does not have the right to present candidates for election to the Tribunal.

Professor Oxman was a member of two arbitral tribunals constituted under Annex VII of the 1982 Convention: *Land Reclamation by Singapore In and Around the Straits of Johor (Malaysia v. Singapore)* (2003)[111] and *The ARA Libertad Arbitration (Argentina v. Ghana)* (2012–13, Judge Mensah was also a member of the Tribunal).[112]

Finally, Professor Oxman was head of a Review Panel established under Article 17 and Annex II of the Convention on the Conservation and Management of High Seas Fishery Resources in the South Pacific Ocean with regard to the Objection by the Russian Federation to the Conservation and Management Measure for *Trachurus murphyi* (CMM 1.01) adopted by the Commission of the South Pacific Regional Fisheries Management Organisation at its First Meeting held from 28 January to 1 February 2013.[113] These were the first proceedings of their kind under the Convention. On 5 July 2013, the Review Panel issued its Findings and Recommendations, and Russia agreed to comply with the Panel's Recommendations.

(1981)," *AJIL*, 76:1 (January 1982), pp. 1–23; Oxman, "La troisième Conférence des Nations Unies sur le Droit de la Mer," in René-Jean Dupuy and Daniel Vignes (eds.), *Traité du Nouveau Droit de la Mer* (Paris: Editions Economica, 1985), pp. 143–216.

105 *Statement of Bernard H. Oxman: Oversight Hearing to Examine the United Nations Convention on the Law of the Sea*, Testimony before the U.S. Senate Committee on Environment and Public Works, 24 March 2004, http://unclosdebate.org/citation/1190/statement-bernard-h-oxman-oversight-hearing-examine-united-nations-convention-law-sea, accessed 8 September 2016.

106 *Statement of Professor Bernard H. Oxman Before the Senate Committee on Foreign Relations*, 4 October 2007, http://www.virginia.edu/colp/pdf/OxmanTestimony071004.pdf, accessed 8 September 2016.

107 *Supra* note 57.

108 https://www.itlos.org/fileadmin/itlos/documents/cases/case_no_12/12_order_081003_en.pdf 8 October 2003, accessed 25 November 2015.

109 *Supra* note 62.

110 http://www.icj-cij.org/en/case/132, accessed 16 March 2018.

111 http://legal.un.org/riaa/cases/vol_XXVII/133-145.pdf, accessed 8 September 2016.

112 https://www.itlos.org/cases/list-of-cases/case-no-20/, accessed 20 November 2015.

113 https://pcacases.com/web/view/33, accessed 30 March 2018.

Questions raised by Professor Oxman during the hearing and audio recordings of the hearing are available on the PCA website.

PROFESSOR PHILIPPE SANDS

A. Education

Professor Sands received his BA from the University of Cambridge in 1982 and his LLM, first class honours, from the same University, in 1983.[114] In the UK, the class of degree is based on the average mark (grade) of the assessed work a candidate has completed. The rough percentage for first class honours is 70%,[115] keeping in mind that grading is much tougher in Europe than in the US (or the Philippines, for that matter). Professor Sands was a Visiting Scholar at Harvard Law School in 1983–84. He has been Member of the Bar of England and Wales since 1985, a Member of the Irish Bar since 2002, and Queen's Counsel since 2003. In the UK, Queen's Counsel (King's Counsel when the sovereign is male) is a barrister who, having practiced law for at least 10 years, is given the honor on the recommendation of the Lord Chancellor to earn the right to wear silk gown ("takes silk" as it is called) and take precedence over other Barristers in the court.[116]

B. Academic Experience

Professor Sands was a Research Fellow at St Catherine's College, University of Cambridge (1984–88), and at Kings College London (1988–91). In 1989, he established the Foundation for International Environmental Law and Development at the School of Oriental and African Studies (SOAS) of the University of London and was Director of Studies at the Foundation until 1989. At SOAS, which describes itself as "the only higher education institution in Europe specialising in the study of Asia, Africa and the Near and Middle East,"[117] he was Lecturer in Law from 1992 to 1996, then Reader in International Law from 1996 to 1999, and finally Professor of International Law from 1996 to 2000. He was Global Professor of Law at the New York University (NYU) School of Law from 1994 to 2003. In 2002, he moved to University College London, University of London, where he is Professor of Laws and Director of the Centre on International Courts and Tribunals.

C. Publications

Professor Sands has a long list of publications to his name. Among specialists, he is probably best known for the standard text, *Principles of International Environmental Law* (1st ed., 3 vols., 1995), which is now in its 3rd edition (2012). Two publications of his that have reached a broader audience are *Torture Team: Deception, Cruelty and the Compromise of Law* (2008, translated into French in 2010) and *Lawless World: America and the Making and Breaking of Global Rules* (2005; translations into Arabic and Chinese in 2006 and 2007, respectively). The latter book was described by a reviewer for the British newspaper *The Observer* as "a

114 See his biography on the Matrix Chambers website: https://www.matrixlaw.co.uk/member/philippe-sands/, accessed 8 September 2016. Unless otherwise indicated, the following information is obtained from this biography.

115 The Student Room, Degree Classifications, 2016, http://www.thestudentroom.co.uk/content.php?r=15857-degree-classifications, accessed 17 November 2015.

116 Business Dictionary, http://www.businessdictionary.com/definition/queen-s-counsel.html, accessed 17 November 2015.

117 https://www.soas.ac.uk/, accessed 17 November 2015.

penetrating, detailed account of the extent to which those who claim to be spreading global values have ridden roughshod over them."[118] It covered such headline-grabbing issues as the detention of General Augusto Pinochet, the former Chilean dictator whose extradition from the UK was requested by the Spanish Judge Baltasar Garzón in 1998 so that he could be tried in Spain for crimes committed in Chile during his brutal dictatorship from 1973 to 1990;[119] the formation of the International Criminal Court, in which the US has refused to participate;[120] the "war on terror"; the US detention centers in Guantánamo, Cuba, where prisoners have been illegally detained without trial for years; and the legal advice that enabled British Prime Minister Blair to commit Britain to the war with Iraq.[121] In the opinion of a reviewer for the British newspaper *The Guardian*, the book is "authoritative and ruthless in its analysis of the conduct of the United States and withering about the role of Britain."[122]

D. Professional Experience

In addition to appearing before English courts, Professor Sands has appeared before many international courts, acting as counsel in maritime boundary disputes in the Caribbean, Atlantic, and Pacific Oceans; international claims relating to natural resources, pollution, and environmental assessment; international trade disputes, including agricultural preferences and genetically modified organisms; cases relating to the immunity of serving and former heads of state from the jurisdiction of national and international courts; international claims relating to the use of force and allegations of torture and genocide and other violations of fundamental human rights; and cases relating to individual violations of international criminal laws.

At the European level, he was counsel for Ireland (2003–05) in *EC Commission v Ireland* and for Greenpeace, in the case *Greenpeace International v EC Commission*, in 1998, in the European Court of Justice (ECJ).[123] The ECJ, one of the main organs of the European Union, has the dual task of "ensuring EU law is interpreted and applied the same in every EU country" and "ensuring countries and EU institutions abide by EU law."[124]

At the World Trade Organization (WTO), he was counsel for St. Lucia, a small Caribbean island whose main export product is bananas, in the long-running case concerning the EU banana regime (US and others v. EU) in 1997[125] and counsel for the EU in the cases concerning Genetically Modified Organisms (US/EU, Argentina/EU, Canada/EU) (2003–06).[126]

---

118 John Kampfner, "These Guilty Men," The Guardian, 6 March 2005, http://www.theguardian.com/politics/2005/mar/06/politicalbooks.iraq, accessed 17 November 2015.

119 Norman Stockwell, "Pinochet's Arrest Remembered," *The Tico Times*, 17 October 2014, http://www.ticotimes.net/l/50287, accessed 17 November 2015.

120 https://www.icc-cpi.int/, accessed 8 September 2016.

121 Attorney General to the Prime Minister, 7 March 2003, Secret, http://news.bbc.co.uk/2/shared/bsp/hi/pdfs/28_04_05_attorney_general.pdf, accessed 8 September 2016.

122 Martin Jacques, "Above the Law," *The Guardian*, 26 March 2005, http://www.theguardian.com/books/2005/mar/26/highereducation.news, accessed 17 November 2015.

123 Judgment of the Court of 2 April 1998. Stichting Greenpeace Council (Greenpeace International) and Others v. Commission of the European Communities, http://eur-lex.europa.eu/legal-content/EN/TXT/?uri=CELEX:61995CJ0321, accessed 17 November 2015.

124 http://europa.eu/about-eu/institutions-bodies/court-justice/index_en.htm, accessed 17 November 2015.

125 Dispute DS105, European Communities—Regime for the Importation, Sale and Distribution of Bananas, https://www.wto.org/english/tratop_e/dispu_e/cases_e/ds105_e.htm, accessed 8 September 2016.

126 US/EU, Dispute DS291, European Communities—Measures Affecting the Approval and Marketing of Biotech Products, https://www.wto.org/english/tratop_e/dispu_e/cases_e/ds291_e.htm; Canada/EU, Dispute DS292, European Communities—Measures Affecting the Approval and Marketing of Biotech Products, https://www.wto.org/english/tratop_e/dispu_e/cases_e/ds292_e.htm; Argentina/EU, Dispute DS293, European Communities—Measures Affecting the Approval and Marketing of Biotech Products, https://www.wto.org/english/tratop_e/dispu_e/cases_e/ds293_e.htm, all accessed 8 September 2016.

Professor Sands has appeared as counsel or adviser in arbitrations between (foreign) investors and States under the rules of the ICSID. In 9 of the 13 cases in which he was involved, he was counsel or adviser for the respondent (Albania, Costa Rica, Mexico, Argentina, and Jordan). He accepted an appointment as ICSID arbitrator, and as a result, since July 2007 he has not accepted new instructions to act as counsel in investment treaty arbitrations.

In the Special Court for Sierra Leone, in the case *Prosecutor v Charles Taylor*, he was appointed as amicus curiae by the Appeals Chamber on Head of State immunity under international law (2003).[127] The Special Court for Sierra Leone was set up in 2002 as the result of a request to the United Nations in 2000 by the Government of Sierra Leone for "a special court" to address serious crimes against civilians and UN peacekeepers committed during the country's decade-long civil war (1991–2002). Its mandate was to try those "bearing the greatest responsibility" for crimes committed in Sierra Leone after 30 November 1996, the date of the failed Abidjan Peace Accord. The Prosecutor of the Special Court was empowered to bring charges for war crimes, crimes against humanity, other serious violations of international humanitarian law, and certain serious violations of Sierra Leonean law. The creation of the Special Court was a landmark in many respects: it was the first modern international tribunal to sit in the country where the crimes took place, the first to have an effective outreach program on the ground, the first to be funded by voluntary contributions, and, in 2013, the first court to complete its mandate and transition to a residual mechanism.[128]

An amicus curia (Latin for "friend of the court") is a "person or group who is not a party to a lawsuit, but has a strong interest in the matter, and who will petition the court for permission to submit a brief in the action with the intent of influencing the court's decision."[129] Rule 74 of the Rules of Evidence and Procedure of the Special Court allows a Chamber of the Court to "invite or grant leave to any State, organization or person to make submissions on any issue specified by the Chamber."[130] One of the conclusions of the submission of Professor Sands to the Special Court was that "a former Head of State is not entitled to claim immunity *ratione materiae* (by reason of the matter involved) before an international criminal court in respect of international crimes."[131]

In the International Criminal Court, Professor Sands represents Libya in *Prosecutor v Saif Al-Islam Gaddafi and Abdullah Al-Senussi, Case ICC-01/11-01/11* (initiated in 2012).[132] The latter case was brought against the son of the late Libyan dictator and the current head of Military Intelligence (the proceedings against Al-Senoussi were terminated in 2014).

Since the mid-1990s, Professor Sands has appeared as counsel before the ICJ in no less than 11 contentious cases and one request for an advisory opinion. Human rights violations allegedly amounting to genocide in the former Yugoslavia were the core of the *Case Concerning the Application of the Genocide Convention (Croatia v. Yugoslavia)* (1999–2008, counsel for

127 Special Court for Sierra Leone, Doc. SCS-03-01-A (10666-11114), Prosecutor against Charles Ghankay Taylor (Case No. SCSL-3-01-A) in the Appeals Chamber, 26 September 2013, http://www.rscsl.org/Documents/Decisions/Taylor/Appeal/1389/SCSL-03-01-A-1389.pdf, accessed 17 November 2015.

128 Special Court for Sierra Leone and Residual Special Court for Sierra Leone, http://www.rscsl.org/, accessed 8 September 2016.

129 Cornell University Law School, Legal Information Institute, *Amicus curiae*, https://www.law.cornell.edu/wex/amicus_curiae, accessed 17 November 2015.

130 http://hrlibrary.umn.edu/instree/SCSL/Rules-of-proced-SCSL.pdf, accessed 8 September 2016.

131 Special Court for Sierra Leone, Doc. SCSL-2003-01-I (3014-3039), Prosecutor against Charles Ghankay Taylor (Case No. SCSL-2003-01-A), Decision on Immunity from Jurisdiction, 31 May 2004, http://www.haguejusticeportal.net/Docs/Court%20Documents/SCSL/Taylor_Decision%20on%20Immunity.pdf, accessed 8 September 2016.

132 https://www.icc-cpi.int/en_menus/icc/situations%20and%20cases/situations/icc0111/related%20cases/icc01110111/pages/icc01110111.aspx, accessed 17 November 2015.

Croatia).[133] Another less dramatic and less catastrophic repercussion of the collapse of the former Yugoslavia was discussed in the case *Violation of Article 11 of the Interim Accord of 13 September 1995 (The Former Yugoslav Republic of Macedonia v. Greece*, 2008–2011, Counsel for FYROM).[134] Two contentious cases dealt with the extremely sensitive issue of the use of force: *Armed Activities on the Territory of the Congo (Democratic Republic of Congo v. Uganda)* (2003–05, Counsel for DRC; Reichler was one of the counsel of Uganda)[135] and *Application of the International Convention on the Elimination of All Forms of Racial Discrimination (Georgia v. Russian Federation)* (2008–2010, counsel for Georgia, together with Reichler).[136] Nuclear testing by France in the South Pacific (*Request for an Examination of the Situation in Accordance With Paragraph 63 of the Court's Judgment of 20 December 1974 in the Nuclear Tests [New Zealand v. France] Case*, 1995, Junior Counsel, Solomon Islands, Samoa, Federated States of Micronesia, Marshall Islands, "intervening" states)[137] was the object of one contentious case, while an advisory opinion was requested on the legality of the use of nuclear weapons (*WHO Advisory Opinion on Legality of Use of Nuclear Weapons and UN General Assembly Opinion Request on Legality of the Use of Nuclear Weapons*, 1995–96, Counsel, Solomon Islands and Samoa).[138]

As is to be expected of the author of the standard text on international environmental law, Professor Sands has appeared before the ICJ in four environmental disputes:

- *Case Concerning Gabcikovo-Nagymaros Project (Hungary/Slovakia)* (1993–97, counsel for Hungary);[139]
- *Case Concerning Pulp Mills (Argentina v. Uruguay)* (2006–10, counsel for Argentina, while Reichler was counsel for Uruguay);[140]
- *Aerial Herbicide Spraying (Ecuador v. Colombia)* (2008–13, counsel for Ecuador, together with Reichler);[141] and
- *Whaling in the Antarctic (Australia v. Japan: New Zealand Intervening)* (2008–14, counsel for Australia; Boyle was counsel for Japan).[142]

Finally, two disputes concerned maritime boundary delimitation in the Caribbean:

- *Territorial and Maritime Dispute Between Nicaragua and Honduras in the Caribbean Sea (Nicaragua v. Honduras)* (1999–2007, counsel for Honduras);[143] and
- *Application for Revision of the Judgment of 11 September 1992 in the Case Concerning the Land, Island and Maritime Frontier Dispute (El Salvador/ Honduras: Nicaragua Intervening) (El Salvador v. Honduras)* (2002–04, counsel for Honduras).[144]

---

133 http://www.icj-cij.org/en/case/118, accessed 16 March 2018.
134 http://www.icj-cij.org/en/case/142, accessed 16 March 2018.
135 *Supra* note 55.
136 *Supra* note 56.
137 http://www.icj-cij.org/en/case/59, accessed 16 March 2018.
138 http://www.icj-cij.org/en/case/95, accessed 16 March 2018.
139 http://www.icj-cij.org/en/case/92, accessed 16 March 2018.
140 *Supra* note 59.
141 *Supra* note 61.
142 http://www.icj-cij.org/en/case/148, accessed 16 March 2018.
143 http://www.icj-cij.org/en/case/120, accessed 16 March 2018.
144 http://www.icj-cij.org/en/case/127, accessed 16 March 2018.

At the ITLOS, Professor Sands was lead counsel for St. Vincent and the Grenadines in the *Case of the M/V Saiga, St. Vincent and the Grenadines v. Guinea Provisional Measures Phase* (Order of 11 March 1998).[145] This was only the second case to be heard by ITLOS; in reality, it was a continuation of the first case. At this time, Judge Mensah was the President of ITLOS, while Judge Wolfrum was its Vice-President. The next case in which Professor Sands appeared, as lead counsel for Ireland, was *The MOX Case, Ireland v. United Kingdom. Provisional Measures* (Order of 3 December 2001).[146] At this time, both Judge Mensah and Judge Wolfrum were members of the Tribunal.

Professor Sands appeared once more before the ITLOS, in the first maritime delimitation case that was submitted to it, the *Dispute Concerning Delimitation of the Maritime Boundary between Bangladesh and Myanmar in the Bay of Bengal (Bangladesh/Myanmar)* (2009–12).[147] In this case, the two judges ad hoc were Judge Mensah (appointed by Bangladesh) and Professor Oxman (appointed by Myanmar). Sands, Reichler, and Boyle were counsel for Bangladesh.

Prior to joining the legal team of the Philippines, Professor Sands appeared as counsel before four arbitral tribunals constituted under Annex VII of the 1982 Convention:

- *Ireland v. United Kingdom ("MOX Plant Case")* (2001–08, counsel for Ireland);[148]
- *Guyana v. Suriname Arbitration* (2004–07, counsel for Guyana; Professors Oxman and Soons were counsel for Suriname);[149]
- *Maritime Boundary Dispute between Bangladesh and India* (2009–14, counsel for Bangladesh, together with Reichler and Martin; Judge Wolfrum was the President of the Tribunal in the first case, with Judges Cot and Mensah as members);[150] and
- *Case Concerning the Chagos Archipelago "Marine Protected Area," Mauritius v. United Kingdom* (2011–15, Counsel for Mauritius, together with Reichler; Judge Wolfrum was a member of the Tribunal).[151]

The *MOX Plant* dispute also gave rise to arbitration between Ireland and the UK regarding Article 9 of the 1992 OSPAR Convention (Convention for the Protection of the Marine Environment of the North-East Atlantic, 2001–03).[152] Professor Sands was once more counsel for Ireland.

Currently, Professor Sands is counsel for Croatia (together with Reichler) in the territorial and maritime dispute between the Republic of Croatia and the Republic of Slovenia (initiated in 2009).[153]

He is on the list of arbitrators in the field of natural resources and the environment maintained by the PCA Secretary General. In June 2011, he was appointed to the panel of

145 https://www.itlos.org/fileadmin/itlos/documents/cases/case_no_2/provisional_measures/order_110398_eng.pdf, accessed 17 November 2015.

146 https://www.itlos.org/fileadmin/itlos/documents/cases/case_no_10/Order.03.12.01.E.pdf, accessed 17 November 2015.

147 *Supra* note 62.

148 https://pcacases.com/web/view/100, accessed 30 March 2018.

149 *Supra* note 57.

150 *Supra* note 63.

151 *Supra* note 64.

152 *Dispute Concerning Access to Information Under Article 9 of the OSPAR Convention Between Ireland and the United Kingdom of Great Britain and Northern Ireland*, Final Award, decision of 2 July 2003, *Reports of International Arbitral Awards*, XXIII (New York: United Nations, 2006), pp. 59–151, http://legal.un.org/riaa/cases/vol_XXIII/59-151.pdf, accessed 9 September 2016.

153 https://pcacases.com/web/view/3, accessed 30 March 2018.

arbitrators of the International Court of Arbitration for Sport (ICAS) and has been appointed as arbitrator in several cases since September 2011.

PROFESSOR ALAN BOYLE

A. Education

Professor Alan Boyle obtained an MA in Jurisprudence[154] and BCL, Bachelor of Civil Law (which, despite its name, is equivalent to the American LLM),[155] both from Pembroke College of the University of Oxford, in 1975 and 1976, respectively.[156] In 1979, he obtained the Diploma of the Hague Academy of International Law, which is granted "to students with a proven advanced knowledge of the field, and who pass an examination in either public or private international law." The Diploma is awarded to only one or two students at the end of each of two periods of the summer courses (private international law and public international law).[157] While the examination is "extremely selective," the Diploma is not a license to practice (international) law in any jurisdiction. In 2005, Professor Boyle received his LLD (Doctor of Laws) from the University of Edinburgh.

B. Academic Experience

Professor Boyle started his academic career in 1978 as a Lecturer (the equivalent of the Assistant Professor in the US system) in the Faculty of Laws of Queen Mary College, University of London, where he was promoted to Senior Lecturer (the equivalent of Associate Professor in the US system) in 1989 and Reader (the equivalent of full professor, without a chair) in 1993. In 1995, he moved to the University of Edinburgh as Professor of Public International Law. He has also taught at University of Texas Law School; William and Mary College Law School, Virginia; the University of Paris II (Panthéon-Assas); the University of Paris X (Paris Ouest Nanterre La Défense); and LUISS (Libera Università Internazionale degli Studi Sociali), a private university in Rome. He was General Editor of the *International and Comparative Law Quarterly* from 1998 until 2006.

C. Publications

Within public international law, Professor Boyle specializes in international environmental law, the law of the sea, the law of treaties, international law-making and the settlement of international disputes. He has a long list of publications: two co-authored books, six co-edited books, ten single-authored articles, one co-authored article, 12 single-authored book chapters, and two co-authored book chapters.[158]

---

154 Oxford University, Faculty of Law, *Magister Juris (MJur)*, https://www.law.ox.ac.uk/admissions/postgraduate/magister-juris, accessed 22 November 2015.

155 Oxford University, Faculty of Law, *Bachelor of Civil Law (BCL)*, https://www.law.ox.ac.uk/admissions/postgraduate/bachelor-civil-law, accessed 22 November 2015.

156 See his biography on the Essex Court Chambers website: http://essexcourt.com/barrister/professor-alan-boyle/, accessed 22 November 2015. Unless otherwise indicated, the following information is obtained from this biography.

157 The Hague Academy of International Law, *Directed Studies and Diploma*, https://www.hagueacademy.nl/programmes/summer-courses/diploma/, accessed 22 November 2015.

158 The list may be found on the University of Edinburgh website: http://www.law.ed.ac.uk/people/alanboyle, accessed 22 November 2015.

D. Professional Experience

Professor Boyle has worked regularly as a consultant or as counsel for various governments, international organizations, and NGOs on general international law, international environmental law, and law of the sea, including maritime boundary delimitation, fisheries conservation and access disputes, jurisdiction over ships, marine pollution and protection of the marine environment, freedom of navigation at sea, international rivers, transboundary environmental impact assessment and environmental damage, state responsibility and liability, and international dispute settlement.

Prior to the *South China Sea Arbitration*, Professor Boyle appeared as counsel in six disputes involving the law of the sea or the environment:

- *Case Concerning the Conservation and Sustainable Exploitation of Swordfish Stocks in the South-Eastern Pacific Ocean (Chile/European Community)*, in the ITLOS (2000, counsel for the EU);[159]
- MOX Plant Arbitration under Annex VII of the 1982 Convention (2002, counsel for the UK; Judge Mensah was the president of the Tribunal);[160]
- *Pulp Mills on the River Uruguay (Argentina v. Uruguay)* in the ICJ (2006–2010, counsel for Uruguay, together with Reichler and Martin);[161]
- *Aerial Herbicide Spraying (Ecuador v. Colombia)* in the ICJ (2008–13, counsel for Ecuador, together with Reichler and Martin);[162]
- *Dispute Concerning Delimitation of the Maritime Boundary between Bangladesh and Myanmar in the Bay of Bengal* in the ITLOS (2009–12, counsel for Bangladesh, together with Reichler and Martin; Judge Mensah was the judge ad hoc for Bangladesh, while Professor Oxman was the judge ad hoc for Myanmar);[163]
- *Whaling in the Antarctic (Australia v. Japan: New Zealand Intervening)* in the ICJ (2010–13, counsel for Japan, while Professor Sands was counsel for Australia);[164]
- *Bay of Bengal Maritime Boundary Arbitration between Bangladesh and India* (ad hoc tribunal under Annex VII of the 1982 Convention, 2009–14, counsel for Bangladesh, together with Reichler and Martin; Judge Wolfrum was President, and Judge Cot, a member of the Tribunal);[165]
- *Chagos Marine Protected Area Arbitration (Mauritius v. United Kingdom)* (ad hoc tribunal under Annex VII of the 1982 UN Convention on the Law of the Sea, 2010–15, counsel for the UK, with Reichler and Sands on the opposing side and Judge Wolfrum as a member of the Tribunal).[166]

Professor Boyle is an arbitrator on the PCA's environmental arbitration list[167] and a special arbitrator under Annex VIII of the 1982 Convention.[168]

---

159 https://www.itlos.org/cases/list-of-cases/case-no-7/, accessed 22 November 2015.

160 *Supra* note 148.

161 *Supra* note 59.

162 *Supra* note 61.

163 *Supra* note 62.

164 *Supra* note 142.

165 *Supra* note 63.

166 *Supra* note 64.

167 Permanent Court of Arbitration, *Panels of Arbitrators and Experts for Environmental Disputes*, https://pca-cpa.org/en/about/structure/panels-of-arbitrators-and-experts-for-environmental-disputes/, accessed 30 March 2018.

168 http://www.un.org/Depts/los/convention_agreements/texts/unclos/annex8.htm, accessed 22 November 2015.

Professor Boyle has been praised in Legal 500 2014, a firm that "assesses the strengths of law firms in 106 jurisdictions," as "a notable and prominent scholar-practitioner in the field," one who "knows the field and the case law." He is described as being "very creative," with "lots of ideas."[169]

In conclusion, there is no doubt that the track record of the legal team is brilliant. The team is characterized by a balance between full-time academics and full-time practitioners. The team's members have represented States in inter-State disputes and investor-State disputes, they have appeared before permanent and ad hoc international tribunals, and they have argued cases ranging from the law of the sea to the international law of the environment and from human rights to the use of force. One could think of no better team to grapple with the legal challenges faced by the Philippines and to present its case persuasively before a Tribunal whose members had combined personal legal experience of 200 years.

---

[169] The Legal 500, *Essex Court Chambers. Prof. Alan Boyle,* http://www.legal500.com/firms/9331/offices/9331/lawyers/61627, accessed 8 September 2016.

6

China Should Emulate Africa in the Area of Peaceful Dispute Settlement[1]

Following the issuance of the Award on Jurisdiction and Admissibility in October 2015, China actively sought international support for its position that the South China Sea dispute with the Philippines should be resolved exclusively by negotiations among the parties directly concerned and thus should not have been submitted to arbitration.[2] Among the 40 States that expressed support for China were several in Africa, including Burundi,[3] Mozambique,[4] Niger,[5] and Togo.[6] China also lobbied Cameroon,[7] Côte d'Ivoire,[8] and Senegal.[9] China justified the need for Africa

1 Earlier versions of this Chapter were published by *The Diplomat*, http://thediplomat.com/2016/06/chinas-south-china-sea-diplomacy-could-use-some-lessons-from-africa/, and *The Foreign Service Institute*, http://www.fsi.gov.ph/wp-content/uploads/2016/06/Vol-03-No-01-June-2016-China-Should-Learn-a-Lesson-or-Two-From-Africa-Robles.pdf.

2 *Foreign Ministry Spokesperson Hua Chunying's Regular Press Conference on May 25, 2016*, http://www.fmprc.gov.cn/mfa_eng/xwfw_665399/s2510_665401/2511_665403/t1366744.shtm l, accessed 26 May 2016.

3 Astere Nduwamungu, "Ambassade de Chine > Présentation de la position de la Chine sur la Mer de Chine méridionale: Pour trouver une solution, la Chine propose une voie de négociation," *Publications de Presse Burundaise*, 11 May 2016, http://www.ppbdi.com/index.php/extras/politique-cooperation-actualite-internationales/4137-ambassade-de-chine-presentation-de-la-position-de-la-chine-sur-la-mer-de-chine-meridionale, accessed 1 June 2016; Xinhua, "La Chine salue le soutien mozambicain, burundais et slovène sur la question de la mer de Chine méridionale," 19 May 2016, http://french.cri.cn/621/2016/05/19/301s479819.htm, accessed 26 May 2016.

4 República de Moçambique, Ministério dos Negócios Estrangeiros e Cooperação, *Moçambique e China estabelecem parceria estratégica para cooperação global*, 20 May 2016, http://www.minec.gov.mz/index.php/imprensa/destaques/91-mocambique-e-china-estabelecem-parceria-estrategica-para-cooperacao-global, accessed 1 June 2016.

5 *Communiqué de presse du Ministère en charge des Affaires Etrangères, relatif au différend entre la République Populaire de Chine et les Philippines en Mer de Chine Méridionale*, 24 May 2016, http://www.nigeriensdebelgique.be/communique-de-presse-du-ministere-en-charge-des-affaires-etrangeres-relatif-au-differend-entre-la-republique-populaire-de-chine-et-les-philippines-en-mer-de-chine-meridionale-le-gouvernement-de-la/, accessed 25 May 2016.

6 "Pékin apprécie la position togolaise," *République Togolaise*, 19 May 2016, http://www.republicoftogo.com/Toutes-les-rubriques/Diplomatie/Pekin-apprecie-la-position-togolaise, accessed 25 May 2016.

7 "Afrique Centrale: Conflit sur la mer de Chine méridionale—La Chine veut le soutien du Cameroun," *Cameroonvoice*, 9 May 2016, http://www.cameroonvoice.com/news/article-news-24297.html, accessed 29 May 2016.

8 "L'arbitrage de la mer de Chine méridionale initié par les Philippines viole le droit international selon Tang Weibin, Ambassadeur de Chine en Côte d'Ivoire," *abidjan.net*, 17 May 2016, http://news.abidjan.net/h/591056.html, accessed 28 May 2016.

9 "L'objection de la Chine contre l'arbitrage concernant la Mer de Chine méridionale s'avère complètement légitime et légale," *Le Soleil*, 26 May 2016, http://www.lesoleil.sn/component/k2/item/50156-l-objection-de-la-chine-contre-l-arbitrage-concernant-la-mer-de-chine-meridionale-s-avere-completement-legitime-et-legale.html, accessed 30 May 2016.

to support it since they had all been "victims of colonization."[10]

Some Western experts dismissed these States as "small, poor and inconsequential." These States allegedly support China because they received massive Chinese assistance. Niger's oil industry was said to be almost totally dependent on Chinese enterprises and the CNPC (China National Petroleum Corporation).[11] Mozambique declared its support during a State visit of its President to China, when the two States agreed to establish a Strategic Partnership for Comprehensive Cooperation and China promised to assist in Mozambique's industrialization and modernization.[12] Nevertheless, as China's spokesperson rightly pointed out on 25 March 2016, the dismissive attitude is "permeated with arrogance, prejudice and snobbishness... all countries, big or small, rich or poor, should be respected as equals.... [It is] particularly preposterous to judge right and wrong based on the size and wealth of a country."[13]

The Philippines should have responded that China could and should learn a lesson or two from the African countries in the area of peaceful dispute settlement. More and more African States now accept the principle of international adjudication, i.e., dispute settlement through international courts, and actually submit specific disputes to the International Court of Justice (ICJ) and the International Tribunal for the Law of the Sea (ITLOS). Moreover, the actual conduct at the ICJ of three African States whose support China sought—Burundi, Senegal, and Niger—is exactly the opposite of that of China in the *South China Sea Arbitration.*

African States Accept International Adjudication

The consent of States parties to a dispute is required before an international court can hear their dispute. A dispute may be submitted to the ICJ if States have given their consent in advance under Article 36(2) of its Statute, through a special agreement, or through a treaty on another subject. States parties to the 1982 UN Convention on the Law of the Sea may also give their consent in advance to submission of their disputes to the ICJ or to ITLOS, which was established by the Convention.

States prefer to resolve their disputes by negotiation, mainly because they believe that they remain in control of the process, without the intervention of third parties. In addition, Socialist States believe that international law is a tool of capitalism; for developing countries, it was an instrument of imperialism. At present, only 72 UN members (about one-third of the total) have given their consent to dispute settlement by the ICJ under Article 36(2) of the Statute.[14]

As a Socialist State, China is viscerally opposed to dispute settlement by international courts.[15] In contrast, the attitudes of developing countries, in particular the African states, have

---

10 Laouali Souleymane, "Conférence de Presse du Directeur général en charge du département Afrique du Ministère des Affaires Etrangères de la République Populaire de Chine: Des clarifications sur la question de la mer de Chine méridionale," *Nigerdiaspora. La communauté virtuelle du Niger*, 20 April 2016, http://www.nigerdiaspora.net/les-infos-du-pays/politique-niger/politique-niger/item/73676-conference-de-presse-du-directeur-general-en-charge-du-departement-afrique-du-ministere-des-affaires-etrangeres-de-la-republique-populaire-de-chine-des-clarifications-sur-la-question-de-la-mer-de-chine-meridionale, accessed 25 May 2016; Eugénio Mateus, "China diz-se soberana sobre as ilhas a Sul," *O País*, 8 April 2016, http://opais.co.ao/china-diz-se-soberana-sobre-as-ilhas-a-sul/, accessed 1 June 2016.

11 Agence France Presse, "Beijing Lines up Diplomatic Battle Groups Over South China Sea," *Philippine Daily Inquirer*, 25 May 2016, http://globalnation.inquirer.net/139665/beijing-lines-up-diplomatic-battle-groups-over-south-china-sea, accessed 25 May 2016.

12 *Moçambique e China estabelecem parceria estratégica*, *supra* note 4.

13 *Hua Chunying's Regular Press Conference on May 25, 2016*, *supra* note 2.

14 ICJ, *Declarations Recognizing the Jurisdiction of the Court as Compulsory*, http://www.icj-cij.org/en/declarations, accessed 16 March 2018

15 The opposition to international adjudication of Socialist States in general and of China in particular is already very well-known and cannot be discussed here. On the former, see for example, Malcolm N. Shaw, *International Law*,

evolved considerably since the 1980s. Before that time, only 12 African States had recognized the Court's compulsory jurisdiction: Botswana, Egypt, Gambia, Kenya, Liberia, Malawi, Mauritius, Somalia, Sudan, Swaziland, Togo, and Uganda. Since then, they have been joined by Cameroon, Côte d'Ivoire, Djibouti, Democratic Republic of Congo (DRC), Equatorial Guinea, Guinea, Guinea-Bissau, Lesotho, Madagascar, Nigeria, and Senegal, bringing the number to 23 (out of 72). This group includes four of the States that officially support China: Cameroon, Côte d'Ivoire, Senegal, and Togo. African States now constitute the second largest group of States that have recognized the Court's compulsory jurisdiction, second only to the group of European States (27). The number of Asian States (six, including the Philippines and Japan, but not China) has not increased at all since the 1980s. Understandably, Africa's role in reconciling the Third World with the ICJ has been described as "considerable."[16]

Of the 23 African States on the list, nine (Cameroon, Democratic Republic of the Congo, Equatorial Guinea, Guinea-Bissau, Kenya, Nigeria, Senegal, Somalia, and Uganda) have been involved in nine cases.[17] Eight cases involving ten African states (Benin, Botswana, Burkina Faso, Chad, Libya, Mali, Namibia, Niger, Republic of the Congo, and Tunisia) have been heard on the basis of a special agreement,[18] while six disputes in which five African states were parties were submitted on the basis of a treaty (Burundi, DRC, Djibouti, Libya, and Rwanda).[19] A total

7th ed. (Cambridge: Cambridge University Press, 2014), pp. 22–27; on the latter, see Julian Ku, "China's Definition of the 'Peaceful Settlement of International Disputes' Leaves out International Adjudication," *opiniojuris.org*, 15 October 2013, http://opiniojuris.org/2013/10/15/obligation-seek-peaceful-settlement-international-disputes-include-international-adjudication/, accessed 5 July 2015.

16 Alain Pellet, "Remarques cursives sur les contentieux 'africains' devant la CIJ," in Maurice Kamga and Makane Moïse Mbengue (eds.), *Liber Amicorum Raymond Ranjeva. L'Afrique et le droit international: variations sur l'organisation internationale* (Paris: Éditions Pedone, 2013), p. 278, http://pellet.actu.com/wp-content/uploads/2015/12/PELLET-2013-M%C3%A9l-Ranjeva.pdf, accessed 3 October 2016.

17 Following is the list:
1–2. *Arbitral Award of 31 July 1989*, http://www.icj-cij.org/en/case/82 (1989–91), and *Maritime Delimitation Between Guinea-Bissau and Senegal (Guinea-Bissau v. Senegal)*, http://www.icj-cij.org/en/case/85 (1991–94).
3–4. *Land and Maritime Boundary Between Cameroon and Nigeria*, http://www.icj-cij.org/en/case/ (1994–98), and *Request for Interpretation of the Judgment of 11 June 1998 (Nigeria v. Cameroon)*, http://www.icj-cij.org/en/case/101 (1998–99).
5. *Arrest Warrant of 11 April 2000 (Democratic Republic of the Congo v. Belgium)*, http://www.icj-cij.org/en/case/121 (2000–02).
6. *Questions Relating to the Obligation to Prosecute or Extradite (Belgium v. Senegal)*, http://www.icj-cij.org/en/case/144 (2009–12).
7. *Armed Activities on the Territory of the Congo (Democratic Republic of the Congo v. Uganda)*, http://www.icj-cij.org/en/case/116, pending.
8. *Maritime Delimitation in the Indian Ocean (Somalia v. Kenya)*, http://www.icj-cij.org/en/case/161, pending.
9. *Immunities and Criminal Proceedings (Equatorial Guinea v. France)*, http://www.icj-cij.org/en/case/163.

18 Following is the list:
1–2. *Continental Shelf (Tunisia/Libyan Arab Jamahiriya)*, http://www.icj-cij.org/en/case/63 (1978–82), and *Application for Revision and Interpretation of the Judgment of 24 February 1982 (Tunisia v. Libyan Arab Jamahiriya)*, http://www.icj-cij.org/en/case/71 (1984–85).
3. *Continental Shelf (Libyan Arab Jamahiriya/Malta)*, http://www.icj-cij.org/en/case/68 (1982–85).
4. *Frontier Dispute (Burkina Faso/Republic of Mali)*, http://www.icj-cij.org/en/case/69 (1983–86).
5. *Territorial Dispute (Libyan Arab Jamahiriya/Chad)*, http://www.icj-cij.org/en/case/83 (1990–94).
6. *Kasikili/Sedudu Island (Botswana/Namibia)*, http://www.icj-cij.org/en/case/98 (1996–99).
7. *Frontier Dispute (Benin/Niger)*, http://www.icj-cij.org/en/case/125 (2002–05).
8. *Frontier Dispute (Burkina Faso/Niger)*, http://www.icj-cij.org/en/case/149 (2010–13).

19 Following is the list:
1–2. *Armed Activities on the Territory of the Congo (Democratic Republic of the Congo v. Rwanda)*, http://www.icj-cij.org/en/case/117 (1999–2001), and *Democratic Republic of the Congo v. Burundi*, http://www.icj-cij.org/en/case/115 (1999–2001).
3–4. *Questions of Interpretation and Application of the 1971 Montreal Convention arising from the Aerial Incident at Lockerbie (Libyan Arab Jamahiriya v. United Kingdom)*, http://www.icj-cij.org/en/case/88 (1992–2003), and *Questions of Interpretation and Application of the 1971 Montreal Convention Arising From the Aerial Incident at*

of 23 African States have thus been involved in 22 out of 83 cases heard by the Court since 1980. The figures might seem very low, but Asian States are arguably even more wary of international courts. Since 1980, the Court has heard only four "Asian" cases, in which three Asian states (Indonesia, Malaysia, and Singapore) were parties.[20]

As for the ITLOS, 36 States, out of 167 parties to the 1982 Convention, have accepted its jurisdiction. Six African States (Angola, Cape Verde, the DRC, Madagascar, Tunisia, and Tanzania) make up the second largest group, together with the Latin American and Caribbean group, that has accepted the Court's jurisdiction, after the European group.

None of the six has been a party to any of the 23 inter-State cases that have been heard by the ITLOS, but five other African States have appeared before it. Ghana and Côte d'Ivoire concluded a special agreement requesting that the Tribunal delimit their maritime boundary.[21] Ghana and three other States (Guinea, Seychelles, and Guinea-Bissau) have appeared in five cases relating to the release of vessels.[22]

Beyond the statistics, the conduct at the ICJ of three African States whose support China is seeking—Burundi, Senegal, and Niger—vividly demonstrates the great differences between Chinese and African attitudes towards international courts.

African States Appear Before the ICJ

Burundi has not accepted ICJ jurisdiction and thus may not be forced to appear before it. Yet, when a case was filed against it, it did not boycott the Court. Senegal, which has accepted ICJ jurisdiction, cannot anticipate when and over what issue another State may bring a case against it. If the issue is sensitive, Senegal might still challenge the Court's jurisdiction. Nevertheless, it chose to appear before the Court when Guinea-Bissau filed two cases against it. Niger, which

Lockerbie (Libyan Arab Jamahiriya v. United States of America), http://www.icj-cij.org/en/case/89 (1992–2003).

5. *Certain Questions of Mutual Assistance in Criminal Matters (Djibouti v. France)*, http://www.icj-cij.org/en/case/136 (2006–08).

6. *Certain Criminal Proceedings in France (Republic of the Congo v. France)*, http://www.icj-cij.org/en/case/1292003-10.

20 Following is the list:

1. *Sovereignty Over Pulau Ligitan and Pulau Sipadan (Indonesia/Malaysia)*, http://www.icj-cij.org/en/case/102 (1998–2002).

2. *Sovereignty Over Pedra Branca/Pulau Batu Puteh, Middle Rocks and South Ledge (Malaysia/Singapore)*, http://www.icj-cij.org/en/case/130 (2003–08).

3. *Application for Revision of the Judgment of 23 May 2008 in the Case Concerning Sovereignty Over Pedra Branca/Pulau Batu Puteh, Middle Rocks and South Ledge (Malaysia/Singapore) (Malaysia v. Singapore)*, http://www.icj-cij.org/en/case/167, pending.

4. *Request for Interpretation of the Judgment of 23 May 2008 in the Case Concerning Sovereignty Over Pedra Branca/Pulau Batu Puteh, Middle Rocks and South Ledge (Malaysia/Singapore) (Malaysia v. Singapore)*, http://www.icj-cij.org/en/case/170, pending.

21 *Dispute Concerning Delimitation of the Maritime Boundary Between Ghana and Côte d'Ivoire in the Atlantic Ocean (Ghana/Côte d'Ivoire)*, https://www.itlos.org/cases/list-of-cases/case-no-23/. Ghana's judge ad hoc in the case, Thomas A. Mensah, was the first president of the ITLOS (1996–99) and was the president of the Tribunal in the *Philippines v. China* arbitration.

22 Following is the list:

1. *Case No. 1: The M/V "SAIGA" Case (Saint Vincent and the Grenadines v. Guinea), Prompt Release*, https://www.itlos.org/cases/list-of-cases/case-no-1/ (1997).

2. *Case No. 2: The M/V "SAIGA" (No. 2) (Saint Vincent and the Grenadines v. Guinea)*, https://www.itlos.org/cases/list-of-cases/case-no-2/ (1998–99).

3. *Case No. 6: The "Monte Confurco" Case (Seychelles v. France), Prompt Release*, https://www.itlos.org/cases/list-of-cases/case-no-6/ (2000).

19. *Case No. 19: The M/V "Virginia G" Case (Panama/Guinea-Bissau)*, https://www.itlos.org/cases/list-of-cases/case-no-19/ (2011–14).

20. *Case No. 20: The "ARA Libertad" Case (Argentina v. Ghana), Provisional Measures*, https://www.itlos.org/cases/list-of-cases/case-no-20/ (2012).

gave its consent by special agreement, could not predict the outcomes of the cases but accepted the risk of unfavorable outcomes after decades of negotiations with two neighbors had failed.

In 1999, Burundi was accused of aggression by the DRC, which had accepted ICJ jurisdiction under Article 36, paragraph 2 of the ICJ Statute. Aggression is one of the gravest violations of international law that may be made against a State, since international law prohibits the use of force in international relations, and the UN's fundamental aim is to maintain international peace and security. No State, big or small, wishes to be accused of aggression. The conduct of Burundi in this case should be instructive to China. As Burundi had not given its consent to ICJ jurisdiction, it could have boycotted the proceedings. Yet, Burundi appointed an agent to represent it in the case, attended a consultation with the DRC and the ICJ over the procedure, and submitted its written arguments by the deadline set by the Court.[23] The case was terminated when the DRC discontinued it in 2001.[24]

Senegal, which accepted ICJ jurisdiction under Article 36, paragraph 2 of the Statute in 1985, was involved between 1985 and 1995 in a less dramatic, but more protracted, process: it was a party to three proceedings before two international tribunals over one issue, maritime delimitation with Guinea-Bissau, which accepted ICJ jurisdiction under Article 36, paragraph 2 of the Statute in 1989. In the first case, an arbitral tribunal held that a 1960 exchange of letters between France and Portugal, the then colonial powers, had determined the boundary between Senegal and Guinea-Bissau, but that it did not delimit their Exclusive Economic Zones.[25] In the second and third cases, Guinea-Bissau, which was dissatisfied with the Tribunal's Award, requested that the ICJ declare that the Award was null and void[26] and delimit the maritime boundaries between the two States.[27] It was arguably not in Senegal's interest to participate in the second case, in view of the fact that the Tribunal's Award was partly favorable to its theses. But both States had accepted ICJ jurisdiction under Article 36, paragraph 2 of the Statute.

Senegal's conduct in this case could not be more different from that of China in the *Philippines v. China* arbitration. Senegal appointed an agent to represent it in the case, participated in consultations on the procedure, submitted its written arguments by the deadline, and took part in all oral proceedings. Senegal denied that Guinea-Bissau's case was admissible. The ICJ did not agree with Senegal,[28] but it ruled that the Award was valid and binding for the two States.[29] The ICJ's judgment paved the way for negotiations between the two States to delimit all maritime areas and the withdrawal of the third case in 1995.[30]

---

23 République du Burundi, *Affaire des activités armées sur le territoire du Congo (République démocratique du Congo c. Burundi). Exceptions préliminaires. Mémoire de la République du Burundi*, 20 April 2000, pp. 5, 6, 21, 33, 34, 52, 67, 68, http://www.icj-cij.org/files/case-related/115/13462.pdf, accessed 29 March 2018.

24 ICJ, *Armed Activities on the Territory of the Congo (Democratic Republic of the Congo v. Burundi) and (Democratic Republic of the Congo v. Rwanda). The Two Cases Are Removed From the List at the Request of the Democratic Republic of the Congo*, Press Release 2001/2 (1 February 2001), http://www.icj-cij.org/files/case-related/115/115-20010201-PRE-01-00-EN.pdf, accessed 29 March 2018

25 *Affaire de la délimitation de la frontière maritime entre la Guinée-Bissau et le Sénégal. Sentence du 31 juillet* 1989, *Reports of International Arbitral Awards*, XX (New York: United Nations, 2006), pp. 127, 153, http://legal.un.org/docs/?path=../riaa/cases/vol_XX/119-213.pdf&lang=O, accessed 4 October 2016.

26 ICJ, *Application Instituting Proceedings of the Government of the Republic of Guinea-Bissau Filed in the Registry of the Court on 23 August 1989 (Arbitral Award of 31 July 1989) (Guinea-Bissau v. Senegal)*, http://www.icj-cij.org/files/case-related/82/11289.pdf, accessed 29 March 2018.

27 ICJ, *Application Instituting Proceedings Filed in the Registry of the Court on 12 March 1991. Maritime Delimitation Between Guinea-Bissau and Senegal (Guinea-Bissau v. Senegal)*, http://www.icj-cij.org/files/case-related/85/6843.pdf, accessed 29 March 2018.

28 *Arbitral Award of 31 July 1989, Judgment, I.C.J. Reports 1991*, p. 63, para. 26, http://www.icj-cij.org/files/case-related/82/082-19911112-JUD-01-00-BI.pdf, accessed 29 March 2018.

29 *Ibid.*, p. 76.

30 Ifesinachi Okafor-Yarwood, "The Guinea-Bissau–Senegal Maritime Boundary Dispute," *Marine Policy*, 61 (November 2015), p. 287; "Le Président de la Cour internationale de justice au Président de la République de

Niger, which has not given its consent to ICJ dispute settlement under Article 36, paragraph 2 of the Statute, has been party to two frontier disputes before the Court, which heard them on the basis of special agreements. Niger and the two other States involved could not have predicted the outcome of the cases; notwithstanding the uncertainty they turned to the ICJ because decades of negotiations following independence from France in 1960 had not yielded any solution. This conduct again contrasts sharply with that of China, which insists on bilateral negotiations despite the fact that they have failed over many years.

Niger's dispute with Benin (2002–05) concerned 25 border islands situated on the delta of the Niger and Mekrou Rivers between them. Although incidents had occurred in 1960, 1993, and 1998, joint commissions meeting in 1961, 1963, and between 1995 and 2000 failed to delimit the border. The two States finally signed an agreement in 2001 to submit the dispute to the ICJ.[31]

African observers believe that the Court's judgment represented a balanced settlement. In one sector of the boundary, the Court accepted Niger's thesis; in another sector, it was Benin's thesis that was followed. Benin thus had title to nine islands situated between the boundary and the right bank of the Niger River, while Niger was granted title to 16 islands situated between the boundary and the River's left bank.[32] Benin lost the largest island, but its area increased by 1118 square kilometers; Niger's area increased by 38 square kilometers.[33]

In the Niger–Burkina Faso (2010–13) dispute, commissions meeting in 1964, 1988, and 1991 had been unable to demarcate the border. In February 2009, the two States finally concluded a special agreement to submit the dispute to the Court.[34] African assessments believe that the Court's judgment split the difference between the two States.[35] It rejected Burkina Faso's request for delimitation in two sectors in the North and the South, while at the same time rejecting Niger's request to modify slightly the delimitation around two localities.[36] The Court's judgment attributed 786 square kilometers of territory occupied by Niger to Burkina Faso, which acquired 14 villages; 277 square kilometers of Burkina territory were returned to Niger, which received 4 villages.[37] A Burkina source implies that Burkina Faso obtained a slight advantage over Niger by being granted greater access to the River Sirba, an affluent of the Niger River, than Niger would have wanted. Yet, Niger's Minister of Justice declared that the two States were winners, because there would be no more disagreement regarding the border.[38]

Guinée-Bissau, 16 mars 1994," *Correspondance*, http://www.icj-cij.org/en/case/85/correspondence, accessed 29 March 2018.

31 *Frontier Dispute (Benin/Niger) Judgment, I.C.J. Reports 2005*, p. 107, paras. 20–22, *supra* note 18.

32 ICJ, *Frontier Dispute (Benin/Niger). The Chamber of the Court Determines the Course of the Whole Boundary Between the Two States*, Press Release 2005/16 (12 July 2005), http://www.icj-cij.org/files/case-related/125/125-20050712-PRE-01-00-EN.pdf, accessed 29 March 2018.

33 Panafrican News Agency, "Le Bénin gagne 9 îles dans le litige frontalier avec le Niger," *Le Blog de Benoît Illassa—Une passion pour le Bénin*, 8 August 2007, http://illassa-benoit.over-blog.com/article-11817649.html, accessed 29 May 2016; "Différend frontalier Bénin-Niger : La paix des braves," *Lefaso net. Actualité du Burkina sur Internet*, 14 July 2005, http://lefaso.net/spip.php?page=impression&id_article=8428, accessed 27 May 2016.

34 *Frontier Dispute (Burkina Faso/Niger), Judgment, I.C.J. Reports 2013*, pp. 62–65, paras. 23–30, *supra* note 18.

35 "Cour internationale de justice: Burkina Faso et Niger se quittent 'bons amis' avec une frontière commune," *zoodomail.com*, 16 April 2013, http://zoodomail.com/spip.php?page=imprimir_articulo&id_article=3858, accessed 29 May 2016.

36 Fulbert Paré, "Différend frontalier Burkina Faso-Niger: la Cour internationale de justice rend une décision mitigée," *Lefaso net. Actualité du Burkina sur Internet*, 17 April 2013, http://lefaso.net/spip.php?article53798, accessed 27 May 2016.

37 Agence France Presse, "Nouvelle frontière Burkina Faso-Niger: 18 communes changeront de pays," *Jeuneafrique.com*, 9 May 2015, http://www.jeuneafrique.com/231107/politique/nouvelle-fronti-re-burkina-faso-niger-18-communes-changeront-de-pays/, accessed 29 May 2016.

38 "Cour internationale de justice: Burkina Faso et Niger se quittent 'bons amis,'" *supra* note 35.

It would seem, then, that the risk of submitting the dispute to the Court was worth running, because the Court gave reasons for satisfaction to both States.[39]

It is sad that China should have to be reminded of the conduct of African States at the ICJ. China cannot dismiss African States' attitudes to and conduct before international courts, alleging that their disputes have low stakes and that they are small countries. China should have stopped canvassing their support for its position and emulated their conduct.

[39] "Verdict de la Cour internationale de justice de la Haye sur le différend frontalier entre le Niger et le Burkina Faso : Une décision unanimement saluée," *Le Sahel*, 16 April 2013, http://lesahel.org/index.php/component/k2/item/2915-verdict-de-la-cour-internationale-de-justice-de-la-haye-sur-le-diff%C3%A9rend-frontalier-entre-le-niger-et-le-burkina-faso--une-d%C3%A9cision-unanimement-salu%C3%A9e, accessed 27 May 2016.

7

The South China Sea Disputes: A View from Togo (West Africa)[1]

Among the African countries that expressed support for the Chinese position on the South China Sea dispute that the dispute must be solved exclusively by negotiations between the States concerned was Togo, a Francophone State in West Africa. On 18 May 2015, the Togolese Ministry of Foreign Affairs issued a communiqué in which it called upon "all of the parties concerned by this crisis to work toward the peaceful settlement of their disputes by means of dialogue and negotiation in accordance with the international laws relating to the sea and more specifically in accordance with Article 298 of the United Nations Convention on the Law of the Sea."[2]

At a press conference on the same day, Chinese Foreign Ministry spokesperson Hong Lei replied the following to a question on Togo's support:

> We have noted the communiqué issued by the government of Togo, which calls on all parties concerned to peacefully resolve differences through dialogue and consultation in accordance with relevant international law such as Article 298 of the UN Convention on the Law of the Sea (UNCLOS), and reaffirms support for countries in the region to build up mutual trust and enhance cooperation through negotiation. It recognizes direct dialogue and negotiation between parties concerned as the only way to achieve fair and equitable settlement of the South China Sea issue and asks all parties concerned to maintain peace and security in the sensitive areas of the South China Sea with joint efforts.
>
> The position held by Togo conforms to the basic fact and the bilateral and regional consensus reached between China and relevant countries on resolving disputes through consultation. It is also in line with international law and universal practice, and reflects the international community's objective and fair opinion on this issue. We commend Togo for safeguarding international fairness and justice on the issue of the South China Sea.[3]

---

1 An earlier version of this Chapter was posted on 9 July 2016 on the blog of the author's sister-in-law, https://www.raissarobles.com/2016/07/09/oops-did-the-chinese-spokesman-read-the-comments-to-togos-press-release-backing-chinas-south-china-sea-stance/.

2 "Pékin apprécie la position togolaise." *République Togolaise*, 19 May 2016, http://www.republicoftogo.com/Toutes-les-rubriques/Diplomatie/Pekin-apprecie-la-position-togolaise, accessed 25 May 2016.

3 *Foreign Ministry Spokesperson Hong Lei's Regular Press Conference on May 18, 2016*, http://www.fmprc.gov.cn/mfa_eng/xwfw_665399/s2510_665401/2511_665403/t1364549.shtml, accessed 10 July 2016.

One wonders if Mr. Hong Lei had the time to read the two comments posted by two readers following the Togolese statement, published on what appears to be an official Togolese website:

> ***togo98***
> ***19/05/2016 12:15***
>
> I have nothing against China, but I believe that it is going too far. It wants to bully small Asian countries in order to take everything, and that is not right. Fortunately, America is there to stop that.
>
> Would you accept a claim by Nigeria, for example, or the Côte d'Ivoire on an island situated, for example, 5 km from the Togolese coast?
> Look at the map of the South China Sea and you will see that China wants to take everything. That is not right. Development does not mean bullying others.[4]
>
> ***Massoteau***
> ***19/05/2016 14:21***
>
> You are right, my dear fellow citizen togo98. China appreciates the position of Togolese diplomacy, based on dialogue. But will it really comply with this rule or will it attempt to resolve the problem by military force, as is its habit? This is China's common practice, in other words, trials of strength. It is one thing to appreciate the advice of friendly countries like Togo, but it is another thing to actually implement it in practice.[5]

Despite the fact that these were only two comments and they were anonymous, it is striking that two readers even took the trouble to make critical remarks on an issue that a priori would be very far removed from their concerns as Togolese and indeed as Africans. One can hardly imagine Filipinos making any type of observation, positive or negative, about territorial conflicts in West Africa.

The distrust of the People's Republic of China and the trust of the US that these two comments express reflect, in uncanny fashion, the feelings of many Filipinos towards the two countries.[6] Perhaps China is concerned only with the views of States, all the more so because it is not clear to what extent the views reflected above are representative of public

4 "Je n'ai rien contre la chine. Mais je trouve que la chine exagère. Elle veut brimer les petits pays de l'asie pour tout prendre et là ce n'est pas normal. heureusement qu'il y a l'amérique pour arrêter ça. Accepteriez vous qu'une ile située par exemple à 5 km des côtes togolaises soit réclamée par le Nigeria par exemple ou la Côte d'ivoire? Regardez la carte de la mer du sud de chine et vous verrez que la chine veut tout prendre. Ce n'est pas normal. Développement ne signifie pas brimer les autres." "Pékin apprécie la position togolaise," *supra* note 2

5 "Vous avez raison cher compatriote togo98. La chine apprécie la position de la diplomatie togolaise fondée sur le dialogue. Mais se conformera-t-elle réellement à cette règle ou tentera-t-elle de résoudre le problème par la force militaire comme elle en a l'habitude? La Chine est coutumière de ce fait, autrement dit, des épreuves de force. Une chose est d'apprécier les conseils de ses pays amis comme le Togo, autre chose est de les mettre effectivement en pratique." *Ibid.*

6 According to a 2014 report by the Pew Center, 83 percent of Filipinos surveyed trusted the US as an ally in the region and considered the People's Republic of China as a threat. Moreover, 90 percent of Filipinos surveyed believed that territorial disputes with China were a big problem for their country. Pew Research Center, *Global Opposition to U.S. Surveillance and drones, but Limited Harm to America's Image* (Washington, D.C., Pew Research Center, 14 July 2014), pp. 38–39, http://assets.pewresearch.org/wp-content/uploads/sites/2/2014/07/2014-07-14-Balance-of-Power.pdf, accessed 13 November 2017. A more recent survey by the Filipino institution Social Weather Station revealed that three out of five Filipinos surveyed distrusted China. "Three of Five Filipinos Distrust China, SWS Says," *Business World Online*, 11 July 2015, http://www.bworldonline.com/content.php?section=Nation&title=three-of-five-filipinos-distrust-china-sws-says&id=111348, accessed 13 November 2017.

opinion. Nevertheless, if China cannot abide any form of public criticism, China might have to make extra efforts in order to convince public opinion, and not just governments, of its good intentions, at least in Togo.

PART II

Understanding the Award of 12 July 2016 and Debating with China

8

Summary of the Award of 12 July 2016

TABLE OF CONTENTS[1]

I.	INTRODUCTION		115	1
II.	PROCEDURAL HISTORY		116	11
	A.	Initiation of the Arbitration	116	11
	B.	Constitution of the Tribunal and Appointment of the PCA as Registry	116	12
	C.	Written Arguments	116	13
	D.	Bifurcation of Proceedings	116	16
	E.	Hearing on Jurisdiction and Admissibility	116	17
	F.	Provisional Scheduling of Hearing on the Merits and Appointment of Expert	116	18
	G.	Issuance of Award on Jurisdiction and Admissibility	116	19
	H.	Hearing on the Merits	117	23
	I.	Post-Hearing Proceedings	117	27
	J.	Further Evidence, Expert Reports, and Communications from China and Others	118	29
	K.	Notification, Publication, and Translation of Award	121	38
	L.	Deposits for Costs of the Arbitration	121	38
III.	RELIEF REQUESTED AND SUBMISSIONS		121	41
IV.	PRELIMINARY MATTERS		123	45
	A.	The Legal and Practical Consequences of China's Non-Participation	123	45
		1. Steps Taken to Ensure Procedural Fairness to Both Parties	123	46

[1] The Table of Contents reproduces that of the Award of 12 July 2016. The first set of numbers refers to the pages in the Summary; the second set, to the pages in the Award itself. All headings and enumerations that are not included in this Table of Contents and that have been supplied by the author are indicated by footnotes.

		2.	Steps Taken by the Tribunal to Satisfy Itself that It Has Jurisdiction and that the Claim is Well Founded in Fact and Law......124	49
		3.	Conclusion on the Legal and Practical Consequences of China's Non-Participation......125	55
	B.	**Summary of the Tribunal's Award on Jurisdiction 125**		**56**
		1.	Preliminary Matters 125	57
		2.	Existence of a Dispute concerning Interpretation and Application of the Convention......125	58
		3.	Involvement of Indispensable Third Parties 125	60
		4.	Preconditions to Jurisdiction 125	60
		5.	Exceptions and Limitations to Jurisdiction 125	62
		6.	Decisions of the Tribunal 125	63
	C.	**The Status and Effect of the Tribunal's Award on Jurisdiction ...125**		**64**
V.	**THE 'NINE-DASH LINE' and CHINA'S CLAIM TO HISTORIC RIGHTS IN THE MARITIME AREAS OF THE SOUTH CHINA SEA (SUBMISSIONS NO. 1 AND 2)...... 126**			**67**
	A.	**Introduction 126**		**67**
	B.	**China's Declarations and Legislation concerning Entitlements to Maritime Zones...... 126**		**68**
	C.	**China's Claims to Historic Rights 126**		**71**
	D.	**The Philippines' Position 127**		**74**
		1.	Jurisdiction 127	79
		2.	China's Claim to Historic Rights 127	80
	E.	**China's Position 128**		**84**
	F.	**The Tribunal's Considerations 128**		**85**
		1.	The Tribunal's Jurisdiction 128	85
			(a) The Nature of China's Claimed Rights in the South China Sea 129	86
			(b) The Scope of the Exception in Article 298(1)(a)(i) of the Convention...... 129	92
		2.	The Merits of the Philippines' Submissions No. 1 and 2...131	97
			(a) The Convention and Prior Claims to Historic Rights and Jurisdiction...... 131	98
			(b) China's Claim to Historic Rights in the South China Sea 135	112
			(c) Whether China has Established Exceptional Rights or Jurisdiction since the Adoption of the Convention......136	115
			(d) Conclusion 136	116

VI.	**THE STATUS OF FEATURES IN THE SOUTH CHINA SEA (SUBMISSIONS NO. 3 TO 7)**			**136**	**119**
	A.	**Introduction**		**136**	**119**
	B.	**The Status of Features as Above/Below Water at High Tide (Submissions No. 4 and 6)**		**137**	**119**
		1.	Introduction	137	119
		2.	Factual Background	137	120
		3.	The Philippines' Position	137	122
		4.	China's Position	138	130
		5.	The Tribunal's Considerations	139	131
		(a)	The Interpretation of Article 13 and the Tribunal's Approach to Submissions No. 4 and 6	139	131
		(b)	Evidence on the Status of Features as Above/Below Water at High Tide	140	137
		(c)	The Status of Particular Features in the South China Sea	142	143
		(d)	Conclusion	144	174
	C.	**The Status of Features as Rocks/Islands (Submissions No. 3, 5, and 7)**		**144**	**175**
		1.	Introduction	144	175
		2.	Factual Background	145	178
		3.	The Philippines' Position	146	181
		(a)	Interpretation of Article 121(3)	146	181
		(b)	Application to Features Identified in Submissions No. 3 and 7	147	186
		(c)	Application to Other Maritime Features	147	187
		4.	China's Position	149	195
		(a)	China's Statements on the Meaning of Article 121(3)	149	197
		(b)	China's Position on the Status of Scarborough Shoal	150	199
		(c)	China's Position on the Status of Itu Aba	150	202
		(d)	China's Position on the Status of Other Features in the Spratly Islands	150	203
		5.	The Tribunal's Considerations	150	204
		(a)	Interpretation of Article 121 of the Convention	150	204
		(b)	Application of Article 121(3) to Scarborough Shoal, Johnson Reef, Cuarteron Reef, Fiery Cross Reef, Gaven Reef (North), and McKennan Reef	155	232

		(c)	Application of Article 121(3) to the Spratly Islands as a Whole	156	235
		(d)	Application of Article 121(3) to Other High-Tide Features in the Spratly Islands	156	237
		(e)	Decision on the Tribunal's Jurisdiction with respect to Submission No. 5	159	254
		(f)	Conclusion	160	259
VII.	**CHINESE ACTIVITIES IN THE SOUTH CHINA SEA (SUBMISSIONS NO. 8 TO 13)**			**161**	**261**
	A.	**Alleged Interference with the Philippines' Sovereign Rights in its EEZ and Continental Shelf (Submission No. 8)**		**161**	**261**
		1.	Introduction	161	261
		2.	Factual Background	161	261
			(a) Actions regarding Non-Living Resources	161	261
			(b) Alleged Interference with Living Resources	162	268
		3.	The Philippines' Position	163	274
			(a) Jurisdiction	163	274
			(b) The Philippines' Rights in the Exclusive Economic Zone	163	275
		4.	China's Position	164	276
		5.	The Tribunal's Considerations	164	277
			(a) The Tribunal's Jurisdiction	164	277
			(b) China's Actions and the Philippines' Sovereign Rights	165	279
			(c) Conclusion	167	286
	B.	**Alleged Failure to Prevent Chinese Nationals from Exploiting the Philippines' Living Resources (Submission No. 9)**		**168**	**287**
		1.	Introduction	168	287
		2.	Factual Background	168	287
		3.	The Philippines' Position	168	288
		4.	China's Position	169	290
		5.	The Tribunal's Considerations	169	291
			(a) The Tribunal's Jurisdiction	169	291
			(b) The Law Applicable to China's Supervision of its Fishing Vessels	169	291
			(c) The Activities of Chinese Fishing Vessels at Mischief Reef and Second Thomas Shoal	169	294
			(d) Conclusion	170	297
	C.	**China's Actions in respect of Traditional Fishing at Scarborough Shoal (Submission No. 10)**		**170**	299
		1.	Introduction	170	299
		2.	Factual Background	170	299

	(a)	Traditional Fishing by Philippine Fishermen at Scarborough Shoal	170	300
	(b)	China's Intermittent Prevention of Fishing by Philippine Vessels at Scarborough Shoal (May 2012 to Present)	171	301
3.		The Philippines' Position	171	304
	(a)	Article 2(3) of the Convention	172	304
	(b)	Articles 51(1) and 62(3) of the Convention	172	308
	(c)	China's Obligation to Act in Good Faith and Settle Disputes by Peaceful Means	172	308
4.		China's Position	173	309
5.		The Tribunal's Considerations	173	301
	(a)	The Law Applicable to Traditional Fishing	173	311
	(b)	The Protection of Traditional Fishing at Scarborough Shoal	174	315
	(c)	Conclusion	175	318
D.		**Alleged Failure to Protect and Preserve the Marine Environment (Submissions No. 11 and 12(B))**	**175**	319
1.		Introduction	175	319
2.		Factual Background	176	321
	(a)	The Marine Environment of the South China Sea	176	321
	(b)	Harmful Fishing Practices and Harvesting of Endangered Species	176	322
	(c)	China's Construction Activities on Seven Reefs in the Spratly Islands	177	329
3.		The Philippines' Position	178	355
	(a)	Harmful Fishing Practices and Harvesting of Endangered Species	179	356
	(b)	China's Construction Activities on Seven Reefs in the Spratly Islands	179	358
	(c)	Interpretation and Application of Part XII of the Convention	180	360
4.		China's Position	180	363
	(a)	Harmful Fishing Practices and Harvesting of Endangered Species	180	363
	(b)	China's Construction Activities on Seven Reefs in the Spratly Islands	181	364
5.		The Tribunal's Considerations	182	369
	(a)	The Tribunal's Jurisdiction	182	369
	(b)	Relevant Provisions of the Convention	182	373
	(c)	Harmful Fishing Practices and Harvesting of Endangered Species	184	378

		(d)	China's Construction Activities on Seven Reefs in the Spratly Islands	186	388
		(e)	Conclusion	188	397
E.	**Occupation and Construction Activities on Mischief Reef (Submission No. 12)**			**188**	**399**
	1.	Introduction		188	399
	2.	Factual Background		188	399
		(a)	China's Initial Activities on Mischief Reef (1995 to 2013)	188	399
		(b)	Island-Building Activities on Mischief Reef (Post-2013)	189	402
	3.	The Philippines' Position		189	404
		(a)	Military Activities and the Tribunal's Jurisdiction	189	404
		(b)	Articles 60 and 80 of the Convention	190	407
		(c)	Attempted Appropriation under the Convention	190	408
	4.	China's Position		190	409
	5.	The Tribunal's Considerations		191	411
		(a)	The Tribunal's Jurisdiction	191	411
		(b)	China's Actions at Mischief Reef and the Philippines' Sovereign Rights	191	413
		(c)	Conclusion	192	415
F.	**Operation of Law Enforcement Vessels in a Dangerous Manner (Submission No. 13)**			**192**	417
	1.	Introduction		192	417
	2.	Factual Background		193	417
		(a)	Near-Collision of Philippine Vessels BRP Pampanga and BRP Edsa II with Chinese Vessel FLEC 310	193	418
		(b)	Near-Collision of Philippine Vessel MCS 3008 with Several Chinese Vessels upon Approach to Scarborough Shoal	193	418
	3.	The Philippines' Position		194	421
		(a)	The Applicability of the COLREGS to China	194	421
		(b)	Exceptions to the COLREGS for Special Circumstances	194	423
		(c)	Application of the COLREGS to Chinese Vessels at Scarborough Shoal	194	423
	4.	China's Position		195	426
	5.	The Tribunal's Considerations		196	428
		(a)	Background on the COLREGS	196	428
		(b)	Report of Tribunal-Appointed Independent Expert	196	429

		(c)	Application of Article 94 of the Convention and the COLREGS	197	431
		(d)	Conclusion	198	435
VIII.	**AGGRAVATION OR EXTENSION OF THE DISPUTE BETWEEN THE PARTIES (SUBMISSION NO. 14)**			**198**	**437**
	A.	**Introduction**		**198**	**437**
	B.	**Factual Background**		**199**	**438**
	1.	Chinese Actions in and around Second Thomas Shoal		199	438
		(a)	China's Objections to the Presence of BRP Sierra Madre at Second Thomas Shoal	199	438
		(b)	China's Interference in the Rotation and Resupply of Philippine Personnel at Second Thomas Shoal	199	441
	2.	China's Dredging, Artificial Island-Building and Construction Activities		200	445
	C.	**The Philippines' Position**		**200**	**445**
	1.	Jurisdiction		200	445
	2.	The Philippines' Rights to Have this Dispute Settled Peacefully		201	447
		(a)	Obligation Not to Engage in Acts that Might Aggravate a Dispute	201	447
		(b)	China's Conduct in relation to the Dispute	202	448
	D.	**China's Position**		**202**	**450**
	1.	Obligation Not to Engage in Acts that Might Aggravate a Dispute		202	450
	2.	China's Conduct in relation to the Dispute		202	451
		(a)	Chinese Activities in and around Second Thomas Shoal	202	451
		(b)	China's Dredging and Construction Activities	202	452
	E.	**The Tribunal's Considerations**		**203**	**452**
	1.	The Tribunal's Jurisdiction		203	452
		(a)	China's Actions in and around Second Thomas Shoal	203	453
		(b)	China's Dredging and Construction Activities	204	456
	2.	The Law Applicable to Conduct in the Course of Dispute Resolution Proceedings		204	457
	3.	The Effect of China's Dredging and Construction Activities on the Parties' Disputes		205	461
	4.	Conclusion		207	464
IX.	**THE FUTURE CONDUCT OF THE PARTIES (SUBMISSION NO. 15)**			**207**	**465**
	A.	**The Philippines' Position**		**207**	**465**
	B.	**China's Position**		**208**	**466**

	C.	**The Tribunal's Considerations**	**208**	**467**
	D.	**Conclusion**	**209**	**469**
X.	**DISPOSITIF**		**209**	**471**

I. INTRODUCTION[2]

The Convention does not address the sovereignty of States over land territory. The Tribunal has not been asked to and does not purport to make any ruling as to which State enjoys sovereignty over any land territory in the South China Sea. None of the Tribunal's decisions is dependent on a finding of sovereignty nor should anything in this Award be understood to imply a view with respect to questions of land sovereignty.

The Convention does contain provisions concerning delimitation of maritime boundaries. In 2006, China made a declaration to exclude maritime boundary delimitation from compulsory dispute settlement, something that the Convention expressly permits for maritime boundaries and certain other matters. Accordingly, the Tribunal has not been asked to and does not purport to delimit any maritime boundaries between the Parties or involving any other littoral States. The Tribunal will address Philippine claims relating to events at particular locations in the South China Sea only insofar as the two States' respective rights and obligations are not dependent on any maritime boundary or where no delimitation of boundary would be necessary because the application of the Convention would not lead to any overlap of the two States' entitlements.

The disputes before the Tribunal fall within four categories:

1. a dispute concerning the sources of maritime rights and entitlements in the South China Sea;
2. a dispute concerning entitlements to maritime zones that would be generated under the Convention by Scarborough Shoal and certain maritime features in the Spratly Islands that are claimed by China and the Philippines;
3. disputes concerning the lawfulness of China's actions in the South China Sea; and
4. the aggravation and extension of the dispute during the arbitration by China.[3]

The Tribunal has taken several steps to satisfy itself of its jurisdiction. It treated China's communications as a plea on jurisdiction. It bifurcated the dispute to have a separate hearing on jurisdiction and admissibility. It probed the Philippines on jurisdictional questions even beyond those in China's Position Paper. It deferred for further consideration seven jurisdictional issues.

In the merits phase, the Tribunal has been particularly vigilant with respect to establishing whether Philippine claims are well founded in fact and in law. For example, it retained independent experts on technical matters raised by Philippine pleadings. It invited comments from both States on materials that were not originally part of the record submitted to the Tribunal by the Philippines. It posed questions to the Philippines before, during, and after the hearing on the merits that was held in The Hague from 24 to 30 November 2015. China was provided with daily transcripts and all documents submitted and was given an opportunity to comment on them.

In addition to a large delegation from the Philippines, representatives from Australia, Indonesia, Japan, Malaysia, Singapore, Thailand, and Viet Nam attended the hearing as observers.

[2] Award of 12 July 2016, pp. 1–9, paras. 1–25, https://pcacases.com/web/sendAttach/2086, accessed 19 March 2018. The summary of Chapter I of the Award covers only content not reported in the summary of the Award on Jurisdiction and Admissibility in Chapter I of this book.

[3] The preceding enumeration has been prepared by the author and does not appear in this form in the original text.

II. PROCEDURAL HISTORY[4]

A. INITIATION OF THE ARBITRATION[5]

B. CONSTITUTION OF THE TRIBUNAL AND APPOINTMENT OF THE PCA AS REGISTRY

C. WRITTEN ARGUMENTS

D. BIFURCATION OF PROCEEDINGS

E. HEARING ON JURISDICTION AND ADMISSIBILITY

F. PROVISIONAL SCHEDULING OF HEARING ON THE MERITS AND APPOINTMENT OF EXPERT

In December 2014, the Tribunal sought the views of the Parties on the utility and timing of the appointment of an expert hydrographer and the appropriate qualifications for the expert. The Philippines responded that it was desirable to appoint as soon as possible a knowledgeable, independent, and impartial hydrographer from whose input many issues in dispute would benefit significantly.

On 21 April 2015, the Tribunal asked the Parties whether it should reserve a period within the next 6 to 12 months for a hearing on the merits and take steps to ascertain the availability of potential experts. The Philippines responded on 11 May that the week of 23 to 27 November would be suitable and that engaging experts would help to avoid unnecessary delay. China did not comment.

On 7 August 2015, the Tribunal informed the Parties that it proposed to appoint Grant Boyes (a national of Australia) as expert hydrographer. The Philippines responded that his terms of reference should clarify that the expert will respect that it is the Tribunal that makes any determination as to legal questions, particularly the application of Article 121(3). China did not comment. With the clarification, the Tribunal appointed Grant Boyes.

On 10 September 2015, the Tribunal invited comments from the Parties on the provisional schedule for a merits hearing and informed them of a request from Singapore for observer status. The Philippines agreed with the schedule and raised no objection to the request from Singapore. China did not comment and returned the correspondence.

G. ISSUANCE OF AWARD ON JURISDICTION AND ADMISSIBILITY

The Award was issued on 29 October 2015.

The Tribunal confirmed that it was ready to proceed in late November with the hearing on the merits. It was willing to make appropriate adjustments to the schedule if China decided to participate. The Philippines confirmed the schedule. China did not comment.

However, on 30 October, the Ministry of Foreign Affairs published a statement declaring that the Award on Jurisdiction and Admissibility was null and void and had no binding effect on China. In addition to repeating the points already raised in China's Position Paper, it declared that the Philippines' unilateral initiation and obstinate pushing forward of the arbitration was

[4] Award of 12 July 2016, pp. 11–39, paras. 26–111, *supra* note 2. In the original text of the Award, there was an error in the numbering of the paragraphs: two paragraphs were numbered 110. The error has since been corrected, so that there are in fact two paragraphs under paragraph 110.

[5] Sections A to E are summarized under the Award on Jurisdiction and Admissibility (Chapter I of this book).

a political provocation under the cloak of law. It was not an effort to settle disputes but an attempt to negate China's territorial sovereignty and maritime rights in the South China Sea. The Philippines and the Tribunal, maliciously evading the 2006 Chinese declaration, were said to have deviated from the Convention's purposes and objectives, abused procedures, and obstinately forged ahead with the Arbitration. China called upon all countries concerned to work together to safeguard the Convention's integrity and authority and declared that the Philippines' attempt to negate China's territorial sovereignty and maritime rights and interests in the South China Sea through arbitration would lead to nothing. It urged the Philippines to return to the track of negotiations and consultations.

On 6 November, the observers were advised of the hearing schedule and informed that they could send up to five representatives. On 10 November, the Tribunal provided an 'Annex of Issues the Philippines May Wish to Present' as guidance for the hearing. The Philippines sought leave to present for examination two experts, Professors Clive Schofield and Kent E. Carpenter (on 6 November), and to present additional documentary and testimonial evidence and legal authorities (on 14 November). The Tribunal invited China's comments by 17 November. On 18 November, not having received any comments, the Tribunal granted the two requests, which were reasonable. The Tribunal asked the Parties whether the 'Annex of Issues' should be provided to the observers (Viet Nam, Malaysia, Thailand, Japan, Indonesia, and Singapore).

The Tribunal forwarded a request from the US to attend the hearing as an observer. On 19 November, the Philippines responded that it had no objection to the provision of the "Annex of Issues" to the observers or to the US request. On 23 November, the Tribunal refused the US request. Only interested States parties to the Convention would be admitted as observers.

The Tribunal received requests from the UK (23 November) and Australia (24 November) to attend the meeting as observers. The Philippines had no objection to the two requests, which were granted. However, the UK did not attend the hearing.

H. HEARING ON THE MERITS

The Hearing, which was not open to the general public, was held in two rounds, on 24–26 and 30 November 2015. The Registry delivered daily transcripts to the Philippines and to China's Embassy in the Netherlands, along with copies of all materials submitted by the Philippines during the Hearing. During the first round, several questions were raised by individual judges. On 27 November, the Tribunal circulated questions for the Philippines to address in the second round, as well as questions for Professors Schofield and Carpenter. Copies of the questions were given to the observers. During the second round, counsel for the Philippines and the two experts responded to written and oral questions.

The Tribunal President invited the Philippines and China to submit their corrections to the transcripts of the Hearing by 9 December. The Philippines had until 18 December 2015 to submit further responses to questions posed during the second round. China was invited to comment on anything said during the Hearing or submitted subsequently by 1 January 2016.

I. POST-HEARING PROCEEDINGS

On 30 November, the Philippines submitted its Final Submissions. On 1 December, the Tribunal noted that the Philippines' Final Submissions reflected three amendments requested by the Philippines during the Hearing.[6]

---

[6] The following enumeration has been prepared by the author and does not appear in this form in the original text.

1. References to Cuarteron Reef, Fiery Cross Reef, Gaven Reef, Johnson Reef, Hughes Reef, and Subi Reef were added to Submission No. 11.
2. References to dredging, artificial island building, and construction activities at Mischief Reef and the six reefs listed above were added to Submission No. 14.
3. In response to the Award on Jurisdiction and Admissibility, the Philippines reframed Submission No. 15 and sought a declaration that 'China shall respect the rights and freedoms of the Philippines under the Convention, including those relevant to the preservation and protection of the marine environment in the South China Sea and shall exercise its rights and freedoms in the South China Sea with due regard to those of the Philippines under the Convention'.

The Tribunal invited comments from China by 9 December.

On 14 December, the Philippines submitted further documents, including electronic versions of the materials displayed by Professor Carpenter, additional legal authorities, observations from R.W. Smith, and EOMAP satellite bathymetry analysis of the nature of certain maritime features between Thitu and Subi Reef. On 16 December, the Tribunal granted leave to the Philippines to make the amendments, announced that the final transcripts would be published on the PCA website, and reminded China that it had the opportunity to submit comments by 1 January 2016. On 18 December, the Philippines filed supplemental responses to Judge Wolfrum's questions on the taking of giant clams and sea turtles and environmental damage to the reefs.

On 21 December, upon the publication of the transcript of the Hearing on the Merits, China's Ministry of Foreign Affairs published a statement. In addition to repeating the points already raised in China's Position Paper, it declared that the Philippines attempted to negate Chinese sovereignty over the Spratly Islands and deny the validity of the Cairo Declaration and the Potsdam Proclamation. It said that it was the Chinese people, rather than any other individuals or institutions, that mastered China's territorial sovereignty. China urged the Philippines to cast aside its illusions.

On 11 January 2016, the Tribunal noted that China had not submitted comments and informed the Parties of a request from Japan for copies of any new documents in relation to the hearing on the merits. The Philippines did not raise any objection to the documents being provided to the observers.

J. FURTHER EVIDENCE, EXPERT REPORTS, AND COMMUNICATIONS FROM CHINA AND OTHERS

On 5 February, the Tribunal wrote to the Parties that in reviewing the evidentiary record and pursuing its deliberations, it had decided that it would benefit from further evidence and clarifications from the Parties and from the views of independent experts. The Tribunal had decided to appoint two experts: one to provide independent opinion on the effects of China's construction activities in the Spratly Islands on the coral reef systems and another to review the materials on navigational safety.

The Tribunal invited comments from the Parties on statements by Chinese officials and the State Oceanic Administration (SOA) regarding the environmental impact of Chinese island-building. China was specifically asked to indicate if it had conducted an environmental impact study under Article 206 of the Convention and, if so, to provide a copy. The Tribunal had decided to appoint two experts: one to provide independent opinion on the effects of China's construction activities in the Spratly Islands on the coral reef systems and another to review the materials on navigational safety. The Tribunal also invited comments on new documents in the public domain about Itu Aba.

The Tribunal proposed (on 26 February) to appoint Capt. Gupreet Singh Singhota (a national of the UK) as expert on navigation safety and (on 29 February) Dr. Sebastian Ferse (a national of Germany) as expert on coral reef issues. The Philippines approved the two appointments, which were confirmed on 15 March.

On 11 March, the Philippines submitted comments on evidence relating to Submissions No. 11 and 12 and materials relevant to the status of features that may generate overlapping entitlements. The comments were accompanied by 30 new annexes, including two new expert reports: one by Ryan T. Bailey, 'Groundwater Resources Analysis of Itu Aba' and the other by Peter P. Motavalli, 'Soil Resources and Potential Self-Sustaining Agricultural Production on Itu Aba.' China did not comment on the appointments, did not supply information about an environmental impact study, and did not comment on the new materials on Itu Aba or those submitted by the Philippines.

On 1 April, the Tribunal sent three letters to the Parties. In the first, it noted that in furtherance of its mandate to satisfy itself that Philippine claims were well founded in fact, the Tribunal considered it appropriate to refer to original records based on direct observation of the maritime features, prior to being subjected to significant human modification. As the most extensive survey work in the South China Sea prior to 1945 had been carried out by the UK Royal Navy, followed closely by the Japanese Navy, it had sought records from the UK Hydrographic Office (UKHO), which also held certain Japanese records captured during World War II. The Tribunal provided these documents to the parties and sought their comments by 22 April. Through the second letter, Dr. Ferse requested clarification from Professor J.W. McManus regarding the extent of reef damage caused by dredging as compared to that caused by clam shell extraction. In the third letter, the Tribunal invited comments on four documents: 'Position Paper on ROC (Republic of China) South China Sea Policy', the Chinese Foreign Ministry Spokesperson's response to it, a document published by the Chinese (Taiwan) Society of International Law, and remarks by former Taiwanese President Ma Ying-jeou at an international conference on Itu Aba.

On 12 April, the Tribunal informed the Parties of its intention to appoint two additional coral reef experts: Professor Peter Mumby (a national of UK/Australia) and Dr. Selina Ward (a national of Australia). The Philippines approved their appointments; China did not comment. On 18 April, the Tribunal sent to the Parties the expert opinion of Capt. Singhota on navigational safety. The Philippines had no comment on the report; China did not respond.

On 25 April, the Philippines filed its comments on Itu Aba. It considered that it would have been within its rights in requesting that the materials should be disregarded. Given the exceptional difficulties that China's non-appearance had created for the Tribunal, it chose not to object to the Tribunal's consideration of Taiwan's most recent materials. The Philippine comments were accompanied by two revised translations and 21 new annexes, including supplemental expert reports from Dr. Bailey and Dr. Motavalli. The Philippines urged the Tribunal to treat with caution Taiwan's newest materials and not to entertain further attempts by Taiwan to influence the Tribunal's deliberations. It argued that Taiwan's submissions proved that Itu Aba had never supported genuine, sustainable human habitation or economic life of its own and that China's remarks made it clear that Taiwan is alone among littoral authorities in claiming that Itu Aba was capable of sustaining human habitation and economic life of its own.

On 26 April, the Philippines filed a response to Dr. Ferse's request for clarification, including a letter and updated report from Professor McManus and a supplementary declaration from Professor Carpenter. On 28 April, the Philippines filed a response to the materials obtained from the UKHO, which confirmed its characterization of the respective features as submerged features, low-tide elevations, or rocks within the meaning of Article 121(3) of the Convention. On 29 April, the Tribunal sent to the Parties the independent expert report of Dr. Ferse, Dr. Mumby, and Dr. Ward, 'Assessment of Potential Environmental Consequences of Construction Activities on Seven Reefs in the Spratly Islands in the South China Sea'. The Philippines had no comments on the report, while China did not respond.

On 12 May, the Director-General of the Chinese Ministry of Foreign Affairs Department of Treaty and Law gave a 'Briefing on the South China Sea Arbitration Initiated by the Philippines'. He argued that four conditions act as bars for States parties to initiate arbitration and for an arbitral tribunal to establish its jurisdiction. A dispute cannot be settled by compulsory arbitration if it does not concern interpretation and application of the Convention. A tribunal has no jurisdiction if a State party has declared that it does not accept compulsory arbitration regarding maritime delimitation and certain other matters, if the Parties have agreed on other means of settlement of their own choice, and if they have not first exchanged views on the means of dispute settlement. By initiating arbitration, the Philippines was said to have violated international law in four respects. The Tribunal was allegedly not objective or just, distorting Convention provisions to embrace the Philippine claims. The Award on Jurisdiction and Admissibility was said not to be convincing or valid. He described the Tribunal as an institution that manifestly lacked jurisdiction and should not have existed in the first place; its opinions were said to be the personal views of arbitrators, at best.

On 20 May, the Chinese Embassy in the Netherlands transmitted the remarks of the Chinese Foreign Ministry's Spokesperson, to the effect that all sides should encourage the Philippines to work with China to resolve disputes peacefully through negotiation.

On 26 May, the Tribunal informed the Parties that it considered it appropriate to consult French materials from the 1930s in order to gain a more complete picture as to the natural conditions of the South China Sea features at the time. It provided them with documents obtained from the *Bibliothèque Nationale de France* (National Library of France) and the *Archives Nationales d'Outremer* (National Overseas Archives) and invited their comments. On 3 June, the Philippines commented and supplied supplementary materials and a further expert report from Dr. Motavalli. China did not comment on the Philippine response.

On 3 June, the Chinese Embassy sent a second letter with a Ministry of Foreign Affairs Spokesperson's statement on Itu Aba, which asserted, among others, that China has, based on the Nansha Islands (Spratly Islands) as a whole, a territorial sea, EEZ, and continental shelf. On 10 June, the Philippines responded that there was no basis in the Convention for China's assertion "based on the Nansha Islands as a whole" to a territorial sea, EEZ, and continental shelf. On 8 and 10 June, letters from the Chinese Embassy repeated the jurisdictional points previously made by China.

In May and June, the Tribunal received copies or was made aware of unsolicited statements and commentaries from Chinese associations and organizations concerning Itu Aba. The statements were not provided by the Chinese government or any other State party to the Convention, were concerned with jurisdictional issues already decided by the Tribunal, and did not offer to assist the Tribunal in the merits phase.

On 23 June, the Malaysian Embassy in the Netherlands sent two Notes Verbales to the Tribunal regarding certain maps in the Award on Jurisdiction and Admissibility and requested that the Tribunal show due regard for Malaysia's rights, although it was not seeking to intervene in the proceedings. On 28 June, the Philippines responded that it had presented the maps in such a way as to preserve its own claim but would leave the issue to the Tribunal's discretion. The question of the rights and interests of third parties had already been dealt with by the Tribunal. Malaysia had been an observer since June 2015, and until now, it had made no effort to raise these concerns. Consequently, Malaysia's communication was without merit and untimely. China did not comment. On 29 June, the Tribunal replied to Malaysia that it had received and taken note of the communication. The Tribunal drew attention to its disclaimer on p. iv of the Award on Jurisdiction and Admissibility regarding the maps published at pages 3 and 9 of the said Award.

K. NOTIFICATION, PUBLICATION, AND TRANSLATION OF AWARD

On 29 June, the Tribunal advised the Parties that it would be issuing the Award on 12 July; authorized the PCA to publish press releases in English, French, and Chinese; and instructed the PCA to arrange for a translation of the two Awards into Chinese. The English version will remain the only authentic version of the Awards.

L. DEPOSITS FOR COSTS OF THE ARBITRATION

The deposits have covered fees and expenses of Tribunal members, the Registry, and experts appointed to assist the Tribunal, as well as all other expenses, including for hearings and meetings, IT support, catering, court reports, deposit administration, archiving, translation, couriers, communication, correspondence, and publication of awards.

The PCA will render an accounting to the Parties of the deposits received and return any expended balance to the Parties after the issuance of the Award.

III. RELIEF REQUESTED AND SUBMISSIONS[7]

112. On 30 November 2015, the Agent for the Philippines presented the Philippines Final Submissions, requesting the Tribunal to adjudge and declare that:

A. The Tribunal has jurisdiction over the claims set out in Section B of these Submissions, which are fully admissible, to the extent not already determined to be within the Tribunal's jurisdiction and admissible in the Award on Jurisdiction and Admissibility of 29 October 2015.

B. (1) China's maritime entitlements in the South China Sea, like those of the Philippines, may not extend beyond those expressly permitted by the United Nations Convention on the Law of the Sea ('UNCLOS' or the Convention');

(2) China's claims to sovereign rights jurisdiction, and to 'historic rights', with respect to the maritime areas of the South China Sea encompassed by the so-called 'nine-dash line' are contrary to the Convention and without lawful effect to the extent that they exceed the geographic and substantive limits of China's maritime entitlements expressly permitted by UNCLOS;

7 Award of 12 July 2016, pp. 41–43, *supra* note 2. Paragraph 112 is a reproduction of Chapter III of the Award.

(3) Scarborough Shoal generates no entitlement to an exclusive economic zone or continental shelf;

(4) Mischief Reef, Second Thomas Shoal and Subi Reef are low-tide elevations that do not generate entitlement to a territorial sea, exclusive economic zone or continental shelf and are not features that are capable of appropriation by occupation or otherwise;

(5) Mischief Reef and Second Thomas Shoal are part of the exclusive economic zone and continental shelf of the Philippines;

(6) Gaven Reef and McKennan Reef (including Hughes Reef) are low-tide elevations that do not generate entitlement to a territorial sea, exclusive economic zone or continental shelf, but their low-water line may be used to determine the baseline from which the breadth of the territorial sea of Namyit and Sin Cowe, respectively, is measured;

(7) Johnson Reef, Cuarteron Reef, and Fiery Cross Reef generate no entitlement to an exclusive economic zone or continental shelf;

(8) China has unlawfully interfered with the enjoyment and exercise of the sovereign rights of the Philippines with respect to the living and non-living resources of its exclusive economic zone and continental shelf;

(9) China has unlawfully failed to prevent its nationals and vessels from exploiting the living resources in the exclusive economic zone of the Philippines;

(10) China has unlawfully prevented Philippine fishermen from pursuing their livelihoods by interfering with traditional fishing activities at Scarborough Shoal;

(11) China has violated its obligations under the Convention to protect and preserve the marine environment at Scarborough Shoal, Second Thomas Shoal, Cuarteron Reef, Fiery Cross Reef, Gaven Reef, Johnson Reef, Hughes Reef and Subi Reef;

(12) China's occupation of and construction activities on Mischief Reef

  (a) violate the provisions of the Convention concerning artificial islands, Installations and structures;

  (b) violate China's duties to protect and preserve the marine environment under the Convention; and

  (c) constitute unlawful acts of attempted appropriation in violation of the Convention;

(13) China has breached its obligations under the Convention by operating its law enforcement vessels in a dangerous manner causing serious risk of collision to Philippine vessels navigating in the vicinity of Scarborough Shoal;

(14) Since the commencement of this arbitration in January 2013, China has unlawfully aggravated and extended the dispute by, among other things:

(a) interfering with the Philippines' rights of navigation in the waters at, and adjacent to, Second Thomas Shoal;

(b) preventing the rotation and resupply of Philippine personnel stationed at Second Thomas Shoal;

(c) endangering the health and well-being of Philippine personnel stationed at Second Thomas Shoal; and

(d) conducting dredging, artificial island-building, and construction activities at Mischief Reef, Cuarteron Reef, Fiery Cross Reef, Gaven Reef, Johnson Reef, Hughes Reef and Subi Reef; and

(15) China shall respect the rights and freedoms of the Philippines under the Convention, shall comply with its duties under the Convention, including those relevant to the protection and preservation of the marine environment in the South China Sea, and shall exercise its rights and freedoms in the South China Sea with due regard to those of the Philippines under the Convention.

The Tribunal notes that China did not file a Counter-Memorial, has not stated its position on the Philippine Submissions, and has not commented on specific substantive submissions when given the opportunity to do so. The Tribunal has sought to take into account China's position to the extent that it is discernible from China's official statements and China's conduct.

IV. PRELIMINARY MATTERS[8]

A. THE LEGAL AND PRACTICAL CONSEQUENCES OF CHINA'S NON-PARTICIPATION

1. Steps Taken to Ensure Procedural Fairness to Both Parties

In addition to the measures listed in the Award on Jurisdiction and Admissibility to safeguard China's procedural rights, the Tribunal invited China to comment on the proposed candidates and the terms of reference for independent experts appointed by the Tribunal as well as on certain materials in the public domain but not already in the case record, made the Registry staff available to Chinese Embassy personnel to answer informal administrative or procedural questions, and conveyed written communications from the Chinese Embassy to individual Tribunal members.

[8] *Ibid.*, pp. 45–65, paras. 116–68. Only the content not summarized under the Award on Jurisdiction and Admissibility will be summarized here.

The Tribunal has also taken measures to safeguard the Philippines' procedural rights. Non-appearance has three possible disadvantages. One is delay. The Tribunal has complied with its duty under Article 10 of the Rules of Procedure to 'conduct the proceedings so as to avoid unnecessary delay and expense and to provide a fair and efficient process for resolving the Parties' dispute' The second disadvantage is that non-appearance would deprive the Philippines of the opportunity to address specific issues that in the Tribunal's view might have been inadequately canvassed (or not at all) by the Philippines. In order to ensure the Parties the opportunity to address specific issues of concern to the Tribunal's decision-making, the Tribunal introduced a procedure in Article 25(2) of the Rules of Procedure and implemented this procedure by issuing a request on 16 December 2014 for further written argument from the Philippines, containing 26 questions. The Tribunal issued further questions on 23 June and on 10 July 2015 and during the Hearing on Jurisdiction and Admissibility. The third disadvantage is that the Philippines would have to guess what China's arguments might be and formulate arguments for both States. The Philippines suggested that the Tribunal discern China's position by consulting statements of China's officials, those associated with China, and academics closely associated with China. The Tribunal has done so, following the practice of international courts and tribunals of taking notice of public statements and informal communications made by non-appearing Parties. The Tribunal has taken note of China's Position Paper, letters from the Chinese Embassy in the Netherlands, and regular press briefings of the Ministry of Foreign Affairs.

At a briefing on 12 May 2016, the Director-General of the Foreign Ministry's Department of Treaty and Law asserted that the Tribunal has failed to fulfill its obligation to establish that it does have jurisdiction. The Tribunal addressed this statement in the next subsection.

2. Steps Taken by the Tribunal to Satisfy Itself that It Has Jurisdiction and that the Claim is Well Founded in Fact and Law

China's non-participation imposes a special responsibility on the Tribunal. There is no system of default judgment under the Convention. The Tribunal does not simply adopt the Philippines' arguments and accept its arguments untested. Under Article 9 of Annex VII of the Convention, the Tribunal must satisfy itself not only that it has jurisdiction over the dispute but also that the claim is well founded in fact and law. As a practical matter, Article 9 of Annex VII has led the Tribunal to test the evidence provided by the Philippines and to augment the record by seeking additional evidence, expert input, and Party submissions relevant to the merits.

The Tribunal

a. asked the Philippines to provide additional historical and anthropological information, as well as detailed geographic and hydrographic information on Itu Aba, Thitu, West York, Northeast Cay, Southwest Cay, Nanshan Island, Sand Cay, Loaita Island, Swallow Reef, Amboyna Cay, Flat Island, Great Discovery Reef, Tizard Bank Reefs, and Union Bank Reefs;
b. appointed independent experts on hydrography, coral reef systems, and navigation;
c. made efforts to understand China's stance on environmental issues by asking Philippine experts to find Chinese statements, asking China to provide a copy of any environmental impact study that it carried out, and taking note of official Chinese statements;

d. invited comments on materials regarding the conditions on features in the South China Sea, including materials from Taiwan;
e. sought the Parties' views on records from the UK Hydrographic Office; and
f. sought French archival records.[9]

3. Conclusion on the Legal and Practical Consequences of China's Non-Participation

Despite China's non-participation in the proceedings, China is a party to the arbitration and is bound under international law by any awards rendered by the Tribunal. In the circumstances of China's non-participation, the Tribunal has taken steps to ensure procedural fairness to both Parties without compromising the efficiency of the proceedings. The Tribunal has taken steps to ascertain China's position on the issues for decision, based on statements made by China's officials publicly and in communications to its members. In addition to a thorough review of the materials placed before it by the Philippines, the Tribunal has taken steps to satisfy itself of its jurisdiction and the legal and factual foundation of the Philippines' claims through obtaining independent expert input, reviewing other materials in the public domain, and inviting further comments from the Parties on these sources.

B. SUMMARY OF THE TRIBUNAL'S AWARD ON JURISDICTION[10]

1. Preliminary Matters

2. Existence of a Dispute concerning Interpretation and Application of the Convention

3. Involvement of Indispensable Third Parties

4. Preconditions to Jurisdiction

5. Exceptions and Limitations to Jurisdiction

6. Decisions of the Tribunal

C. THE STATUS AND EFFECT OF THE TRIBUNAL'S AWARD ON JURISDICTION

The Tribunal's Award on Jurisdiction and Admissibility is an 'Award of the Tribunal' for purposes of Annex VII of the Convention. It is final and without appeal.

The Tribunal is conscious that China continues to assert that the Tribunal lacks jurisdiction for the same reasons set out in its Position Paper and that the Philippines' initiation of arbitration is a typical abuse of compulsory dispute settlement procedures stipulated in the Convention. The Tribunal considers that each of these objections has been fully addressed and decided in the Award on Jurisdiction and Admissibility. For the avoidance of doubt, the Tribunal hereby reaffirms in full and incorporates by reference the conclusions and reasoning set out in the Award on Jurisdiction and Admissibility.

---

9 This enumeration has been prepared by the author and does not appear in this form in the original text.
10 For the contents of this section, please see Chapter I of this book.

V. THE 'NINE-DASH LINE' AND CHINA'S CLAIM TO HISTORIC RIGHTS IN THE MARITIME AREAS OF THE SOUTH CHINA SEA (SUBMISSIONS NO. 1 AND 2)[11]

A. INTRODUCTION

The Tribunal recalls its characterization of Submissions No. 1 and 2 in the Award on Jurisdiction and Admissibility. The Tribunal deferred a decision on its jurisdiction because the decision is dependent on the nature of any historic rights claimed by China, which might be covered by exclusions from jurisdiction concerning "historic bays or titles" (Article 298, Optional exceptions to applicability of section 2).

B. CHINA'S DECLARATIONS AND LEGISLATION CONCERNING ENTITLEMENTS TO MARITIME ZONES

In the 1930s, China, under the control of its Republican government, issued a decree declaring a 3-nautical-mile territorial sea. On 4 September 1958, China issued a Declaration on China's Territorial Sea, which provided for a 12-nautical-mile territorial sea. The Law of 25 February 1992 on the Territorial Sea and the Contiguous Zone declared a 12-nautical-mile territorial sea and a 12-nautical-mile contiguous zone. A Declaration of 15 May 1996 set out certain coordinates for the baselines from which China's territorial sea would be measured. On 7 June 1996, in conjunction with its ratification of the Convention, China declared an EEZ. On 26 June 1998, China adopted a Law on the EEZ and Continental Shelf. Its Article 14 declared that the law's provisions would not 'affect any rights that the People's Republic of China has been enjoying ever since the days of the past.'

C. CHINA'S CLAIMS TO HISTORIC RIGHTS

The resolution of the dispute is complicated by the ambiguity in China's position. China has never expressly clarified the nature or scope of its claimed historic rights or its understanding of the meaning of the 'nine-dash line'.

The line, which originally featured 11 dashes, first appeared in a privately produced map in 1933 and in an official map in 1948. In 1953, two dashes in the Gulf of Tonkin were removed, and since then, the line has appeared consistently in the 'nine-dash form'.

The map depicting the 'nine-dash line' was appended to two Notes Verbales dated 7 May 2009 and sent by China to the UN Secretary-General in response to Malaysia and Viet Nam's Joint Submission to the Commission on the Limits of the Continental Shelf. The Notes prompted objections from Viet Nam and Malaysia in 2009, from Indonesia in 2010, and from the Philippines in 2011. The last claimed sovereignty over the 'Kalayaan Island Group' and asserted that the 'nine-dash' claim would have no basis under international law. China responded that 'China's sovereignty and related rights and jurisdiction in the South China Sea are supported by abundant historical and legal evidence', a formula that it has repeated in diplomatic correspondence and official statements. China has expressly linked the 'nine-dash line' to its claims to rights 'formed over a (sic) long course of history'.

---

[11] Award of 12 July 2016, pp. 67–117, paras. 161–278, *supra* note 2.

D. THE PHILIPPINES' POSITION

1. Jurisdiction

China's statements since 2009 make two distinctions: the first between 'claims to sovereignty' and 'claims to sovereign rights and jurisdiction', and the second between 'islands in the South China Sea and adjacent waters' and 'relevant waters'. In effect, China is asserting sovereignty over the South China Sea islands and their adjacent waters and claiming sovereign rights and jurisdiction, short of sovereignty, in the waters that lie between the territorial sea claimed by China and the 'nine-dash line'.

China's conduct confirms that

a. it is claiming sovereign rights and jurisdiction, by banning fishing by other States within the 'nine-dash line', by interfering with Philippine petroleum exploration activities, and by offering concessions to petroleum blocks within the 'nine-dash line'; and

b. it is not claiming sovereignty over the entire area within the 'nine-dash line', repeatedly asserting that it respects freedom of navigation and overflight in the South China Sea.[12]

The exception to jurisdiction in Article 298 refers to "historic bays or titles". The concept of 'historic title' is limited only to near-shore areas of sea that are susceptible to a claim of sovereignty. Because China's claims fall short of sovereignty over the maritime areas of the South China Sea, its claims of historic rights are not covered by Article 298(1)(a)(1). There is a consistent distinction between China's use of 'historic rights' in its Exclusive Economic Zone and Continental Shelf Act and "historic rights" in Article 198. Even if China's claims were to historic title, Article 298 applies only to disputes over the delimitation of historic bays and titles.

2. China's Claim to Historic Rights

On the merits, the Philippines' argument is twofold.[13]

a. Prior to the adoption of the Convention, international law did not accept the assertion of historic rights over such vast areas as China claims.

The sea was subject only to two principles: the freedom of the seas, which prohibited appropriation by any State, and control over a limited area by the immediately adjacent coastal State, which prohibited appropriation by any other State. China's claim is inconsistent with both.

States parties to the Convention carefully specified the nature of prior uses of the sea that were protected, the nature of the protections and the areas in which the protections applied. Where the Convention made no express exception for prior rights or uses, these historic rights would not have survived as derogations from the sovereignty, sovereign rights, and high seas freedoms of other States. At the Third UN Conference on the Law of the Sea, distant-water

12 This enumeration has been prepared by the author and does not appear in this form in the original text.

13 The following enumeration has been prepared by the author and does not appear in this form in the original text.

fishing States failed to obtain recognition in the EEZ of historic fishing rights. China was a vocal supporter of developing countries' demands for exclusive jurisdiction over resources in the EEZ and continental shelf and did not attempt to secure an exception protecting historic rights. Any historic rights that China may have had in the South China Sea's maritime areas beyond the rights provided for in the Convention were extinguished by China's accession to the Convention.

b. China never had historic rights in the waters of the South China Sea.

China first claimed the existence of 'historic rights' on 7 May 2009. Since 1136 AD, Chinese maps show that China's territory extended no further than Hainan Island. From the 14th to the 16th centuries, China prohibited maritime trade by Chinese subjects or suppressed maritime activities. China did not protest against navigation by European States in South China Sea or against the colonization of Southeast Asia. Taiwanese archives do not show evidence of Chinese official activities in the South China Sea features until the beginning of the 20th century.

As late as 1932, a Chinese note to the French Ministry of Foreign Affairs stated that the Paracel Islands formed the southernmost part of Chinese territory. China had so little involvement or connection with the South China Sea features that when it sought to assert its claim over them after World War II, it had to develop Chinese names for them. French archival materials obtained by the Tribunal show that France did not consider China to have claims over the Spratly Islands or to the waters of the South China Sea that were so far removed from China's mainland coast. After World War II, France retained its claim to these features, which the US and the UK wished to protect in the Cairo Declaration and the Potsdam Proclamation.

Until 2009, any Chinese claims to the South China Sea features did not include claims to the waters beyond the territorial sea. The 1958 Declaration on the Territorial Sea declared that the Spratly Islands are 'separated from the mainland and the coastal islands by the high seas.' At the Second UN Conference on the Law of the Sea in 1960, China supported the proposal for a 3-nautical-mile territorial sea.

Consequently, China has no historic rights within the 'nine-dash line'.

E. CHINA'S POSITION

In addition to earlier statements, a briefing on 12 May 2016 by the Director- General of the Foreign Ministry's Treaty and Law Department asserted that the line incorporated in a 1948 map was a confirmation of China's rights in the South China Sea formed through history, instead of the creation of new claims. The line came into existence earlier than the Convention, which does not cover all aspects of the law of the sea. For a long time, no State questioned the legitimacy of the line. The real motives of the attack on the line are to intentionally confuse territorial disputes with disputes over maritime delimitation, to deny China's sovereignty over the South China Sea Islands and their adjacent waters, and to cover up other States' illegal invasion and occupation of part of the Spratly Islands' maritime features.

F. THE TRIBUNAL'S CONSIDERATIONS

1. The Tribunal's Jurisdiction

The first exception in Article 298(1)(a)(i) concerns sea boundary delimitations. The Tribunal has already found this exception inapplicable.

The second exception applies to disputes involving historic bays or titles. Since the South China Sea is not a bay, the question is whether China potentially claims historic titles in the South China Sea. The most insightful formulation by China of its claim, beyond a claim to sovereignty over the islands and adjacent waters, is as a claim to 'relevant rights in the South China Sea, formed in the long historical course.' In the absence of a more specific indication from China, it is the Tribunal that has to ascertain, on the basis of conduct, whether China's claim amounts to 'historic title'.

(a) The Nature of China's Claimed Rights in the South China Sea

China's statements indicate that it understands its rights to extend beyond the rights expressly described in the Convention. Much of the area encompassed by the 'nine-dash line' would fall within China's claim to an EEZ or a continental shelf drawn from Spratly Islands features. The mere assertion by China of rights in the South China Sea does not indicate that the rights derive from the 'nine-dash line'. Where China has asserted rights to areas beyond the maximum entitlement that could be claimed under the Convention, these assertions indicate a claim to rights arising independently of the Convention.

There are at least three instances when China appears to have asserted such rights.[14]

(1) In June 2012, China National Oil Company (CNOC) issued notice of open blocks for exploration, one of which (BS 16) lies beyond 200 nautical miles from any feature in the South China Sea claimed by China.
(2) In March 2001, July 2010, and July 2011, China objected to the Philippine award of petroleum blocks within the 'nine-dash line', based on Chinese rights to petroleum resources that stemmed from historic rights.
(3) In May 2012, China announced a summer ban on marine fishing in the South China Sea maritime space.

At the same time, China has unequivocally stated that it respects freedom of navigation and overflight in the South China Sea. Since the Convention does not provide for such freedoms in the territorial sea, China's commitment establishes that it does not consider Chinese areas within the 'nine-dash line' to be equivalent to its territorial sea or internal waters. Moreover, China declared baselines for the territorial sea surrounding Hainan Island and the Paracel Islands. It would not have done so if the waters within and beyond 12 nautical miles of these islands already formed part of China's territorial sea or internal waters by virtue of claims to historic rights.

On the basis of China's conduct, the Tribunal understands that China claims rights to the living and non-living resources within the 'nine-dash line' but does not consider that those waters form part of its territorial sea or internal waters.

(b) The Scope of the Exception in Article 298(1)(a)(i) of the Convention

The Tribunal does not agree with the Philippines that the exception can be dispensed with because the exception applies only to maritime delimitation involving historic bays or titles. Even if the English text of the Convention is potentially ambiguous, no comparable ambiguity is to be found in the Chinese, French, Russian, or Spanish texts of the Convention, which

[14] The following enumeration has been prepared by the author and does not appear in this form in the original text.

are equally authentic. The broader exception within these other texts, for disputes involving historic bays or titles, best reconciles the different authentic versions of the Convention.

The ordinary meaning of 'historic titles' implies the notion of property, but reference to it should be understood in the context of the evolution of the law of the sea. Historic bays were discussed at the 1930 League of Nations Codification Conference, at The Hague. In 1951, the ICJ defined historic waters as waters that are treated as internal waters but that would not have that character were it not for the existence of historic titles. In 1957, a UN Secretariat Memorandum noted that historic rights are claimed with respect to bays, archipelagic waters, straits, and estuaries. The first reference to historic title appeared in the 1958 Geneva Convention on the Territorial Sea and the Contiguous Zone, which provided that Article 12 on the delimitation of the territorial sea would not apply "where it is it necessary by reason of historic title or other special circumstances to delimit the territorial seas of the two States in a way which is at variance with this provision."

A 1962 UN Secretariat memorandum considered the term *historic waters* as equivalent to 'historic title'. It defined the formation of historic title as a process of acquiring a historic right. To determine whether a title to "historic waters" exists, three factors should be taken into consideration (i) the authority exercised over the area by the State claiming it, (ii) the continuity of such exercise of authority, and (iii) the attitude of foreign States.

At the Third UN Conference on the Law of the Sea, Article 12 of the 1958 Convention was adopted as Article 15 of the 1982 Convention, without significant discussion. In recent years, the ICJ has distinguished between historic fishing rights and historic title that would bear on the entitlement to maritime zones.

This extended recitation emphasizes that within the law of the sea context, there exists a cognizable usage among terms for rights deriving from historical process.[15]

(1) The term 'historic rights' is general and can describe any rights that a State may possess that would not normally arise under general international law, absent particular historical circumstances. The historic rights may include sovereignty or more limited rights (e.g., fishing rights).
(2) 'Historic title' refers to historical sovereignty to land or maritime areas.
(3) 'Historic waters' is a term for historic title over maritime areas.
(4) 'Historic bay' is a bay in which a State claims historic waters.

This usage was understood by the drafters of the Convention. Accordingly, the reference to historic titles in Article 298(1)(a)(i) is a reference to claims of sovereignty over maritime areas derived from historical circumstances. This accords with the only other direct usage of historical title in the Convention, Article 15 on the delimitation of the territorial sea. Other 'historic rights' are nowhere mentioned in the Convention. The Tribunal sees nothing to suggest that Article 298(1)(a)(i) was intended also to exclude jurisdiction over a broad and unspecified category of possible claims to historic rights falling short of sovereignty. It should be noted, as the Philippines pointed out, that in Chinese, the terminological distinction between historic rights and historic title also exists. The only inconsistency in Chinese usage appears in a Note Verbale dated 6 July 2011, but this inconsistency probably reflects an error in translation or imprecise drafting.

The dispositive proof that China's claim is not one to historic title lies in China's conduct, which respects the freedom of navigation and overflight over the waters of the South China Sea.

15 The following enumeration has been prepared by the author and does not appear in this form in the original text.

This conduct is incompatible with a claim that these waters constitute China's territorial waters or internal waters. As the exception to jurisdiction in Article 298(1)(a)(i) is limited to disputes involving historic titles, the Tribunal has jurisdiction to consider Submissions No. 1 and 2 of the Philippines.

2. The Merits of the Philippines' Submissions No. 1 and 2

The Convention's provisions (Articles 2–32 on the Territorial Sea, Articles 55–75 on the EEZ, Articles 76–85 on the continental shelf, Articles 86–120 on the high seas, and Article 133–91 on the Area) provide and define limits within a comprehensive system of maritime areas that is capable of encompassing any area of the sea or seabed.

China's claims raise three issues.

(a) The Convention and Prior Claims to Historic Rights and Jurisdiction

The question is whether the Convention preserves rights to living and non-living resources in the EEZ and continental shelf that are at variance with the Convention and that may have been established prior to the Convention's entry into force, by agreement or unilateral act.

To answer the question, it is necessary to examine the relationship between the Convention and other possible sources of rights under international law. The Convention's relationships with other international agreements and with other norms of international law are set out in Articles 311 (Relation to other conventions and international agreements) and 293(1) (Applicable law), respectively. These provisions mirror general rules of international law concerning the interaction of different bodies of law, which provide that the intent of the Parties to a convention will control its relationship with other instruments.

The application of these rules leads to four propositions:

(a) Where the Convention expressly permits or preserves other international agreements, the latter shall remain unaffected (Article 311(5)).
(b) Where the Convention does not expressly permit or preserve a prior agreement, a customary rule, or historic right, those norms will not be incompatible with the Convention where their operation does not conflict with any Convention provision or where interpretation indicates that the Convention intended these prior agreements, rules, or rights to continue in operation.
(c) Where rights and obligations arising independently of the Convention are not incompatible with its provisions, their operation shall remain unaltered (Article 311(2)).
(d) Where independent rights and obligations have arisen prior to the Convention's entry into force and are incompatible with its provisions, the Convention shall prevail over the earlier incompatible rights or obligations (Article 293).

No Convention article expressly provides for or permits the existence of historic rights to living or non-living resources of the EEZ. Nothing in the Convention expressly provides for States to maintain historic rights over the living and non-living resources of the continental shelf, high seas, or the Area. The question is whether the Convention nevertheless intended the continued operation of such historic rights.

(i) *The Text and Context of the Convention*

Article 58 (Rights and duties of other States in the exclusive economic zone) of the Convention limits the rights of States other than the coastal State in the EEZ to navigation and overflight, the laying of submarine cables and pipelines, and lawful uses of the sea related to these freedoms. Under Article 62 (Utilisation of the living resources), the coastal State is only obliged to permit fishing in its EEZ by foreign nationals that have habitually fished in these areas when the coastal State lacks the capacity to harvest the entire allowable catch. Even then, historical fishing is only one of the criteria to be applied in allocating access, and foreign fishing is subject to the coastal State's laws and regulations.

As a matter of text alone, the Tribunal considers that the Convention is clear in according sovereign rights over the living and non-living resources of the EEZ to the coastal State alone. The notion of sovereign rights over the living and non-living resources is generally incompatible with another State having historic rights to the same resources, particularly if such rights are considered exclusive. As a matter of ordinary interpretation, (1) the express inclusion of articles setting out the rights of other States and (2) the attention given to the rights of other States in the allocation of excess catch exclude the possibility that the Convention intended for other States to have rights in the EEZ in excess of those specified.[16]

The same considerations apply with respect to the coastal State's sovereign rights over the continental shelf (Article 77, Rights of the coastal State over the continental shelf). Other States' rights are limited to the laying of cables and pipelines and the freedoms to which they are otherwise entitled in the superjacent waters. The Convention is even more explicit that the rights to the living and non-living resources pertain to the coastal State exclusively.

The context of EEZ rights is the system of maritime zones created by the Convention, which was intended to be comprehensive and to cover any area of the sea or seabed. The intention was expressed in the Preamble and reflected in the limitation of exceptions to the greatest extent possible (Article 309 on Reservations or exceptions). In October 2015, China asserted that its relevant rights in the South China Sea formed in the long historical course are "protected under international law, including the Convention." If these rights comprise claims to living and non-living resources within the 'nine-dash line', which would partially comprise the Philippine EEZ or continental shelf, then the Tribunal cannot agree with this position. The Convention does not include any express provisions preserving or protecting historic rights that are at variance with the Convention. On the contrary, the Convention supersedes earlier, incompatible rights and agreements. The Convention is comprehensive in setting out the nature of the EEZ and the continental shelf and the rights of other States in these zones. China's claim to historic rights is not compatible with these provisions.

The text and context of the Convention are clear in superseding any historic rights that a State may once have had in areas that now form part of the EEZ and the continental shelf of another State. There is no ambiguity here that would call for the Tribunal to have recourse to supplementary rules of interpretation. In light of the sensitivity of the issues, it is warranted to recall the origin of and purpose behind the Convention's provisions on the EEZ and the continental shelf.

(ii) *The Negotiation of the Convention and the Creation of the Exclusive Economic Zone*

16 This enumeration bas been prepared by the author and does not appear in this form in the original text.

The principal failure of the First and Second UN Conferences on the Law of the Sea was the lack of agreement on the breadth of the territorial sea and the extent of coastal States' jurisdiction over resources.[17] In the 1960s, many newly independent States, faced with the lack of international agreement on the breadth of the territorial sea and the growing capabilities of the long-distance fishing fleets of developed countries, declared exclusive fishing zones or 200-nautical-mile territorial seas. Such claims were opposed by traditional maritime States. In the 1970s, Latin American and African States organized around assertions of greater control over coastal resources. The EEZ was a compromise—it offered a standardized form of coastal State jurisdiction over living and non-living resources, but it stopped short of extending the territorial sea beyond 12 nautical miles.

At the Third UN Conference on the Law of the Sea, Japan and the USSR, which possessed the largest distant sea fishing fleets, sought to preserve the status quo.[18] China was resolutely opposed to their suggestion that coastal States should be obliged to share EEZ resources with other States that had historically fished in their waters. China accused the superpowers of wantonly plundering the resources of developing coastal States. The Chinese position during the negotiations is incompatible with the claim that China would be entitled to historic rights to living in non-living resources in the South China Sea that would take precedence over other littoral States' rights in the EEZ. China never advanced that claim during the negotiations, notwithstanding the fact that the South China Sea and sovereignty over the Spratly Islands were raised by the Philippines in 1972 and Viet Nam in 1974.

The Convention's negotiating history sheds light on the intent for the Convention to serve as a comprehensive agreement and the importance of the prohibition on reservations (Article 309). The Convention was negotiated on the basis of consensus, and the final text represented a package deal. The prohibition on reservations was essential to prevent States from clawing back through reservations those portions of the final compromise that they had opposed during the negotiations. China and other States were opposed to a complete ban on reservations. The compromise permitted certain reservations and prohibited others. China was entitled to and activated the reservations on dispute settlement, but it is not entitled to except itself from the system of compulsory settlement generally. It is simply inconceivable that the drafters of the Convention could have gone to such lengths to forge a consensus text and to prohibit any but a few express reservations while, at the same time, anticipating that the resulting Convention would be subordinate to broad claims of historic rights.

(iii) Rights in the Exclusive Economic Zone in other Disputes concerning the Law of the Sea

In the *Delimitation of the Maritime Boundary in the Gulf of Maine (Canada v. US)* (ICJ, 1981–84), the US had argued that the delimitation line should take account of the longstanding use of Georges Bank by US fishermen.[19] The ICJ rejected this argument and pointed out that the

17 The First UN Conference on the Law of the Sea was held at Geneva, from 24 February to 27 April 1958. See United Nations Codification Division Publications, *Diplomatic Conferences. United Nations Conference on the Law of the Sea (Geneva, 24 February–27 April 1958)* (2018), http://legal.un.org/diplomaticconferences/1958_los/vol7.shtml, accessed 20 March 2018. The Second UN Conference on the Law of the Sea was held at Geneva, from 17 March to 26 April 1960. See United Nations Second Codification Division Publications, *Diplomatic Conferences. United Nations Conference on the Law of the Sea (Geneva, 17 March–26 April 1960)*, 2018, http://legal.un.org/diplomaticconferences/1960_los/, accessed 20 March 2018.

18 The Third United Nations Conference on the Law of the Sea held 11 sessions between 1973 and 1982. See United Nations Second Codification Division Publications, *Diplomatic Conferences. Third United Nations Conference on the Law of the Sea (1973–1982)*, 2018, http://legal.un.org/diplomaticconferences/1973_los/, accessed 20 March 2018.

19 The documents of the case are available at the ICJ website, http://www.icj-cij.org/en/case/67, accessed 17 March 2018.

declaration of exclusive fishery zones had radically altered the situation. The US acquired a legal monopoly in areas where US nationals had been factually predominant; conversely, any predominance enjoyed by US nationals in areas where Canada acquired a legal monopoly could no longer be a valid ground for US claims.

While the Tribunal has no doubt that Chinese fishermen have long made use of the waters of the South China Sea, the acceptance of the EEZ and China's adherence to the Convention altered the situation. Through the Convention, China gained additional rights in the areas adjacent to its coasts that became part of the EEZ. It necessarily follows that China also relinquished the rights that it may have held in the waters allocated by the Convention to the EEZs of other States.

The ICJ Judgments in the *Fisheries Jurisdiction Cases (UK v. Iceland; Federal Republic of Germany v. Iceland)* (1972–74) do not constitute a contrary indication.[20] Although the Court declared that Iceland could not extinguish the rights of other States to have habitually fished in Iceland's 50-mile exclusive fishing zone, it should be noted that in the early 1970s, international law permitted an exclusive fishing zone of only 12 nautical miles. Moreover, the UK and the Federal Republic of Germany had never asserted that their historic fishing superseded Iceland's declaration of a fisheries zone and had merely claimed rights of access. China, on the other hand, considers that its "historic rights" effectively negate the EEZ rights of other littoral States in the South China Sea. The Tribunal considers that the ICJ's reasoning in the cases would be inapplicable under the present law of the sea, which permits EEZs.

The Arbitral Tribunal in *Eritrea v. Yemen* (1996–99) emphasized the importance of preserving traditional fishing practices in the Red Sea that had been carried on for centuries without regard for maritime boundaries.[21] But the Philippines correctly pointed out that the applicable law in this case was different—it was not an arbitration under Annex VII of the Convention, and the arbitration agreement empowered the Tribunal to go beyond the law on traditional fishing under the Convention.

The Arbitral Tribunal in *Chagos Marine Protected Area (Mauritius v. UK)* (2010–15) held that Mauritius had rights in the EEZ declared by the UK around the Chagos Archipelago, but these were not fishing rights.[22] These rights were the right to an eventual return of the Archipelago when it was no longer necessary for defense and the right to the benefit of any oil or minerals discovered in or around the Archipelago. The rights originated in UK assurances given in 1968. The UK also emphasized that the marine protected area it created was not for purposes beyond fisheries and environmental protection.

The Tribunal concludes that China's claim to historic rights to the living and non-living resources is incompatible with the Convention to the extent that it exceeds the limits of China's maritime zones as provided for by the Convention. This is apparent in the text of the Convention and reinforced by the negotiating record. Upon China's accession to the Convention, any historic rights that it may have had were superseded as a matter of law and as between the Philippines and China, by the limits of the maritime zones provided for by the Convention. This is not unexceptional or unexpected. As a package, the Convention could not and did not fully reflect any State's prior understanding of its rights. Accession to the Convention reflects

[20] The documents of the cases between the UK and Iceland and between the Federal Republic of Germany and Iceland are available on the ICJ website, http://www.icj-cij.org/en/case/55 and http://www.icj-cij.org/en/case/56, respectively, accessed 17 March 2018.

[21] The text of the Award may be found in *Reports of International Arbitral Awards*, XXII (New York: United Nations, 2006), pp. 335–410, http://legal.un.org/docs/?path=../riaa/cases/vol_XXII/335-410.pdf&lang=O, accessed 20 March 2018.

[22] The text of the Award may be found on the PCA website, https://files.pca-cpa.org/pcadocs/MU-UK%20 20150318%20Award.pdf, accessed 20 March 2018.

a commitment to bring incompatible claims into alignment with the Convention and the Convention's continued operation necessarily calls for compromise by States with prior claims in excess of Convention limits.

(b) China's Claim to Historic Rights in the South China Sea

The above conclusion would suffice to decide the question whether China had, prior to the Convention's entry into force, historic rights over living and non-living resources in the waters of the South China Sea beyond the limits of the territorial sea (Submissions No. 1 and 2). For the sake of completeness, it is important to distinguish between China's claims that are in excess of and incompatible with the Convention and those that are not. In ratifying the Convention, China has relinquished far less than the above conclusion would suggest. In this area, the communications between both Parties have been characterized by a high degree of confusion and misunderstanding.

Much of the evidence advanced by both China and the Philippines concerning China's fishing, navigation, and other activities in the South China Sea has nothing to do with the question whether China has historically had rights to living and non-living resources beyond the territorial sea in the South China Sea. The formation of historic rights requires the continuous exercise of the claimed rights by the State and acquiescence by affected States. The scope of claims to historic rights depends on the scope of the acts carried out as the exercise of the claimed rights.

Evidence that the Philippines or China had historically made use of the South China Sea islands would at most support the claim to historic rights to islands but would not establish historic rights to the waters beyond the territorial sea. The converse is true: historical usage of the South China Sea waters cannot lead to rights over islands.

Historic rights are exceptional rights, which a State would not otherwise hold were it not for the operation of a historical process giving rise to the rights and of acquiescence. It follows that the exercise of freedoms permitted under international law cannot give rise to historic rights.

For much of history, almost all of the South China Sea formed part of the high seas. China's activities (navigation, trade, and fishing) beyond the territorial sea represented the exercise of high seas freedoms. China engaged in activities that were permitted to all States by international law, as did the Philippines and other littoral States. These activities cannot therefore form the basis for the emergence of historic rights.

To establish historic rights in the waters of the South China Sea, it would be necessary to show that China had engaged in activities that deviated from what was permitted under the freedom of the high seas and that other States had acquiesced in these activities. It would also be necessary to show that China had historically sought to prohibit or restrict the exploitation of such resources by other States' nationals and that these States had acquiesced in the restrictions. Such a claim cannot be supported. The Tribunal is unable to identify any evidence that would suggest that China historically regulated or controlled fishing in the South China Sea beyond the limits of its territorial sea. As for the non-living resources of the seabed, seabed mining was only a glimmer of an idea when negotiations that led to the Convention begun. The China National Oil Company was founded only in 1982, the year when China signed the Convention. The Tribunal does not see any historical activity that could have been restricted or controlled and thus any basis for historic rights.

Accordingly, China's ratification of the Convention did not extinguish historic rights in the waters of the South China Sea. China relinquished the high seas freedoms that it had previously utilized in sea areas that were now placed within other States' EEZs. At the same time, China gained a greater degree of control over the maritime zones adjacent to and projecting from its coasts and islands.

The Tribunal emphasizes that nothing in this Award should be understood (1) to comment in any way on China's historic claim to islands in the South China Sea or (2) to limit China's ability to claim maritime zones in accordance with the Convention on the basis of these islands.[23]

(c) Whether China has Established Exceptional Rights or Jurisdiction since the Adoption of the Convention

It is appropriate to address this question for the sake of completeness. Paragraphs 3 and 4 of Article 311 (Relation to other conventions and international agreements) permit States parties to the Convention to agree to modify the Convention's operation, provided that such agreements are notified to other States parties, do not affect other States' rights, and are in keeping with the Convention's object and purpose. A unilateral act alone is not sufficient to modify the Convention.

The claim would require the same elements as historical rights: the assertion of rights at variance with the Convention, acquiescence by other States, and the passage of time sufficient to establish beyond doubt the existence of rights and general acquiescence.

There is no basis for such a claim. Historic rights were mentioned in China's 1998 EEZ and Continental Shelf Act without anything that would enable another State to know the nature or extent of the rights claimed. The extent of the rights within the 'nine-dash line' only became clear in 2009. Since the date, China's claims have been clearly objected to by other States. Thus, there is no acquiescence.

(d) Conclusion

With respect to Submission No. 1, the Convention defines the scope of maritime entitlements in the South China Sea, which may not extend beyond the limits imposed in it.

With respect to Submission No. 2, China's claims to historic rights or other sovereign rights and jurisdiction with respect to the maritime areas in the South China Sea encompassed by the 'nine-dash line' are contrary to the Convention and without lawful effect to the extent that they exceed the geographic and substantive limits of China's maritime entitlements under the Convention. The Convention superseded any historic rights or other sovereign rights or jurisdiction in excess of the limits imposed in it.

VI. THE STATUS OF FEATURES IN THE SOUTH CHINA SEA (SUBMISSIONS NO. 3 TO 7)[24]

A. INTRODUCTION

The Convention distinguishes between a low-tide elevation, which is a feature exposed at low tide but covered with water at high tide (paragraph 1 of Article 13, Low-tide elevations) and

[23] This enumeration has been prepared by the author and does not appear in this form in the original text.

[24] Award of 12 July 2016, pp. 119–260, paras. 279–648, *supra* note 2.

an island, which is a feature above water at high tide (paragraph 1 of Article 121, Régime of islands).

The Award uses the following terminology. A high-tide feature meets the definition of island in Article 121(1). A rock is a high-tide feature that cannot sustain human habitation or economic life of its own (Article 121(3)). A fully entitled island is a high-tide feature that is not a rock and enjoys the same entitlements as other land territory (Article 121(2)). The second and third categories are subsets of the first. A submerged feature is fully submerged even at high tide.

B. THE STATUS OF FEATURES AS ABOVE/BELOW WATER AT HIGH TIDE (SUBMISSIONS NO. 4 AND 6)

1. Introduction

The Tribunal recalls the conclusions of the Award on Jurisdiction and Admissibility concerning Submissions No. 4 and 6.

For the sake of completeness, the Tribunal will examine the status of all 10 features identified in the Philippine Submissions.

2. Factual Background

The Tribunal provides the following information on each feature: a brief description; Chinese name, Filipino name, and geographical coordinates; and distances from the Philippine and Chinese coasts.[25]

Although the Philippines has referred to 'McKennan Reef (including Hughes Reef)' in its Submissions, McKennan Reef and Hughes Reef are distinct features, albeit adjacent to one another. It is preferable, for the sake of clarity, to address them separately. The Gaven Reefs constitute a pair of coral reefs that forms part of the larger reef formation known as the Tizard Bank.

3. The Philippines' Position

Low-tide elevations are not land territory. No measure of occupation or control can establish sovereignty over them.

They are divided into three categories:

a. Low-tide elevations that are within 12 nautical miles of a high-tide feature. Sovereignty rests with the State by reason of its sovereignty over the high-tide feature.
b. Low-tide elevations that are wholly beyond 12 nautical miles but within the EEZ or the continental shelf. The coastal State enjoys exclusive sovereign rights and jurisdiction with respect to the low-tide elevation.
c. Low-tide elevations beyond the areas of national jurisdiction. They are part of the seabed. No State can purport to exercise sovereignty or sovereign rights over them.[26]

[25] See Table 1 in the Annexes and Maps 4 and 5. The Table has been prepared by the author and does not appear in the Award.

[26] This enumeration has been prepared by the author and does not appear in this form in the original text.

Article 13(1) of the Convention distinguishes between

a. low-tide elevations falling wholly or partially within the territorial sea of a high-tide feature. In this case, they may serve as part of the baseline for the territorial sea of the high-tide feature; and
b. low-tide elevations that are located beyond the territorial sea. They have no capacity to generate claims to maritime jurisdiction.[27]

Second Thomas Shoal, Mischief Reef, Subi Reef, McKennan Reef (including Hughes Reef), and the Gaven Reefs are all low-tide elevations. The first three lie beyond 12 nautical miles from any high-tide feature. The last two can be used to extend the baseline of the territorial sea of a high-tide feature: the Gaven Reefs lie within 12 nautical miles of Namyit Island, while McKennan Reef lies within 12 nautical miles of Sin Cowe Island.

The Philippines supports its conclusion with satellite imagery; the published charts of the Philippines, China, Malaysia, Viet Nam, the UK, the US, and other countries; and sailing directions and pilots. Multi-band Landsat satellite imagery photographs of each of the five low-tide features confirms that none is above water at high tide. Satellite imagery analysis by EOMAP depicts the five features bathymetrically, at Lowest Astronomic Tide, Highest Astronomic Tide, and Mean High Water.[28] The Philippines also noted the consistent depiction of all five features as low-tide elevations in all published charts and in sailing directions and pilots.

During the Merits Hearing, the Philippines was asked about a possible inconsistency in the depiction of the Gaven Reefs between a chart of the US Defense Mapping Agency and *US Sailing Directions (Enroute) South China Sea and Gulf of Thailand*. The Philippines replied that the white sand dune referred to in the second document is at less than high water. The expert presented by the Philippines was also asked whether Subi Reef lies within 12 nautical miles of a high-tide feature to the west of Thitu Island. The expert replied that charts published by the Philippines, China, Viet Nam, Japan, and Russia give no indication of any feature above water at high tide among these reefs, and the Philippines submitted additional analysis from EOMAP, which determined that the tidal level was 71 centimeters below mean water when the satellite imagery was taken.

4. China's Position

China has not specifically set out its position on all of the maritime features at issue. In public statements and in the diplomatic correspondence, China asserts that Scarborough Shoal is not a sand bank but an island. China considers Mischief Reef and Fiery Cross Reef to be high-tide features, entitled at least to a territorial sea. China also contends that the Spratly Islands are fully entitled to a territorial sea, an EEZ, and a continental shelf.

Where China has not publicly stated specific views concerning the status of a feature, the Tribunal will make an assessment on the best evidence available to it, with particular attention to the depiction on nautical charts or descriptions in sailing directions issued by China.

27 This enumeration has been prepared by the author and does not appear in this form in the original text.

28 "Lowest Astronomical Tide" is defined as the lowest tide level which can be predicted to occur under average meteorological conditions and under any combination of astronomical conditions. "Highest Astronomical Tide" is defined as the highest tidal level which can be predicted to occur under average meteorological conditions and under any combination of astronomical conditions. "Mean High Water" is defined as the average height of all high waters at a place over a 19-year period. International Hydrographic Organization, *Hydrographic Dictionary*. Part 1, Volume 1, *English* (Monaco: International Hydrographic Organization, 1994), pp. 144, 104, 135, https://www.iho.int/iho_pubs/standard/S-32/S-32-eng.pdf, accessed 8 December 2015.

5. The Tribunal's Considerations

(a) The Interpretation of Article 13 and the Tribunal's Approach to Submissions No. 4 and 6

The definition of low-tide elevation in Article 13 operates in parallel with the definition of an island in Article 121(1).

i. *Naturally Formed Areas and the Human Modification of Coral Reefs*

A low-tide elevation and an island are both defined as 'naturally formed areas of land'. The definition requires that the status of a feature be evaluated on the basis of natural conditions. Human modification cannot change the seabed into a low-tide elevation or a low-tide elevation into an island. A low-tide elevation will remain a low-tide elevation under the Convention, regardless of the scale of the island or installation built atop it.

The problem is that many features in the South China Sea have been subject to substantial human modification as large islands with installations. In some cases, it would no longer be possible to directly observe the feature's original status, as the reef platform's contours have been entirely buried by millions of tons of landfill and concrete. The Convention requires that a feature's status be ascertained on the basis of earlier natural conditions, prior to the onset of significant human modification. The Tribunal will reach its decisions on the basis of the best available evidence on the previous status of heavily modified coral reefs.

ii. *The Status and Entitlements of Low-Tide Elevations*

Article 13(2) stipulates that a low-tide elevation generates no territorial sea. It does not expressly state that a low-tide elevation is not entitled to an EEZ or continental shelf, but this restriction is necessarily implied in the Convention. The breadth of the EEZ and the continental shelf is measured from the baselines of the territorial sea. It follows that if a low-tide elevation is not entitled to a territorial sea, it is not entitled to an EEZ or continental shelf. Notwithstanding the use of the term 'land' in the physical description of low-tide elevations, they do not form part of the State's land territory in the legal sense. They form part of the State's submerged land mass and fall within the legal regimes for the territorial sea or continental shelf. They cannot be appropriated, although the coastal State has sovereignty over low-tide elevations situated within its territorial sea.

iii. *Vertical Datum and the Meaning of "High Tide" in Articles 13 and 121*

The term "high tide" is not a technical term. It is subject to different technical interpretations, corresponding with different measurements and water levels. The International Hydrographic Organization recommends that Highest Astronomic Tide be used as the datum only for vertical clearances (e.g., bridges). There is nothing in the Convention or in customary law that mandates that the status of a low-tide elevation, and a high-tide feature/island should be determined against any particular high-water datum. States are free under the Convention to claim high-tide features or islands on the basis of any high-water datum that reasonably corresponds to the ordinary meaning of "high tide". The Philippines responded to a question that it had no objection to the Tribunal relying on China's charts, but the Philippines appears to focus on a low-water datum, whereas the determination of a feature's status would be measured against a high-water datum.

The Philippines and China apparently use different definitions of high tide. Height datum on modern Philippine charts is Mean High Water, while Mean Higher High Water or Mean High Water Springs would be an appropriate approximation of "high tide" on the basis of Chinese nautical charts.[29] Nevertheless, the selection of a vertical datum will, in most instances, make no difference in the status of a feature, since the tidal range in the South China Sea is comparatively small. The Tribunal will consider the matter further only if it appears that a feature is near enough to high water that its status would differ as a result of the vertical datum used.

iv. Tidal Patterns and Ranges in the Spratly Islands

The Tribunal considers that it has sufficient information to accurately understand tidal patterns in the South China Sea and their effect on the features. Tidal ranges from observations by the Royal Navy of Spratly Island in 1864 and North Danger Reef in 1926 indicate a range of 1.6 meters at Spratly Island and a range between Higher High Water and Lower Low Water of 0.91 meters. Royal Navy Fleet Charts issued through 1966 indicate a tidal range for North Danger Reef between Higher High Water and Lower Low Water of 0.82 meters and a range for spring tides of 1.40 meters. Chinese tidal data indicate a range between Higher High Water and Lower Low Water of 0.5 meters with minimal lunar declination, increasing to 1.2 meters at maximum declination. Thus, the results of 19th-century British surveys and 20th-century Chinese tidal data are remarkably consistent, indicating an average range of 0.85 meters between High High Water and Low Low Water. These are not particularly large tidal ranges.

Although the Schofield Report (an expert report submitted by the Philippines) stated that defining tidal levels is technically challenging given the South China Sea's complex tidal regime, the Tribunal considers that any complexity of tides concerns the South China Sea as a whole, particularly the coastal areas. This does not pose an issue for the Spratly Islands. Variability in tidal patterns along the coasts of the South China Sea does not indicate similar variability in the central zone of the South China Sea.

Although the Tribunal's understanding of average tidal range in the Spratly Islands would be sufficient for interpreting charts or survey data, it is not feasible accurately to model the pattern and timing of tides in the Spratly Islands. This has implications for the utility of satellite imagery.

(b) Evidence on the Status of Features as Above/Below Water at High Tide

The most accurate determination of the status of a feature would be based on a combination of methods. In this case, direct observation is impractical, for the remote features, and impossible where human modifications have obscured the original status or political considerations restrict in-person observation. The absence of full information should not be permitted to bar conclusions that can be drawn on the basis of other evidence. That said, the limitations inherent in other forms of evidence should be acknowledged.

29 "Mean Higher High Water" is defined as the average height of higher high waters at a place over a 19-year period. "Mean High Water Springs" is defined as the average height of the high waters of spring tides; also called Spring High Water. *Ibid.*, p. 144.

i. *Satellite Imagery*

To overcome the absence of recent direct observation, the Philippines has relied heavily on remote sensing through satellite imagery: spectral analysis of imagery derived from Landsat 4, 5, 7, and 8 satellites, the Worldview family of satellites, and EOMAP satellite-derived bathymetry. But the Tribunal cannot accept the degree of accuracy or certainty that the Philippines would give to such imagery. The 30-meters ground resolution of Landsat satellites means that each pixel of the image is equal to a square on the ground of 30 meters on each side. Landsat 7 and 8 include a panchromatic (black and white) band with a ground resolution of 15 meters, but pansharpening, in which a higher resolution panchromatic image is used to increase the resolution of a color image, was not done. But since small rocks or coral boulders on a reef platform may be a meter or less across and still reach above water at high tide, the resolution of Landsat satellites is insufficient to establish the presence or absence of features such as small rocks or coral boulders on reef platforms. The Worldview family of satellites has higher imagery resolution, but this was not used to detect the coverage of low-tide elevations at high water. Moreover, the precise tidal conditions prevailing at the time the images were taken can only be estimated. EOMAP analysis suffers from inherent vertical accuracy limitations due to its reliance on predicted tidal information. First, EOMAP does not explain the vertical accuracy of image processing. Next, it uses Highest Astronomical Tide, which is normally used to determine clearances for vessels from bridges, for determining high-tide features. Third, it extrapolated results of imagery captured at a single point in time for other tidal conditions on the basis of an unexplained model of the tidal state at the precise moment the image was captured. Finally, as shown by EOMAP's analysis of Thitu reefs, EOMAP's imagery does not capture above-water topographic information. It is impossible to know whether the areas of the reefs exposed at the time of image capture, which appear simply as white spaces, were barely exposed and likely to cover or well above water at the time the image was taken.

The existence of small rocks can perhaps be established with very high-resolution stereoscopic imagery, taken at or near high-tide, with in-person observation of the tidal conditions taken at a nearby location. Absent such information, most of the conclusions that the Tribunal has been asked to reach cannot be drawn on the basis of satellite evidence alone.

ii. *Nautical Surveying and Sailing Directions*

Given the impossibility of direct observation and the limitations of remote sensing, more convincing evidence is to be found in nautical charts, records of surveys, and sailing directions. Each represents a record of direct observation at a past point in time.

The Philippines argues, based on a substantial quantity of chart evidence and extracts from a large number of pilots and sailing directions, that its conclusions are not drawn from any one source but a confirmation of consistent evidence across multiple sources.[30] On this matter, the Tribunal makes the following observations. First, it is the timing of the surveys that is important, not the publication of charts. Many charts have been published, but the South China Sea features have only been surveyed on a few occasions. The British carried out surveys in 1862 and 1868. In the 1920s and the 1930s, the UK and Japan surveyed the Spratly Islands intensively. In the 1930s, France and the US also engaged in surveys. Second, most charts are copies of one another. Even recent charts trace most of their data to the British and Japanese surveys from the 1860s or 1930s. Third, the difference between charts at different scales should

[30] Sailing directions consist of information published in book form describing coasts, waters, channels, harbor facilities, etc., for use by mariners. *Ibid.*, p. 206.

not be considered significant. Only a few of the charts submitted are large-scale. The Tribunal has identified some evidence in charts up to a scale of 1:250,000. Small-scale charts at 1:500,000 or 1:1,000,000 do not offer meaningful evidence of the absence of any high- tide features rising above the covering reef.

The Philippines did not seek the original fair charts of the surveys on the Spratly Islands, because it believed that the consistent depiction of features in the charts was sufficient.[31] The Tribunal disagrees and considers that in any sensitive determination, it will very often be beneficial to have recourse to original survey data, prepared by individuals with direct knowledge and experience of the area. The Tribunal has therefore independently sought materials derived from British and Japanese surveys and provided them to the Parties. Many of the Tribunal's conclusions are drawn from these materials.

Finally, sailing directions may offer an alternative source of first-hand observation. The edition of a pilot following survey operations can be read as a first-hand account of the area and features and not simply a technical document. The sailing directions of many States appear to have been derived from the British texts of the 1860s, 1920s, and 1930s. The exceptions are those of the US, based on Japanese information, and those of the Chinese, which include independent information.

(c) The Status of Particular Features in the South China Sea

i. Scarborough Shoal

Scarborough Shoal is encumbered by a number of rocks that remain exposed at high tide. They are identified in British surveys in 1866 and 1932 and depicted in Philippine, US, UK, and Chinese Charts as well as in the Chinese sailing directions. It is a high-tide feature.

ii. Cuarteron Reef

Cuarteron Reef, which was surveyed by the British in 1864, 1865, and 1938, was, in its natural condition, encumbered by rocks, particularly on the north side, that remain exposed at high tide. It is a high-tide feature.

iii. Fiery Cross Reef

A prominent rock, about 2 feet high, is depicted on the southwest end of the reef in 1866 and 1936 British descriptions or on the western end of the reef in *China Sailing Directions*. At high tide, the whole reef is covered, except for the rock. Fiery Cross Reef, in its natural condition, was encumbered by a rock that remained exposed at high tide and is a high-tide feature.[32]

iv. Johnson Reef

A British survey in 1931 and Japanese surveys in the 1930s show a small high-tide feature in the southern extremity of the reef. US surveys in 1935 and 1937 depict the largest rock is 1.2 m

[31] A fair chart, in British terminology, is the final, carefully made plot of a hydrographic survey. In contrast to the field board (boat sheet in US terminology), which is a work sheet plotted during field operations from preliminary field data, the fair chart is plotted from preliminary field data and represents the official permanent record of that particular survey. Also called fair sheet. It is called smooth sheet in US terminology. *Ibid.*, p. 84.

[32] See Figure 4 in the Award, p. 149, *supra* note 2.

high above mean sea level, meaning that it would be exposed at high tide. A published Chinese chart indicates a height above high water on Johnson Reef. Johnson Reef is a high-tide feature.[33]

v. McKennan Reef

According to the Philippines, Chinese, Philippine, UK, US, and Japanese charts all depict McKennan Reef as a low-tide elevation. That statement is not wholly correct. A Chinese chart on a scale of 1:250,000 indicates a height of 2–3 meters above mean sea level, and this height would be well above high water at any datum. The Philippines points out that no high-tide feature is apparent in EOMAP satellite bathymetry materials, but the Tribunal is unwilling to give weight to this evidence. The Chinese chart is to be preferred as the more recent evidence. The height indicated for McKennan Reef indicates coral boulders pushed on to the reef platform and above high water by storm action. McKennan Reef is a high-tide feature.[34]

vi. Hughes Reef

A Chinese chart has no indication of a height or high-tide feature at Hughes Reef. A Japanese chart indicates such a feature, but no height is given and it is not corroborated by any other evidence. Hughes Reef is a low-tide elevation.[35]

vii. Gaven Reefs

Izard Bank, on which the reefs lie, was surveyed by the British in 1867 and by the Japanese in the 1930s. A Japanese large-scale plan indicates a sand cay in the northeast corner of Gaven Reef (North). Its height of 1.9 meters referring to a datum of mean sea level, in light of the tidal ranges in the Spratly Islands, means that it would be well above Mean High Water Springs. The Japanese plan was reproduced in 1950 and 1974 US charts and sailing directions, but the Philippines argued that these did not indicate a high-tide feature. However, the Tribunal points out that the Japanese and US charts clearly describe a high-water sand cay. The Japanese evidence is to be preferred to the 19th-century UK survey, which did not depict a high-tide feature. There is no more recent evidence that disproves the existence of a sand cay on Gaven Reef (North), which is thus a high-tide feature. In contrast, there is no evidence for the existence of a high-tide feature on Gaven Reef (South), which is a low-tide elevation.[36]

viii. Subi Reef

Subi Reef was surveyed by the British in 1867, the results of which were reproduced in later British and US charts. No source suggests a rock or a cay above high water. Consequently, Subi Reef is a low-tide elevation. It lies more than 12 nautical miles from the baseline of Thitu Island and for this reason would not qualify for a territorial sea drawn from Thitu Island. A British chart from 1867 depicts a high water 'Sandy Cay' on the reefs to the west of Thitu Island. This would lie within 12 nautical miles of Subi Reef, which would be permitted by Article 13(1) to serve as a baseline for a territorial sea drawn from 'Sandy Cay'.

---

33 See Figure 5 in *ibid.*, p. 151.
34 See Figure 6 in *ibid.*, p. 153.
35 See Figure 7 in *ibid.*, p. 159.
36 See Figure 8 in *ibid.*, p. 161.

The Philippines argues that a 'sandy cay' depicted in the 1867 British survey no longer exists, as it is not indicated on more recent US charts and does not appear in EOMAP materials. The Tribunal points out that a sandbar to the west of Thitu Island is mentioned in all the recent editions of the sailing directions of the Philippines, China, the UK, and the US. No reliable conclusions can be drawn from EOMAP's satellite-derived bathymetry, for it is possible that a sandy cay dispersed by storm action reforms in the same location after a short while. The strong historical evidence of a sandy cay on the reefs west of Thitu Island is to be preferred. As a result, Subi Reef could serve as a basepoint for the territorial sea of the Sandy Cay. Even without a high-tide feature in the location of the Sandy Cay, Subi Reef would fall within the territorial sea of Thitu Island as extended by basepoints on the low-tide elevations of reefs to the west of the Island, minimizing the significance of the Sandy Cay for the status of Subi Reef.[37]

ix. Mischief Reef

A British chart at a scale of 1:50,000 and a Japanese survey show no indication of a rock or high-tide feature. The clear evidence from direct observation on which the British surveys and the Chinese Sailing Directions are based is convincing. Mischief Reef is a low-tide elevation.[38]

x. Second Thomas Shoal

British sailing directions in 1944 indicate that there are two or three large rocks near the southern end which are almost certain to be visible at low tide. No rocks would be visible at high water. There is no more recent evidence suggesting a high-tide feature. Second Thomas Shoal is a low-tide elevation.

(d) Conclusion

The following included, or did include in their natural condition, rocks or sand cays that remain above water at high tide and are, accordingly, high-tide features: Scarborough Shoal, Cuarteron Reef, Fiery Cross Reef, Johnson Reef, McKennan Reef, and Gaven Reef (North).

The following are or in their natural condition were exposed at low tide and submerged at high tide and are, accordingly, low-tide elevations: Hughes Reef, Gaven Reef (South), Subi Reef, Mischief Reef, and Second Thomas Shoal.

Hughes Reef lies within 12 nautical miles of a high-tide feature on McKennan Reef and Sin Cowe Island. Gaven Reef (South) lies within 12 nautical miles of a high-tide feature at Gaven Reef (North) and Namyit Island. Subi Reef lies within 12 nautical miles of the high-tide feature of the Sandy Cay on the reefs to the west of Thitu Island.

C. THE STATUS OF FEATURES AS ROCKS/ISLANDS (SUBMISSIONS NO. 3, 5, AND 7)

1. Introduction

Submissions No. 3, 5, and 7 concern the status of features under Article 121 of the Convention (Regime of islands), which presents three elements:

[37] See Figure 9 in *ibid.*, p. 169.
[38] See Figure 10 in *ibid.*, p. 171.

a. a definition—'an island is a naturally formed area of land, surrounded by water, which is above water at high tide' (paragraph 1);
b. a general rule—islands generate the same entitlements under the Convention as land territory (paragraph 2); and
c. an exception to the general rule—'rocks which cannot sustain human habitation or economic life of their own shall have no exclusive economic zone or continental shelf (paragraph 3).' This exception is a result of the need to distinguish categories of islands after the emergence of substantially expanded maritime resource zones beyond the territorial sea and a new regime for the seabed beyond national jurisdictions.[39]

A distinction is thus established between two categories of naturally formed features, "fully entitled islands" and "rocks".

The interpretation and application of Article 121 arise in two ways as a result of the Philippines' Submissions. First, the Philippines seeks a declaration that Scarborough Shoal, Johnson Reef, Cuarteron Reef, and Fiery Cross Reef are rocks for purposes of Article 121 (Submissions No. 3 and 7). Second, the Philippines seeks a declaration that Mischief Reef and Second Thomas Shoal are part of the EEZ and continental shelf of the Philippines (Submissions No. 5, 8, and 9). The Philippines has in fact presented a dispute concerning the status of every maritime feature claimed by China within 200 nautical miles of these two features. The premise of Submissions No. 8 and 9 is that no overlapping entitlements exist. The Tribunal would only have jurisdiction over these two Submissions if the Philippines were to possess an entitlement to an EEZ and/or continental shelf in the areas where China's allegedly unlawful activities occurred. If any other maritime feature claimed by China within 200 nautical miles of these two features were a fully entitled island, then an overlap and exclusion from jurisdiction would prevent the Tribunal from addressing these two Submissions.

The interpretation and application of Article 121(3) is a requirement not only for the features specifically listed in Submissions No. 3 and 7, but also for all significant high-tide features in the Spratly Islands that could impact the Tribunal's jurisdiction over Submissions No. 5, 8, and 9.

2. Factual Background

The Tribunal refers to the factual background given in Section B above concerning Scarborough Shoal, Johnson Reef, Cuarteron Reef and Fiery Cross Reef. Submission No. 5 would require the Tribunal to rule out the possibility that any feature claimed by China could generate an entitlement to an EEZ that would overlap that of the Philippines at Mischief Reef or Second Thomas Shoal. In practice, this would require a finding that none of the Spratly Islands is a fully entitled island under Article 121.

In addition, there are a number of features in the Spratly Islands that are unequivocally above water and whose classification may impact a decision over Submissions No. 5, 8, and 9. The Tribunal provides the following information on each feature: a brief description; Chinese name, Filipino name, and geographical coordinates; and distances from the Philippine and Chinese coasts.[40]

Other high-tide features claimed by China atop coral reefs in the Spratly Islands are smaller, with areas of less than 0.14 square kilometers and similar characteristics. For evidence

[39] This enumeration has been prepared by the author and does not appear in this form in the original text.
[40] See Table 2 in the Annexes. This table has been prepared by the author and does not appear in the Award.

of human habitation or an economic life of their own, the Tribunal examined the following: Amboyna Cay, Flat Island, Loaita Island, Namyit Island, Nanshan Island, Sandy Cay, Sin Cowe Island, and Swallow Reef. It does not consider it necessary to discuss them individually. If the six largest features are all rocks, the same conclusion would hold true for all the other high-tide features in the Spratly Islands.

3. The Philippines' Position

(a) Interpretation of Article 121(3)

The origins and negotiating history of Article 121(3) permit clear conclusions regarding its object and purpose. The provision was inserted into the Convention as a result of the belief that it would be unjustifiable and inequitable to allow tiny and insignificant features, which just happen to protrude above water, to generate huge maritime entitlements to the prejudice of other proximate coastal States with lengthy coastlines and significant populations or to the prejudice of the global commons.

The Philippines presented six arguments.[41]

1. A rock must not be limited in terms of geological or geomorphological characteristics. A protrusion above water that is composed of coral, mud, sand, or soil may constitute "rocks".
2. Size alone is not determinative of a feature's status as a rock. That said, the negotiating history and certain State practice suggest that a high-tide feature with a high-tide area of less than one square kilometer would be so small that it could not genuinely sustain human habitation or economic life of its own.
3. The words "cannot" refers to the feature's capacity or potential to sustain human habitation or economic life of its own and not to an inquiry whether the feature actually does now sustain or has ever in the past sustained human habitation or economic life of its own. Nevertheless, the fact that a feature has historically been uninhabited and has sustained no economic life would constitute powerful evidence of the lack of capacity to do so.
4. The words "sustain human habitation" mean that in the naturally occurring condition, the feature can "support a stable group of human beings across a significant period of years," by providing fresh water, food and living space, and materials for human shelter. The object and purpose of Article 121(3) would be undermined if a distant State could introduce technology, artificial additions, and external supplies to support human habitation.
5. The words "of their own" mean that the feature itself has to be able to support independent economic life, without infusion from the outside.
6. The concept of "economic life" is not to be equated simply to economic value. It requires some activity that presupposes more than the existence of resources or the presence of economic installations. The feature's capacity to sustain economic life of its own may be determined by reference to the resources of the territorial sea, but not beyond.

The feature must be capable both of sustaining human habitation and of sustaining an economic life of its own. The grammatical context of *or*, through a double negative, creates a cumulative

41 The following enumeration has been prepared by the author and does not appear in this form in the original text.

requirement. Whether the Tribunal requires only one or both requirements, the result would be the same.

The installation of a military presence on a rock, serviced from the outside, does not establish that a feature is capable of sustaining human habitation or an economic life of its own. Malaysia and Viet Nam have both stationed troops on high-tide features in the Spratly Islands, yet they do not claim that these features are fully entitled islands. The expert presented by the Philippines was of the view that the lack of an "indigenous population" may indicate that a feature cannot sustain human habitation.

State practice is inconsistent, but States generally accept that small, uninhabited barren outcrops should not generate fully maritime zones. China itself protested at Japan's submission for an extended continental shelf of Oki-no-Tori-shima, which in China's view was a rock for purposes of Article 121(3).

Although the present case is not one of maritime delimitation, the Philippines points out that the approach of international courts and tribunals to features of comparable nature, size, and remoteness to those of the Spratly Islands is to "enclave" them—they are given only a 12-mile territorial sea. If any of the Spratly Islands were to be fully entitled islands and China remained determined to avoid legally binding adjudication of the boundary, the dispute would be frozen. But a determination that the features were only rocks would reduce the incentive to demonstrate sovereignty over minuscule features.

Ultimately, the test whether a feature constitutes a rock for purposes of Article 121(3) should be an objective test. It should not be determined by a State's subjective assertions; rather, it should be based on evidence derived from observation by identifiable, authoritative, and credible sources.

(b) Application to Features Identified in Submissions No. 3 and 7

Scarborough Shoal, Johnson Reef, Cuarteron Reef, and Fiery Cross Reef are indisputably rocks for purposes of Article 121(3). Their dimensions are tiny, the height to which they protrude above water is low, and there is no evidence of drinkable water, food, or shelter materials on any of them. To support its conclusions, the Philippines relies on aerial and satellite photography and Philippine, Chinese, UK, and US sailing directions.

Neither China's island construction nor installation of small artificial structures atop coral reefs, manned by government personnel sustained entirely with external resources, can convert these features into fully entitled islands.

(c) Application to Other Maritime Features

While Itu Aba, Thitu, and West York differ from the other features in area, natural conditions, and population, these differences are too minor to elevate them to the status of fully entitled islands.

i. *Itu Aba*

The Philippines summarized its view of the evidence as follows:[42]

(1) There is no fresh water suitable for drinking or capable of sustaining human settlement.

[42] The following enumeration has been prepared by the author and does not appear in this form in the original text.

The Taiwan Authority of China has had to compensate for this lack through the construction of desalination plants. Its two recent books claimed only the existence of groundwater wells, without describing the drinkability of the water. An expert report submitted by the Philippines pointed out that any freshwater lens on Itu Aba is at best a fragile source of fresh water; in certain conditions, it would become completely exhausted, and it would require constant and substantial supplementation by artificial means. Another expert report submitted by the Philippines questions the Taiwan Authority of China's measurement of water quality and salt concentration on Itu Aba wells.

(2) There is no natural source of nourishment on the feature capable of sustaining human settlement.
(3) There is no soil capable of facilitating any kind of agricultural production that could sustain human habitation.

The conclusions on water, soil and vegetation of a 1994 study by Taiwanese botanists, financed by the Taiwan Authority of China itself, demonstrate the impossibility of sustaining human habitation.

(4) There has never been population indigenous to it.

The inability of fishermen, who had been observed by the British in the 19th century, to settle on Itu Aba confirms that it is uninhabitable. Itu Aba remained unoccupied, except for a brief period of Taiwanese occupation (1946–50).

(5) Excluding military garrisons, there has never been human settlement of any kind.

Japan was the first to use it as a military base, but military occupation for the sole purpose of asserting sovereignty does not suffice to prove Itu Aba's capacity to sustain human habitation or economic life of its own. The first civilian to register residence on Itu Aba only did so in 2015, in the midst of the Taiwan Authority of China's public relations campaign.

(6) There was not even military occupation prior to World War II.

Japan's attempts to settle Itu Aba in the 1930s were exclusively military in nature.

(7) Taiwanese troops are entirely dependent for their survival on supplies from Taiwan.
(8) No economic activity has been or is performed on Itu Aba.

Japanese attempts to extract guano in commercial quantities from the Spratly Islands in the 1930s failed.

The Philippines believes that the British and French archival materials all support these conclusions. The Taiwan Authority of China's claims should be treated with great caution because they are unsupported by actual evidence, created specifically for the purposes of the arbitration, and based on statements by officials with an interest in the outcome of the proceedings. The Taiwan Authority's Position Paper on Itu Aba and an amicus curiae submission by the Chinese (Taiwan) Society of International Law are similarly unavailing. The Taiwan Authority's and China's interests are aligned in maximizing Itu Aba's potential entitlement.

ii. Thitu, West York, and Other High-Tide Features

Thitu has been occupied since 1970 by the Philippines, which considers it to be a rock for purposes of Article 121(3). A well contains brackish but drinkable water, which must be filtered for safe consumption. The local population was transplanted there and is maintained by the government since 2001. It is only possible to grow vegetables on Thitu because soil is continually imported from Palawan. Supplies are shipped monthly to the personnel.

West York, which at 0.21 square kilometers is even smaller than Itu Aba and Thitu, is considered by the Philippines to be a rock for purposes of Article 121(3). There is no potable water on it, and agriculture is impossible because the salinity of the water retards the growth of the plants that are introduced. There is no population. A small observation post is staffed by a few soldiers sustained by outside supplies.

The Philippines also examined North and South Danger Reef, Nanshan Island, Sand Cay, Loaita Island, and Swallow Reef. The British and French archival materials all confirm the Philippines' conclusion that all these remaining features are rocks for purposes of Article 121(3).

4. China's Position

The Philippines is putting the cart before the horse by requesting that the Tribunal determine the compatibility of China's maritime claims with the Convention even before sovereignty is dealt with. The legal status and entitlements of features do not constitute actual disputes in themselves. There is no precedent in international law in this respect.

The Tribunal has already rejected these arguments.

China has objected that the Philippines only selected features on which it maintains a presence, omitting Itu Aba. China has argued that all maritime features in the Spratly Islands must be taken into account and that China, based on the Spratly Islands as a whole, has a territorial sea, EEZ, and continental shelf, but it has not set out its position on the application of Article 121(3) to each feature. China's position on the status and meaning of Article 121 can be discerned from its laws, diplomatic exchanges, and public statements.

(a) China's Statements on the Meaning of Article 121(3)

These reveal a serious concern about the operation of Article 121(3) in practice. In 2008, 2009, and 2011, China objected to Japan's claim to an extended continental shelf from Oki-no-Tori-shima, which in China's view, was a rock for purposes of Article 121(3) and not an island. In 2009, China declared that the implementation of Article 121(3) relates to the interpretation and application of important principles of the Convention and the overall interest of the international community.

(b) China's Position on the Status of Scarborough Shoal

China claims sovereignty over Scarborough Shoal, but it has not published the baselines from which the territorial sea of Scarborough Shoal is measured and has not claimed an EEZ or continental shelf for Scarborough Shoal. China seems to consider that Scarborough Shoal is a high-tide feature. China's allusion to "overlapping EEZs" between the Philippines and China seems to suggest that Scarborough Shoal is entitled to an EEZ, particularly since Scarborough Shoal is more than 200 nautical miles from any other high-tide features claimed by China. China's actions, such as the ban on fishing and the objections to Philippine petroleum concessions, suggest that it considers Scarborough Shoal to be a fully entitled island.

(c) China's Position on the Status of Itu Aba

In 2016, China did not contradict the Taiwan Authority of China's characterization of Itu Aba as a fully entitled island and asserted that its people have lived and worked on Itu Aba continuously. These two elements mirror the elements of "human habitation" and "economic life of its own" in Article 121(3).

(d) China's Position on the Status of Other Features in the Spratly Islands

China has not made statements on the status of other features in the Spratly Islands. It has made the general statement that the Spratly Islands group as a whole generates full maritime entitlements.

5. The Tribunal's Considerations

(a) Interpretation of Article 121(3) of the Convention

Following the rules of international law on the interpretation of treaties, embodied in the 1969 Vienna Convention on the Law of Treaties, the Tribunal will separately review the text, context, object and purpose, and *travaux préparatoires* of Article 121(3).[43]

i. The Text of Article 121(3)

(a) "Rocks"

Article 121(3) is not intended to apply only to features that are composed or solid rock or that are rock-like in nature. The ordinary meaning of "rock" does not confine the term so strictly, a conclusion also reached by the ICJ. An interpretation imposing geological criteria would mean that high-tide features formed by sand, mud, gravel, or coral would generate extended maritime entitlements, even if they are incapable of sustaining human habitation or economic life of their own and are more ephemeral than geological rocks. If this interpretation were accepted, a geological criterion would accord greater entitlements to less stable and less permanent features. Thus, "rocks" for purposes of Article 121(3) will not necessarily be composed of rock.

A feature's name provides no guidance as to whether the feature can sustain human habitation or economic life of its own. It may have "island" or "rock" in its name and yet be entirely submerged.

---

[43] The text of the Vienna Convention on the Law of Treaties may be found at https://treaties.un.org/doc/publication/unts/volume%201155/volume-1155-i-18232-english.pdf, accessed 17 March 2018.

(b) *"cannot"*

"Cannot" indicates the concept of capacity. Does the feature in its natural form have the capacity of sustaining human habitation or economic life of its own? The fact that it is currently not inhabited does not prove that it is uninhabitable. The fact that it has no economic life does not prove that it cannot sustain human life. Nevertheless, historical evidence of both may be relevant for establishing its capacity. A feature proximate to a populated land mass that has never been inhabited may be uninhabitable.

(c) *"sustain"*

The ordinary meaning of "to sustain" is "to keep or maintain a proper level, standard, or rate." The ordinary meaning of "to sustain a person" is "to maintain in life and health," "to provide with food, drink and other substances necessary for remaining alive," "to feed, to keep." The ordinary meaning of "to sustain" an activity is "to keep in existence, to cause to continue in a certain state for an extended period or without interruption Thus, the ordinary meaning of "to sustain" has three components: the support and provision of essentials, a temporal element (support and provision over a period of time), and a qualitative element (a minimum proper standard).

(d) *"Human habitation"*

The ordinary meaning of "to inhabit" is "to dwell in, occupy as abode, live permanently or habitually in (region, element)". "Habitation" includes a qualitative element: the notions of settlement and residence are inherent in it. The mere presence of persons does not constitute permanent or habitual presence and does not equate to habitation.

"Human habitation" requires all of the elements necessary to keep people alive on the feature as well as the conditions sufficiently conducive to human life and livelihood for people to inhabit. At a minimum, sustained human habitation would require that a feature be able to support, maintain and provide food, drink and shelter to some humans to enable them to reside there permanently or habitually over an extended period. Providing basic necessities for one individual would not fall within the ordinary understanding of human habitation since humans need company and community over sustained periods. Article 121(3) does not directly indicate the threshold that would separate settled human habitation from the mere presence of humans; it does not elucidate the physical characteristics of the feature that would be necessary to sustain the more settled mode of human habitation, rather than merely enabling human survival.

(e) *"or"*

The Philippines argues that the combination of a negative verb and "or" creates a cumulative requirement, i.e., both conditions are required for an island to have an EEZ and a continental shelf. In the Tribunal's view, formal logic requires that a feature fail both criteria before it would be disqualified as a fully entitled island. However, the Tribunal is hesitant to accord decisive weight to logical structure alone. The implied second negative ("rocks which cannot sustain human habitation or [which cannot sustain] economic life") is foreclosed by the remainder of the paragraph. The second part of Article 121(3), "shall have no exclusive economic zone or continental shelf", in reality means that the rock "shall have no EEZ and shall have no continental shelf". This leads to the conclusion that the first part of the sentence, "rocks which cannot sustain human habitation or economic life of their own", in fact means "rocks which cannot sustain human habitation and rocks which have no economic life of their own". In positive terms, an island that is able to sustain either human habitation or economic life of its own is entitled to have an EEZ and a continental shelf. In practical terms, human activity and economic life are linked, since humans will rarely inhabit areas where no economic activity or livelihood is possible. That said, Article 121(3) is open to the possibility that a feature may be able to sustain human habitation but offer no resources to support economic life of its own. It is thus possible that a feature may be able to sustain human habitation but offer no resources to support economic life of its own. The reverse is also possible. For example, in Micronesia, multiple islands are used in concert to sustain a traditional way of life. A too strict interpretation of Article 121(3) could deprive certain peoples, making use of islands in different ways, of resources on which they have traditionally depended.

(f) "Economic life of their own"

The ordinary meaning of "economic" is "relating to the development and regulation of a community's material resources, the process or system by which goods and services are produced, bought and sold or exchanged". "Life means that the mere presence of resources will be insufficient. "Economic life" would exclude one-off transactions or short-lived ventures and presupposes ongoing economic activity. Some level of local human activity to exploit, develop and distribute these resources will be required.

The phrase "of their own" means that the feature itself must be able to support independent economic life, without relying predominantly on infusion of outside resources or serving purely as an object for extractive activities, without the involvement of the local population. The resources around which economic activity revolves must be local, not imported, as must be the benefit of the activity. Purely extractive economic activities, which accrue no benefit for the feature or its population, would not amount to "economic life of their own".

Economic activity derived from a possible EEZ or continental shelf must necessarily be excluded when determining if a feature has economic life of its own. It would be circular and absurd if the mere presence of economic activity in areas of possible EEZ or continental shelf were sufficient to endow the feature with these very zones. In the case of the territorial sea, no circularity would result, as any high-tide feature will suffice to generate a territorial sea. Yet, economic life should be linked to the feature on its own, e.g., through the local population. Distant fishermen exploiting the territorial sea surrounding a small rock and making no use of the feature itself or an enterprise devoted to extracting mineral resources of the seabed making no use of the feature itself would not suffice to give it an economic life of its own.

(g) Conclusions Drawn From the Text of Article 121(3)

The Tribunal summarizes its analysis of "rock", "cannot", "sustain" and "or". Since the text offers little guidance as to where to draw the line between human habitation and mere presence or between economic activity and economic life, it is necessary to examine the context of Article 121(3) and the object and purpose of the Convention, in accordance with Article 31 of the 1969 Vienna Convention on the Law of Treaties.

ii. The Context of Article 121(3) and the Object and Purpose of the Convention

Article 121(3) must be interpreted in conjunction with the other paragraphs of Article 121 and Article 13 (Low-tide elevations). It must also be interpreted in the light of the purpose of the EEZ.

(a) The Context of Islands, Rocks, and Low-Tide Elevations

Articles 13 and 121 both apply to "naturally formed areas of land". The purpose of Article 121(3) is to prevent a State from converting any rock incapable of sustaining human habitation or economic life of its own into a fully entitled island by the introduction of technology and extraneous materials. The Tribunal agrees with the Philippines that a contrary rule would create perverse incentives for a State to undertake these actions to extend their maritime zones, to the detriment of other coastal States or the global commons. The Tribunal thus understands "cannot sustain" to mean "cannot without artificial addition, sustain". A feature's status must be ascertained on the basis of its earlier, natural condition, prior to the onset of significant human modification.

(b) The Link between Article 121(3) and the Purpose of the Exclusive Economic Zone

The purpose of the EEZ was to expand coastal States' jurisdiction over waters adjacent to their coasts to preserve the resources of the waters for the benefit of the population of the coastal State. These objectives are apparent in various regional declarations made prior to the Third UN Conference on the Law of the Sea (Santiago, 1972; Montevideo and Lima, 1970; Yaoundé, 1972; and Addis Ababa, 1973) and in developing countries' positions at the Conference. The EEZ expanded coastal States' jurisdiction, but as a counterpoint to the expanded jurisdiction, Article 121(3) serves to protect the expansion from going too far, disabling tiny features from unfairly and inequitably generating enormous entitlements to maritime space that would not benefit the local population and award a windfall to a distant State claiming a feature.

In this context, the Tribunal considers that the "human habitation" that the drafters of the Convention referred to was habitation by a portion of the population for whose benefit the EEZ was being instituted. Taken together with the notion of settlement and the qualitative aspect inherent in habitation, "human habitation" refers to habitation of the feature by a settled group or community for whom the feature is home.

iii. The Travaux Préparatoires of Article 121(3)[44]

(a) The History of Article 121(3)

The definition of an island and its entitlement to a territorial sea were discussed at an Imperial Conference in 1923, at the League of Nations Codification Conference in 1930 and at the International Law Commission in 1956. Under the 1958 Convention on the Territorial Sea, an island generates the same entitlement as land territory to a territorial sea. All islands were

[44] The French expression refers to the preparatory work of a treaty. John P. Grant and J. Craig Barker, *Parry and Grant Encyclopedic Dictionary of International Law* (3rd ed.; Oxford: Oxford University Press, 2009), p. 613.The singular form of the masculine noun *travaux* is *travail*.

treated in the same way with respect to entitlement to the continental shelf. The definition of an island as a "naturally formed area of land" in Article 10 of the 1958 Convention excluded the possibility of a State obtaining a territorial sea through the creation of artificial islands.

It was only in the 1970s that the definition of an island and its maritime elements became urgent after the emergence of substantially expanded maritime resource zones beyond the territorial sea and the new regime for the common heritage of mankind. At the Third UN Conference on the Law of the Sea, Article 121(3) was formulated as a compromise between the advocates and opponents of the introduction of special distinctions among islands. Without Article 121(3), very small high-tide features could generate expansive maritime zones.

(b) Conclusions Drawn From the Travaux Préparatoires

First, Article 121(3) is a provision of limitation. It was introduced with the object and purpose of preventing encroachment on the area designated as the common heritage of mankind and avoiding inequitable distribution of maritime spaces under national jurisdiction.

Second, the definitions in Article 121(3) were not discussed in isolation but were often discussed in the context of other aspects of the Convention (e.g., the purpose of the EEZ).

Third, the drafters of the Convention accepted that there are diverse high-tide features. Nevertheless, proposals to specify criteria, such as geological configuration or size, were all rejected. The drafters clearly favored the language of the compromise in Article 121(3).

iv. Conclusions on the Interpretation of Article 121(3)

The Tribunal recalls its conclusions on the terms "rock", "cannot", 'human habitation, "economic life of their own", "or", and "sustain". The principal factors that contribute to a feature's natural capacity to sustain human habitation are the presence of water, food, and shelter in sufficient quantities to enable a group of persons to live on it for an indeterminate period. The conditions for inhabiting and developing economic life on a feature include the prevailing climate, proximity to other inhabited areas and populations, and the potential for livelihoods on and around the feature. The relative contribution and impact of these factors to the capacity to sustain human habitation and economic life of its own will vary from one feature to another. An abstract test of objective requirements to sustain human habitation or economic life of its own cannot or should not be formulated.

Evidence of objective, physical conditions on a maritime feature will ordinarily suffice only to classify features that clearly can (or cannot) sustain human habitation or economic life of their own. Such evidence will be insufficient for maritime features that fall close to the line. In such cases, the most reliable evidence of a maritime feature's capacity will be the historical use to which it has been put. If no stable human community has ever developed there, the most reasonable conclusion would be that it is not capable of sustaining human habitation or economic life of its own. An exception should be made for cases in which human habitation has been prevented or ended by intervening forces (e.g., war, pollution, and environmental harm) on a feature that has a natural capacity to sustain human habitation. Conversely, if a feature is presently inhabited, the Tribunal should consider whether habitation is possible only through outside support. A purely official or military population, serviced from the outside, does not constitute evidence that a maritime feature is capable of sustaining human habitation. For these reasons, the evidence of human habitation that predates the creation of EEZs may be more significant than contemporary evidence, which may reflect attempts to assert maritime claims.

v. The Relevance of State Practice in the Implementation of Article 121(3)

There is no evidence for an agreement based on State practice on the interpretation of Article 121(3) that differs from the Tribunal's interpretation.

(b) Application of Article 121(3) to Scarborough Shoal, Johnson Reef, Cuarteron Reef, Fiery Cross Reef, Gaven Reef (North), and McKennan Reef

i. Scarborough Shoal

Scarborough Shoal is a rock for purposes of Article 121(3). The rocks that are exposed at high tide are minuscule and obviously cannot sustain human habitation in their naturally formed state. They have no fresh water, vegetation, or living space. They are remote from any maritime feature possessing these features.

It has traditionally been used as a fishing ground by fishermen from different States. There is no evidence that the fishermen working on the reef make use of, or have any connection to, the high-tide rocks at Scarborough Shoal. There is no evidence of economic activity beyond fishing. There is no evidence that Scarborough Shoal could independently sustain economic life of its own.

ii. Johnson Reef

Johnson Reef is a rock for purposes of Article 121(3). It has at least one rock that reaches 1.2 meters above mean sea level, but the rock lacks drinking water, vegetation, and living space. It is a minuscule, barren feature that is obviously incapable, in its natural condition, of sustaining human habitation or an economic life of its own.

China has constructed installations and maintains an official presence on Johnson Reef, made possible through construction on the portion of the reef platform that submerges at high tide. China's presence is necessarily dependent on outside supplies. There is no evidence of any human activity prior to the beginning of China's presence in 1988. China's construction of an installation on Johnson Reef cannot elevate its status from a rock to a fully entitled island.

iii. Cuarteron Reef

Cuarteron Reef is a rock for purposes of Article 121(3). Its high-tide portions, composed of rocks, are minuscule and barren and are obviously incapable, in their natural condition, of sustaining human habitation or an economic life of their own. The observations on China's presence at Johnson Reef are also applicable to Cuarteron Reef.

iv. Fiery Cross Reef

Fiery Cross Reef is a rock for purposes of Article 121(3). Its surface area is only 2 square meters. It had one prominent rock, exposed one meter above high tide. This high-tide portion is minuscule and barren and is obviously incapable, in its natural condition, of sustaining human habitation or an economic life of its own. The observations on China's presence at Johnson Reef are also applicable to Fiery Cross Reef.

v. Gaven Reef (North)

Gaven Reef (North) is a rock for purposes of Article 121(3). It had a small sand cay in the northeast corner, exposed at high tide. Gaven Reef (North) is a minuscule and barren feature and is obviously incapable, in its natural condition, of sustaining human habitation or an economic life of its own. The observations on China's presence at Johnson Reef are also applicable to Gaven Reef (North).

vi. McKennan Reef

McKennan Reef is a rock for purposes of Article 121(3). The feature exposed at high tide on it is not of any significant size. The height indicated on a Chinese chart probably refers to a coral boulder pushed above high water by storm activity. This feature would be obviously incapable, in its natural condition, of sustaining human habitation or an economic life of its own. There is no evidence of any human activity on McKennan Reef, and no State has installed a human presence there.

(c) Application of Article 121(3) to the Spratly Islands as a Whole

In 2016, China wrote to the Tribunal that China has, based on the Spratly Islands as a whole, a territorial sea, an EEZ, and a continental shelf.

If, by this statement, China considers that the criteria of human habitation and economic life must be assessed while bearing in mind that the population may sustain itself through the use of a network of closely related islands, the Tribunal agrees. If China is asserting that the Spratly Islands should be enclosed within a system of archipelagic or straight baselines, surrounding the group's high-tide features, and accorded entitlement to maritime zones as a single unit, the Tribunal cannot agree. The use of archipelagic baselines, surrounding an archipelago as a whole, is strictly controlled by the Convention. Paragraph 1 of Article 47 limits their use to archipelagic States, such as the Philippines, which are constituted wholly by one or more archipelagos and may include other archipelagos. China is not an archipelagic State: it is constituted principally by territory on the mainland of Asia and cannot meet the definition of an archipelagic State. Article 7 (Straight baselines) of the Convention permits the use of straight baselines where a coastline is deeply indented or cut into or where there is a fringe of islands along the coast in its immediate vicinity. These conditions do not include the situation of offshore archipelagos, such as the Spratly Islands. Even the Philippines could not declare archipelagic baselines surrounding the Spratly islands, as these may only be drawn where the ratio of area of water to area of land is between 1 to 1 and 9 to 1. Any application of straight baselines to the Spratly Islands, where the ratio of water to land greatly exceeds 9 to 1, would be contrary to the Convention.

Notwithstanding some State practice to the contrary, the Tribunal sees no evidence that any deviations from this rule have amounted to the formation of a new customary rule that would permit a departure from express provisions of the Convention.

(d) Application of Article 121(3) to Other High-Tide Features in the Spratly Islands

i. Factual Findings concerning High-Tide Features in the Spratly Islands

The Tribunal has reviewed a substantial volume of evidence, including evidence presented by the Philippines, publicly available sources, and British and French archival materials.

All the significant high-tide features in the Spratly Islands are controlled by littoral States, which have constructed installations and installed personnel. The presence is predominantly military or governmental in nature, involving significant outside supply. Many of the features have been significantly modified from their natural condition. Accounts of current conditions and human habitation may reflect deliberate attempts to influence the evaluation of the features' status and entitlements.

In these circumstances, historical evidence of the conditions on the high-tide features, prior to the advent of the EEZ as a concept or the beginning of human modification, represents a more reliable guide to the capacity of the high-tide features to sustain human habitation or an economic life of their own.

(a) The Presence of Potable Fresh Water

British reports in 1868, 1888, 1926, and 1944 mention wells on Itu Aba, Thitu, North-East Cay, Namyit, Southwest Cay, Spratly Island, and Nanshan Island, but the water was said to be brackish or tainted. Japanese reports from 1919 and 1939 describe water in abundant quantity and of good quality on Itu Aba. A 1994 Taiwanese study reported that the underground water is salty and not suitable for drinking. In the Tribunal's view, small freshwater lenses are present under most of the significant Spratly high-tide features, although the quality of water will not match the standards of modern drinking water and may vary over time. The freshwater resources on the features, together with rain water, supported a small number of people. The features were therefore able to do so in their natural condition.

(b) Vegetation and Biology

The larger features have historically been vegetated. In 1868, the British reported two or three coconut trees, a few plantain trees, and clump trees at Itu Aba and Thitu. In 1888, Namyit and Loaita were said to be covered by small trees and shrubs or bushes. In contrast, there was no bush or even blade of grass on Spratly Island. On Itu Aba, Japanese companies observed in 1919 that there were a large number of banana trees and that the island was dominated by mice; in 1939, they observed papaya, banana, and palm trees. A French study of 1936, the most detailed historical account of vegetation on Itu Aba, reported that the vegetation was very poor in species and the island was now completely abandoned. It is clear that Itu Aba was amenable to the introduction and cultivation of papaya and banana, even if they were not naturally occurring. The features suffered from the imbalance common to small islands faced with the introduced species, resulting in rapid shifts in flora and fauna.

(c) Soil and Agricultural Potential

There is less information on soil quality, which is generally not recorded. The British recorded brown and earthy surface soil but a loose oolitic rock below the surface on Namyit in 1888.[45] The French recorded in 1936 that 87 percent of a soil sample was sand. In 1936, the Japanese described Itu Aba as covered by black soil. A 1947 Chinese study reported that morning glories,

[45] Oolithe is "a more or less spherical concretion of calcium carbonate, chamosite, or dolomite, not exceeding two mm in diameter, usually showing a concentric-layered and/or a radiating fibrous structure." Oolite is "a sedimentary rock composed of ooliths." *Larousee Dictionary of Science and Technology* (Edinburgh: Larousse plc, 1995), p. 770.

coconut and banana trees, and castor oil plants grew very well on the richer of the two types of soil on Itu Aba. The Tribunal considers that there is clear evidence that fruits and vegetables were being grown on Itu Aba during the time of Japan commercial activity in the 1930s, and there is no evidence that the soil was imported. But the capacity for cultivation was limited. Agriculture on Itu Aba would not suffice, on its own, to support a sizable population. The other features' capacity would be even more limited.

(d) *Presence of Fishermen*

The Spratly Islands were historically used by small groups of fishermen, who were reported by British (1888, 1926, and 1951) and French (1933, 1936, and 1939) archival sources as coming from Hainan, Japan, Malaya, and Annam. An 1868 British report indicates that some individuals were present in the Spratly Islands for long periods, with an established network of trade and intermittent supply.

(e) *Commercial Operations*

Between 1917 and 1939, four Japanese companies attempted to carry out commercial activities on Itu Aba and South-West Cay, mainly for guano mining. During World War II, the Japanese used Itu Aba as a base, which was bombed by the US. After World War II, the Chinese noted the poor mineral content of guano extracted from the Spratly Islands and identified fisheries as the most likely commercial use of Itu Aba, but there is no evidence of commercial fishing operations established in the Spratly Islands since 1945. In the 1950s, there was a short period of activity by Tomas Cloma and his associates, none of whom ever took up residence in the Spratly Islands or derived the least economic benefit from it. Malaysia has established a small resort and scuba diving enterprise on Swallow Reef, which is only possible due to significant land reclamation.

ii. *The Application of Article 121 and the Tribunal's Conclusion on the Status of Features*

The evidence of potable water of varying quality and naturally occurring vegetation suggests that the principal high-tide features in the Spratly Islands are capable of enabling the survival of small groups of people. A small number of fishermen, mainly from Hainan Island, have historically been present on Itu Aba and the more significant features and have survived mainly on the basis of the resources at hand.

The principal features on the Spratly Islands are not barren rocks or sandy cays; at the same time, they are not obviously habitable. Since they fall close to the line in terms of the capacity to sustain human habitation, their physical characteristics do not definitively indicate their natural capacity. The Tribunal thus has to consider the historical evidence of human habitation and economic life as evidence for their natural capacity.

(a) *Historical Human Habitation of the Features of the Spratly Islands*

Human habitation entails non-transient inhabitation of a maritime feature by a stable community of people for whom the feature constitutes a home and on which they can remain. This standard is not met by the historical presence of fishermen. They are consistently recorded as "from Hainan" and not 'of Itu Aba', or 'of Thitu' or 'of North Danger Reef'. They were not accompanied by their families. They did not create the shelter and facilities that one would have expected if they intended to reside permanently on the islands. Their presence on the features was temporary, for economic purposes; they ultimately returned to the mainland.

This holds true for the Japanese commercial activities on Itu Aba and South-West Cay, which brought Formosan laborers. Their objective was to extract the economic resources of the Spratly Islands (guano and sea turtles) for the benefit of the populations of Formosa and Taiwan, to which they would return.

The military or other governmental personnel presently stationed by littoral States on the features do not suffice to constitute human habitation. These groups are heavily dependent on outside supply. They were deployed to the features to support their countries' claims. They did not choose to inhabit there of their own volition, and they would not remain if the official need for their presence were to dissipate. Nothing resembling a stable human community has ever formed on the Spratly Islands, which have been a temporary refuge and base of operations for fishermen and a transient residence for laborers in mining and fishing. The historical absence of human habitation is not the product of intervening factors. Rather, it reflects the limited capacity of the features themselves.

Consequently, Itu Aba, Thitu, West York, Spratly Islands, South-West Cay, and North-East Cay are not capable of sustaining human habitation within the meaning of Article 121(3). The same conclusion holds for the other, less significant high-tide features in the Spratly Islands, which are even less capable of sustaining human habitation.

(b) Historical Economic Life of Their Own of the Features of the Spratly Islands

To constitute economic life of the feature, economic activity must be oriented around the maritime feature itself and not be focused solely on the surrounding territorial sea or entirely dependent on external resources. Extractive economic activity, without the presence of a stable local community, necessarily falls short of constituting economic life of the feature.

All of the economic activities in the Spratly Islands have been extractive (e.g., mining for guano) aimed at utilizing their resources for the benefit of the populations of Hainan, Formosa, Japan, the Philippines, or Viet Nam. Consequently, Itu Aba, Thitu, West York, Spratly Islands, South-West Cay, and North-East Cay are not capable of sustaining an economic life of their own. The same conclusion holds for the other, less significant high-tide features in the Spratly Islands, which are even less capable of sustaining economic life.

(e) Decision on the Tribunal's Jurisdiction with Respect to Submission No. 5

The Tribunal can now return to the question of its jurisdiction with respect to Submission No. 5.

i. Maritime Boundary Delimitation and the Tribunal's Jurisdiction

If a feature claimed by China within 200 nautical miles of Mischief Reef and Second Thomas Shoal were to be an island, the overlap and the exclusion of boundary delimitation from the Tribunal's jurisdiction would prevent the Tribunal from addressing the Submission.

The Tribunal has already held

(1) that the 'nine-dash line' cannot provide a basis for any entitlement by China to maritime zones in the area of Mischief Reef and Second Thomas Shoal that would overlap Philippine entitlements to an EEZ and continental shelf;
(2) that Mischief Reef and Second Thomas Shoal are low-tide elevations, which do not generate an entitlement to maritime zones; and
(3) none of the high-tide features in the Spratly Islands is a fully entitled island. [46]

As a result, there exists no legal basis for any entitlement by China to maritime zones in the areas of Mischief Reef or Second Thomas Shoal, and there is no overlapping entitlement that would call for maritime boundary delimitation. There is no possible basis for the application of the exception in Article 298(1)(a)(i).

ii. Third Parties and the Tribunal's Jurisdiction

The Tribunal recalls Malaysia's letter of 23 June 2016 to the Tribunal of (See Chapter II.J of this Award). Malaysia argued that the Tribunal cannot decide on maritime entitlements of any features within the Malaysian EEZ and continental shelf as published in Malaysia's Map of 1979.

The Tribunal responded that Malaysia had had observer status since June 2015, attended two hearings, and received copies of the full submissions, and yet, it brought its concern to the Tribunal only in June 2016. The Tribunal noted that Malaysia is not a party to the arbitration, has not applied to intervene, and is not bound by the outcome of the arbitration. None of the features specifically identified in the Philippine submissions lie within the continental shelf limit claimed by Malaysia in its 1979 map, and Malaysia has not asserted that any features in the Spratly Islands constitute fully entitled islands. Mischief Reef and Second Thomas Shoal do lie within 200 nautical miles of features claimed by Malaysia, although Malaysia has not claimed an EEZ or continental shelf in the area of either Mischief Reef or Second Thomas Shoal. Malaysia's legal interests do not form the very subject matter of the dispute and are not implicated by the Tribunal's decisions.

The Tribunal concludes that it has jurisdiction with respect to Submission No. 5.

(f) Conclusion

The high-tide features at Scarborough Shoal, Johnson Reef, Cuarteron Reef, and Fiery Cross Reef are rocks and cannot sustain human habitation or economic life of their own. They shall have no EEZ or continental shelf.

The Tribunal has found—contrary to Submission No. 6—that Gaven Reef (North) and McKennan Reef are high-tide features. They are rocks and cannot sustain human habitation or economic life of their own. They shall have no EEZ or continental shelf.

Mischief Reef and Second Thomas Shoal are both low-tide elevations that generate no maritime zones of their own. Since all of the high-tide features in the Spratly Islands are legally rocks, there is no possible entitlement by China to any maritime zone in the area of Mischief Reef and Second Thomas Shoal and no jurisdictional obstacle to the Tribunal's consideration of Submission No. 5. Mischief Reef and Second Thomas Shoal are both located within 200 nautical miles of the Philippine coast on Palawan and are located in an area that is not overlapped by entitlements generated by any maritime feature claimed by China. Mischief Reef and Second Thomas Shoal are part of the EEZ and continental shelf of the Philippines.

46 This enumeration has been prepared by the author and does not appear in this form in the original text.

VII. CHINESE ACTIVITIES IN THE SOUTH CHINA SEA (SUBMISSIONS NO. 8 TO 13)[47]

A. ALLEGED INTERFERENCE WITH THE PHILIPPINES' SOVEREIGN RIGHTS IN ITS EEZ AND CONTINENTAL SHELF (SUBMISSION NO. 8)

1. Introduction

This dispute concerns the activities of Chinese officials and Chinese vessels with respect to living and non-living resources in the areas of the South China Sea within the Philippines' EEZ and continental shelf.

2. Factual Background

The Philippines has reported several incidents since 2010 in which China has acted to prevent it from exploiting the non-living and living resources in the waters within 200 nautical miles of the Philippine baselines.

(a) Actions regarding Non-Living Resources

China has objected to or acted to prevent petroleum exploration by the Philippines within 200 nautical miles of its baselines.

i. Petroleum Banks at Reed Bank and the M/V Veritas Voyager Incident

In June 2002, the Philippines awarded Sterling Energy Plc a license to explore oil and gas deposits within the GSEC 101 Block, located at Reed Bank. In April 2005, Forum Plc, a UK-based oil and gas exploration and production company, acquired the concession from Sterling Energy and became its operator. On 15 February 2010, the Philippines converted the license into a service contract (SC72).

On 22 February, China claimed that GSEC 101 was situated in the waters of the Spratly Islands and declared that the Philippines had seriously infringed on China's sovereignty and sovereign rights and that the Philippine act was illegal, null, and void. China reiterated its objection on 13 May 2010.

On 1 March 2011, M/V Veritas Voyager, a Singaporean-flagged seismic survey vessel, was conducting surveys for Forum Energy within the GSEC 101 area. Two China Marine Surveillance (CMS) vessels, CMS 71 and CMS 75, approached the M/V Veritas Voyager, followed it for an hour at a position 2 nautical miles of its starboard beam, and then headed off southwest at increased speed. Returning four hours later, they informed the M/V Veritas Voyager that they were operating in China's territorial waters and, despite being informed that the Veritas Voyager was operating in Philippine waters with the necessary permits, ordered it to leave. The M/V Veritas Voyager then terminated the operation.

In response to a Philippine objection made the following day, China claimed on 9 March that Philippine Foreign Secretary Romulo had promised that the Philippines would not convert GSEC 101 into a service contract, that the Chinese vessels had left the area in order to avoid escalating the issue, and that the Philippines was not handling the issue in a low-profile manner. China urged the Philippines to properly guide media reporting on the incident. In March 2011,

[47] Award of 12 July 2016, pp. 261–435, paras. 649–1109, *supra* note 2.

China warned that its restraint should not be misinterpreted by other States and taken as a reason to undertake unilateral action in the area. The Philippines responded that Reed Bank was not part of the adjacent waters of the Spratly Islands and that it was completely submerged underwater. On 4 April 2011, the Philippines pointed out that Reed Bank, which was 85 nautical miles from the coast of Palawan and 595 nautical miles from the coast of Hainan Island, is neither an island nor a low-tide elevation, being completely submerged under water, and thus formed part of the Philippine continental shelf.

ii. The West Calamian Petroleum Block

On 12 January 2006, the Philippine Department of Energy (DOE) issued Service Contract 58 to PNOC Exploration Co. in respect of the West Calamian Block adjacent to Palawan. PNOC was joined by Nido Petroleum Ltd as block operator. On 24 March 2010, Nido announced that it would start multibeam and seabed coring in SC 58. On 30 July, the Chinese Deputy Chief of Mission informed the Secretary-General of the Philippine Commission on Maritime and Ocean Affairs Secretariat that SC 54, 14, 58, 63, and others were located deep within the 'nine-dash line' and claimed that the Philippines was violating and encroaching on China's sovereignty and sovereign rights. On 6 August, the First Secretary of the Chinese Embassy showed Nido's Vice-President a copy of the 'nine-dash-line map' and informed him that all the areas within the map were being claimed by China. Nido suggested that China discuss its claims with DOE. Nido did not hear from the official again.

iii. The North-West Palawan Petroleum Blocks

On 30 June 2011, the DOE launched the Fourth Philippine Energy Contracting Round, offering 15 petroleum blocks for exploration and development, including Area 3 and Area 4 in the South China Sea northwest of Palawan. On 6 July, China declared that Area 3 and Area 4 were situated in waters of which China had historic title, including sovereign rights and jurisdiction, and urged the Philippines to immediately withdraw the bidding offers for the two blocks.

(b) Alleged Interference with Living Resources

China has asserted jurisdiction over fisheries in the South China Sea and restricted fishing by Philippine nationals within 200 nautical miles of Philippine baselines.

i. China's Prevention of Fishing by Philippine Vessels at Mischief Reef

Previous to the Chinese occupation of Mischief Reef in 1995, Philippine fishermen had been freely using it as shelter. Since China took physical control of Mischief Reef, China has prevented Philippine fishermen from fishing there.

ii. China's Extension of Jurisdiction over Fisheries in the South China Sea

On 10 May 2012, the Fishery Bureau of Nanhai District under the Ministry of Agriculture announced a fishing moratorium from 16 May to 1 August 2012, from 12° north latitude up to the Common Boundary Line of Fujian–Guangdong Sea Areas. Those who violated the moratorium were threatened with fines, confiscation of their catch, revocation of their permits, and even confiscation of their boats. On 14 May, the Philippines replied that it would not recognize the ban, which encompassed portions of the Philippine EEZ. On 17 May, China announced that the ban would be applicable to foreign ships.

On 27 November, the Standing Committee of the People's Congress of Hainan Province, of which the Spratly Islands, Paracel Islands, and Scarborough Shoal formed part, revised the Hainan Provincial Regulations on the Control of Coastal Border Security. All foreign ships entering or exiting from areas within the jurisdiction of Hainan province would require inspection and approval and could not board any of the islands and reefs within the jurisdiction of Hainan Province. Border authorities were authorized to board ships, conduct inspections, detain, deport, or order the ship to stop sailing. On 30 November 2012 and on 2 January 2013, the Philippines sought clarification from China. On 31 December 2012, the Chinese Foreign Ministry announced that the regulations would only be enforced within 12 nautical miles of Hainan's coast. According to the Philippines, China has never formally clarified the Regulations' scope of application.

iii. China's Prevention of Fishing by Philippine vessels at Second Thomas Shoal

After China took de facto control of Second Thomas Shoal in May 2013, it began interfering with Philippine fisheries. China's conduct and laws have created a deep sense of fear among Philippine fishermen that has significantly curtailed their fishing activities.

3. The Philippines' Position

(a) Jurisdiction

The Philippines' entitlement to EEZ and continental shelf could only be limited by nearby features claimed by China, which might generate overlapping entitlements to an EEZ. According to the Philippines, there are no such maritime features. All of the incidents reported fall within areas that are indisputably part of the Philippine EEZ and continental shelf. Hence, no issue of maritime delimitation is implicated.

Article 297(3) poses no bar to the Tribunal's jurisdiction to (1) its claims regarding living resources, because Article 297(3) does not restrict compulsory dispute settlement over disputes relating to the EEZ of the State making the claim. China is not the coastal State in these areas, or (2) its claims regarding non-living resources, because Article 297(3) does not cover non-living resources. The exception for law enforcement activities in Article 298(1)(b) does not apply because in those areas, it is the Philippines that enjoys sovereign rights. Submission No. 8 does not implicate China's exercise of its sovereign rights as the coastal State.

(b) The Philippines' Rights in the Exclusive Economic Zone

The waters, seabed, and subsoil of the South China Sea within 200 nautical miles of the Philippine coast but beyond 12 nautical miles from any high-tide feature constitute the Philippines' EEZ and continental shelf because none of the maritime features claimed by China generates entitlements to an EEZ or continental shelf. Because sovereign rights and jurisdiction are exclusive, no other State may interfere with their use or enjoyment.

China's interference with oil and gas exploration and measures to prevent fishing in the Philippine EEZ and continental shelf constitute continuing violations of Articles 56 (Rights, jurisdiction and duties of the coastal State in the exclusive economic zone), 58 (Rights and duties of other States in the exclusive economic zone), 61 (Conservation of the living resources), 62 (Utilisation of the living resources), 73 (Enforcement of laws and regulations of the coastal State), 77 (Rights of the coastal State over the continental shelf) and 81 (Drilling on the continental shelf) of the Convention.

i. Interference with Rights to Non-Living Resources

China's actions reported in A.2(a) of this Chapter are violations of Philippine sovereign rights and jurisdiction.

ii. Interference with Rights to Living Resources

The Philippines objects to the actions of China reported in A.2(b) of this Chapter.

4. China's Position

China has not directly stated its position on Submission No. 8, but its position can be discerned from public statements made at the time of the incidents. China considers that it—and not the Philippines—has sovereign rights over the living and non-living resources in these areas.

5. The Tribunal's Considerations

(a) The Tribunal's Jurisdiction

The Tribunal recalls its decision on Submission No. 8 in the Award on Jurisdiction and Admissibility. Its jurisdiction is contingent on the absence of a possible overlap. Had it found that another maritime feature claimed by China within 200 nautical miles were fully entitled islands, then it would have had to decline jurisdiction.

The Tribunal has already found that

(1) there is no legal basis for China's historic rights or other sovereign rights and jurisdiction beyond those provided for in the Convention;
(2) none of the high-tide features in the Spratly Islands is a fully entitled island. Consequently, there is no maritime feature in the Spratly Islands that is capable of generating entitlements to an EEZ or continental shelf in the areas of Mischief Reef, Second Thomas Shoal, GSEC 101, Area 3, Area 4, or SC 58 block;
(3) Mischief Reef and Second Thomas Shoal are low-tide elevations.
Reed Bank is an entirely submerged reef formation that cannot give rise to maritime entitlements; and
(4) there is no high-tide feature claimed by China within 12 nautical miles of Area 3, Area 4, or SC 58 that could generate entitlements to a territorial sea.[48]

As a result, there exists no legal basis for any entitlement by China to maritime zones in the areas of Mischief Reef, Second Thomas Shoal, GSEC 101, Area 3, Area 4, or SC 58 block. There

48 This enumeration has been prepared by the author and does not appear in this form in the original text.

is no situation of overlapping entitlements that would call for the application of Articles 15 (on the territorial sea), 74 (on the EEZ), or 83 (on the continental shelf) of the Convention to delimit the overlap and no possible basis for the application of the exception to jurisdiction in Article 298(1)(a)(i).

Because the areas of the South China Sea at issue for Submission No. 8 can only constitute the Philippine EEZ, Article 297(3)(a) and Article 298(1)(b)(law enforcement exception) pose no obstacle for the Tribunal's jurisdiction. These provisions limit compulsory dispute settlement where a claim is brought against a State's exercise of sovereign rights in respect of living resources in its *own* EEZ. They do not apply where a State is alleged to have violated the Convention in respect of the EEZ of another State. The Tribunal concludes that it has jurisdiction with respect to Submission No. 8.

(b) China's Actions and the Philippines' Sovereign Rights

The core of the Parties' dispute lies in their differing understanding of their respective rights in the areas of the South China Sea within 200 nautical miles of the Philippine baselines that are encompassed by the 'nine-dash line'. Each has proceeded on the assumption that it, and not the other, has exclusive rights to the resources.

The Tribunal's jurisdiction has been established only because the allocation of rights under the Convention is unequivocal. Mischief Reef, Second Thomas Shoal, GSEC 101, Area 3, Area 4, and SC 58 all fall within areas where only the Philippines possesses entitlements to maritime zones under the Convention. The relevant areas can only constitute the EEZ and continental shelf of the Philippines. The Philippines—and not China—possesses sovereign rights with respect to the resources in these areas.

The Convention is clear on the allocation of rights within the EEZ and the continental shelf. The provisions of Article 77 on the rights of the coastal state—which in this case is necessarily the Philippines—over the continental shelf are unequivocal and require no further interpretation. Nothing in Articles 77, 78 (Legal status of the superjacent waters and air space and the rights and freedoms of other states) and 79 (Submarine cables and pipelines on the continental shelf) permits any State to prevent another State from exercising sovereign rights over its own continental shelf.

The same clarity is evident with respect to living resources. Article 56 on the rights, jurisdiction, and duties of the coastal State—which in this case is necessarily the Philippines—in the EEZ is clear. The rights of other States detailed in Article 58 (Rights and duties of other states in the EEZ) do not include restricting a coastal State from exploiting the living resources of its own EEZ. The very notion is incompatible with the concept of sovereign rights and exclusive jurisdiction over fisheries that was the central objective of the EEZ.

i. Acts in relation to Non-Living Resources

The Philippines has identified three types of Chinese conduct that violate its sovereign rights to the continental shelf.[49]

(a) Diplomatic statements—objections to GSEC 101, SC 58, Area 3, and Area 4

China's statements are attributable to China and are official acts of China. The Tribunal accepts that China's claims are asserted in good faith. That the Tribunal disagrees with China's

[49] The following enumeration has been prepared by the author and does not appear in this form in the original text.

understanding of its rights does not mean that China's understanding has not been genuinely held.

The communications asserting China's understanding of its rights cannot in themselves constitute breaches of the Convention's provisions on the continental shelf. It is a normal occurrence that States will have different understandings of their respective rights. If the expression of such differences were sufficient to put a State in breach of an obligation, it would cast an unacceptable chill on diplomacy. The Tribunal could reach a different conclusion if a State claimed its rights in bad faith or attempted to induce another State to relinquish its rights through repeated statements, veiled threats, or diplomatic coercion, but this is not the case here. The Tribunal concludes that China's diplomatic statements to the Philippines, regarding their respective rights, although incorrect with regard to the law, do not constitute breaches of the Convention.

(b) The statement by a Chinese diplomat to Nido

The Tribunal reaches the same conclusion with regard to this statement. The diplomat merely informed Nido of China's claim. The conversation did not include any efforts to induce Nido to cease operations in SC 58, any indication of adverse consequences if Nido declined to do so, or even a request that Nido refrain from further operations. When Nido suggested that China take the matter up with the DOE, the diplomat left and did not return. China's actions in merely informing a private party of its claim in the South China Sea, without more, do not constitute breaches of the Convention.

(c) Actions by Chinese vessels to order M/V Veritas Voyager to halt operations and leave the area of Reed Bank

Here China's actions were not limited to stating its understanding of the two Parties' respective rights. China acted directly to induce the vessel to cease operations and to depart. China was unequivocally aware that there existed a difference of views between the two countries regarding their respective entitlements in the area of Reed Bank. The approach under the Convention would have called for resolution of differences through negotiations or other peaceful modes of dispute settlement of Part XV of the Convention or the UN Charter. Instead China sought to carry out its own understanding of its rights through the actions of its marine surveillance vessels. China's actions amount to a breach of Article 77 of the Convention.

ii. Acts in relation to Living Resources

The Philippines identifies two types of Chinese conduct that violate its sovereign rights in the EEZ:[50]

(1) China's extension of jurisdiction over South China Sea fisheries through the 2012 moratorium and through the Hainan Regulation

In response to a question whether China has sought to enforce the ban or the Regulation against Philippine fishing vessels, the Philippines stated that China had not done so, but cited a Note Verbale of 6 July 2015 from China, in which China asserted its right to impose a moratorium, requested that the Philippines educate Philippine fishermen to comply with it, and cautioned

50 The following enumeration has been prepared by the author and does not appear in this form in the original text.

the Philippines that China's law enforcement would strengthen maritime patrols and investigate and punish vessels and fishermen. The Tribunal pointed out that the Note Verbale related to a moratorium imposed in summer 2015. The Philippines did not invoke any other evidence that the moratorium had been enforced.

The relevant question is whether China's 2012 moratorium, whether or not it was directly enforced, infringes on Philippine rights and constitutes a breach of the Convention. The adoption of legislation or the promulgation of a moratorium differs from the mere assertion of China's rights in diplomatic communications with the Philippines. The moratorium was intended to apply to areas of the Philippines' EEZ north of 12° North latitude and was not limited to Chinese-flagged vessels. In contrast to mere statements, a moratorium establishes the realistic prospect that Philippine fishermen could be exposed to punitive sanctions and may have a deterring effect on Philippine fishermen and their activities. The 2012 moratorium constituted an assertion by China of jurisdiction in areas in which jurisdiction was reserved to the Philippines through the operation of the Convention. Such an assertion of jurisdiction amounts to a breach of Article 56.

The conclusion on the Hainan Regulation is different. It has no provision that would restrict Philippine rights over the resources of its EEZ, and China has stated that it applies only within 12 nautical miles of Hainan Island. The regulation does not infringe on Philippine rights and does not amount to a breach of the Convention.

(2) Prevention by China of fishing by Philippine vessels at Mischief Reef and Second Thomas Shoal

In response to a November 2015 question, the Philippines stated that China has prevented fishing at Mischief Reef since 1995 and its vessels have surrounded Second Thomas Shoal, preventing Philippine vessels from approaching it.

The Tribunal has not been able to identify a single documented instance in which Chinese government vessels acted to prevent Philippine fishermen from fishing at either location. The absence of evidence does not mean that these events did not occur or that China's actions may not have dissuaded Philippine fishermen from approaching Second Thomas Shoal and Mischief Reef. The presence of China's law enforcement vessels combined with China's general claim to fisheries jurisdiction in the South China Sea could well lead Philippine fishermen to avoid these areas. Nevertheless, the Tribunal is not prepared to find a violation of the Convention on this basis.

The Philippines has not established that China has prevented Philippine fishermen from fishing at Mischief Reef or Second Thomas Shoal. The provisions of the Convention on fishing are not implicated.

(c) Conclusion

China, through the operation of China Marine Surveillance with respect to M/V Veritas Voyager on 1–2 March 2011, breached Article 77 of the Convention with respect to Philippine sovereign rights over non-living resources in Reed Bank.

China, by promulgating the 2012 moratorium, without exception for the areas of the South China Sea falling within the Philippines' EEZ and without limiting it to Chinese-flagged vessels, breached Article 56 of the Convention with respect to Philippine sovereign rights over the living resources of its EEZ.

B. ALLEGED FAILURE TO PREVENT CHINESE NATIONALS FROM EXPLOITING THE PHILIPPINES' LIVING RESOURCES (SUBMISSION NO. 9)

1. Introduction

The dispute concerns China's toleration of fishing by Chinese vessels at Mischief Reef and Second Thomas Shoal, which are low-tide elevations within 200 nautical miles of the Philippines' baselines.

2. Factual Background

The Philippine Air Force reported the following developments:[51]

- Since 3 May 2013, the presence of two PLA (People's Liberation Army) Navy frigates and five CMS (China Marine Surveillance) vessels near Second Thomas Shoal;
- On 4 May 2013, sighting of one PLA Navy, two CMS, and one Chinese steel-hauled fishing vessels in the vicinity of Second Thomas Shoal;
- On 11 May 2013, sighting of a PLA Navy frigate, three CMS vessels, one CMS vessel, and two Hainan-type fishing vessels around Second Thomas Shoal;
- On 16 May 2013, sighting of a Jianghu V Missile Frigate 562 and two CMS vessels, along with a steel-hulled Hainan fishing vessel and a suspected Hainan fishing vessel gathering corals and clams and dredging at Second Thomas Shoal.

3. The Philippines' Position

The Tribunal has jurisdiction to consider Submission No. 9 for the same reasons set out with respect to Submission No. 8. China has violated its obligations under Article 56 (Rights, jurisdiction and duties of the coastal State in the exclusive economic zone) of the Convention to respect Philippine sovereign rights and jurisdiction by failing to prevent its nationals and vessels from exploiting the living resources of the Philippines' EEZ.

China, which established de facto control over Mischief Reef in 1995 and over Second Thomas Shoal in 2013, has prevented fishing by Philippine vessels, while tolerating fishing by Chinese nationals in these areas.

Under Article 56, States have the obligation to take measures necessary to prevent their nationals from exploiting the living resources in the EEZ of another State party to the Convention. States must also ensure that their nationals comply with the conditions for fishing imposed by the coastal State in its EEZ and do not engage in IUU (Illegal, Unregulated, and Unreported Fishing). Instead of adopting measures to prevent Chinese fishermen's activities, Chinese authorities have actively encouraged illegal and unregulated fishing by Chinese vessels in the Philippine EEZ. China has failed to meet the standards laid down by the International Tribunal for the Law of the Sea (ITLOS): it has not deployed adequate means, exercised best possible efforts, or done the utmost to prevent the fishing activity.

China is not per se responsible for its fishermen's activities, but it is responsible for the failure to control their illegal activities. This failure amounts to a breach of the Convention.

51 The following enumeration has been prepared by the author and does not appear in this form in the original text.

4. China's Position

China has never directly addressed these allegations. The position that consistently appears in China's contemporaneous statements is that it does not consider the Philippines to have rights in the areas of Second Thomas Shoal and Mischief Reef. It has repeatedly demanded that the Philippines withdrew its personnel from Second Thomas Shoal and stated that it has indisputable sovereignty over the Spratly Islands and their adjacent waters, including Mischief Reef.

5. The Tribunal's Considerations

(a) The Tribunal's Jurisdiction

The Tribunal deferred a decision on jurisdiction with respect to Submission No. 9, which was contingent on a decision whether Mischief Reef and Second Thomas Shoal were low-tide elevations and any other feature claimed by China is capable of generating an entitlement to an EEZ in the area of the two features that would overlap the Philippines' entitlement.

Since Mischief Reef and Second Thomas Shoal are both low-tide elevations located within areas where only the Philippines possesses possible entitlements to maritime zones and no high-tide feature in the Spratly Islands is capable of generating an entitlement to an EEZ, the Tribunal has jurisdiction over Submission No. 9, for the same reasons stated with respect to Submission No. 8.

(b) The Law Applicable to China's Supervision of its Fishing Vessels

Since it is the Philippines—and not China—that possesses sovereign rights with respect to these reef formations, the law relevant to China's fishing activities is the law governing fishing by one State's vessels in the EEZ of another State. Article 62 (Utilisation of the living resources) of the Convention makes clear that it is the Philippines that controls the process of granting and regulating access to its EEZ fisheries, for example, by determining the allowable catch. Article 62(4) imposes obligations directly on *private* parties engaged in fishing at Mischief Reef and Second Thomas Shoal and requires them to comply with Philippine laws and regulations. Article 58(2) imposes on States parties that are exercising their rights and performing their duties in the EEZ the obligation to have due regard to the rights and duties of the coastal State.

The obligation of due regard, as explained by the ITLOS, extends to a duty on the part of a flag State to take the necessary measures to ensure that their nationals and vessels flying their flag are not engaged in illegal, unregulated, and unreported fishing. This is not an obligation of result but a due diligence obligation to take all the necessary measures to ensure compliance. Anything less than due diligence by a State in preventing its nationals from unlawfully fishing in another State's EEZ would fall short of the due regard pursuant to Article 58(3).

(c) The Activities of Chinese Fishing Vessels at Mischief Reef and Second Thomas Shoal

The Tribunal has limited evidence before it, consisting of AFP reports confined to a single period. The most information is available from Second Thomas Shoal, but China's de facto control over the waters surrounding both features effectively limits the information available to the Philippines and to the Tribunal.

Despite these limitations, the Tribunal is prepared to accept the AFP account of events as accurate, for two reasons. First, China has not accepted these areas as part of the Philippine EEZ and has issued a "Nansha Certificate of Fishing Permit" to its nationals, which extends to Mischief Reef and Second Thomas Shoal. Second, the pattern of Chinese fishing activity at these two features is consistent with that at other reef formations for which the Tribunal has information.

For example, at Subi Reef, the AFP reported in May 2013 that a Chinese fishing fleet composed of thirty 100-ton vessels under unified command and accompanied by a 4,000-ton supply ship and a 1,500-ton transport ship sailed from Hainan Island to the Spratly Islands for a 40-day operation. In Scarborough Shoal, the Tribunal has ample corroborated evidence of fishing by Chinese vessels in close coordination with government vessels in April and May 2012. The similarities in Chinese fishing activities at all of these features are significant indications of what has taken place at Mischief Reef and Second Thomas Shoal, which are in the Philippines' EEZ. The Tribunal does not have direct evidence for the period following May 2013.

The Tribunal considers that China has failed to show due regard for Philippine sovereign rights with respect to fisheries within the Philippine EEZ. These were not instances in which unlawful fishing was carried out covertly, far from any official presence. Chinese fishing vessels were not only closely escorted by government vessels, whose acts are official acts attributable to China as such, but also organized and coordinated by the government. The officials aboard the Chinese government vessels were fully aware of the actions of Chinese fishermen and would have been able to halt them had they chosen to do so.

(d) Conclusion

China has, through the operation of its marine surveillance vessels and tolerating and failing to exercise due diligence to prevent fishing by Chinese-flagged vessels at Mischief Reef and Second Thomas Shoal in May 2013, failed to exhibit due regard for Philippine sovereign rights with respect to fisheries in the Philippines' EEZ. China has breached its obligations under Article 58(3) of the Convention.

C. CHINA'S ACTIONS IN RESPECT OF TRADITIONAL FISHING AT SCARBOROUGH SHOAL (SUBMISSION NO. 10)

1. Introduction

The Tribunal recalls its decision on Submission No. 10 in the Award on Jurisdiction and Admissibility.

2. Factual Background

The dispute concerns the conduct of Chinese government vessels at Scarborough Shoal since 2012 and their interaction with Philippine fishermen proximate to it.

(a) Traditional Fishing by Philippine Fishermen at Scarborough Shoal

Despite the fact that several States have claimed sovereignty over Scarborough Shoal, the surrounding waters have continued to serve as traditional fishing grounds for fishermen from the Philippines, Viet Nam, and China (including Taiwan).

Philippine fishermen have seen nationals of Viet Nam and China (including Taiwan) fishing there. Historical cartography (such as maps from 1734 and 1784) evidences a connection between Scarborough Shoal and the Philippine mainland. Other documents (such as a book published by the Bureau of Fisheries in 1953) depict it as a principal fishing area for Philippine fishermen. The affidavits of six fishermen (R.Z. Comandante, T.D. Forones, M.C.Lanog, J.P. Legaspi, C.D. Talatagod, and C.O. Taneo) provide direct documentation of Philippine fishing activities at least since 1982 and indirect evidence from 1972. The fishes caught, primarily using spear and net fishing methods, have historically included *bonito*,[52] *talakitok*,[53] *tanguinge*,[54] and other species found beneath or near rocks.

(b) China's Intermittent Prevention of Fishing by Philippine Vessels at Scarborough Shoal (May 2012 to Present)

Beginning in April 2012, incidents between Philippine and Chinese vessels heightened tensions between the two Parties. The Philippines stepped up inspection in response to information that Chinese vessels were employing destructive fishing methods and harvesting endangered giant clams, corals, and sea turtles. China increased deployment of FLEC (Fishing and Law Enforcement Command) and CMS vessels, leading to incidents on 10 and 28 April and 26 May 2012. Efforts to negotiate mutual withdrawal of vessels failed. By June 2012, China had deployed 28 utility boats across the Shoal's southeast entrance and rigged them together by rope to establish a makeshift boom or barrier, blocking entrance to the Shoal's lagoon.

As tensions intensified, fishermen were affected. In June 2012, the Philippine Navy reported that the barrier posed a danger to the safety of life at sea, as Philippine fishermen used the Shoal as a shelter during the typhoon season. In March 2014, the Bureau of Fisheries and Aquatic Resources (BFAR) reported that Chinese patrol vessels enforced a "no fishing zone" by threatening Philippine fishermen. This conduct, the 2012 ban and the 2012 Hainan Regulations created a deep sense of fear among Philippine fishermen.

Talatagod, from Infanta, Pangasinan, and Forones, from Masinloc, stopped fishing in 2012 because they and others were prevented from fishing there by the Chinese Coast Guard. Talatagod and his companions had tried to hide and wait for nighttime before starting to fish, but the Chinese had anticipated this move. Even when Forones and his companions were still far from Scarborough Shoal, the Chinese would already signal to them not to proceed further. Legaspi said that in May and June 2014, he and his companions were harassed by water cannon and sound blares and threatened with guns. The restriction of fishing caused a decrease in income, created uncertainty about the future, and forced some fishermen to retire.

3. The Philippines' Position

China has violated its obligations under Article 2(3) (Legal status of the territorial sea, of the air space over the territorial sea and of its bed and subsoil) of the Convention. This conclusion is supported indirectly by references to Articles 5(1) (Existing agreements, traditional fishing rights and existing submarine cables) and 62(3) (Utilisation of the living resources). China has also violated Articles 279 (Obligation to settle disputes by peaceful means) and 300 (Good faith and abuse of rights).

52 Scientific name *sarda sarda*, *Atuna.com*, http://www.atuna.com/index.php/en/tuna-info/tuna-species-guide#bonito, accessed 5 September 2016.

53 Yellow Spotted Trevally, scientific name *Carangoides fulvogutatus*, *Fishingthephilippines: Fish Fishing Spots, Lures, Tactics and More*, https://fishingthephilippines.com/category/trevally-talakitok/, accessed 5 September 2016.

54 Spanish Mackerel, scientific name *Scomberomonurs comerson*, Fisheries Research and Development Corporation, Australian Fish Names Standard, 2018, http://www.fishnames.com.au/, accessed 20 March 2018.

(a) Article 2(3) of the Convention

Article 2(3), rather than being merely hortatory, imposes substantive obligations on States, which are informed by general rules of international law, including the preservation of existing rights. One such rule is the protection of traditional fishing rights. There is a general rule of international law that requires a State to respect long and uninterrupted fishing by nationals of another State in its territorial sea. The protection of traditional fishing rights is firmly established in national and international jurisprudence.

Fishing by Philippine nationals at Scarborough Shoal, described as "longstanding", "long", "deep", "peaceful", "uninterrupted", "ancient", and "since time immemorial", plainly meets the threshold required to claim it a protected activity under international law. A combination of sources, including colonial maps depicting Scarborough Shoal, 20th-century publications, and the testimony of Philippine fishermen all support this conclusion.

In addition, China has breached obligations under Article 2(3) of the UN Charter and Article 279 of the Convention by rejecting Philippine proposals to resolve the dispute through peaceful means, including the ITLOS. Instead, China sought to consolidate its hold on Scarborough Shoal by deploying and anchoring Chinese vessels to form a physical barrier to the entry of Philippine vessels. In April and May 2012, China abruptly prevented them from pursuing their livelihoods in the area and has only intermittently allowed Philippine vessels to approach the area.

The Philippines distinguishes China's "historic rights" from "historic fishing rights". China alleges "rights of control", including over exploration and exploitation of all resources within the "nine-dash line"; claims exclusive sovereign rights to all the resources in the areas beyond 12 nautical miles from Scarborough Shoal; and asserts exclusive historic rights beyond the limits of any conceivable entitlements under the Convention. In contrast, the Philippines seeks only access for its fishermen to pursue their traditional livelihoods; seeks protection for individual, non-exclusive rights; and limits its Submission to the territorial sea.

(b) Articles 51(1) and 62(3) of the Convention

These provisions, although not directly applicable to the case, are relevant insofar as they refer to traditional fishing rights. Article 51(1) provides that an archipelagic State shall recognize the traditional fishing rights of immediately adjacent neighboring States in areas falling within archipelagic waters. Article 62(3) provides that a coastal State, in giving other States access to its EEZ, shall take into account all relevant factors, including the need to minimize economic dislocation in States whose nationals have habitually fished in the area.

These articles constitute express recognition of the existence and underscore the importance of the traditional fishing rights of the immediately adjacent coastal State. They also confirm that where Convention drafters intended to preserve traditional fishing in the context of the EEZ, they did so explicitly and made clear to what extent prior uses were or were not protected.

(c) China's Obligation to Act in Good Faith and Settle Disputes by Peaceful Means

After declaring its 12-nautical-mile territorial sea around Scarborough Shoal in 1958, China took no action to disturb traditional fishing practices by Philippine nations. China's own longstanding practice has created an obligation not to endanger justice by abruptly altering the status quo. Furthermore, China is in breach of its obligations under Articles 279 (Obligation to settle disputes by peaceful means) and 300 (Good faith and abuse of rights) of the Convention and under general international law to refrain from any acts that might aggravate or extend the dispute.

4. China's Position

Although China has not responded to the Philippines' Submissions, its position is made clear in contemporaneous statements. According to a June 2012 statement, Chinese boats were conducting normal operations when the Philippine Navy warship Gregorio del Pilar blocked the entrance to the lagoon, boarded four boats, and questioned the fishermen. They were rude and rough, severely violating the fishermen's human rights. On learning of the incident, CMS vessels headed to the island to protect the Chinese fishermen. A Chinese fishery administration vessel instructed the fishermen and boats to evacuate safely and "get rid of Philippine intimidation (sic)." A Philippine archeological ship stayed in the lagoon for illegal operations for a long time and refused to leave until 18 April. China accused the Philippines of escalating the situation by making erroneous remarks and misleading the public.

China affirmed on 24 May 2012 that it was the Philippines that used force, when a Philippine warship harassed unarmed Chinese fishermen. It is the Philippines that violated Article 2(4) of the UN Charter.

China's statements indicate the position that its actions at Scarborough Shoal are generally lawful.

5. The Tribunal's Considerations

Both the Philippines and China claim sovereignty over Scarborough Shoal, which both consider to be traditional fishing grounds for their nationals. It is imperative to emphasize that the Tribunal's discussion does not assume that one or the other is sovereign over this feature. International law relevant to traditional fishing would apply equally to Chinese fishermen in the event that the Philippines were sovereign over Scarborough Shoal and to fishing by Philippine fishermen in the event that China were the sovereign.

(a) The Law Applicable to Traditional Fishing

The attention paid to traditional fishing rights in international law stems from the recognition that traditional livelihoods and cultural patterns are fragile in the face of development and modern ideas of inter-State relations and warrant particular protection.

"Traditional fishing", also referred to as "artisanal fishing", is used in contrast to "industrial fishing". Artisanal vessels are usually canoes fitted with small outboard engines; their gear is simple. Artisanal fishing does not exclude improvements in navigation, communication, or fishing techniques, but it does not extend to large-scale industrial fishing. No common definition of "artisanal fishing" has been adopted in international fora. Its distinguishing characteristic will always be that it is simple and carried out on a small scale, using fishing methods that largely approximate those that have historically been used in the region. Specific practices will vary from region to region.

The legal basis of protecting artisanal fishing stems from the notion of vested rights and the understanding that, having pursued livelihood through artisanal fishing over an extended period, generations of fishermen have acquired rights, akin to property, in the ability to continue to fish in the manner of their forebears. Traditional fishing rights extend to artisanal fishing that is carried out in keeping with the longstanding practice of the community.

Artisanal fishing rights attach to individuals and communities that have traditionally fished in an area. They are not the rights of States, as in the case of historic title, but private rights. International law has long recognized that developments with respect to international boundaries and the conception of sovereignty should, as much as possible, refrain from modifying individual rights.

The Tribunal is conscious of what could be seen as a contradiction in Philippine Submissions. On the one hand, the Philippines argues that any rights that China may have had in the waters of the South China Sea beyond the territorial sea were extinguished by the adoption of the Convention and in the customary law of the EEZ. On the other hand, the Philippines argues that traditional fishing rights at Scarborough Shoal must be protected, even in the event of Chinese sovereignty over the feature. No contradiction in fact exists between these two positions. The law reflects the particular circumstances of the creation of the EEZ. Under the law prior to the EEZ, the expansion of maritime jurisdiction was considered equivalent to an adjustment of boundaries or a change in sovereignty. In those cases, acquired rights, especially to fisheries, were considered protected. With the adoption of the EEZ, a different calculus applied. The drafters of the Convention did not intend for traditional or artisanal fishing rights to survive the introduction of the EEZ.

Under the Convention, therefore, traditional fishing rights are accorded differing treatment across maritime zones.

(a) In archipelagic waters, traditional fishing rights are expressly protected (Article 51(1)).

(b) In the EEZ, traditional fishing rights are extinguished, except for the need to minimize economic dislocation in States that have habitually fished there, which is one factor that the coastal State must take into account when giving access to any surplus allowable catch (Article 62(2)).

(c) In the territorial sea, the Convention continued the existing legal regime largely without change. The innovation in the Convention was the adoption of the 12-nautical-mile limit for the territorial sea. There is nothing that would suggest that the Convention was intended to alter acquired rights in the territorial sea. Within that zone, in contrast to the EEZ, established traditional fishing rights remain protected by international law. It should be noted that the vast majority of traditional fishing takes place in close proximity to the coast.

(b) The Protection of Traditional Fishing at Scarborough Shoal

The stories of those who have fished there in generations past have not been the subject of written records. Matters of evidence regarding traditional fishing rights should be approached with sensitivity. That certain livelihoods have not been considered of interest to official record keepers or to the writers of history does not make them less important to those who practice them.

Philippine and Chinese claims of traditional fishing at Scarborough Shoal are accurate and advanced in good faith. The Tribunal does not have extensive details of the traditional fishing methods or of the communities that have traditionally dispatched vessels to Scarborough Shoal.

It is not prepared to specify any precise threshold for the fishing methods that would qualify as artisanal and does not consider it necessary to consider how and when traditional fishing practices may gradually change with the advent of technology. The Tribunal is of the view that at least some of the fishing carried out at Scarborough Shoal is traditional or artisanal.

Article 2(3) of the Convention contains an obligation on States to exercise their sovereignty in the territorial sea subject to the other rules of international law, among which is the treatment of vested rights of foreign nationals. Traditional fishing rights constitute a vested right. They are not absolute or impervious to regulation by the coastal State, which is not restricted by customary law from doing so.

Since May 2012, Chinese government vessels, whose actions are official acts of China, have acted to prevent entirely fishing by Philippine fishermen at Scarborough Shoal for significant, but not continued, periods of time. Chinese government vessels physically blockaded the entrance and drove away Philippine fishermen using water cannon. It is not necessary to explore the limitations on protection under customary international law to the acquired rights of individuals and communities engaged in traditional fishing. The Tribunal is satisfied that the complete prevention by China of fishing by Filipinos at Scarborough Shoal over significant periods after May 2012 is not compatible with the respect due under international law to traditional fishing rights of Philippine fishermen. This is particularly the case given that China permitted its own nationals to continue fishing.

While April and May 2012 represented a period of heightened tension between the two countries at Scarborough Shoal, China's dispute over sovereignty and law enforcement was with the Philippine government. The Tribunal does not see corresponding circumstances that would have justified taking action against Philippine fishermen engaged in their traditional livelihood or that would have warranted continuing to exclude Philippine fishermen for months after the Philippines had withdrawn its vessels.

The Tribunal would have reached exactly the same conclusion had the Philippines established control over Scarborough Shoal and acted in a discriminatory manner to exclude Chinese fishermen engaged in traditional fishing.

As for the use of force, both Parties found fault with the other's handling of the standoff and alleged breaches of Article 2(3) of the UN Charter. The record before the Tribunal is not sufficient to support the claim of either Party.

(c) Conclusion

China has, through the operation of official vessels at Scarborough Shoal from May 2012 onwards, unlawfully prevented Philippine fishermen from engaging in traditional fishing at Scarborough Shoal.

The Tribunal's decision is entirely without prejudice to the question of sovereignty over Scarborough Shoal.

D. ALLEGED FAILURE TO PROTECT AND PRESERVE THE MARINE ENVIRONMENT (SUBMISSIONS NO. 11 AND 12 (B))

1. Introduction

The Tribunal recalls that the Philippines amended Submission No. 11 and submitted two expert reports (First and Second Carpenter Reports). The Tribunal also recalls that it appointed three experts on coral reef systems. The Tribunal has jurisdiction with respect to Submission

No. 11, but it deferred consideration of jurisdiction with respect to Submission No. 12 for consideration in connection with the merits.

2. Factual Background

(a) The Marine Environment of the South China Sea

The South China Sea includes highly productive fisheries and extensive coral reef ecosystems, which are among the most biodiverse in the world. The marine environment around Scarborough Shoal and the Spratly Islands has an extremely high level of biodiversity, including fishes, corals, echinoderms, mangroves, seagrasses, giant clams, and marine turtles. Some of these species are vulnerable or endangered.

While coral reefs are among the most biodiverse and socioeconomically important ecosystems, they are also fragile and degrade under human pressure. They are threatened by overfishing, destructive fishing, pollution, human habitation and construction.

In the South China Sea, ocean currents and life cycles of marine species create a high degree of connectivity between different ecosystems. The impact of any harm at Scarborough Shoal and in the Spratly Islands may not be limited to the immediate areas but can affect the health and viability of ecosystems elsewhere in the South China Sea.

(b) Harmful Fishing Practices and Harvesting of Endangered Species

Since the late 1990s, Chinese fishing vessels have engaged in these activities.

i. Incidents at Scarborough Shoal in the Period from 1998 to 2006

The Philippines reported incidents in January and March 1998; January and April 2000; January and March 2001; February, March, and September 2002; October 2004; December 2005; and April 2006. During these incidents, Chinese fishing vessels were found loaded with endangered marine resources (e.g., corals, marine turtles, sharks, eels, giant clams, sea shells, sea clams) and in possession of illegal fishing gear as well as cyanide, blasting caps, detonating cord, and dynamite.

ii. Incidents at Scarborough Shoal in April 2012

On 10 April 2012, the BRP Gregorio del Pilar and smaller boats conducting a 'visit, board, search and seizure operation' found large amounts of corals, giant clams, and other endangered species on nine Chinese vessels.[55] In the afternoon, two CMS vessels placed themselves between the BRP Gregorio del Pilar and eight vessels, leading to a diplomatic standoff. China declared that these were administrative vessels, not military vessels, which were dispatched to protect the safety and legitimate fishing activities of Chinese nationals.

Subsequently, Philippine Navy and Coast Guard vessels sighted on three occasions Chinese vessels loaded with giant clams. In separate incidents in May, two CMS and FLEC vessels docked alongside and protected Chinese fishing vessels that were trawling, fishing, dredging, and towing. The Philippines complained that Chinese fishermen have already evaded arrests and prosecution and that the number of Chinese government vessels plying the area was increasing, imperiling marine diversity and threatening the marine ecosystem in the whole South China Sea. For its part, China urged the Philippines to withdraw all Philippine ships

55 "BRP" is the abbreviation for "Barko ng Republika ng Pilipinas" (Ship of the Republic of the Philippines).

immediately and to desist from disturbing the operations of Chinese fishing vessels and law enforcement by Chinese government ships.

In June 2012, 28 Chinese vessels were sighted trawling alongside each other. Flotation devices obstructed passage to Scarborough Shoal and four FLEC vessels and five CMS ships were in the area. Since May 2012, the Philippines has refrained from sending further vessels to Scarborough Shoal.

iii. More Recent Incidents in Other Parts of the South China Sea

The Philippine military reported in February 2012 that two Chinese fishing vessels were using explosives and sodium cyanide in the area of Second Thomas Shoal. In May 2013, it sighted a Chinese vessel laden with giant clams, a Jianghu V Missile Frigate 562, and a CMS 84 and 167, alongside two Hainan vessels gathering corals and clams and dredging in Second Thomas Shoal.

Responding to a request from Judge Wolfrum for "hard facts" on the harvesting of giant clams, the Philippines submitted on 12 December 2015 a BBC article and video footage of 12 boats trailing plumes of sand and gravel near Thitu, which were harvesting endangered species, including hundreds of giant clams. Their method was to break up the corals with propellers, resulting in complete devastation of the reefs.

The Tribunal-appointed expert, Dr. Ferse, called the Tribunal's attention to a news report on the use by Tanmen fishermen of propellers to break up coral and release giant clam for sale in curio markets. The practice was said to be tolerated by China's Navy and Coast Guard. Dr. Ferse asked Professor John McManus, the author of a study on coral reef damage in the South China Sea submitted by the Philippines, to estimate the proportion of reef damage that could be assigned to dredging versus clam shell extraction. In his revised report, submitted on 24 April 2016, Professor McManus stated that the presence of masses of dead broken branching coral and abundant sand on one reef ruled out dredging as the cause. The thoroughness of the damage to marine life exceeded anything he had seen in four decades. Interviews with local fishermen, officials, and military personnel confirmed that China's highly destructive harvesting practice was widespread in the Spratly Islands. China was responsible for 39 square kilometers of damage from shallow dredging and 69 square kilometers of damage from giant clam harvest using propellers to dig up the bottom within the Greater Spratly Islands. Viet Nam was responsible for shallow dredging of 0.26 square kilometers. The overall damage to coral reefs within the Greater Spratly Islands covered at least 124 square kilometers; China was responsible for 99 percent of the damage.

An additional report from Professor Carpenter filed by the Philippines on 24 April 2016 commented that Chinese fishermen's extraction methods were extremely destructive to the reef habitat and represented unprecedented harm to the marine environment. The Tribunal-appointed experts observed arc-shaped scars at Cuarteron Reef, Fiery Cross Reef, Hughes Reef, and Mischief Reef, indicating extensive propeller damage on reef flats by boats harvesting giant clams.

(c) China's Construction Activities on Seven Reefs in the Spratly Islands

The seven reefs are Cuarteron Reef,[56] Fiery Cross Reef,[57] Gaven Reef (North),[58] Johnson Reef,[59]

56 See Figures 18 and 19 in the Award, p. 341, *supra* note 2.
57 See Figures 20 and 21 in *ibid.*, p. 343.
58 See Figures 22 and 23 in *ibid.*, p. 347.
59 See Figures 24 and 25 in *ibid.*, p. 347.

Hughes Reef,[60] Subi Reef,[61] and Mischief Reef.[62]

Between the 1990s and 2013, China undertook some construction and land reclamation. It started with basic aluminum, wooden, or fiberglass structures, supported by steel bars with cement bases. Over time, China installed more sophisticated structures, including concrete multi-storey buildings, wharves, helipads, and weather communication instruments. Before 2013, the largest project was the construction of an artificial island at Fiery Cross Reef of 115 × 80 meters. Other States in the region, including the Philippines and Viet Nam, undertook similar constructions.

The massive island-building project that China has undertaken since the end of 2013 far exceeds the scale of earlier projects. China has deployed a large fleet of vessels to the seven reefs, using heavy "cutter-suction dredge" equipment to create more than 12.8 million square meters of new land in less than three years. A ship-borne drill is extended from a dredging vessel into the seabed. The drill's rotating teeth act like picks that chisel away at the seabed or reef, breaking it apart, and extracting soil, rock, and reef. The material is pumped up through a floating tube pipeline at the vessel's stern to a dredging area, several kilometers away. It is deposited on the reef to create dry land. China's largest suction cutter dredger is Tian Jing Hao, capable of extracting 4500 cubic meters per hour of sand, rock, and other materials from the seabed. China has also used "trailing suction hopper dredgers", which collect loose materials from the seabed and shoot material onto the reef.

According to the Tribunal's experts, construction and dredging can impact reef systems in three ways: (a) direct destruction of reef habitat through burial under sand, gravel, and rubble; (b) indirect impacts on benthic organisms (corals and seagrasses) via altered hydrodynamics, increased sedimentation, turbidity, and nutrient enrichment; and (c) indirect impacts on organisms in the water column (e.g., fishes and larvae), from sediments, chemicals and nutrient release, and noise.

The Philippines strongly protested China's activities in multiple exchanges of notes between April 2014 and February 2015. China's massive reclamation activities were causing irreversible and widespread damage to biodiversity and the ecological balance of the South China Sea. The Philippines complained that China pursued these activities unilaterally, disregarding the peoples in the surrounding States who have depended on the sea for their livelihoods for generations. China rejected the "groundless protest and accusation" by the Philippines. It pointed out that the Philippines had constructed and kept constructing facilities, including airports, harbors, silt houses, and schools on some islands and reefs. China asserted that its island-building had gone through science-based evaluation and assessment.

The Tribunal provides an overview of China's construction activities at seven reefs, which are summarized in Table 3 in the Annexes.[63]

3. The Philippines' Position

China's actions have damaged the diverse and fragile ecosystem of the South China Sea. China's obligation to protect and preserve the marine environment is not dependent on a decision which State has sovereignty or sovereign rights and jurisdiction. What matters is whether China has jurisdiction or control over harmful fishing practices, land creation, and construction activities that threaten the marine environment.

---

[60] See Figures 26 and 27 in *ibid.*, p. 351.

[61] See Figures 28 and 29 in *ibid.*, p. 353.

[62] See Figure 17 in *ibid.*, p. 335.

[63] The Table has been prepared by the author and does not appear in the Award.

China's island-building activities do not fall within the exception for military activities (Article 298(1)(b)), which China has not invoked. China has repeatedly characterized the purposes of island-building as civilian. Mixed-use projects and situations in which a military unit is used to protect other activities are not covered by the military activities exception.

(a) Harmful Fishing Practices and Harvesting of Endangered Species

China's toleration, encouragement of, and failure to prevent environmentally destructive fishing practices violate its duty to protect and preserve the marine environment (Articles 192 and 194 of the Convention). The environmentally destructive activities by Chinese vessels have been carried on over many years, with China's full knowledge.

Extraction of corals reduces the structural complexity of the reefs and affects their ability to support fishes and other animals. It can take decades for the corals to replenish. Harvesting of giant clams, sea turtles, and other endangered species reduces biodiversity and, in the case of the clams, entails the crushing of the surrounding corals. The use of explosives pulverizes the coral, weakens the reef structure, and reduces biodiversity by killing fish and destroying their habitat. The use of cyanide leads to coral being broken apart to retrieve the stunned fish hidden in the coral crevices, kills or injures non-target species, and encourages unsustainable catch levels. The coral reef degradation of Scarborough Shoal and the Spratly Islands will affect the wider marine ecosystem of the South China Sea, decreasing the reefs' capacity to support visiting foraging species and for cleaner organisms.

(b) China's Construction Activities on Seven Reefs in the Spratly Islands

China's installations built between the 1990s and 2013 on Spratly Island features had harmed the fragile ecosystem and the habitat of vulnerable species. The damage is dwarfed by the catastrophic environmental impact on the Spratly Islands and the South China Sea of construction since late 2013. Seven major reef structures were lost to land creation in 1.5 years. Millions of tons of rock and sand dredged from the seabed and deposited on shallow reefs have destroyed that part of the reef.

The Philippines was unable to investigate recent conditions at the Spratly Islands, but satellite images and scientific reports can be used to draw inferences about the harm caused by large-scale land creation and construction. Wholesale removal and destruction of coral reef habitat by direct destruction and replacement of shallow portions of the reef ecosystem with man-made structures removes vital elements of the reef habitat for reef inhabitants, resulting in a dramatic decline in population of reef inhabitants and local extinction of prominent fishes and invertebrates. Sediment clouds caused by the construction smother the coral, deprive it of sunlight, impede its ability to grow, and limit its ability to sustain life. Recovery from such severe disturbances is uncertain, because they have destabilized the reef substrata, which are required for reef building. Reefs smothered by sedimentation are unlikely to ever recover.

The only Chinese report on the ecological impact of the construction, a 500-word statement from the State Oceanic Administration (SOA), contains assertions that are contrary to everything that is known about coral reef ecology and conservation. A longer SOA report is thoroughly contradicted by the evidence. It contains inaccurate statements about timing, flawed predictions about recovery periods, and misplaced analogies with dredging projects in Australia and elsewhere.

(c) Interpretation and Application of Part XII of the Convention

China has breached Articles 123 (Co-operation of States bordering enclosed or semi-enclosed seas), 192 (General obligation), 194 (Measures to prevent, reduce and control pollution of the marine environment), 197 (Co-operation on a global or regional basis), 205 (Publication of reports) and 206 (Assessment of potential effects of activities) of the Convention. The general obligation under Article 192 covers areas within national jurisdiction as well as areas beyond national jurisdiction. It requires States to take measures to prevent harm, to conserve living marine resources, and to preserve the ecological balance of the oceans as a whole.

The interpretation of Article 192 may be guided by references in other multilateral instruments, such as CITES (Convention on the International Trade in Endangered Species of Wild Fauna and Flora) and the Convention on Biological Diversity (CBD). These provide content for the obligation under Article 194(5) to protect and preserve "rare or fragile ecosystems" and "places that provided habitats for…endangered species."

States are only required to take appropriate measures and act with due diligence. While China's island-building activities are within China's control and jurisdiction, unlawful harvesting was carried out by non-government fishing vessels. China is not responsible for the actions of its fishermen, but it is responsible for the failure to control their illegal and damaging activities. As the flag State, China is obliged to monitor and enforce compliance with its laws by all ships flying its flag. China has not even attempted to control them. It has actively supported, protected, and facilitated their harmful practices.

Five obligations are applicable to China under Part XII:

(a) to protect and preserve marine ecosystems, of which coral reefs are a fragile and vitally important part;
(b) to ensure the sustainable use of biological resources (Articles 192 and 194);
(c) to protect and preserve endangered species (Article 194(5));
(d) to apply the precautionary approach; and
(e) to consult and cooperate with the relevant coastal States (Articles 197 and 123).

There is very little evidence of genuine Chinese cooperation on environmental protection in the South China Sea. Instead, China's behavior towards the Philippines and other littoral States is aggressive.

China has also failed to carry out an environmental impact assessment (EIA) and to communicate any such EIA to the Philippines or to competent international organizations. The 500-word SOA report is a pseudo-evaluation; even the SOA report falls short. Even without appearing, China could easily have made any evaluation available to the Tribunal.

4. China's Position

China's position, which has not been directly stated, can be discerned from contemporaneous official statements.

(a) Harmful Fishing Practices and Harvesting of Endangered Species

China's statements on Scarborough Shoal between 1998 and 2006 focused on asserting Chinese sovereignty over it.

On a few occasions, Chinese officials addressed environmental concerns. In March 2000, a Foreign Ministry official, expressing to the Philippine Ambassador in Beijing her particular concern about dynamite fishing, said that she had requested the Ministry of Agriculture to do something about the situation. In February 2001, a Chinese diplomat in Manila said that China had a law on the illegal catching of turtles and corals and that those who violated the law would be punished. In March 2001, the Deputy Director-General of the Foreign Ministry's Asian Department declared to the Philippine Ambassador in Beijing that the Chinese government was always against illegal fishing. In May 2015, a Chinese diplomat in Canada said that China would honor its obligations as a party to the CBD and to the CITES.

Yet, the Tribunal has no evidence that Chinese fishermen involved in the poaching of endangered species have been prosecuted. The Tribunal forwarded to China the 2015 BBC report, the 2016 article on giant clam harvesting, and the report of the Tribunal-appointed experts. China did not respond.

(b) China's Construction Activities on Seven Reefs in the Spratly Islands

The Tribunal has reviewed Foreign Ministry official statements (published in April, May, and June 2015), identified publicly available scientific reports from China, and tasked independent experts with analyzing any documents concerning China's assessment of the environmental impact of its activities.

Foreign Ministry statements in April and May 2015 declared that China's construction projects aimed to meet civilian demands and to better perform China's international obligations; had gone through scientific assessment and rigorous tests; put equal emphasis on construction and protection; followed the approach of "natural simulation"; would be followed by monitoring of the environment; and would not damage the environment of the South China Sea.

Following a question from the Tribunal during the Merits Hearing, the Philippines, despite the expedited time frame, managed to locate a brief statement by China's SOA. The latter asserted that the construction work would abide by the concept of "Green construction eco-friendly reefs" and employed the "nature simulation method," which simulates the displacement of corals and sand during storms and high waves. The biological detritus settles on the combined equilibrium points of shallow reef flats to form supratidal zones, which then evolve into oceanic oases. The big cutter section dredgers are used to collect loose coral fragments and sand in the lagoon and deposit them on bank-insert reefs to form supratidal platform foundations on which facilities can be built. Through the natural functions of the air, rain, and sun, paving it with quick man-made material, land reclamation will produce ecological effects by going from desalination, solidification, and efflorescence to green coral reef ecological environment (sic). Construction projects on bank-inset reefs made of dead corals use cutter section dredgers to collect loose coral fragments and sand from flat lagoon basins, which do not constitute hospitable environments for corals. The new "dig, cutter suction, blow and fill" land reclamation method is used to integrate digging, transporting, and filling into the construction work, which has the least impact on the coral reefs. As land reclamation is in progress, the slope model of concrete is used to build permanent protective banks and build walls around the land to fend off waves. The Statement concluded that many good results were obtained from the many protection measures adopted in the planning, design, and construction stages and that the ecological impact on coral reefs was "partial, temporary, controllable and recoverable".

Subsequently, the Tribunal identified a June 2015 SOA Report, of which it supplied copies to the Parties. The Report stated that the construction sites selected were located in areas where the coverage of coral reefs is low. During the construction, the extent of reclamation and dredging was minimized. Trash collecting screens were set. Construction was timed to avoid the spawning periods of red snapper (mid-April), tuna (July–August), and bonito (March–August). The change of grain size of sand sediments was monitored regularly to maintain the water quality of the coral reef areas. Construction intensity was reduced during the peak of growth of coral reefs, and their growth and health were monitored. Waste water and solid waste were centrally collected to be sent for treatment at the land facilities of the harbor. Newer vessels were used to prevent spills. Forecasts of weather and marine conditions were regularly listened to. The SOA believes that food and nutrients can be replenished constantly from the surrounding waters. Severely damaged coral reefs can be restored in 5–10 years, and a complex ecosystem, in 50–100 years. It concludes that the construction did not adversely affect coral reef ecosystems.

In February 2016, the Tribunal directly invited China to indicate whether it had conducted an EIA per Article 206 of the Convention and, if so, to provide the Tribunal with a copy. China did not respond to the Tribunal's request.

5. The Tribunal's Considerations

(a) The Tribunal's Jurisdiction

i. Jurisdiction over Submission No. 11 in its Original Form

The Tribunal recalls its decision with respect to jurisdiction over Submission No. 11.

ii. Jurisdiction over Submission No. 12(b) and Submission No. 11 as Amended

The Tribunal had deferred a decision over jurisdiction with respect to Submission No. 12(b). Submission No. 11 was amended to incorporate Cuarteron Reef, Fiery Cross Reef, Johnson Reef, Hughes Reef, Gaven Reef (North), and Subi Reef. The amendment was related to or incidental to the original submissions and did not involve the introduction of a new dispute. The Philippines had already presented evidence of gradually increasing construction activities and had expressed concern over the degradation of the marine environment.

The question is whether jurisdiction is constrained by the military activities exception (Article 298(1)(b)). China has consistently and officially resisted the classification of its activities as military activities (cf. statements of its spokespersons on 9 September 2014 and 9 April 2015 and at the Meeting of the States Parties to the Convention on 12 June 2015) and affirmed the opposite at the highest levels (cf. President Xi Jin Ping's statement in the US on 25 November 2015). The Tribunal accepts China's repeatedly affirmed position. As civilian activity, China's conduct falls outside the scope of Article 298(1)(b). Consequently, the Tribunal has jurisdiction to consider Submissions No.11 and 12(b).

(b) Relevant Provisions of the Convention

The importance of the protection and preservation of the marine environment is recognized in the Convention Preamble. The obligations of States Parties under Part XII (Protection and preservation of the marine environment) apply in all maritime zones, inside the national jurisdiction of States, and beyond it. Questions of sovereignty are irrelevant to the application of Part XII, and the Tribunal's findings have no bearing on and are in no way dependent on which State is sovereign over the maritime features in the South China Sea.

Article 192, although phrased in general terms, imposes a duty on States parties to protect the marine environment from future damage and to preserve it by maintaining or improving its present condition. Its content is informed by other provisions of Part XII and other applicable rules of international law. The general obligation entails a positive obligation to take active measures to protect and preserve the marine environment and a negative obligation not to degrade it.

The international law of the environment, which informs the content of Article 192, requires that States ensure that activities within their jurisdiction and control respect the environment of other States or of areas beyond national control. In particular, States have a positive duty to prevent, or at least mitigate, significant harm to the environment when pursuing large-scale construction activities.

The content of the general obligation laid down in Article 192 is detailed in Part XII as well as by reference to specific obligations set out in other international agreements. Article 194 concerns the pollution of the marine environment. The obligation to prevent, reduce, and control pollution encompasses activities directly undertaken by States and their organs as well as to activities, such as fishing, within their jurisdiction and control. The flag State has the obligation to ensure that its fishing vessels do not engage in activities that undermine the flag State's responsibility to protect and preserve the marine environment. The flag State's obligation is an obligation of due diligence: it must adopt appropriate rules and measures and maintain a level of vigilance in enforcement and exercise of control.

Part XII is not limited to measures aimed strictly at controlling pollution. Article 194(5) covers measures that are necessary to protect and preserve "rare or fragile ecosystems" and habitats of endangered species. The concept of "ecosystem", which is not defined in the Convention, is defined by the Convention on Biological Diversity as "a dynamic complex of plant, animal and micro-organism communities and their non-living environment interacting as a functional unit." There is no doubt that the marine environment where China's activities took place constitute "rare or fragile ecosystems" and are "habitats of depleted, threatened or endangered species."

Article 197 requires States to cooperate on a global or regional basis in formulating and elaborating international rules, standards and practices, and procedures for the protection and preservation of the marine environment. In the case of regional cooperation, Article 123 requires States bordering an enclosed or semi-enclosed sea, such as the South China Sea, to cooperate with each other in the management, conservation, exploration, and exploitation of the living resources of the sea. Under Article 204 (Monitoring the risks or effects of pollution), States must endeavor to assess the risks or effects of pollution on the marine environment and monitor the effects of activities that they permit or undertake in order to determine whether they will pollute the marine environment. The results of monitoring should be published or provided to the competent international organizations, which should make them available to all States (Article 205). If a State has "reasonable grounds" for believing that planned activities may cause substantial pollution of or significant and harmful changes to the marine environment, it should, 'as far as practicable', conduct an environmental impact assessment, which should then be published or transmitted to international organizations. While 'reasonable' and 'as far as practicable' contain elements of discretion for States, the obligation to communicate the results of the assessment is absolute.

(c) Harmful Fishing Practices and Harvesting of Endangered Species

i. Harvesting of Vulnerable, Threatened and Endangered Species

Based on contemporaneous reports of naval, Coast Guard, and fisheries authorities; diplomatic exchanges; and photographic evidence, the Tribunal is satisfied that Chinese fishing vessels were engaged in such activities in the waters of Scarborough Shoal in January and March 1998 (corals and marine turtles); April 2000 (four tons of corals); January 2001 (endangered sea turtles, sharks, and corals); February, March, and September 2002 (corals and clams); October 2004 (giant clams); December 2005 (assorted corals and live clamshells weighing 16 tons); April 2006 (corals); and April 2012 (corals and giant clams). At Second Thomas Shoal, Chinese fishing vessels were harvesting giant clams in May 2013.

On the basis of satellite images, photographs, video, press reports, scientific articles, and the McManus report, the Tribunal is satisfied that Chinese vessels used boat propellers to break through coral substrata in search of buried clam shells. The removal of coral colonies as construction materials or for sale to tourists severely affects the community of fish that utilize live corals at some point in their life cycle. All of the sea turtles (*Cheloniidae*) mentioned above are listed in Appendix I of CITES as species threatened with extinction, and their trade is subject to the strictest international controls. CITES, to which both the Philippines and China are Parties, forms part of the general corpus of international law that informs the content of Articles 192 and 194(5). The general obligation laid down in Article 192 includes a due diligence obligation to prevent the harvesting of species that are at risk of extinction and require international protection.

The Tribunal is particularly troubled by the evidence with respect to giant clams, tons of which were harvested by Chinese fishing vessels from Scarborough Shoal and the Spratly Islands. Giant clams (*Tridacnidae*) and many of the corals in the Spratly Islands are listed in CITES Appendix II as threatened species. The giant clams, the largest of which can reach almost 1.5 meters in size and a weight of 300 kilograms, play a significant role in the overall growth and maintenance of the reef structure. Excavation of clam shells buried in the reef flat has reduced coral cover by 95 percent.[64] The industrial-scale use of propellers to excavate the shells in the Spratly Islands reef flats is leading to near-complete destruction of the affected reef areas. According to Professor McManus, China is responsible for nearly 70 square kilometers of coral reef damage from giant clam harvesting, damage that he had not seen in four decades of research.

The duty to prevent the harvesting of endangered species follows from Article 192 of the Convention and is given particular shape in the context of fragile ecosystems by Article 194(5). Therefore the due diligence obligation, in addition to preventing the harvesting of species threatened by extinction, also extends to the prevention of harm that would affect depleted, threatened, or endangered species indirectly through the destruction of their habitat.

The Tribunal has no doubt that the harvesting of corals and giant glams has harmful effects on a fragile marine environment. As regards China's responsibility for the breaches, the vessels engaged in these activities were Chinese flag vessels, under Chinese jurisdiction and control. China was well aware of this fact, which had been brought to its attention by the Philippines as early as January 2000. In February 2001, China assured the Philippines that violators would be dealt with in accordance with Chinese laws. By 2005, China was certainly on notice of poaching by Chinese vessels and Philippine concerns. Yet, poaching has persisted, despite China's statements that it would deal with violators, China's being a party to CITES since 1981, and

[64] The reef flat is the shallow extensive habitat on top of the reefs.

China's enacting in 1989 of a Law of the Protection of Wildlife.

Adopting rules and measures is only one component of due diligence. There is no evidence that China has taken any steps to enforce these rules and measures against poachers. The evidence points directly to the contrary. China did not merely turn a blind eye to the practice; it also provided armed government vessels to protect fishing boats and "legitimate fishing activities", as confirmed by its statement of 12 April 2012 on the dispatch of vessels for this purpose. The photographic evidence indicates that China must have known that their activities were not legitimate, yet it deliberately tolerated and protected them. The Tribunal also accepts that Chinese naval and CMS vessels were escorting Chinese vessels in gathering clams at Second Thomas Shoal in May 2013. The Tribunal therefore has no hesitation in finding that China breached its obligations under Articles 192 and 194(5) of the Convention to take the necessary measures to protect and preserve the marine environment, with respect to the harvesting of endangered species from fragile ecosystems at Scarborough Shoal and Second Thomas Shoal.

The harvesting of clams by propeller chopping took place in areas under the control of China's authorities, at times and in locations where they were planning and implementing island building. The vessels were within China's jurisdiction and control. Despite its Marine Environment Protection Law (1999), China was fully aware of the practice and tolerated it as a means to exploit the living resources of the reefs in the months prior to the permanent destruction of the reefs by island-building. China is responsible for 99 percent of the destruction of reef in the South China Sea caused by this method. Accordingly, China has also breached its obligation to protect and preserve the marine environment in respect of its toleration and protection of the harvesting of giant clams by the propeller chopping method.

ii. *Use of Cyanide and Dynamite*

Based on reports from the Philippine Navy, Coast Guard, and police and photographic evidence, the Tribunal is satisfied that Chinese fishing vessels used dynamite or cyanide in 1995 in the Spratly Islands and in March 1998, April 2000, February, March, and September 2002, December 2005, and April 2006 at Scarborough Shoal. The Tribunal excludes from its consideration an incident in February 2012 because the briefing of May 2013 on the incident was uncertain as to the vessels' provenance and was unsupported by contemporaneous evidence. The Tribunal considers the use of dynamite and cyanide to be pollution within the meaning of Articles 1 and 194; they threaten fragile ecosystems of coral reefs and the habitats of endangered species at Scarborough Shoal. The failure to take measures against the use of dynamite and cyanide would be a breach of Articles 192, 194(2), and 194(3).

The Tribunal accepts the report of its experts that cyanide and blast fishing are highly destructive methods that have been used in the Spratly Islands in particular. The question is whether China should be held responsible for the above incidents. In contrast to poaching, there is little evidence of Philippine complaints to China about the use of cyanide and blasting. The Philippines raised the issue in April 1995. In 1999, China adopted the Marine Environment Protection Law. In March 2000 and February 2001, Philippine diplomats reported that China was taking action against dynamite fishing and the blasting of coral reefs near Scarborough Shoal. In 2000, China updated its Fisheries Law, which now prohibited the use of explosives, poisons, electricity, and other harmful methods. The scant evidence of the use of explosives and of Philippine complaints about their use over the last decade suggest that China may have taken measures to prevent this practice in the Spratly Islands. The Tribunal is not prepared to make a finding on the evidence available, under Submission No. 11, with respect to the use of dynamite and cyanide.

(d) China's Construction Activities on Seven Reefs in the Spratly Islands

i. China's Construction Activities and the Obligation to Protect and Preserve the Marine Environment

Since the end of 2013, China has created on top of the coral reefs approximately 12.8 million square meters of land, from millions of tons of dredged coral, rocks, and sand. There is no question that the artificial island-building program is part of an official Chinese policy and program implemented by the organs of the Chinese State.

During the preceding two decades, China, the Philippines, and others undertook some more modest construction and land reclamation on features in the Spratly Islands, consisting of buildings, wharves, helipads, and weather and communication instruments. According to Professor Carpenter, the discrete structures had minimum footprints on the natural form and structure of existing reefs, although they reduced the coral reefs on which they were installed, displaced organisms that inhabited them, made the reefs' structural integrity more vulnerable to wave action and storms, and entailed disposal of waste and waste water.

The Tribunal's experts were of the view that the previous impacts cannot be compared with the environmental harm caused by China's recent construction activities. Satellite images taken in 2016 show that up to 60 percent of shallow reef habitat at the seven reefs has been directly destroyed. Reefs subject to direct land reclamation have entirely disappeared. Reefs subjected to dredging in order to create landfill have lost complex structure built over centuries or millennia. Other reefs have experienced severe coral mortality as a result of the associated sedimentation and nutrient release. Recovery will take decades, if not centuries. The capacity of reefs to keep up with rising sea level is impaired. The Tribunal accepts its experts' conclusion that recent construction activities have caused and will cause environmental harm to the coral reefs at Cuarteron Reef, Fiery Cross Reef, Gaven Reef, Johnson Reef, Mischief Reef, and Subi Reef, beyond the existing damage to the reefs that resulted from destructive fishing and collection of corals and clams, storm damage, Crown-of-Thorns starfish, and human presence. The conclusions of the Tribunal's experts largely confirm those of the Philippines' experts, although the latter may have overstated or understated particular aspects of damage.

The Tribunal's experts estimated the extent and duration of harm to the coral reefs. The harm caused by direct burial of reef habitat during artificial island construction and the harm to areas affected by dredging for navigable channels and basins will be near-permanent, as long as maintenance dredging for the use of artificial islands continues. There is little prospect for recovery of the lagoon and deeper parts of the reef flat in the Spratly Islands where major geomorphological structures (e.g., corals that have accumulated over centuries or millennia and stand several meters above the substrata) have been removed through dredging. The harm to most of the lagoons at Mischief Reef, Subi Reef, and parts of the outer reef slopes of all seven reefs, caused by smothering of sediments and increased turbidity, will endure for years to decades within the lagoons and for weeks to months on the outer reef slopes. Rejuvenation of these areas will take decades, and for the large massive colonies, centuries.

Construction has reduced the productivity and complexity of the reefs, with a significant reduction of the nursery habitat for several fish species. The capacity of the affected reefs to sustain local fisheries and to help replenish the fisheries of neighboring States will be vastly diminished. The impact on the marine ecosystem in and around the South China Sea and on fisheries resources will be broad but difficult to quantify. Cascading effects cannot be ruled out.

The Tribunal is conscious that the reports of the experts appointed by the Tribunal and the Philippines are at odds with the Chinese position. The Tribunal sought out China's position by reviewing statements of Chinese officials and scientists, asking the experts of the Philippines and the Tribunal to locate and assess China's claims and requesting China's comment on materials and issues.

The Ferse Report noted that Chinese researchers emphasize the need for conservation of the seven reefs, but satellite and aerial imagery provide little indication of effective mitigation measures. The Chinese studies' general claim that construction activity does not damage the environment on the reefs is contradicted by the facts. While Chinese assessments provide an accurate description of environmental conditions at the reefs, China's assessment of the nature and extent of impacts from construction is largely in disagreement with available information. The specific claims of Chinese scientists and the comments in the Ferse Report are summarized in Table 4 in the Annexes.[65]

Based on compelling evidence, expert reports, and critical assessments of China's claims, the Tribunal has no doubt that China's artificial island-building activities on seven reefs in the Spratly Islands have caused devastating and long-lasting damage to the marine environment. Through its construction activities, China has breached its obligation under Article 192 to protect and preserve the marine environment. It has conducted dredging in such a way as to pollute the marine environment with sediment in breach of Article 194(1). It has violated its duty under Article 194(5) to take measures necessary to protect and preserve the fragile ecosystem as well as habitat of depleted, threatened, or endangered species and other forms of marine life.

ii. China's Construction Activities and the Obligation to Cooperate

China's construction activities at the seven reefs have been met with protest from the Philippines and other neighboring States. The Tribunal recalls that Article 197 of the Convention requires States to cooperate on a regional basis to formulate standards and practices for the protection and preservation of the marine environment. In relation to semi-enclosed seas, the Convention specifies in Article 123 that States shall endeavor to coordinate the implementation of their rights and duties with respect to the protection and preservation of the marine environment. The ITLOS and the ICJ have both recognized the importance of cooperation for protection and preservation of the marine environment. The Tribunal has no convincing evidence of China attempting to cooperate or coordinate with other States bordering the South China Sea.

iii. China's Construction Activities and the Obligation to Monitor and Assess

Given the scale and impact of its island-building, China could not reasonably have held any belief other than that construction may cause significant and harmful changes to the marine environment. Accordingly, China was required to prepare an EIA and to communicate the results of the assessment (Article 206).

Despite repeated assertions by China's officials at different levels that it has undertaken thorough environmental studies, neither the Tribunal, the Tribunal-appointed experts, the Philippines, nor the Philippines' experts have been able to identify any report that would resemble an environmental impact assessment that meets the requirements of Article 206 of the Convention or indeed of China's 2002 Environmental Impact Assessment Law. The latter requires that the EIA must be objective, open, and impartial; comprehensively consider the impacts on various environmental factors and the ecosystem that they form after the

---

65 The Table has been prepared by the author and does not appear in the Award.

implementation of the plan or construction project; and provide a scientific basis for decision-making. The EIA for construction projects must include analysis, projection, and evaluation of the project's environmental impacts and suggestions on the implementation of environmental monitoring. The SOA Statement and the SOA Report are far less comprehensive than the EIAs reviewed by other international courts and tribunals or those filed for construction projects to which the SOA referred.

The Tribunal cannot make a definitive finding that China has prepared (or failed to prepare) an EIA, but such a finding is not necessary in order to find a breach of Article 206. To fulfill its obligations under Article 206, a State must not only prepare an EIA but also communicate it. The Tribunal directly asked China on 5 February and 15 March 2016 for a copy of any EIA that it had prepared. China did not provide one. Although China is not participating in the arbitration, China has found occasions and means to communicate statements by its officials or by others writing in line with China's interests. Had it wished to draw attention to the existence and content of an EIA, the Tribunal has no doubt that it could have done so. China has assured States parties to the Convention that construction has followed high environmental standards but has delivered no assessment in writing to them or to any other international body. China has not fulfilled its duties under Article 206.

(e) Conclusion

China has, through its toleration and protection of and failure to prevent Chinese fishing vessels engaging in harmful harvesting activities of endangered species at Scarborough Shoal, Second Thomas Shoal, and other features in the Spratly Islands, breached Articles 192 and 194(5) of the Convention.

China has, through its island-building at Cuarteron Reef, Fiery Cross Reef, Gaven Reef (North), Johnson Reef, Hughes Reef, Subi Reef, and Mischief Reef, breached Articles 192, 194(1), 194(5), 197, 123, and 206 of the Convention.

E. OCCUPATION AND CONSTRUCTION ACTIVITIES ON MISCHIEF REEF (SUBMISSION NO. 12)

1. Introduction

This Section addresses Submissions No. 12(a) and (c). To avoid duplication, the Tribunal has addressed Submission No. 12(b) in connection with Submission No. 11.

2. Factual Background

(a) China's Initial Activities on Mischief Reef (1995 to 2013)

In 1995, fiberglass structures flying the Chinese flag were seen at four locations on the reef platform. An estimated 1000 uniformed men were aboard Chinese vessels and in the structure.

China had denied building a base on the feature. In February 1995, the Philippines expressed serious concern about the presence of large warships and five smaller vessels on the feature, the construction of certain structures, and the detention of Philippine fishermen by the Chinese military. China's action violated the 1992 ASEAN Declaration on the South China Sea. The Philippines requested the immediate removal of the vessels. In March 1995, China's Vice Premier declared that the structures were typhoon shelters constructed by the

Chinese authorities to protect Chinese fishermen. The structures were civilian and did not pose a threat to any State. Between October 1998 and February 1999, China substantially enlarged two structures while removing two others. In October 1998 China informed the Philippines that it planned to renovate and reinforce the structures, which had deteriorated due to exposure to the elements. China would give consideration to the use of the facilities by other States, including the Philippines, after the completion of renovation and enforcement. China added a concrete platform supporting a three-story building at each site.

In November 1998, the Philippines demanded that China cease and desist from further improvements over illegal structures and dismantle any repair works, renovations, reinforcements, fortifications, and/or improvements. China responded that the activities were the work of local fishing authorities undertaking repair and renovation. A spokesperson later added that the structures were solely for fishermen's shelter and that the scale of the work was small. There was said to be no change in the civilian nature of the facilities. By February 1999, the two sites were equipped with a helipad, new communications equipment, and two wharves.

(b) Island-Building Activities on Mischief Reef (Post-2013)

Between 1999 and 2013, construction was limited. In January 2015, construction on Mischief Reef was resumed, involving 32 dredger vessels, 32 cargo ships, and 3 ocean tugs. In February 2015, the Philippines strongly protested land reclamation, pointing out that Mischief Reef was a low-tide elevation located in the Philippine EEZ and on its continental shelf. It demanded that China desist from reclamation. China responded that the development of any facility in the Spratly Islands fell within the scope of China's sovereignty.

An aerial photo taken in October 2015 shows that an artificial island now covers the northern half of the reef.[66] By November 2015, China's construction had created 5,580,000 square meters of new land on Mischief Reef. China had added fortified seawalls, temporary loading piers, cement plants, and a 250-meter-wide channel to allow transit into the lagoon by larger vessels. An area 3000 meters in length had been cleared and flattened along the reef's northern rim, suggesting an intention to build an airstrip.[67] The Foreign Ministry declared that construction activities are completely lawful, reasonable, and justified.

3. The Philippines' Position

China's activities violate Articles 60 (Artificial islands, installations and structures in the exclusive economic zone) and 80 (Artificial islands, installations and structures on the continental shelf) of the Convention and constitute unlawful acts of attempted appropriation.

(a) Military Activities and the Tribunal's Jurisdiction

The Tribunal's jurisdiction to consider Submission No. 12 is not constrained by the military activities exception, which was not invoked in China's Position Paper. China has repeatedly told the Philippines that the facilities on Mischief Reef were being built for civilian use. The Tribunal should accept China's characterization of its own activities.

The context of the exception requires that the nature and purpose of the activity be military, to the exclusion of other activities or purposes that are more than purely incidental. "Mixed-use projects" and situations in which a military unit is used to protect other activities

66 See Figures 30, 31, and 32 in the Award, pp. 402 and 405, *supra* note 2.

67 See Figure 17 in *ibid.*, p. 335.

are not covered by the exception. The involvement of military personnel in land reclamation does not necessarily mean that the activity purpose is military. The logistical capabilities of the armed forces are at times engaged for civilian purposes in different parts of the world. The People's Liberation Army (PLA) of China is expressly tasked by the Constitution to participate in national reconstruction. Subsequent Chinese statements cannot change the nature of the activities it has undertaken, which is determined at the time the activity occurred, not two to five years after the proceedings were started.

(b) Articles 60 and 80 of the Convention

Under Article 60, coastal States enjoy the "exclusive right" to authorize or regulate the construction of artificial islands, installations, and structures in the EEZ, a principle that is extended to the continental shelf by Article 80.

Mischief Reef is located within 200 nautical miles of the Philippines and is not within 200 nautical miles of any other maritime feature claimed by China that is capable of generating an EEZ or a continental shelf. The Philippines is the only beneficiary of Articles 60 and 80 with respect to Mischief Reef. China did not seek and receive authorization from the Philippines to build the artificial islands, installations, and structures on Mischief Reef. It thereby violated Articles 56(1)(b)(i) (Rights, jurisdiction and duties of the coastal State), 60(1), and 80. Since the Convention requires similar authorization for the operation and use of structures that have already been built, China's violation is a continuing one.

(c) Attempted Appropriation under the Convention

China's construction constitutes acts of attempted and unlawful appropriation. In view of China's assertions of sovereignty and the presence of the Chinese flag, it is beyond dispute that China claims to have appropriated Mischief Reef.

The Philippines recalls its arguments with respect to low-tide elevations in Chapter VI.B.3 of this Award.

4. China's Position

Although China is not participating in the proceedings, China's statements concerning the nature and purpose of the activities provide an indication of its position regarding the activities on the reef. China has characterized its activities on Mischief Reef as civilian. In 1995, 1998, and 1999, China stressed that the structures were not military structures but wind shelters for local fishermen. The so-called radar facilities were dish-type TV satellite antennae.

In April 2015, the Ministry of Foreign Affairs stated that China had been carrying out maintenance and construction work on some of the garrisoned Spratly Islands to optimize their functions, improve the living and working conditions of the personnel, better safeguard territorial sovereignty and maritime rights and interests, and better perform China's international rights and obligations in relation to search and rescue, disaster prevention and mitigation, marine scientific research, meteorological observation, environmental protection, navigation safety, and fishery production services. The construction, which was said to be reasonable, justified, and lawful, was well within China's sovereignty. It did not target or impact any State, and it was beyond reproach. After construction, the islands and reefs would be able to provide all-round and comprehensive services to meet civilian demands besides satisfying the needs of military defense.

The South China Sea maritime areas, where shipping lanes criss-cross (sic) and fishing grounds scatter around (sic), are far away from the landmass. These areas are prone to marine accidents due to the influence of typhoons and monsoons. Civilian construction and facilities will be included in construction for ships to take shelter and for navigation, search and rescue facilities for maritime emergencies, marine meteorological observation and forecast, fishery services, and administrative services so as to provide services to the ships of China, neighboring States, and other States that sail across the South China Sea. In August 2015, China announced the completion of land reclamation at a meeting of the ASEAN Regional Forum (ARF). China would next build facilities mainly for public good purposes, including a multi-functional lighthouse, search and rescue facilities for maritime emergencies, a meteorological observatory, a maritime science and research center, and medical and first aid facilities.

5. The Tribunal's Considerations

(a) The Tribunal's Jurisdiction

Since Mischief Reef is a low-tide elevation and no high-tide feature in the Spratlys is a fully entitled island, there exists no legal basis for any entitlement by China to maritime space in the area of Mischief Reef, nor is there a situation of overlapping entitlements calling for maritime delimitation. The remaining question is whether China's activities at Mischief Reef constitute military activities. The Tribunal takes note of China's repeated statements that its installations and island construction are intended to fulfill civilian purposes. The Tribunal will not deem activities to be military in nature when China itself has consistently resisted this classification and affirmed the opposite at the highest level. As civilian activities, China's conduct falls outside the scope of Article 298(1)(b). Accordingly, the Tribunal has jurisdiction to consider the Philippine Submission.

(b) China's Actions at Mischief Reef and the Philippines' Sovereign Rights

The dispute concerning Submission No. 12 appears to stem from the Parties' divergent understandings of their respective rights in the areas of the South China Sea within 200 nautical miles of Philippine baselines that are encompassed by the 'nine-dash line', including Mischief Reef. Each Party has evaluated its affairs from the premise that it, and not the other Party, has sovereign rights over Mischief Reef.

However much these beliefs have been held in good faith, Mischief Reef is a low-tide elevation that falls within the area where only the Philippines possesses possible entitlements to maritime zones. Mischief Reef can only be a constituent part of the Philippines' EEZ and continental shelf. It does not lie within any entitlement that could be generated by any feature claimed by China (or any other State).

i. Acts in Relation to the Installations and the Construction of Islands at Mischief Reef

The Convention is clear with respect to the law governing artificial islands, installations and structures. Article 56(1) provides that, within the EEZ, the coastal State enjoys jurisdiction with regard to the establishment and use of artificial islands, installations and structures. Article 60 elaborates on this provision, by providing that the coastal State shall have the exclusive right to construct and to authorize and regulate the construction, operation and use of artificial islands, installations, and structures and that it shall have exclusive jurisdiction over them. Notice must be given of the construction of artificial islands, installations, and structures. Those that are abandoned or disused must be removed. The coastal State also has the power to establish reasonable safety zones around artificial islands, installations, and structures. Article 60(6) makes clear that artificial islands, installations, and structures do not possess the status of islands and therefore do not have a territorial sea of their own. Article 80 applies these provisions to the continental shelf.

These provisions speak for themselves. They endow the coastal State—which in this case is necessarily the Philippines—with exclusive decision-making and regulatory power over the construction or operate artificial islands, installations, and structures. The Tribunal takes China at its word that the original purpose of the installations and structures was to provide shelter for fishermen. This is an economic purpose. The original structures, which China declined to permit fishermen from the Philippines to use, had the potential to interfere with the Philippines' exercise of its rights in the EEZ. Only the Philippines could construct or authorize these structures.

China is now engaged in island-building. It has elevated the reef platform submerged at high tide into a permanently exposed island, which is undoubtedly an artificial island for purposes of Article 60. It is equally clear that China has proceeded without receiving or even seeking the permission of the Philippines. Indeed, China's conduct has taken place in the face of Philippine protests. Article 60 is unequivocal in permitting only the coastal State to construct or authorize such islands. China's violation of its obligations is manifest.

ii. Acts in relation to Appropriation

Low-tide elevations do not form part of a State's land territory in the legal sense. They form part of a State's submerged landmass and thus fall within the legal regime of the continental shelf. As distinct from land territory, they cannot be appropriated.

Mischief Reef is a low-tide elevation and is incapable of appropriation. The Tribunal has already held that China's actions at Mischief Reef (Submissions No. 8 and 9) have unlawfully interfered with the Philippines' enjoyment of its sovereign rights. The Tribunal sees no reason to address Submission No. 12(c).

(c) Conclusion

China has, through the construction of islands, installations and structures at Mischief Reef, without the Philippines' authorization, breached Articles 60 and 80 of the Convention, with respect to the Philippines' sovereign rights in its EEZ and continental shelf. As a low-tide elevation, Mischief Reef is not capable of appropriation.

F. OPERATION OF LAW ENFORCEMENT VESSELS IN A DANGEROUS MANNER (SUBMISSION NO. 13)

1. Introduction

The Tribunal recalls its decision on jurisdiction in the Award on Jurisdiction and Admissibility.

2. Factual Background

(a) Near-Collision of Philippine Vessels BRP Pampanga and BRP Edsa II with Chinese Vessel FLEC 310

On 28 April 2012, BRP Pampanga, a coast guard ship on maritime patrol and law enforcement in the area of Scarborough Shoal, was to be relieved of its duties by BRP Edsa II. At 09:00, after the Edsa II Captain and Commander had boarded Pampanga, the latter was approached by FLEC 310 from port to almost dead ahead, at a distance of 600 yards and speed of 20.3 knots. At 09:15, FLEC 310 approached Edsa II, passing from starboard quarter to the ship's port side at a distance of 200 yards and speed of 20.6 knots. FLEC 310 maneuver created 2-meter-high waves in its wake, which battered two Philippine boats transferring personnel. Pampanga II turned over the area to Edsa II at 09:25.

(b) Near-Collision of Philippine Vessel MCS 3008 with Several Chinese Vessels upon Approach to Scarborough Shoal

On 26 May 2012, MCS 3008, a vessel of the Philippine Bureau of Fisheries and Aquatic Resources (BFAR), approached Scarborough Shoal to resupply the BRP Corregidor, a coast guard vessel. At 15:50, when it was within 7 miles from Scarborough Shoal, MCS 3008 was approached by CMS 71. The latter increased speed and at less than 100 yards from MCS 3008 attempted to cross the latter's port bow. In order to evade the impact, MCS 3008 increased its speed to 20 knots, altered the course to starboard, and passed to the rear of CMS 71. CMS 71 again swung to its starboard and attempted to cross MCS 3008's starboard bow. To avoid a collision, MCS 3008 immediately maneuvered hard port and passed through the rear of CMS 71.

MCS 3008 was then approached by FLEC 303, which started towards it and aimed to cross its starboard bow. MCS 3008 increased speed to 22 knots and swerved toward the rear of FLEC 303. MCS 3008 was pursued by FLEC 303, CMS 71, and CMS 84 until it approached BRP Corregidor. As MCS 3008 and Corregidor were side by side, CMS 84 passed through the starboard side of MCS 3008 at a distance of less than 100 yards, eventually stopped, and positioned on the port quarter at a distance of less than 500 yards; FLEC 303 was stationed at port beam with a distance of 1000 yards. As MCS 3008 pulled away from the Corregidor to head towards the lagoon of Scarborough Shoal, CMS 84 again began to chase it, aiming to cross through its bow. MCS 3008 increased speed and left behind CMS 84, but it was approached by FLEC 303, CMS 71, and FLEC 306. When FLEC 303 was 50 yards from MCS 3008, FLEC 303 immediately altered course, as if it were crossing to MCS 3008's starboard bow. When FLEC 303 was dead head of MCS 3008, it decreased speed and established a blocking position. MCS 3008 swerved towards the rear of FLEC 303 to avoid a possible impact. Meanwhile, CMS 71 was moving fast toward it but was able to approach it at only a distance of 70 yards on its portside.

At the lagoon entrance, MCS 3008, which was still being pursued by CMS 71, CMS 84, and FLEC 303, encountered FLEC 306, with three Chinese fishing vessels in blocking position. A few yards from the entrance of the Shoal, MCS 3008 decided to enter the Shoal's basin by passing between the three fishing vessels and FLEC 306 but sighted two mooring lines planted by the fishing vessels to impede movement towards the basin. MCS 3008 stopped its engines and maneuvered backward, at which point the crew of all the Chinese vessels cheered and clapped. Although FLEC 306 was already in blocking position by this time, MCS 3008 increased its speed, maneuvered hard to starboard and swerved toward FLEC 306. The latter, which was

10 meters away from the portside of MCS 3008, intended to ram it. MCS 3008 maneuvered left to dodge FLEC 306 and to avoid a shallow area 25 yards on the starboard side. It was only then that MCS 3008 was able to enter the Shoal's basin.

3. The Philippines' Position

China has breached its obligations relating to safe navigation under Articles 94 (Duties of the flag State) and 121 (Laws and regulations of the coastal State relating to innocent passage) of the Convention and the 1972 COLREGS (Convention on the International Regulations for Preventing Collisions at Sea).

(a) The Applicability of the COLREGS to China

As the flag State, China has general obligations under Article 94 of the Convention, wherever its ships are located at any particular time. Article 94(3) requires the flag State to take measures necessary to ensure safety at sea, including the use of signals, maintenance of communication, and prevention of collision. In taking such measures, the flag State must conform to generally accepted international regulations, procedures, and practices and take steps to secure their observations. The COLREGS are among the "generally accepted regulations" to which flag States are required to conform, and are recognized as such by the International Maritime Organisation (IMO).

Article 21(4) (Laws and regulations of the coastal State relating to innocent passage) also refers to international regulations relating to the prevention of collisions at sea. While Article 21(4) technically applies only to foreign ships in innocent passage in the territorial sea, a coastal State's failure to ensure that its vessels respect the COLREGS will endanger navigation for foreign ships in the territorial sea. The coastal State would then be violating its duties under Article 24 (Duties of the coastal State) to refrain from hampering innocent passage and to publicize dangers to navigation.

(b) Exceptions to the COLREGS for Special Circumstances

The COLREGS are legally binding and apply to the high seas, the EEZ, the territorial sea, archipelagic waters and sea lanes, and straits used for international navigation. They bind China with respect to its vessels operating in the vicinity of Scarborough Shoal.

COLREGS Rule 2(b) recognizes special circumstances in which departure from the Rules may be "necessary to avoid immediate danger". National courts limit the exception only to circumstances raising "immediate danger", and not "generic special circumstances". In any event, the exception is inapplicable in the present case.

(c) Application of the COLREGS to Chinese Vessels at Scarborough Shoal

China has violated Rules 2, 6, 7, 8, 15, and 16 of the COLREGS.

The Philippines relies on the expert opinion of Professor Craig Allen, who considers China to have violated Rules 2, 6, 8, and 16 of the COLREGS on both occasions. Under Rule 2, relating to the general principle of responsibility for the prevention of collisions, any vessel, owner, master, or crew is responsible for any negligence in complying with the COLREGS or of any precaution which may be required by the ordinary practice of seamanship or by the special circumstances of the case. In compliance with the Rules, due regard should be had to all dangers of navigation and collision and to any special circumstances, which may make a departure from the Rules necessary to avoid immediate danger. The conduct of the Chinese vessels in April and May 2012 intentionally endangered another vessel through high speed "blocking" or harassment maneuvers. They demonstrated serious and apparently intentional breaches of the requirement that ships take precautions required by the ordinary practice of seamen and showed flagrant disregard for the tenets of good seamanship.

Rule 6 requires vessels to proceed at a safe speed so that they can take proper and effective action to avoid collision. The Chinese vessels breached Rule 6 by passing BRP Pampanga and Edsa II at distances of 600 and 200 yards and speeds of more than 20 knots. Although "safe speed" is not specified in the COLREGS, there is little doubt that China failed to ensure that its vessels proceeded at safe speed. The failure was aggravated by the size of the Chinese vessels and the wake created by the maneuvers.

The Chinese vessels breached Rules 7 and 8, governing the risk of collision and the avoidance of collision. Rule 8 requires evasive action to have "due regard to the observance of good seamanship" and achieve passing at a "safe distance". While "safe distance" is not specified, it implies that the passing distance must be large enough to leave a margin of error and to allow for the unexpected, such as human error or mechanical malfunction. The Chinese vessels not only failed to take action to avoid collision; they also took actions that made collision substantially more likely. That no collision actually occurred does not diminish China's culpability, since the Rules impose obligations of conduct, rather than obligations of result.

Finally, Rules 15 and 16 have been violated. Rule 15 requires that the vessel on the left turn away. When CMS 71 approached MCS 3008 from the left, it was the "give-way" vessel. Yet, CMS 71 attempted to cross ahead of MCS 3008, rather than avoid the maneuver. Rule 15 requires that a vessel "so far as possible, take early and substantial action to keep well clear". Yet, the Chinese vessels intentionally closed in on MCS 3008 to attempt to block progress toward Scarborough Shoal.

Rule 2(b) permits only limited exceptions from Rule 16, "to avoid immediate danger". In the two incidents, no "immediate danger" justified departure from the Regulations. They involved intentional violations of the most basic rules for preventing collisions at sea and would be condemned by all professional mariners.

4. China's Position

China has made no statements as to the incidents raised in Submission No. 13. However, it has made statements concerning the presence of Chinese vessels at Scarborough Shoal, generally and in response to Philippine protests. In April 2012, the Philippines had expressed grave concern over the provocative and extremely dangerous maneuvers and requested that China instruct its ships to observe the COLREGS. China, rejecting the Philippine protests, stated that the conduct of the Chinese vessels was justified and completely within China's sovereignty. It urged the Philippines to immediately pull out all Philippine ships from the waters of Scarborough Shoal and to desist from disturbing the operations of Chinese fishing boats and of law enforcement vessels.

In the Position Paper, China, referring only to the incident on 10 April, declared that the presence of Philippine naval vessels at Scarborough Shoal was a "provocation" that forced China to take measures to safeguard its sovereignty. More generally, China has stated that the legality of its actions in the Spratly Islands and the waters of Scarborough Shoal rests on its sovereignty over the features and the maritime rights derived from them. China's statements indicate that it considers its actions at Scarborough Shoal to have been generally lawful.

5. The Tribunal's Considerations

(a) Background on the COLREGS

The COLREGS entered into force on 15 July 1977. One hundred fifty-six States representing more than 98 percent of the world's tonnage are party to it. China has been a party to COLREGS since 1980. Although the Philippines did not become a party to it until 2013, the Tribunal considers the COLREGS to bind both States relating to the conduct of their vessels by virtue of Article 94 (Duties of the flag State) of the Convention.

Article 94(1) requires flag States to effectively exercise their jurisdiction and control in administrative, technical, and social matters over ships flying their flag. Article 94(3) clarifies the scope of the flag State's duties, requiring them to take measures necessary to ensure safety at sea, including the use of signals, maintenance of communications, and the prevention of collisions. In taking these measures, States must conform to generally accepted international regulations, procedures, and practices (Article 94(5)). Consequently, Article 94 incorporates COLREGS into the Convention, which are binding on China. A violation of COLREGS as generally accepted international regulations constitutes a violation of the Convention.

(b) Report of Tribunal-Appointed Independent Expert

China has breached its obligations under Rules 2, 6, 8, 15, and 16 of COLREGS.

FLEC 310's high-speed maneuvering in the vicinity of BRP Pampanga on 28 April violated Rule 2(a). Veering away at a distance of 0.32 nautical miles from Pampanga exemplifies unprofessional ship handling totally inconsistent with the practice of good seamanship. A momentary decision-making lapse could have resulted in a catastrophic collision. FLEC 310's high speed at the time of its encounters with Pampanga and Edsa II (20.3 and 20.6 knots, respectively) also constitutes a breach of Rule 6 relating safe speed in the prevailing situations. FLEC 310's closing in, within 600 yards (0.296 nautical miles) and 200 yards (0.098 nautical miles) of the Philippine vessels fell short of the requirement of Rule 8 that give-way vessels "take timely action to keep clear" and to maintain a safe distance from the other ship and of the requirement of Rule 16 that give-way vessels take "early and substantial action" to maintain a safe distance.

The high-speed blocking maneuvers on 26 May of CMS 71, FLEC 303, and FLEC 306, and particularly CMS 71's attempt to cut across the bow of MCS 3008 at a distance of less than 100 yards (0.049 nautical miles) breached Rules 2, 6, and 8 of the COLREGS. CMS 71 "unnecessarily" attempting to cut across the bow of MCS 3008 is a violation of Rule 15, an unseamanlike maneuver and negligent conduct. The Chinese vessels' actions created a situation that required them to assume the role of give-way vessel and to take early and substantial action to keep well clear. The Chinese maneuvers on 26 April and 28 May demonstrated complete disregard for the observance and practice of good seamanship, including the ordinary practice of seamen, but, most importantly, total disregard for the observance of the collision regulations.

(c) Application of Article 94 of the Convention and the COLREGS

The conduct of the Chinese vessels (CMS 71, CMS 84, FLEC 303, 306, and 310) is attributable to China. All the Chinese-flagged vessels in the incidents belonged to CMS or FLEC. Because the conduct was committed by vessels directly under the Chinese government's command and control, the vessels' behavior constitutes official acts of China. Their conduct is automatically attributable to China as such.

The Chinese vessels' activities constituted violations of the COLREGS. Rule 2(a) of the COLREGS was breached by each incident. FLEC 310 passed within 200 yards of BRP Edsa II and within 600 yards of BRP Pampanga at speeds of more than 20 knots. Similar conduct occurred on 26 April. CMS 71 and FLEC 303 attempted to cut across the bow of MCS 3008 on three occasions, once at a distance of less than 100 yards. Their conduct is irreconcilable with the obligation of responsible navigation. The Tribunal accepts its expert's characterization of their conduct as being "in total disregard of good seamanship and neglect of any precaution."

The exception posed by Rule 2 (b), where "necessary to avoid immediate danger" is inapposite to the case. The high threshold established by the exception cannot apply to the facts. If anything, it was the Chinese maneuvers themselves that created immediate danger, rather than having been undertaken in response to a pre-existing threat. The Tribunal is aware that for China its actions were justified as part of law enforcement in the vicinity of a feature that it considers to be part of its territory. Yet, where operational requirements of law enforcement ships stand in tension with the COLREGS, the latter must prevail. The Tribunal can find no danger justifying departure from Rule 2(b).

The actions of Chinese vessels breached Rule 6, which requires that to avoid collisions, every vessel must all times proceed at a safe speed, so that she can take proper action to avoid collision and be stopped within a distance appropriate to the prevailing circumstances and conditions. On 28 April, FLEC 310 passed by BRP Pampanga at 20.3 knots and BRP Edsa II at 20.6 knots. The COLREGS do not define "safe speed", whose meaning and application remain dependent on the facts of each case, including the vessels' size and the probability of harm. In this instance, the Tribunal's and the Philippines' experts consider the incidents to have occurred at unsafe speeds, and the Tribunal concurs with that view.

Rule 7(a) provides that every vessel must "use all available means appropriate to the prevailing circumstances and conditions to determine if a risk of collision exists. If there is any doubt, such risk will be deemed to exist." The Tribunal considers that the "risk" identified under Rule 7 to have been clearly established. FLEC 303 closed in at high speed within 600 yards of BRP Pampanga and passed BRP Edsa II within 200 yards; CMS 71, FLEC 303, and CMS 84 passed Philippine vessels at distances of 100 yards or less. FLEC nearly rammed MCS 3008.

Once a risk is established, Rule 8 requires that action to avoid collision must be positive, made in ample time and with due regard to the observance of good seamanship. Action taken to avoid collision with another vessel will be such as to result in passing at a safe distance, which is not defined in Rule 8. In addition to the Philippine-appointed expert's definition of "safe distance", the Tribunal's expert considers that safe distance must allow for "human error on the bridge and engine or (for) steering gear failure at a critical phase of the maneuver" as well as for any incidental effects of the interaction between the passing vessels. In any evident, the conduct of the Chinese vessels falls short of any reasonable definition of a safe distance. Far from avoiding collision, their conduct made the possibility of collision substantially more likely. This fact alone—independent of the question as to whether collision was ultimately avoided—suffices to demonstrate violation of the COLREGS. The Tribunal considers that the other requirement of Rule 8 (due regard to the observance of good seamanship) has also been violated.

Rules 15 and 16 concern right of way. Both incidents constituted a breach of the COLREGS. On 28 April, FLEC 310 approached BRP Pampanga to within 60 yards. Fifteen minutes later, it passed BRP Edsa II from starboard quarter to the port side at a distance of barely 200 yards. Rather than keeping out of way and avoiding the other ship, FLEC 310 did the opposite. On 26 May, CMS 71 attempted to cut across MCS 3008's bow from port side at a distance of merely 100 yards.

The Tribunal considers China to have repeatedly violated the COLREGS, as described by the crew of the Philippine vessels and as credibly assessed in two expert reports. Where Chinese vessels were under the obligation to yield, they persisted. Where the regulations called for a safe distance, they infringed it. These actions are not suggestive of occasional negligence in failing to adhere to the COLREGS, but rather conscious disregard of international regulations. The violations are underscored by other factors, such as the large disparity in size of the Chinese and Philippine vessels, the shallow waters in which the incidents took place, and the creation of a 2-meter high wake causing additional risk to the Philippines' crew.

The operational requirements of law enforcement vessels may sometimes stand in tension with the obligations imposed by COLREGS, but this does not diminish their binding force. After considering possible circumstances precluding wrongfulness, the Tribunal has found no convincing evidence that the violations are excusable by any mitigating circumstances.

The Tribunal's determination does not depend upon and does not involve any finding of sovereignty over Scarborough Shoal and its waters. The same conclusions about violations of the navigational safety provisions of the Convention would be reached, irrespective of which State has sovereignty over Scarborough Shoal.

(d) Conclusion

China has, by virtue of the conduct of Chinese law enforcement vessels in the vicinity of Scarborough Shoal, created serious risk of collision and danger to Philippine vessels and personnel. China has violated Rules 2, 6, 7, 8, 15, and 16 of the COLREGS and is in breach of Article 94 of the Convention.

VIII. AGGRAVATION OR EXTENSION OF THE DISPUTE BETWEEN THE PARTIES (SUBMISSION NO. 14)[68]

A. INTRODUCTION

The initial formulation of Submission No. 14 comprised paragraphs (a) to (c), concerning China's interaction with the AFP at Second Thomas Shoal. In light of China's extensive land reclamation since the start of the arbitration, the Philippines sought at the Merits Hearing to amend Submission No. 14 to include paragraph (d) (dredging, artificial island-building, and construction at Mischief Reef, Cuarteron Reef, Fiery Cross Reef, Gaven Reef, Johnson Reef, Hughes Reef, and Subi Reef). On 16 December 2015, after inviting China's comments, the Tribunal gave leave to the Philippines to amend the Submission.

B. FACTUAL BACKGROUND

[68] Award of 12 July 2016, pp. 437–64, paras. 1110–81, *supra* note 2.

1. Chinese Actions in and around Second Thomas Shoal

On 7 May 1999, the Philippine Navy grounded BRP Sierra Madre on Second Thomas Shoal, where it has remained. The BRP Sierra Madre, built by the US in 1944 and transferred to the Philippines in 1976, is a ship designed for offloading tanks and other heavy equipment onto an unimpeded beach. Since May 1999, the Philippines has maintained on board the Sierra Madre a detachment of seven marines that is resupplied and rotated regularly. The Philippines commenced the arbitration on 22 January 2013.

(a) China's Objections to the Presence of BRP Sierra Madre at Second Thomas Shoal

Beginning in February 2013, the AFP reported the repeated presence of Chinese government vessels and unidentified aircraft in the vicinity of Second Thomas Shoal. On 11, 16, and 17 April, China objected to the presence of the Sierra Madre. On 17 April, the Chinese Vice Foreign Minister objected that the Sierra Madre, on the pretext of being stranded, was illegally grounded on the Shoal and that the Philippines had promised that it would immediately remove the vessel but still had not done so.

Beginning 3 May, the AFP reported a significant increase in the presence of Chinese government vessels at the Shoal, including two navy frigates and five Civilian Maritime Law Enforcement Agency vessels on a rotation basis. On 8 May, the Philippines objected to the "provocative and illegal presence" of Chinese vessels on Second Thomas Shoal and reiterated its call for China to participate in the arbitration. On 22 May, the Chinese Foreign Ministry declared that the Shoal was part of the Spratly Islands and that official Chinese vessels have conducted normal patrols in these waters.

On 28 May, a PLA official gave a TV interview in which he described the measures to seal and control the areas around Scarborough Shoal as constituting a "cabbage strategy." In the outer ring, Navy ships conduct normal patrols; in the area around the island, fishing administration ships and marine surveillance ships conduct the patrols. If the Philippines' vessels wanted to go in, they would have to go through the two rings or layers. Chinese fishermen would thus be able to fish safely. A cabbage strategy around small islands without food or drinking water would prevent resupply, forcing troops stationed on the islands to leave them within one or two weeks and preventing them from ever coming back.

On 10 June, the Philippines protested that these statements amounted to a threat to use force to prevent the Philippines from delivering essential supplies to its personnel at Second Thomas Shoal. The Philippines had no obligation to notify China of its naval or other maritime activities in the vicinity of Second Thomas Shoal or in any other area in which the Philippines had sovereignty or sovereign rights. However, to avoid conflict and misunderstanding of its intentions, the Philippines voluntarily informed China that it would deliver supplies that week to its personnel at Second Thomas Shoal. The vessel would seek to avoid contact with any Chinese vessels in the vicinity. The Philippines once again called on China to participate in the arbitration.

(b) China's Interference in the Rotation and Resupply of Philippine Personnel at Second Thomas Shoal

On 7 March 2014, China objected to any Philippine plans for large-scale construction at Second Thomas Shoal. China accused the Philippines of illegally running aground the Sierra Madre on the Shoal and of failing on its promise to tow away the ship. China urged the Philippines to tow it away and warned that it would not sit idly by while the Philippines ignored Chinese objections, insisted on construction, severely violated China's sovereign rights, and pushed China's bottom line. Rather, it would take resolute measures and actions, the consequences of which would be borne by the Philippines. Finally, China accused the Philippines of distorting the facts, misguiding the public, and covering up the truth.

On 9 March, two Chinese Coast Guard Vessels approached two Philippine vessels at distances of 400 and 200 yards and prevented them from proceeding to Second Thomas Shoal. Near Hasa-Hasa Shoal, one of the Chinese vessels warned the Philippine ships to leave the area. Subsequently, one of the two Philippine vessels suffered a mechanical breakdown and had to be towed back to Balabac, Palawan; the planned resupply and personnel rotation operations were aborted. On 11 March, the Philippines rejected the Chinese accusation that the vessels were carrying construction materials to Second Thomas Shoal. China's actions constituted a dramatic and dangerous departure from the status quo. Since these actions occurred three weeks before the submission of the Philippine Memorial, the Philippines concluded that they were intended as retaliation for the Philippines' initiation of the arbitration. China refused to accept the protest, declaring that it would never accept Philippine illegal occupation of Second Thomas Shoal in any form.

On 18 March, the Philippines informed the Tribunal that it had been able to provide some supplies to its personnel by airdrop but it had not been able to rotate them and its capacity to deliver supplies by air was limited. On 29 March 2014, a BFAR supply vessel attempted to resupply Second Thomas Shoal. Two Chinese Coast Guard vessels blocked the Philippine vessel and demanded that it turn around or "take full responsibility" for its actions. The Chinese vessels' maneuvers created a grave risk of collision, in violation of the COLREGS and Article 94 (Duties of the Flag State) of the Convention. The BFAR vessel was able to complete its rotation and supply mission by changing course, increasing its speed and navigation into the shallow waters of Second Thomas Shoal.

2. China's Dredging, Artificial Island-Building and Construction Activities

Since the commencement of the arbitration, China has greatly intensified its program of building artificial islands and installations at Mischief Reef, Cuarteron Reef, Fiery Cross Reef, Gaven Reef (North), Johnson Reef, Hughes Reef, and Subi Reef. The Philippines informed the Tribunal of these activities on 30 July 2014 and 27 April 2015.

C. THE PHILIPPINES' POSITION

1. Jurisdiction

The Philippines argues that Articles 297 (Limitations on applicability of section 2) and 298 (optional exceptions to applicability of section 2) of the Convention do not exclude the Tribunal's jurisdiction to consider the Submission. In the alternative, the Philippines argues that the exceptions do not apply to conduct that aggravates a dispute pending arbitration.

The military activities exception in Article 298(1)(b) does not exclude jurisdiction because the conduct complained of in paragraphs (a) to (c) of the Submission is not military. They are more appropriately considered to be law enforcement activities. They were largely carried out by CCG and CMS vessels, seeking to enforce China's jurisdiction. Where military vessels were used, they were used for civilian or law enforcement purposes. In the case of the construction, China has repeatedly stated that their purpose was civilian, not military. There is no basis to conclude that they are military activities, whose nature and purpose must be exclusively military, to the exclusion of all other incidental activities and purposes. The involvement of military units in construction projects does not change their nature or purpose.

The exception for law enforcement activities does not apply to the Submission. Pursuant to Article 297(2) and (3), the exception applies only to claims concerning marine scientific research or fishing in the EEZ, neither of which is addressed by the Submission. Moreover, Second Thomas Shoal is a low-tide elevation that is located more than 12 nautical miles from any high-tide feature. It is subject to Philippine sovereign rights. China is not the coastal State that is entitled to invoke the law enforcement activities exception in Second Thomas Shoal.

In the event that the Tribunal considers the activities to be military, the Philippines argues that the Tribunal's jurisdiction would remain unaffected. China's activities in and around Second Thomas Shoal give rise to a distinct dispute under Article 300 (Good faith and abuse of rights), which establishes obligations regarding good faith and abuse rights, and out of the inherent obligation of a party to refrain from aggravating or extending a dispute that is *sub judice*.[69] An act that constitutes an aggravation of a dispute need not arise from a breach of any substantive duty under the Convention. Thus, the restrictions on jurisdiction over disputes arising from these duties are irrelevant.

2. The Philippines' Rights to Have this Dispute Settled Peacefully

Corresponding to a Philippine right to have a dispute settled peacefully is China's obligation not to aggravate or extend the dispute pending its resolution.

(a) Obligation Not to Engage in Acts that Might Aggravate a Dispute

The Philippines and China are under an obligation to settle their disputes by peaceful means (Article 297, Obligation to settle disputes by peaceful means). A long-recognized corollary of this obligation is the prohibition of any acts that might aggravate or extend the dispute. Referring to the basic principles of good faith and abuse of rights (Article 300), the Philippines argues that a State must behave with restraint with a view to narrowing and not widening the differences between them. The aggravation and extension of a dispute are inconsistent with Articles 279 and 300. They prejudice the integrity of the adjudicative process and the ability of the Tribunal to render effective relief.

The Permanent Court of International Justice (PCIJ) recognized in 1939 the universally accepted principle that parties in a case must refrain from aggravating the dispute. The principle is commonly invoked by a State requesting provisional measures, but there is nothing in the Convention or international law that limits the application of the principle to provisional measures, that requires a Party to seek provisional measures in order to invoke it, or that restricts its application to situations in which it may be appropriate to prescribe provisional measures.

(b) China's Conduct in relation to the Dispute

China has dramatically and dangerously altered the *status quo pendente lite*[70] by aggressively challenging the Philippines' long-standing presence at Second Thomas Shoal and unlawfully

[69] Under or before a judge or court; under judicial consideration. Henry Campbell Black, *Black's Law Dictionary* (3rd ed.; St. Paul, MN: West Publishing Co., 1979), p. 1278.

[70] Pending the suit; during the actual progress of a suit during litigation. *Ibid.*, p. 1020.

preventing routine and supply missions that the Philippines has been conducting since 1999. These actions stem from violations of the exclusive rights and jurisdiction of the Philippines under Articles 56 (Rights, duties and jurisdiction of the coastal State in the exclusive economic zone) and 77 (Rights of the coastal State over the continental shelf) of the Convention. China's actions at Second Thomas Shoal were intended as a reprisal for the Philippine decision to move forward with arbitration.

China has greatly intensified its program of building artificial islands and installations since the commencement of the arbitration. After thousands of years of development, the coral reefs are no longer in the condition in which they were found at the time the dispute was submitted to arbitration. Direct evidence of the natural state of the features has been destroyed or covered over, and this following China's rejection of a site visit by the Tribunal. As a result, the Tribunal's capacity to render effective relief has been prejudiced. China has presented the Tribunal with a *fait accompli* of unprecedented proportions.

D. CHINA'S POSITION

1. Obligation Not to Engage in Acts that Might Aggravate a Dispute

On 6 February 2015, China, writing to the Tribunal's members, referred to its consistent and steadfast efforts to uphold and contribute to international law. Upholding the rule of law requires adherence to the fundamental principles of respect for sovereignty and territorial integrity. Efforts should be made to maintain international peace and stability rather than to instigate or even exacerbate disagreements and disputes in the name of the international rule of law.

In the Position Paper, China called attention to Article 300 (Good faith and abuse of rights) and accused the Philippines of unilaterally initiating arbitration while being fully aware that Philippine claims dealt with sovereignty and that China has never accepted any compulsory procedure in respect of these claims. China also described the Philippines' recent call on the Parties to the DOC to comply with it as a selective and self-contradictory tactic that violates the good faith principle. Good faith, which touches every aspect of international law, requires all States to honestly interpret their agreements with others and not to misinterpret them in disregard of their authentic meaning in order to obtain an unfair advantage.

2. China's Conduct in Relation to the Dispute

(a) Chinese Activities in and around Second Thomas Shoal

China's two principal objections to the conduct of the Philippines at Second Thomas Shoal refer to the Philippines' refusal to fulfill its commitment of towing away the vessel that it illegally run aground in May 1999, on the pretext of technical difficulties, and the aggravation of the situation by carrying out illegal activities in an attempt to permanently occupy Second Thomas Shoal.

(b) China's Dredging and Construction Activities

On 16 June 2015, China declared that its activities were "reasonable, justified and lawful" and well within its sovereignty. They were not targeted at any other State, did not affect the freedom of navigation and overflight enjoyed by all States, and had not caused or would not cause damage to the marine environment in the South China Sea. The main purpose was to meet various civilian demands and better perform China's international obligations and responsibilities, such as maritime search and rescue, disaster prevention and mitigation, marine scientific research, meteorological observation, conservation, navigation safety, and fishery production services. After land reclamation, China would start to build facilities to meet functional requirements.

E. THE TRIBUNAL'S CONSIDERATIONS

1. The Tribunal's Jurisdiction

In the Award on Jurisdiction and Admissibility, the Tribunal held that its jurisdiction to address the unamended Submission No. 14 may depend on the status of Second Thomas Shoal and on the nature of Chinese activities. Since the Philippines amended the Submission following the Award on Jurisdiction and Admissibility, the Tribunal has not yet considered its jurisdiction in respect of the amended Submission.

(a) China's Actions in and around Second Thomas Shoal

The Tribunal has now decided that Second Thomas Shoal is a low-tide elevation (see Chapter VI.B.5 of this Award). The Tribunal's jurisdiction is still contingent on the application of the military activities exception (Article 298(1)(b), which China's 2006 Declaration activated.

On its face, the Declaration excludes consent to jurisdiction in respect of disputes concerning military activities. Nevertheless, the Philippines considers that two limitations restrict the scope of Article 298(1)(b) and render it inapplicable. First, if China has not specifically invoked Article 298(1)(b) in the proceedings, the Tribunal need not look further into its application. The Tribunal cannot agree with this proposition. The formulation of Article 298(1) stands in stark contrast to the more optional formulation employed in Article 297(2) and (3), which provided that a State "will not be obliged to accept the submission of a dispute...". In contrast to an objection under Article 297, the Tribunal sees nothing to suggest that Article 298(1) must be specifically invoked. Once made, a declaration under Article 298(1) excludes the consent of the declaring State to compulsory settlement of the specified category of disputes, and the declaration stands until it is modified or withdrawn. The absence of any mention of Article 298(1)(b) from China's public statements does not obviate the Tribunal's need to consider the applicability of the provision.

Second, the Philippines argues that Submission No. 14 addresses only breaches of the obligation not to aggravate or extend a dispute and jurisdiction over the latter is the only requirement for jurisdiction over the Submission. The obligation not to aggravate a dispute that concerns events subsequent to commencement of proceedings is not separately subject to the limitations on dispute settlement set out in the Convention. The Tribunal points out that Article 298(1)(b) applies to disputes concerning military activities and not to "military activities" as such. In a situation in which one Party initiates compulsory dispute settlement over a dispute that does not concern military activities and the other Party employs its military in relation to the dispute during the proceedings, Article 298(1)(b) would not apply. Nor would it limit the Tribunal's jurisdiction to prescribe provisional measures in respect of military activities taking place in relation to a dispute that does not concern military activities. If the claim of aggravation or extension of a dispute is made in connection with substantive claims, it is necessary for a Tribunal to consider whether the claim depends on an underlying dispute or whether the claim constitutes a distinct dispute to which the military activities exception would be applicable.

The Philippines has never clearly identified the dispute that it considers to have been aggravated by China's actions at Second Thomas Shoal. Rather, when pressed to elaborate on the existence of the dispute, the Philippines argued that China's interference with the navigation and the prevention of rotation and resupply of Philippine troops gives rise to a distinct legal dispute under Article 300 (Good faith and abuse of rights) of the Convention. It follows that China's activities in and around Second Thomas Shoal and its interaction with Philippine military forces stationed there constitute a distinct matter, irrespective of their effect in potentially aggravating other disputes before the Tribunal.

The Tribunal finds that the essential facts at Second Thomas Shoal concern the deployment of a detachment of Philippine armed forces that is engaged in a standoff with a combination of ships from China's Navy, Coast Guard, and other government agencies. Chinese vessels have attempted to prevent the resupply and rotation of Philippine troops on at least two occasions. Although these vessels were not military vessels, Chinese military vessels were reported to be in the vicinity. This represents a quintessential military situation, involving the military forces of one side and a combination of military and paramilitary forces on the other, arrayed in opposition to one another. As these facts fall well within the military activities exception, it is not necessary to explore the outer bounds of what would or would not constitute military activities for purposes of Article 298(1)(b).

Accordingly, the Tribunal finds that it lacks jurisdiction to consider Submissions No. 14(a) to (c).

(b) China's Dredging and Construction Activities

The Tribunal has already discussed its jurisdiction with respect to its activities on seven maritime features in connection with Submissions No. 11 and 12 (see Chapter VI.D.5(a) and Chapter VI.E.5(a) of this Award). The Tribunal accepts China's repeatedly affirmed position that civilian use comprises the primary motivation underlying the works on these maritime features. Accordingly, the Tribunal need not discuss whether Submission No. 14(d) constitutes a dispute distinct from those that the Philippines alleges to have been aggravated or extended and considers that it has jurisdiction with respect to Submission No.14(d).

2. The Law Applicable to Conduct in the Course of Dispute Resolution Proceedings

Based on the extensive jurisprudence of the PCIJ and the ICJ on provisional measures, there exists a duty on parties engaged in a dispute settlement procedure to refrain from aggravating or extending the dispute during the pendency of the settlement process. The duty exists independently of any order from a court or tribunal to refrain from aggravating or extending the dispute and stems from the purpose of dispute settlement and the status of States in the proceedings. It is a duty that exists by virtue of the parties' involvement in the proceedings. The duty, which is included in bilateral and multilateral conventions and has been underlined by UN General Assembly Resolution 2625, is inherent in the central role of good faith in international legal relations.

The obligation is no less applicable to the provisions of a treaty relating to dispute settlement. Where the treaty provides for compulsory dispute settlement, good faith performance of the treaty requires the cooperation of the parties with the applicable procedure. The premise of compulsory settlement is that the final result will be binding on the parties and implemented by them. The very purpose of dispute settlement procedures would be frustrated by the actions of any part that had the effect of aggravating or extending the dispute, thereby rendering it less amenable to settlement.

The same principles are to be found in the Convention. Article 279 (Obligation to settle disputes by peaceful means) requires States to resolve their disputes by peaceful means. In carrying out the dispute settlement procedures, the Parties are under an obligation, pursuant to Article 300 (Good faith and abuse of rights), to fulfill in good faith their obligations and to exercise their rights, jurisdiction, and freedoms in a manner that would not constitute an abuse of right. The final and binding nature of the decision (Article 296 and Article 11 of Annex VII of the Convention) has an impact on the permissible conduct of parties in the course of proceedings. Actions by either Party to aggravate or extend the dispute would be incompatible with the recognition and performance in good faith of these obligations. There is no need to go beyond the Convention's text to identify the source of the law applicable to the Parties' conduct, but if it were necessary to do so, the Tribunal considers that the duty to abstain from any step that might aggravate or extend the dispute is one of the other rules of international law referred to in Article 293 (Applicable law).

3. The Effect of China's Dredging and Construction Activities on the Parties' Disputes

A necessary first step is to identify clearly the dispute that is alleged to have been aggravated or extended. Neither the Convention nor international law imposes a legal duty on States to refrain from aggravating generally their relations with one another. Actions must have a specific nexus with the rights and claims making up the dispute in order to fall foul of the limits applicable to Parties engaged in dispute settlement proceedings.

China's dredging, artificial island-building, and construction at Cuarteron Reef, Fiery Cross Reef, Johnson Reef, Hughes Reef, Gaven Reef (North), Subi Reef, and Mischief Reef bear on a number of disputes submitted by the Philippines.

a. In relation to Submissions No. 4, 6, and 7 (see Chapter VI.B.5(a) and (b) and Chapter VI.C.5(a) and (d) of this Award), China's activities have obscured the evidence of the natural status of these maritime features.
b. With respect to Submissions No. 5, 8, 9, and 12 (see Chapters VI.C, VII.A, VII.B, and VII.E of this Award), Chinese activities have obscured the evidence of the natural status of Mischief Reef. China's construction of a very large artificial island has an effect on the implementation of the Tribunal's decision and the future exercise by the Philippines of its sovereign rights in the area of Mischief Reef.
c. With respect to Submissions No. 11 and 12(d) (see Chapter VII.D of this Award), China's construction of a large artificial island has an effect on the implementation of the Tribunal's decision and the practical possibility of avoiding harm to the marine environment.

A party may aggravate a dispute

a. when it continues with actions that are alleged to violate the rights of the other Party, rendering the alleged violations more serious;
b. when it takes actions that would frustrate the effectiveness of the potential decision, rendering its implementation significantly more difficult; and

c. when it undermines the integrity of the proceedings themselves, for example, by rendering the work of the tribunal significantly more onerous or taking other actions that decrease the likelihood of the proceedings leading to the resolution of the dispute.[71]

China's intensified construction of artificial islands on the seven features in the Spratly Islands during the proceedings has unequivocally aggravated the dispute.[72]

a. China has effectively created a fait accompli at Mischief Reef by constructing a large artificial island on this low-tide elevation located within the Philippine EEZ. The implementation of the Tribunal's decision will be significantly more difficult. Mischief Reef cannot be returned to its original state, before China's construction work began.
b. China has caused irreparable harm to the coral reef habitat at Cuarteron Reef, Fiery Cross Reef, Gaven Reef (North), Johnson Reef, Hughes Reef, Subi Reef, and Mischief Reef (see Chapter VII.D.5(c) to (e) of this Award). Neither this decision nor any action that either Party may take in response can undo the permanent damage that has been done to the coral reef habitat in the South China Sea. The marine environment at Cuarteron Reef, Fiery Cross Reef, Gaven Reef (North), Johnson Reef, Hughes Reef, and Subi Reef did not form part of the Philippines' claims prior to the Merits Hearing. It is China's actions that have extended that dispute to encompass additional features that became sites of large-scale construction while the arbitration was ongoing.
c. China has undermined the integrity of the proceedings and rendered the task of the Tribunal more difficult. At the same time that the Tribunal was called on to determine the status of maritime features in the Spratly Islands, China has permanently destroyed evidence of the natural status of these features. Small rocks and sand cays that determine whether a feature constitutes a low-tide elevation or a high-tide feature are now literally buried under millions of tons of sand and concrete. The Tribunal, using the best available evidence and drawing heavily on historical sources, is satisfied that its decisions are well founded in fact, but the decisions were rendered significantly more difficult by China's works at these maritime features.

The Tribunal notes that China has refused to participate in the proceedings and continues to reject the Tribunal's jurisdiction, notwithstanding the Award on Jurisdiction and Admissibility.

> China has been free to represent itself in these proceedings in the manner it considered most appropriate, including by refraining from any formal appearance.... The decision of how best to represent China's position is a matter for China, not the Tribunal. China is not free, however, to act to undermine the integrity of these proceedings or to frustrate the effectiveness of the Tribunal's decisions. The Convention and general international law limit the actions a party may take in the course of ongoing dispute resolution proceedings. China has fallen short of its obligations in this respect.

71 The preceding enumeration has been prepared by the author and does not appear in this form in the original text.

72 The following enumeration has been prepared by the author and does not appear in this form in the original text.

4. Conclusion

While these proceedings were ongoing,

(a) China has aggravated the Parties' dispute concerning their respective rights and entitlements in the area of Mischief Reef by building a large artificial island on a low-tide elevation located in the EEZ of the Philippines;
(b) China has aggravated the Parties' dispute concerning the protection and preservation of the marine environment at Mischief Reef by inflicting permanent, irreparable harm to the coral reef habitat of that feature;
(c) China has extended the Parties' dispute concerning the protection and preservation of the marine environment by commencing large-scale island-building and construction works at Cuarteron Reef, Fiery Cross Reef, Gaven Reef (North), Johnson Reef, Hughes Reef, and Subi Reef;
(d) China has aggravated the Parties' dispute concerning the status of maritime features in the Spratly Islands and their capacity to generate entitlements to maritime zones by permanently destroying evidence of the natural condition of Mischief Reef, Cuarteron Reef, Fiery Cross Reef, Gaven Reef (North), Johnson Reef, Hughes Reef, and Subi Reef;
(e) China has extended the Parties' dispute concerning the protection and preservation of the marine environment by commencing large-scale island-building and construction works at Cuarteron Reef, Fiery Cross Reef, Gaven Reef (North), Johnson Reef, Hughes Reef, and Subi Reef; and
(f) China has aggravated the Parties' dispute concerning the status of maritime features in the Spratly Islands and their capacity to generate entitlements to maritime zones by permanently destroying evidence of the natural condition of Mischief Reef, Cuarteron Reef, Fiery Cross Reef, Gaven Reef (North), Johnson Reef, Hughes Reef, and Subi Reef.

IX. THE FUTURE CONDUCT OF THE PARTIES (SUBMISSION NO. 15)[73]

The Philippines reframed Submission No. 15 in response to the Award on Jurisdiction and Admissibility. The Tribunal gave the Philippines leave to amend it, noting that the amendment was related to or incidental to the Philippine original submission and did not involve the submission of a new dispute.

A. THE PHILIPPINES' POSITION

The focus of the Submission is prospective. The record of China's significant, persistent and continuing violations of the Philippines rights and China's statements and conduct provide ample justification for ordering China to respect the Philippines' rights and freedoms in the future and to honor its environmental obligations. The Submission is linked to the "due regard" requirement, which is one of the organizing principles of the Convention and should be given broad application.

The Philippines concentrated its arguments on a hypothetical situation that would result from a Tribunal finding any feature in the Spratly Islands to be a fully entitled island and the uncertainty, tension, and perverse effects that would potentially result from the finding. Chaos

[73] Award of 12 July 2016, pp. 465–69, pp. 1182–1201, *supra* note 2.

and insecurity had resulted in the past year and a half from unilateral actions in the absence of a precisely defined legal order.

There are no obstacles to the Tribunal's jurisdiction to address the Submission. Due to China's 2006 declaration, the Tribunal could not proceed to delimitation. However, the Tribunal would retain jurisdiction in respect of the rights and obligations of the Parties in the area of overlap pending a delimitation. Paragraph 3 of Articles 74 (Delimitation of the exclusive economic zone between States with opposite or adjacent coasts) and 83 (Delimitation of the continental shelf between States with opposite or adjacent coasts) are not maritime delimitation provisions to which Article 298(1)(a) applies. Rather, it invites structuring of a binding code of conduct pending delimitation. As such, it is a specific manifestation of the obligation to settle disputes peacefully (Article 279) and of the prohibition of the abuse of rights (Article 300). Article 298(1)(a) does not apply to these articles, as they are not specifically mentioned and they are not delimitation provisions.

B. CHINA'S POSITION

China has not directly stated its position with respect to the amended Submission. Chinese officials have made statements on the importance of good faith and the duties incumbent on States pursuant to the Convention. On 19 May 2016, the Foreign Minister declared that China acts in accordance with law and safeguards the sanctity of the Convention.

C. THE TRIBUNAL'S CONSIDERATIONS

There are three components to the Submission, which asks the Tribunal to adjudge and declare that

1. China shall respect the rights and freedoms of the Philippines under the Convention;
2. China shall comply with its duties under the Convention, including those relevant to the protection and preservation of the marine environment in the South China Sea; and
3. China shall exercise its rights and freedoms in the South China Sea with due regard to those of the Philippines under the Convention.[74]

All these propositions fall within the basic rule of "*pacta sunt servanda*", expressed in Article 26 of the 1969 Vienna Convention on the Law of Treaties as "Every treaty in force is binding upon the parties to it and must be performed by them in good faith." In essence, the Philippines is requesting a declaration that China shall do what it is already obliged by the Convention to do (Article 300).

Various provisions of the Convention make clear that States are under a duty to resolve their disputes peacefully (Article 279) and to have "due regard" to the rights and obligations of other States. There is, however, no dispute between the Parties that these general obligations define and regulate their conduct. The root of the disputes presented by the Philippines lies not in any intention on the part of China or the Philippines to infringe on the legal rights of the other, but rather in fundamentally different understandings of their respective rights under the Convention in the waters of the South China Sea. In these circumstances, the purpose of dispute resolution is to clarify the Parties' respective rights and obligations and thereby to

74 The following enumeration has been prepared by the author and does not appear in this form in the original text.

facilitate their future relations in accordance with the general obligations of good faith that both States unequivocally recognize.

To the extent that the matters presented by the Philippines have fallen within its jurisdiction, the Tribunal has already acted, through this Award, to clarify the Parties' respective rights and obligations. Much of the Philippine concern reflected in the Submission is connected with the hypothetical situation of potentially overlapping entitlements to maritime zones and the absence of an interim regime pending maritime delimitation. The Tribunal's findings with respect to Submissions No. 3, 5, and 7 and its conclusion that there is no possible overlap of entitlements that would require delimitation render that concern purely hypothetical and no basis for further action by the Tribunal.

Going forward, it is a fundamental principle of international law that bad faith is not presumed. Article 11 of Annex VII provides that the Award shall be complied with by both Parties. It goes without saying that both are obliged to resolve their disputes peacefully and to comply with the Convention and the Award in good faith.

D. CONCLUSION

It is beyond dispute that both Parties are obliged to comply with the Convention, including its provisions regarding the resolution of disputes and to respect the rights and freedoms of other States under the Convention. Neither Party contests this; the Tribunal is therefore not persuaded that it is necessary or appropriate for it to make any further declaration.

X. DISPOSITIF[75]

1202. The Tribunal recalls and incorporates the following findings reached unanimously in its Award on Jurisdiction and Admissibility of 29 October 2015:

A. that the Tribunal was properly constituted in accordance with Annex VII to the Convention;

B. that China's non-appearance in these proceedings does not deprive the Tribunal of jurisdiction;

C. that the Philippines' act of initiating this arbitration did not constitute an abuse of process;

D. that there is no indispensable third party whose absence deprives the Tribunal of jurisdiction;

E. that the 2002 China–ASEAN Declaration on Conduct of the Parties in the South China Sea, the joint statements of the Parties referred to in paragraphs 231 to 232 of the Tribunal's Award on Jurisdiction and Admissibility of 29 October 2015, the Treaty of Amity and Cooperation in Southeast Asia, and the Convention on Biological Diversity do not preclude, under Articles 281 or 282 of the Convention, recourse to the compulsory dispute settlement procedures available under Section 2 of Part XV of the Convention;

F. that the Parties have exchanged views as required by Article 283 of the Convention; and

[75] This chapter reproduces Chapter XI of the Award, pp. 471–77, paras. 1202–03.

G. that the Tribunal has jurisdiction to consider the Philippines' Submission Nos. 3, 4, 6, 7, 10, 11, and 13, subject to the conditions noted in paragraphs 400, 401, 403, 404, 407, 408, and 410 of the Tribunal's Award on Jurisdiction and Admissibility of 29 October 2015.

1203. For the reasons set out in this Award, the Tribunal unanimously, and without prejudice to any questions of sovereignty or maritime boundary delimitation, decides as follows:

A. In relation to its jurisdiction, the Tribunal:

(1) FINDS that China's claims in the South China Sea do not include a claim to 'historic title', within the meaning of Article 298(1)(a)(i) of the Convention, over the waters of the South China Sea and that the Tribunal, therefore, has jurisdiction to consider the Philippines' Submissions No. 1 and 2;

(2) FINDS, with respect to the Philippines' Submission No. 5,

a. that no maritime feature claimed by China within 200 nautical miles of Mischief Reef or Second Thomas Shoal constitutes a fully entitled island for the purposes of Article 121 of the Convention and therefore that no maritime feature claimed by China within 200 nautical miles of Mischief Reef or Second Thomas Shoal has the capacity to generate an entitlement to an exclusive economic zone or continental shelf;

b. that Mischief Reef and Second Thomas Shoal are low-tide elevations and, as such, generate no entitlement to maritime zones of their own;

c. that there are no overlapping entitlements to an exclusive economic zone or continental shelf in the areas of Mischief Reef or Second Thomas Shoal; and

d. that the Tribunal has jurisdiction to consider the Philippines' Submission No. 5;

(3) FINDS, with respect to the Philippines' Submissions No. 8 and 9:

a. that no maritime feature claimed by China within 200 nautical miles of Mischief Reef or Second Thomas Shoal constitutes a fully entitled island for the purposes of Article 121 of the Convention and therefore that no maritime feature claimed by China within 200 nautical miles of Mischief Reef or Second Thomas Shoal has the capacity to generate an entitlement to an exclusive economic zone or continental shelf;

b. that Mischief Reef and Second Thomas Shoal are low-tide elevations and, as such, generate no entitlement to maritime zones of their own;

c. that Reed Bank is an entirely submerged reef formation that cannot give rise to maritime entitlements;

d. that there are no overlapping entitlements to an exclusive economic zone or continental shelf in the areas of Mischief Reef or Second Thomas Shoal or in the areas of the Philippines' GSEC101, Area 3, Area 4, or SC58 petroleum blocks;

e. that Article 297(3)(a) of the Convention and the law enforcement exception in Article 298(1)(b) of the Convention are not applicable to this dispute; and

f. that the Tribunal has jurisdiction to consider the Philippines' Submissions No. 8 and 9;

(4) FINDS that China's land reclamation and/or construction of artificial islands, installations, and structures at Cuarteron Reef, Fiery Cross Reef, Gaven Reef (North), Johnson Reef, Hughes Reef, Subi Reef, and Mischief Reef do not constitute "military activities", within the meaning of Article 298(1)(b) of the Convention, and that the Tribunal has jurisdiction to consider the Philippines' Submission No. 11 and 12(b);

(5) FINDS, with respect to the Philippines' Submission Nos. 12(a) and 12(c):

a. that no maritime feature claimed by China within 200 nautical miles of Mischief Reef or Second Thomas Shoal constitutes a fully entitled island for the purposes of Article 121 of the Convention and therefore that no maritime feature claimed by China within 200 nautical miles of Mischief Reef or Second Thomas Shoal has the capacity to generate an entitlement to an exclusive economic zone or continental shelf;

b. that Mischief Reef and Second Thomas Shoal are low-tide elevations and, as such, generate no entitlement to maritime zones of their own;

c. that there are no overlapping entitlements to an exclusive economic zone or continental shelf in the areas of Mischief Reef or Second Thomas Shoal; and

d. that the Tribunal has jurisdiction to consider the Philippines' Submissions No. 12(a) and 12(c);

(6) FINDS with respect to the Philippines' Submission No. 14:

a. that the dispute between China and the Philippines concerning the stand-off between the Philippines' marine detachment on Second Thomas Shoal and Chinese military and paramilitary vessels involves "military activities", within the meaning of Article 298(1)(b) of the Convention, and that the Tribunal has no jurisdiction to consider the Philippines' Submissions No. 14(a) to (c); and

b. that China's land reclamation and/or construction of artificial islands, installations, and structures at Cuarteron Reef, Fiery Cross Reef, Gaven Reef (North), Johnson Reef, Hughes Reef, Subi Reef, and Mischief Reef do not constitute "military activities", within the meaning of Article 298(1)(b) of the Convention, and that the Tribunal has jurisdiction to consider the Philippines' Submission No. 14(d);

(7) FINDS, with respect to the Philippines' Submission No. 15, that there is not a dispute between the Parties such as would call for the Tribunal to exercise jurisdiction; and

(8) DECLARES that it has jurisdiction to consider the matters raised in the Philippines' Submission Nos. 1, 2, 3, 4, 5, 6, 7, 8, 9, 10, 11, 12, 13, and 14(d) and that such claims are admissible.

B. In relation to the merits of the Parties' disputes, the Tribunal:

(1) DECLARES that, as between the Philippines and China, the Convention defines the scope of maritime entitlements in the South China Sea, which may not extend beyond the limits imposed therein;

(2) DECLARES that, as between the Philippines and China, China's claims to historic rights or other sovereign rights or jurisdiction with respect to the maritime areas of the South China Sea encompassed by the relevant part of the 'nine-dash line' are contrary to the Convention and without lawful effect to the extent that they exceed the geographic and substantive limits of China's maritime entitlements under the Convention and further DECLARES that the Convention superseded any historic rights or other sovereign rights or jurisdiction in excess of the limits imposed therein;

(3) FINDS, with respect to the status of features in the South China Sea:

a. that it has sufficient information concerning tidal conditions in the South China Sea such that the practical considerations concerning the selection of the vertical datum and tidal model referenced in paragraphs 401 and 403 of the Tribunal's Award on Jurisdiction and Admissibility of 29 October 2015 do not pose an impediment to the identification of the status of features;

b. that Scarborough Shoal, Gaven Reef (North), McKennan Reef, Johnson Reef, Cuarteron Reef, and Fiery Cross Reef include or, in their natural condition, did include naturally formed areas of land, surrounded by water, which are above water at high tide, within the meaning of Article 121(1) of the Convention;

c. that Subi Reef, Gaven Reef (South), Hughes Reef, Mischief Reef, and Second Thomas Shoal are low-tide elevations, within the meaning of Article 13 of the Convention;

d. that Subi Reef lies within 12 nautical miles of the high-tide feature of Sandy Cay on the reefs to the west of Thitu;

e. that Gaven Reef (South) lies within 12 nautical miles of the high-tide features of Gaven Reef (North) and Namyit Island; and

f. that Hughes Reef lies within 12 nautical miles of the high-tide features of McKennan Reef and Sin Cowe Island;

(4) DECLARES that, as low-tide elevations, Mischief Reef and Second Thomas Shoal do not generate entitlements to a territorial sea, exclusive economic zone, or continental shelf and are not features that are capable of appropriation;

(5) DECLARES that, as low-tide elevations, Subi Reef, Gaven Reef (South), and Hughes Reef do not generate entitlements to a territorial sea, exclusive economic zone, or continental shelf and are not features that are capable of appropriation but may be used as the baseline for measuring the breadth of the territorial sea of high-tide features situated at a distance not exceeding the breadth of the territorial sea;

(6) DECLARES that Scarborough Shoal, Gaven Reef (North), McKennan Reef, Johnson Reef, Cuarteron Reef, and Fiery Cross Reef, in their natural condition, are rocks that cannot sustain human habitation or economic life of their own, within the meaning of Article 121(3) of the Convention and accordingly that Scarborough Shoal, Gaven Reef (North), McKennan Reef, Johnson Reef, Cuarteron Reef, and Fiery Cross Reef generate no entitlement to an exclusive economic zone or continental shelf;

(7) FINDS with respect to the status of other features in the South China Sea:

a. that none of the high-tide features in the Spratly Islands, in their natural condition, are capable of sustaining human habitation or economic life of their own within the meaning of Article 121(3) of the Convention;

b. that none of the high-tide features in the Spratly Islands generate entitlements to an exclusive economic zone or continental shelf;

and

c. that therefore there is no entitlement to an exclusive economic zone or continental shelf generated by any feature claimed by China that would overlap the entitlements of the Philippines in the area of Mischief Reef and Second Thomas Shoal; and

DECLARES that Mischief Reef and Second Thomas Shoal are within the exclusive economic zone and continental shelf of the Philippines;

(8) DECLARES that China has, through the operation of its marine surveillance vessels in relation to M/V Veritas Voyager on 1 and 2 March 2011 breached its obligations under Article 77 of the Convention with respect to the Philippines' sovereign rights over the non-living resources of its continental shelf in the area of Reed Bank;

(9) DECLARES that China has, by promulgating its 2012 moratorium on fishing in the South China Sea, without exception for areas of the South China Sea falling within the exclusive economic zone of the Philippines and without limiting the moratorium to Chinese flagged vessels, breached its obligations under Article 56 of the Convention with respect to the Philippines' sovereign rights over the living resources of its exclusive economic zone;

(10) FINDS, with respect to fishing by Chinese vessels at Mischief Reef and Second Thomas Shoal:

a. that, in May 2013, fishermen from Chinese flagged vessels engaged in fishing within the Philippines' exclusive economic zone at Mischief Reef and Second Thomas Shoal;

b. that China, through the operation of its marine surveillance vessels, was aware of, tolerated, and failed to exercise due diligence to prevent such fishing by Chinese flagged vessels; and

c. that therefore China has failed to exhibit due regard for the Philippines' sovereign rights with respect to fisheries in its exclusive economic zone; and

DECLARES that China has breached its obligations under Article 58(3) of the Convention;

(11) FINDS that Scarborough Shoal has been a traditional fishing ground for Fishermen of many nationalities and DECLARES that China has, through the operation of its official vessels at Scarborough Shoal from May 2012 onwards, unlawfully prevented fishermen from the Philippines from engaging in traditional fishing at Scarborough Shoal;

(12) FINDS, with respect to the protection and preservation of the marine environment in the South China Sea:

a. that fishermen from Chinese flagged vessels have engaged in the harvesting of endangered species on a significant scale;
b. that fishermen from Chinese flagged vessels have engaged in the harvesting of giant clams in a manner that is severely destructive of the coral reef ecosystem; and
c. that China was aware of, tolerated, protected, and failed to prevent the aforementioned harmful activities and

DECLARES that China has breached its obligations under Articles 192 and 194(5) of the Convention;

(13) FINDS further, with respect to the protection and preservation of the marine environment in the South China Sea:

a. that China's land reclamation and construction of artificial islands, installations, and structures at Cuarteron Reef, Fiery Cross Reef, Gaven Reef (North), Johnson Reef, Hughes Reef, Subi Reef, and Mischief Reef has caused severe, irreparable harm to the coral reef ecosystem;

b. that China has not cooperated or coordinated with the other States bordering the South China Sea concerning the protection and preservation of the marine environment concerning such activities; and

c. that China has failed to communicate an assessment of the potential effects of such activities on the marine environment, within the meaning of Article 206 of the Convention, and

DECLARES that China has breached its obligations under Articles 123, 192, 194(1), 194(5), 197, and 206 of the Convention;

(14) With respect to China's construction of artificial islands, installations, and structures at Mischief Reef:

a. FINDS that China has engaged in the construction of artificial islands, installations, and structures at Mischief Reef without the authorisation of the Philippines;

b. RECALLS (i) its finding that Mischief Reef is a low-tide elevation, (ii) its declaration that low-tide elevations are not capable of appropriation, and (iii) its declaration that Mischief Reef is within the exclusive economic zone and continental shelf of the Philippines; and

c. DECLARES that China has breached Articles 60 and 80 of the Convention with respect to the Philippines' sovereign rights in its exclusive economic zone and continental shelf;

(15) FINDS, with respect to the operation of Chinese law enforcement vessels in the vicinity of Scarborough Shoal:

a. that China's operation of its law enforcement vessels on 28 April 2012 and 26 May 2012 created serious risk of collision and danger to Philippine ships and personnel; and

b. that China's operation of its law enforcement vessels on 28 April 2012 and 26 May 2012 violated Rules 2, 6, 7, 8, 15, and 16 of the Convention on the International Regulations for Preventing Collisions at Sea, 1972; and

DECLARES that China has breached its obligations under Article 94 of the Convention; and

(16) FINDS that, during the time in which these dispute resolution proceedings were ongoing, China:

a. has built a large artificial island on Mischief Reef, a low-tide elevation located in the exclusive economic zone of the Philippines;

b. has caused—through its land reclamation and construction of artificial islands, installations, and structures—severe, irreparable harm to the coral reef ecosystem at Mischief Reef, Cuarteron Reef, Fiery Cross Reef, Gaven Reef (North), Johnson Reef, Hughes Reef, and Subi Reef; and

c. has permanently destroyed—through its land reclamation and construction of artificial islands, installations, and structures—evidence of the natural condition of Mischief Reef, Cuarteron Reef, Fiery Cross Reef, Gaven Reef (North), Johnson Reef, Hughes Reef, and Subi Reef; and

FINDS further that China:

d. has aggravated the Parties' dispute concerning their respective rights and entitlements in the area of Mischief Reef;

e. has aggravated the Parties' dispute concerning the protection and preservation of the marine environment at Mischief Reef;

f. has extended the scope of the Parties' dispute concerning the protection and preservation of the marine environment to

Cuarteron Reef, Fiery Cross Reef, Gaven Reef (North), Johnson Reef, Hughes Reef, and Subi Reef; and

g. has aggravated the Parties' dispute concerning the status of maritime features in the Spratly Islands and their capacity to generate entitlements to maritime zones; and

DECLARES that China has breached its obligations pursuant to Articles 279, 296, and 300 of the Convention, as well as pursuant to general international law, to abstain from any measure capable of exercising a prejudicial effect in regard to the execution of the decisions to be given and in general, not to allow any step of any kind to be taken which might aggravate or extend the dispute during such time as dispute resolution proceedings were ongoing.

9

Reading the Award of 12 July 2016[1]

The Award of 12 July 2016 issued by the Arbitral Tribunal constituted under Annex VII of the UN Convention on the Law of the Sea may have taken Filipinos by surprise first of all because of its length. The file consists of 501 pages, of which the text of the Award itself is 479 pages long, and comprises 1,203 paragraphs. The length is perhaps not that surprising, given the fact that the Philippines had made 15 submissions that the Tribunal had to consider. Nevertheless, reading the Award poses a challenge to anyone who wishes to familiarize himself/herself not only with the conclusions but also with the reasoning of the Tribunal.[2]

In its length, the Award is nearly double the length of a normal scholarly book (200 pages, 100,000 words). Like a scholarly book, it contains preliminary matter:

- List of representatives of the Parties (the Parties are the Philippines and China, p. i of the Award, p. 3 of the file);
- Table of Contents (pp. iii–viii of the Award, pp. 5–10 of the file);
- Table of Maps (p. ix of the Award, p. 11 of the file);
- Table of Figures (p. xi of the Award, p. 13 of the file);
- Glossary of Defined Terms (pp. xiii–xvii of the Award, pp. 15–19 of the file); and
- Glossary of Geographic Names mentioned in the Award (in English, Chinese, and Filipino, pp. xix–xx of the Award, pp. 21–22 of the file).

Like a book, the Award itself is divided into Chapters, which may be classified into two groups. Chapters I to IV deal with the background and the history of the arbitration. Although most of this has already been covered in the Award on Jurisdiction and Admissibility,[3] these chapters have naturally been updated to take account of developments since the issuance of that Award. Chapter I is the Introduction and is quite brief (pp. 1–9, pp. 23–31 of the file, paras. 1–9). Chapter II covers the Procedural History (pp. 11–40, pp. 33–61 of the file, paras. 26–39). Developments since the issuance of the first Award are recounted on pp. 19–39 (pp. 31–61 of

[1] An earlier version of this Chapter was posted on 13 July 2016 on the blog of the author's sister-in-law, https://www.raissarobles.com/2016/07/13/how-to-read-the-501-page-tribunal-ruling-on-the-south-china-sea/. The text of the Award can be found at the PCA website, https://pcacases.com/web/sendAttach/2086, accessed 26 March 2018.

[2] The ICJ Judgment in the extremely complex and sensitive *Application of the Convention on the Prevention and Punishment of the Crime of Genocide (Bosnia and Herzegovina v. Serbia and Montenegro)*, which dealt with alleged genocide (popularly known as "ethnic cleansing") in the former Yugoslavia, consisted of 201 pages and 471 paragraphs), http://www.icj-cij.org/files/case-related/91/091-20070226-JUD-01-00-BI.pdf, accessed 26 March 2018.

[3] http://www.pcacases.com/web/sendAttach/1506, accessed 30 March 2018.

the file, paras. 60–111). Chapter III, Relief Requested and Submissions (pp. 41–43, pp. 63–65 of the file, paras. 112–15), simply reproduces the 15 Philippine submissions and summarizes China's position. Half of Chapter IV, Preliminary Matters (pp. 45–55, pp. 67–77 of the file, paras. 116–68), discusses the consequences of China's non-participation; much of this ground was already covered in the first Award. The other half of the Chapter summarizes the Award on Jurisdiction and Admissibility (pp. 56–65, pp. 78–87 of the file, paras. 145–68).

The merits are examined in Chapters V to IX, constituting the bulk of the Award. The Philippines made 15 Submissions, but these are not discussed in numerical order. Rather, they have been classified into four main groups of disputes. Within each group (or sub-group), the Tribunal first gives the factual background and then summarizes the positions of the Philippines and China, before discussing its considerations. The use of the innocuous word "considerations" should not deceive the reader, for it is in this section that the Tribunal discusses the bases of its decision. If the Tribunal deferred its decision on jurisdiction for consideration together with the merits, it first discusses jurisdiction (for example, in Chapter V, pp. 85–97, pp. 107–119 of the file, paras. 202–29) and assuming it concludes that it has jurisdiction, it examines the merits (in Chapter V, pp. 97–117, paras. 119–39 of the file, paras. 230–78). In the last section of each Chapter (or part of a chapter), the Tribunal states its conclusion.

China's claim to "historic rights," as embodied in the "nine-dash line," constitutes the first group of submissions (Submissions No. 1 and 2) and is discussed in Chapter V (pp. 67–117 of the Award, pp. 89–139 of the file, paras. 169–278).

The second group of submissions (Submissions No. 3 to 7) refers to the disputes over the status of certain features in the South China Sea. The Tribunal's reasoning is carried out in two steps. The Tribunal first determines (on pp. 119–74, pp. 141–96 of the file, paras. 279–384) whether the features are low-tide elevations (above water at low tide and submerged at high-tide) or high-tide features (above water at all times) (Submission No. 4, Mischief Reef, Second Thomas Shoal, and Subi Reef, and Submission No. 6, Gaven Reef and McKennan Reef). The distinction is important, because a low tide elevation is not entitled to any maritime zone; if it is within a coastal State's territorial sea, the low-tide elevation's low water line may be used as the baseline for measuring the State's territorial sea.

If the Tribunal determines that a feature is a high-tide feature, it then proceeds to determine (on pp. 175–260, pp. 197–282 of the file, paras. 385–648, covering Submission No. 3, on Scarborough Shoal, Submission No. 5, on Mischief Reef and Second Thomas Shoal, and Submission No. 7, on Johnson Reef, Cuarteron Reef, and Fiery Cross Reef) whether it is a rock as defined by Article 121, paragraph 3 of the Convention ("rocks which cannot sustain human habitation or economic life of their own") or a fully entitled island. Again, the distinction is crucial, as a rock for purposes of Article 121 paragraph 3 is entitled only to a 12-nautical-mile territorial sea, whereas a fully entitled island, as the name implies, is entitled to all maritime zones: (1) territorial sea, (2) contiguous zone (24 nautical miles from the baselines of the territorial sea, i.e., 12 nautical miles from the outer limit of the territorial sea), (3) an EEZ (200 nautical miles from the baselines of the territorial sea),[4] and (4) a continental shelf (200 nautical miles from the baselines of the territorial sea).[5]

The third group of Submissions refers to China's activities in the South China Sea and is the object of the longest Chapter in the Award (Chapter VII, pp. 261–435 of the Award, pp. 283–457 of the file, paras. 649–1101). Chapter VII is further subdivided into six sections, each corresponding to one of China's unlawful activities, as identified by Philippine Submissions.

4 It should be noted that the outer limit of the EEZ is not measured from the outer limit of the territorial sea, as erroneously indicated in some Philippine publications.

5 It should be noted that the outer limit of the continental shelf is not measured from the outer limit of the territorial sea, as erroneously indicated in some Philippine publications.

The first section of Chapter VII examines Submission No. 8, China's alleged interference with the Philippines' sovereign rights in the EEZ and the Continental Shelf (Submission No. 8, pp. 261–86, pp. 283–308 of the file, paras. 649–716). This interference extends to non-living resources (oil and gas) and living resources (e.g., fish). The second section of Chapter V discusses Submission No. 9, China's failure to prevent Chinese nationals from exploiting the Philippines' living resources (pp. 287–97, pp. 309–19 of the file, paras. 717–57). The third section, Submission No. 10, examines China's prevention of traditional fishing by Filipinos at Scarborough Shoal (Submission No. 10, pp. 299–318, pp. 321–40 of the file, paras. 758–814). The longest section in Chapter VII (nearly 90 pages, pp. 319–97, pp. 341–419 of the file, paras. 815–993) examines in great detail the allegation that China, by allowing harmful fishing practices and harvesting of endangered species and undertaking construction on seven reefs in the Spratly Islands, has failed to preserve and protect the marine environment (Submissions No. 11 and 12(b)). The last two sections of Chapter VII are fairly brief. The fifth section examines China's occupation of and construction on one reef, Mischief Reef (Submission No. 12, pp. 399–415, pp. 420–35, paras. 994–1043). The sixth and last section examines China's operation of its law enforcement vessels in a dangerous manner (Submission No. 13, pp. 417–35, pp. 439–57, paras. 1044–109).

The fourth main set of disputes concerns the aggravation or extension of the dispute between China and the Philippines (Submission No. 14, pp. 437–64, pp. 459–86 of the file, paras. 1110-81). The Philippines complained that China prevented the rotation and resupply of Philippine personnel at Second Thomas Shoal. The Tribunal decided that the "military activities" exception was applicable to this claim and that as a result it did not have jurisdiction over the claim. The Tribunal agreed with the Philippines that China's dredging, artificial island-building, and construction since the initiation of the arbitration did aggravate or extend the dispute between the Philippines and China.

As to Submission No. 15, the Future Conduct of the Parties (Chapter IX, pp. 465–70, pp. 487–91 of the file, paras. 1182–201), the Tribunal decided not to take any action.

The last chapter, Chapter X, is entitled "Dispositif" (pp. 471–77 of the Award, pp. 493–99 of the file, paras. 1202–03). In French legal language, *dispositif* means "the final formulation of a judgment that contains the decision of the tribunal (as opposed to the 'reasons' of the judgment)."[6] This French term is widely used in English with the same meaning. The last page (p. 479, p. 501 of the file) contains the signatures of the five members of the Arbitral Tribunal and the Registrar of the Case, who is a staff member of the Registry in the case, the Permanent Court of Arbitration (PCA).

It is noteworthy that the Award has been adopted unanimously (p. 471 of the Award, p. 493 of the file, para. 1203). No separate opinion, dissenting opinion, or even declaration is attached to it. At the International Court of Justice (ICJ), a judge who agrees with the dispositif but disagrees with aspects of the reasoning that led to the dispositif may write a separate opinion. A judge who disagrees not just with the reasoning but also with the conclusions in the dispositif may append a dissenting opinion to the Judgment. A declaration may be made by a judge who wishes to express agreement or dissent without providing reasons.[7]

6 Paul Robert, *Dictionnaire alphabétique et analogique de la langue française* (Paris: S.N.L., Dictionnaire Le Robert, 1978), p. 553. A French legal dictionary defines *dispositif* as "the part of a judgment containing the solution to the dispute and to which attaches 'l'autorité de la chose jugée' [res judicata]." "[Res judicata] does not exist for the reasons of the judgment that support the decision." Raymond Guillien and Jean Vincent (eds.), *Lexique de termes juridiques* (5th ed.; Paris: Dalloz, 1981), pp. 75–76. "The sum and substance of the whole rule [res judicata] is that a matter, once judicially decided, is finally decided." Henry Campbell Black, *Black's Law Dictionary* (5th ed.; St. Paul, MN: West Publishing House, 1979), p. 1174.

7 ICJ, *Rules of Court (1978) Adopted on 14 April 1978 and Entered Into Force on 1 July 1978*, Article 95, para. 2, http://

The absence of a separate opinion, a dissenting opinion, or a declaration will confer great moral authority on the Award. Separate or dissenting opinions, or even a declaration, could have been exploited by China to undermine the reasoning or the conclusions of the Award itself. In the case of the maritime delimitation between Senegal and Guinea-Bissau, the latter, which was dissatisfied with the Award,[8] used the Declaration of the Tribunal's President, appended to the Award[9] to argue that the Award was non-existent and null and void. On this basis, Guinea-Bissau filed a case with the ICJ requesting that the latter invalidate the Award.[10] The result was further delays in maritime delimitation and additional expenses for two of the poorest countries on the planet.

In the *South China Sea Arbitration*, delays, if not indefinite postponement, in implementing the Award have not been due to any decision of the Tribunal but to the intransigence of China and the tergiversation of the Philippines.

---

www.icj-cij.org/en/rules, accessed 29 March 2018.

8 *Affaire de la délimitation de la frontière maritime entre la Guinée-Bissau et le Sénégal. Sentence du 31 juillet* 1989, *Reports of International Arbitral Awards*, XX (New York: United Nations, 2006), pp. 119–213, http://legal.un.org/riaa/cases/vol_XX/119-213.pdf, accessed 13 July 2016.

9 *Ibid.*, p. 154.

10 ICJ, *Application Instituting Proceedings Filed in the Registry of the Court on 12 March 1991. Maritime Delimitation between Guinea-Bissau and Senegal (Guinea-Bissau v. Senegal)*, http://www.icj-cij.org/files/case-related/82/6667.pdf, accessed 26 March 2018.

10

Are You Going to Scarborough Shoal?[1]

The Arbitral Tribunal's decisions on the "nine-dash line" and the entitlements of various features in the South China Sea will probably sound abstruse, abstract, and far-removed to many Filipinos, but the decision on Submission No. 10 has concrete consequences for particular fishing communities. In that Submission, the Philippines had argued that "China has unlawfully prevented Philippine fishermen from pursuing their livelihoods by interfering with traditional fishing activities at Scarborough Shoal."

Agreeing with the Philippines, the Tribunal found that Scarborough Shoal had been a traditional fishing ground for fishermen of many nationalities and declared that China through the operation of its official vessels at Scarborough Shoal from May 2012 onwards, had unlawfully prevented fishermen from the Philippines from engaging in traditional fishing at Scarborough Shoal.[2]

The Philippines emphasized that the dispute was not about China's sovereignty claim over Scarborough Shoal or China's claim to a 12-nautical-mile territorial sea or to historic sovereign rights or fishing in another State's EEZ or fishing in an area of overlapping EEZs. Rather, the dispute was about the protection of longstanding prior use in and only in the territorial sea around Scarborough Shoal.[3] The thrust of the Philippine argument is that even if China were the sovereign over Scarborough Shoal, Filipino fishermen would enjoy traditional fishing rights in the territorial sea around it. This Chapter examines two sets of concepts that help us to understand the concept of "traditional fishing rights." The first is the distinction between these rights and "historic rights" that the Philippines clarified. The second is the conception of "traditional fishing rights" as "vested rights," which was the basis of the Tribunal's reasoning.

Traditional Fishing Rights, Not Historic Rights

The differences between Philippine and Chinese positions can be expressed in terms of the differences between traditional fishing rights and "historic rights." The Philippines was obliged to make this distinction; otherwise, it could have been accused of denying China's claim to

1 An earlier version of this chapter was posted on 16 July 2016 of the blog of the author's sister-in-law, https://www.raissarobles.com/2016/07/16/are-you-going-to-scarborough-shoal/.

2 Award of 12 July 2016, p. 475, para. 1203.B(11), https://pcacases.com/web/sendAttach/2086, accessed 26 March 2018.

3 *South China Sea Arbitration, Hearing on the Merits and Remaining Issues of Jurisdiction and Admissibility, Transcript, Day 2* (25 November 2015), p. 163, https://pcacases.com/web/sendAttach/1548, accessed 30 March 2018.

"historic rights" within the nine-dash line, while claiming "historic (fishing) rights" for itself in Scarborough Shoal's territorial sea.

The Philippines based its claim of Chinese illegal actions on Article 2(3) of the UN Convention on the Law of the Sea, supported indirectly by reference to Articles 51(1) and 62(3) of the Convention. Turning to Article 2(3), one might be in for a surprise, as there is no explicit reference to fishing in the article, entitled "Legal status of the territorial sea, of the air space over the territorial sea and of its bed and subsoil." Article 2(3) simply says, "The sovereignty over the territorial sea is exercised subject to this Convention and to other rules of international law."

Citing the *Chagos Marine Protected Area Arbitration* between Mauritius and the UK (2010–15),[4] the Philippines argued that the phrase "other rules of international law" was not merely descriptive. On the contrary, it imposed substantive obligations. Among the rules that it encompassed was the general rule that required States to respect long and uninterrupted fishing by nationals of another State in its territorial sea. In other words, even if China had sovereignty over Scarborough Shoal, it was still under a duty to respect traditional fishing rights of nationals of adjacent States in the 12-nautical-mile territorial sea of Scarborough Shoal. It did not matter, either, whether Scarborough Shoal were an island or a rock: the latter, as a category of island, would be entitled to a 12-nautical-mile territorial sea.[5]

The Philippines cited several cases as precedents for the general rule that it was invoking: the *Paquete Habana* case, decided by the US Supreme Court in 1900;[6] the *Eritrea/Yemen* arbitration (1998–99);[7] and even the *Abyei* Arbitration (2008–09) between the Government of Sudan and the Sudan People's Liberation Movement/Army (SPLM/A).[8] The first case is well-known for exempting from prize capture in wartime "a poor and industrious order of people." In the second case, the parties had directed the Tribunal to resolve the issues on the basis of "historic tiles" in general international law. The reference to the third case might be more surprising, since it did not involve maritime entitlements. However, what was significant for the Philippines was the fact that "the tribunal applied the same rule even to the delimitation of a land boundary to protect traditional grazing rights."[9]

The waters surrounding Scarborough Shoal have been traditional fishing grounds for fishermen from several adjacent coastal States, such as the Philippines, Vietnam, and China (including Taiwan). To support its claim that Filipinos had a long and deep connection to Scarborough Shoal, the Philippines referred to traditional Filipino names for the Shoal and provided colonial-era maps, direct documentation of fishing since 1982, indirect evidence of fishing since 1972, and the testimony of fishermen.[10] Among the fish species that Filipinos caught were *bonito*, *talakitok*, and *tanguinge*, which are thus immortalized in an international judicial document.[11] Since 2012, the activities of fishermen have been disrupted, resulting in declines in income for some, the retirement of others, and uncertainty about the future for all.[12]

---

4 https://pca-cpa.org/en/cases/11/, accessed 26 March 2018.

5 Award of 12 July 2016, pp. 304–05, paras. 773–74, *supra* note 2.

6 US Supreme Court, The Paquete Habana, 175 U.S. 677 (1900), The Paquete Habana. Nos. 895–896 Argued 7–8 November 1899, https://supreme.justia.com/cases/federal/us/175/677/case.html, accessed 16 July 2016.

7 *Reports of International Arbitral Awards* (*RIAA*), XXII (New York: United Nations, 2006), pp. 334–410, http://legal.un.org/riaa/cases/vol_XXII/335-410.pdf, accessed 16 July 2016.

8 https://pca-cpa.org/en/cases/92/, accessed 26 March 2018.

9 *South China Sea Arbitration, Merits Hearing Transcript, Day 2*, p. 166, *supra* note 3.

10 *Ibid.*, pp. 175–76.

11 Award of 12 July 2016, pp. 301–02, paras. 762–63. See Chapter VIII of this book, footnotes 52, 53, and 54 for the scientific names of these species.

12 *Ibid.*, p. 304, para. 770.

The Tribunal was conscious of a possible contradiction in Philippine arguments. On the one hand, the Philippines argued that China's historic rights were extinguished by the Convention on the Law of the Sea; on the other hand, it asserted that traditional fishing rights had to be protected.[13] It therefore asked the Philippines during the Merits Hearing how the compatibility of traditional fishing rights with the Convention differed from the compatibility of any Chinese historic rights with the Convention.[14] In response, the Philippines explained that the traditional fishing rights that it was claiming for its nationals differed from the historical rights that China was claiming for itself in the South China Sea in three ways:

- First, China was asserting rights of control and jurisdiction, while the Philippines merely sought "access for its fishermen to pursue their traditional livelihood."
- Second, China claimed "exclusive sovereign rights," whereas the Philippines acknowledged that its fishing rights were "non-exclusive." The traditional fishing rights of Filipino fishermen would not prevent fishermen from China, or indeed from other adjacent States, like Vietnam, from fishing in Scarborough Shoal's territorial sea.
- Third, the Philippine claim was limited to the territorial sea, in contrast with China's expansive claims in the South China Sea beyond the territorial sea and, indeed, beyond any conceivable entitlement under the Convention.[15]

As for Articles 51(1) and 62(3) of the Convention on the Law of the Sea, the Philippines admitted that they were not directly applicable to the case. Article 51(1) provides that "an archipelagic State…shall recognize traditional fishing rights and other legitimate activities of the immediately adjacent neighbouring States in certain areas falling within archipelagic waters." Article 62(3) provides that, "[i]n giving access to other States to its exclusive economic zone under this article, the coastal State shall take into account all relevant factors, including, inter alia,…the need to minimize economic dislocation in States whose nationals have habitually fished in the zone." The importance of these provisions lay in the fact that they constituted express recognition of the existence of traditional fishing and its importance for the nationals of immediately adjacent coastal States. Moreover, the two articles confirmed that, where the drafters of the Convention intended to "preserve traditional fishing in the context of the new legal regimes they created," they did so "explicitly" and "made clear to what extent such prior uses were or were not protected."[16]

In its Award of 12 July 2016, the Tribunal further specified the notion of "traditional fishing rights" by characterizing them as "vested rights."

Traditional Fishing Rights as Vested Rights

At the outset, the Tribunal clarified that its discussion did not assume that either the Philippines or China enjoyed sovereignty over Scarborough Shoal. We may recall that the Tribunal's jurisdiction did not allow it to rule on sovereignty over any of the features in the South China Sea. The Tribunal's reasoning would apply whoever was the sovereign. If the Philippines had sovereignty over Scarborough Shoal, then the Tribunal's decision would also be applicable to fishing by Chinese nationals in the Shoal's territorial sea. This means that if the Philippines had sovereignty, Chinese fishermen would still be able to fish in Scarborough Shoal.[17]

[13] *Ibid.*, p. 313, para. 800.

[14] *South China Sea Arbitration, Merits Hearing, Transcript, Day 2*, p. 172, *supra* note 3.

[15] *Ibid.*, pp. 172–73; Award of 12 July 2016, p. 307, para. 781, *supra* note 2.

[16] Award of 12 July 2016, p. 308, paras. 782–83, *supra* note 1.

[17] *Ibid.*, pp. 310–11, para. 793.

The Tribunal's reasoning was divided into two parts. First, it discussed in general the law applicable to traditional fishing, which is part of traditional livelihoods and cultural patterns that are fragile and for this reason deserve attention. Traditional fishing had been extensively discussed in the arbitration between Yemen and Eritrea. The difficulty confronting the Tribunal in the latter arbitration as well as the Tribunal in the *South China Sea Arbitration* was the lack of a common definition of traditional fishing, also known as artisanal fishing, at the international level. The latter Tribunal nevertheless identified some common elements of a definition. Artisanal fishing is simple, carried out on a small scale, and uses methods that are similar to those that have historically been used in the region. Moreover, artisanal fishing is to be contrasted with industrial fishing.[18]

In the Tribunal's view, the legal basis for protecting artisanal fishing was the notion of vested rights. Vested or acquired rights are well-known in domestic law and international law. A brief definition of a "vested right" is that it is "a right complete and consummated, and of such character that it cannot be divested without the consent of the person to whom it belongs, and fixed or established, and no longer open to controversy."[19] In international law, vested rights are "private rights, acquired either by nationals or by aliens, under the existing law of a given State which, according to traditional international law, do not cease on a change of sovereignty, and in the event of State succession must be respected by the successor State."[20] The concept of vested (or acquired) rights has been applied to fur seal fishing by Indians living on the coasts of US or British territory in the Behring Sea,[21] to the acquired rights of German settlers who owned or leased land under contracts with the Prussian government and who found themselves living in territories that were ceded by Germany to Poland after World War I,[22] and to the traditional rights to graze cattle and move across the Abyei Area.[23]

Applying the notion of vested rights to fishing in the territorial sea, the Tribunal explained that "generations of fishermen who have pursued a livelihood through artisanal fishing have acquired a right, akin to property, in the ability to continue to fish in the manner of their forebears."[24] To avoid confusion with China's "historic rights" claim, the Tribunal stressed that artisanal fishing rights are rights of individuals and communities that have traditionally fished in an area. They are not the historic rights of States; rather, they are private rights.[25]

The Tribunal accepted the Philippine argument that "traditional fishing rights" were to be distinguished from China's claimed "historic rights" in the South China Sea and therefore found that there was no contradiction in the Philippine positions.[26] Before the notion of EEZ was widely adopted in the 1970s, any expansion of jurisdiction by coastal States over maritime areas was treated as functionally equivalent to a boundary adjustment, in which case acquired

18 *Ibid.*, pp. 311–12, para. 797.

19 Henry Campbell Black, *Black's Law Dictionary* (5th ed.; St. Paul, MN: West Publishing Co., 1978), p. 1402.

20 John P. Grant and J. Craig Barker, *Parry & Grant Encyclopedic Dictionary of International Law* (Oxford: Oxford University Press, 2009), p. 5.

21 *Award Between the United States and the United Kingdom Relating to the Rights of Jurisdiction of United States in the Bering's Sea and the Preservation of Fur Seals (United Kingdom v. United States), Award of 15 August 1893, RIAA*, XXVIII (New York: United Nations 2008), p. 271. http://legal.un.org/docs/?path=../riaa/cases/vol_XXVIII/263-276.pdf&lang=O, accessed 26 November 2017.

22 *Questions Relating to Settlers of German Origin in Poland, Advisory Opinion of 10 September 1923*, PCIJ Series B, No. 6, p. 36. http://www.icj-cij.org/files/permanent-court-of-international-justice/serie_B/B_06/Colons_allemands_en_Pologne_Avis_consultatif.pdf, accessed 26 November 2017.

23 *Abyei Arbitration (Government of Sudan v. Sudan People's Liberation Movement/Army), Final Award of 22 June 2009, RIAA*, vol. XXX (New York: United Nations, 2012), p. 412, para. 766, http://legal.un.org/riaa/cases/vol_XXX/145-416.pdf, accessed 11 July 2017.

24 Award of 12 July 2016, p. 312, para. 798, *supra* note 2.

25 *Ibid.*

26 *Ibid.*, p. 313, paras. 800–01.

rights, particularly those relating to fisheries, were protected. With the widespread adoption of EEZs by coastal States, the Tribunal believed that the States participating in the Third UN Conference on the Law of the Sea, which drafted the Convention, did not intend traditional fishing rights to survive the introduction of the EEZ.[27]

As a result, the Convention treats traditional fishing rights differently, depending on the maritime area:

- in archipelagic waters, they are protected;
- in the EEZ, they are extinguished, with a possible minor exception specified in Article 62(3); and
- in the territorial sea, the existing legal regime continued largely without change.[28]

The importance of the last cannot be underestimated, given that most traditional fishing takes place close to the coast, and can be expected to take place within the 12-nautical-mile territorial sea.[29]

In the second part of the Tribunal's reasoning, the protection of traditional fishing at Scarborough Shoal was examined. The Tribunal agreed with the Philippines—and, for that matter, with China—that the waters surrounding Scarborough Shoal had been traditional fishing grounds for nationals of many countries, including the Philippines, China (and Taiwan), and Vietnam. Although the Tribunal did not have extensive details of Filipino or Chinese fishing methods or of the fishing communities concerned, the available evidence was sufficient to convince it that at least some of the fishing carried out at Scarborough Shoal was traditional (artisanal) in nature.[30]

The way that the Tribunal dealt with the paucity of evidence evinces great understanding of and sympathy for the condition of traditional fishermen:

> The stories of most of those who have fished at Scarborough Shoal in generations past have not been the subject of written records, and the Tribunal considers that traditional fishing rights constitute an area where matters of evidence should be approached with sensitivity. That certain livelihoods have not been considered of interest to official record keepers or the writers of history does not make them less important to those who practice them.[31]

Adopting this perspective, the Tribunal had no trouble in accepting that Philippine and Chinese claims to have traditionally fished at the Shoal are "accurate and advanced in good faith."[32]

The Tribunal agreed with the Award in the *Chagos Marine Protected Area Arbitration* that Article 2(3) of the Convention imposed on the coastal State the obligation to exercise its sovereignty subject to other rules of international law. Among these were the rules on the treatment of the vested rights of foreign nationals, which also encompassed traditional fishing rights. The respect for traditional fishing rights does not prevent a coastal State from

27 *Ibid.*, pp. 313–14, para. 803. For the documents of the conference, see United Nations Codification Division Publications, *Third United Nations Conference on the Law of the Sea (1973–1982)* (2018), http://legal.un.org/diplomaticconferences/1973_los/, accessed 20 March 2018.

28 Award of 12 July 2016, p. 314, para. 804, *supra* note 2.

29 *Ibid.*

30 *Ibid.*, p. 315, paras. 805–07.

31 *Ibid.*, para. 805.

32 *Ibid.*

adopting reasonable regulation, for example, for purposes of conservation and restricting environmentally harmful practices.[33]

In view of the documentary evidence submitted by the Philippines, the Tribunal had no difficulty in finding that China had prevented entirely fishing by Filipino fishermen at Scarborough Shoal for significant periods of time. The fact that the vessels that resorted to blocking the entrance to the Shoal and using water cannon were official Chinese government vessels meant that under the rules for international responsibility, these acts constituted official acts of the State itself, and that the consequences of these acts were attributable to the Chinese State.[34] The Tribunal also pointed out that China's dispute with the Philippines over sovereignty and law enforcement was with the Philippine Government. The existence of the inter-State dispute could not justify action against Filipino fishermen, who were simply engaging in their traditional livelihood, or continued exclusion of Filipino fishermen from Scarborough Shoal for months, even after the Philippines had withdrawn its vessels.[35]

Although the Tribunal's decision should have been good news for Filipino fishermen (and for Vietnamese fishermen, for that matter), in the immediate aftermath of the issuance of the Award, it was reported that Chinese vessels continued to block access by Filipino fishermen to Scarborough Shoal.[36] With the change in administration in the Philippines in May 2016 and an appeal from newly elected President Duterte, China was said to be willing to open Scarborough Shoal to Filipino fishermen, even if the exact date of implementation of the policy could not be specified.[37] Filipino fishing at Scarborough Shoal was discussed during the State visit of President Duterte to China from 18 to 21 October 2016, the apparent consequence of which was that Chinese coast guard vessels stopped harassing Filipino fishermen at Scarborough Shoal.[38] The new Philippine ambassador to China went further and declared that China was complying with the Award, although it did not acknowledge the fact.[39] While China's conduct may be consistent with the Tribunal's decision, Filipino fishermen will only be able to tell whether China is truly complying with the Award when the winds of change start to blow and push Filipino and Chinese foreign policies in different directions.

---

33 *Ibid.*, p. 316, paras. 808–09.

34 *Ibid.*, pp. 316–17, paras. 810–12.

35 *Ibid.*

36 ABS-CBN News, "Two Days After Tribunal's Ruling, Filipino Fishermen Still Get Driven Away from Scarborough Shoal," *South China Sea Research: Facts and Legal Aspects*, 14 July 2016, https://seasresearch.wordpress.com/2016/07/14/two-days-after-tribunals-ruling-filipino-fishermen-still-get-driven-away-from-scarborough-shoal/, accessed 26 November 2017.

37 Desiree Sison, "China Opens Scarborough Shoal to Filipino Fishermen," *chinatopix.com*, 31 August 2016, http://www.chinatopix.com/articles/99686/20160831/china-opens-scarborough-shoal-to-filipino-fishermen.htm, accessed 26 November 2017.

38 Philippine News Agency, "Filipino Fishermen No Longer Intercepted at Scarborough Shoal," 28 October 2016, https://www.update.ph/2016/10/filipino-fishermen-no-longer-intercepted-at-scarborough-shoal/10591, accessed 26 November 2017.

39 Manuel Mogato, "New Philippine Ambassador Says China Is Complying With Arbitration Ruling," *Reuters*, 8 November 2016, https://www.yahoo.com/news/philippine-ambassador-says-china-complying-arbitration-ruling-105654168.html, accessed 26 November 2017.

11

Territorial and Maritime Claims in Multilateral Forums: The Example of China

A year after the issuance of the Award of 12 July 2016, the Philippine Department of Foreign Affairs (DFA) declared that the Duterte Administration's approach to the territorial dispute in the South China Sea sought to resolve it "in a manner consistent with the spirit of good neighbourly relations."[1] Remarkably, it is only in the title of the DFA Statement that the Arbitral Award is mentioned; one searches in vain for any reference to it in the statement itself. It is equally striking that the fact that Filipino fishermen are said to be able to fish once more at Scarborough Shoal is attributed to "the adoption of positive neighbourly relations," rather than to China's compliance with a legal obligation that it had violated for years. Other recent official statements of the Philippines concerning the negotiations for a Code of Conduct in the South China Sea studiously avoid any reference to the arbitration with China.[2] One could argue in the Administration's defense that the silence on the arbitration accurately reflects the change in policy implemented by the Duterte Administration but that it has unambiguously declared that its "commitment to protect our country's territorial claims and maritime entitlements" is "unwavering."[3] Nevertheless, the present Administration seems to forget very easily this allegedly unwavering commitment, as demonstrated by its failure to use the forums offered by the United Nations in order to explain its foreign policy to the international community. This

1 *Statement on the First Anniversary of the Arbitral Tribunal Award*, 12 July 2017, https://www.dfa.gov.ph/newsroom/statements-and-advisoriesupdate/13302-statement-on-the-first-anniversary-of-the-arbitral-tribunal-award, accessed 15 November 2017.

2 *Joint Press Release for the First Meeting of the Philippines–China Bilateral Consultation Mechanism for the First Meeting of the Philippines–China Bilateral Consultation Mechanism on the South China Sea*, 19 May 2017, https://www.dfa.gov.ph/newsroom/dfa-releasesupdate/12694-joint-press-release-for-the-first-meeting-of-the-philippines-china-bilateral-consultation-mechanism-on-the-south-china-sea, accessed 15 November 2017; *Statement on Claims by CSIS-AMTI of Ongoing Reclamation Activities in the South China Sea*, 11 August 2017, https://www.dfa.gov.ph/newsroom/statements-and-advisoriesupdate/13565-statement-on-claims-by-csis-amti-of-ongoing-reclamation-activities-in-the-south-china-sea, accessed 15 November 2017; *DFA Convenes ASEAN–China Seminar on Cooperation in South China Sea*, 28 August 2017, https://www.dfa.gov.ph/newsroom/dfa-releasesupdate/13731-dfa-convenes-asean-china-seminar-on-cooperation-in-south-china-sea?tmpl=component&print=1, accessed 15 November 2017; *DFA Convenes ASEAN–China Meeting to Assess DOC Implementation, Discuss COC Negotiations*, 30 August 2017, https://www.dfa.gov.ph/newsroom/dfa-releasesupdate/13781-dfa-convenes-asean-china-meeting-to-assess-doc-implementation-discuss-coc-negotiations?tmpl=component&print=1, accessed 15 November 2017.

3 *Statement on the First Anniversary*, *supra* note 1.

forgetfulness (to put it charitably) does not merely offer a sharp contrast with the attitudes of other UN Member States who are involved in territorial and/or maritime disputes with other UN Member States. It is also in stark contrast with the strategy of China, which itself took advantage of the opportunities offered by different UN forums to object to Japan's claim to an extended continental shelf.

The South China Sea Territorial Claims and Maritime Entitlements: The Forgotten Commitment of the Duterte Administration at the UN

Two forums are available to the Philippines at the UN to present its policy orientations and strategies concerning the country's territorial claims and maritime entitlements: the General Assembly and the Meeting of the States Parties to the UN Convention on the Law of the Sea. In both forums, the Duterte Administration failed to even allude to the country's territorial claims and maritime entitlements in the South China Sea.

The annual session of the General Assembly begins in the third week of September with what is called a "general debate." Each State presents its foreign policy in a few minutes; other Member States have the right of reply, which may be followed by a response from the State concerned. The solemnity of the occasion is highlighted by the fact that very often, heads of state or government or foreign ministers travel to New York specifically for the purpose of participating in the general debate.[4] The "general debate" constitutes a unique opportunity for each UN Member State to present a comprehensive overview of its foreign policy to the entire international community. An exposition of the country's foreign policy before the UN General Assembly would go some way towards compensating the handicap suffered by the Philippines vis-à-vis China, arising from the fact that its network of embassies in the world is much less extensive than that of China (59 versus 166).[5]

The Duterte Administration failed to take advantage of this unparalleled opportunity to reaffirm its alleged "unwavering commitment to protect our country's territorial claims and maritime entitlements" to an audience composed of all UN Members. The Philippine Foreign Secretary's speech went on at some length to discuss the war against illegal drugs, counterterrorism and violent extremism, the role of law, human rights and the rule of law, peace and security, sustainable development, and disarmament and non-proliferation. [6] In a nine-page speech, only two sentences were devoted to the South China Sea:

[4] In 2017, on the first day alone of the debate (19 September 2017), the General Assembly was addressed by the heads of State of Brazil, the US, Guinea, Switzerland, Slovakia, Nigeria, the Czech Republic, Liberia, France, Colombia, Tajikistan, Zambia, Lithuania, Qatar, Turkey, Mali, Monaco, Poland, Egypt, Uzbekistan, Armenia, Costa Rica, Uganda, Sri Lanka, Estonia, Guatemala, Afghanistan, the Gambia, Bolivia, and Honduras; the Prime Minister of Israel; and the Foreign Ministers of Mauritania and Austria. General Assembly of the United Nations, General Debate of the 72nd Session, 19–25 September 2017, https://gadebate.un.org/en, accessed 26 November 2017.

[5] China has 22 embassies in Asia, 23 in West Asia and North Africa, 40 in Africa, 12 in Europe–Central Asia, 36 in Europe, 11 in North America and Oceania, and 21 in Latin America. The list may be found in Ministry of Foreign Affairs of the People's Republic of China, *Chinese Embassies*, http://www.fmprc.gov.cn/mfa_eng/wjb_663304/zwjg_665342/2490_665344/, accessed 11 September 2016. The comparable figures for the Philippines are 17, 14, 2, 1, 16, 5, and 4. To these may be added 67 consulates general in countries in which it has no embassy (2, 2, 14, 5, 17, 5, and 22 in the different regions). These consulates general are headed by honorary consuls, who may be Filipinos residing in the country or nationals of the country who have special ties with the Philippines. Department of Foreign Affairs, *PHL Embassies and Consulates General*, http://www.dfa.gov.ph/about-us/phl/embassies-and-consulates, accessed 11 September 2016. Honorary consuls are not professional diplomats, do not exercise the functions of diplomats, and do not normally receive a salary from the State that appoints them.

[6] *Statement of Secretary Alan Peter S. Cayetano at the 72nd Session of the UN General Assembly High Level General Debate*, 23 September 2017, https://www.dfa.gov.ph/newsroom/statements-and-advisoriesupdate/14062-statement-of-secretary-alan-peter-s-cayetano-at-the-72th-session-of-the-un-general-assembly-high-level-general-debate, accessed 15 November 2017.

> The Philippines, as ASEAN Chairman this year, looks forward to successful negotiations on the long-overdue code of conduct in West Philippine Sea/South China Sea. We thank fully our ASEAN neighbours, the individual ASEAN states, and China for their utmost cooperation in this endeavor.[7]

These brief sentences cannot but surprise the reader, Filipino or foreign. It may have been too much to expect the Foreign Secretary to raise China's non-compliance with the Award of 12 July 2016. One might also with a little bit of effort gloss over the expression of gratitude to China for its cooperation in negotiating an eventual Code of Conduct in the South China Sea, even if that country had for three years verbally abused the Philippines and the Arbitral Tribunal for conducting the arbitral proceedings. One could always defend these oversights with the reminder that the Duterte Administration has changed the tack of Philippine foreign policy. But one can by no stretch of the imagination argue that these two sentences constitute an affirmation of the Administration's allegedly "unwavering commitment to protect our country's territorial claims and maritime entitlements."

One only has to glance at the speeches made at this year's general debate by other Member States that are involved in territorial and/or maritime disputes with other UN Member States to realize that States do not fail to reassert their territorial claims, even if only briefly, out of concern that silence might be interpreted as a change in policy. This observation applies equally to developed and developing States, in all regions.[8] The foreign minister of Spain, which has claimed sovereignty over Gibraltar since the Treaty of Utrecht of 1713, was quoted as saying that Spain made a proposal that "combines the unwavering claim of Spanish sovereignty over the colony with a statute that benefits the Rock's inhabitants so that they may continue to enjoy the advantages of European Union membership."[9] The Vice-President of Argentina, whose sovereignty claim over the Malvinas Islands dates back to the beginning of British occupation in 1833, emphasized her country's sovereignty over the Malvinas, South Georgia Islands, and South Sandwich Islands and the surrounding maritime spaces. She expressed the hope that the "new phase" in Argentina's relationship with the United Kingdom would help convince the latter to enter into negotiations and resolve that protracted dispute.[10] The Minister for Foreign Affairs of the United Arab Emirates affirmed his country's solid position and legitimate right to sovereignty over the three islands of Greater Tunb, Lesser Tunb, and Abu Musa, which were allegedly occupied by Iran in violation of international law and the Charter.[11] The Minister for Foreign Affairs of Morocco reaffirmed his country's readiness to work with the UN Secretary-General and his Special Envoy towards a peaceful settlement on the former Spanish colony of Western Sahara, which would maintain Moroccan sovereignty and territorial integrity.[12] Nothing would have prevented the Duterte Administration from restating briefly Philippine

---

7 *Ibid.*, p. 6.

8 The author, wishing to obtain the full text of the statement of China's permanent representative during the General Debate, visited the website of China's Permanent Mission to the UN on 16 November 2017. As a result of this visit, his hard disk was attacked by two viruses, crashed, and had to be reformatted. This was the second time in the course of his research that the author's hard disk had been attacked by viruses originating from official Chinese websites. One cannot help but wonder if official Chinese websites are programmed to attack computers with IP addresses in the Philippines.

9 H.E. Mr. Alfonso Dastis Quecedo, Minister for Foreign Affairs, 21 September 2017, https://gadebate.un.org/en/72/spain, accessed 15 November 2017.

10 Argentina, H.E. Ms. Marta Gabriela Michetti Illia, Vice-President, 20 September 2017, https://gadebate.un.org/en/72/argentina, accessed 15 November 2017.

11 United Arab Emirates, H.H. Sheikh Abdullah Bin Zayed Al Nahyan, Minister for Foreign Affairs, 22 September 2017, https://gadebate.un.org/en/72/united-arab-emirates, accessed 16 November 2017.

12 Morocco, H.E. Mr. Nasser Bourita, Minister for Foreign Affairs, 20 September 2017, https://gadebate.un.org/en/72/morocco, accessed 16 November 2017.

territorial claims, in the same way that these countries did, if its commitment had been truly "unwavering."

The June 2017 meeting of the States Parties to the UN Convention on the Law of the Sea was another lost opportunity to remind the international community of the "unwavering" commitment of the Philippines. Meetings of States parties to the Convention may be convened by the UN Secretary-General, in accordance with Article 319, paragraph 2(e) of the Convention, upon the request of any State party and for purposes of elections and organizations. Elections are held every three years for the International Tribunal for the Law of the Sea (ITLOS), every five years for the Commission on the Limits of the Continental Shelf (CLCS), for a vacancy to ITLOS, and for discussions on remuneration of ITLOS members and ITLOS expenses. Since the entry into force of the Convention in 1994, 27 such meetings have been held.

Between 2013 and 2016, the Aquino Administration called the attention of the States parties to the conduct of the arbitral proceedings. The Reports of the Meetings do not identify the States parties by name, but it is safe to assume that the Philippines was one of the States that informed the 2013 Meeting of incidents in the South China Sea, which had affected fishermen's livelihoods, and reminded States parties of their right to have recourse to dispute settlement mechanisms under Part XV of the Convention.[13] In 2014, the Philippines was probably one of the State parties that urged other State parties to respect the rights and interests of other States parties in their respective maritime zones and to resolve maritime disputes peacefully under the Convention.[14]

At the 25th meeting of the States parties in 2015, the Philippines stressed that

> China's expansionist policy claiming almost all of the South China Sea should concern the international community as a whole…China's increasingly aggressive rhetoric and action in the South China Sea [threatened] the integrity of the Convention, our constitution for the oceans.[15]

On the sidelines of the Meeting, the Philippines organized a forum entitled "UNCLOS and the Protection of the Marine Environment," which highlighted the fact that the South China Sea was already in a state of environmental crisis.[16] At the 26th meeting, held three weeks before the issuance of the Award on 12 July 2016, the Philippines underscored the obligation of States parties to participate in the mandatory dispute settlement mechanism established in the Convention when disputes arose. It also emphasized the role of arbitration in resolving disputes under the Convention.[17]

A year after the issuance of the Award of 12 July 2016, the Philippine Mission to the UN in New York does not appear to have made any reference to the arbitral proceedings at the 27th

13 *Report of the Twenty-Third Meeting of States Parties*, Doc. SPL0S/263 (8 July 2013), pp. 14–15, para. 85, https://documents-dds-ny.un.org/doc/UNDOC/GEN/N13/386/14/PDF/N1338614.pdf?OpenElement, accessed 18 July 2016.

14 *Report of the Twenty-Fourth Meeting of States Parties*, Doc. SPLOS/277 (14 July 2014), p. 19, para. 115, https://documents-dds-ny.un.org/doc/UNDOC/GEN/N14/467/74/PDF/N1446774.pdf?OpenElement, accessed 18 July 2016.

15 Philippines Permanent Mission to the United Nations, *PH to UN: South China Sea Disputes of Global Concern*, 12 June 2015, https://www.un.int/philippines/activities/ph-un-south-china-sea-disputes-global-concern, accessed 7 August 2016.

16 *Ibid.*, *Philippines Raises Concern on Environmental Crisis in South China Sea, Calls for Regional and Global Cooperation*, 10 June 2015, https://www.un.int/philippines/activities/philippines-raises-concern-environmental-crisis-south-china-sea-calls-regional-and-global, accessed 7 August 2016.

17 *Report of the Twenty-Sixth Meeting of States Parties*, Doc. SPLOS/303 (2 August 2016), p. 19, para. 110, https://documents-dds-ny.un.org/doc/UNDOC/GEN/N16/245/62/PDF/N1624562.pdf?OpenElement, accessed 30 November 2016.

Meeting of the States Parties. The only reference to the South China Sea in the Report of the Meeting cannot be attributed with certainty to any particular littoral State, given its generic character:

> With regard to the South China Sea region, one delegation called upon all relevant parties to refrain from actions that might further complicate the geopolitical situation and escalate tension, to implement the Declaration on the Conduct of Parties in the South China Sea and to conclude a legally binding code of conduct. That delegation recalled, in that context, the importance of the principles of international law, such as freedom of navigation and overflight, as well as the obligation to settle disputes peacefully.[18]

A search through the website of the Philippine Permanent Mission to the UN in New York does not yield any statement made by any Philippine representative concerning not so much the Award or the arbitration—that would have been too much to expect—but at the very least a reaffirmation of the so-called unwavering commitment of the Duterte Administration "to protect our country's territorial claims and maritime entitlements."

The Duterte Administration's failure to take advantage of the opportunities offered to it by UN forums to reaffirm its "unwavering commitment" stands in marked contrast to China's use of multilateral forums to protest against certain maritime claims of Japan.

China's Protests in Multilateral Forums Against Japan's Maritime Claims

Throughout the arbitral proceedings, China consistently declared that negotiations are "the most direct, effective and universally used means for peaceful dispute settlement."[19] Yet, if one reads carefully the Award of 12 July 2016, we discover that China, the staunch advocate of a bilateral approach to resolving the South China Sea disputes, saw the virtues of presenting its challenge to the status of the maritime feature known as Okinotorishima at meetings of the State parties of the Convention and of the International Seabed Authority, a body created by the 1982 Convention.[20]

China's dispute with Japan began in 2008, when Japan made a submission to the Commission on the Outer Limits of the Continental Shelf (CLCS), regarding the outer limits of its continental shelf.[21] The function of the CLCS, which was established under Article 76, paragraph 8, and Annex II of the 1982 Convention and is composed of 21 members who are experts in geology, geophysics, or hydrography, is to make recommendations, on the basis of data and other material submitted to it, to coastal States that wish to establish the outer limits of their continental shelves beyond 200 nautical miles.[22]

18 *Report of the Twenty-Seventh Meeting of States Parties*, Doc. SPLOS/316 (10 July 2017), p. 19, para. 104, https://documents-dds-ny.un.org/doc/UNDOC/GEN/N17/209/81/PDF/N1720981.pdf?OpenElement, accessed 16 November 2017.

19 *Official Position Paper of the Government of the People's Republic of China on the Matter of Jurisdiction in the South China Sea Arbitration Initiated by the Republic of the Philippines, 2014/12/07*, para. 87, http://www.fmprc.gov.cn/mfa_eng/zxxx_662805/t1217147.shtml, accessed 15 December 2014.

20 Award of 12 July 2016, pp. 197–99, para. 452–58, https://pcacases.com/web/sendAttach/2086, accessed 26 March 2018.

21 The following draws heavily on Xue Guifang (Julia), "How Much Can a Rock Get? A Reflection From the Okinotorishima Rocks," in Myron H. Nordquist, John Norton Moore, Alfred A.H. Soons, and Hak-so Kim (eds.), *The Law of the Sea Convention: US Accession and Globalization* (Leiden: Martinus Nijhoff Publishers, 2012), pp. 342–43.

22 The continental shelf comprises "the seabed and subsoil of the submarine areas that extend beyond its territorial sea

Three of the seven regions in Japan's submission were based on a maritime feature known as Okinotorishima. The latter, which a few decades ago had five protrusions, consists at present of only two rocks, extending 4.5 kilometers from east to west and 1.7 kilometers from north to south. The rocks' area is 5 square kilometers within the rim of a reef, most of which is submerged even at low tide. If Okinotorishima was considered as a fully entitled island, then it would be entitled to all the maritime zones of fully entitled islands: a 12-nautical-mile territorial sea, a 24-nautical-mile contiguous zone measured from the baselines of the territorial sea, a 200-nautical-mile EEZ measured from the baselines of the territorial sea, and a 200-nautical-mile continental shelf measured from the baselines of the territorial sea. Japan's continental shelf would have an area of 740,000 square kilometers, twice the size of Japan's land territory (378,000 square kilometers). If these were considered rocks within the meaning of Article 121(3) of the UN Convention on the Law of the Sea (i.e., islands with no human habitation and no economic life of their own) and therefore entitled merely to a territorial sea, Japan's claim to an EEZ and continental shelf would be reduced by 430,000 square kilometers. The problem for Japan's claim that the Okinotorishima rocks are fully entitled islands, which must be permanently above water at high tide, is that typhoons and erosion threaten the reef's existence. To stop the rocks from disappearing and to keep them above water at high tide, Japan has spent $600 million since the late 1980s to build steel breakers and concrete casings.[23]

Since 2004, China has constantly objected to Japan's jurisdiction over marine scientific research around Okinotorishima, which Japan would have the right to regulate, authorize, and conduct if Okinotorishima were entitled to an EEZ and a continental shelf, pursuant to Article 246, paragraph 1 of the Convention. China does not claim the rocks, but it believes that the legal status of the surrounding waters is that of the high seas, which are traditional fishing grounds for fishermen from China, Taiwan, and South Korea.

As the Award of 12 July 2016 points out, China, in a Note Verbale to the UN Secretary-General on 6 February 2009, objected to the Japanese submission to the CLCS, on the grounds that Japan's submission was illegally encroaching on the International Seabed Area.[24] The Area, which comprises those parts of the ocean beyond national jurisdiction as well as their resources, is declared by the Convention to be the common heritage of mankind (Article 136). As such, it is not subject to any claim or exercise of sovereignty or sovereign rights (Article 137). Activities in the Area are to be carried out for the benefit of mankind as a whole, with the Convention providing for a mechanism for the equitable sharing of financial and other economic benefits derived from activities in the Area (Article 140).

China was not satisfied with expressing its objection to Japan's submission concerning Okinotorishima at the CLCS and went one step further. In 2009, a few months before the 19th Meeting of States Parties to the Convention, China proposed that the Meeting discuss the relationship between the International Seabed Area and claims of island status. It argued that

> coastal States should comply fully with the Convention, taking into account the overall interests of the international community, and should not interpret the Convention in a biased way, nor put their own interest above the overall interests of the international community, nor encroach upon the Area as the common heritage of mankind.[25]

---

throughout the natural prolongation of its land territory to the outer edge of the continental margin," which may extend beyond 200 nautical miles. UN Convention on the Law of the Sea, Article 76(1) and (4), http://www.un.org/depts/los/convention_agreements/texts/unclos/unclos_e.pdf, accessed 15 July 2015.

23 Justin McCurry, "Japan to Spend Millions on Tiny Islands 1,000 Miles South of Tokyo," *The Guardian*, 3 February 2016, https://www.theguardian.com/world/2016/feb/03/japan-spend-billions-yen-tiny-okinotori-islands-1000-miles-south-of-tokyo, accessed 5 August 2016.

24 Award of 12 July 2016, p.197, para. 452, *supra* note 20.

25 *Ibid.*, p. 198, para. 453.

Without naming Japan, China accused some States of failing to comply with the Convention by making claims to continental shelf with an isolated rock in the ocean as base point.[26] The Meeting decided not to include the matter as a new agenda item but did discuss it under another agenda item.[27]

Almost simultaneously, at the 15th session of the International Seabed Authority in June 2009, China raised the issue of rocks and continental shelf submissions. Japan objected that the Authority's session was not the appropriate forum for discussion of individual continental shelf submissions, since the Authority had no jurisdiction on the matter.[28] China refuted Japan, arguing that the Authority was the right forum to discuss the issue, as the Authority had the mandate to protect the Common Heritage of Mankind.[29]

If China, the fervent advocate of bilateral approaches to the resolution of the South China Sea disputes, is not averse to multilateral approaches to law of the sea disputes when it finds it convenient to do so, then there is no reason why the Philippines should not have emulated China's pragmatic approach. The Duterte Administration stands a better chance of convincing a Filipino audience that its commitment to Philippine territorial claims and maritime entitlements is "unwavering," rather than vacillating, when it seizes all the opportunities available to it in all appropriate international forums to assert them firmly.

---

26 *Ibid.*, p. 198, para. 454.

27 *Report of the Nineteenth Meeting of the States Parties*, Doc. SPLOS/203 (24 July 2009), pp. 3–4, 12–13, paras. 11–13, 14, 70–78, https://documents-dds-ny.un.org/doc/UNDOC/GEN/N09/424/12/PDF/N0942412.pdf?OpenElement, accessed 18 July 2016.

28 International Seabed Authority, *Seabed Adopts Recommendations of Finance Committee; Completes Debate on Secretary-General's Report and Considers Commonwealth Secretariat's Request for Observer Status*, Doc. SB/15/14 (4 June 2009), p. 3, https://www.isa.org.jm/sites/default/files/files/documents/sb-15-14.pdf, accessed 8 August 2016.

29 Award of 12 July 2016, pp. 198–199, para. 456, *supra* note 20.

12

Memo to Taiwan: Beijing Is (Almost Always) to Blame

Immediately after the release to the public on 12 July 2016 of the Award in the *South China Sea Arbitration*, the Ministry of Foreign Affairs (MOFA) of the Republic of China (ROC) issued a thunderous statement.[1]

The very first sentence echoed Beijing's rejection of the Award, but its imprecision provides a foretaste of the lack of rigor of the legal arguments put forward by Taiwan in the rest of the press release: "The award rendered by the tribunal at the Permanent Court of Arbitration in the South China Sea arbitration is completely unacceptable to the government of the Republic of China." We now know that the Award was issued by an Annex VII Tribunal and that the Tribunal did not hold a public sitting for the rendering of the award.[2]

In the second sentence of the statement, Taiwan asserted that "[t]he tribunal's decisions have no legally binding force on the ROC." It went on to give two reasons, but the attentive reader will realize that in fact there are three separate reasons. These will be discussed in order of increasing gravity: the designation of Taiwan as "the Taiwan Authority of China"; the failure to invite Taiwan to the proceedings; and the expansion of the Tribunal's authority.

The Designation of Taiwan as the "Taiwan Authority of China"

Taiwan complains that "[i]n the text of the award, the ROC is referred to as 'Taiwan Authority of China,' and that this inappropriate designation is demeaning to the status of the ROC as

---

1 Ministry of Foreign Affairs, Republic of China (Taiwan), *ROC Position on the South China Sea Arbitration*, 12 July 2016, http://www.mofa.gov.tw/en/PrintContent.aspx?n=1EADDCFD4C6EC567&t=FB01D469347C76A7, accessed 14 July 2016.

2 In the Press Release on 29 June 2016 announcing the date of issuance of the Award, the Tribunal specified that "[t]here will be no in-person meeting or ceremony for the rendering of the Award." PCA, Tribunal Sets Date for Issuance of Final Award, Tenth Press Release, 29 June 2016, https://pcacases.com/web/sendAttach/1782, accessed 30 March 2018. The practice of the International Court of Justice is different. It always holds a public sitting, in which the President reads the dispositif of the Judgment. Statute of the International Court of Justice, Article 58, http://legal.un.org/avl/pdf/ha/sicj/icj_statute_e.pdf, accessed 11 September 2016. But the Arbitral Tribunal, which was not bound by the ICJ Statute, decided not to hold a public sitting. This procedural decision was important in the Philippine context, as the attendance of a large Philippine delegation at the jurisdictional hearing in July 2015 had been criticized in the press and on social media. Louis Bacani, "Palace Hits Lawyer for Questioning Big Hague Delegation," *The Philippine Star*, 8 July 2015, http://www.philstar.com/headlines/2015/07/08/1474653/palace-hits-lawyer-questioning-big-hague-delegation, accessed 28 November 2017; Christine F. Herrera, "The Hague Delegation 'Meant to Impress,'" *The Manila Standard*, 10 July 2015, http://manilastandard.net/news/top-stories/181937/the-hague-delegation-meant-to-impress-.html, accessed 28 November 2017.

a sovereign state." It is true that the Philippines and the Tribunal referred to Taiwan as the "Taiwan Authority of China."[3] The expression is an unfamiliar one even to those who know that Taiwan is classified as an economy in APEC and is described as "Separate Customs Territory of Taiwan, Penghu, Kinmen and Matsu (Chinese Taipei)" at the WTO.[4] One might be puzzled by Taiwan's complaint when one discovers, upon reading the footnotes of the Award of 12 July 2016, that the Tribunal uses "Republic of China" whenever it cites official documents published by the ROC. For example, footnote 443 on p. 190 refers the reader to three publications of the "Ministry of the Interior of the Republic of China": *A Frontier in the South China Sea: Biodiversity of Taiping Island, Nansha Islands, Compilation of Historical Archives on the Southern Territories of the Republic of China*, and *Compilation of Historical Archives on the Southern Territories of the Republic of China.*

Why then did the Tribunal use the term "Taiwan Authority of China" to designate Taiwan in the text proper of the Award? As the title of this essay suggests, all one has to do is to look across the Taiwan Strait to Beijing for the answer. In paragraph 22 of the Position Paper of the People's Republic of China of 7 December 2014, one finds the following sentence:

> ...the Philippines has deliberately excluded from the category of the maritime features "occupied or controlled by China" the largest island in the Nansha Islands, Taiping Dao, which is currently controlled by the Taiwan authorities of China.[5]

This sentence makes clear that if there is any actor to blame for the designation "demeaning to the status of the Republic of China," it is Beijing. The Tribunal and the Philippines merely adopted the expression used to refer to the "renegade province" (i.e., Taiwan) by the government of the People's Republic of China. The latter is recognized by the overwhelming majority of members of the international community recognizes as the sole legitimate representative of China. According to Taiwan's MOFA, only 24 States in the world recognize the ROC as a State.[6] The most that the Tribunal can be accused of is that it used the expression "Taiwan Authority" rather than "Taiwan Authorities." If anything, Taiwan should be grateful to the Tribunal for the use of the singular (*authority*), as it suggests a degree of unity that the word "authorities" does not.

The Failure to Invite Taiwan to the Proceedings

Taiwan's second objection sounds very serious: "The arbitral tribunal did not formally invite the ROC to participate in its proceedings, nor did it solicit the ROC's views." Unfortunately, the objection is based on a flawed assumption and portrays only a partial picture of the Tribunal's conduct.

The flawed assumption is that Taiwan should have been invited to the proceedings. Taiwan

3 For examples, see Award of 12 July 2016, p. 190, paras. 432–34, https://pcacases.com/web/sendAttach/2086, accessed 26 March 2018.

4 WTO, *Member Information. Separate Customs Territory of Taiwan, Penghu, Kinmen and Matsu (Chinese Taipei) and the WTO*, 2016, https://www.wto.org/english/thewto_e/countries_e/chinese_taipei_e.htm, accessed 11 September 2016.

5 http://www.fmprc.gov.cn/mfa_eng/zxxx_662805/t1217147.shtml, accessed 15 December 2014.

6 According to Taiwan's MOFA, the ROC currently maintains diplomatic relations with six States in the South Pacific (Kiribati, Nauru, Palau, the Marshall Islands, Solomon Islands, and Tuvalu), three States in Africa (Burkina Faso, São Tomé e Principe, and Swaziland), one State in Europe (The Holy See), and 12 States in Latin America and the Caribbean (Belize, the Dominican Republic, El Salvador, Guatemala, Haiti, Honduras, Nicaragua, Panama, Paraguay, Saint Kitts and Nevis, St. Lucia, and Saint Vincent and the Grenadines). *Diplomatic Allies*, 2014, http://www.mofa.gov.tw/en/AlliesIndex.aspx?n=DF6F8F246049F8D6&sms=A76B7230ADF29736, accessed 11 September 2016.

does not explain why it should have been invited to participate in the proceedings. It is not a party to the UN Convention on the Law of the Sea. Observers from Australia, Japan, Malaysia, Singapore, Thailand, and Vietnam were permitted to attend the Hearing on the Merits as observers because they are parties to the Convention.[7] The US request to attend the Hearing as an observer was refused, on the grounds that the US was not a party to the Convention.[8] There is no reason why Taiwan should have been treated any differently than the US.

Unlike the US, Taiwan could not have and still could not become a party to UN Convention on the Law of the Sea because Taiwan is not a UN member. Taiwan occupied the seat of China at the UN from 1945 to 1971. In the latter year, the UN General Assembly adopted Resolution 2758, by a vote of 76 for, 35 against, with 17 abstentions. The second paragraph of the preamble declared that the representatives of the government of the People's Republic of China are "the only lawful representatives of China to the UN." Accordingly, the General Assembly decided "to restore all its rights to the People's Republic of China," to recognize "the representatives of its government as the only legitimate representatives of China to the UN," and "to expel forthwith the representatives of Chiang Kai-shek from the place which they unlawfully occupy at the United Nations and in all the organizations related to it."[9] Since the government of the People's Republic of China is the only legitimate representative of China to the UN, Taiwan was not (and could not have been) invited to the UN Conference on the Law of the Sea (1973–82), which drafted the Convention.[10] Since Taiwan is not a UN member and is not recognized as a State by most UN members, it does not belong to the category of entities that could become party to the Convention.[11] One can only imagine the fury of Beijing, which had refused to appear before the Arbitral Tribunal, if the latter had invited Taiwan, which is not recognized as a State by most UN members, is not a UN member, and is not a party to the Convention, to participate in the proceedings.

The second part of the objection, to the effect that the Tribunal did not solicit Taiwan's views, is only a partial description of the Tribunal's conduct towards Taiwan. There is

---

7 Award of 12 July 2016, p. 22, para. 65; pp. 24–25, para. 70, *supra* note 3.

8 *Ibid.*, p. 22, paras. 65 67.

9 UN General Assembly Resolution 2758 (XXVI), "Restoration of the Lawful Rights of the People's Republic of China in the United Nations," http://www.un.org/en/ga/search/view_doc.asp?symbol=A/RES/2758(XXVI), accessed 9 August 2016.

10 United Nations Second Codification Division Publications, *Third United Nations Conference on the Law of the Sea (1973–1982)* (2018), http://legal.un.org/diplomaticconferences/1973_los/, accessed 20 March 2018.

11 Article 305(1) of the Convention provides the following:

> 1. This Convention shall be open for signature by:
> (a) all States;
> (b) Namibia, represented by the United Nations Council for Namibia;
> (c) all self-governing associated States which have chosen that status in an act of self-determination supervised and approved by the United Nations in accordance with General Assembly resolution 1514 (XV) and which have competence over the matters governed by this Convention, including the competence to enter into treaties in respect of those matters;
> (d) all self-governing associated States which, in accordance with their respective instruments of association, have competence over the matters governed by this Convention, including the competence to enter into treaties in respect of those matters;
> (e) all territories which enjoy full internal self-government, recognized as such by the United Nations, but have not attained full independence in accordance with General Assembly resolution 1514 (XV) and which have competence over the matters governed by the Convention, including the competence to enter into treaties in respect of those matters; and
> (f) international organisations, in accordance with Annex IX.

United Nations Convention on the Law of the Sea, adopted 10 December 1982. https://treaties.un.org/doc/Publication/UNTS/Volume%201833/v1833.pdf, accessed 16 July 2016.

no denying that Taiwan was not requested to submit a Counter-Memorial or any other submissions. However, the Tribunal, once it became aware of Taiwan's publications in early 2016, took cognizance of them. In January 2016, a first set of publications consisted of a 23 January 2016 press release from Taiwan's Ministry of Foreign Affairs and President Ma Ying-jeou's public remarks dated 28 January 2016.[12] In March 2016, three further publications by Taiwan came to the Tribunal's attention: "Position Paper on ROC South China Sea Policy Republic of China (Taiwan)" (21 March 2016); remarks by President Ma Ying-jeou at an international press conference "regarding Taiping Island in Nansha Islands" (23 March 2016); and "Amicus Curiae Submission by the Chinese (Taiwan) Society of International Law" (23 March 2016), accompanied by 39 exhibits.[13] On both occasions, the Tribunal did not reject outright the documentation that Taiwan submitted. Rather, it transmitted them to China and the Philippines for their comments. Consistent with its policy of non-participation, China did not respond to the Tribunal's invitation for comments, but the Philippines did, as we shall see below. Suffice it to say for the moment that although the Tribunal did not solicit Taiwan's views, it did not ignore them when the Tribunal became aware of them and sought the Parties' comments on them.

The Alleged Expansion of the Tribunal's Authority

The final and most serious ground that Taiwan invoked for the nullity of the Award is based on the Tribunal's decision that Itu Aba (Taiping Island), presently occupied by Taiwan, is a rock for purposes of Article 121(3) of the Convention, i.e., it is not capable of sustaining human habitation or economic life of its own. One can understand Taiwan's reaction to the Tribunal's decision. If Itu Aba had been declared a fully entitled island, it would have been entitled to a 12-nautical-mile territorial sea, a 200-nautical-mile EEZ measured from the baselines of the territorial sea, and a 200-nautical-mile continental shelf measured from the baselines of the territorial sea. As a rock that is not capable of sustaining human habitation or economic life of its own, Itu Aba is entitled to only a 12-nautical-mile territorial sea.

Taiwan objected to the very fact that Taiping Island was considered in the decision:

> Taiping Island was not originally included in the Philippines' submissions for arbitration. However, the tribunal took it upon itself to expand its authority, declaring ROC-governed Taiping Island, and other features in the Nansha (Spratly)

12 Ministry of Foreign Affairs of the Republic of China (Taiwan), "Taiping Island Is an Island, Not a Rock, and the ROC Possesses Full Rights Associated with an Exclusive Economic Zone and Continental Shelf in Accordance with UNCLOS" (23 January 2016), Annex 875, *Responses of the Philippines to the Tribunal's 2 February 2016 Request for Written Comments (11 March 2016) (Annexes 864–892)*, pp. 216–52, https://files.pca-cpa.org/pcadocs/The%20Philippines%27%20Written%20Responses%20%2811%20March%202016%29%20%28Annexes%20864-892%29.pdf, accessed 30 March 2018; Office of the President of the Republic of China, "Remarks by President Ma on Taiping Island" (28 January 2016), http://english.president.gov.tw/Default.aspx?tabid=491&itemid=36616&rmid=2355, accessed 9 March 2016); also Annex 876, *ibid.*, pp. 253–61; *South China Sea Arbitration, Responses of the Philippines to the Tribunal's 5 February 2016 Request for Comments* (11 March 2016), p. 17, paragraph 43, https://pcacases.com/web/sendAttach/1849, accessed 28 November 2017; Award of 12 July 2016, p. 31, para. 89(c), *supra* note 3.

13 Republic of China (Taiwan), Position Paper on ROC South China Sea Policy (21 March 2016), http://multilingual.mofa.gov.tw/web/web_UTF-8/South/Position%20Paper%20on%20ROC%20South%20China%20Sea%20Policy.pdf, accessed 28 November 2017; Office of the President of the Republic of China, "President Ma's Remarks at International Press Conference Regarding Taiping Island in Nansha Islands" (23 March 2016), https://www.mac.gov.tw/en/News_Content.aspx?n=FE07F9DA122E29D4&sms=3A4E63FA5107487D&s=F3B2B90AA560D22F, accessed 28 November 2017; *Amicus Curiae Submission by the Chinese (Taiwan) Society of International Law* (23 March 2016), http://csil.org.tw/home/wp-content/uploads/2016/03/SCSTF-Amicus-Curiae-Brief-final.pdf, accessed 27 October 2016.

> Islands occupied by Vietnam, the Philippines, and Malaysia, all to be rocks that "do not generate an exclusive economic zone."[14]

Taiwan is here implying, in so many words, that the Tribunal had committed *excès de pouvoir*, which is defined in French administrative law as "action exceeding legal power" or "decision of a judge that exceeds his jurisdiction."[15] In international arbitral practice, it is translated as "excessive exercise of power" and

> may consist, not only in deciding a question not submitted to the arbitrators, but also in misinterpreting the express provisions of the agreement in respect of the way in which they are to reach their decisions, notably with regard to the legislation or the principles of law to be applied.[16]

The excessive exercise of power may be a ground for invoking the invalidity of an arbitral award. If Taiwan's objection is tantamount to a charge of *excès de pouvoir*, it is a grave one, indeed.

One can readily agree with the first part of Taiwan's objection. One will search in vain for a reference to Taiping (Itu Aba) in the Philippines' Submissions No. 3 (Scarborough Shoal), 4 (Mischief Reef, Second Thomas Shoal, and Subi Reef), 5 (Mischief Reef and Second Thomas Shoal), 6 (Gaven Reef and McKennan Reef [including Hughes Reef]), and 7 (Johnson Reef, Cuarteron Reef, and Fiery Cross Reef).[17] It might thus seem legitimate to ask why the Tribunal considered the issue whether Taiping Dao (Itu Aba) is a fully entitled island or a rock that is not capable of sustaining human habitation or an economic life of its own and whether the Tribunal did "[take] it upon itself to expand its authority." To answer these questions, one must again look to Beijing.

In its 2014 Position Paper, China complained that the Philippines, by requesting that the Tribunal rule on the status of particular features, had not taken the Spratly Islands as a whole and dissected them:

> The Philippines, by requesting the Arbitral Tribunal to determine the maritime entitlements of only what it describes as the maritime features "occupied or controlled by China," has in effect dissected the Nansha Islands [Spratly Islands]. It deliberately makes no mention of the rest of the Nansha Islands, including those illegally seized or claimed by the Philippines. Its real intention is to gainsay China's sovereignty over the whole of the Nansha Islands, deny the fact of its illegal seizure of or claim on several maritime features of the Nansha Islands, and distort the nature and scope of the China–Philippines disputes in the South China Sea.[18]

An additional reason for China's objection to the Philippine approach was the fact that

---

14 *ROC Position on the South China Sea Arbitration*, 12 July 2016, *supra* note 1.

15 Paul Robert, *Dictionnaire alphabétique et analogique de la langue française* (Paris: S.N.L., Dictionnaire Le Robert. 1978), p. 723.

16 "Award of the Tribunal of Arbitration Constituted Under an Agreement signed at Caracas, February 13, 1909, Between the United States of America and the United States of Venezuela. The Hague, October 25, 1910," in James Brown Scott (ed.), *The Hague Court Reports* (New York: Oxford University Press, 1916), p. 232. See also Santiago Benadava, "La 'competencia de la competencia' y el exceso de poder en la justicia arbitral," in Calixto A. Armas Barea et al. (eds.), *Liber Amicorum 'In Memoriam' of Judge José María Ruda* (The Hague: Kluwer Law International, 2000), pp. 221–30.

17 Award of 12 July 2016, p. 41, para. 112, *supra* note 3.

18 *Supra* note 6, para. 22.

> ...the Philippines has deliberately excluded from the category of the maritime features "occupied or controlled by China" the largest island in the Nansha Islands, Taiping Dao, which is currently controlled by the Taiwan authorities of China.[19]

These quotations demonstrate without any room for doubt that it was not the Tribunal that first raised the issue of Taiping Dao (Itu Aba); it was the People's Republic of China.

Taiwan must share some of the blame with the People's Republic of China for the inclusion of Itu Aba in the proceedings, through its publications in 2015 and early 2016 that came to the Tribunal's attention. The Philippines' responses to both sets of documents, which were transmitted to it by the Tribunal, are worth noting. In relation to the first set, the Philippines argued that Taiwan's public declarations constituted an explicit attempt to rebut the Philippine case. In the Philippine view, the materials were created specifically for the purpose of making a legal case, after the case had already been fully pleaded and after the close of the Merits Hearing. They were prepared for the specific purpose of influencing the Tribunal's ongoing deliberations after the record had been closed. They should be considered "self-serving evidence" specially created for the purposes of litigation. Contemporary evidence from persons with direct knowledge; evidence that has not been, before litigation, challenged by impartial persons for correctness of content; and statements from government officials or other knowledgeable sources that acknowledge unfavorable facts are sources of evidence considered as inherently more probative by international courts and tribunals.[20] As for the substance of the claims concerning Itu Aba, the Philippines pointed out that Taiwan's assertions about Itu Aba were unsupported by actual evidence and did not withstand scrutiny. For example, President Ma's claim that Itu Aba had a rich supply of ground water was not supported by any evidentiary source of any kind.[21] As for the publications that appeared in March 2016, the Philippines identified serious shortcomings in the documentation that accompanied the amicus curiae submission of the Chinese (Taiwan) Society of International Law. The translations provided of certain documents were only partial; other documents cited in the text were not annexed at all. When the Philippines obtained full translations of the former and copies of the latter, it turned out that these flatly contradicted the assertions made in the submission.

The Philippines believed that given the late date at which the documents were published—nearly four months after the close of the oral hearings and at a time when the Tribunal's deliberations were already advanced—the Philippines would be well within its rights in requesting that the Taiwanese materials should be disregarded. Nevertheless, the Philippines recognized the exceptional difficulties that China's non-appearance had created for the Tribunal and chose not to object to the Tribunal's consideration of Taiwan's most recent materials. That said, the Philippines requested that the Tribunal not entertain any further efforts by Taiwan to interfere in the proceedings.[22]

Once Taiwan's publications had come to the Tribunal's attention, the Tribunal could hardly ignore them. Once it was asked to react to them, the Philippines could hardly ignore the Tribunal's request. Once Taiwan's arguments for and the Philippines' arguments against had been examined, the Tribunal could hardly avoid ruling on them. The Tribunal gives other, cogent reasons that explain why it ruled on the status as fully entitled islands or "rocks which

19 *Ibid.*

20 *Responses of the Philippines to the Tribunal's 5 February 2016 Request for Comments*, p. 18, para. 47; p. 20, para. 52; p. 21, paras. 55–56, *supra* note 12.

21 *Ibid.*, p. 19, paras. 48, 50.

22 *Responses of the Philippines to the Tribunal's 1 April 2016 Request for Comments on Additional Materials Regarding the Status of Itu Aba* (25 April 2016), p. 2, paras. 5–8, https://pcacases.com/web/sendAttach/1850, accessed 17 September 2016; Award of 12 July 2016, p. 190, para. 434, *supra* note 3.

cannot sustain human habitation or economic life of their own" of Taiwan-occupied Itu Aba and the more significant high-tide features in the Spratly Islands, rather than confining itself to the features identified by the Philippines.[23] The discussion so far should suffice to prove that the Tribunal did not "(take) it upon itself to expand its authority," with the implication that the Tribunal had exceeded its power.

As the Philippines pointed out, China and Taiwan share an interest in having Itu Aba declared a fully entitled island. This common interest seems to have caused Taiwan to forget what one would have thought was a maxim of its domestic and foreign policy: Beijing is (almost always) to blame.

---

23 *Ibid.*, pp. 237–60, paras. 577–648, *supra* note 3.

13

The Binding Force of the Award of 12 July 2016

Following the issuance of the Award of 12 July 2016, China orchestrated a propaganda campaign, led by no less than the Vice-Minister of Foreign Affairs, whose aim was to deny the validity of the Award.[1] The campaign was part of an undertaking to "tear down" [sic][2] the veil of the Arbitral Tribunal, as if China were revealing some secret or unlocking some mystery that the Philippines and/or the Tribunal had deliberately kept from the public.[3] The campaign exploited the public's lack of understanding of a number of basic principles of international law. First, the Chinese government argued that since the Permanent Court of Arbitration (PCA) is neither permanent nor a court, "its award (on the merits) has nothing to do with justice." But China was setting up a straw man, since it is no secret that the PCA is not a court strictly speaking.[4] Second, China contended that because the arbitral tribunal is not part of a system of permanent international courts, it cannot be an international court. Undoubtedly, the Arbitral Tribunal is not part of a system of permanent international courts. Yet, it is an integral element of the system of dispute settlement entailing binding procedures enshrined in the UN Convention on the Law of the Sea. Finally and most importantly, China argued that the Award was invalid because the Tribunal is not a court; even if it were, the Award was not binding on China because China had refused to participate in the proceedings. This argument ignores the principles that awards of international arbitral tribunals are binding and that non-appearance of one of the parties has no effect on the binding force of an award. Each of these arguments will be dealt with in turn in this chapter, beginning with the critique based on the observation that the PCA is not a court.

---

1 The text of the Award may be found on the PCA website, https://pcacases.com/web/sendAttach/2086, accessed 27 March 2018.

2 The translator seems to have confused three expressions. One tears apart a veil and one tears down a building, but one does not tear down a veil. One can also "pierce" a veil. It should also be noted that the past participle of "to tear" is "torn."

3 Ministry of Foreign Affairs of the People's Republic of China, *Veil of the Arbitral Tribunal Must Be Tore (sic) Down—Vice Foreign Minister Liu Zhenmin Answers Journalists' Questions on the So-Called Binding Force of the Award Rendered by the Arbitral Tribunal of the South China Sea Arbitration Case, 2016/07/13*, http://www.fmprc.gov.cn/mfa_eng/wjbxw/t1381879.shtml, accessed 18 July 2016.

4 A straw man is "a weak argument or opposing view set up by a politician, debater, etc. so as to be able to attack it and gain an easy, showy victory." *Collins English Dictionary*, https://www.collinsdictionary.com/dictionary/english/straw-man, accessed 30 November 2017.

The Permanent Court of Arbitration as the Registry in the Arbitration

Chinese international law scholars correctly stated that "the PCA in nature is neither a specialized agency for intergovernmental legal issues, nor an experienced organization for territorial disputes."[5] But anyone who has taken a basic course in international law can readily agree that the PCA is neither a permanent nor a court.[6] This has been public knowledge since the establishment of the PCA in 1899, i.e., for nearly 120 years now. The PCA was established by the Convention for the Pacific Settlement of International Disputes concluded at The Hague during the first Hague Peace Conference.[7] Article 1 explicitly declares that the PCA was organized "with the object of facilitating an immediate recourse to arbitration for international differences." The PCA merely facilitates arbitrations by maintaining a list of qualified arbitrators, nominated by the States parties to the 1899 Convention (Article 23). States that wish to organize arbitration would then be able to choose arbitrators from the list (Article 24).

China's critique of the PCA as neither "permanent" nor a court is not even as severe as that of some scholars. The late Charles Rousseau (1902–93), author of a five-volume treatise on international law, totaling 3071 pages, published between 1970 and 1983, described the PCA as follows:

> This pseudo-permanent Court does not deserve its name to any degree: it is not a court, and it is not permanent…It is…an ephemeral tribunal in a permanent framework….The PCA is not, strictly speaking, a court of justice: it is merely a list of persons that have been designated in advance in order to exercise arbitral functions.[8]

Despite the well-known facts concerning the nature of the PCA, China implies that the PCA actually settled disputes by declaring that "[a]t the beginning of the PCA, it only made arbitration on the disputes between nation-states."[9] China further insinuates that the PCA was engaged in empire-building, accusing it of extending "its arbitration realm to disputes between nation-states and international organizations as well as disputes between nation-states and private sectors." The aim would have been to "maintain its existence," after a long period during which States refrained from recourse to its services."[10]

The expression "arbitration realm" is patently inaccurate, if it is used to refer to the putative jurisdiction of the PCA. The PCA maintains list of arbitrators from which States may choose arbitrators once they have decided to submit a dispute to arbitration.[11] The jurisdiction of the

5 "Permanent Court of Arbitration Neither Permanent nor a Court," *xinhuanet.com*, 16 July 2016, http://news.xinhuanet.com/english/2016-07/16/c_135518252.htm, accessed 18 July 2016.

6 In fact, the author usually had one question asking whether the PCA was a court in his short-answer examinations at the undergraduate and graduate levels. There were always some who were misled by the word *court* in the PCA's name.

7 See the text of the Convention on the PCA website: https://pca-cpa.org/wp-content/uploads/sites/175/2016/01/1899-Convention-for-the-Pacific-Settlement-of-International-Disputes.pdf, accessed 30 March 2018.

8 "Cette pseudo-Cour permanente ne mérite à aucun degré son nom: ce n'est pas une Cour, et elle n'est pas permanente. C'est…un tribunal éphémère dans un cadre permanente…La C.P.A. n'est pas…à proprement parler, une Cour de justice: c'est une simple liste de personnes désignées d'avance pour exercer des fonctions arbitrales." Charles Rousseau, *Droit international public* (8th ed.; Paris: Éditions Dalloz, 1976), p. 315. For a brief biography of Rousseau, see the article by Marie Duclaux de l'Estoille on the website of the *Société française pour le droit international*, http://www.sfdi.org/internationalistes/rousseau-charles/, accessed 30 November 2017.

9 "Permanent Court of Arbitration Neither Permanent nor a Court," *supra* note 3.

10 *Ibid.*

11 The Chinese Vice Foreign Minister, Liu Zhenmin, who led the attack on the validity of the Award of 12 July 2016, has been on the list of arbitrators maintained by the PCA since 2014. PCA, *Members of the Permanent Court of Arbitration* (2017), https://pca-cpa.org/wp-content/uploads/sites/175/2017/07/Current-List-Annex-1-Members-

particular arbitral tribunal will depend on the agreement under which it was established and will therefore vary from case to case. The jurisdiction is that of the tribunal and not of the PCA.

As explained in the Award on Jurisdiction and Admissibility, the five members of the Arbitral Tribunal were appointed by the President of the International Tribunal for the Law of the Sea (ITLOS), pursuant to Articles 3(c), 3(d), and 3(e) of Annex VII of the Convention.[12] These provisions require that the arbitrators be drawn from a list of arbitrators maintained by the UN Secretary-General under Article 2(1) of Annex VII of the UN Convention on the Law of the Sea, rather than from the list of arbitrators maintained by the PCA. One might thus ask why the case had a PCA case number and why the Press Releases carried the logo of the PCA. The explanation is simple: the Arbitral Tribunal designated the PCA as the Registry in the case. The Tribunal did so after consulting China, which refused to comment, and the Philippines, which approved the designation. The PCA website very clearly explains that in addition to maintaining lists of arbitrators, it also offers services to arbitrations between States as well as arbitrations between States and private entities (investor–State arbitrations).

If designated as the Registry in either type of case, the PCA will

- transmit oral and written communications from the parties to the arbitral tribunal and vice-versa and between the parties;
- maintain an archive of filings and correspondence;
- make all arrangements concerning the amounts of the arbitrators' fees and advance deposits on the fees;
- hold the party deposits and disbursing tribunal fees and expenses;
- assist the arbitral tribunal in establishing the date, time, and place of hearings;
- give advance notice of the hearings to the parties;
- make its hearing and meeting rooms in the Peace Palace or elsewhere available to the parties and the arbitral tribunal at no charge in PCA-administered proceedings (costs relating to catering, court reporting, or other support associated with hearings or meetings at the Peace Palace or elsewhere are borne by the parties);
- make arrangements for transcription, recording, interpretation, translation, catering, or other support associated with hearings or meetings at the Peace Palace or elsewhere, the costs of which are borne by the parties;
- assist with travel and hotel reservations, as well as procurement of visas; and
- carry out any other tasks entrusted to it by the parties or the arbitral tribunal.[13]

The venerable PCA, caught in the crossfire, explained the nature of its functions in the *South China Sea Arbitration*:

> PCA undertook financial management of the case, which involved collecting payment from both parties, and paying fees to arbitrators, experts, technical support, court reporters, among others….According to the "Rules of Procedures" of the tribunal, the functions of the registry…included maintaining an archive of the arbitral proceedings…publishing information about the arbitration and issuing press releases, and organizing hearings at the Peace Palace, the seat of the PCA.[14]

of-the-Court-update-20180320.pdf, accessed 28 March 2018. In theory, therefore, he may be chosen as an arbitrator by States parties to a dispute who wish to settle their disputes by arbitration.

12 Award on Jurisdiction and Admissibility, p. 16, paras. 30–31, https://pcacases.com/web/sendAttach/1506, accessed 30 March 2018.

13 PCA, *Case Administration*, https://pca-cpa.org/en/services/arbitration-services/case-administration/, accessed 30 March 2018.

14 Xinhua, "Permanent Court of Arbitration Clarifies Role in South China Sea Case," *xinhuanet.com*, 16 July 2016,

Why did the Tribunal need a registry? Again, the answer is simple: the Tribunal, which was constituted under Annex VII of the Convention, is ad hoc. It was established to resolve this dispute, and only this dispute; once it has issued its Award(s), it is dissolved. Unlike a permanent court, such as the International Court of Justice (ICJ), with headquarters in The Hague, and the ITLOS, with headquarters in Hamburg, Annex VII Tribunals, by definition, do not have headquarters or facilities or permanent staff. They would thus have to rent facilities where the Tribunal could carry out its work, particularly the hearings. They would also need to hire staff who could perform all of the administrative tasks involved in the Tribunal's work, from drafting press releases to renting halls where hearings can take place. The advantage of the PCA is that it already possesses the facilities and the staff required for these tasks. The PCA does need to be remunerated for services. But facilities rented and services rendered in connection with the arbitration would have had to be paid for anyway. The resulting cost would probably have been much higher if the Tribunal had had to rent facilities on its own and recruit staff from scratch. It is for this reason that most of the Annex VII Tribunals that have been established to settle disputes regarding interpretation and application of the Convention have turned to the PCA for its registry services. The selection of the PCA as Registry did not have anything to do, as Xinhua claimed, with the desire "to be bound to the PCA because of its long history and international authority and credibility."[15]

Why then was the case not brought to ITLOS or the ICJ, which have permanent facilities and staff? This option was impossible, as neither the Philippines nor China has made a declaration under Article 287 of the Convention accepting the jurisdiction of either ITLOS or the ICJ for the settlement of their disputes concerning interpretation and application of the UN Convention on the Law of the Sea. The Philippines has accepted the ICJ's compulsory jurisdiction under Article 36(2) of the ICJ Statute since 18 January 1972, but China has not.[16] Had the Philippines attempted to file a case against China, the ICJ would simply have refused to entertain it, given China's non-acceptance of the ICJ's jurisdiction. In view of the fact that neither the Philippines nor China has accepted the jurisdiction of either the ICJ or the ITLOS for the settlement of their disputes concerning interpretation and application of the Convention, they are deemed, by virtue of Article 287, paragraph 3 of the Convention, to have accepted arbitration under Annex VII of the Convention for the settlement of their disputes concerning interpretation and application of the Convention.

The fact that the PCA is neither permanent nor a court has nothing to do with the binding force of the Award of 12 July 2016 or the earlier Award on Jurisdiction and Admissibility. Neither does the fact that the Arbitral Tribunal was not part of any system of permanent international courts or tribunals. Arbitration is an essential element in the dispute settlement system of the UN Convention on the Law of the Sea.

The Arbitral Tribunal as an International Court

One astounding tactic that China adopted in order to impugn the Award of 12 July 2016 consisted in denying that the Arbitral Tribunal was an international court. No less than Chinese Vice Foreign Minister Liu Zhenmin made this astonishing assertion.[17] The bases of the allegation are three factually accurate statements, but the conclusion that the Vice Foreign

http://news.xinhuanet.com/english/2016-07/16/c_135517684.htm, accessed 30 November 2017.

15 "UN Court Denies Involvement in South China Sea Arbitration," *xinhuanet.com*, 15 July 2016, http://news.xinhuanet.com/english/2016-07/15/c_135515567.htm, accessed 18 July 2016.

16 The text of the declaration is on the ICJ website: http://www.icj-cij.org/en/declarations/ph, accessed 27 March 2018.

17 This is all the more astonishing because the Vice Foreign Minister, as mentioned in note 11, is on the list of arbitrators maintained by the PCA.

Minister draws from them is a non sequitur.[18]

He pointed out that the Arbitral Tribunal had "nothing to do with the International Court of Justice (ICJ) under the United Nations (UN) system in The Hague."[19] It is impossible to argue with this point. Any confusion on this point in the public mind is to be attributed to the carelessness of the media and so-called experts, who often call the Tribunal a "UN-backed tribunal." Anyone who takes the trouble to read the documents of the Arbitration will notice that from the very start, the Tribunal was described as a "Tribunal constituted under Annex VII to the United Nations Convention on the Law of the Sea."

The second factual statement is that the Arbitral Tribunal "has a certain relationship with the International Tribunal for the Law of the Sea (ITLOS) in Hamburg, but it is not a part of the ITLOS."[20] This is another unimpeachable statement. ITLOS is a tribunal established by the UN Convention on the Law of the Sea; its Statute constitutes Annex VI of the Convention.[21] Arbitration under the Convention is governed by Annex VII of the Convention.

The third factual statement is that the Arbitral Tribunal "is not in the system of the Permanent Court of Arbitration (PCA) in The Hague either, but they can be related just because the PCA provided secretarial service [sic] for the Arbitral Tribunal. The Arbitral Tribunal also used the hall of the PCA to carry out the court trail [sic] and that is all."[22] Filipinos and others would do well to remember this point. There is nothing more annoying than to read that it was PCA that rendered the judgment.[23]

Unfortunately, the Vice Foreign Minister's conclusion that for these reasons the Arbitral Tribunal is not an international court is a non sequitur. As unambiguously explained in the Award on Jurisdiction and Admissibility, arbitration is one of the methods of dispute settlement entailing binding decisions provided for in the Convention. Assuming that States parties to a dispute have failed to resolve a dispute by means of their own choosing (Article 281) or by recourse to general, regional, or bilateral agreements in force between them (Article 282), any State party to the dispute may submit the dispute to a settlement procedure (i.e., without the consent of the other State party to the dispute) that entails binding decisions (Article 286). The Convention provides States parties the choice among the ICJ, the ITLOS, arbitration under Annex VII of the Convention, and Special Arbitration under Annex VIII of the Convention. If the States parties to a dispute have not made a choice among these four procedures, then they are deemed to have accepted arbitration under Annex VII of the Convention (Article 287). The Tribunal acknowledged that recourse to these compulsory procedures entailing binding decisions is subject to exceptions, but these exceptions, which are spelled out in the Convention itself, are limited. If these exceptions are inapplicable, then the arbitral tribunal has jurisdiction to hear and decide the dispute.[24]

If there is no doubt that the Arbitral Tribunal is a court, there is no doubt either that it is an "international" court for the following reasons:

---

18 A non sequitur is a statement, remark, or conclusion that does not follow naturally or logically from what has just been said. *Collins English Dictionary*, *supra* note 4.

19 *Veil of the Arbitral Tribunal Must Be Tore [sic] Down*, *supra* note 3.

20 *Ibid.*

21 *Statute of the International Tribunal for the Law of the Sea (Annex VI of the United Nations Convention on the Law of the Sea)*, https://www.itlos.org/fileadmin/itlos/documents/basic_texts/statute_en.pdf, accessed 31 August 2016.

22 *Veil of the Arbitral Tribunal Must Be Tore [sic] Down*, *supra* note 3.

23 At times, even Philippine representatives seemed to be confused on this point. For example, the opening statement of the Philippines at the Hearing on Jurisdiction and Admissibility in July 2015 was entitled "Statement Before the Permanent Court of Arbitration." See http://www.dfa.gov.ph/newsroom/dfa-releases/6795-statement-before-the-permanent-court-of-arbitration, accessed 8 July 2015. The error was repeated in the Concluding Remarks, http://www.dfa.gov.ph/newsroom/dfa-releases/8087-concluding-remarks-of-secretary-albert-f-del-rosario-before-the-permanent-court-of-arbitration-peace-palace-the-hague-netherlands, accessed 2 October 2016.

24 Award on Jurisdiction and Admissibility, p. 37, para. 107, *supra* note 12.

- It was established under Annex VII of a multilateral treaty (a treaty with more than two States parties), the 1982 United Nations Convention on the Law of the Sea;[25]
- The Convention was negotiated by the Third UN Conference on the Law of the Sea from 1973 to 1982, under the auspices of the United Nations;[26]
- A total of 164 States, among them China, attended the 11 sessions of the Conference from 1973 to 1982;
- The Convention was adopted by a vote of 130 States for, four against, and 17 abstentions;[27]
- As of November 2017, 168 States and entities, among them China and the Philippines, had ratified the Convention;[28] and
- The States parties to the Convention meet every year at UN headquarters.[29]

Since the above reasons that China put forward for purposes of denying the binding force of the arbitral award are themselves invalid, the only remaining question is the basis for the binding force of the two Awards issued by the Arbitral Tribunal.

The Binding Force of International Arbitral Awards Under International law

The binding force of international arbitral awards is an established principle of international law, one that was explicitly confirmed by Annex VII of the Convention.

Although arbitration as a dispute settlement procedure goes back to ancient Greece, the modern law of international arbitration may be traced to the late 18th century.[30] On 19 November 1794, the United States and Great Britain (as it was known at the time) concluded the Treaty of Amity Commerce and Navigation, widely known as Jay's Treaty or the Jay Treaty, after the US negotiator, Supreme Court Chief Justice John Jay.[31] The aim of the Treaty was to settle outstanding issues between the two states that had been left unresolved since the American War of Independence (1776–83). Articles 5, 6, and 7 of the Treaty established three joint commissions, composed of US and British representatives.[32]

25 *Annex VII, Arbitration*, http://www.un.org/depts/los/convention_agreements/texts/unclos/annex7.htm, accessed 31 August 2016.

26 For a brief history of UNCLOS III, see United Nations Office of Legal Affairs, Codification Division Publications, Diplomatic Conferences, Third United Nations Conference on the Law of the Sea (1973–1982) (2017), http://legal.un.org/diplomaticconferences/1973_los/, accessed 30 November 2017.

27 *Final Act of the Third United Nations Conference on the Law of the Sea*, http://www.un.org/depts/los/convention_agreements/texts/final_act_eng.pdf, accessed 31 August 2016.

28 United Nations, Division for Ocean Affairs and the Law of the Sea, *Chronological Lists of Ratifications of, Accessions and Successions to the Convention and the related Agreements* (2017), http://www.un.org/depts/los/reference_files/chronological_lists_of_ratifications.htm, accessed 27 March 2018.

29 United Nations, Division for Ocean Affairs and the Law of the Sea, *Meetings of States Parties to the 1982 United Nations Convention on the Law of the Sea*, http://www.un.org/depts/los/meeting_states_parties/meeting_states_parties.htm, accessed 18 July 2016.

30 For the origins of arbitration, see A. Ræder, *L'arbitrage international chez les hellènes* (Kristiania: H. Aschehoug and Co. [W. Nygaard], 1912), https://ia601600.us.archive.org/9/items/larbitrageintern00raed/larbitrageintern00raed.pdf, accessed 23 October 2017; Baron Michel De Taube, "Les origines de l'arbitrage international. Antiquité et Moyen Âge," *Recueil des Cours de l'Académie de Droit International de La Haye*, t. 42 (1932-IV), pp. 1–116; Luisa Bussi, "Mediazione e arbitrati fra medioevo ed età moderna," *Diritto@Storia*, 4 (2005), pp. 1–27, http://eprints.uniss.it/223/1/Bussi_L_Articolo_2005_Mediazione.pdf, accessed 30 November 2017.

31 US Department of State, Office of the Historian, *John Jay's Treaty 1794–95*, https://history.state.gov/milestones/1784-1800/jay-treaty, accessed 18 July 2016.

32 The following is taken from John Bassett Moore, *The United States and International Arbitration* (Boston: The American Peace Society, 1896), pp. 3–6, https://archive.org/details/unitedstatesand00moorgoog, accessed 27 March 2018.

The joint commission under Article 5 was to determine which river was intended to be the River St. Croix, which had been specified in the 1783 Treaty ending the War of Independence as part of the US northeastern boundary with Canada, then under British rule. Under Article 5 of the Treaty, the US and Great Britain undertook the following commitment:

> And both parties agree to consider such decision as final and conclusive, so as that the same shall never thereafter be called into question, or made the subject of dispute or difference between them.[33]

The two States thus agreed that the award of this joint commission would be binding.

The joint commission organized under Article 6 was to determine compensation to be paid by the US to British subjects who had failed to recover debts owed to them as a result of actions by States that later became part of the US. The US committed itself to complying with the award of the commission:

> The award of the said Commissioners or of any three of them as aforesaid shall in all Cases be final and conclusive both as to the Justice of the Claim, and to the amount of the Sum to be paid to the Creditor or Claimant. And the United States undertake to cause the Sum so awarded to be paid in Specie to such Creditor or Claimant without deduction; and at such Time or Times, and at such Place or Places, as shall be awarded by the said Commissioners, and on Condition of such Releases or assignments to be given by the Creditor or Claimant as by the said Commissioners may be directed; Provided always that no such payment shall be fixed by the said Commissioners to take place sooner than twelve months from the Day of the Exchange of the Ratifications of this Treaty.[34]

The joint commission organized under Article 7 was to determine compensation to be paid by Great Britain to American merchants and citizens whose vessels had been irregularly or illegally captured or condemned by the British in the course of the French Revolutionary Wars. Great Britain undertook the following commitment:

> The award of the said Commissioners or any such three of them as aforesaid, shall in all Cases be final and conclusive both as to the Justice of the Claim and the amount of the Sum to be paid to the Claimant; and His Britannick [sic] Majesty undertakes to cause the same to be paid to such Claimant in Specie, without any Deduction, at such place or places, and at such Time or Times as shall be awarded by the said Commissioners and on Condition of such releases or assignments to be given by the Claimant, as by the said Commissioners may be directed.[35]

The cumulative effect of these three provisions was that the awards of the three joint commissions were binding on the two States.

As a growing number of States in Europe and outside Europe submitted their disputes to arbitration in the 19th century, there was practically no discussion concerning the binding force of international arbitral awards. Digests of such awards observed variations in procedure relating primarily to the type of special agreement that was the basis of the arbitral proceedings, the composition of the organ, and the mode of designation of the umpire (the fifth or the

[33] Yale Law School, Lillian Goldman Law Library, *The Jay Treaty, November 17, 1794*, http://avalon.law.yale.edu/18th_century/jay.asp, accessed 20 July 2016.

[34] *Ibid.*

[35] *Ibid.*

"neutral" arbitrator) but do not record any controversy over the binding force of the awards themselves.[36] Indeed, it could be argued that satisfactory arrangements in these three areas were essential precisely because the outcome of the proceedings would be binding. Advocates of the general recourse to arbitration as a dispute settlement procedure were at pains to stress that arbitration differed from mediation, in that the outcome of the former was binding, while that of the latter was non-binding.[37]

The more widespread acceptance of international arbitration made it possible to conclude the Convention for the Pacific Settlement of International Disputes in 1899, at the First Hague Peace Conference. Article 54 of the Convention provides that "[t]he Award, duly pronounced and notified to the agents of the parties at variance, puts an end to the dispute definitively and without appeal."[38] Article 56 stipulates that "[t]he Award is only binding on the parties who concluded the 'Compromis.'"[39] The Award is binding only on the parties, but it is binding on them.

China ratified the 1899 Convention on 21 November 1904.[40] At the time, as Xinhua pointed out, the Qing Dynasty (1644–1912) still ruled China.[41] Despite the many momentous changes in China's political regime since then, China has apparently never denounced the 1899 Convention. In fact, China ratified on 26 January 2010 the 1907 Convention for the Pacific Settlement of International Disputes, which reproduces almost verbatim the text of Articles 54 and 56 of the 1899 Convention in Articles 81 and 84, respectively.[42] Even if China had

---

36 H. La Fontaine (ed.), *Pasicrisie internationale 1794–1900. Histoire documentaire des arbitrages internationaux* (Berne: Imprimerie Stampfli & Cie, 1902), pp. viii–xvi, https://ia600205.us.archive.org/9/items/pasicrisieinter00fontgoog/pasicrisieinter00fontgoog.pdf, accessed 13 October 2017; Albert Geouffre de Lapradelle and Nicolas Politis (eds.), *Recueil des arbitrages internationaux*, I, *1798–1855* (Paris: A. Pedone Éditeur, 1905), pp. xxxviii, https://ia600309.us.archive.org/19/items/recueildesarbit01lapr/recueildesarbit01lapr.pdf, 21 May 2016; Lapradelle and Politis (eds.), *Recueil des arbitrages internationaux*, II, *1856–1872* (Paris: A. Pedone Éditeur, 1923), pp. i xxxviii, https://ia802607.us.archive.org/3/items/recueildesarbitr02lapruoft/recueildesarbitr02lapruoft.pdf, accessed 21 May 2016.

37 See, for example, M. E. Rouard de Card, *L'arbitrage international dans le passé, le présent et l'avenir* (Paris: A. Durand et Pedone-Lauriel, Éditeurs, 1877), pp. 28–76, https://ia902706.us.archive.org/14/items/droitinternatio01cardgoog/droitinternatio01cardgoog.pdf, accessed 23 October 2017; L. Kamarowsky, *Le tribunal international*, trans. Serge de Westman (Paris: A. Durand et Pedone-Lauriel, Éditeurs, 1887), pp. 73–107, https://ia902700.us.archive.org/26/items/letribunalinter00lacogoog/letribunalinter00lacogoog.pdf, accessed 23 October 2017.

38 *Supra* note 7.

39 A *compromis* is "an agreement to refer to arbitration or to judicial settlement some matter or matters in dispute, these being defined more clearly in the compromis." Lord Gore-Booth, *Satow's Guide to Diplomatic Practice*, 4th ed. (London: Longman Group UK Ltd., 1979), p. 263. It is normally translated into English as "special agreement." Article 31 of the 1899 Convention (*supra* note 3) explains that in a "compromise," "the subject of the difference is clearly defined, as well as the extent of the Arbitrators' powers." Article 52 of the 1907 Convention on the Pacific Settlement of International Disputes provides a more detailed explanation of the contents of the "compromise."

> The Powers which have recourse to arbitration sign a "Compromis," in which the subject of the dispute is clearly defined, the time allowed for appointing Arbitrators, the form, order, and time in which the communication referred to in Article 63 must be made, and the amount of the sum which each party must deposit in advance to defray the expenses.
>
> The "Compromis" likewise defines, if there is occasion, the manner of appointing Arbitrators, any special powers which may eventually belong to the Tribunal, where it shall meet, the language it shall use, and the languages the employment of which shall be authorized before it, and, generally speaking, all the conditions on which the parties are agreed.

See the text of the 1907 Convention on the PCA website: https://pca-cpa.org/wp-content/uploads/sites/175/2016/01/1907-Convention-for-the-Pacific-Settlement-of-International-Disputes.pdf, accessed 20 July 2016.

40 PCA, *Member States*, https://pca-cpa.org/en/about/introduction/member-states/, accessed 20 July 2016.

41 "Permanent Court of Arbitration Neither Permanent nor a Court," *supra* note 1.

42 See the text of the 1907 Convention, *supra* note 39.

denounced either or both Conventions following the issuance of the Award of 12 July 2016, the denunciation would have had no effect on the binding force of the latter or of the earlier Award on Jurisdiction and Admissibility, for two reasons. First, the denunciation cannot have a retroactive effect; second, and even more importantly, the principle that awards of international arbitral tribunals are binding is so fundamental that denunciation of either or both Conventions cannot relieve China of the obligation to comply with the two Awards in the *South China Sea Arbitration*.

Annex VII Arbitral Tribunals, despite the fact that they are ad hoc, are no less courts than permanent international tribunals. As such, they have the power to issue binding awards. Article 6(2) of the Rules of Procedure of the *South China Sea Arbitration*, adopted on 27 July 2013, is explicit on this point: "Pursuant to Article 11 of Annex VII to the Convention, the award shall be final and without appeal, unless the Parties agree in advance to an appellate procedure. It shall be complied with by the Parties."[43]

China might retort that the Rules of Procedure adopted by a Tribunal that it refuses to recognize could hardly confer binding force on the Tribunal's Awards. The reference by the Rules of Procedure to the Convention makes it more difficult to sustain this objection. Article 11 of Annex VII of the Convention reads as follows:

> Article 11
>
> Finality of award
>
> The award shall be final and without appeal, unless the parties to the dispute have agreed in advance to an appellate procedure. It shall be complied with by the parties to the dispute.[44]

China, as a State party, is indisputably bound by the UN Convention on the Law of the Sea. The latter, as a treaty, confers rights and imposes obligations on China and on other States parties to it. State parties may exercise the rights conferred on them by the Convention, but they must comply with the obligations that it imposes on them.

China's Vice-Minister for Foreign Affairs seemed to argue that because the Arbitral Tribunal decided that it had jurisdiction in spite of China's non-participation, it could not exist as a tribunal. Understanding this argument is a bit more problematic, as it seems that the remarks of the Vice Foreign Minister were mistranslated. According to the text distributed by the Foreign Ministry, "this case was the first of its kind that led to the establishment of the temporary arbitration tribunal in *self-alleged accordance* [italics supplied] of the Annex VII of the United Nations Convention on the Law of the Sea (UNCLOS) since the UNCLOS took effect."

One commentator believes that he meant by this that "UNCLOS arbitration is some sort of aberration that has never happened before, unlike the more established ICJ or ITLOS systems."[45] Assuming that this is the idea that the Vice Foreign Minister had in mind, then the affirmation is certainly incorrect. By the time the Award in the *Philippines v. China* arbitration

43 Rules of Procedure, 27 August 2013, https://pcacases.com/web/sendAttach/233, accessed 30 March 2018.

44 Annex VII, http://www.un.org/depts/los/convention_agreements/texts/unclos/annex7.htm, accessed 12 September 2016.

45 Julian Ku, "China's Vice-Minister for Foreign Affairs Casually Slanders the South China Sea Arbitral Tribunal," *opiniojuris.org*, 26 July 2016, http://opiniojuris.org/2016/07/26/chinas-vice-minister-for-foreign-affairs-casually-slanders-the-south-china-sea-arbitral-tribunal/, accessed 31 August 2016.

had been issued, there had already been nine arbitrations under Annex VII of the Convention.[46]

However, reading the complete sentence, including the badly translated phrase, suggests a different interpretation. The mysterious (and non-existent in English) expression "self-alleged accordance" prompts the suspicion that the Vice Foreign Minister may have said (or wished to say) that "this is the first temporary tribunal THAT ACCORDED JURISDICTION TO ITSELF." Now, Article 288, paragraph 1 of the Convention provides that "[a] court or tribunal referred to in article 287 shall have jurisdiction over any dispute concerning the interpretation or application of this Convention which is submitted to it in accordance with this Part."[47] If the interpretation proposed here of the mistranslated sentence is accurate, the real reason for China's objection to the Tribunal's declaration of its jurisdiction would be that it did so without China's participation. From China's point of view, the Tribunal could not legally exist; consequently, its award is null and void.

If this were indeed the intended message, then the Vice Foreign Minister's objection, though partly correct, is irrelevant. It is partly correct, in that China rejected the Philippines' request for arbitration in February 2013, approximately eight months before Russia rejected the request of the Netherlands for arbitration over Russia's handling of the Greenpeace vessel Arctic Sunrise in Russia's EEZ. China thus has the doubtful honor of being the first State party to the Convention to refuse to participate in arbitration under Annex VII of the Convention. But the Tribunal in the *Arctic Sunrise* arbitration declared that it had jurisdiction in November 2014, nearly a year before the Tribunal in the *South China Sea Arbitration* issued its Award on Jurisdiction and Admissibility.[48] Consequently, the *Arctic Sunrise* case enjoys the dubious distinction of being the first in which an Annex VII Tribunal declared that it had jurisdiction despite the non-appearance of one party.

---

46 Ku erroneously counted only seven. The nine arbitrations that had been organized prior to the *South China Sea Arbitration* are the following:

1. *M.V. Saiga (St. Vincent & the Grenadines v. Guinea)* (1997–99), https://www.itlos.org/fileadmin/itlos/ documents/cases/case_no_2/merits/Judgment.01.07.99.E.pdf;
2. *Southern Bluefin Tuna (Australia and New Zealand v. Japan), Reports of International Arbitral Awards (RIAA)*, XXIII (New York: United Nations, 2006), pp. 1–57, http://legal.un.org/riaa/cases/vol_XXIII/1-57.pdf;
3. *MOX Plant (Ireland v. United Kingdom)* (2001–08), https://pcacases.com/web/view/100;
4. *Land Reclamation by Singapore in and Around the Straits of Johor (Malaysia v. Singapore)* (2003–05), *RIAA*, XXVII (New York: United Nations, 2008), pp. 133–45, http://legal.un.org/riaa/cases/vol_XXVII/133-145.pdf;
5. *Maritime Delimitation Between Barbados and Trinidad & Tobago (Barbados v. Trinidad & Tobago)* (2004–06), *RIAA*, XXVII (New York: United Nations, 2008), pp. 147–251, http://legal.un.org/riaa/cases/vol_XXVII/147-251.pdf;
6. *Maritime Delimitation Between Guyana and Suriname (Guyana v. Suriname)* (2004–07), *RIAA*, XXX (New York: United Nations, 2012), pp. 1–144, http://legal.un.org/riaa/cases/vol_XXX/1-144.pdf;
7. *Chagos Marine Protected Area Arbitration (Mauritius v. United Kingdom)* (2010–15), https://pcacases.com/web/view/11;
8. *The Atlanto-Scandian Herring Arbitration (The Kingdom of Denmark in Respect of the Faroe Islands v. The European Union)* (2013–14), https://pcacases.com/web/view/25; and
9. *The Arctic Sunrise Arbitration (Netherlands v. Russia)* (2013–15), https://pcacases.com/web/view/21, all accessed 31 August 2016.

For a survey of the first six cases, see Shabtai Rosenne, "Arbitrations Under Annex VII of the United Nations Convention on the Law of the Sea," in Tafsir Malick Ndiaye and Rüdiger Wolfrum (eds.), *Law of the Sea, Environmental Law and Settlement of Disputes. Liber Amicorum Judge Thomas A. Mensah* (Leiden: Martinus Nijhoff Publishers, 2007), pp. 989–1006.

47 United Nations Convention on the Law of the Sea, http://www.un.org/depts/los/convention_agreements/texts/unclos/unclos_e.pdf, accessed 31 August 2016.

48 Award on Jurisdiction dated 26 November 2014, https://pcacases.com/web/sendAttach/1325, accessed 31 August 2016.

More importantly, an objection to the Tribunal's decision on jurisdiction relying on China's non-participation is irrelevant because Article 9 of Annex VII of the Convention anticipates the situation in which a State party to a dispute refuses to appear before the Arbitral Tribunal, as the Tribunal stressed in the two Awards. Each sentence of Article 9 deserves careful attention.

> If one of the parties to the dispute does not appear before the arbitral tribunal or fails to defend its case, the other party may request the tribunal to continue the proceedings and to make its award.

In its Memorial, the Philippines declared that "[f]or the avoidance of any doubt, the Philippines here requests that these proceedings continue."[49] The next sentence reads as follows:

> Absence of a party or failure of a party to defend its case shall not constitute a bar to the proceedings.

The Tribunal expressly quoted this provision in its Award on Jurisdiction and Admissibility, before declaring that "the non-participation of China does not bar the Tribunal from proceeding with the arbitration."[50] The last sentence reads as follows:

> Before making its award, the arbitral tribunal must satisfy itself not only that it has jurisdiction over the dispute but also that the claim is well founded in fact and law.

The Tribunal did not automatically rule in favor of the Philippines simply because China refused to appear.[51] To satisfy itself that it had jurisdiction over the dispute, the Tribunal treated China's Position Paper as a preliminary objection to its jurisdiction and bifurcated the proceedings, notwithstanding Philippine opposition to bifurcation.[52] In its Award on Jurisdiction and Admissibility, the Tribunal declared that it had jurisdiction over seven of the Philippine submissions but postponed consideration of its jurisdiction in conjunction with the merits for seven others and asked the Philippines to reformulate the last submission.[53] To satisfy itself that the Philippine submissions were well founded in fact and in law, the Tribunal took a whole series of measures, which are detailed in the Procedural History section of the Award of 12 July 2016.[54] Although the Award was favorable to most of the Philippine theses, the Tribunal did not accept the Philippine claim that McKennan Reef and Gaven Reef (North) were low-tide elevations, declared that it had no jurisdiction over the Philippine submission relating to the standoff between the military of the Philippines and China at Second Thomas Shoal, and declined to take action over the reformulated Submission No. 15.

As the reader can see, disproving China's contentions that the Arbitral Tribunal is not an international court and that its decision is not binding requires very little effort. It certainly does not require lifting or piercing any veil of any kind.

49 *Arbitration Under Annex VII of the United Nations Convention on the Law of the Sea. Republic of the Philippines v. People's Republic of China, Memorial of the Philippines, 30 March 2014*, vol. I, p. 6, para. 1.21, p. 230, para. 7.39, http://www.pcacases.com/pcadocs/Memorial%20of%20the%20Philippines%20Volume%20I.pdf, accessed 30 March 2018.

50 Award on Jurisdiction and Admissibility, p. 11, para. 11, *supra* note 12.

51 *Ibid.*, p. 11, para. 12.

52 *Ibid.*, p. 22, para. 63.

53 *Ibid.*, p. 149, para. 413 G, H, and I.

54 Award of 12 July 2016, pp. 49-55, paras. 129–42, *supra* note 1.

14

Unraveling China's Conspiracy Theory of International Arbitration

A conspiracy theory is defined as "a belief that an unpleasant event or situation is the result of a secret plan made by powerful people."[1] A conspiracy theory is said to be a staple of American popular culture, widely reflected in the movies and television,[2] but conspiracy theories are by no means confined to the US. Indeed, the contemporary period has often been described as "the age of conspiracism."[3] They raise the question for policy-makers whether they should be ignored or rebutted. Underlying this dilemma is the observation that conspiracy theories are extremely difficult to combat: "they have a self-sealing quality, rendering them particularly immune to challenge."[4] Nevertheless, given the conspiracy tradition's long legacy of harmful influence and its noted "affinity" for bad causes, a plausible argument can be made for combating them.[5] A further question then arises, relating to the appropriate strategy. Whether a narrow or broad strategy is adopted, an essential component will be the provision of factual and logical grounds for disconfirming the theory.[6] The rebuttal should probably be directed not so much to those who have created the conspiracy theory, but to the theory's intended audience.

A new chapter might have to be added to histories of conspiracy theory as China creatively adapts it to international arbitration. This conspiracy theory, which was unveiled to the world following China's realization that the Tribunal had upheld most of the Philippine claims, has several strands. It claims that the appointment of the majority of judges in the Arbitral Tribunal was the product of political manipulation, allegedly master-minded by the President of the International Tribunal for the Law of the Sea (ITLOS) in 2013. This manipulation allegedly resulted in the appointment of a Tribunal that was said to lack knowledge of Asia and to have

1 *Cambridge Dictionary*, http://dictionary.cambridge.org/dictionary/english/conspiracy-theory, accessed 12 September 2016.

2 Gordon B. Arnold, *Conspiracy Theory in Film, Television, and Politics* (New York: Praeger, 2008), p. 1.

3 Jovan Byford, *Conspiracy Theories: A Critical Introduction* (Houndmills, Basingstoke, Hampshire: Palgrave Macmillan, 2011), p. 3.

4 Cass R. Sunstein and Adrian Vermeule, "Conspiracy Theories: Causes and Cures," *The Journal of Political Philosophy*, 17:1 (2009), p. 204, http://www.ask-force.org/web/Discourse/Sunstein-Conspiracy-Theories-2009.pdf, accessed 1 December 2017.

5 Jovan, p. 152, *supra* note 3.

6 *Ibid.*, p. 156.

rendered an Award favorable to the Philippines in exchange for the Philippines payment of the costs of the arbitration. These two charges would prompt the conclusion that the members of the Arbitral Tribunal lacked the qualities required of judges, namely, fairness, competence, and integrity. Finally, the conspiracy theory alleges that the arbitration was manipulated by the United States.

Providing the logical and factual background to these issues very easily leads to the unraveling of the theory. The ITLOS President was merely fulfilling an institutional role; knowledge of any particular region is not a requirement for appointment of members of the Arbitral Tribunal; the latter were required to meet the same criteria of fairness, competence, and integrity as ITLOS judges; and the Tribunal's decision to refuse the US request to attend the merits hearing as an observer contradicts the assertion that the US manipulated the Tribunal. No illusion that China will be convinced by the factual and logical evidence, which is addressed to an audience that seeks the truth, is entertained here.

The Institutional Role of the ITLOS President

China alleges that the establishment of the Arbitral Tribunal was "the result of political manipulation."[7] Yet, the only reason for the appointment of four of the five members of the Arbitral Tribunal by the ITLOS President was China's own failure to appoint its judge and to agree with the Philippines on the appointment of the remaining judges.

This charge could not possibly be directed against Judge Rüdiger Wolfrum, who was appointed by the Philippines in conformity with Article 3 of Annex VII of the Convention.[8] The latter stipulates that the State party to the Convention that institutes the proceedings should appoint one arbitrator and include the arbitrator's name in the Notification and Statement of Claim, which initiates the arbitration.

China charge is based on the fact that the four other members of the Arbitral Tribunal were appointed by then ITLOS President, Judge Yanai, a Japanese national. Judge Yanai is described by a Chinese Vice Foreign Minister as follows:

> Who is Shunji Yanai? He is a judge of the ITLOS now and before as well as the Chairman of Advisory Panel on Reconstruction of the Legal Basis for Security set by the Shinzo Abe administration. He plays an important role in helping Shinzo Abe with the lifting of the ban on collective self-defense and challenging the international order after World War II. He was also former Japanese Ambassador to the US.[9]

This recapitulation of Judge Yanai's professional background is a model of restraint and sobriety compared to the abuse that has been heaped on Judge Yanai by Chinese journalists. One has even characterized him as a "manipulator."[10]

China's representatives conveniently fail to mention that it is Annex VII of the UN

---

7 Ministry of Foreign Affairs of the People's Republic of China, *Veil of the Arbitral Tribunal Must Be Tore [sic] Down—Vice Foreign Minister Liu Zhenmin Answers Journalists' Questions on the So-Called Binding Force of the Award Rendered by the Arbitral Tribunal of the South China Sea Arbitration Case, 2016/07/13*, http://www.fmprc.gov.cn/mfa_eng/wjbxw/t1381879.shtml, accessed 18 July 2016

8 *Annex VII, Arbitration*, http://www.un.org/depts/los/convention_agreements/texts/unclos/annex7.htm, accessed 31 August 2016.

9 *Veil of the Arbitral Tribunal Must Be Tore (sic) Down, supra* note 7.

10 "Shunji Yanai, Manipulator Behind Illegal South China Sea Arbitration," *xinhuanet.com*, 17 July 2016, http://news.xinhuanet.com/english/2016-07/17/c_135519215.htm, 18 July 2016.

Convention on the Law of the Sea that confers an institutional role, under certain conditions, on the ITLOS President in the appointment of members of Arbitral Tribunals. Under Article 3(e) of Annex VII,

> Unless the parties agree that any appointment under subparagraphs (c) and (d) be made by a person or a third State chosen by the parties, the President of the International Tribunal for the Law of the Sea shall make the necessary appointments.

Paragraph (c) refers to the appointment of a second arbitrator by the other party to the dispute within 30 days of receipt of the notification and statement of claim initiating the arbitration. If the second party fails to appoint its arbitrator within the specified period, the first party may request that the appointment be made in accordance with the procedure laid down in paragraph (e). Paragraph (d) refers to the appointment of the other three members of the Arbitral Tribunal by the two parties. If the two parties are unable to reach an agreement, either one may request that the appointment be made in accordance with paragraph (e). The ITLOS President is prevented from proceeding with the appointment(s) only if for some reason he or she is unable to act or is a citizen of one of the parties to the dispute. In either case, the appointment will be made by the next senior member of the Tribunal.

The purpose of this type of provision is to prevent a Party to a dispute from paralyzing compulsory dispute settlement by refusing to nominate its judge or arbitrator. This type of provision is found in two other annexes of the Convention. Annex IV of the Convention, which governs conciliation, and Annex VIII of the Convention, which provides for special arbitration relating to fisheries, protection and concerning preservation of the marine environment, marine scientific research, or navigation, assign a similar role to the Secretary-General of the United Nations.[11]

Judge Yanai performed the same function in the *Arctic Sunrise Arbitration*, initiated by the Netherlands against Russia in 2013. Russia refused to participate in the proceedings and to appoint its arbitrator. In conformity with Article 3(e) of Annex VII, the Netherlands then requested that the ITLOS President nominate the second arbitrator and, subsequently, the three remaining arbitrators.[12] Despite Russia's boycott of the proceedings, it seems that Russia understood that Judge Yanai was merely performing an institutional function, as there appears to be no record of any criticism on the part of Russia regarding the constitution of the Tribunal or the role of the ITLOS President in the appointment of the four arbitrators.

Judge Yanai's predecessor in the Presidency, Judge José Luis Jesus of Cape Verde (2008–11), was called upon to perform a similar function in the *Chagos Marine Protected Area* arbitration. The two Parties, Mauritius and the UK, after having nominated their respective arbitrators, were unable to agree on the appointment of the three other arbitrators. Thus, upon the request of Mauritius, the ITLOS President appointed two more members and the President of the Tribunal.[13]

If for some reason Judge Yanai had been unable to perform his duty under Article 3(e) of Annex VII, the next senior member of the ITLOS would have proceeded with the appointment.

11 Article 3(c), (d), and (e) of Annex V, http://www.un.org/depts/los/convention_agreements/texts/unclos/annex5.htm, and Article 3(e) of Annex VIII, http://www.un.org/depts/los/convention_agreements/texts/unclos/annex8.htm, accessed 12 September 2016.

12 One indicator of the reputation of the President of the *South China Sea* Arbitral Tribunal is that Judge Yanai also appointed Judge Mensah as the President of this Tribunal. *The Arctic Sunrise Arbitration (Netherlands v. Russia)*, Award on Jurisdiction and Admissibility, pp. 3–4, paras. 14–16, https://pcacases.com/web/sendAttach/1325, accessed 26 September 2015.

13 *Chagos Marine Protected Area*, Award of 18 March 2015, p. 5, paras. 16–17, https://files.pca-cpa.org/pcadocs/MU-UK%2020150318%20Award.pdf, accessed 30 March 2018.

In 2013, the next two senior members of the ITLOS were Judge Vincente Marotta Rangel from Brazil (judge, 1996–2015) and Judge L. Dolliver Nelson from Grenada (judge, 1996–2014).[14] Had either of the two been called on to appoint the members of the Arbitral Tribunal, China would have in all likelihood raised against them the same objection that it raised against the Tribunal that was finally constituted: as judges from Latin American and the Caribbean, they had no understanding of Asia or the South China Sea dispute.

The requirements for election to the ITLOS should in themselves offer guarantees of fairness, integrity, and competence on the part of the Tribunal's President (and of all its members, for that matter). The Statute of ITLOS requires that judges be "elected from among persons enjoying the highest reputation for fairness and integrity and of recognized competence in the field of the law of the sea."[15] Judge Yanai, who is a lawyer by training, served for over 50 years in the Japanese Foreign Ministry (1961–2002). In the Home Office, almost all of his assignments were in the Legal Affairs Division (1977–78) or Treaties Division (1977–80, 1987, 1990–92). In matters of the law of the sea, his experience is quite extensive. He was a member of the Committee that drafted Japan's Law on the Territorial Sea (1977) and a Japan–South Korea Joint Committee on the Continental Shelf. He participated in fisheries negotiations with Indonesia, South Korea, and the USSR (1978–80) and represented Japan at the Third United Nations Conference on the Law of the Sea, which drafted the Convention.[16]

Judge Yanai was elected to the ITLOS in 2005, receiving votes from 113 States parties out of 147 votes cast, with the majority required for election being 80 States.[17] He was reelected for a second nine-year term in 2014, when 142 States voted for him, out of a total of 159 States, the majority required for election being 105 States.[18] Judge Yanai was elected to the post of ITLOS President for the period 2011–14 by the other members of the Tribunal.[19] If Judge Yanai had not enjoyed "the highest reputation for fairness and integrity and of recognized competence in the field of the law of the sea," he would not have been elected to the ITLOS by States Parties to the Convention and by the other ITLOS judges to the post of President.[20] China at no time objected to the election or reelection of Judge Yanai to the ITLOS or his election to the post of ITLOS President.

Had China harbored doubts about Judge Yanai's fairness and integrity at the time that the Philippines initiated the arbitration in 2013, all it had to do in order to prevent Judge Yanai from performing his institutional function was to appoint its arbitrator. As China chose not to do so, its criticism of the appointing authority is completely unjustified. The real reason for China's objection to Judge Yanai is that he performed his institutional role and made possible the constitution of the tribunal, which China wished to prevent by boycotting the proceedings.

---

14 *Annual Report of the International Tribunal for the Law of the Sea for 2011*, Doc. SPLOS/241 (9 April 2012), p. 5, para. 5, https://www.itlos.org/fileadmin/itlos/documents/annual_reports/annualreport_2011.pdf, accessed 13 September 2016.

15 Article 2, para. 1, *Statute of the International Tribunal for the Law of the Sea (Annex VI of the United Nations Convention on the Law of the Sea)*, https://www.itlos.org/fileadmin/itlos/documents/basic_texts/statute_en.pdf, accessed 31 August 2016.

16 *Curricula Vitae of Candidates Nominated by States Parties for Election to the International Tribunal for the Law of the Sea. Note by the Registrar*, Doc. SPLOS/125 (30 March 2005), https://documents-dds-ny.un.org/doc/UNDOC/GEN/N05/291/03/IMG/N0529103.pdf?OpenElement, accessed 18 July 2016.

17 *Report of the Fifteenth Meeting of the States Parties*, Doc. SPLOS/135 (25 July 2005), https://documents-dds-ny.un.org/doc/UNDOC/GEN/N05/439/16/PDF/N0543916.pdf?OpenElement, accessed 18 July 2016.

18 *Report of the Twenty-Fourth Meeting of States Parties*, Doc. SPLOS/277 (14 July 2015), p. 17, footnote 10, https://documents-dds-ny.un.org/doc/UNDOC/GEN/N14/467/74/PDF/N1446774.pdf?OpenElement, accessed 18 July 2016.

19 Article 11, para. 6, *Rules of the Tribunal*, Doc. ITLOS/8, dated 17 March 2009, https://www.itlos.org/fileadmin/itlos/documents/basic_texts/Itlos_8_E_17_03_09.pdf, accessed 31 August 2016.

20 The functions of the ITLOS President are described in Chapter IV.

Any other ITLOS judge performing that role would not have escaped China's criticism.

The next strand of the conspiracy theory disparaged the experience and competence of the five members of the Tribunal, for allegedly lacking knowledge of Asia.

The Competence of the Members of the Arbitral Tribunal

China's allegation that the members of the Tribunal were not knowledgeable about Asia is irrelevant, for two reasons. First, the members of the Tribunal complied with the same criteria as those required for ITLOS judges, and second, the criteria emphasize fairness, competence, and integrity, rather than knowledge of any particular region.

It is worthwhile quoting at length China's strictures:

> there are big problems in the composition of the Arbitral Tribunal…four of them come from Europe….The fifth judge is from Ghana…but he lived in Europe permanently. So does a court like this have any representativeness?….[N]one of the five judges of the Arbitral Tribunal is from Asia, let alone China. Do they know Asia? Do they understand Asian cultures? Do they know the South China Sea issue? Do they understand the complicated geographical politics in Asia? Do they know the history of the South China Sea? On what basis can they make a fair award?[21]

It is true that none of the five judges of the Arbitral Tribunal is from Asia, let alone China. The Philippines appointed Judge Wolfrum rather than a Filipino national, because there is no Filipino national who possesses the educational, academic, publication, and professional record of Judge Wolfrum. The reason that there is no judge from Asia or China is simple: China refused to appoint its arbitrator. If China had truly wanted a judge from Asia or China, China should have appointed one, within 30 days of receipt of the Notification of the Statement and Claim sent by the Philippines, in accordance with Article 3(c) of Annex VII of the Convention. China would have been free to appoint anyone that it wanted. China refused to do so. Even if the ITLOS President could theoretically have appointed the judge of Chinese nationality at the ITLOS, Judge Gao,[22] the latter, given the Chinese government's refusal to participate in the Arbitration, would surely have refused.

China's objection is that the five judges did not know Asia nor understand Asian cultures. Judge Yanai had originally appointed M.C.W Pinto, a Sri Lankan national, as member and president of the Tribunal, but as explained in Chapter IV, Mr. Pinto resigned because his wife is Filipina. Despite Pinto's resignation, three of the four other judges appointed by the ITLOS President had varying degrees of experience in relation to Asia. Judge Pawlak, before being elected to the ITLOS, had a long and distinguished career as a diplomat, with various assignments to different Asian countries, and as a scholar, having authored several works on US foreign policy towards China. Judge Cot had written on a dispute between Cambodia and Thailand over the Preah Vihear Temple and became a judge ad hoc 50 years later in the case regarding the judgment's interpretation. Professor Soons, for his part, participated in law of the sea projects with Indonesia.

That being said, trying to prove that one or more of the judges had knowledge and/or experience of Asia concedes too much ground to China. Annex VII of the Convention lays

21 *Veil of the Arbitral Tribunal Must Be Tore [sic[Down*, *supra* note 7.

22 See the biography of Judge Gao on the ITLOS website: https://www.itlos.org/the-tribunal/members/judge-zhiguo-gao/, accessed 18 July 2016.

down three criteria for the appointment by the two parties of the five members of the Arbitral Tribunal:

1. All of the arbitrators should be preferably chosen from a list of arbitrators drawn up and maintained by the UN Secretary-General.
2. The members so appointed shall be of different nationalities.
3. They may not be in the service of, ordinarily resident in the territory of, or nationals of any of the parties to the dispute.[23]

If it is the ITLOS President that makes the appointments, i.e., where one party fails to appoint its arbitrator and/or the two parties fail to agree on the appointment of the three remaining arbitrators, the appointments must be made from the list of arbitrators drawn up and maintained by the UN Secretary-General. Clearly, there is no requirement that the judges have knowledge of any particular geographic region.

The last two requirements listed above are self-explanatory. It is the first criterion that sets the bar very high, as the arbitrators, to be put on the list, must possess qualifications that are equivalent to those required for election to the ITLOS. Article 2(1) of Annex VII stipulates that each arbitrator nominated for the list "shall be a person experienced in maritime affairs and enjoying the highest reputation for fairness, competence and integrity." The assumption is that the experience and the reputation for fairness, competence, and integrity will enable them to bring to bear the principles and rules of the law of the sea on specific problems in particular geographic regions. China's attack on the experience, fairness, competence, and integrity of the five members of the Tribunal is an indirect attack against all of those whose names appear on the list and casts doubt on the judgment of all those States that nominated them or indeed hired them in the past as counsel or judges for cases before the International Court of Justice, the ITLOS, or arbitral tribunals constituted under Annex VII of the Tribunal.

A quick glance at the list of arbitrators and conciliators maintained by the UN Secretary-General would make clear that anyone who casts aspersions on the experience, fairness, competence, and integrity of the five arbitrators would be foolhardy indeed. The list includes eight present and former ITLOS judges, two ICJ judges, one member of the European Court of Human Rights, and twenty-five well-known professors of international law. Judge Mensah, Professor Soons, and Judge Pawlak were nominated by their respective countries. Interestingly, Judges Cot and Wolfrum were both nominated by Mongolia.[24] China did not nominate anyone.

While it is not a requirement for the two parties to the dispute to choose arbitrators from the list, the ITLOS President, if called upon to appoint arbitrators, must choose them from the list. This requirement considerably narrows the field. Mr. Pinto's name was on the list; replacing him with arbitrators from Asia would have obliged the ITLOS President to choose from a field composed of nationals of Indonesia, Japan, Lebanon, the Republic of Korea, and Singapore. An arbitrator from Japan or the Republic of Korea would never have been acceptable to China, in spite of China's non-participation in the proceedings, because these two countries have maritime and/or territorial disputes with China. The arbitrators from Indonesia and Singapore,

23 *Annex VII, supra* note 8.

24 The list may be found on the UN website, *United Nations Convention on the Law of the Sea, Montego Bay, 10 December 1982*, https://treaties.un.org/Pages/ViewDetailsIII.aspx?src=TREATY&mtdsg_no=XXI-6&chapter=21&Temp=mtdsg3&clang=_en, accessed 31 August 2016. Professor Sands, one of the members of the legal team of the Philippines, was nominated by Mauritius.

who are well-known specialists of the law of the sea, did not have experience either as counsel or as judges that was as extensive as that of Pinto or any of the five members of the Tribunal.[25] In addition, they are nationals of member states of the Association of Southeast Asian Nations (ASEAN), like the Philippines.

One can affirm without fear of contradiction that all five members of the Tribunal, quite apart from the fact that they had among them 200 years of personal professional experience, as explained in Chapter IV, met the requirements of fairness, competence, and integrity set for ITLOS judges or for arbitrators, because they had been elected to the ITLOS or their names were on the list of arbitrators maintained by the UN Secretary-General or both. There is also no doubt that all five satisfied the second and third criteria. The requirement that the ITLOS President appoint the remaining members of the Tribunal from the list would have prevented Judge Yanai from appointing the non-Chinese scholars who have defended China's case, such as German scholar Stefan Talmon, whose name does not appear on the list.[26] As for the Chinese scholar Sienho Yee, even assuming that his name had been on the list, he would have been eliminated by the requirement that none of the remaining arbitrators "be in the service of, ordinarily resident in the territory of, or nationals of, any of the parties to the dispute."[27]

Again, it is interesting to note that Russia, which had refused to appear in the *Arctic Sunrise Arbitration*, refrained from attacking the members of the Arbitral Tribunal on the basis of their alleged lack of knowledge of Russia or Eastern Europe.[28]

For the sake of completeness (to use an expression that appears frequently in the Award of 12 July 2016), China also launched an assault on the fairness and integrity of members of the Tribunal.

The Fairness and Integrity of the Members of the Arbitral Tribunal

China's diatribe targeted individual members and the Arbitral Tribunal as a whole. One member was attacked for agreeing to a reasoning of the Tribunal that was apparently at variance with his previously expressed views. This criticism deliberately ignores the cogent reason given by the Tribunal for adopting the finding that it did adopt. The attack on the Tribunal as a whole, bordering on slander, accused it of upholding most of the Philippine claims for pecuniary reasons. This line of attack was wholly unjustified, for it is in the nature of arbitration that the costs of the proceedings are borne by the parties. As a result, in case of non-appearance of one party, the other is obliged to shoulder the costs for both if it wishes the proceedings to continue.

Without mentioning any name, China's Vice Foreign Minister charged that one member of the Tribunal had changed his well-known academic views: "Original viewpoints of some judges convinced people that they would safeguard relevant interests, but during the proceedings of the Arbitral Tribunal, these judges turned their backs on the academic opinions they once held on to."[29] A Xinhua article makes it clear that the Vice Foreign Minister is referring to Professor Soons.[30] The article quotes Wang Hanling and Peng Sixiang, researchers with the Chinese

25 The arbitrator nominated by Lebanon is a judge at the ITLOS.

26 Stefan Talmon, "The South China Sea Arbitration: Is There a Case to Answer?," in Stefan Talmon and Bing Bing Jia (eds.), *The South China Sea Arbitration: A Chinese Perspective* (Oxford: Hart Publishing, 2014), pp. 15–79.

27 *Annex VII*, Art. 3(e), *supra* note 8. Sienho Yee is Changjiang Xuezhe Professor of International Law and Chief Expert, Wuhan University Institute of Boundary and Ocean Studies and Institute of International Law. See his website http://www.sienhoyee.org/, accessed 18 July 2016.

28 The members of the Tribunal were nationals of Ghana (President), Australia, Poland, the Netherlands, and Mexico. *The Arctic Sunrise Arbitration (Netherlands v. Russia)*. Award on Jurisdiction and Admissibility, pp. 3–4, paras. 14–16, *supra* note 13.

29 *Veil of the Arbitral Tribunal Must Be Tore [sic] Down*, *supra* note 7.

30 "Major Chinese Newspapers Slam South China Sea Arbitration," *xinhuanet.com*, 11 July 2016, http://english.cri.

Academy of Social Sciences, who described Soons as a "chameleon" for allegedly reversing a position expressed in his scholarly work:

> Soons has expressed his opinion publicly at least twice over the years that when two countries have overlapping claims over waters, issues about the legal status and maritime rights of islands and reefs cannot be separated from the maritime delimitation disputes between the two countries, and they form an integral part of maritime delimitation.

A quick perusal of the Award on Jurisdiction and Admissibility will clarify the issue. On page 61, paragraph 155 of the Award, the Tribunal declares that it "agrees with China that maritime delimitation is an integral and systemic process"—this is supposedly the view espoused by Professor Soons in his earlier research. However, the Tribunal goes on to point out that in the process of maritime delimitation, many issues may have to be considered in order to meet the requirements of an "equitable solution," "special circumstances" in respect of the territorial sea, and relevant circumstances in relation to the Exclusive Economic Zone and/or the continental shelf. Separate disputes may exist over each of these issues in a context that is different from that of maritime delimitation. The fact that a dispute exists over any one of these issues does not automatically transform the issue into a dispute over maritime delimitation itself. To quote the Tribunal, "It does not follow that a dispute over an issue that may be considered in the course of maritime delimitation constitutes a dispute over maritime delimitation itself."[31]

Not satisfied with questioning the fairness and integrity of one member of the Tribunal, China tarred them all with the same brush:

> Who supported the Arbitral Tribunal? The arbitrators are paid by certain parties, but who? Maybe by the Philippines or other countries. This system is completely different from the ICJ or the ITLOS. Judges of the ICJ or the ITLOS receive salaries from the UN for the sake of independence and impartiality. But these five judges of the Arbitral Tribunal are doing it for a profit, and their payments come from the Philippines and probably others, too. We are unsure about the details but they do provide paid services.[32]

The implication that the judges were bribed is so grave that one American writer deemed it tantamount to "defamation"[33] and another equated it with "slander."[34]

This "character assassination,"[35] as Julian Ku describes it, deliberately ignores the fundamental difference between a permanent international tribunal, such as the ICJ or the ITLOS, and an ad hoc international tribunal. In proceedings before both types of tribunals, each party naturally pays its own expenses, e.g., costs for preparation of the pleadings, the fees of its legal counsel, and the costs of travel to the seat of the ICJ or ITLOS. In the case of an arbitral tribunal, which is established by the two parties to the dispute for the sole purpose of resolving a particular dispute, it is an established principle that each party pays an equal

cn/12394/2016/07/11/3521s933802.htm, accessed 1 September 2016.

31 Award on Jurisdiction and Admissibility, https://pcacases.com/web/sendAttach/1506, accessed 30 March 2018.

32 *Veil of the Arbitral Tribunal Must Be Tore [sic] down, supra* note 7.

33 Jerome A. Cohen, "South China Sea Ruling and Defamation," *jeromecohen.net*, 20 July 2016, http://www.jeromecohen.net/jerrys-blog/2016/7/20/south-china-sea-ruling-and-defamation, accessed 31 August 2016.

34 Julian Ku, "China's Vice-Minister for Foreign Affairs Casually Slanders the South China Sea Arbitral Tribunal," *opiniojuris.org*, 26 July 2016, http://opiniojuris.org/2016/07/26/chinas-vice-minister-for-foreign-affairs-casually-slanders-the-south-china-sea-arbitral-tribunal/, accessed 31 August 2016.

35 *Ibid.*

share of the expenses of the tribunal. This principle was laid down in Article 57 of the 1899 Convention for the Pacific Settlement of International Disputes and in Article 85 of the 1899 Convention for the Pacific Settlement of International Disputes, to both of which China is a party.[36] Article 7 of Annex VII of the Convention merely reaffirms this principle:

> Article 7
>
> Expenses
>
> Unless the arbitral tribunal decides otherwise because of the particular circumstances of the case, the expenses of the tribunal, including the remuneration of its members, shall be borne by the parties to the dispute in equal shares.[37]

This provision applies to all arbitrations under Annex VII of the Convention.

It is carried over into Article 31, para. 1 of the Rules of Procedure of the *South China Sea Arbitration.*[38] The reason that the Philippines paid for the expenses of the two Parties to the dispute is the same as the reason for the appointment by the ITLOS President of four members of the Tribunal: China's refusal to participate in the arbitration. The Netherlands found itself in the same situation when Russia refused to appear in the *Arctic Sunrise Arbitration* and thus failed to pay its share of the deposit toward the costs of the arbitration.[39] It is remarkable that Russia, in its critique of the final Award in the arbitration, refrained from attributing the Tribunal's decision, which found Russia in breach of UN Convention on the Law of the Sea, to pecuniary motives on the part of the judges.[40]

The Philippines (and China, if it had appeared before the Tribunal) could have avoided the obligation to shoulder the expenses of the Arbitral Tribunal and the Registry if they had recognized the jurisdiction of either the ICJ or the ITLOS, for the settlement of their disputes concerning interpretation and application of the Convention. Both are permanent tribunals. As such, the compensation of ICJ members is paid for by the United Nations and that of the ITLOS members, by the States parties to the Convention and the International Seabed Authority. As explained in Chapter XIII, the Philippines has recognized the compulsory jurisdiction of the ICJ, but China has not. Had the Philippines filed an application with the ICJ, the latter would have dismissed it, for lack of jurisdiction. Neither the Philippines nor China has recognized the jurisdiction of ITLOS, which thus lacks jurisdiction to hear the case. The Philippines and China could have concluded a special agreement (*compromis*) by which they would have submitted the dispute to either the ICJ or ITLOS. Yet, China's intransigence would have ruled out this last possibility. In these circumstances, arbitration under Annex VII is deemed under Article 287(3) of the Convention to be the mode of dispute settlement that the two Parties to the dispute have chosen. This mode of dispute settlement inevitably carries with it the corresponding obligation to assume responsibility for the expenses of the Tribunal.

---

36 1899 Convention for the Pacific Settlement of International Disputes, https://pca-cpa.org/wp-content/uploads/sites/175/2016/01/1899-Convention-for-the-Pacific-Settlement-of-International-Disputes.pdf, accessed 30 March 2018; 1907 Convention for the Pacific Settlement of International Disputes, https://pca-cpa.org/wp-content/uploads/sites/175/2016/01/1907-Convention-for-the-Pacific-Settlement-of-International-Disputes.pdf, accessed 30 March 2018.

37 *Annex VII, supra* note 8.

38 *Rules of Procedure*, 27 August 2013, p. 13, https://pcacases.com/web/sendAttach/233, accessed 30 March 2018.

39 *The Arctic Sunrise Arbitration (Netherlands v. Russia), supra* note 10.

40 Interfax, "Russian Foreign Ministry: Arctic Sunrise Arbitration Court Lacks Proper Jurisdiction," *Russia Beyond the Headlines*, 25 August 2015, http://rbth.com/news/2015/08/25/russian_foreign_ministry_arctic_sunrise_arbitration_court_lacks_proper_j_48720.htm, accessed 12 September 2015.

The last strand in China's conspiracy theory of international arbitration is as unfounded as the first three.

The Alleged Role of the US in the Arbitration

The charge of a US-led conspiracy conjures up all sorts of images.[41] One imagines the US acting behind the scenes in any or all of the following phases of the proceedings: the decision to initiate arbitration, the hiring of the lawyers, the drafting of the memorials, the appointment of the experts, the bifurcation of the proceedings, or the preparation of the strategy and tactics during the oral proceedings.[42] One is almost disappointed to learn that China's charge is limited to the alleged US role in the timing of the release of the Award. This alleged US manipulation of the Tribunal, for which no evidence is provided, is belied by the undisputable fact that the Tribunal refused to grant permission for the US to attend the Merits Hearing as an observer.

China alleges that the issuance of the Award, which was said to have been originally set for 7 July, was reset to 12 July through US pressure, the aim being supposedly to show support for the Administration of President Duterte, who was elected in May 2016.[43] To this damp squib, one might reply that China provides no evidence whatsoever that the date of release of the Award was postponed.[44] Perhaps China is unwilling to reveal the source of its information, because it was obtained through a conspiracy or a secret intelligence operation? Even assuming that the date of release was indeed postponed, it is hard to see how the delay could be construed as a form of support for the new Philippine administration. Was the delay intended to give the new administration more time to think of pretexts for rejecting the Award? After all, it would probably have wished that the arbitration had never taken place and preferred that no decision ever be released. This fictional scenario imagined by the Chinese would have to explain why the US would find it in its interest to delay the issuance of the Award. The US was in all likelihood hoping for decisions that rejected China's theses, particularly the "nine-dash line," and would have been eager to see the Award issued as soon as possible.

The strongest counter-argument to the idea of US manipulation of the Tribunal is that the latter refused to allow it to attend the Hearing on the Merits, held in November 2015, as an observer. China's excessive maritime claims and artificial island-building that has been so damaging to the marine environment have aroused so much concern among the littoral States in the South China Sea and beyond that the arbitration inevitably sparked great interest. One unexpected manifestation of this interest was that five States requested and were granted permission to attend the Hearing on Jurisdiction and Admissibility as observers—Indonesia, Japan, Malaysia, Thailand, and Vietnam.[45] Such a phenomenon is without precedent in international arbitration. Unlike oral hearings at the ICJ, which are open to the public,[46] arbitral tribunals normally conduct the oral phase of the proceedings behind closed doors. Prior to the hearing on the Merits, these five States once more requested permission to attend as observers; similar requests to attend the hearing were made by Australia, Singapore, the UK, and the US.

41 Wang Xiaohui, "S. China Sea Arbitration: A US-Led Conspiracy Behind the Farce," *China.org.cn*, 12 July 2016, http://www.china.org.cn/opinion/2016-07/12/content_38864239.htm, accessed 18 July 2016.

42 The appointment of the members of the Tribunal would be excluded, for that responsibility was already attributed to the ITLOS President.

43 *Ibid.*

44 A damp squib is something intended but failing to impress. *Collins English Dictionary*, https://www.collinsdictionary.com/dictionary/english/damp-squib, accessed 27 March 2018.

45 Award on Jurisdiction and Admissibility, pp. 29–30, para. 86, https://pcacases.com/web/sendAttach/1506, accessed 18 July 2016.

46 *Statute of the International Court of Justice*, Article 46, http://legal.un.org/avl/pdf/ha/sicj/icj_statute_e.pdf, accessed 11 September 2016.

All were granted permission, except the US.[47]

The US had justified its request by explaining that

> [as] a major coastal and maritime State, and as a State that is continuing to pursue its domestic constitutional processes to accede to the United Nations Convention on the Law of the Sea, the United States has a keen interest in the proceedings in light of the important legal issues relating to the law of the sea that are the subject of the arbitration.[48]

The Tribunal forwarded the request to the Philippines and China. True to form, China did not respond. The Philippines, which had already agreed to the requests from Vietnam, Malaysia, Thailand, Japan, Indonesia, and Singapore and later agreed to similar requests by the UK and Australia, had no objection to the US request. However, on 23 November, the Tribunal informed the Philippines, China, and the US that it had decided that "only interested States parties to the United Nations Convention on the Law of the Sea will be admitted as observers" and that it could not accede to the US request.[49] The fact is all the other States that had requested permission to attend the hearings as observers were States parties to the Convention.

Why did the Tribunal refuse to allow the US to attend the Hearings? The US, which has not ratified the Convention, is not a State party to it. A State party is defined by the Vienna Convention on the Law of Treaties as "a State which has consented to be bound by the treaty and for which the treaty is in force."[50] As a matter of fact, the US was one of only four countries (the other three being Israel, Turkey, and Venezuela) that had voted against the adoption of the Convention on 30 April 1982, at the 11th and last session of the Third United Nations Conference on the Law of the Sea; 130 States voted for, and 18 States abstained.[51] The main reason for the US negative vote was the opposition to the Convention's provisions on deep seabed mining (Part XI of the Convention), as explained by President Ronald Reagan in a declaration on 10 March 1983.[52] More than 30 years later, the US is still not bound by the rules laid down in the Convention, with the exception of rules that may be deemed part of customary international law.[53] In relation to the Convention, the US remains a "third State" as defined by the Vienna Convention on the Law of Treaties—"'Third State' means a State not a party to the treaty."[54]

Now, the object of the dispute between the Philippines and China is the interpretation and application of the UN Convention on the Law of the Sea; as a third State in relation to the latter, the US could not have any legal interest in the interpretation and application of

47 Award of 12 July 2016, pp. 21–22, paras. 62, 65, 67, 68, https://pcacases.com/web/sendAttach/2086, accessed 27 March 2018.

48 *Ibid.*, p. 22, para. 65.

49 *Ibid.*, p. 22, para. 66. The Tribunal's decision was reported by Niña P. Calleja, "US Request to Send Observers in PH Case vs China Denied," *Philippine Daily Inquirer*, 1 December 2015, http://globalnation.inquirer.net/133103/us-request-to-send-observers-in-ph-case-vs-china-denied, accessed 6 August 2016.

50 Article 2, paragraph 1(g) of the Vienna Convention on the Law of Treaties, adopted on 23 May 1969, https://treaties.un.org/doc/publication/unts/volume%201155/volume-1155-i-18232-english.pdf, accessed 13 September 2016.

51 United Nations Office of Legal Affairs, Codification Division, *Diplomatic Conferences, Third United Nations Conference on the Law of the Sea, 1973–1982*, http://legal.un.org/diplomaticconferences/1973_los/, accessed 27 March 2018.

52 *Statement on United States Oceans Policy, March 10, 1983*, https://www.reaganlibrary.archives.gov/archives/speeches/1983/31083c.htm, accessed 16 August 2016.

53 "Customary international law envisages two principal elements: a concordant practice of a number of States acquiesced in by others, and a conception that the practice is required by or consistent with the prevailing law (*opinio juris*)." John P. Grant and J. Craig Barker, *Parry and Grant Encyclopedic Dictionary of International Law* (Oxford: Oxford University Press, 2009), p. 137.

54 Article 2, paragraph 1(h) of the Vienna Convention on the Law of Treaties, *supra* note 50.

the Convention. The interpretation of a treaty's provisions has been defined by the Italian scholar Adolfo Maresca as a logical and legal operation that seeks to determine the meaning of the treaty's provisions, to specify their scope, and to clarify the points that may appear to be obscure or ambiguous.[55] The specific purpose of interpretation is to apply a treaty norm to a concrete fact or situation. The fact or situation is confronted with the norm, the fact or situation is assessed, and the legal consequences that the norm attributes to the fact or situation are established.[56] Interpretation of a treaty is essential because no treaty, no matter how detailed its provisions, can possibly anticipate all situations that may arise in the future and to which its norms could conceivably apply. Interpretation is carried out at the international level by State bodies acting jointly (e.g., a joint commission, composed of representatives of the States parties to the treaty), by the organs of international organizations (e.g., the Secretary-General of the organization), or by international organs strictly speaking (an arbitral tribunal or a permanent international court).[57]

It goes without saying that only States parties to a treaty can have a legal interest in the interpretation and application of the treaty. The latter creates rights and obligations exclusively for them, unless it specifically contains provisions for the benefit of third States (Part III, Section 4 of the Vienna Convention on the Law of Treaties, Treaties and Third States). In a concrete situation and particularly if the situation is confused, it may be very tempting for a State party to interpret a treaty in a way that enhances the enjoyment of its rights and minimizes the burden of its obligations under the treaty. As the other State party (in the case of a bilateral treaty) or other State parties (in the case of a multilateral treaty) may be expected to behave in the same way, it is imperative to interpret the relevant provisions of the treaty and to determine their precise meaning. Obviously, States that are not parties to the treaty, which have not agreed to be bound by the treaty, cannot have any legal stake in the interpretation of the treaty. This point is so basic that it does not even appear in Part III (Observance, Interpretation, and Application of Treaties) of the Vienna Convention on the Law of Treaties.[58]

One might ask whether the refusal of the US request injured any US legal or political interest. The observers permitted to attend the Hearings were not allowed to take the floor; hence, even if the US had been allowed to observe the proceedings, it would not have been able to address the Tribunal. The US was probably hoping or expecting that the arguments presented at the Hearing would confirm its own arguments against China's "nine-dash line" or even provide it with new ones that it could immediately incorporate into its own policy positions and exploit in the court of world public opinion.[59] The Tribunal's refusal, which contradicted the position

55 Adolfo Maresca, *Il Diritto dei trattati. La Convenzione codificatrice di Vienna del 23 maggio 1969* (Milano: Dott. A. Giuffrè Editore, 1971), p. 333. The chair of the Drafting Committee of the Vienna Conference on the Law of Treaties (1968–69), which drafted the Vienna Convention on the Law of Treaties, defined interpretation as "the intellectual operation that aims to understand the treaty, to clarify its meaning and to determine its scope." Mustafa Kamil Yasseen, "L'interprétation des traités d'après la Convention de Vienne sur le droit des traités," *Recueil des Cours de l'Académie de Droit International de La Haye*, t. 151 (1976-III), p. 9.

56 Maresca, p. 334, *supra* note 55.

57 *Ibid.*, p. 335.

58 *Supra* note 50.

59 US Department of State, Bureau of Oceans and International Environmental and Scientific Affairs, Office of Ocean and Polar Affairs, *China: Maritime Claims in the South China Sea*, 5 December 2014, http://www.state.gov/documents/organization/234936.pdf, accessed 8 August 2016.

of the Philippines, deprived the US of these opportunities, something that the Tribunal would never have done if it had been truly manipulated by the US. The latter was forced to wait a few weeks until the transcripts of the Merits Hearing were uploaded to the PCA website.

Of course, China could always argue that the Tribunal's decision was deliberately staged by the US with the aim of masking US manipulation of the Tribunal. For this kind of imagination, no remedy has yet been discovered.

To conclude, the four strands of China's conspiracy theory of international arbitration do not stand up to critical scrutiny. Of course, as recommended by the scholarly literature, the rebuttals have been addressed to the audience of the conspiracy theory, and not to its authors, in the hope that if and when the vicissitudes of Chinese and Philippine foreign policies prompt China to revive its conspiracy theory, the audience will be very easily able to break its flimsy threads.

ANNEXES

TABLE 1

MARITIME FEATURES THAT ARE THE OBJECT OF SUBMISSIONS NO. 3 TO 7

International Name/ Chinese Name/ Philippine Name	Location and Brief Description	Distance from a Philippine Archipelagic Baseline	Distance from a Chinese Baseline
Scarborough Shoal/ Huangyan Dao/ Panatag Shoal or Bajo de Masintoc	Coral reef located at 15°09′16″ N, 117°45′58″ E	116.2 NM from Luzon baseline	448.2 NM from baseline point 29 (Jiapengliedao) near Hong Kong
Cuarteron Reef/ Huayang Jiao/ Calderon Reef	Coral reef located at 08°51′41″ N, 112°50′08″ E; easternmost of London Reefs on western edge of Spratlys	245.3 NM from Palawan baseline	585.3 NM from baseline point 39 (Dongzhou (2)) adjacent to Hainan
Fiery Cross Reef/ Yongshiu Jiao/ Kagitingan Reef	Coral reef located at 09°33′00″ N, 112°53′25″ E, to north of Cuarteron Reef and along western edge of Spratlys	254.2 NM from Palawan baseline	547.7 NM from baseline point 39 (Dongzhou (2)) adjacent to Hainan
Johnson Reef/ Chigua Jiao/ Mabini Reef	Coral reef that forms part of Union Bank in center of Spratlys; located at 9°43′00″ N, 114°16′55″ E	184.7 NM from Palawan baseline	570.8 NM from baseline point 39 (Dongzhou (2)) adjacent to Hainan
McKennan Reef/ Ximen Jiao/ Chigua Reef	Coral reef that forms part of Union Bank in center of Spratlys; located at 09°54′13″ N, 114°27′53″ E	181.3 NM from Palawan baseline	566.8 NM from baseline point 39 (Dongzhou (2)) adjacent to Hainan
Hughes Reef/ Dongmen Jiao/ Chigua Reef	Coral reef that forms part of Union Bank in center of Spratlys; located at 09°54′48″ N, 114°29′48″ E	180.3 NM from Palawan baseline	567.2 NM from baseline point 39 (Dongzhou (2)) adjacent to Hainan
Gaven Reef (North)/ Nanxun Jiao/ Burgos Reef	One of a pair of coral reefs that forms part of Tizard Bank, directly to North of Union Bank; located at 10°12′27″ N, 114°13′21″ E	203.0 NM from Palawan baseline	544.1 NM from baseline point 39 (Dongzhou (2)) adjacent to Hainan
Gaven Reef (South)/ Nanxun Jiao/ Burgos Reef	One of a pair of coral reefs that forms part of Tizard Bank, directly to North of Union Bank; located at 10°09′42″ N, 114°15′09″ E	200.5 NM from Palawan baseline	547.4 NM from baseline point 39 (Dongzhou (2)) adjacent to Hainan
Subi Reef/ Zhubi Jiao/ Zamora Reef	Coral reef located to north of Tizard Bank and short distance to south-west of Thitu Island and Thitu reefs; located at 10°55′22″ N, 114°05′04″ E, on northwestern edge of Spratlys	231.9 NM from Palawan baseline	502.2 NM from baseline point 39 (Dongzhou (2)) adjacent to Hainan
Mischief Reef/ Meiji Jiao/ Panganiban Reef	Coral reef located in the center of the Spratlys, to the east of Union Bank and to the southeast of Tizard Bank; located at 09°54′17″ N, 115°31′59″ E	125.4 NM from Palawan baseline	589.1 NM from baseline point 39 (Dongzhou (2)) adjacent to Hainan
Second Thomas Shoal/ Ren'ai Jiao/ Ayungin Shoal	Coral reef located in the center of the Spratlys, to the east of Union Bank and to the southeast of Tizard Bank; located at 09°54′17″ N, 115°51′49″ E	104.0 NM from Palawan baseline	616.2 NM from baseline point 39 (Dongzhou (2)) adjacent to Hainan

Source: Award of 12 July 2016, pp. 120–22, paras. 284–90. This Table has been prepared by the author and is not to be found in this form in the original text.

TABLE 2

SOUTH CHINA SEA MARITIME FEATURES REFERRED TO IN CHAPTER VI.C OF THE AWARD OF 12 JULY 2016

International Name/ Chinese Name/ Philippine Name	Location and Brief Description	Distance from Palawan Archipelagic Baseline (in NM)	Distance from Chinese Baseline Point 39 (Dongzhou (2)) Adjacent to Hainan (in NM)
Itu Aba/ Taiping Dao/ Ligaw	Largest high-tide feature in Spratlys; surface area app. 0.43 km²; located at 10°22'38" N, 114°21'56" E, lying atop northern edge of Tizard Bank; surrounded by coral reef and shallow water; controlled by Taiwan	200.6	539.6
Thitu/ Zhongye Dao/ Pagasa	Surface area app. 0.41 km²; located at 11°03'19" N, 114°17'08" E, atop west-side shoal of two adjacent coral reefs separated by a narrow deep channel, surrounded by drying coral reef; controlled by the Philippines	227.4	502.1
West York/ Xiyue Dao/ Likas	Surface area app. 0.21 km²; located atop a coral reef at 11°05'01" N, 115°01'26" E; surrounded by white sand cay, outside of which there is a coral reef basin; controlled by the Philippines	195.0	524.9
Spratly Island/ Nanwei Dao/ Lagos	Surface area app. 0.17 km²; located atop a coral bank at 8°38'41" N, 111°55'15" E; has a margin of white sand and broken coral, surrounded by drying rocky ledges; controlled by Vietnam	298.2	584.3
North-East Cay/ Beizi Dao/ Parola	Surface area app. 0.15 km²; located in larger complex of features known as "North Danger Reef"; located at 11°27'14" N, 114°21'14" E; surrounded by belt of coral sand, lies on drying reef; controlled by the Philippines	293.3	484.3
South-West Cay/ Nanzi Dao/ Pugad	Surface area app. 0.15 km²; located in larger complex of features known as "North Danger Reef"; located at 11°25'49" N, 114°19'52" E; surrounded by drying reef	239.6	484.8

Source: Award of 12 July 2016, pp. 178–80, paras. 397–406. This Table has been prepared by the author and is not to be found in this form in the original text.

TABLE 3
OVERVIEW OF CHINA'S CONSTRUCTION ACTIVITIES
IN THE SPRATLY ISLANDS

Date of Observation	Cuarteron Reef	Fiery Cross Reef	Gaven Reef (North)
1988		Small naval post, followed by oceanographic observation post, pier and other buildings	Start of Chinese presence
1989			
1992	3 small buildings		
1994			
1995			
1996			Outpost with barracks, 2 octagonal structures
1997	More buildings, wharves, communication facilities		
1999			
2005			3-story concrete building with communication equipment
2006	3-story building, concrete platforms, helipad		
2011			Further enhancements
2013	More concrete buildings, solar panels, weather and communication instruments, observation towers, temporary pier	Communication system and lighthouses, complete complex of buildings with significant communication and defense and military features, greenhouse	
2014	Start of more substantial land reclamation	Runway being built	Intense reclamation work began
2015	Land reclamation intensified	Land reclamation intensified	
May	Permanent pier, ceremony to mark the start of construction of a 50-m lighthouse		
November	231,000 sq.m of new land, channel 125 m wide for large vessels to access and berth within a harbor cut out of the reef platform	2,740,000 sq.m of new land created, sand and rock dredged from seabed covered the entire platform of southwest reef flat; artificial island is 300 times larger than preexisting installations, which covered 11,000 m^2; 3-km runway, 630,000-m^2 harbor; cement plants; support buildings; temporary loading pier; communication facilities; defense equipment, 2 lighthouses; green- house; 2 helipads; multi-level administrative facility	Gaven Reef was an artificial island 300 × 250 m, created from 136,000 sq.m of materials dredged from the seabed

Source: Award of 12 July 2016, pp. 337-55, paras. 863-90. This Table has been prepared by the author and is not to be found in this form in the original text.

Table 3 continued...

Johnson Reef	Hughes Reef	Subi Reef	Mischief Reef
	Start of Chinese presence		
		Start of Chinese presence	
Heavily fortified area with observation tower			
		5 buildings, wharf, helipad	
			Construction of typhoon shelters
			Multi-storey structures, communication equipment, wharves, helipad
3-story concrete building, communication equipment, solar panels, helipads	3-story concrete building, helipad	4-storey concrete building	
		More concrete structures, lighthouse, communication equipment	
Intense reclamation work began	Start of large-scale land reclamation		
		Dredging intensified	Intense reclamation work began
More buildings, solar panels, paved roads, piers ceremony to mark the start of construction of a lighthouse	Permanent pier, massive onshore construction of 6-story building		
Johnson Reef was an artificial island, with an area of 109,000 sq.m, 1,000 times larger than the previous structure	Hughes Reef was an artificial island, with an area of 75,000 sq.m, coastal fortifications, defensive towers, multi-level facility; reef entrance enlarged to create 118-m-wide access channel for larger vessels	Artificial island 3,950,000 sq. m^2. covering most of the reef; start of 3-km runway, multi-level facility, reinforced sea walls, towers, communication facilities; created 230-m-wide access channel; almost the entire atoll has been transformed into an artificial island.	Total land area created was 5,580,000 sq. m^2 southern entrance was widened from 110 m to 275 m

TABLE 4

COMPARISON OF THE ASSESSMENT OF THE ENVIRONMENTAL IMPACT OF CHINA'S CONSTRUCTION ACTIVITIES IN THE SPRATLY ISLANDS BY CHINA'S SOA AND BY THE TRIBUNAL'S EXPERTS

State Oceanic Administration	Ferse Report
Timing of works: construction tried to avoid the spawn periods of red snapper (mid-April), tuna (June–August), and bonito (March–August).	Land construction occurred during the spawning periods and during the suspected spawning time of reef corals.
Water quality: China avoided fine sand going into the reclamation areas to maintain the water quality of the coral reef areas.	Satellite and aerial imagery clearly shows water quality in the vicinity of each construction site was affected by increasing sediment and turbidity from dredging.
Selection of sites containing dead coral: construction sites contained dead coral.	Even deep lagoon basins containing fewer live corals than other reef habits constitute vital habitat for molluscs, echinoderm, and crustaceans; On reefs lacking deep lagoon (Cuarteron Reef, Hughes Reef, Gaven Reef, Johnson Reef), material for land reclamation was gathered from shallow reef habitat; and Sediment plumes affected both the lagoon and the outer reef slope habitats.
Use of nature simulation method: going from desalination, solidification, efflorescence to green coral reef ecological environment [sic].	This overlooks the importance of biogenic sediment production: rather than simulating the natural process of island development, the construction process increases the erosion of reefs by shifting the balance between carbonate accretion and erosion and thus increases the risk of drowning the reef as sea levels continue to rise.
Replenishment: nutrients and food organisms can be replenished constantly from surrounding waters.	There is very limited support for the potential for replenishment from outside the Spratly Islands, in light of larval connectivity patterns within the South China Sea.
Impact on reef structure: Due to strong currents and waves, photosynthesis of corals is largely unaffected; the sites are in areas where coverage of coral reefs is low; and The overall community structure of coral reefs and the physical and chemical living environment of the coral reefs remain unaltered.	Sediment plumes generated by dredging have altered the community structure of affected coral reefs; Construction has permanently altered hydrodynamics; and An elevated level of sediments is likely for months to years in those parts of the reefs that are well-flushed by open ocean waters and for years to decades in areas with less flushing (e.g., Mischief Reef and Subi Reef lagoons).
Impact on reef health: Reef status is sub-healthy before and after construction; and Construction neither affected ecosystem health nor harmed coral reef ecosystem.	Available evidence leaves little doubt that coral reef ecosystems of the seven reefs have suffered significant and extensive harm as a result of construction.
Restoration and transplantation: Restoration of coral reef communities will take 5–10 years and of complex and complete ecosystems, 50–100 years; and Transplantation will better protect coral reefs.	Restoration will not succeed if stressors persist and if ecological connectivity and larval supply are disturbed; Large parts of the seven reefs have been permanently destroyed by construction; For the remaining reefs, recovery is uncertain; If it occurs, it will take more than a century; Restorative activities are extremely expensive and have only been attempted on much smaller scales; Transplantation will not be suitable on the scale of the impacts as it would risk impacting other reefs in the region; and Transplantation involves prohibitive labor and costs.
Recovery: good results have been obtained; the ecological impact is partial, temporary, controllable and recoverable.	The ecological impacts affected large parts of the reefs; The effects are permanent (for reclaimed reef flats and excavated channels) and long-lasting (for sediment resuspension in the lagoons); extensive sediment plumes that remained near the construction sites for weeks render the amount of control over the potential impacts doubtful; and For large areas of the reefs affected, recovery is unlikely or may take decades or centuries.

Source: Award of 12 July 2016, pp. 337–55, paras. 863–90. This Table has been prepared by the author and is not to be found in this form in the original text.

References

BOOKS, JOURNAL ARTICLES, NEWSPAPER ARTICLES, BLOG POSTS

ABS-CBN News. "Two Days After Tribunal's Ruling, Filipino Fishermen Still Get Driven Away From Scarborough Shoal." *South China Sea Research: Facts and Legal Aspects*, 14 July 2016, https://seasresearch.wordpress.com/2016/07/14/two-days-after-tribunals-ruling-filipino-fishermen-still-get-driven-away-from-scarborough-shoal/, accessed 26 November 2017.

"Afrique Centrale: Conflit sur la mer de Chine méridionale—La Chine veut le soutien du Cameroun." *Cameroonvoice*, 9 May 2016, http://www.cameroonvoice.com/news/article-news-24297.html, accessed 29 May 2016.

Agence France Presse. "Beijing Lines up Diplomatic Battle Groups Over South China Sea." *Philippine Daily Inquirer*, 25 May 2016, http://globalnation.inquirer.net/139665/beijing-lines-up-diplomatic-battle-groups-over-south-china-sea, accessed 25 May 2016.

__________. "Nouvelle frontière Burkina Faso-Niger: 18 communes changeront de pays." *Jeuneafrique.com*, 9 May 2015, http://www.jeuneafrique.com/231107/politique/nouvelle-fronti-re-burkina-faso-niger-18-communes-changeront-de-pays/, accessed 29 May 2016.

American Bar Association. *Model Code of Judicial Conduct*. Chicago: American Bar Association, 2011, http://www.americanbar.org/groups/professional_responsibility/publications/model_code_of_judicial_conduct/model_code_of_judicial_conduct_canon_2/rule2_9expartecommunications.html, accessed 5 July 2015.

"Andrew B. Loewenstein." *superlawyers*, 2016, http://profiles.superlawyers.com/massachusetts/boston/lawyer/andrew-b-loewenstein/7b399d78-0651-41f9-bf3c-b96a2bdd4e5f.html, accessed 2 September 2016.

"L'arbitrage de la mer de Chine méridionale initié par les Philippines viole le droit international selon Tang Weibin, Ambassadeur de Chine en Côte d'Ivoire." *abidjan.net*, 17 May 2016, http://news.abidjan.net/h/591056.html, accessed 28 May 2016.

Arnold, Gordon B. *Conspiracy Theory in Film, Television, and Politics*. New York: Praeger, 2008.

Associated Press. "Philippine Warship in Standoff with China Vessels." *The Guardian*, 11 April 2012, https://www.theguardian.com/world/2012/apr/11/philippines-china-stand-off-south-china-sea, accessed 16 July 2016.

Bacani, Louis. "Palace Hits Lawyer for Questioning Big Hague Delegation." *The Philippine Star*, 8 July 2015, http://www.philstar.com/headlines/2015/07/08/1474653/palace-hits-lawyer-questioning-big-hague-delegation, accessed 28 November 2017.

Benadava, Santiago. "La 'competencia de la competencia' y el exceso de poder en la justicia arbitral." *Liber Amicorum 'In Memoriam' of Judge José María Ruda*, pp. 221–30. Eds. Calixto A. Armas Barea et al. The Hague: Kluwer Law International, 2000.

Black, Henry Campbell. *Black's Law Dictionary*, 3rd ed. St. Paul, MN: West Publishing Co., 1979.

Bussi, Luisa. "Mediazione e arbitrati fra medioevo ed età moderna." *Diritto@Storia*, 4 (2005), pp. 1–27, http://eprints.uniss.it/223/1/Bussi_L_Articolo_2005_Mediazione.pdf, accessed 30 November 2017.

Byford, Jovan. *Conspiracy Theories: A Critical Introduction*. Houndmills, Basingstoke, Hampshire: Palgrave Macmillan, 2011.

Calleja, Niña P. "US Request to Send Observers in PH Case vs China Denied." *Philippine Daily Inquirer*, 1 December 2015, http://globalnation.inquirer.net/133103/us-request-to-send-observers-in-ph-case-vs-china-denied, accessed 6 August 2016.

Calonzo, Andreo. "Palace Defends Hiring of Foreign Lawyers for PHL Arbitration Case vs. China." *Philippine Daily Inquirer*, 8 July 2015, http://www.gmanetwork.com/news/story/518286/news/nation/palace-defends-hiring-of-foreign-lawyers-for-phl-arbitration-case-vs-china, accessed 24 September 2015.

Cambridge Dictionary. Cambridge: Cambridge University Press, 2016, http://dictionary.cambridge.org/dictionary/english/conspiracy-theory, accessed 12 September 2016

Centre d'histoire de Sciences Po. *Cot, Pierre*. Paris: Fondation Nationale des Sciences Politiques, n.d., http://chsp.sciences-po.fr/fond-archive/cot-pierre, accessed 12 November 2015.

Centre for Maritime Research (MARE). *Curriculum vitae Alfred H.A. Soons*. Amsterdam, MARE, 2015, http://www.marecentre.nl/people_and_the_sea_2/documents/CVSoons.pdf, accessed 12 November 2015.

Chambers and Partners. *Foley Hoag LLP*. London: Chambers and Partners, 2015, http://www.chambersandpartners.com/15649/96/editorial/2/1, accessed 17 November 2015.

"Cleary Gottlieb Takes Over Treaty Case against Bolivia." *Latin Lawyer Online*, 27 July 2009, http://doclink.demarest.com.br/fds/fds.aspx?lib=BIBLIOTECA&doc=63088, accessed 18 November 2015.

Collins English Dictionary. Glasgow: HarperCollins Publishers, 2018, https://www.collinsdictionary.com/, accessed 29 March 2018.

Cornell University Law School. Legal Information Institute. *Amicus curiae*. Ithaca, NY: Legal Information Institute, Cornell Law School, 2015, https://www.law.cornell.edu/wex/amicus_curiae, accessed 17 November 2015.

Cot, Jean-Pierre. "Affaire des Essais nucléaires (Australie c. France et Nouvelle-Zélande c. France). Demandes en indication de mesures conservatoires. Ordonnances du 22 juin 1973." *Annuaire Français de Droit International*, 19 (1973), pp. 252–71, http://www.persee.fr/doc/afdi_0066-3085_1973_num_19_1_2213?q=Jean-Pierre%20Cot%20essais%20nucl%C3%A9aires, accessed 11 November 2015.

__________. "Appearing 'for' or 'on Behalf of' a State': The Role of Private Counsel Before International Tribunals." *Liber Amicorum Judge Shigeru Oda*, II, pp. 835–48. Eds. Nisuke Ando, Edward McWhinney, and Rüdiger Wolfrum. The Hague: Kluwer Law International, 2002.

__________. "L'arrêt de la Cour internationale de Justice dans l'affaire du temple Préah Vihéar (Cambodge c/Thaïlande). Exceptions préliminaires." *Annuaire Français de Droit International*, 7 (1961), pp. 229–51, http://www.persee.fr/web/revues/home/prescript/article/afdi_0066-3085_1961_num_7_1_1087, accessed 12 November 2015.

__________. "L'arrêt de la Cour internationale de Justice dans l'affaire du temple de Préah Vihéar (Cambodge c. Thaïlande - Fond)." *Annuaire Français de Droit International*, 8 (1962), pp. 217–47, http://www.persee.fr/web/revues/home/prescript/article/afdi_0066-3085_1962_num_8_1_969, accessed 12 November 2015.

__________. *La conciliation internationale*. Paris: Éditions Pedone, 1968.

__________, Mathias Forteau and Alain Pellet. *La Charte des Nations Unies, commentaire article par article*, 3rd ed. Paris: Éditions Economica, 2005.

__________ and Jean-Pierre Mounier. *Pour une sociologie politique*. 2 vols. Paris: Éditions du Seuil, 1975.

"Cour internationale de justice: Burkina Faso et Niger se quittent 'bons amis' avec une frontière commune." *zoodomail.com* (Burkina Faso), 16 April 2013, http://zoodomail.com/spip.php?page=imprimir_articulo&id_article=3858, accessed 29 May 2016.

De Taube, Baron Michel. "Les origines de l'arbitrage international. Antiquité et Moyen Âge." *Recueil des Cours de l'Académie de Droit International de La Haye*, t. 42 (1932-IV), pp. 1–116.

del Callar, Michaela. "For Having Pinay Wife, Sri Lankan Judge in PHL Arbitral Proceedings vs China Resigns." *Philippine Daily Inquirer*, 7 June 2013, http://www.gmanetwork.com/news/story/311870/news/nation/for-having-pinay-wife-sri-lankan-judge-in-phl-arbitral-proceedings-vs-china-resigns, accessed 27 July 2015.

"Différend frontalier Bénin-Niger: La paix des braves." *Lefaso net. Actualité du Burkina sur Internet* (Burkina Faso), 14 July 2005, http://lefaso.net/spip.php?page=impression&id_article=8428, accessed 27 May 2016.

Duclaux de l'Estoille, Marie. *Charles Rousseau. Société française pour le droit international*, 2017, http://www.sfdi.org/internationalistes/rousseau-charles/, accessed 30 November 2017.

Esmaquel, Paterno II. "PH Faces Major Hurdle in China Case." *rappler.com*, 12 March 2014, http://www.rappler.com/nation/52764-philippines-china-arbitral-tribunal-jurisdiction, accessed 26 July 2015.

Essex Court Chambers. *Professor Alan Boyle*, n.d. http://essexcourt.com/barrister/professor-alan-boyle/, accessed 22 November 2015.

European Parliament. *MEPs. Jean-Pierre Cot*, n.d. http://www.europarl.europa.eu/meps/en/1027/JEAN-PIERRE_COT_home.html, accessed 12 November 2015.

European University Institute. *Germany, Academic Career Structure*. 30 July 2015, http://www.eui.eu/ProgrammesAndFellowships/AcademicCareersObservatory/AcademicCareersbyCountry/Germany.aspx, accessed 12 November 2015.

Fisheries Research and Development Corporation. *Australian Fish Names Standard*. Canberra: Fisheries Research and Development Corporation, 2018, http://www.fishnames.com.au/ accessed 20 March 2018.

Foley Hoag LLP. *History*. Boston: Foley Hoag, 2015, http://www.foleyhoag.com/our-firm/history, accessed 18 November 2015.

__________. *Our People. Andrew B. Loewenstein*. Boston: Foley Hoag 2016, http://foleyhoag.com/people/loewenstein-andrew, accessed 2 September 2016.

__________. *Our People. Lawrence H. Martin*. Boston: Foley Hoag, 2015, http://www.foleyhoag.com/people/martin-lawrence, accessed 25 November 2015.

__________. *Our People. Paul S. Reichler*. Boston: Foley Hoag, 2015, http://www.foleyhoag.com/people/reichler-paul, accessed 18 November 2015.

"Foley Hoag Helps Uruguay Secure Landmark Victory Over Philip Morris; Arbitral Tribunal Affirms Uruguay's Sovereign Right to Regulate Tobacco." *BusinessWire.com*, 8 July 2016, http://www.businesswire.com/news/home/20160708005865/en/Foley-Hoag-Helps-Uruguay-Secure-Landmark-Victory, accessed 2 September 2016.

"Foley Hoag Wins Historic Victory for the Philippines in the South China Sea." *BusinessWire*, 12 July 2016, https://www.businesswire.com/news/home/20160712006548/en/Foley-Hoag-Wins-Historic-Victory-Philippines-South, accessed 29 March 2018.

Gore-Booth, Lord. *Satow's Guide to Diplomatic Practice*, 4th ed. London: Longman Group UK Ltd., 1979.

Grant, John P., and J. Craig Barker. *Parry & Grant Encyclopedic Dictionary of International Law*, 3rd ed. Oxford: Oxford University Press, 2009.

Guillien, Raymond, and Jean Vincent (eds.). *Lexique de termes juridiques*, 5th ed. Paris: Dalloz, 1981.

The Hague Academy of International Law. *Directed Studies and Diploma*. The Hague: The Hague Academy of International Law, 2015, https://www.hagueacademy.nl/programmes/summer-courses/diploma/, accessed 22 November 2015.

Herrera, Christine F. "The Hague Delegation 'Meant to Impress.'" *The Manila Standard*, 10 July 2015, http://manilastandard.net/news/top-stories/181937/the-hague-delegation-meant-to-impress-.html, accessed 28 November 2017.

Indiana University. Robert H. McKinney School of Law. *Judicial Clerkship Guide*. Indianapolis, IN: Robert H. McKinney School of Law, Indiana University, 2016, http://mckinneylaw.iu.edu/careers/judicial-clerkships-guide.html, accessed 2 September 2016.

International Hydrographic Organization. *Hydrographic Dictionary*. Part 1, Volume 1, *English*. Monaco: International Hydrographic Organization, 1994, https://www.iho.int/iho_pubs/standard/S-32/S-32-eng.pdf, accessed 8 December 2015.

Jacques, Martin. "Above the Law." *The Guardian*, 26 March 2005, http://www.theguardian.com/books/2005/mar/26/highereducation.news, accessed 17 November 2015.

"Judge Thomas A. Mensah: Biographical Note." *Law of the Sea, Environmental Law and Settlement of Disputes. Liber Amicorum Judge Thomas A. Mensah*, pp. xiv–xvi. Eds. Tafsir Malick Ndiaye and Rüdiger Wolfrum. Leiden: Martinus Nijhoff Publishers, 2007.

Kampfner, John. "These Guilty Men." *The Guardian*, 6 March 2005, http://www.theguardian.com/politics/2005/mar/06/politicalbooks.iraq, accessed 17 November 2015.

Kamarowsky, L. *Le tribunal international*. Translated by Serge de Westman. Paris: A. Durand et Pedone-Lauriel, Éditeurs, 1887, https://ia902700.us.archive.org/26/items/letribunalinter00lacogoog/letribunalinter00lacogoog.pdf, accessed 23 October 2017.

Ku, Julian. "China's Definition of the 'Peaceful Settlement of International Disputes' Leaves Out International Adjudication." *opiniojuris.org*, 15 October 2013, http://opiniojuris.org/2013/10/15/obligation-seek-peaceful-settlement-international-disputes-include-international-adjudication/, accessed 5 July 2015.

__________. "China's Vice-Minister for Foreign Affairs Casually Slanders the South China Sea Arbitral Tribunal." *opiniojuris.org*, 26 July 2016, http://opiniojuris.org/2016/07/26/chinas-vice-minister-for-foreign-affairs-casually-slanders-the-south-china-sea-arbitral-tribunal/, accessed 31 August 2016.

La Fontaine, H. (ed.). *Pasicrisie internationale 1794–1900. Histoire documentaire des arbitrages internationaux*. Berne: Imprimerie Stampfli & Cie, 1902, https://ia600205.us.archive.org/9/items/pasicrisieinter00fontgoog/pasicrisieinter00fontgoog.pdf, accessed 13 October 2017.

Lapradelle, Albert Geouffre de, and Nicolas Politis (eds.). *Recueil des arbitrages internationaux*. I, *1798–1855*. Paris: A. Pedone Éditeur, 1905, https://ia600309.us.archive.org/19/items/recueildesarbit01lapr/recueildesarbit01lapr.pdf, accessed 21 May 2016.

__________ (eds.). *Recueil des arbitrages internationaux*. II, *1856–1872*. Paris: A. Pedone Éditeur, 1923, https://ia802607.us.archive.org/3/items/recueildesarbitr02lapruoft/recueildesarbitr02lapruoft.pdf, accessed 21 May 2016.

Larousse Dictionary of Science and Technology. Edinburgh: Larousse plc, 1995.

The Legal 500. *Essex Court Chambers. Prof. Alan Boyle. The Legal 500*, 2016, http://www.legal500.com/firms/9331/offices/9331/lawyers/61627, accessed 8 September 2016.

"L'objection de la Chine contre l'arbitrage concernant la Mer de Chine méridionale s'avère complètement légitime et légale." *Le Soleil*, 26 May 2016, http://www.lesoleil.sn/component/k2/item/50156-l-objection-de-la-chine-contre-l-arbitrage-concernant-la-mer-de-chine-meridionale-s-avere-completement-legitime-et-legale.html, accessed 30 May 2016.

Loewenstein, Andrew B. "An Interview With Stephanie Morin and Amanda Nagai. Reflections on Darfur: A Personal and Political Account." *Brown Journal of World Affairs*, 11:2 (Winter/Spring 2005), pp. 235–41.

__________. "Words Fail." *New Republic*, 14 May 2006, https://newrepublic.com/article/62957/words-fail, accessed 2 September 2016.

Maresca, Adolfo. *Il Diritto dei trattati. La Convenzione codificatrice di Vienna del 23 maggio 1969*. Milano: Dott. A. Giuffrè Editore, 1971.

Mateus, Eugénio. "China diz-se soberana sobre as ilhas a Sul." *O País* (Luanda), 8 April 2016, http://opais.co.ao/china-diz-se-soberana-sobre-as-ilhas-a-sul/, accessed 1 June 2016.

Matrix Chambers. *Philippe Sands. Matrix Chambers*, 2015, https://www.matrixlaw.co.uk/uploads/other/21_05_2015_02_42_50_Philippe%20Sands%20CV%202013.pdf, accessed 8 November 2015.

Max-Planck-Gesellschaft. *Organisational Structure of the Max Planck Society*. München: Max-Planck-Gesellschaft, 2015, http://www.mpg.de/183267/organisation, accessed 12 November 2015.

Max Planck Institute for Comparative Public Law and International Law. *About Us*. Heidelberg: Max Planck Institute for Comparative Public Law and International, 2015, www.mpil.de/en/pub/news.cfm, accessed 12 November 2015.

McCurry, Justin. "Japan to Spend Millions on Tiny Islands 1,000 Miles South of Tokyo." *The Guardian*, 3 February 2016, https://www.theguardian.com/world/2016/feb/03/japan-spend-billions-yen-tiny-okinotori-islands-1000-miles-south-of-tokyo, accessed 5 August 2016.

Mensah, Thomas A. "Provisional Measures in the International Tribunal for the Law of the Sea (ITLOS)." *Zeitschrift für ausländisches öffentliches Recht und Völkerrecht*, 63 (2002), pp. 43–54, http://www.zaoerv.de/62_2002/62_2002_1_a_43_54.pdf, accessed 14 November 2015.

__________, and Christopher H. Zimmerli. "L'activité réglementaire de l'OMCI." *L'élaboration du droit international public*, pp. 31–47. Société Française pour le Droit International. Colloque de Toulouse. Paris: Éditions A. Pedone, 1975.

Mogato, Manuel. "New Philippine Ambassador Says China Is Complying with Arbitration Ruling." *Reuters*, 8 November 2016, https://www.yahoo.com/news/philippine-ambassador-says-china-complying-arbitration-ruling-105654168.html, accessed 26 November 2017.

Moore, John Bassett. *The United States and International Arbitration*. Boston: The American Peace Society, 1896, https://archive.org/details/unitedstatesand00moorgoog, accessed 27 March 2018.

National Geospatial Intelligence Agency. *Vertical Datums, Elevations and Heights*. Springfield, VA: NGA, 2011, http://earth-info.nga.mil/GandG/publications/vertdatum.html, accessed 4 September 2016.

Nduwamungu, Astere. "Ambassade de Chine > Présentation de la position de la Chine sur la Mer de Chine méridionale: Pour trouver une solution, la Chine propose une voie de négociation." *Publications de Presse Burundaise* (Bujumbura), 11 May 2016, http://www.ppbdi.com/index.php/extras/politique-cooperation-actualite-internationales/4137-ambassade-de-chine-presentation-de-la-position-de-la-chine-sur-la-mer-de-chine-meridionale, http://www.ppbdi.com/, accessed 1 June 2016.

Okafor-Yarwood, Ifesinachi. “The Guinea-Bissau–Senegal Maritime Boundary Dispute.” *Marine Policy*, 61 (November 2015), pp. 284–90.

Oxford University. Faculty of Law. *Bachelor of Civil Law (BCL)*. Oxford: Faculty of Law Oxford University, 2015, https://www.law.ox.ac.uk/admissions/postgraduate/bachelor-civil-law, accessed 22 November 2015.

__________. *Magister Juris (MJur)*. Oxford: Faculty of Law Oxford University, 2015, https://www.law.ox.ac.uk/admissions/postgraduate/magister-juris, accessed 22 November 2015.

Oxman, Bernard H. "The Third United Nations Conference on the Law of the Sea: The 1976 New York Sessions." *American Journal of International Law*, 71:2 (April 1977), pp. 247–69.

__________. “The Third United Nations Conference on the Law of the Sea: The 1977 New York Session.” *American Journal of International Law*, 72:1 (January 1978), pp. 57–83.

__________. “The Third United Nations Conference on the Law of the Sea: The Seventh Session (1978).” *American Journal of International Law*, 73:1 (January 1979), pp. 1–41.

__________. “The Third United Nations Conference on the Law of the Sea: The Eighth Session (1979).” *American Journal of International Law*, 74:1 (January 1980), pp. 1–47.

__________. “The Third United Nations Conference on the Law of the Sea: The Ninth Session (1980).” *American Journal of International Law*, 75:2 (April 1981), pp. 211–56.

__________. “The Third United Nations Conference on the Law of the Sea: The Tenth Session (1981).” *American Journal of International Law*, 76:1 (January 1982), pp. 1–23.

__________. “La troisième Conférence des Nations Unies sur le Droit de la Mer.” *Traité du Nouveau Droit de la Mer*, pp. 143–216. Eds. René-Jean Dupuy and Daniel Vignes. Paris: Éditions Economica, 1985.

__________. “Twenty Years of the United Nations Convention on the Law of the Sea.” *International Oceanographic Commission Annual Report 2002*, pp. 16–17, http://unesdoc.unesco.org/images/0013/001351/135127e.pdf, accessed 8 September 2016.

__________. “The United States and the Future of International Law.” Celebration in Honor of the Appointment of Bernard H. Oxman to the Richard A. Hausler Chair University of Miami, 5 March 2008, http://media.law.miami.edu/faculty-administration/pdf/bernard-oxman/hausler-chair-lecture.pdf, accessed 25 November 2015.

Panafrican News Agency. “Le Bénin gagne 9 îles dans le litige frontalier avec le Niger.” *Le Blog de Benoît Illassa—Une passion pour le Bénin*, 8 August 2007, http://illassa-benoit.over-blog.com/article-11817649.html, accessed 29 May 2016.

Paré, Fulbert. “Différend frontalier Burkina Faso–Niger: la Cour internationale de justice rend une décision mitigée.” *Lefaso net. Actualité du Burkina sur Internet* (Burkina Faso), 17 April 2013, http://lefaso.net/spip.php?article53798, accessed 27 May 2016.

Pellet, Alain. “Remarques cursives sur les contentieux ‘africains’ devant la CIJ.” *Liber Amicorum Raymond Ranjeva. L’Afrique et le droit international: variations sur l’organisation internationale*, pp. 277–95. Eds. Maurice Kamga and Makane Moïse Mbengue. Paris: Éditions Pedone, 2013, http://pellet.actu.com/wp-content/uploads/2015/12/PELLET-2013-M%C3%A9l-Ranjeva.pdf, accessed 2 October 2016.

__________. “Remarques sur le ‘métier’ de conseil devant la Cour internationale de Justice.” *Collection of Essays by Legal Advisers of States, Legal Advisers of International Organizations and Practitioners in the Field of International Law*, pp. 451–54. United Nations Office of Legal Affairs. New York: United Nations, 1999, http://legal.un.org/cod/books/CollectionOfEssaysByLegalAdvisers.pdf, accessed 19 November 2015.

Pew Research Center. *Global Opposition to U.S. Surveillance and Drones, but Limited Harm to America’s Image*. Washington, DC: Pew Research Center, 14 July 2014, http://assets.

pewresearch.org/wp-content/uploads/sites/2/2014/07/2014-07-14-Balance-of-Power.pdf, accessed 13 November 2017.

Philippine News Agency. "Filipino Fishermen No Longer Intercepted at Scarborough Shoal." *Update Philippines*, 28 October 2016, https://www.update.ph/2016/10/filipino-fishermen-no-longer-intercepted-at-scarborough-shoal/10591, accessed 26 November 2017.

Quismundo, Tarra. "PH Hails Hague Court Ruling to Take up Arbitration Case vs China." *Philippine Daily Inquirer*, 30 October 2015, http://globalnation.inquirer.net/130174/ph-hails-hague-court-ruling-to-take-up-arbitration-case-vs-china, accessed 30 October 2015.

Ræder, A. *L'arbitrage international chez les hellènes*. Kristiania: H. Aschehoug and Co. (W. Nygaard), 1912, https://ia601600.us.archive.org/9/items/larbitrageintern00raed/larbitrageintern00raed.pdf, accessed 23 October 2017.

Ranjeva, Raymond. "Le règlement des différends." *Traité du Nouveau Droit de la Mer*, pp. 1105–68. Eds. René-Jean Dupuy and Daniel Vignes. Paris: Editions Economica, 1985.

Robert, Paul. *Dictionnaire alphabétique et analogique de la langue française*. Paris: Société du Nouveau Littré, Dictionnaire Le Robert, 1978.

Rosenbaum, David E. "Abram Chayes, John Kennedy Aide, Dies at 77." *New York Times*, 18 April 2000, http://www.nytimes.com/2000/04/18/us/abram-chayes-john-kennedy-aide-dies-at-77.html, accessed 17 November 2015.

Rosenne, Shabtai. "Arbitrations Under Annex VII of the United Nations Convention on the Law of the Sea." *Law of the Sea, Environmental Law and Settlement of Disputes. Liber Amicorum Judge Thomas A. Mensah*, pp. 989–1006. Eds. Tafsir Malick Ndiaye and Rüdiger Wolfrum. Leiden: Martinus Nijhoff Publishers, 2007.

Rouard de Card, M. E. *L'arbitrage international dans le passé, le présent et l'avenir*. Paris: A. Durand et Pedone-Lauriel, Éditeurs, 1877, https://ia902706.us.archive.org/14/items/droitinternatio01cardgoog/droitinternatio01cardgoog.pdf, accessed 23 October 2017.

Rousseau, Charles. *Droit international public*, 8th ed. Paris: Éditions Dalloz, 1976.

Sánchez Rodríguez, Luis Ignacio. "Litigation Practice before the International Court of Justice: Some Specific Problems of Developing and Small Countries." *Collection of Essays by Legal Advisers of States, Legal Advisers of International Organizations and Practitioners in the Field of International Law*, pp. 459–78. United Nations Office of Legal Affairs. New York: United Nations, 1999, http://legal.un.org/cod/books/CollectionOfEssaysByLegalAdvisers.pdf, accessed 19 November 2015.

Sands, Philippe. "Sir Ian Brownlie Obituary." *The Guardian*, 11 January 2010, http://www.theguardian.com/theguardian/2010/jan/11/sir-ian-brownlie-obituary, accessed 17 November 2015.

Santos, Matikas. "Key Points of the Arbitral Tribunal's First Ruling in Philippines vs China Case." *Philippine Daily Inquirer*, 31 October 2015, http://globalnation.inquirer.net/130215/south-china-sea-arbitration-philippines-china-spratly-islands-west-philippine-sea, accessed 31 October 2015.

__________. "UN Tribunal Ruling 'Null, Void, Nonbinding'—China." *Philippine Daily Inquirer*, 30 October 2015, http://globalnation.inquirer.net/130235/un-tribunal-ruling-null-and-void-china, accessed 30 October 2015.

Shaw, Malcolm N. *International Law*, 7th ed. Cambridge: Cambridge University Press, 2014.

Shi Jiangtao. "Is Beijing Courting Disaster by Shunning South China Sea Tribunal?" *South China Morning Post*, 19 June 2016, http://www.scmp.com/news/china/diplomacy-defence/article/1977418/beijing-courting-disaster-shunning-south-china-sea, accessed 21 June 2016.

Shykles, Oliver. *Foley Hoag Wins Key Victory for Government of Bolivia in Investor Dispute.* Brussels: Corporate Europe Observatory, 1 August 2008, http://lists.noticias.nl/pipermail/eti-l/2008-August/000283.html, accessed 18 November 2015.

Sison, Desiree. "China Opens Scarborough Shoal to Filipino Fishermen." *chinatopix.com*, 31 August 2016, http://www.chinatopix.com/articles/99686/20160831/china-opens-scarborough-shoal-to-filipino-fishermen.htm, accessed 26 November 2017.

Souleymane, Laouali. "Conférence de Presse du Directeur général en charge du département Afrique du Ministère des Affaires Etrangères de la République Populaire de Chine: Des clarifications sur la question de la mer de Chine méridionale." *Nigerdiaspora. La communauté virtuelle du Niger*, 20 April 2016, http://www.nigerdiaspora.net/les-infos-du-pays/politique-niger/politique-niger/item/73676-conference-de-presse-du-directeur-general-en-charge-du-departement-afrique-du-ministere-des-affaires-etrangeres-de-la-republique-populaire-de-chine-des-clarifications-sur-la-question-de-la-mer-de-chine-meridionale, accessed 25 May 2016.

"Staatsexamen (auch: Staatsprüfung)." *Studisonline*, 21 January 2016, http://www.studis-online.de/StudInfo/studienabschluesse.php#stex, accessed 7 September 2016.

Stevenson, John R., and Bernard H. Oxman. "The Preparations for the Law of the Sea Conference." *American Journal of International Law*, 68:1 (January 1974), pp. 1–32.

__________. "The Third United Nations Conference on the Law of the Sea: The 1974 Caracas Session. "*American Journal of International Law*, 69:1 (January 1975), pp. 1–30.

__________. "The Third United Nations Conference on the Law of the Sea: The 1975 Geneva Session." *American Journal of International Law*, 69:4 (October 1975), pp. 763–97.

Stockwell, Norman. "Pinochet's Arrest Remembered." *The Tico Times*, 17 October 2014, http://www.ticotimes.net/l/50287, accessed 17 November 2015.

The Student Room. *Degree Classifications.* 2016, http://www.thestudentroom.co.uk/content.php?r=15857-degree-classifications, accessed 17 November 2015.

Sunstein, Cass R., and Adrian Vermeule. "Conspiracy Theories: Causes and Cures." *The Journal of Political Philosophy*, 17:1 (2009), pp. 202–27, http://www.ask-force.org/web/Discourse/Sunstein-Conspiracy-Theories-2009.pdf, accessed 1 December 2017.

Talmon, Stefan A. G. "The South China Sea Arbitration: Is There a Case to Answer?" *The South China Sea Arbitration: A Chinese Perspective*, pp. 15–79. Eds. Stefan Talmon and Bing Bing Jia. Oxford: Hart Publishing, 2014.

ThreatConnect Intelligence Research Team (TCIRT), *China Hacks the Peace Palace: All Your EEZ's Are Belong [sic] to Us*, 20 July 2015, https://www.threatconnect.com/blog/china-hacks-the-peace-palace-all-your-eezs-are-belong-to-us/, accessed 26 July 2015.

"Three of Five Filipinos Distrust China, SWS Says." *Business World Online* (Manila), 10 July 2015, http://www.bworldonline.com/content.php?section=Nation&title=three-of-five-filipinos-distrust-china-sws-says&id=111348, accessed 13 November 2017.

Timm, Leo. "How China Tried, and Failed, to Influence The Hague on the South China Sea Dispute." *Epoch Times*, 11 July 2016, https://www.theepochtimes.com/how-china-tried-and-failed-to-influence-the-hague-on-the-south-china-sea-dispute_2112535.html, accessed 30 March 2018.

__________. "Cómo China trató manipular la decisión de La Haya sobre el Mar de China Meridional." *La gran época*, 12 July 2016, https://www.lagranepoca.com/china/regimen-chino/73137-como-china-trato-manipular-la-decision-de-la-haya-sobre-el-mar-de-china-meridional.html, accessed 30 March 2018.

"Tuna Species Guide." *Atuna.com*, http://www.atuna.com/index.php/en/tuna-info/tuna-species-guide#bonito, accessed 5 September 2016.

Universität Heidelberg. *Professor Dr. Dr. h.c. Rüdiger Wolfrum*. Heidelberg: Universität Heidelberg, 2015, https://www.rzuser.uni-heidelberg.de/~p00/down/cv_wolfrum_en.pdf, accessed 6 November 2015.

Universiteit Utrecht. Staff Law, Economics and Governance. *Prof. Mr. Fred Soons*. Utrecht: Universiteit Utrecht, 2015, http://www.uu.nl/staff/default.aspx?lng=NL&Profielpagina=AHASoons&t=0, accessed 6 November 2015.

University of Edinburgh. Edinburgh Law School. *Professor Alan Boyle*. Edinburgh: Edinburgh Law School, University of Edinburgh, 2016, http://www.law.ed.ac.uk/people/alanboyle, accessed 22 November 2015.

University of Miami School of Law. *Bernard H. Oxman*. Miami: University of Miami School of Law, 2015, http://www.law.miami.edu/faculty/bernard-h-oxman, accessed 25 November 2015.

University of Warsaw. Faculty of Political Science and International Studies. Institute of International Relations. *Prof. Stanisław Pawlak*. Warsaw: Institute of International Relations, Faculty of Political Science and International Studies, University of Warsaw, 2015, http://www.en.ism.uw.edu.pl/prof-stanislaw-pawlak/, accessed 9 November 2015.

"Verdict de la Cour internationale de justice de la Haye sur le différend frontalier entre le Niger et le Burkina Faso: Une décision unanimement saluée." *Le Sahel* (Niamey), 16 April 2013, http://lesahel.org/index.php/component/k2/item/2915-verdict-de-la-cour-internationale-de-justice-de-la-haye-sur-le-diff%C3%A9rend-frontalier-entre-le-niger-et-le-burkina-faso--une-d%C3%A9cision-unanimement-salu%C3%A9e, accessed 27 May 2016.

Walker, George K. *Definitions for the Law of the Sea: Terms Not Defined by the Convention*. Leiden: Martinus Nijhoff Publishers, 2012.

"Was genau ist eine Habilitation?" *bild.de*, 2015, http://www.bild.de/infos/studium/studium/habilition-10692372.bild.html, accessed 12 November 2015.

"Washington, DC's Best Lawyers: Civil Defense." *Washingtonian*, 4 November 2015, https://www.washingtonian.com/2015/11/04/washington-dcs-best-lawyers-civil-defense/, accessed 8 September 2016.

"Washington Talk. Nicaragua Peace Talks; American Sitting Opposite U.S.-Backed Rebels." *New York Times*, 19 February 1988, http://www.nytimes.com/1988/02/19/us/washington-talk-nicaragua-peace-talks-american-sitting-opposite-us-backed-rebels.html?pagewanted=print, accessed 15 November 2015.

Wolfrum, Rüdiger. "The Admissibility of Land-based Tourism in Antarctica Under International Law." *Zeitschrift für ausländisches öffentliches Recht und Völkerrecht*, 65 (2005), pp. 735–40, http://www.zaoerv.de/65_2005/65_2005_3_b_735_740.pdf, accessed 12 November 2015.

__________. "The Principle of the Common Heritage of Mankind." *Zeitschrift für ausländisches öffentliches Recht und Völkerrecht*, 43 (1983), pp. 312–37, http://www.zaoerv.de/43_1983/43_1983_2_a_312_337.pdf, accessed 12 November 2015.

__________. "The Problems of Limitation and Prohibition of Military Use of Outer Space." *Zeitschrift für ausländisches öffentliches Recht und Völkerrecht*, 44 (1984), pp. 784–805, http://www.zaoerv.de/44_1984/44_1984_4_a_784_805.pdf, accessed 12 November 2015.

__________. "The Protection of Indigenous Peoples in International Law." *Zeitschrift für ausländisches öffentliches Recht und Völkerrecht*, 59 (1999), pp. 369–82, http://www.zaoerv.de/59_1999/59_1999_2_a_369_382.pdf, accessed 12 November 2015.

Xue Guifang (Julia). "How Much Can a Rock Get? A Reflection From the Okinotorishima Rocks." *The Law of the Sea Convention: US Accession and Globalization*, pp. 341–68. Eds. Myron H. Nordquist, John Norton Moore, Alfred A.H. Soons, and Hak-so Kim. Leiden: Martinus Nijhoff Publishers, 2012.

Yasseen, Mustafa Kamil. "L'interprétation des traités d'après la Convention de Vienne sur le droit des traités." *Recueil des Cours de l'Académie de Droit International de La Haye*, t. 151 (1976-III), pp. 1–114.

"Yellow Spotted Trevally, Scientific Name *Carangoides fulvoguttatus*." *fishingthephilippines: fish fishing spots, lures, tactics and more*, https://fishingthephilippines.com/category/trevally-talakitok/, accessed 5 September 2016.

OFFICIAL DOCUMENTS

Burundi

République du Burundi. *Affaire des activités armées sur le territoire du Congo (République démocratique du Congo c. Burundi). Exceptions préliminaires. Mémoire de la République du Burundi.* 20 April 2000, http://www.icj-cij.org/files/case-related/115/13462.pdf, accessed 29 March 2018.

China

"China Doesn't Accept or Recognize the South China Sea Arbitration." *chinausfocus.com*, 20 April 2016, http://www.chinausfocus.com/uncategorized/china-doesnt-accept-or-recognize-the-south-china-sea-arbitration/, accessed 8 September 2016.

Foreign Ministry Spokesperson Hong Lei's Regular Press Conference on May 18, 2016, http://www.fmprc.gov.cn/mfa_eng/xwfw_665399/s2510_665401/2511_665403/t1364549.shtml, accessed 10 July 2016.

Foreign Ministry Spokesperson Hua Chunying's Remarks on the Release of the Transcript of the Oral Hearing on Jurisdiction by the South China Sea Arbitral Tribunal Established at the Request of the Philippines, 2015/08/24, http://www.fmprc.gov.cn/mfa_eng/xwfw_665399/s2510_665401/2535_665405/t1290752.shtml, accessed 2 November 2015.

Foreign Ministry Spokesperson Hua Chunying's Regular Press Conference on May 25, 2016, http://www.fmprc.gov.cn/mfa_eng/xwfw_665399/s2510_665401/2511_665403/t1366744.shtml, accessed 26 May 2016.

Ministry of Foreign Affairs. *Chinese Embassies*. http://www.fmprc.gov.cn/mfa_eng/wjb_663304/zwjg_665342/2490_665344/, accessed 11 September 2016.

__________. *Position Paper of the Government of the People's Republic of China on the Matter of Jurisdiction in the South China Sea Arbitration Initiated by the Republic of the Philippines*. 7 December 2014. http://www.fmprc.gov.cn/mfa_eng/zxxx_662805/t1217147.shtml, accessed 15 December 2014.

__________. *Veil of the Arbitral Tribunal Must Be Tore [sic] Down—Vice Foreign Minister Liu Zhenmin Answers Journalists' Questions on the So-Called Binding Force of the Award Rendered by the Arbitral Tribunal of the South China Sea Arbitration Case*. 13 July 2016, http://www.fmprc.gov.cn/mfa_eng/wjbxw/t1381879.shtml, accessed 18 July 2016.

Wang Xiaohui. "S. China Sea arbitration: A US-Led Conspiracy Behind the Farce." *China.org.cn*, 12 July 2016, http://www.china.org.cn/opinion/2016-07/12/content_38864239.htm, accessed 18 July 2016.

Wang Xu. "Diplomat Slams 'Biased' Nansha Arbitration Panel." *China Daily USA*, 18 April 2016, http://usa.chinadaily.com.cn/epaper/2016-04/18/content_24631887.htm, accessed 1 July 2016.

Xinhua. "La Chine salue le soutien mozambicain, burundais et slovène sur la question de la mer de Chine méridionale." *Radiochineinternationale*, 19 May 2016, http://french.cri.cn/621/2016/05/19/301s479819.htm, accessed 26 May 2016.

__________. "Permanent Court of Arbitration Clarifies Role in South China Sea Case." *xinhuanet.com*, 16 July 2016, http://news.xinhuanet.com/english/2016-07/16/c_135517684.htm, accessed 18 July 2016.

__________. "Permanent Court of Arbitration Neither Permanent nor a Court." *xinhuanet.com*, 16 July 2016, http://news.xinhuanet.com/english/2016-07/16/c_135518252.htm, accessed 18 July 2016.

__________. "Shunji Yanai, Manipulator Behind Illegal South China Sea Arbitration." *xinhuanet.com*, 17 July 2016, http://news.xinhuanet.com/english/2016-07/17/c_135519215.htm, 18 July 2016.

__________. "UN Court Denies Involvement in South China Sea Arbitration," *xinhuanet.com*, 15 July 2016, http://news.xinhuanet.com/english/2016-07/15/c_135515567.htm, accessed 18 July 2016.

Convention on Biological Diversity

Convention on Biological Diversity, 5 June 1992, https://www.cbd.int/doc/legal/cbd-en.pdf, accessed 8 August 2016.

European Union

Judgment of the Court of 2 April 1998. Stichting Greenpeace Council (Greenpeace International) and Others v. Commission of the European Communities, http://eur-lex.europa.eu/legal-content/EN/TXT/?uri=CELEX:61995CJ0321, accessed 17 November 2015.

France

Ministère de l'Éducation nationale, de l'Enseignement Supérieur et de la Recherche. *Les concours nationaux d'agrégation*. Paris: Ministère de l'Éducation nationale, de l'Enseignement Supérieur et de la Recherche, 2015, http://www.enseignementsup-recherche.gouv.fr/cid22721/les-concours-nationaux-d-agregation.html, accessed 12 November 2015.

International Arbitral Awards

Affaire de la délimitation de la frontière maritime entre la Guinée-Bissau et le Sénégal. Sentence du 31 juillet 1989. Reports of International Arbitral Awards, XX (New York: United Nations, 2006), pp. 119–213, http://legal.un.org/docs/?path=../riaa/cases/vol_XX/119-213.pdf&lang=O, accessed 3 October 2016.

Arbitration Between the Republic of Croatia and the Republic of Slovenia, https://pcacases.com/web/view/3, accessed 9 September 2016.

Award Between the United States and the United Kingdom Relating to the Rights of Jurisdiction of United States in the Bering's Sea and the Preservation of Fur Seals (United Kingdom v. United States), Award of 15 August 1893. Reports of International Arbitral Awards, XXVIII (New York: United Nations, 2007), pp. 273–76, http://legal.un.org/docs/?path=../riaa/cases/vol_XXVIII/263-276.pdf&lang=O, accessed 26 November 2017.

Award of the Tribunal of Arbitration Constituted Under an Agreement Signed at Caracas, February 13, 1909, between the United States of America and the United States of Venezuela. The Hague, October 25, 1910. The Hague Court Reports, pp. 226–74. Ed. James Brown Scott. New York: Oxford University Press, 1916, https://ia801604.us.archive.org/17/items/in.ernet.dli.2015.179316/2015.179316.The-Hague-Court-Reports.pdf, accessed 30 March 2018.

Award of the Arbitral Tribunal in the Second Stage of the Proceedings Between Eritrea and Yemen (Maritime Delimitation), Decision of 17 December 1999. Reports of International Arbitral Awards, XXII (New York: United Nations, 2006), pp. 335–410, http://legal.un.org/riaa/cases/vol_XXII/335-410.pdf, accessed 13 September 2016.

Dispute Concerning Access to Information Under Article 9 of the OSPAR Convention between Ireland and the United Kingdom of Great Britain and Northern Ireland, Final Award, Decision of 2 July 2003. Reports of International Arbitral Awards, XXIII (New York: United Nations, 2006), pp. 59–151, http://legal.un.org/riaa/cases/vol_XXIII/59-151.pdf, accessed 9 September 2016.

The Government of Sudan/The Sudan People's Liberation Movement/Army (Abyei Arbitration), https://pcacases.com/web/view/92, accessed 16 July 2016.

Tax Regime Governing Pensions Paid to Retired UNESCO Officials Residing in France (France/UNESCO). Reports of International Arbitral Awards, XXV (York: United Nations, 2006), pp. 231–66, http://legal.un.org/riaa/cases/vol_XXV/231-266.pdf, accessed 12 November 2015.

International Centre for the Settlement of Investment Disputes

Philip Morris Brands SARL, Philip Morris Products S.A. and Abal Hermanos S.A. (The Claimants) and Oriental Republic of Uruguay (The Respondent) (ICSID Case No. ARB/10/7). *Decision on Jurisdiction, 2 July 2013*, http://www.italaw.com/sites/default/files/case-documents/italaw1531.pdf, accessed 18 November 2015.

Philip Morris Brand Sàrl (Switzerland), Philip Morris Products S.A. (Switzerland) and Abal Hermanos S.A. (Uruguay) v. Oriental Republic of Uruguay (ICSID Case No. ARB/10/7). Award of 8 July 2016, https://www.italaw.com/sites/default/files/case-documents/italaw7417.pdf, https://www.italaw.com/cases/460, accessed 30 March 2018.

International Court of Justice

Aerial Herbicide Spraying (Ecuador v. *Colombia)*, http://www.icj-cij.org/en/case/138, accessed 29 March 2018.

Application of the International Convention on the Elimination of All Forms of Racial Discrimination (Georgia v. Russian Federation), http://www.icj-cij.org/en/case/140, accessed 29 March 2018.

Application for Revision and Interpretation of the Judgment of 24 February 1982 (Tunisia v. Libyan Arab Jamahiriya), http://www.icj-cij.org/en/case/71, accessed 29 March 2018.

Application for Revision of the Judgment of 11 September 1992 in the Case Concerning the Land, Island and Maritime Frontier Dispute (El Salvador/Honduras: Nicaragua Intervening) (El Salvador v. Honduras), http://www.icj-cij.org/en/case/127, accessed 29 March 2018.

Application Instituting Proceedings of the Government of the Republic of Guinea-Bissau filed in the Registry of the Court on 23 August 1989 (Arbitral Award of 31 July 1989) (Guinef-Bissau v. Senegal), http://www.icj-cij.org/files/case-related/82/11289.pdf, accessed 29 March 2018.

Application Instituting Proceedings Filed in the Registry of the Court on 12 March 1991. Maritime Delimitation between Guinea-Bissau and Senegal (Guinea-Bissau v. Senegal), http://www.icj-cij.org/files/case-related/85/6843.pdf, accessed 29 March 2018.

Application of the Convention on the Prevention and Punishment of the Crime of Genocide (Bosnia and Herzegovina v. Serbia and Montenegro), http://www.icj-cij.org/en/case/91, accessed 29 March 2018.

Arbitral Award of 31 July 1989 (Guinea-Bissau v. Senegal), http://www.icj-cij.org/files/case-related/82/082-19911112-JUD-01-00-BI.pdf, accessed 29 March 2018.

Armed Activities on the Territory of the Congo (Democratic Republic of the Congo v. *Burundi)*, http://www.icj-cij.org/en/case/115, accessed 29 March 2018.

Armed Activities on the Territory of the Congo (Democratic Republic of the Congo v. Rwanda), http://www.icj-cij.org/en/case/115, accessed 29 March 2018.

Armed Activities on the Territory of the Congo (Democratic Republic of the Congo v. Uganda), http://www.icj-cij.org/en/case/116, accessed 29 March 2018.

Armed Activities on the Territory of the Congo (Democratic Republic of the Congo v. Burundi) and (Democratic Republic of the Congo v. Rwanda). The Two Cases Are Removed From the List at the Request of the Democratic Republic of the Congo. Press Release 2001/2 (1 February 2001), http://www.icj-cij.org/files/case-related/115/115-20010201-PRE-01-00-EN.pdf, accessed 29 March 2018.

Arrest Warrant of 11 April 2000 (Democratic Republic of the Congo v. Belgium), http://www.icj-cij.org/en/case/121, accessed 29 March 2018.

Case Concerning Gabcikovo-Nagymaros Project (Hungary/Slovakia), http://www.icj-cij.org/en/case/92, accessed 29 March 2018.

Certain Activities carried out by Nicaragua in the Border Area (Costa Rica v. Nicaragua). http://www.icj-cij.org/en/case/150, accessed 29 March 2018.

Certain Criminal Proceedings in France (Republic of the Congo v. France), http://www.icj-cij.org/en/case/129, accessed 29 March 2018.

Certain Questions of Mutual Assistance in Criminal Matters (Djibouti v. France), http://www.icj-cij.org/en/case/136, accessed 29 March 2018.

Construction of a Road in Costa Rica Along the San Juan River (Nicaragua v. Costa Rica), http://www.icj-cij.org/en/case/152, accessed 29 March 2018.

Continental Shelf (Libyan Arab Jamahiriya/Malta), http://www.icj-cij.org/en/case/68, accessed 29 March 2018.

Continental Shelf (Tunisia/Libyan Arab Jamahiriya), http://www.icj-cij.org/en/case/63, accessed 29 March 2018.

Declarations Recognizing the Jurisdiction of the Court as Compulsory, http://www.icj-cij.org/en/declarations, accessed 29 March 2018.

Delimitation of the Maritime Boundary in the Gulf of Maine (Canada v. US), http://www.icj-cij.org/en/case/67, accessed 29 March 2018.

Dispute regarding Navigational and Related Rights (Costa Rica v. Nicaragua), http://www.icj-cij.org/en/case/133, accessed 29 March 2018.

Fisheries Jurisdiction Case (Federal Republic of Germany v. Iceland), http://www.icj-cij.org/en/case/56, accessed 29 March 2018.

Fisheries Jurisdiction Case (UK v. Iceland), http://www.icj-cij.org/en/case/55, accessed 29 March 2018.

Frontier Dispute (Benin/Niger), http://www.icj-cij.org/en/case/125, accessed 29 March 2018.

Frontier Dispute (Benin/Niger). The Chamber of the Court Determines the Course of the Whole

Boundary between the Two States. Press Release 2005/16 (12 July 2005), http://www.icj-cij.org/files/case-related/125/125-20050712-PRE-01-00-EN.pdf, accessed 29 March 2018.

Frontier Dispute (Burkina Faso/Niger), http://www.icj-cij.org/en/case/149, accessed 29 March 2018.

Frontier Dispute (Burkina Faso/Republic of Mali), Judgment, I.C.J. Reports 1986, p. 554, http://www.icj-cij.org/files/case-related/69/069-19861222-JUD-01-00-BI.pdf, accessed 29 March 2018.

Judges Ad Hoc, http://www.icj-cij.org/en/judges-ad-hoc, accessed 29 March 2018.

Kasikili/Sedudu Islands (Botswana/Namibia), Judgment, I. C. J. Reports 1999, p. 1045, http://www.icj-cij.org/en/case/98, accessed 29 March 2018.

Land and Maritime Boundary between Cameroon and Nigeria (Cameroon v. *Nigeria: Equatorial Guinea intervening), Judgment, I. C. J. Reports 2002*, p. 303, http://www.icj-cij.org/en/case/94, accessed 29 March 2018.

Maritime Delimitation Between Guinea-Bissau and Senegal (Guinea-Bissau v. Senegal), http://www.icj-cij.org/en/case/85, accessed 29 March 2018.

Maritime Delimitation in the Black Sea (Romania v. *Ukraine)*, http://www.icj-cij.org/en/case/132, accessed 29 March 2018.

Maritime Delimitation in the Caribbean Sea and the Pacific Ocean (Costa Rica v. Nicaragua), http://www.icj-cij.org/en/case/157, accessed 29 March 2018.

Maritime Delimitation in the Indian Ocean (Somalia v. Kenya), http://www.icj-cij.org/en/case/161, accessed 29 March 2018.

Military and Paramilitary Activities in and Against Nicaragua (Nicaragua v. United States of America), Jurisdiction and Admissibility, Judgment, I.C.J. Reports 1984, p. 392, http://www.icj-cij.org/files/case-related/70/070-19841126-JUD-01-00-BI.pdf, accessed 20 March 2018.

Military and Paramilitary Activities in and against Nicaragua (Nicaragua v. United States of America), Merits, Judgment, I.C.J. Reports 1986, p. 14, http://www.icj-cij.org/files/case-related/70/070-19860627-JUD-01-00-BI.pdf, accessed 20 March 2018.

"Le Président de la Cour internationale de justice au Président de la République de Guinée-Bissau, 16 mars 1994." *Correspondance*, http://www.icj-cij.org/en/case/85/correspondence, accessed 29 March 2018.

Pulp Mills on the River Uruguay (Argentina v. Uruguay), http://www.icj-cij.org/en/case/135, accessed 29 March 2018.

Questions of Interpretation and Application of the 1971 Montreal Convention arising From the Aerial Incident at Lockerbie (Libyan Arab Jamahiriya v. United Kingdom), http://www.icj-cij.org/en/case/88, accessed 29 March 2018.

Questions of Interpretation and Application of the 1971 Montreal Convention arising From the Aerial Incident at Lockerbie (Libyan Arab Jamahiriya v. United States of America), http://www.icj-cij.org/en/case/89, accessed 29 March 2018.

Questions Relating to the Obligation to Prosecute or Extradite (Belgium v. Senegal), http://www.icj-cij.org/en/case/144, accessed 29 March 2018.

Questions Relating to the Seizure and Detention of Certain Documents and Data (Timor-Leste v. *Australia)*, http://www.icj-cij.org/en/case/156, accessed 29 March 2018.

Request for an Examination of the Situation in Accordance With Paragraph 63 of the Court's Judgment of 20 December 1974 in the Nuclear Tests (New Zealand v. France) Case, http://www.icj-cij.org/en/case/97, accessed 29 March 2018.

Request for Interpretation of the Judgment of 11 June 1998 (Nigeria v. Cameroon), http://www.icj-cij.org/en/case/101, accessed 29 March 2018.

Rules of Court (1978) Adopted on 14 April 1978 and Entered Into Force on 1 July 1978, http://www.icj-cij.org/en/rules, accessed 29 March 2018.

Sovereignty Over Pedra Branca/Pulau Batu Puteh, Middle Rocks and South Ledge (Malaysia/Singapore), http://www.icj-cij.org/en/case/130, accessed 29 March 2018.

Sovereignty over Pulau Ligitan and Pulau Sipadan (Indonesia/Malaysia), http://www.icj-cij.org/en/case/102, accessed 29 March 2018.

Statute of the International Court of Justice, http://www.icj-cij.org/en/statute, accessed 29 March 2018.

Temple of Preah Vihear, Interpretation (Cambodia v. Thailand), http://www.icj-cij.org/en/case/151, accessed 29 March 2018.

Territorial and Maritime Dispute (Nicaragua v. Colombia), Judgment, I.C.J. Reports 2012, p. 624, http://www.icj-cij.org/en/case/124, accessed 29 March 2018.

Territorial and Maritime Dispute Between Nicaragua and Honduras in the Caribbean Sea (Nicaragua v. Honduras), http://www.icj-cij.org/en/case/74, accessed 29 March 2018.

Territorial Dispute (Libyan Arab Jamahiriya/Chad), Judgment, I. C. J. Reports 1994, p. 6, http://www.icj-cij.org/files/case-related/83/083-19940203-JUD-01-00-BI.pdf, accessed 29 March 2018.

Violation of Article 11 of the Interim Accord of 13 September 1995 (The Former Yugoslav Republic of Macedonia v. Greece), http://www.icj-cij.org/en/case/142, accessed 29 March 2018.

Whaling in the Antarctic (Australia v. Japan: New Zealand Intervening), http://www.icj-cij.org/en/case/148, accessed 29 March 2018.

WHO Advisory Opinion on Legality of Use of Nuclear Weapons and UN General Assembly Opinion Request on Legality of the Use of Nuclear Weapons, http://www.icj-cij.org/en/case/93, accessed 29 March 2018.

International Criminal Court

Prosecutor v. Saif Al-Islam Gaddafi and Abdullah Al-Senussi, Case ICC-01/11-01/11. https://www.icc-cpi.int/en_menus/icc/situations%20and%20cases/situations/icc0111/related%20cases/icc01110111/pages/icc01110111.aspx, accessed 17 November 2015.

International Tribunal for the Law of the Sea

Annual Report of the International Tribunal for the Law of the Sea for 2011. Doc. SPLOS/241 (9 April 2012), https://www.itlos.org/fileadmin/itlos/documents/annual_reports/annualreport_2011.pdf, accessed 13 September 2016.

"ARA Libertad" Case (Argentina v. Ghana), Provisional Measures, https://www.itlos.org/cases/list-of-cases/case-no-20/, accessed 20 November 2015.

"ARA Libertad" Case (Argentina v. Ghana), Provisional Measures, Separate Opinion of Judge Chandrasekhara Rao. https://www.itlos.org/fileadmin/itlos/documents/cases/case_no.20/C20_Ord_15_12_2012_SepOp_Ch_Rao_E_.pdf, accessed 25 November 2015.

Arbitrators Appointed in the Arbitral Proceedings Instituted by the Republic of the Philippines Against the People's Republic of China. Doc. ITLOS/Press 191 (25 April 2013), https://www.itlos.org/fileadmin/itlos/documents/press_releases_english/PR_191_E.pdf, accessed 12 October 2015.

Case Concerning the Conservation and Sustainable Exploitation of Swordfish Stocks in the South-Eastern Pacific Ocean (Chile/European Union), https://www.itlos.org/cases/list-of-cases/case-no-7/, accessed 12 November 2015.

Case Concerning Land Reclamation by Singapore in and around the Straits of Johor (Malaysia v. Singapore), Provisional Measures, https://www.itlos.org/fileadmin/itlos/documents/cases/case_no_12/12_order_081003_en.pdf 8 Oct 03, accessed 25 November 2015.

Case of the M/V Saiga (St Vincent and the Grenadines v. Guinea). Provisional measures phase, Order of 11 March 1998, https://www.itlos.org/fileadmin/itlos/documents/cases/case_no_2/provisional_measures/order_110398_eng.pdf, accessed 17 November 2015.

Dispute Concerning Delimitation of the Maritime Boundary between Bangladesh and Myanmar in the Bay of Bengal (Bangladesh/Myanmar), https://www.itlos.org/cases/list-of-cases/case-no-16/, accessed 20 November 2015.

Dispute Concerning Delimitation of the Maritime Boundary between Ghana and Côte d'Ivoire in the Atlantic Ocean (Ghana/Côte d'Ivoire). https://www.itlos.org/cases/list-of-cases/case-no-23/, accessed 20 November 2015.

Judge Jean-Pierre Cot. https://www.itlos.org/the-tribunal/members/judge-jean-pierre-cot/, accessed 11 November 2015.

Judge Stanisław Pawlak, https://www.itlos.org/the-tribunal/members/judge-stanislaw-michal-pawlak/, accessed 12 November 2015.

Judge Zhiguo Gao, https://www.itlos.org/the-tribunal/members/judge-zhiguo-gao/, accessed 18 July 2016.

The "Monte Confurco" Case (Seychelles v. France), Prompt Release, https://www.itlos.org/cases/list-of-cases/case-no-6/, accessed 17 November 2015.

The MOX Plant Case, Ireland v. United Kingdom. Provisional Measures, Order of 3 December 2001, https://www.itlos.org/fileadmin/itlos/documents/cases/case_no_10/Order.03.12.01.E.pdf, accessed 17 November 2015.

The M/V "SAIGA" (No. 2) (Saint Vincent and the Grenadines v. Guinea), https://www.itlos.org/cases/list-of-cases/case-no-2/, accessed 20 November 2015.

The M/V "Virginia G" Case (Panama/Guinea-Bissau), https://www.itlos.org/cases/list-of-cases/case-no-19/, accessed 20 November 2015.

New Arbitrator and President Appointed in the Arbitral Proceedings Instituted by the Republic of the Philippines Against the People's Republic of China. Doc. ITLOS/Press 197, 24 June 2013, https://www.itlos.org/fileadmin/itlos/documents/press_releases_english/PR_197_E.pdf, accessed 8 July 2015.

Resolution on the Internal Judicial Practice of the Tribunal. Doc. ITLOS/10 (27 April 2005), https://www.itlos.org/fileadmin/itlos/documents/basic_texts/Itlos.10.E.27.04.05.pdf, accessed 24 November 2015.

Statute of the International Tribunal for the Law of the Sea, https://www.itlos.org/fileadmin/itlos/documents/basic_texts/statute_en.pdf, accessed 16 September 2016.

Mozambique

República de Moçambique. Ministério dos Negócios Estrangeiros e Cooperação. *Moçambique e China estabelecem parceria estratégica para cooperação global*. 20 May 2016, http://www.minec.gov.mz/index.php/imprensa/destaques/91-mocambique-e-china-estabelecem-parceria-estrategica-para-cooperacao-global, accessed 1 June 2016.

Niger

Communiqué de presse du Ministère en charge des Affaires Etrangères, relatif au différend entre la

République Populaire de Chine et les Philippines en Mer de Chine Méridionale. 24 May 2016, http://www.nigeriensdebelgique.be/communique-de-presse-du-ministere-en-charge-des-affaires-etrangeres-relatif-au-differend-entre-la-republique-populaire-de-chine-et-les-philippines-en-mer-de-chine-meridionale-le-gouvernement-de-la/, accessed 25 May 2016.

Permanent Court of Arbitration

Case Administration. https://pca-cpa.org/en/services/arbitration-services/case-administration/, accessed 30 March 2018.

Members of the Permanent Court of Arbitration, 2017, https://pca-cpa.org/wp-content/uploads/sites/175/2017/07/Current-List-Annex-1-Members-of-the-Court-update-20180320.pdf, accessed 28 March 2018.

Member States, https://pca-cpa.org/en/about/introduction/member-states/, accessed 30 March 2018.

Panels of Arbitrators and Experts for Environmental Disputes, 2018, https://pca-cpa.org/en/about/structure/panels-of-arbitrators-and-experts-for-environmental-disputes/, accessed 30 March 2018.

Permanent Court of International Justice

Questions relating to Settlers of German Origin in Poland, Advisory Opinion of 10 September 1923, PCIJ Series B, No. 6, p. 6, http://www.icj-cij.org/files/permanent-court-of-international-justice/serie_B/B_06/Colons_allemands_en_Pologne_Avis_consultatif.pdf, accessed 26 November 2017.

Philippines

Arbitration Under Annex VII of the United Nations Convention on the Law of the Sea. Republic of the Philippines v. People's Republic of China, Memorial of the Philippines. 30 March 2014. Vol. I, http://www.pcacases.com/pcadocs/Memorial%20of%20the%20Philippines%20Volume%20I.pdf, accessed 30 March 2018.

Department of Foreign Affairs. *PHL Embassies and Consulates General*, http://www.dfa.gov.ph/about-us/phl/embassies-and-consulates, accessed 11 September 2016.

__________. *Concluding Remarks of Secretary Albert F. del Rosario Before the Permanent Court of Arbitration, Peace Palace, The Hague, Netherlands. Permanent Court of Arbitration. Republic of the Philippines v. People's Republic of China*. 30 November 2015, http://www.dfa.gov.ph/newsroom/dfa-releases/8087-concluding-remarks-of-secretary-albert-f-del-rosario-before-the-permanent-court-of-arbitration-peace-palace-the-hague-netherlands, accessed 2 October 2016.

__________. *DFA Convenes ASEAN–China Meeting to Assess DOC Implementation, Discuss COC Negotiations*. 30 August 2017, https://www.dfa.gov.ph/newsroom/dfa-releasesupdate/13781-dfa-convenes-asean-china-meeting-to-assess-doc-implementation-discuss-coc-negotiations?tmpl=component&print=1, accessed 15 November 2017.

__________. *DFA Convenes ASEAN–China Seminar on Cooperation in South China Sea*. 28 August 2017, https://www.dfa.gov.ph/newsroom/dfa-releasesupdate/13731-dfa-convenes-asean-china-seminar-on-cooperation-in-south-china-sea?tmpl=component&print=1, accessed 15 November 2017.

__________. *Joint Press Release for the First Meeting of the Philippines–China Bilateral Consultation Mechanism for the South China Sea*. 19 May 2017, https://www.dfa.gov.ph/newsroom/dfa-releasesupdate/12694-joint-press-release-for-the-first-meeting-of-the-philippines-china-bilateral-consultation-mechanism-on-the-south-china-sea, accessed 15 November 2017.

__________. "Philippine Position on Bajo de Masinloc (Scarborough Shoal) and the Waters Within Its Vicinity." *Official Gazette of the Republic of the Philippines*, 18 April 2012, http://www.gov.ph/2012/04/18/philippine-position-on-bajo-de-masinloc-and-the-waters-within-its-vicinity/, accessed 16 July 2016.

__________. *Statement Before the Permanent Court of Arbitration. Peace Palace, The Hague, Netherlands. Why the Philippines Brought This Case to Arbitration and Its Importance to the Region and the World. Republic of the Philippines v. People's Republic of China. Hon. Albert F. Del Rosario, Secretary of Foreign Affairs*. 7 July 2015, http://www.dfa.gov.ph/newsroom/dfa-releases/6795-statement-before-the-permanent-court-of-arbitration, accessed 8 July 2015.

__________. *Statement on Claims by CSIS-AMTI of Ongoing Reclamation Activities in the South China Sea*. 11 August 2017, https://www.dfa.gov.ph/newsroom/statements-and-advisoriesupdate/13565-statement-on-claims-by-csis-amti-of-ongoing-reclamation-activities-in-the-south-china-sea, accessed 15 November 2017.

__________. *Statement on the First Anniversary of the Arbitral Tribunal Award*. 12 July 2017, https://www.dfa.gov.ph/newsroom/statements-and-advisoriesupdate/13302-statement-on-the-first-anniversary-of-the-arbitral-tribunal-award, accessed 15 November 2017.

Notification and Statement of Claim. 22 January 2013, http://www.philippineembassy-usa.org/uploads/pdfs/embassy/2013/2013-0122-Notification%20and%20Statement%20of%20Claim%20on%20West%20Philippine%20Sea.pdf, accessed 7 September 2016.

Philippines Permanent Mission to the United Nations. *PH to UN: South China Sea Disputes of Global Concern*. 12 June 2015, https://www.un.int/philippines/activities/ph-un-south-china-sea-disputes-global-concern, accessed 7 August 2016.

__________. *Philippines Raises Concern on Environmental Crisis in South China Sea, Calls for Regional and Global Cooperation*. 10 June 2015, https://www.un.int/philippines/activities/philippines-raises-concern-environmental-crisis-south-china-sea-calls-regional-and-global, accessed 7 August 2016.

Statement of the Foreign Affairs Secretary: PH Files Memorial Under UNCLOS Against China. 30 March 2014, http://www.gov.ph/2014/03/30/statement-of-the-secretary-of-foreign-affairs-ph-files-memorial-under-unclos-against-china/, accessed 19 November 2015.

Statement of Secretary Alan Peter S. Cayetano at the 72nd Session of the UN General Assembly High Level General Debate. 23 September 2017, https://www.dfa.gov.ph/newsroom/statements-and-advisoriesupdate/14062-statement-of-secretary-alan-peter-s-cayetano-at-the-72th-session-of-the-un-general-assembly-high-level-general-debate, accessed 15 November 2017.

Republic of China (Taiwan)

Amicus Curiae Submission by the Chinese (Taiwan) Society of International Law. 23 March 2016, http://csil.org.tw/home/wp-content/uploads/2016/03/SCSTF-Amicus-Curiae-Brief-final.pdf, accessed 27 October 2016.

Ministry of Foreign Affairs. *Diplomatic Allies*. 2014, http://www.mofa.gov.tw/en/AlliesIndex.aspx?n=DF6F8F246049F8D6&sms=A76B7230ADF29736, accessed 11 September 2016.

———. *ROC Position on the South China Sea Arbitration.* 12 July 2016, http://www.mofa.gov.tw/en/PrintContent.aspx?n=1EADDCFD4C6EC567&t=FB01D469347C76A7, accessed 14 July 2016.

———. "Taiping Island Is an Island, Not a Rock, and the ROC Possesses Full Rights Associated With an Exclusive Economic Zone and Continental Shelf in Accordance With UNCLOS" (23 January 2016). Annex 875, *Responses of the Philippines to the Tribunal's 2 February 2016 Request for Written Comments (11 March 2016) (Annexes 864–892)*, pp. 216–52, https://files.pca-cpa.org/pcadocs/The%20Philippines%27%20Written%20Responses%20%2811%20March%202016%29%20%28Annexes%20864-892%29.pdf, accessed 1 November 2016.

Office of the President of the Republic of China. *Remarks by President Ma on Taiping Island.* (28 January 2016), http://english.president.gov.tw/Default.aspx?tabid=491&itemid=36616&rmid=2355, accessed 9 March 2016); also Annex 876, *Responses of the Philippines to the Tribunal's 2 February 2016 Request for Written Comments (11 March 2016) (Annexes 864–892)*, pp. 253–61, https://files.pca-cpa.org/pcadocs/The%20Philippines%27%20Written%20Responses%20%2811%20March%202016%29%20%28Annexes%20864-892%29.pdf, accessed 1 November 2016.

———. *President Ma's Remarks at International Press Conference regarding Taiping Island in Nansha Islands.* 23 March 2016, https://www.mac.gov.tw/en/News_Content.aspx?n=FE07F9DA122E29D4&sms=3A4E63FA5107487D&s=F3B2B90AA560D22F, accessed 28 November 2017.

The South China Sea Arbitration

Arbitration between the Republic of the Philippines and the People's Republic of China. The Tribunal Renders Award on Jurisdiction and Admissibility; Will Hold Further Hearings. Seventh Press Release, 29 October 2015, https://pcacases.com/web/sendAttach/1503, accessed 30 March 2018.

The Republic of the Philippines v. The People's Republic of China. Award on Jurisdiction and Admissibility. 29 October 2015, https://pcacases.com/web/sendAttach/1506, accessed 30 March 2018.

———. Award of 12 July 2016, https://pcacases.com/web/sendAttach/2086, accessed 29 March 2018.

———. *Hearing on the Merits and Remaining Issues of Jurisdiction and Admissibility. Final Transcript. Day 4, Monday, 30th November 2015.* https://pcacases.com/web/sendAttach/1550, accessed 16 February 2016.

Responses of the Philippines to the Tribunal's 2 February 2016 Request for Written Comments (11 March 2016) (Annexes 864–892), pp. 216–52, https://files.pca-cpa.org/pcadocs/The%20Philippines%27%20Written%20Responses%20%2811%20March%202016%29%20%28Annexes%20864-892%29.pdf, accessed 30 March 2018.

Responses of the Philippines to the Tribunal's 5 February 2016 Request for Comments. 11 March 2016, https://pcacases.com/web/sendAttach/1849, accessed 28 November 2017.

Responses of the Philippines to the Tribunal's 1 April 2016 Request for Comments on Additional Materials Regarding the Status of Itu Aba. 25 April 2016, https://pcacases.com/web/sendAttach/1850, accessed 17 September 2016.

Rules of Procedure. 27 August 2013, https://pcacases.com/web/sendAttach/233, accessed 30 March 2018.

Tribunal Sets Date for Issuance of Final Award. Tenth Press Release 29 June 2016, https://pcacases.com/web/sendAttach/1782, accessed 30 March 2018.

The South China Sea Arbitration (The Republic of the Philippines v. The People's Republic of China). The Tribunal Renders Its Award. Eleventh Press Release, 12 July 2016, https://pcacases.com/web/sendAttach/1801, accessed 30 March 2018.

Special Court for Sierra Leone

Rules of Procedure. http://hrlibrary.umn.edu/instree/SCSL/Rules-of-proced-SCSL.pdf, accessed 8 September 2016.

Special Court for Sierra Leone, Doc. SCSL-2003-01-I (3014-3039), Prosecutor against Charles Ghankay Taylor (Case No. SCSL-2003-01-A), Decision on Immunity from Jurisdiction. 31 May 2004, http://www.haguejusticeportal.net/Docs/Court%20Documents/SCSL/Taylor_Decision%20on%20Immunity.pdf, accessed 8 September 2016.

Special Court for Sierra Leone, Doc. SCS-03-01-A (10666-11114), Prosecutor against Charles Ghankay Taylor (Case No. SCSL-3-01-A) in the Appeals Chamber. 26 September 2013, http://www.rscsl.org/Documents/Decisions/Taylor/Appeal/1389/SCSL-03-01-A-1389.pdf, accessed 17 November 2015.

Special Court for Sierra Leone, Doc. SCSL-2003-01-I (3014-3039), Prosecutor against Charles Ghankay Taylor (Case No. SCSL-2003-01-A), Decision on Immunity from Jurisdiction, 31 May 2004, http://www.haguejusticeportal.net/Docs/Court%20Documents/SCSL/Taylor_Decision%20on%20Immunity.pdf, accessed 8 September 2016.

Togo

"Pékin apprécie la position togolaise." *République Togolaise,* 19 May 2016, http://www.republicoftogo.com/Toutes-les-rubriques/Diplomatie/Pekin-apprecie-la-position-togolaise, accessed 25 May 2016.

Treaties

Agreement for Cooperation in Dealing With Pollution of the North Sea by Oil, 9 June 1969, http://www.bonnagreement.org/about/history, accessed 12 November 2015.

Convention on the Law of Treaties Between States and International Organizations or Between International Organizations, 21 March 1986, http://legal.un.org/ilc/texts/instruments/english/conventions/1_2_1986.pdf, accessed 9 November 2015.

Convention for the Pacific Settlement of International Disputes, 29 July 1899, https://pca-cpa.org/wp-content/uploads/sites/175/2016/01/1899-Convention-for-the-Pacific-Settlement-of-International-Disputes.pdf, accessed 30 March 2018.

Convention for the Pacific Settlement of International Disputes, 18 October 1907, https://pca-cpa.org/wp-content/uploads/sites/175/2016/01/1907-Convention-for-the-Pacific-Settlement-of-International-Disputes.pdf, accessed 30 March 2018.

Convention for the Prevention of Marine Pollution by Dumping From Ships and Aircraft, 15 February 1972, http://sedac.ciesin.org/entri/texts/marine.pollution.dumping.ships.aircraft.1972.html, accessed 12 November 2015.

Convention on the Prevention of Marine Pollution by Dumping of Wastes and Other Matter, 13 November 1972, http://www.imo.org/en/OurWork/Environment/LCLP/Pages/default.aspx, accessed 12 November 2015.

Convention on Protection of Pollock Resources in the Bering Sea, 16 June 1994, http://www.jus.uio.no/english/services/library/treaties/06/6-05/pollock-resources-bering.xml, accessed 12 November 2015.

Vienna Convention on the Law of Treaties, 23 May 1969, https://treaties.un.org/doc/publication/unts/volume%201155/volume-1155-i-18232-english.pdf, accessed 13 September 2016.

Yale Law School. Lillian Goldman Law Library. *The Jay Treaty, November 17, 1794.* http://avalon.law.yale.edu/18th_century/jay.asp, accessed 20 July 2016.

UNESCO

Election of Members of the Executive Board. Curriculum Vitae. Mr. Jean-Pierre Cot (France). Doc. 22 C/NOM/29 (30 August 1983), http://www.unesdoc.unesco.org/images/0015/001532/153214eo.pdf, accessed 11 November 2015.

United Kingdom

Attorney General to the Prime Minister, 7 March 2003, Secret, http://news.bbc.co.uk/2/shared/bsp/hi/pdfs/28_04_05_attorney_general.pdf, accessed 8 September 2016.

United Nations

General Debate of the 72nd Session, 19–25 September 2017. Argentina. H.E. Ms. Marta Gabriela Michetti Illia, Vice-President. 20 September 2017, https://gadebate.un.org/en/72/argentina, accessed 15 November 2017.

__________. Morocco, H.E. Mr. Nasser Bourita, Minister for Foreign Affairs. 20 September 2017, https://gadebate.un.org/en/72/morocco, accessed 16 November 2017.

__________. Spain. H.E. Mr. Alfonso Dastis Quecedo, Minister for Foreign Affairs. 21 September 2017, https://gadebate.un.org/en/72/spain, accessed 15 November 2017.

__________. United Arab Emirates. H.H. Sheikh Abdullah Bin Zayed Al Nahyan, Minister for Foreign Affairs. 22 September 2017, https://gadebate.un.org/en/72/united-arab-emirates, accessed 16 November 2017.

United Nations Convention on the Law of the Sea

Agreement for the Implementation of the Provisions of the United Nations Convention on the Law of the Sea of 10 December 1982 Relating to the Conservation and Management of Straddling Fish Stocks and Highly Migratory Fish Stocks, 4 August 1995, http://www.un.org/Depts/los/convention_agreements/convention_overview_fish_stocks.htm, accessed 12 November 2015.

Annex V, Conciliation, http://www.un.org/depts/los/convention_agreements/texts/unclos/annex5.htm, accessed 12 September 2016.

Annex VI, Statute of the International Tribunal for the Law of the Sea, http://www.un.org/depts/los/convention_agreements/texts/unclos/annex7.htm, accessed 12 September 2016.

Annex VII, Arbitration, http://www.un.org/depts/los/convention_agreements/texts/unclos/annex8.htm, accessed 12 September 2016.

Arctic Sunrise Arbitration (Netherlands v. Russia). Award on Jurisdiction, 26 November 2014, https://pcacases.com/web/sendAttach/1325, accessed 30 March 2018.

Arctic Sunrise Arbitration (Netherlands v. Russia). Award on the Merits, 14 August 2015, https://

pcacases.com/web/sendAttach/1438, accessed 30 March 2018.

Atlanto-Scandian Herring Arbitration (The Kingdom of Denmark in respect of the Faroe Islands v. The European Union), https://pcacases.com/web/view/25, accessed 31 August 2016.

Bay of Bengal Maritime Boundary Arbitration Between Bangladesh and India, https://pcacases.com/web/view/18, accessed 12 November 2015.

Chagos Marine Protected Area Arbitration (Mauritius v. United Kingdom), 18 March 2015, https://files.pca-cpa.org/pcadocs/MU-UK%2020150318%20Award.pdf, accessed 20 March 2018.

Curricula Vitae of Candidates Nominated by States Parties for Election to the International Tribunal for the Law of the Sea. Note by the Registrar. Doc. SPLOS/125 (30 March 2005), https://documents-dds-ny.un.org/doc/UNDOC/GEN/N05/291/03/IMG/N0529103.pdf?OpenElement, accessed 18 July 2016.

Curricula Vitae of Candidates Nominated by States Parties for Election to the International Tribunal for the Law of the Sea. Note by the Secretary-General. Doc. SPLOS/11 (25 June 1996), https://documents-dds-ny.un.org/doc/UNDOC/GEN/N96/158/21/PDF/N9615821.pdf?OpenElement, accessed 18 July 2016.

Division for Ocean Affairs and the Law of the Sea. *Oceans and the Law of the Sea. Declarations and Statements.* 2013, http://www.un.org/Depts/los/convention_agreements/convention_declarations.htm, accessed 30 October 2015.

The Duzgit Integrity Arbitration (Malta v. São Tomé and Príncipe), https://pcacases.com/web/view/53, accessed 2 October 2016.

Final Act of the Third United Nations Conference on the Law of the Sea, http://www.un.org/depts/los/convention_agreements/texts/final_act_eng.pdf, accessed 31 August 2016.

Guyana v. Suriname. Reports of International Arbitral Awards, XXX (New York: United Nations, 2012), pp. 1–144, https://pcacases.com/web/view/9, http://legal.un.org/riaa/cases/vol_XXX/1-144.pdf, accessed 1 September 2016.

International Seabed Authority. *Seabed Adopts Recommendations of Finance Committee; Completes Debate on Secretary-General's Report and Considers Commonwealth Secretariat's Request for Observer Status.* Doc. SB/15/14 (4 June 2009), https://www.isa.org.jm/sites/default/files/files/documents/sb-15-14.pdf, accessed 8 August 2016.

Land Reclamation by Singapore in and around the Straits of Johor (Malaysia v. Singapore). Reports of International Arbitral Awards, XXVII (New York: United Nations, 2008), pp. 133–45, http://legal.un.org/riaa/cases/vol_XXVII/133-145.pdf, accessed 8 September 2016.

Maritime Delimitation Between Barbados and Trinidad & Tobago (Barbados v. Trinidad & Tobago). Reports of International Arbitral Awards, XXVII (New York: United Nations, 2008), pp. 147–251, http://legal.un.org/riaa/cases/vol_XXVII/147-251.pdf, accessed 31 August 2016.

MOX Plant Case (Ireland v. The United Kingdom), https://pcacases.com/web/view/100, accessed 31 August 2016.

Report of the Fifth Meeting of States Parties. Doc. SPLOS/14 (20 September 1996), https://documents-dds-ny.un.org/doc/UNDOC/GEN/N96/249/47/PDF/N9624947.pdf?OpenElement), accessed 18 July 2016.

Report of the Fifteenth Meeting of States Parties. Doc. SPLOS/135 (25 July 2005), https://documents-dds-ny.un.org/doc/UNDOC/GEN/N05/439/16/PDF/N0543916.pdf?OpenElement, accessed 18 July 2016.

Report of the Nineteenth Meeting of States Parties. Doc. SPLOS/203 (24 July 2009), https://documents-dds-ny.un.org/doc/UNDOC/GEN/N09/424/12/PDF/N0942412.pdf?OpenElement, accessed 18 July 2016.

Report of the Twenty-Third Meeting of States Parties. Doc. SPL0S/263 (8 July 2013), https://documents-dds-ny.un.org/doc/UNDOC/GEN/N13/386/14/PDF/N1338614.pdf?OpenElement, accessed 18 July 2016.

Report of the Twenty-Fourth Meeting of States Parties. Doc. SPLOS/277 (14 July 2014), https://documents-dds-ny.un.org/doc/UNDOC/GEN/N14/467/74/PDF/N1446774.pdf?OpenElement, accessed 18 July 2016.

Report of the Twenty-Fifth Meeting of States Parties. Doc. SPLOS/287 (13 July 2015), https://documents-dds-ny.un.org/doc/UNDOC/GEN/N15/217/42/PDF/N1521742.pdf?OpenElement, accessed 18 July 2016.

Report of the Twenty-Seventh Meeting of the States Parties. Doc. SPL0S/316 (10 July 2017), https://documents-dds-ny.un.org/doc/UNDOC/GEN/N17/209/81/PDF/N1720981.pdf?OpenElement, accessed15 November 2017.

Rules of Procedure for Meetings of States Parties. Doc. SPLOS/2/Rev.4 (24 January 2005), https://documents-dds-ny.un.org/doc/UNDOC/GEN/N05/217/77/PDF/N0521777.pdf?OpenElement, accessed 5 August 2016.

Southern Bluefin Tuna (Australia and New Zealand v. Japan). Reports of International Arbitral Awards, XXIII (New York: United Nations, 2006), pp. 1–57, http://legal.un.org/riaa/cases/vol_XXIII/1-57.pdf, accessed 31 August 2016.

United Nations, Division for Ocean Affairs and the Law of the Sea. *Meetings of States Parties to the 1982 United Nations Convention on the Law of the Sea.* http://www.un.org/depts/los/meeting_states_parties/meeting_states_parties.htm, accessed 18 July 2016.

United Nations Codification Division. *Diplomatic Conferences. United Nations Conference on the Law of the Sea (Geneva, 24 February–27 April 1958).* 2018, http://legal.un.org/diplomaticconferences/1958_los/vol7.shtml, accessed 20 March 20

__________. *Diplomatic Conferences. United Nations Conference on the Law of the Sea (Geneva, 17 March–26 April 1960).* 2018, http://legal.un.org/diplomaticconferences/1960_los/, accessed 20 March 2018.

__________. *Diplomatic Conferences. Third United Nations Conference on the Law of the Sea, 1973–1982.* 2018, http://legal.un.org/diplomaticconferences/1973_los/, accessed 20 March 2018.

United Nations Convention on the Law of the Sea, 10 December 1982, https://treaties.un.org/doc/Publication/UNTS/Volume%201833/v1833.pdf, accessed 16 July 2016.

United States

28 U.S.C. United States Code, 2011 Edition. Title 28—Judiciary and Judicial Procedure. Part IV—Jurisdiction and Venue. Chapter 97—Jurisdictional Immunities of Foreign States, http://www.gpo.gov/fdsys/pkg/USCODE-2011-title28/html/USCODE-2011-title28-partIV-chap97.htm, accessed 18 November 2015.

Department of State. Bureau of Oceans and International Environmental and Scientific Affairs. Office of Ocean and Polar Affairs. *China: Maritime Claims in the South China Sea.* 5 December 2014, http://www.state.gov/documents/organization/234936.pdf, accessed 8 August 2016.

__________. Office of the Historian. *John Jay's Treaty 1794–95*, https://history.state.gov/milestones/1784-1800/jay-treaty, accessed 18 July 2016.

Statement of Bernard H. Oxman: Oversight Hearing to Examine the United Nations Convention on the Law of the Sea. Testimony before the U.S. Senate Committee on Environment &

Public Works, March 24, 2004, http://unclosdebate.org/citation/1190/statement-bernard-h-oxman-oversight-hearing-examine-united-nations-convention-law-sea, accessed 8 September 2016.

Statement of Professor Bernard H. Oxman Before the Senate Committee on Foreign Relations. 4 October 2007, http://www.virginia.edu/colp/pdf/OxmanTestimony071004.pdf, accessed 8 September 2016.

Statement on United States Oceans Policy. 10 March 1983. https://www.reaganlibrary.archives.gov/archives/speeches/1983/31083c.htm, accessed 16 August 2016.

Supreme Court. The Paquete Habana, 175 U.S. 677 (1900), the Paquete Habana. Nos. 895–896, Argued November 7–8, 1899, https://supreme.justia.com/cases/federal/us/175/677/case.html, accessed 16 July 2016.

World Trade Organization

Argentina/EU, Dispute DS293, European Communities—Measures Affecting the Approval and Marketing of Biotech Products, https://www.wto.org/english/tratop_e/dispu_e/cases_e/ds293_e.htm, accessed 8 September 2016.

Canada/EU, Dispute DS292, European Communities—Measures Affecting the Approval and Marketing of Biotech Products, https://www.wto.org/english/tratop_e/dispu_e/cases_e/ds292_e.htm, accessed 8 September 2016.

Dispute DS105, European Communities—Regime for the Importation, Sale and Distribution of Bananas, https://www.wto.org/english/tratop_e/dispu_e/cases_e/ds105_e.htm, accessed 8 September 2016.

Member Information. Separate Customs Territory of Taiwan, Penghu, Kinsmen and Matsu (Chinese Taipei) and the WTO. 2016, https://wwwJo.wto.org/english/thewto_e/countries_e/chinese_taipei_e.htm, accessed 11 September 2016.

US/EU, Dispute DS291, European Communities—Measures Affecting the Approval and Marketing of Biotech Products, https://www.wto.org/english/tratop_e/dispu_e/cases_e/ds291_e.htm, accessed 8 September 2016.

WEBSITES OF SCHOLARLY JOURNALS

African Yearbook of International Law, https://brill.com/view/journals/afyo/afyo-overview.xml (subscription required), accessed 1 April 2018.

Annuaire Français de Droit International, http://www.persee.fr/collection/afdi (five-year embargo), accessed 30 March 2018.

Anuario Argentino de Derecho Internacional, http://www.aadi.org.ar/index.php?acc=4, accessed 30 March 2018.

Anuário Brasileiro de Direito Internacional, http://centrodireitointernacional.com.br/publicacoes/anuario-brasileiro-de-direito-internacional/, accessed 30 March 2018.

Anuario Mexicano de Derecho Internacional, https://revistas.juridicas.unam.mx/index.php/derecho-internacional, accessed 30 March 2018.

Archiv des Völkerrechts, https://www.mohr.de/en/journals/archiv-des-voelkerrechts-avr (subscription required), accessed 1 April 2018.

Asian Journal of International Law, https://www.cambridge.org/core/journals/asian-journal-of-international-law (subscription required), accessed 1 April 2018.

Asian Yearbook of International Law, https://brill.com/view/title/34781 (subscription required), accessed 1 April 2018.

British Yearbook of International Law, https://academic.oup.com/bybil (subscription required), accessed 30 March 2018.

Chinese Journal of International Law, https://academic.oup.com/chinesejil/pages/About (subscription required), accessed 1 April 2018.

German Yearbook of International Law, http://www.gyil.org (subscription required), accessed 1 April 2018.

Indian Journal of International Law, http://www.isil-aca.org/publication.htm (subscription required), accessed 30 March 2018.

Japanese Yearbook of International Law, http://www.ilajapan.org/jyil/ (subscription required), accessed 1 April 2018.

Journal du Droit International, http://www.lexisnexis.fr/droit-document/numeros/journal-droit-international-clunet-.htm (subscription required), accessed 1 April 2018.

Korean Journal of International and Comparative Law, https://brill.com/view/journals/kjic/kjic-overview.xml (subscription required), accessed 1 April 2018.

Netherlands International Law Review, https://www.cambridge.org/core/journals/netherlands-international-law-review/all-issues (subscription required), accessed 1 April 2018.

Netherlands Yearbook of International Law, http://www.springer.com/series/8913 (subscription required), accessed 1 April 2018.

Revista Brasileira de Direito Internacional, http://revistas.ufpr.br/dint, accessed 30 March 2018.

Revista Colombiana de Derecho Internacional, http://revistas.javeriana.edu.co/index.php/internationallaw/index, accessed 30 March 2018.

Revista Eletrônica de Direito Internacional, http://centrodireitointernacional.com.br/publicacoes/revista-eletronica/, accessed 30 March 2018.

Revista Española de Derecho Internacional, http://www.revista-redi.es/ (subscription required), accessed 1 April 2018.

Revue Belge de Droit International, http://rbdi.bruylant.be/public/index.php?module_id=00000000009&rec_id=00000107432_00000011782, archives 1965–99, accessed 30 March 2018.

Revue Générale de Droit International Public, http://www.rgdip.com (subscription required), accessed 30 March 2018.

Rivista di Diritto Internazionale, https://www.iusexplorer.it/Rivista/Rivista_di_Diritto_Internazionale?area=riv_internazionale (subscription required), accessed 1 April 2018.

Zeitschrift für ausländisches öffentliches Recht und Völkerrecht, http://www.zaoerv.de/, archives 1929–2015, accessed 30 March 2018.

Index

A

abuse of legal process
arbitration as, 16-17, 116-17
Abyei Arbitration
and traditional grazing rights, 223
ACP Group *See* African, Caribbean and Pacific Group
Addis Ababa regional declaration on the law of the sea, 153
Advanced Persistent Threat (APT)
attack on PCA website, 51, n. 3
Administrative Directive
formalizes appointment of PCA as Registry, 8
African, Caribbean and Pacific Group (ACP), 62
African Yearbook of International Law, 75
AFP *See* Armed Forces of the Philippines
Agreement for Cooperating in Dealing with Pollution of the North Sea by Oil (Bonn Agreement), 67
Allen, Craig
expert opinion on Submission No. 13, 194-95
Amboyna Cay
examined by the Tribunal, 146
Amended Statement of Claim, 11-12
American Bar Association
Model Code of Judicial Conduct, 52
American Journal of International Law, 84
American War of Independence
and the Jay Treaty, 247-48
amicus curiae
Arbitral Tribunal requests parties' views on, 9
China opposes, 9
definition, 9 n. 9
Special Court for Sierra Leone, 88
submission of Chinese (Taiwan) Society of International Law, 149, 238
Annam
fishermen in the Spratly Islands from, 158
Annex II *See* United Nations Convention on the Law of the Sea
Annex IV *See* United Nations Convention on the Law of the Sea
Annex V *See* United Nations Convention on the Law of the Sea
Annex VII *See* United Nations Convention on the Law of the Sea
Annex VIII *See* United Nations Convention on the Law of the Sea
Antarctic Treaty (1959), 71
Annuaire Français de Droit International 60, 75
Anuario Argentino de Derecho Internacional, 75
Anuário Brasileiro de Direito Internacional, 75
Anuario Mexicano de Derecho Internacional, 75
APEC *See* Asia-Pacific Economic Cooperation
APT *See* Advanced Persistent Threat
Aquino Administration
and Meetings of the States parties to the Convention, 231
Arbitration
binding force of awards, 247-52
definition, 55
history of, 247-50
archipelagic baselines
and the Philippines, 156
and the Spratly Islands, 156
archipelagic State
and archipelagic baselines, 156
and traditional fishing rights, 172, 174, 224
China not archipelagic State, 156
Philippines as archipelagic State, 156
Archiv des Völkerrechts, 76
Archives Nationales d'Outremer
documents on South China Sea features obtained from, 120
Area
Convention articles on, 131

Japanese submission to CLCS encroaching on, 233
Area 3 Petroleum Block, 162
Area 4 Petroleum Block, 162
Argentina
sovereignty claim over Malvinas Islands, 230
at UN General Assembly general debate 2017, 230
Armed Forces of the Philippines (AFP)
interaction with China at Second Thomas Shoal, 198, 199
reports on fishing at Mischief Reef and Second Thomas Shoal, 169-70
artificial islands, installations and structures
and Submission No. 12, 14, 48, 190,191
and Submission No. 14, 202
at Mischief Reef, 14, 48, 190, 191
See also construction activities
ASEAN *See* Association of Southeast Asian Nations
Asian Journal of International Law, 75
Asian Yearbook of International Law, 75
Asia-Pacific Economic Cooperation (APEC)
designation of Taiwan at, 236
Association of Southeast Asian Nations (ASEAN)
and China, 10
and the DOC, 24
ASEAN Regional Forum, 191
Declaration on the South China Sea, 188
the Philippines a member of, 259
See also Declaration on the Conduct of the Parties in the South China Sea, Declaration on the South China Sea, Treaty on Amity and Cooperation in Southeast Asia
Australia
at hearing on the merits, 115, 117, 237, 262, 263

B

Bailey, Ryan T.
expert report on Itu Aba groundwater resources by, 119
BBC *See* British Broadcasting Corporation
Benin
party to a case before the ICJ, 96, 99
BFAR *See* Bureau of Fisheries and Aquatic Resources
Bibliothèque Nationale de France
documents on South China Sea features obtained from, 120
biodiversity
around Scarborough Shoal and Spratly Islands, 176
effects of harvesting of endangered species on, 179
See also Convention on Biological Diversity, construction activities, corals, coral reefs, echinoderms, ecosystem, eels, giant clams, mangroves, seagrasses, seaturtles, sharks
Bifurcation
Arbitral Tribunal decides, 9, 16, 115
Philippines opposes, 9
bonito
fish species caught at Scarborough Shoal, 171, 223
scientific name of, 171 n. 52
spawn period and timing of construction activities, 272
See also red snapper tuna
Bonn Agreement *See* Agreement for Cooperation in Dealing with Pollution of the North Sea by Oil
Botswana
accepts ICJ compulsory jurisdiction, 96
party to a case before the ICJ, 96
Boyes, Grant
appointment as expert hydrographer, 116
Boyle, Alan
academic experience, 91
education, 91
professional experience, 90, 92-93
publications, 91
British Broadcasting Corporation (BBC)
report forwarded to China, 181
video of harvesting of endangered species near Thitu Island, 177
British Yearbook of International Law, 76
BRP Edsa II
near-collision with Chinese vessels, 193, 195, 196, 197, 198
BRP Gregorio del Pilar
at Scarborough Shoal, 173, 176
BRP Pampanga
near-collision with Chinese vessels, 193, 195, 196, 197, 198
BRP Sierra Madre
grounding at Second Thomas Shoal, 199
Philippines resupplies and rotates detachment at, 199
Brownlie, Ian, 77
Brunei Darussalam
access to documents granted, 11
requests copies of hearing transcripts, 10
Bureau of Fisheries (Philippines)
book on fishing at Scarborough Shoal, 171
Bureau of Fisheries and Aquatic Resources (Philippines)(BFAR)

attempts to resupply BRP Sierra Madre, 200
report on China's "no fishing zone," 171
Burkina Faso
party to a case before the ICJ, 96, 99
Burundi
party to a case before the ICJ, 96, 97, 98
supports China's position, 94

C

Cairo Declaration
China claims violation of, 118
protects French claim to Spratly Islands, 128
Cambodia
dispute with Thailand over Preah Vihear temple, 257
Cameroon
accepts ICJ compulsory jurisdiction, 96
lobbied by China, 94, 96
party to a case before the ICJ, 96
Carpenter, Kent E.
expert reports, 175, 186
presented by the Philippines as expert, 117, 118
supplementary declaration by, 120
CBD *See* Convention on Biological Diversity
CCG *See* China Coast Guard
Chad
party to a case before the ICJ, 96
Chagos Marine Protected Area Arbitration
and appointment of arbitrators, 255
and Article 2(3), 223
and Article 297, 35
and rights of Mauritius, 134
Chayes, Abram, 77
China
accession to Convention, 126, 134, 136
accession to TAC, 27
abuses the Arbitral Tribunal, 51, 55, 252-65
ambassador to the UK requests meeting with President of the Arbitral Tribunal, 8, 52, 53, 55
arbitration as abuse of legal process, 16-17, 117
cannot pick and choose portions of Convention, 15
comments sought by Arbitral Tribunal from, 8, 9, 10, 11, 16, 116, 117, 118, 119, 120, 121, 123
continental shelf law, 126, 136
Declaration (2006), 117
and Article 298, 36, 40
activates optional exceptions, 15
and Submission No. 14, 203
excludes maritime boundary delimitation, 6
excludes military activities, 48
Embassy to the Netherlands discusses procedural questions with the PCA, 8, 53
EEZ declaration, 126
EEZ law, 126, 136
Environmental Impact Assessment Law, 187-88
fails to appoint arbitrator, 8, 55, 66
fails to file Counter-Memorial, 9, 123
fails to make deposits for costs of the arbitration, 11, 121
Filipinos' distrust of, 102
informal participation in the arbitration, 51-54
Marine Environment Protection Law, 185
negotiated boundaries with Vietnam as example of peaceful negotiations, 22
"nine-dash line", 6, 7, 11, 13, 47, 48, 121, 126-36
no protest against navigation or colonization of Southeast Asia, 128
not an archipelagic State, 156
opposed to dispute settlement by international courts, 95
prohibition of maritime trade, 128
protest at Japan's submission of extended continental shelf of Oki-no-Tori-shima, 147, 149
ratification of 1899 Convention for the Pacific Settlement of International Disputes, 249
ratification of 1907 Convention for the Pacific Settlement of International Disputes, 249
receives all materials on the arbitration, 10, 16, 42, 117
rejects arbitration, 7, 8, 120
seeks African support, 94-95, 101
statements on the arbitration, 120, 121, 128, 181, 190
statement on the Award on Jurisdiction and Admissibility, 116
statement on the publication of transcripts of hearings, 11, 51, 118
support for exclusive rights and jurisdiction at UNCLOS III, 128, 133
support for 3-nautical-mile territorial sea at UNCLOS II, 128
territorial sea decree, 126, 172
writes to the Arbitral Tribunal, 9, 10, 202
See also China Coast Guard, China Marine

Surveillance, China National Oil Company, China National Petroleum Corporation, Chinese Navy, Civilian Maritime Law Enforcement Agency, conspiracy theory, construction activities, default of appearance, Fisheries Law and Enforcement Command, historic rights, "nine-dash line", non-appearance, Position Paper, Submission Nos. 1 to 15
China Coast Guard (CCG)
and Article 298, 38, 200
and Submission No. 14, 200
vessels prevent Philippine vessels from proceeding to Second Thomas Shoal, 200
tolerates breaking up of coral with propellers, 177
China Marine Surveillance (CMS)
and Article 298, 38
and fishing by Chinese vessels at Scarborough Shoal, 173, 176, 177
and fishing by Philippine vessels at Scarborough Shoal, 171
and harvesting of giant clams, 176, 177, 185
and Submission No. 14, 200
near-collision with Philippine vessels, 193-94, 195, 196-98
near Second Thomas Shoal, 168
terminates M/V Veritas Voyager seismic survey, 61, 167
China National Oil Company (CNOC)
founded in 1982, 135
issues notice of open blocks for exploration, 129
China National Petroleum Corporation (CNPC)
in Niger, 95
Chinese Journal of International Law, 75
Chinese Navy
tolerates breaking up of coral with propellers, 177
Chinese (Taiwan) Society of International Law
amicus curiae submission by, 119, 149, 238, 240
CITES *See* Convention on the International trade in Endangered Species
Civilian Maritime Law Enforcement Agency (China)
at Second Thomas Shoal, 199
Cloma, Tomas
activity in Spratly Islands, 158
CMS *See* China Marine Surveillance
CNOC *See* China National Oil Company
CNPC *See* China National Petroleum Corporation
Code of Conduct
negotiations for, 24, 25, 228, 230
COLREGS *See* Convention on the International Regulations for Preventing Collisions at Sea
Comandante, R.Z.
affidavit on fishing at Scarborough Shoal by, 71
See also traditional fishing
Commission on the Limits of the Continental Shelf
elections to, 231
Japan's submission to, 232-33
Malaysia's submission to, 126
"nine-dash line map" and, 126
Viet Nam's submission to, 126
compulsory conciliation
under the CBD, 29
conspiracy theory
China's conspiracy theory of international arbitration, 253-76
combating, 253, 265
definition, 253
in American culture, 253
construction activities
and Submission No. 11, 177-78, 179, 181-82, 186-88
and Submission No. 12, 4, 43, 48, 188-90, 191-92
and Submission No. 14, 118, 198, 200-01, 202, 204, 205, 206, 207, 212
appointment of expert on effects of, 118
at Second Thomas Shoal, 198
decision on the merits, 215, 216
impact on reef health, 272
impact on reef structure, 272
impact on reef systems, 178, 272
in Amended Statement of Claim, 11
overview of, 270-71
Philippines writes to Tribunal about China's land reclamation, 9
recovery, 272
replenishment, 272
restoration and transplantation, 272
selection of sites, 272
timing of works, 272
use of cutter-suction dredge equipment, 178
use of nature simulation method, 272
water quality, 272
See also coral reefs, Cuarteron Reef, ecosystems, Fiery Cross Reef, Gaven Reef, Johnson Reef, Hughes Reef, marine environment, Subi Reef
contiguous zone
China's rights under the Convention, 11
China's territorial sea and contiguous zone declaration, 126

entitlement of fully entitled island to, 219, 233
Geneva Convention on the Territorial Sea and Contiguous Zone, 130
continental shelf
and Article 297, 35-36
and Article 298, 37, 38
and low-tide elevations, 48
and Submission No. 3, 13, 40-41, 46, 122
and Submission No. 4, 13, 46, 122
and Submission No. 5, 20, 41, 48, 122
and Submission No. 6, 122
and Submission No. 7, 14, 46, 122
and Submission No. 8, 20, 42, 48, 49, 122
and Submission No. 9, 20, 42, 48
China's rights under the Convention, 11
China's support for exclusive rights and jurisdiction at UNCLOS III, 128
Convention articles on, 131
entitlement of fully entitled island to, 219, 233
entitlement of Spratly Islands to, 20, 120
Mischief Reef on Philippine continental shelf, 12
no entitlement of Cuarteron Reef to, 14, 213
no entitlement of Fiery Cross Reef to, 14, 213
no entitlement of Gaven Reef (North) to, 213
no entitlement of Gaven Reef (South) to, 213
no entitlement of Hughes Reef to, 213
no entitlement of Johnson Reef to, 14, 213
no entitlement of McKennan Reef to, 213
no entitlement of Scarborough Shoal to, 13, 213
no entitlement of Subi Reef to, 213
overlapping entitlements to, 20, 21, 36, 37, 40, 41, 42, 48, 49, 145, 163, 164, 165, 210, 211, 214
Philippine rights under the Convention, 12
Convention for the Pacific Settlement of International Disputes, 1899
and the binding force of international arbitral awards, 249
and costs of arbitration, 261
definition of arbitration, 55
establishes PCA, 243
ratified by China, 249
Convention for the Pacific Settlement of International Disputes, 1907
and costs of arbitration, 261
ratified by China, 249
Convention for the Protection of the Marine Environment of the North-East Atlantic (OSPAR Convention), 90
Convention for the Prevention of Marine Pollution by Dumping from Ships and Aircraft (Oslo Dumping Convention), 67
Convention on Biological Diversity (CBD)
Article 27 of, 29
and Article 281, 28-30, 44, 209
and Article 282, 31-32, 44, 209
and Philippine Submissions, 21, 29
and Submission No. 11, 180
and Submission No. 12(b), 180
and the Vienna Convention on the Law of Treaties, 29
China's compliance with, 181
definition of ecosystem in, 183
decision on jurisdiction and admissibility, 44, 209
Convention on Protection of Pollock Resources in the Bering See, 65
Convention on the International Regulations for Preventing Collisions at Sea (COLREGS)
and Article 24, 194
and Article 94, 194, 196
as "generally accepted regulations", 194
China as party to, 196
decision on the merits, 216
exceptions for "special circumstances" under, 194, 195, 197
the Philippines as party to, 196
violation by China of Rule 2, 194, 196, 198, 216
violation by China of Rule 6, 194, 195, 196, 197, 198, 216
violation by China of Rule 7, 194, 195, 197, 198, 216
violation by China of Rule 8, 194, 195, 196, 197, 198, 216
violation by China of Rule 15, 194, 195, 196, 198, 216
violation by China of Rule 16, 194, 195, 196, 198, 216
violation by Chinese vessels at Second Thomas Shoal, 200
Convention on the International Trade in Endangered Species (CITES)
and Submission No. 11, 180
and Submission No. 12(b), 180
China's compliance with, 181, 182-83
corals listed in Appendix II, 184
giant clams listed in Appendix II, 184
Convention on the Law of Treaties between States and International Organizations or between International Organizations, 65
Convention on the Protection and Management of High Seas Fishery Resources in the South Pacific Ocean, 85

coral reefs
breaking up with propellers of, 177
decision on the merits, 215, 216
degradation at Scarborough Shoal and Spratly Islands of, 179
effects of construction activities on, 178, 179, 181, 186-87, 206, 207
effects of harvesting of endangered species on, 177, 184-85, 186-87
experts on, 119, 120, 175, 177, 272
human habitation of, 139
human modification of, 139
impact of construction activities on reef health, 272
impact of construction activities on reef structure, 272
impact of construction activities on reef systems, 178, 272
in the Spratly Islands, 145
Judge Wolfrum's question on, 118
recovery, 272
replenishment, 272
restoration and transplantation, 272
selection of sites, 272
SOA report on impact of construction on coral reefs, 179, 180, 182, 272
SOA statement on impact of construction on, 179, 180, 181, 272
timing of works, 272
use of cutter-suction dredge equipment, 178
use of nature simulation method, 272
water quality, 272
See also biodiversity, construction activities, corals, Cuarteron Reef, Fiery Cross Reef, ecosystem, experts, explosives, Gaven Reef, giant clams, Hughes Reef, Johnson Reef, McKennan Reef, marine environment, Mischief Reef, Subi Reef
corals
around Scarborough Shoal and Spratly Islands, 176
China's law on illegal catching of, 181
effects of extraction of, 179
harvested by Chinese vessels ,171, 184
listed in Appendix II of CITES, 184
See also coral reefs, eels, giant clams, sharks
costs of arbitration deposits for, 8, 11
equal share of parties in, 260-61
in case of non-appearance, 261
Netherlands pays for, 261
no criticism from Russia for Netherlands for payment of, 261
Philippines pays for, 11, 121, 261
Rules of Procedure, 11
Solicitor General opposes bifurcation, 47
Cot, Jean-Pierre
academic experience, 60
appointed to the Arbitral Tribunal, 8
education, 60
signs Declaration on Independence and Impartiality, 8
nominated for the list of arbitrators maintained by the UN secretary-General, 258
professional experience, 60, 61, 85, 90, 92, 257
publications, 60, 74, 76, 257
Côte d'Ivoire
accepts ICJ compulsory jurisdiction, 96
lobbied by China, 94, 96
Council of Europe, 65
Cuarteron Reef
and Submission No. 7, 14, 41, 46, 122, 219, 239
and Submission No. 11, 118, 122
and Submission No. 14, 123, 200, 205, 206, 207, 212
as high-tide feature, 142, 144
as "rock" under Article 121(3) of the Convention, 12, 145, 147, 155, 160
Chinese name, 268
construction activities at, 177, 177 n. 56, 186, 215, 270
decision on the merits, 213, 215, 216
description, 142, 155, 268
distance from a Chinese baseline, 268
distance from Palawan, 268
incapable of sustaining economic life of their own, 155, 160
incapable of sustaining human habitation, 153, 160
no entitlement to EEZ or continental shelf, 14, 122
Philippine name, 268
Philippines writes to Arbitral Tribunal about China's land reclamation on, 9
propeller damage caused by harvesting of giant clams, 177
customary international law
and the Convention, 263
and the US, 263
definition, 263 n. 53
cyanide
and Article 1, 185
Chinese vessels in possession of, 176, 177
effects on coral reefs of use of, 179
use as pollution, 185

use in Scarborough Shoal, 185
use in Spratly Islands, 185

D

Declaration on Independence and Impartiality
signed by arbitrators, 8
Declaration on the Conduct of the Parties in the South China Sea (DOC)
and Article 281, 21, 23-25, 44, 209
and Article 282, 30-31, 44
and Submission No. 14, 202, 209
China's position on, 7, 23, 25
China's violations of, 23, 24
decision on jurisdiction and admissibility, 24-26, 44, 209
in exchanges of views, 33
in Memorial of the Philippines, 13
no bar to Tribunal's exercise of jurisdiction, 13
Philippine position on, 23-24
as political document, 25
reaffirms obligations under UN Charter and Convention, 24
and recourse to Part XV procedures, 25
Tribunal's decision on, 24-26
declarations
absence in Award of 12 July 2016, 220-21
appended to ICJ judgments, 220
default of appearance
imposes special responsibility on the Tribunal, 7
no system of default judgment, 7
not a bar to the proceedings, 6
in Annex VII, 6
See also Non-appearance
Del Rosario, Albert P.
at hearing on jurisdiction and admissibility, 73
at hearing on the merits, 49-50, 73
Democratic Republic of the Congo (DRC)
accepts ICJ compulsory jurisdiction, 96
party to a case before the ICJ, 96, 98
Department of Energy (Philippines)
issues service contract on West Calamian Block, 162
offers Area 3 and Area 4 petroleum blocks, 162
dispositif
definition, 220
dispute
about interaction of the Convention with another instrument or body of law, 21
definition, 19, 20
based on examination of conduct ,21
evaluated objectively, 21
ICJ jurisprudence on existence of, 21
dissenting opinion
absence in Award of 12 July 2016, 220-21
appended to ICJ judgments, 220
appended to Arbitral Award Guinea-Bissau and Senegal, 221, 221 n. 8, 9 and 10
Djibouti
accepts ICJ compulsory jurisdiction, 96
party to a case before the ICJ, 96
DOC *See* Declaration on the Conduct of the Parties in the South China Sea
DRC *See* Democratic Republic of the Congo
dredging *See* construction activities, Cuarteron Reef, Fiery Cross Reef, Gaven Reef, Johnson Reef, Hughes Reef, Subi Reef
due diligence obligation
and Submission No. 9, 169
and Submission No. 11, 180, 184, 185
and Submission No. 12(b), 18 184, 185
due regard obligation
and fishing by Chinese vessels at Mischief Reef and Second Thomas Shoal, 214
and Submission No. 9, 169, 170
and Submission No. 15, 208
ITLOS standards on 168, 169
Duterte administration
appeal to China to open Scarborough Shoal to Filipino fishermen, 227
commitment to protect territorial claims and maritime entitlements, 227
fails to reaffirm commitment to territorial claims and maritime entitlements at UN General Assembly, 229-30
statement a year after the issuance of the Award of 12 July 2016, 228
state visit to China, 227
dynamite
China's expression of concern about use in fishing, 181
Chinese vessels in possession of, 176
use in Scarborough Shoal, 185
use in Spratly Islands, 185

E

ECJ *See* European Court of Justice
echinoderms
in the South China Sea, 176
"economic life of their own"
and "rocks", 152, 154
Cuarteron Reef, 155
Fiery Cross Reef, 155
Gaven Reef (North), 156
Itu Aba, 148-49

Johnson Reef, 155
McKennan Reef, 155
Philippine position on, 146-47
Scarborough Shoal, 155
See also human habitation, islands, United Nations Convention on the Law of the Sea Article 121, United Nations Convention on the Law of the Sea Article 121(3)

ecosystems
connectivity of, 176
decision on the merits, 215, 216
definition of, 183
effects of coral reef degradation on, 179
of South China Sea, 176
See also CBD, corals, coral reefs, eels, giant clams, marine environment, sea turtles

eels
harvested by Chinese vessels, 176

EEZ *See* exclusive economic zone

Egypt
accepts ICJ compulsory jurisdiction, 96

EIA *See* Environmental Impact Assessment

Environmental Impact Assessment (EIA)
China's failure to carry out, 180, 187
China's failure to communicate, 180, 187
decision on the merits, 215
duty to carry out, 183
duty to communicate, 183
requested from China by Arbitral Tribunal, 118, 182, 188

Environmental Impact Assessment Law (China)
requirements of, 187-88

EOMAP satellite bathymetry analysis
as evidence for status of maritime features, 118, 138, 141, 143, 144

Equatorial Guinea
party to a case before the ICJ, 96

equality of the parties
in Rules of Procedure, 52

Eritrea v. Yemen
and historic titles, 223
and preservation of traditional fishing practices, 134, 225

estoppel
definition, 27
no evidence, 27
question to the Philippines on, 27

excès de pouvoir
definition, 239
Tawan implies on the part of the Tribunal, 239

exchange of views
at the UN, 21
bilateral, 19, 32-33
decision on jurisdiction and admissibility, 44, 209
in Memorial of the Philippines, 13
required by Article 283, 22, 209
See also United Nations Convention on the Law of the Sea Article 283

exclusive economic zone (EEZ)
and 2012 fishing moratorium, 214
and Article 297, 35-36
and Article 298, 37, 38
and Canada, 134
and low-tide elevations, 48
and Submission No. 1, 132-34
and Submission No. 2, 132-34
and Submission No. 3, 13, 40-41, 46, 122
and Submission No. 4, 13, 46, 122
and Submission No. 5, 20, 41, 48, 122
and Submission No. 6, 122
and Submission No. 7, 14, 46, 122
and Submission No. 8, 20, 42, 48, 122
and Submission No. 9, 20, 42, 48, 122
and the US, 133-34
as a compromise, 133
China's EEZ declaration, 126
China's EEZ law, 126
China's rights under the Convention, 11
China's support for exclusive rights and jurisdiction at UNCLOS III, 128
Convention articles on, 131
entitlement of fully entitled island to, 219, 233
entitlement of Spratly Islands to, 20, 120
fishing by foreign nationals in, 132
historical fishing in, 132
Mischief Reef in Philippine EEZ, 13
negotiation at UNCLOS III, 132-33
no entitlement of Cuarteron Reef to, 14, 213
no entitlement of Fiery Cross Reef to, 14, 213
no entitlement of Gaven Reef (North) to, 213
no entitlement of Gaven Reef (South) to, 213
no entitlement of Hughes Reef to, 213
no entitlement of Johnson Reef to, 14, 213
no entitlement of McKennan Reef to, 213
no entitlement of Mischief Reef to, 213
no entitlement of Scarborough Shoal to, 13, 213
no entitlement of Second Thomas Shoal to, 213,
no entitlement of Subi Reef to, 213
overlapping entitlements to, 20, 21, 36, 37, 40, 41, 42, 43, 48, 49, 145, 150, 163, 164, 165, 210, 211, 214
Philippine rights under the Convention, 12

purpose of, 132-33, 153
Spratly Islands entitled to, 20
traditional fishing rights extinguished by, 174
exclusive fishing zones
declarations in the 1970s, 133
See also Federal Republic of Germany, Iceland, United Kingdom
European Court of Justice (ECJ), 87
European Development Fund, 62
European Parliament, 61
European Union, 61
ex parte communications
definition, 52
Parties should refrain from 8, 52
experts
appointment of, 118-19, 123
coral reefs, 119, 120, 175, 177, 178, 185, 186-87, 272
hydrographer, 116
Itu Aba groundwater resources, 119
navigational safety, 119, 194-95, 196
reports of, 120, 148, 272
See also Bailey, Ryan T.; Boyes, Grant; Carpenter, Kent E.; Ferse, Sebastian; McManus, John W.; Motavalli, Peter B.; Mumby, Peter; Singhota, Gupreet, Singh; Smith, R.W.; Ward, Selina
explosives
effects on coral reefs of use of, 179

F

Falung Gong
newspaper picks up blog post, 51 n. 1
Federal Republic of Germany
claim of access to Iceland's exclusive fishing zone, 134
Ferse, Sebastian
appointment as independent coral reef expert, 119
calls Tribunal's attention to use of propellers to break up coral, 177
Philippine response to request for clarification by, 120, 177
report submitted by, 120, 187, 271
request for clarification from J.W. McManus by, 119, 177
Fiery Cross Reef
and Submission No. 7, 14, 41, 46, 122, 219, 239
and Submission No. 11, 118, 122, 188
and Submission No. 14, 18, 123, 198, 200, 205, 206, 207, 212
as high-tide feature, 138, 142, 144
as "rock" under Article 121(3) of the Convention,12, 145, 147, 155, 160
Chinese name, 268
construction activities at, 177, 177 n. 57, 178, 270
decision on the merits, 213, 215, 216
description, 142, 155, 268
distance from a Chinese baseline, 268
distance from Palawan, 268
incapable of sustaining economic life of their own, 155, 160
incapable of sustaining human habitation, 155, 160
no entitlement to EEZ or continental shelf, 14, 122, 160
Philippine name, 268
propeller damage caused by harvesting of giant clams, 177
See also islands, low-tide elevations, United Nations Convention on the Law of the Sea Article 121, United Nations Convention on the Law of the Sea Article 121(3)
First United Nations Conference on the Law of the Sea (UNCLOS I)
failure to agree on the breadth of the territorial sea, 133
Fisheries Law (China)
prohibits use of explosives, 185
Fishery Bureau Nanhai District
announces fishing moratorium, 162
fishing activities
and 2012 moratorium, 129, 162-63, 166-67, 171, 214
and Article 298, 36. 38
and Submission No. 8, 42
and Submission No. 9, 14, 42
and Submission No. 10, 14, 42, 47
and Submission No. 14, 201
by Philippine vessels at Mischief Reef 162, 167
by Philippine vessels at Second Thomas Shoal 163, 167
China's failure to prosecute fishermen involved in poaching, 180
harmful fishing practices employed by Chinese vessels, 171, 176-77, 179, 180-81, 184-85, 215
harvesting of endangered species by Chinese vessels, 171, 176-77, 179, 180-81, 184-85, 215
See also China Coast Guard, China Marine Surveillance, corals, eels, Fisheries Law Enforcement Command, giant

clams, sharks, traditional fishing
Fisheries Law Enforcement Command (FLEC)
and Article 298, 38
and fishing by Philippine vessels at Scarborough Shoal, 171
and fishing by Chinese vessels at Scarborough Shoal, 176, 177
near collision with Philippine vessels, 193-94, 195, 196-98
flag State
duties under Part XII, 183
duties under Article 94, 194
Flat Island
examined by the Tribunal,146
FLEC *See* Fisheries Law Enforcement Command
Forones, T.D.
affidavit on fishing at Scarborough Shoal by, 171
See also traditional fishing
Forum Plc
acquires concession from Sterling Energy, 161
France
did not consider China to have claims over the Spratly Islands, 128
retained claim to Spratly Islands after World War II, 128
ROC note to Ministry of Foreign Affairs (1932), 128
study of vegetation and biology on Itu Aba, 157
surveys of the South China Sea, 141
freedom of navigation
and Submission No. 1, 127, 135
and Submission No. 2, 127, 135
and Submission No. 14, 202
China's respect of, 27, 129. 130-31, 202
in the EEZ, 132
freedom of overflight
and Submission No. 1, 127, 135
and Submission No. 2, 127, 135
and Submission No. 14, 202
China's respect of, 127, 129, 130-31
in the EEZ, 132
freedom of the seas
China's claim to historic rights inconsistent with, 127
exercise cannot give rise to historic rights, 135

G

Gambia
accepts ICJ compulsory jurisdiction, 96
Gao, Zhiguo
ITLOS judge, 257
Gaven Reef
and Submission No. 6, 122, 143, 219
and Submission No. 11, 118
and Submission No. 14, 118, 198, 200
as high-tide elevation, 49, 143
description, 137, 143
as low-tide elevation, 12, 41 46, 122, 252
in Amended Statement of Claim, 12
Philippines writes to Arbitral Tribunal about, 9
See also islands, low-tide elevations, United Nations Convention on the Law of the Sea Article 121, United Nations Convention on the Law of the Sea Article 121(3)
Gaven Reef (North)
and Submission No. 11, 188
as high-tide feature, 143, 144
and Submission No. 14, 123, 300, 205, 206, 207, 212
Chinese name, 268
construction activities at, 177, 177 n. 58, 186, 270
decision on the merits, 213, 215, 216
description, 143, 268
distance from a Chinese baseline, 268
distance from Palawan, 268
incapable of sustaining economic life of their own, 156
incapable of sustaining human habitation, 156
Philippine name, 268
See also islands, low-tide elevations, United Nations Convention on the Law of the Sea Article 121, United Nations Convention on the Law of the Sea Article 121(3)
Gaven Reef (South)
and Gaven Reef (North), 213
as low-tide elevation, 143, 144, 213
Chinese name, 268
description, 143, 268
distance from a Chinese baseline, 268
distance from Palawan, 268
Philippine name, 268
See also islands, low-tide elevations, United Nations Convention on the Law of the Sea Article 121, United Nations Convention on the Law of the Sea Article 121(3)
Geneva Convention on the Territorial Sea and Contiguous Zone (1958)
definition of island, 154
historic titles in, 130

maritime entitlements of islands, 153-54
German Yearbook of International Law, 76
giant clams
around Scarborough Shoal and Spratly Islands, 176
effects of harvesting of, 179, 184
decision on the merits, 214
extraction by propellers, 177, 184
harvested by Chinese vessels, 171, 176, 177, 184, 185
Judge Wolfrum's question on, 118
listed in Appendix II of CITES, 184
See also biodiversity, British Broadcasting Corporation, coral reefs, ecosystem, eels, Ferse, Sebastian, McManus, J.W., sharks
Gibraltar
Spain's sovereignty claim over, 230
good faith
and Submission No. 14, 201, 202, 204-05
UN General Assembly Resolution 2625 on, 204
Great Britain
and the Jay Treaty, 247-48
Greater Tunb, Lesser Tunb, and Abu Musa
United Arab Emirates sovereignty claim over, 230
Greenpeace
and *Arctic Sunrise Arbitration (Netherlands v. Russia)*, 59, 251
Greenpeace International v. EC Commission, 87
GSEC 101
allegedly in the waters of the Spratly Islands, 161
license to explore oil and gas deposits within, 161
no overlapping entitlements to exclusive economic zone or continental shelf in the area of, 211
Guinea
accepts ICJ compulsory jurisdiction, 96
party to a case before the ICJ, 96
Guinea-Bissau
accepts ICJ compulsory jurisdiction, 96
party to a case before the ICJ, 96, 97, 98
Gulf of Fonseca
and Article 298, 38
Gulf of Tonkin
two dashes removed in, 126

H

Hague Academy of International Law, 69, 91
Hainan island
fishermen in the Spratly Islands from, 158, 159
fishing vessels near Second Thomas Shoal from, 168
limit of China's territory on maps, 128
Hainan Provincial Regulations on the Control of Coastal Border Security
revised in 2012, 163
summer ban on fisheries, 162-63, 167, 171
Hasa Hasa Shoal
Chinese vessels warn Philippine vessels to leave, 200
hearing on jurisdiction and admissibility *See* procedural history
hearing on the merits *See* procedural history
Higher High Water
at Spratly Island, 140
at North Danger Reef, 140
definition, 140 n. 29
Highest Astronomic Tide
as vertical datum, 139
definition, 137 n. 28
satellite imagery analysis at, 138, 141
high seas
Convention articles on, 131
high-tide
and vertical datum, 139-40
high-tide feature
definition, 137
Fiery Cross Reef as, 138
in the Spratly Islands, 145
Mischief Reef as, 138
historic bays
and Article 298, 36, 37
and Submission No. 1, 40, 126, 128, 130
and Submission No. 2, 40, 126, 128
at the 1930 League of Nations Codification Conference, 130
at UNCLOS III, 130
defined by the Arbitral Tribunal, 130
See also historic fishing rights, historic titles, historic waters, "Nine-dashline", Submission No. 1, Submission No. 2, traditional fishing
historic fishing rights
distinguished from historic rights, 172
distinguished from historic titles by ICJ, 130
non-recognition at UNCLOS III of, 127
See also historic bays, historic fishing rights, historic titles, historic waters, "Nine-dash line", Submission No. 1, Submission No. 2, traditional fishing
historic rights
and Article 297, 39

and Article 298, 36, 37, 39
"nine-dash line", 17
and Submission No. 1, 17-18, 39, 40, 47, 48, 126-36, 219
and Submission No. 2, 13, 17-18, 39, 40, 47, 48, 121, 126-36, 219
at UNCLOS III, 130
decision on jurisdiction and admissibility, 210
decision on the merits, 212
defined by the UN Secretariat, 130
defined by Tribunal, 130
distinction between artisanal fishing rights and, 174
distinction between historic fishing rights and, 172, 222-24
exception for historic rights not sought by China at UNCLOS III, 127, 133
in Amended Statement of Claim, 13
nature and scope not clarified by China, 20, 21, 126
not accepted by international law prior to adoption of Convention, 127
See also historic bays, historic fishing rights, historic titles, historic waters, "Nine-dash line", Submission No. 1, Submission No. 2, traditional fishing

historic titles
and Article 298, 36, 37, 38
and Submission No. 1, 40, 126, 130
and Submission No. 2, 13, 40, 126, 130
and 1958 Geneva Convention on the Territorial Sea 130
at UNCLOS III, 130
defined by the Arbitral Tribunal, 130
distinguished from historic fishing rights by ICJ, 130
limited to near-shore areas of sea, 127
See also historic bays, historic fishing rights, historic rights, historic waters, "Nine-dash line", Submission No. 1, Submission No. 2, traditional fishing

historic waters
at UNCLOS III, 130
defined by the ICJ, 130
defined by the Arbitral Tribunal, 130
defined by the UN Secretariat, 130
See also historic bays, historic fishing rights, historic rights, historic titles, "Nine-dash line", Submission No. 1, Submission No. 2, traditional fishing

Hughes Reef
and Sin Cowe Island, 213
and Submission No. 6, 13, 14, 122, 239
and Submission No. 11, 118, 122, 188
and Submission No. 14, 118, 122, 198, 200, 123, 205, 206, 207, 212
as low-tide elevation, 138, 143, 144, 213
Chinese name, 268
construction activities at, 178, 178 n. 60, 271
decision on the merits, 213, 215, 216
description of, 143, 268
distance from a Chinese baseline, 268
distance from Palawan, 268
distinct from McKennan Reef, 13, 137, 144
Philippine name, 268
propeller damage caused by harvesting of giant clams, 177
See also islands, low-tide elevations, United Nations Convention on the Law of the Sea Article 121, United Nations Convention on the Law of the Sea Article 121(3)

human habitation
Cuarteron Reef, 155
Fiery Cross Reef, 155
Gaven Reef (North), 156
Itu Aba, 147-49
Johnson Reef, 155
McKennan Reef,156
of coral reefs, 139
Philippine position on, 146-47
"rocks" and, 151, 154
Scarborough Shoal, 155
See also "economic life of their own", islands, low-tide elevations, United Nations Convention on the Law of the Sea Article 121, United Nations Convention on the Law of the Sea Article 121(3)

I

ICC *See* International Chamber of Commerce, International Criminal Court

Iceland
sets up 50-mile exclusive fishing zone, 134

ICJ *See* International Court of Justice

ICSID *See* International Centre for the Settlement of Investment Disputes

IHO *See* International Hydrographic Organization

Illegal, Unregulated and Unreported Fishing (IUU)
and Article 56, 168, 169

IMCO *See* International Maritime Consultative Organization

IMO *See* International Maritime Organization

Imperial Conference (1923)
definition of islands at, 153

Indian Journal of International Law, 75
Indonesia
and hearing on jurisdiction and admissibility, 7, 10, 262
and hearing on the merits, 115, 262, 263
objection to China's "nine-dash line", 126
receives copies of pleadings, 22
party to a case before the ICJ, 96
party to the TAC, 27
innocent passage
and Submission No. 13, 194
International Atomic Energy Agency (IAEA), 57
International Centre for the Settlement of Investment Disputes (ICSID), 78, 80, 82, 88
International Chamber of Commerce (ICC), 68, 78
International Commission for the Protection of the Rhine, 68
International Court of Justice (ICJ)
acceptance by States of compulsory jurisdiction, 95, 245, 261
and Annex VII Tribunals, 246
and cooperation for the protection and preservation of the marine environment, 187
as permanent international court, 55, 245
cases
Aerial Herbicide Spraying (Ecuador v. Colombia), 62, 79, 83, 89, 92
Application of the International Convention on the Elimination of All Forms of Racial Discrimination (Georgia v. Russian Federation), 78, 83, 89
Application for Revision and Interpretation of the Judgment of 24 February 1982 (Tunisia v. Libyan Arab Jamahiriya), 96 n. 18
Application for Revision of the Judgment of 11 September 1992 in the Case concerning the Land, Island and Maritime Frontier Dispute (El Salvador/Honduras: Nicaragua intervening) (El Salvador v. Honduras), 89
Application for Revision of the Judgment of 23 May 2008 in the Case concerning Sovereignty over Pedra Branca/Pulau Batu Puteh, Middle Rocks and South Ledge (Malaysia/Singapore) (Malaysia v. Singapore), 97 n. 20
Application of the Convention on the Prevention and Punishment of the Crime of Genocide (Bosnia and Herzegovina v. Serbia and Montenegro), 218 n. 1
Arbitral Award of 31 July 1989 (Guinea-Bissau v. Senegal), 96 n. 17, 98, 221
Armed Activities on the Territory of the Congo (Democratic Republic of the Congo v. Burundi), 62, 98 n. 23, 24
Armed Activities on the Territory of the Congo (Democratic Republic of the Congo v. Rwanda), 96 n. 19, 98 n. 24
Armed Activities on the Territory of the Congo (Democratic Republic of the Congo v. Uganda), 78, 89, 96 n. 17
Arrest Warrant of 11 April 2000 (Democratic Republic of the Congo v. Belgium), 96 n. 17
Case Concerning Application of the Genocide Convention (Croatia v. Yugoslavia), 88
Case Concerning Gabcikovo-Nagymaros Project (Hungary/Slovakia), 89
Certain Activities carried out by Nicaragua in the Border Area (Costa Rica v. Nicaragua), 79, 83
Certain Criminal Proceedings in France (Republic of the Congo v. France), 97 n. 19
Certain Questions of Mutual Assistance in Criminal Matters (Djibouti v. France), 96 n. 19
Construction of a Road in Costa Rica along the San Juan River (Nicaragua v. Costa Rica), 79, 80
Continental Shelf (Libyan Arab Jamahiriya/Malta), 96 n. 18
Continental Shelf (Tunisia/Libyan Arab Jamahiriya), 96 n. 18
Delimitation of the Maritime Boundary in the Gulf of Maine (Canada v. US), 133-34
Dispute regarding Navigational and Related Rights (Costa Rica v. Nicaragua), 78, 80
Fisheries Jurisdiction case (Federal Republic of Germany v. Iceland), 134
Fisheries Jurisdiction case (UK v. Iceland), 134
Frontier Dispute (Benin/Niger), 96 n. 18, 99
Frontier Dispute (Burkina Faso/Niger), 96 n. 18, 99
Frontier Dispute (Burkina Faso/Republic of Mali), 61, 96 n. 18

Immunities and Criminal Proceedings (Equatorial Guinea v. France), 96 n. 17
Kasikili/Sedudu Islands (Botswana/ Namibia), 61, 96 n. 18
Land and Maritime Boundary between Cameroon and Nigeria (Cameroon v. Nigeria: Equatorial Guinea intervening), 62, 96 n. 17
Maritime Delimitation between Guinea Bissau and Senegal (Guinea-Bissau v. Senegal), 96 n. 17, 98
Maritime Delimitation in the Black Sea (Romania v. Ukraine), 62, 85
Maritime Delimitation in the Caribbean Sea and the Pacific Ocean (Costa Rica v. Nicaragua), 79
Maritime Delimitation in the Indian Ocean (Somalia v. Kenya), 79, 96. n. 17
Military and Paramilitary Activities in and against Nicaragua (Nicaragua v. United States of America), 47-48, 77-78
Pulp Mills on the River Uruguay (Argentina v. Uruguay), 79, 80, 83, 89, 92
Questions of Interpretation and Application of the 1971 Montreal Convention arising from the Aerial Incident at Lockerbie (Libyan Arab Jamahiriya v. United Kingdom), 96 n. 19
Questions of Interpretation and Application of the 1971 Montreal Convention arising from the Aerial Incident at Lockerbie (Libyan Arab Jamahiriya v. United States of America), 96 n. 19
Questions relating to the Obligation to Prosecute or Extradite (Belgium v. Senegal), 96 n. 17
Questions relating to the Seizure and Detention of Certain Documents and Data (Timor-Leste v. Australia), 62
Request for an Examination of the Situation in Accordance with Paragraph 63 of the Court's Judgment of 20 December 1974 in the Nuclear Tests (New Zealand v. France) Case, 89
Request for Interpretation of the Judgment of 11 June 1998 (Nigeria v. Cameroon), 96 n. 17
Request for Interpretation of the Judgment of 23 May 2008 in the Case concerning sovereignty over Pedra Branca/Pulau Batu Puteh, Middle Rocks and South Ledge (Malaysia/ Singapore)(Malaysia v. Singapore), 97 n. 20
Sovereignty over Pedra Branca/Pulau Batu Puteh, Middle Rocks and South Ledge (Malaysia/Singapore), 97 n. 20
Sovereignty over Pulau Ligitan and Pulau Sipadan (Indonesia/Malaysia), 62, 68, 97 n. 20
Tax regime governing pensions paid to retired UNESCO officials residing in France (France/UNESCO), 62
Temple of Preah Vihear, Interpretation (Cambodia v. Thailand), 62
Territorial and Maritime Dispute (Nicaragua v. Colombia), 59, 60, 62, 79
Territorial and Maritime Dispute between Nicaragua and Honduras in the Caribbean Sea (Nicaragua v. Honduras), 89
Territorial Dispute (Libyan Arab Jamahiriya/Chad), 61, 96, n. 18
Violation of Article 11 of the Interim Accord of 13 September 1995 (The former Yugoslav Republic of Macedonia v. Greece), 89
Whaling in the Antarctic (Australia v. Japan: New Zealand intervening,) 89, 92
WHO Advisory Opinion on Legality of Use of Nuclear Weapons and UN General Assembly Opinion Request on Legality of the Use of Nuclear Weapons, 89
characterization of dispute by, 19
compensation of judges, 260, 261
declarations appended to judgments, 220
dispute settlement under the Convention, 32
dissenting opinions, 220
distinguishes historic fishing rights and historic title, 130
"exclusively preliminary character test", 39
jurisprudence on provisional measures, 201, 204
jurisprudence on the existence of a dispute, 21
practice on preliminary objections, 47
separate opinions, 220
Statute, 95

International Criminal Court (ICC)
 Prosecutor v Saif Al-Islam Gaddafi and Abdullah Al-Senussi, 88
International Hydrographic Organization (IHO)
 recommendation on Highest Astronomic Tide as vertical datum, 139
International Law Commission
 definition of islands, 153
International Maritime Consultative Organization (IMCO), 57
International Maritime Organization (IMO), 57, 68
 and the COLREGS, 194
International Oceanographic Commission, 68
International Seabed Area *See* Area
International Seabed Authority
 created by the Convention, 233
International Tribunal for the Law of the Sea (ITLOS)
 and Annex VII Tribunals, 246
 and cooperation for the protection
 and preservation of the marine environment, 187
 and Submission No. 10, 172
 as permanent international court, 55, 245
 cases
  "ARA Libertad" Case (Argentina v. Ghana), Provisional Measures, 59, 97 n. 22
  Case concerning the Conservation and Sustainable Exploitation of Swordfish Stocks in the South-Eastern Pacific Ocean (Chile/European Union), 71, 92
  Case concerning Land Reclamation by Singapore in and around the Straits of Johor (Malaysia v. Singapore), Provisional Measures, 85
  Dispute Concerning Delimitation of the Maritime Boundary between Bangladesh and Myanmar in the Bay of Bengal (Bangladesh/Myanmar), 59, 79, 80, 90, 92
  Dispute Concerning Delimitation of the Maritime Boundary between Ghana and Côte d'Ivoire in the Atlantic Ocean (Ghana/Côte d'Ivoire), 59, 71, 79, 97 n. 21
  The "Monte Confurco" Case (Seychelles v. France), Prompt Release, 97 n. 22
  The MOX Plant Case (Ireland v United Kingdom), Provisional Measures, 90
  The M/V "SAIGA" (No. 2) (Saint Vincent and the Grenadines v. Guinea), 90, 97 n. 22
  M/V "Virginia G" Case (Panama/ Guinea-Bissau), 97 n. 22
 Chamber for Marine Environment Disputes, 71
 compensation of judges, 260, 261
 composition of, 58
 elections to, 231
 established by the UN Convention on the Law of the Sea, 58
 Judge Mensah as first President, 58
 President appoints arbitrators, 8, 253-57
 qualifications of members, 256
 role of President, 58, 244
 standards for due regard, 168, 169
island-building *See* construction activities, coral reefs, Cuarteron Reef, Fiery Cross Reef, Gaven Reef, Johnson Reef, Hughes Reef, marine environment, Subi Reef Submission No. 11, Submission No. 12
islands
 definition, 137, 145, 146-47, 149, 153
 entitlement to contiguous zone, 6, 238
 entitlement to continental shelf, 6, 238
 entitlement to EEZ, 6, 238
 entitlement to territorial sea, 6, 238
 fully entitled, 145, 155, 210, 211, 219, 233, 253
 maritime features in Philippine requests to Tribunal, 6
 See also Low-tide elevations, Submission No. 3, Submission No. 5, Submission No. 7, Submission No. 8, Submission No. 9, United Nations Convention on the Law of the Sea Article 121, United Nations Convention on the Law of the Sea Article 121(3)
Israel
 votes against the Convention at UNCLOS III, 263
ITLOS, *See* International Tribunal for the Law of the Sea
Itu Aba
 and the Taiwan Authority of China, 147-49, 238-41
 as "rock", 238, 240-41
 Chinese name, 269
 description, 147-49, 269
 distance from a Chinese baseline, 269
 distance from Palawan, 269
 EOMAP satellite bathymetry analysis of, 118
 human habitation on, 148, 149, 158-59
 incapable of sustaining economic life of their own, 159
 Japanese economic activity on, 149, 158, 159

Japanese military occupation of, 149, 158
Philippine name, 269
Philippine position, 119, 147-49, 240
Position Paper on, 239
presence of fishermen, 158, 159
presence of potable fresh water, 147-48, 157, 240
remarks by President Ma Ying-jeou on, 119, 240
shared interest of Taiwan and Beijing on, 149, 241
unsolicited statements from Chinese associations and organizations on, 120
soil and agricultural potential, 148, 157-58
vegetation and biology, 157

IUU *See* Illegal, Unregulated and Unreported Fishing

Izard Bank
Gaven Reefs on, 137

J

Japan
accepts ICJ's compulsory jurisdiction, 96
and negotiation of EEZ at UNCLOS III, 33
and hearing on jurisdiction and admissibility, 7, 10, 262
and hearing on the merits, 115, 237, 262, 263
attempts to extract guano from the Spratly Islands, 148, 158
attempts to settle Itu Aba for military purposes, 148, 158
fishermen in the Spratly Islands from, 158
Navy surveys
of Itu Aba, 157
of Johnson Reef, 142
of Mischief Reef, 144
of the South China Sea, 119, 141-42
request for copies of documents, 118
submission of extended continental shelf of Oki-no-Tori-shima, 147, 232-34

Japanese Yearbook of International Law, 75

Jay, John
and Jay Treaty, 247

Jay Treaty
and the origins of modern arbitration, 247

Jesus, José Luis
appoints arbitrators in *Chagos Marine Protected Area Arbitration*, 255

Johnson Reef
and Submission No. 7, 14, 41, 46, 122, 219, 239
and Submission No. 11, 118, 122, 188
and Submission No. 14, 118, 123, 198, 200, 205, 206, 207, 212
as high-tide feature, 143, 144
as "rock" under Article 121(3) of the Convention, 12, 145, 147, 155, 160
China's interference with exploitation of living resources, 12
Chinese name, 268
construction activities at, 177, 177 n. 59, 186, 271
decision on the merits, 213, 215, 216
description, 142-43, 155, 268
distance from a Chinese baseline, 268
distance from Palawan, 268
incapable of sustaining economic life of their own, 160
incapable of sustaining human habitation, 155, 160
no entitlement to EEZ or continental shelf, 14, 122, 160
Philippine name, 268

Journal du Droit International, 76

judge *ad hoc*
definition, 59

Jurisdiction and admissibility *See* Submissions No. 1 to 15

K

Kenya
accepts ICJ compulsory jurisdiction, 96
party to a case before the ICJ, 96

Korean Journal of International and Comparative Law, 75

Ku, Julian
on China's character assassination of the judges, 260

L

La gran época
picks up blog post, 51, n. 1

land reclamation *See* construction activities, coral reefs, Cuarteron Reef, ecosystem, Fiery Cross Reef, Gaven Reef, Johnson Reef, Hughes Reef, marine environment, Mischief Reef, Subi Reef

Lanog, L.C.
affidavit on fishing at Scarborough Shoal by, 171

law enforcement activities
and Article 298, 37, 38
and Submission No. 8, 165
and Submission No. 9, 42
and Submission No. 14, 201, 220

League of Nations Codification conference (1930)
definition of islands, 153
Legaspi, J.P.
affidavit on fishing at Scarborough Shoal by, 171
See also traditional fishing
Lesotho
accepts ICJ compulsory jurisdiction, 96
Liberia
accepts ICJ compulsory jurisdiction, 96
Libya
party to a case before the ICJ, 96
Liu Zhenmin
on the list of arbitrators maintained by the PCA, 243 n. 11, 246 n. 18
orchestrates China's propaganda campaign against the Award of 12 July 2016, 243, 245-46
Loaita Island
examined by the Tribunal, 146
vegetation and biology, 157
Loewenstein, Andrew B.
education, 81
publications ,81
professional experience, 81-82
London Convention on the Prevention of Marine Pollution by Dumping Wastes and Other Matter (London Dumping Convention), 67
London Dumping Convention *See* London Convention on the Prevention of Marine Pollution by Dumping Wastes and Other Matter, 67
Lowest Astronomic Tide
definition of, 138 n. 28
as vertical datum, 138
low-tide elevations
and Submission No. 4, 13, 41, 47, 122
and Submission No. 6, 13, 41, 47, 122
definition, 48, 136, 137, 138
Gaven Reef (South) as, 13, 41, 47, 138, 213
Hughes Reef as, 13, 41, 138, 213
McKennan Reef as, 13, 41, 47, 138
Mischief Reef as, 13, 41, 47, 138, 160, 210, 211, 213
no entitlement to continental shelf, 139, 219
no entitlement to EEZ, 139, 219
Second Thomas Shoal as, 13, 47, 138, 160, 210, 211, 213
Subi Reef as, 13, 47, 138, 213
and territorial sea, 138, 139, 219
See also islands, United Nations Convention on the Law of the Sea Article 13, United Nations Convention on the Law of the Sea, Article 121

M

McKennan Reef
and Submission No. 6, 13, 122, 143, 144, 219, 239
as high-tide elevation, 49
as high-tide feature, 143, 144
as "rock", 213
Chinese name, 268
description, 143, 268
distance from a Chinese baseline, 268
distance from Palawan, 268
distinct from Hughes Reef, 137
in Amended Statement of Claim, 11, 12
incapable of sustaining economic life, 156
incapable of sustaining human habitation, 156
part of Philippine continental shelf, 11
Philippine name, 268
Philippines writes to Arbitral Tribunal about, 9
whether low-tide elevation, 13, 122, 138, 252
See also islands, low-tide elevations, United Nations Convention on the Law of the Sea Article 121, United Nations Convention on the Law of the Sea Article 121(3)
McManus, J.W.
estimate of reef damage caused by clam shell extraction, 177, 184
request from S. Ferse for estimate of reef damage caused by dredging, 119
updated report by, 120, 177
Madagascar
accepts ICJ compulsory jurisdiction, 96
Malawi
accepts ICJ compulsory jurisdiction, 96
Malaya
fishermen in the Spratly Islands from, 158
Malaysia
and Mischief Reef, 160
and Second Thomas Shoal, 160
and Spratly Islands, 160
and the Tribunal's jurisdiction, 160
at hearing on jurisdiction and admissibility, 7, 262
at hearing on the merits, 115, 237, 262, 263
communication to the Arbitral Tribunal, 120-21, 160
nautical charts as evidence for status of maritime features, 138
no claim that high-tide features are fully-entitled islands, 147
objection to China's "nine-dash line", 126

party to a case before the ICJ, 97
party to the TAC, 27
requests copies of pleadings, 10, 22
resort on Swallow Reef, 158
submission to Commission on the Limits of the Continental Shelf, 126
Mali
party to a case before the ICJ, 96
Malvinas Islands
Argentina's sovereignty claim over, 230
mangroves
in the South China Sea, 176
See also biodiversity, corals, coral reefs, echinoderms, ecosystem
Maresca, Adolfo
definition of treaty interpretation, 264
marine environment
and Article 192, 21, 29, 42, 179, 180, 182-83, 188
and Article 194, 21, 29, 42, 179, 180, 188
and Submission No. 11, 14, 42, 122, 220
and Submission No. 12, 14, 42, 122, 220
and Submission No. 14, 202-03
decision on the merits, 215, 216, 217
in Amended Statement of Claim, 6
of South China Sea, 176
Philippine statement on the sidelines of the Meeting of the States parties, 231
the Philippines writes to the Arbitral Tribunal about, 10
See also biodiversity, CBD, construction activities, corals, coral reefs, Cuarteron Reef, cyanide, dynamite, echinoderms, ecosystem, eels, Fiery Cross Reef, Gaven Reef (North), Gaven Reef (South), giant clams, Hughes Reef, mangroves, McKennan Reef, Mischief Reef, Scarborough Shoal, seagrasses, sea turtles, Second Thomas Shoal, sharks, Subi, Reef Submission No. 11, Submission No. 12, Submission No. 14
Marine Environment Protection Law (China), 185
marine scientific research
and Article 298, 36, 38
and Submission No. 14, 201
marine turtles *See* sea turtles
maritime delimitation
and Article 298, 36, 126
and Submission No. 1, 128
and Submission No. 2, 128
and Submission No. 3, 41
and Submission No. 4, 41
and Submission No. 5, 18, 41, 48, 159-60
and Submission No. 6, 41
and Submission No. 7, 41
and Submission No. 8, 18, 41, 48
and Submission No. 9, 42, 48
and Submission No. 10, 42, 43
and Submission No. 11, 42
and Submission No. 12, 43
and Submission No. 13, 42
and Submission No. 14, 42
between States with opposite or adjacent coasts, 20
conflated by China with maritime entitlement, 19
dispute over maritime entitlement not dispute over, 20, 260
enclaves islands, 147
excluded from compulsory dispute settlement by Chinese Declaration, 6, 7, 18, 36, 48, 49, 115
entitlement issues are not necessarily integral part of, 19
integral and systemic process, 20, 260
not proper characterization of dispute, 20
not requested by the Philippines, 6, 115
Marotta Rangel, Vicente
ITLOS judge, 256
Martin, Lawrence M.
education, 80
professional experience, 79, 80-81, 83, 92
Mauritius
accepts ICJ compulsory jurisdiction, 96
and *Chagos Marine Protected Area Arbitration*, 223
requests appointment of arbitrators, 255
right of return to the Chagos Archipelago, 134
Mean High Water
definition, 137 n. 28
height datum on Philippine charts, 140
satellite imagery analysis at, 138
Mean Higher High Water
definition, 139 n. 29
height datum on Chinese charts, 140
Mean High Water Springs
and Gaven Reefs, 143
definition, 139 n. 29
height datum on Chinese charts, 140
Memorial of the Philippines
and Article 283, 33
and Article 297, 35
assumed that there would be only one phase, 49
China's actions at Second Thomas Shoal before filing, 200
copy sent to the Chinese Embassy in the Netherlands, 8

submissions in, 12-13
Philippines submits, 8
requests that proceedings continue, 16
Tribunal sets date for submission, 8
Mensah, Thomas A.
academic experience, 57
appointed to Arbitral Tribunal, 8, 55
appointed as President, 8, 55
education, 57
nominated for the list of arbitrators maintained by the UN secretary-General, 258
professional experience, 57-58, 85, 90, 92, 97 n. 21
publications, 57
signs Declaration on Independence and Impartiality, 8
Micronesia
use of multiple islands to sustain traditional way of life in, 152
military activities
and Article 298, 36, 37, 38, 43
and Submission No. 12, 40, 43
and Submission No. 11, 129, 182
and Submission No. 12, 189-90, 191
and Submission No. 12(b), 129, 182
and Submission No. 14, 40, 43-44, 48, 49, 200, 201, 212, 220
excluded by Chinese Declaration, 48, 49, 203
Mischief Reef
and Article 298, 36-37, 38
and Malaysia, 160
and Submission No. 4, 13, 41, 47, 122, 144, 219, 239
and Submission No. 5, 13, 41, 47, 48, 122, 145, 159, 210, 219, 239
and Submission No. 8, 145, 164, 165, 167, 192
and Submission No. 9, 145, 168-70, 192
and Submission No. 12, 14, 122, 143, 188, 211, 220
and Submission No. 14, 114, 118, 205, 206, 207, 212
as low-tide elevation, 13, 41, 47, 48, 138, 160, 164, 188, 192, 211, 213, 215
as part of Philippine continental shelf, 11, 21, 145, 160, 165, 169, 214, 215
as part of Philippine EEZ, 13, 21, 145, 160, 165, 169, 214, 215
construction activities at, 178, 178 n. 62, 186, 271
decision on the merits, 213, 214, 215, 216
distance from Palawan, 48, 160
fishing by Chinese vessels at, 168-70, 214
fishing by Philippine vessels at 162, 167, 168
in Amended Statement of Claim, 11, 12
propeller damage caused by harvesting of giant clams, 177
whether high-tide feature, 138
See also islands, low-tide elevations, United Nations Convention on the Law of the Sea Article 121, United Nations Convention on the Law of the Sea Article 121(3)
Model Code of Judicial Conduct
definition of *ex parte* communication, 52
Mongolia
nominates Judges Cot and Wolfrum for the list of arbitrators maintained by the UN secretary-General, 258
Morocco
sovereignty claim over Western Sahara, 230
at UN General Assembly general debate 2017, 230
Motavalli, Peter P.
expert report on Itu Aba soil resources, 119, 120
Mozambique
supports China's position, 94, 95
Mumby, Peter
appointment as coral reef expert, 119
report submitted by, 120
M/V Veritas Voyager
seismic survey terminated by Chinese vessels, 161, 166, 167, 214

N

Namibia
party to a case before the ICJ 96
Namyit Island
and Gaven Reef (South), 213
and Hughes Reef, 144
examined by the Tribunal, 146
presence of potable fresh water, 147-48, 157
soil and agricultural potential, 157
use of low-water line to determine baseline of Gaven Reef and McKennan Reef, 13, 122, 138
vegetation and biology, 157
Nanshan Island
examined by the Tribunal,146
presence of potable fresh water, 157
nautical charts as evidence for status of maritime features, 138, 141-44
China, 138, 142, 143
Japan, 138, 143
Malaysia, 138

the Philippines, 138, 142, 143
Russia, 138
the UK, 138, 142, 143
the US, 138, 142, 143
Viet Nam, 138
nautical mile
definition, 12 n. 11
navigational safety
appointment of expert on, 118
expert report on, 19, 196
See also Convention on the International Regulations for Preventing Collisions at Sea, Submission No. 13
Nelson, L. Dolliver M.
ITLOS judge, 256
Netherlands
pays for Russia's share of the costs of arbitration, 261
requests appointment of arbitrators, 255
requests arbitration with Russia, 251
requests bifurcation in *Arctic Sunrise Arbitration (Netherlands v. Russia)*, 59
Netherlands International Law Review, 76
Netherlands Yearbook of International Law, 76
Nicaragua
and Reichler, 77-78
Military and Paramilitary Activities in and against Nicaragua, 47
preliminary objections in, 46-47
Nido Petroleum Co.
and statement by Chinese diplomat, 162, 166
as block operator of Service Contract,58 , 162
Niger
supports China's position, 94, 95
party to a case before the ICJ 96, 97, 99
Nigeria
accepts ICJ compulsory jurisdiction, 96
party to a case before the ICJ, 96
"Nine-dash line"
and China's "historic rights", 6, 17
and historic fishing rights, 172
and Submission No. 1, 11, 17, 47, 48, 121, 126-36, 219
and Submission No. 2, 13, 47, 48, 126-36, 219
and Submission No. 8, 165
China's claim exceeds potential entitlement under Convention, 18
claim to sovereign rights and jurisdiction, 127
maps, 126, 128, 162
nature and scope not clarified by China, 20, 21, 126
origin, 126, 128
Philippine Service Contracts allegedly within, 162
rejected by Viet Nam, 9
sent to UN Secretary General, 126
See also historic bays, historic fishing rights, historic titles, historic waters, "Nine-dash line", Submission No. 1, Submission No. 2, traditional fishing
Non-appearance
and Annex IV of the Convention, 248
and Annex VIII of the Convention, 248
and Submission No. 14, 206
Arctic Sunrise Arbitration (Netherlands v. Russia), 59, 245, 251, 255, 259, 261
consequences of China's non-participation, 16, 35, 44, 123-25
disadvantages for the Philippines, 16, 124
exceptional difficulties created by China's, 119, 240
no effect on Tribunal's jurisdiction, 13, 209
no system of default judgment, 16, 124
public statements or informal communications treated as preliminary objections in case of, 9
steps taken to ensure procedural fairness, 16, 123-25
See also Default of appearance
North-East Cay
Chinese name, 269
description, 269
distance from a Chinese baseline, 269
distance from Palawan, 269
incapable of sustaining economic life of their own, 159
incapable of sustaining human habitation, 159
Philippine name, 269
presence of potable fresh water, 157
North Danger Reef
Royal Navy survey of, 140
tidal range in, 140
Notification and Statement of Claim
initiation of arbitration by, 7
Philippines appoints judge, 8, 56, 254
rejected and returned by China, 7

O

OAS *See* Organization of American States
OECD *See* Organisation for Economic Co-operation and Development
oil and gas exploration
China's interference with Philippine, 21, 42, 48, 128, 161-62, 220
CNOC notice of open blocks for exploration, 128

in the area of Mischief Reef, 164, 165
in the area of Reed Bank, 161-62
in the area of Second Thomas Shoal, 164, 165
interference as claim to sovereign rights and jurisdiction, 127
See also Submission No. 8
Oki-no-Tori-shima
as "rock", 147, 149
Japan's submission of extended continental shelf of, 147, 149, 232-33
China's protest at CLCS, 147, 149, 233-35
China's protest at meeting of the International Seabed Authority, 234
China's protest at Meeting of the States parties to the Convention, 233
Organisation for Economic Co-operation and Development (OECD), 68
Organization of American States (OAS), 79
OSPAR Convention *See* Convention for the Protection of the Marine Environment of the North-East Atlantic
Oslo Dumping Convention, 67
overlapping entitlements *See* continental shelf, exclusive economic zone
Oxman, Bernard H.
academic experience, 83
education, 83
professional experience, 84, 90
publications, 84

P

pacta sunt servanda
and Submission No. 15, 208
Palawan
distance of Cuarteron Reef from, 268
distance of Fiery Cross Reef from, 268
distance of Gaven Reef from, 268
distance of Hughes Reef from, 268
distance of Itu Aba from, 269
distance of Johnson Reef from, 268
distance of McKennan Reef from, 268
distance of Mischief Reef from, 48, 160, 268
distance of North-East Cay from, 269
distance of Reed Bank from, 162
distance of Scarborough Shoal from, 268
distance of Second Thomas Shoal from, 48, 160, 268
distance of South-East Cay from, 269
distance of Spratly Island from, 268
distance of Subi Reef from, 268
distance of Thitu from, 269
distance of West York from, 269
West Calamian Block adjacent to, 162
Paquete Habana case
and traditional fishing, 223
Paracel Islands
as southern limit of China's territory, 128
baselines declared by China, 129
Pawłak, Stanisław
academic experience, 63
appointed to the Arbitral Tribunal, 8, 55
education, 63
nominated for the list of arbitrators maintained by the UN secretary-General, 258
professional experience, 64-65, 257
publications, 63-64
signs Declaration on Independence and Impartiality, 8
PCA *See* Permanent Court of Arbitration
PCIJ *See* Permanent Court of International Justice
Pellet, Alain, 74, 77
Peng Sixiang
criticizes Professor Soons, 259-60
People's Liberation Army (PLA)
in national reconstruction, 190
interview on "cabbage strategy" at Second Thomas Shoal, 199
Navy frigates near Second Thomas Shoal, 168
Permanent Court of Arbitration (PCA)
and Annex VII Tribunals, 245, 246
as a court, 242, 243, 244
as Registry, 7, 52, 220, 244, 245
attack on website by Chinese APT, 51
discusses procedural questions with China's Embassy in the Netherlands, 8, 53
publication of final transcripts on PCA website, 118
staff made available to China for administrative or procedural questions, 16, 123
Permanent Court of International Justice (PCIJ)
and obligation not to engage in acts that might aggravate a dispute, 201
jurisprudence on provisional measures, 201, 204
Questions Relating to Settlers of German Origin in Poland, 225 n. 22
Philip Morris
arbitration with Uruguay, 82
Philippine Air Force
reports on fishing at Mischief Reef and Second Thomas Shoal, 168
Philippine Daily Inquirer, 46
Philippine Coast Guard
and fishing by Chinese vessels at Scarborough Shoal, 176

Philippine Commission on Maritime and Ocean Affairs
China's interference in West Calamian Petroleum Block, 162
Philippine Navy
report on danger to safety of life at sea, 171
and fishing by Chinese vessels at Scarborough Shoal, 176
Philippines
accepts ICJ's compulsory jurisdiction, 96, 245, 261
Amended Statement of Claim, 11-12
and observers' requests to attend hearings, 10, 117, 263
and requests for copies of documents, 8, 9, 11, 117, 118
as archipelagic State, 156
proposes publication of hearing records and opening of hearing to the public, 10
raises sovereignty claim over Spratly Islands at UNCLOS III, 133
requests appointment of arbitrators, 8, 55
requests leave to amend Statement of Claims, 8
requests that proceedings continue, 16
response to communications from Malaysia, 120
response to communications from Viet Nam, 9
submits additional documents, 9, 10-11, 118-19
writes to the Tribunal, 8, 9, 10
writes to the Tribunal on China's activities in the South China Sea, 9, 10
See also bifurcation, costs, default of appearance, non-appearance, procedural history, Submissions No. 1 to 15
Pinto, Moragodage Christopher Walter
appointed to Arbitral Tribunal, 8, 55, 257
on the list of arbitrators maintained by the UN Secretary-General, 258
withdraws from Arbitral Tribunal, 8, 55, 257
PNOC Exploration Co.
issued Service Contract 58 on West Calamian Block, 162
pollution
use of cyanide and dynamite as, 185
Position Paper (China)
and Article 192, 31
and Article 194, 31
and Article 282, 30, 31
and Article 297, 35
and Article 298, 36
and the CBD, 31
as plea concerning jurisdiction, 7, 9, 15, 39
hearing on jurisdiction not limited to, 10
on incident at Scarborough Shoal, 195-96
on Spratly Islands, 239
published by China. 7, 9
taken into account by the Arbitral Tribunal, 124
PLA *See* People's Liberation Army
Potsdam Declaration
China claims violation of, 118
protects French claim to Spratly Islands ,128
Preah Vihear Temple
dispute between Thailand and Cambodia, 257
Preliminary objections
China's statements as, 9, 15, 39, 115
in *Military and Paramilitary Activities in and against Nicaragua*, 47-48
nature, 47
practice of ICJ, 39, 47
practice of international courts and tribunals, 9
Procedural history
adoption of Administrative Orders, 8, 9
adoption of Procedural Orders, 8, 9
appointment of independent experts, 9, 115, 116, 118, 119, 124
appointment of PCA as Registry, 8
appointment of members of Arbitral Tribunal, 8, 44, 209, 254-57
archival documents obtained, 119, 120, 125, 142
bifurcation of proceedings, 9, 16
comments from parties requested, 9, 10, 115, 118, 119
grant of Philippine request to amend Statement of Claims, 8
meetings of Arbitral Tribunal, 8, 9
notification of issuance of Award of 12 July 2016, 121
publication of the Award of 12 July 2016, 121
publication of transcripts, 118
questions to the Philippines 10, 11, 16, 28, 29, 30, 35, 37, 48-49, 115, 117, 124, 138, 139, 166, 167, 175, 177
reminder to China on participation, 9, 16, 118
reminder to parties to refrain from *ex parte* communications, 8, 52-53
requests from observers, 10, 116, 17, 262-63
requests from third States for copies of documents, 8, 9, 11, 117, 118
request for further information or written

arguments from the Philippines 9, 11, 16, 124
scheduling of hearings, 9, 10, 116
See also China, costs, default of appearance, experts, non-appearance, Philippines, procedural orders
Procedural Order
adopts Rules of Procedure, 8
bifurcates proceedings, 9
considers China's statements as preliminary objections, 9, 15
copies sent to China, 2, 52
copy requested by Viet Nam, 9
on scope of jurisdiction, 38
requests further written arguments from the Philippines, 9

Q

Qing Dynasty
and ratification of the 1899 Convention for the Pacific Settlement of International Disputes, 249

R

red snapper
spawn period and timing of construction activities, 272
See also bonito, construction activities, tuna
Reed Bank
and Article 77, 214
as submerged feature, 162, 211
award of license to explore and oil deposits at, 161
China's actions at, 161-62, 166
distance from Hainan Island, 162
distance from Palawan, 162
Reichler, Paul S.
and *Nicaragua* case, 77-78
education, 77
professional experience, 77-79, 80, 83, 89, 90, 92
Republic of China (ROC)
no evidence of official Chinese activities the South China Sea in archives of, 128
Position Paper on ROC South China Sea Policy, 119
remarks by President Ma Ying-jeou, 119
Republic of the Congo
party to a case before the ICJ, 96
Revista Brasileira de Direito Internacional, 75
Revista Colombiana de Derecho Internacional, 75
Revista Eletrônica de Direito Internacional, 7
Revista Española de Derecho Internacional, 76
Revue Belge de Droit International, 75-76
Revue Egyptienne de Droit International, 75
Revue Générale de Droit International Public, 76
Rivista di Diritto Internazionale, 76
"rocks"
and Article 121(3), 150-59, 219, 238
and Submission No. 3, 145
and Submission No. 7, 41, 145
and Submission No. 12, 43
definition, 137, 145
entitlement to territorial sea, 238
in Amended Statement of Claim, 12
Itu Aba as, 238
Philippine position, 146
See also Cuarteron Reef, Fiery Cross Reef, Johnson Reef, Gaven Reef (North), McKennan Reef, Scarborough Shoal, Subi Reef
Romulo, Albert
and M/V Veritas Voyager incident, 161
Rousseau, Charles
on the PCA as a court, 243
Rules of Procedure, 53
adopted by Procedural Order, 8
and the binding force of awards, 250
copy sent to China, 52
introduce procedure taking into account Philippine concerns, 16
on scope of jurisdiction, 38
Russia
appointment of arbitrators by ITLOS President in place of, 255
no criticism on the appointment of arbitrators by ITLOS President from, 255
no criticism on the composition of arbitral tribunal from, 259
no criticism of the judges for pecuniary reasons from, 261
non-appearance in *Arctic Sunrise Arbitration (Netherlands v. Russia)*, 59, 251, 255
Rwanda
party to a case before the ICJ, 96

S

Sailing Directions
and Gaven Reefs ,138
as evidence for status of maritime features, 138, 142-44, 147
definition, 141 n. 30
Sánchez Rodríguez, Luis Ignacio, 74
Sands, Philippe

academic experience, 86
education, 86
professional experience, 79, 87-91, 92
publications, 86-87
Sandy Cay
and Subi Reef, 143-44, 213
examined by the Tribunal, 146
Santiago regional declaration on the law of the sea, 153
satellite imagery
as evidence for harvesting of corals using propellers, 184
as evidence for status of maritime features, 138, 141, 147
as evidence of construction activities, 186, 187
EOMAP, 138, 141
Multi-band Landsat, 138, 141
SC 58 *See* Service Contract 58
Scarborough Shoal
and Article 297, 35-36
and Submission No. 2, 40
and Submission No. 3, 13, 40, 46, 122, 219, 239
and Submission No. 5, 13
and Submission No. 10, 10, 42, 46, 122, 170-75
and Submission No. 11, 10, 14, 42-43, 122
and Submission No. 13, 10, 43, 45, 46
as high-tide feature, 142, 144
as "rock" under Article 121(3) of the Convention, 12, 145, 147, 155, 160
China's actions based on sovereignty, 18, 180
China's position on the status of, 150
Chinese name, 268
coral reef degradation at, 179
description, 142, 155, 268
distance from a Chinese baseline, 268
distance from Luzon baseline, 268
fishermen from China at, 170, 171, 223, 225
in Amended Statement of Claim, 12,
incapable of sustaining human habitation, 153
marine environment around, 176
near-collision of Chinese and Philippine vessels at, 193-94, 195, 196-98, 216
no entitlement to continental shelf, 13, 122, 150
no entitlement to EEZ, 13, 122, 150, 160
Philippine name, 268
traditional fishing at, 14, 170-75, 214, 220, 226, 227
use of cyanide at, 185
use of dynamite at, 185
use of force in waters of, 23, 173, 174
SCC *See* Stockholm Chamber of Commerce
Schofield, Clive
presented by the Philippines as expert, 117
report submitted by, 140
seabed mining
and Submission No. 1, 135
seagrasses
in the South China Sea, 176
seal fishing in the Behring Sea
arbitration between the US and the UK, 225 n. 21
sea shells
harvested by Chinese vessels, 176
sea turtles
around Scarborough Shoal and Spratly Islands, 176
China's law on illegal catching of, 181
effects of harvesting of, 179
harvested by Chinese vessels, 171, 176, 184-85
Judge Wolfrum's question on, 118
See also biodiversity, corals, coral reefs, ecosystems, marine environment
Second Thomas Shoal
and Article 297, 35
and Article 298, 37, 41
and Malaysia, 160
and Submission No. 4, 13, 41, 46, 122, 219, 239
and Submission No. 5, 3, 41, 47, 48, 122, 159, 210, 219
and Submission No. 8, 63, 164, 165, 167
and Submission No. 9, 168, 169, 170
and Submission No. 11, 14, 42, 43, 122, 211
and Submission No. 14, 14, 43-44, 48, 123, 198-204, 212, 220
as low-tide elevation, 13, 123, 138, 144, 160, 164, 210, 213
as part of Philippine continental shelf, 11, 13, 160, 165, 169, 214
as part of Philippine EEZ, 13, 160, 165, 169, 214
construction activities, 202-03, 204, 205, 206
Chinese name, 268
decision on the merits, 212, 213, 214, 215
description, 144, 268
distance from a Chinese baseline, 268
distance from Palawan, 48, 160, 268
endangering health and well-being of Philippine personnel stationed at 14, 123
fishing by Chinese vessels at,168-70, 214
fishing by Philippine vessels at, 62, 167, 168
interaction of AFP with China at, 198

in Amended Statement of Claim, 11, 12
Philippine name, 268
Philippine request to determine the status of, 8
Philippine letter about China's actions on, 8
Philippine rights of navigation, 14, 123
rotation and resupply of Philippine personnel at, 14, 123, 199-204
Second United Nations Conference on the Law of the Sea (UNCLOS II)
China's support for 3-nautical-mile territorial sea at, 128
failure to agree on the breadth of the territorial sea, 133
seismic survey
China's interference with Philippine, 21, 42, 48, 161, 166, 167
Senegal
accepts ICJ compulsory jurisdiction, 96
lobbied by China, 94
party to a case before the ICJ, 96, 97, 98
separate opinions
absence in Award of 12 July 2016, 220-21
appended to ICJ judgments, 220
Service Contract 58 (SC 58) petroleum block
deep within "nine-dash line", 162
no overlapping entitlements to exclusive economic zone or continental shelf in the area of, 211
sharks
harvested by Chinese vessels, 176, 184
See also eels, corals, giant clams, sea turtles
Sin Cowe Island
and Hughes Reef, 144, 213
examined by the Tribunal, 146
use of low-water line to determine baseline of Gaven Reef and McKennan Reef, 13, 122, 138
Singapore
at hearing on the merits, 115, 116, 117, 237, 262, 263
party to a case before the ICJ, 97
party to the TAC, 27
Singhota, Capt. Gupreet Singh
appointment as expert on navigational safety, 119
report submitted by, 19, 196
Smith, R.W.
presented by the Philippines as expert, 118
SOA *See* State Oceanic Administration (China)
Société Française pour le Droit International
and article of Judge Mensah, 57
Solicitor General (Philippines)
at the Hearing on the Merits, 73
opposes bifurcation to save money, 47
statement on the Award on Jurisdiction and Admissibility, 46
Somalia
accepts ICJ compulsory jurisdiction, 96
party to a case before the ICJ, 96
Soons, Alfred H.A.
academic experience, 66-67
appointed to Arbitral Tribunal, 8, 55
criticized by Wang Hanling and Peng Sixiang, 259-60
education, 66
nominated for the list of arbitrators maintained by the UN secretary-General, 258
professional experience, 67-68, 90, 257
signs Declaration on Independence and Impartiality, 8
publications, 67
South China Sea
area, 6
connectivity of ecosystems, 179
ecosystem of, 176, 179
fishing ground, 6
oil and gas reserves, 6
semi-enclosed sea, 6
shipping lane, 6
tidal patterns and ranges, 140
South-East Cay
presence of potable fresh water, 157
South-West Cay
Chinese name, 269
description, 269
distance from a Chinese baseline, 269
distance from Palawan, 269
incapable of sustaining economic life of their own, 159
Japanese commercial activities on, 158, 159
Philippine name, 269
presence of potable fresh water, 157
South Pacific Forum Fisheries Agency, 68
South Pacific Regional Fisheries Management Organisation, 85
sovereignty
and Submission No. 1, 17, 128
and Submission No. 2, 17, 128
and Submission No. 3, 17, 41, 149
and Submission No. 4, 17, 41
and Submission No. 5, 17, 18, 41, 49, 149
and Submission No. 6, 17, 41
and Submission No. 7, 17, 41, 149
and Submission No. 8, 18, 41, 49
and Submission No. 9, 42, 49, 169
and Submission No. 10, 42, 175
and Submission No. 11, 42, 178, 183
and Submission No. 12, 43
and Submission No. 12(b), 178, 183

and Submission No. 13, 42, 195
and Submission No. 14, 42, 202
and traditional fishing at Scarborough Shoal, 222, 224
as basis for assumption of China's unlawful conduct, 19
as premise to approach Philippine submissions, 20
claims not impediments to determination of maritime entitlements, 18
distinction between "claims to sovereignty" and "claims to sovereign rights and jurisdiction", 127
not addressed by Convention, 115
not appropriate characterisation of Philippine claims, 19
not required for determination of maritime entitlement, 19
not required by Philippine Submissions, 18, 115
over land territory as basis for maritime rights, 17
Philippine claim over Kalayaan Island Group, 126
See also Argentina, Morocco, Spain, United Arab Emirates

Spain
sovereignty claim over Gibraltar, 230
at UN General Assembly general debate 2017, 230

Special Court for Sierra Leone
Prosecutor v. Charles Taylor, 88

Spratly Island
Royal Navy survey of, 140
presence of potable fresh water, 157
soil and agricultural potential, 157
tidal range in, 140

Spratly Islands
and archipelagic baselines, 156
and Article 47, 156
and Article 121(3), 40, 145, 156-59, 213-14
and straight baselines, 156
"as a whole", 120, 149, 156
baselines declared by China, 129
China's actions based on sovereignty, 18, 169, 190, 195
construction activities in, 118, 177-78, 181-82, 186-88, 189, 206, 270-71
coral reef degradation at, 179
decision on the merits, 213, 217 217
economic life, 156
effects of China's construction activities in, 178, 179, 181-82, 186-87
entitlement to continental shelf, 20, 37, 128, 138, 149, 213-14
entitlement to EEZ, 10, 37, 128, 138, 149, 213-14
entitlement to territorial sea, 20, 37, 128, 138, 149
fishing by Chinese vessels at, 170
incapable of sustaining economic life of their own, 159
incapable of sustaining human habitation, 159
Japan's attempts to extract guano from, 148
marine environment of, 176
number of maritime features in, 19
Position Paper on, 239
used by fishermen, 158, 159
separated from mainland in China's Declaration on Territorial Sea, 128
tidal range in, 140
use of cyanide in, 185
use of dynamite in, 185
See also historic rights, "nine-dash line", sovereignty

State Oceanic Administration (China)(SOA)
impact on reef health, 272
impact on reef structure, 272
impact on reef systems, 178, 272
parties' comments on study, 118
recovery, 272
replenishment, 272
report on impact of construction on coral reefs, 179, 180, 182, 188, 272
restoration and transplantation, 272
selection of sites, 272
statement on impact of construction on coral reefs, 179, 180, 181, 188, 272
timing of works, 272
use of cutter-suction dredge equipment, 178
use of nature simulation method, 272
water quality, 272

State practice
and Article 121(3), 55, 156

Sterling Energy Plc
awarded license to explore and oil deposits at Reed Bank, 161

Stockholm Chamber of Commerce (SCC), 78

Subi Reef
and Sandy Cay, 143-44
and Submission No. 4, 13, 41, 46, 219, 239
and Submission No. 11, 118, 188
and Submission No. 14, 118, 198, 200, 205, 206, 207, 212
and Thitu Island, 138, 143-44
as low -tide elevation, 13, 138, 143
as submerged feature, 12

Chinese name, 268
construction activities at, 178, 178 n. 61, 186, 188-89, 191-92, 271
description, 143-44, 268
decision on the merits, 213, 215, 216, 217
distance from a Chinese baseline, 268
distance from Palawan, 268
EOMAP satellite bathymetry analysis of, 118, 144
fishing by Chinese vessels at, 170
in Amended Statement of Claim, 12
Philippine name, 268
See also islands, low-tide elevations, United Nations Convention on the Law of the Sea Article 121, United Nations Convention on the Law of the Sea Article 121(3)

submarine cables and pipelines
and Submission No. 8, 165
laying in EEZ, 132, 165
laying on continental shelf. 132, 165

submerged feature
definition, 137
Reed Bank as, 162

Submission No. 1
and Article 297, 39, 40
and Article 298, 39, 40, 126, 127, 128, 130, 131
as dispute over source of entitlements, 21
China's objections to jurisdiction and admissibility, 17, 128
China's position, 128
decision on jurisdiction, 40, 45, 47, 48, 49, 126, 128-31, 210
decision on the merits, 131-36
Final Submission, 13, 121
Philippine position, 27, 127-28

Submission No. 2
and Article 297, 39, 40
and Article 298, 39, 40
as dispute over source of entitlements, 21
China's objections to jurisdiction and admissibility, 17
China's position, 128
decision on jurisdiction, 40, 45, 47, 48, 49, 128-31, 210
decision on the merits, 131-36
Final Submission, 13, 121
Philippine position, 27, 127-28

Submission No. 3
and Article 121, 40, 144-60
and Article 297, 40, 41
and Article 298, 40, 41
as dispute over status of maritime features and source of entitlements, 21
China's objections to jurisdiction and admissibility, 17, 149-50
decision on jurisdiction, 40, 45, 46, 210
decision on the merits, 160
Final Submission, 13, 122
Philippine position, 146-49

Submission No. 4
and Article 13, 41, 139, 143
and Article 121(1), 41, 139, 143
and Submission No. 14, 205
as dispute over status of maritime features and source of entitlements, 21, 219
China's objections to jurisdiction and admissibility, 17
China's position, 138
decision on jurisdiction, 41, 45, 46, 137, 210
decision on the merits, 144
Final Submission, 122
Philippine position, 137-38

Submission No. 5
and Article 121(3), 40, 144-60
and Submission No. 14, 205
as dispute over status of maritime features and source of entitlements, 21
based on premise that feature is in Philippine EEZ or continental shelf, 20
China's objections to jurisdiction and admissibility, 17
China's position, 149-50
decision on jurisdiction, 41, 45, 47, 48, 159-60, 210
decision on the merits, 139-41
Final Submission, 13, 122
Philippine position, 146-49

Submission No. 6
and Article 13, 41, 143
and Submission No. 14, 205
as dispute over status of maritime features and source of entitlements, 21, 219
China's objections to jurisdiction and admissibility 17
China's position, 138
decision on jurisdiction, 41, 45, 47, 137, 159-60, 210
decision on the merits, 139-44
Final Submission, 13, 122
Philippine position, 137-38

Submission No. 7
and Article 121(3), 144-60
and Submission No. 14, 205
as dispute over status of maritime features
and source of entitlements, 21
China's objections to jurisdiction and

admissibility, 18, 149-50
China's position, 149
decision on jurisdiction, 41, 45, 46, 210
decision on the merits, 139-44
Philippine position, 146-49
Submission No. 8
and Article 15, 165
and Article 56, 163, 165, 167
and Article 58, 164, 165
and Article 61, 164
and Article 62, 164
and Article 73, 164
and Article 74, 165
and Article 77, 164, 165
and Article 78, 165
and Article 81, 164
and Article 83, 165
and Article 121, 40
and Article 297, 163, 165
and Article 298, 40, 42, 47, 48, 163, 164, 165
and Submission No. 14, 205
and "nine-dash line", 165
as dispute on Chinese activities, 21
based on premise that feature is in Philippine EEZ or continental shelf, 20
China's objections to jurisdiction and admissibility, 18
China's position, 164
decision on jurisdiction, 42, 45, 47, 49, 164, 165, 168, 169, 210-11
decision on the merits, 167
Final Submission, 14, 122
Philippine position, 163-64
Submission No. 9
and Article 56, 168
and Article 58, 169
and Article 62, 169
and Article 121, 40
and Article 298, 40
and Submission No. 14, 205
as dispute on Chinese activities, 21
based on premise that feature is in Philippine EEZ or continental shelf, 20
China's objections to jurisdiction and admissibility, 18
China's position, 169
decision on jurisdiction, 42, 45, 47, 47, 168, 169, 210-11
decision on the merits, 170
Final Submission, 14, 122
Philippine position, 168
Submission No. 10
and Article 2, 171, 172
and Article 5, 171, 172, 174
and Article 62, 171, 172, 174
and Article 297, 171, 173
and Article 298, 40
and Article 300, 171-72
as dispute on Chinese activities, 21, 220
China's objections to jurisdiction and admissibility,18
China's position, 173
decision on jurisdiction, 42, 45, 46, 170, 210
decision on the merits, 175
Final Submission, 14, 122
Philippine position, 171-72
Submission No. 11 and Submission No. 12(b)
amendment of, 118, 182
and Article 123, 180
and Article 192, 180, 184, 185
and Article 194, 180, 184, 185
and Article 197, 180, 183
and Article 205, 180, 183
and Article 206, 180, 187, 188
and Submission No. 14, 205
and CITES, 180
and EIA, 180, 187
and the CBD, 21, 32
and the SOA, 118, 179, 180, 181, 188, 272
as dispute on Chinese activities, 21
China's objections to jurisdiction and admissibility, 18
China's position, 180-182
decision on jurisdiction, 42-43, 45, 47, 182, 210, 211
decision on the merits, 188
Final Submission, 114, 22
Philippine comments on evidence, 119
Philippine position, 178-80
Submission No. 12
and Article 56, 191
and Article 60, 189, 190
and Article 80, 189, 190
and Article 298, 43, 191
and Submission No. 14, 205
and the CBD, 21, 32
as dispute on Chinese activities, 21
China's objections to jurisdiction and admissibility, 18
China's position, 180-182, 190
decision on jurisdiction, 43, 45, 47, 49, 182, 211
decision on the merits, 188
Final Submission, 14, 122
Philippine comments on evidence, 119
Philippine position, 178-80, 189-90
Submission No. 13
and Article 21, 194

and Article 94, 194, 196, 198
and Article 298, 40
as dispute on Chinese activities, 21
China's objections to jurisdiction and admissibility, 18
China's position, 195-96
decision on jurisdiction, 43, 45, 46, 192, 210
Final Submission, 14, 124
Philippine position, 194
Submission No. 14
amendment of, 118, 198
and Annex VII, 205
and Article 56, 202
and Article 77, 202
and Article 279, 205
and Article 293, 205
and Article 296, 205
and Article 297, 200, 201, 203
and Article 298, 200, 203, 204
and Article 300, 202, 204, 205
as dispute on Chinese activities, 21
China's objections to jurisdiction and admissibility, 18
China's position, 202-03
decision on jurisdiction, 43-44, 45, 47, 48, 14, 203-04, 212
Final Submission, 14, 124
Philippine position, 201-02
Submission No. 15
and Annex VII, 209
and Article 74, 208
and Article 83, 208
and Article 279, 208
and Article 298, 208
and Article 300, 208
China's objections to jurisdiction and admissibility, 18
China's position, 208
decision on jurisdiction, 44, 45, 47, 49, 208-09, 212, 252
Final Submission, 14, 124
Philippine position, 207-08
Sudan
accepts ICJ compulsory jurisdiction, 96
Supplemental Written Submissions
Tribunal requests, 9
Philippines submits, 9
Swallow Reef
examined by the Tribunal, 146
Malaysian resort on, 158
Swaziland
accepts ICJ compulsory jurisdiction, 96

T

TAC *See* Treaty on Amity and Cooperation in Southeast Asia
Taiwan
fishermen at Scarborough Shoal from, 170, 171, 223, 225
See also Republic of China (ROC), Taiwan Authority of China
Taiwan Authority of China
amicus curiae submission, 237
and Itu Aba, 148-49
designation at APEC, 236
designation at the WTO, 236
designation of Taiwan by China as, 236
designation of Taiwan by the Tribunal as, 236
not a party to the Convention, 237
not a UN member, 237
not invited to UNCLOS III, 237
Philippine response to submissions by, 119-20, 240
Position Paper on Itu Aba, 149, 150
Position Paper on ROC South China Sea Policy, 238
press release from Ministry of Foreign Affairs, 238
remarks by President Ma Ying-jeou, 119, 238
statement on the Award of 12 July 2016, 235-41
Taiwan's complaint at designation as, 235-36
talakitok
fish species caught at Scarborough Shoal, 171, 223
scientific name, 171 n.
Talatagod, C.D.
affidavit on fishing at Scarborough Shoal by, 171
See also traditional fishing
Talmon, Stefan
defends China's case, 259
Taneo, C.O.
affidavit on fishing at Scarborough Shoal by, 171
tanguinge
fish species caught at Scarborough Shoal, 171, 223
scientific name of, 171 n.
territorial sea
and Article 297, 35
and low-tide elevations, 48
and Submission No. 4, 13, 47
and Submission No. 10, 42
and Submission No. 11, 43
and Submission No. 13, 43
and traditional fishing rights, 174

China's rights to, 11
China's territorial sea decree/declaration, 125, 128, 172
Convention articles on, 131
declaration of 200-mile territorial sea, 133
entitlement of fully entitled island to, 219, 233, 238
entitlement of "rock" to, 238
entitlement of Scarborough Shoal to, 223
entitlement of Spratly Islands to, 20, 120
Geneva Convention on the Territorial Sea and Contiguous Zone, 130, 153-54
no entitlement of Gaven Reef (South) to, 213
no entitlement of Hughes Reef to, 213
no entitlement of Mischief Reef to, 213
no entitlement of Second Thomas Shoal to, 213
no entitlement of Subi Reef to, 213
overlapping entitlements to, 164, 165
Philippine rights under the Convention, 12

territorial sovereignty
and arbitration's subject matter, 7, 17
not required for determination of maritime entitlements, 20, 22, 260
Philippines not asking the Tribunal to rule on, 6, 20
See also sovereignty, Submission No. 1, Submission No. 2

Thailand
and hearing on jurisdiction and admissibility, 7, 10, 262
and hearing on the merits, 115, 117, 237, 262
dispute with Cambodia over Preah Vihear Temple, 257, 263
party to the TAC, 27

The Epoch Times
picks up blog post, 51 n. 1

third parties
whether indispensable to proceedings, 22
See also Malaysia, Viet Nam

Third United Nations Conference on the Law of the Sea (UNCLOS III)
adopted by majority vote, 247
and adoption of EEZ, 226
attended by, 247
China's support for exclusive jurisdiction in EEZ and continental shelf, 128, 133
historic titles at, 130
negotiation of Convention at, 247
negotiation of EEZ at, 132-33
non-recognition of historic fishing rights at, 127-28
Oxman at, 84
Pinto at, 56
regional declarations on the law of the sea before, 153
sovereignty claim over Spratly Islands raised at, 133
vote on the Convention at, 263
Wolfrum at, 71

Thitu Island
and Subi Reef, 138, 143-44, 213
Chinese name, 269
description of, 147, 149, 269
distance from a Chinese baseline, 269
distance from Palawan, 269
EOMAP analysis of, 141
harvesting of endangered species near, 177
incapable of sustaining economic life of their own, 159
incapable of sustaining human habitation, 159
Philippine name, 269
soil and agricultural potential, 157
vegetation and biology, 157

tidal model
and Submission No. 4, 41, 140
and Submission No. 6, 41, 140
decision on the merits, 212

Togo
accepts ICJ compulsory jurisdiction, 96
comments of netizens on China's position, 102
supports China's position, 94, 96, 101

traditional fishing
and acquired rights, 174
and Submission No. 10, 14, 42, 47, 122, 222
and the *Chagos Marine Protected Area Arbitration*, 223, 226
and the EEZ, 174, 226
and the territorial sea, 174
at Scarborough Shoal, 14, 42, 170-75, 214, 222-27
decision on the merits, 214
description of, 173
distinction between traditional fishing rights and historic rights, 222-24
in archipelagic waters, 226
in the territorial sea, 171, 172, 174, 223, 226
prior to adoption of EEZ, 225
vested rights and, 173-74, 224-227
See also bonito, Comandante, R.Z., Forones, T.D., Legaspi, J.P., *talakitok*, Talatagod, C.D., *tanguinge*,

translation of the Award of 12 July 2016, 121

travaux préparatoires
definition, 153 n. 44
of Article 121(3), 153-54

Treaty on Amity and Cooperation in Southeast Asia (TAC)
and Article 281, 27-28, 44, 209
and Article 282, 44, 209
decision on jurisdiction and admissibility, 28, 44, 209
High Council, 28
Philippine position on, 28
tuna
spawn period and timing of construction activities, 272
See also bonito, construction activities, red snapper
Tunisia
party to a case before the ICJ, 96
Turkey
votes against the Convention at UNCLOS III, 263

U

Uganda
accepts ICJ compulsory jurisdiction, 96
party to a case before the ICJ, 96
UNCLOS I *See* First United Nations Conference on the Law of the Sea
UNCLOS II *See* Second United Nations Conference on the Law of the Sea
UNCLOS III *See* Third United Nations Conference on the Law of the Sea
UNESCO *See* United Nations Educational, Scientific and Cultural Organization
Union of Soviet Socialist Republics (USSR)
and negotiation of EEZ at UNCLOS III, 133
United Arab Emirates
sovereignty claim over Greater Tunb, Lesser Tunb, and Abu Musa, 230
at UN General Assembly general debate 2017, 230
United Kingdom
and *Chagos Marine Protected Area Arbitration*, 134, 223
and hearing on the merits, 117, 262, 263, 264
appoints arbitrators, 255
claim of access to Iceland's exclusive fishing zone, 134
Hydrographic Office (UKHO), 119
nautical charts as evidence for status of maritime features, 138
protects French claim to Spratly Islands, 128
Royal Navy surveys
Cuarteron Reef, 142
Fiery Cross Reef, 142
Gaven Reefs, 143
Itu Aba, 157
Johnson Reef, 142
Namyit, 157
Nanshan Island, 157
North-East Cay, 157
Scarborough Shoal, 142
South-East Cay, 157
Spratly Island, 157
Spratly Islands,158
Subi Reef, 143
the South China Sea, 119, 141-42
Thitu, 157
Sailing Directions, 144, 147
United Nations
Charter and Submission No. 8, 168
Charter and Submission No. 10, 172, 174, 175
Charter obligations reaffirmed by DOC, 24
exchanges of views at, 21
General Assembly, 229-30
general debate at, 229-30
no requirement of prior negotiations, 33
United Nations Committee to Study the Peaceful Seas of the Sea-bed and the Ocean Floor beyond the Limits of National Jurisdiction, 84
United Nations Committee on the Peaceful Seas of the Sea-bed and the Ocean Floor beyond the Limits of National Jurisdiction, 84
United Nations Compensation Commission (UNCC), 57
United Nations Convention on the Law of the Sea
Agreement for the Implementation of the Provisions of the United Nations Convention on the Law of the Sea of 10 December 1982 relating to the Conservation and Management of Straddling Fish Stocks and Highly Migratory Fish Stocks, 65
and the CBD, 28–30
Annex II
and the CLCS, 33
Annex IV
and non-appearance, 255
Annex V
List of Arbitrators, 65
Annex VII
acceptance of arbitration under, 15, 245
and the binding force of awards, 247-52
and the ICJ, 246
and the ITLOS, 246
and appointment of arbitrators, 244, 254-56
and non-participation, 6, 16, 252

and Notification and Statement of Claim, 7
and number of arbitrators, 55
and the PCA as registry, 245, 246
cases
Arctic Sunrise Arbitration (Netherlands v. Russia), 59, 68, 251 n. 6, 255
Atlanto-Scandian Herring Arbitration (The Kingdom of Denmark in respect of the Faroe Islands v. The European Union), 59, 72
Bay of Bengal Maritime Boundary Arbitration between Bangladesh and India, 63, 72, 80, 90, 92
Chagos Marine Protected Area Arbitration (Mauritius v. United Kingdom), 35, 72, 79, 83, 90, 92, 134, 223, 226, 256
The Duzgit Integrity Arbitration (Malta v. São Tomé and Príncipe), 68
Guyana v. Suriname, 68, 78, 80, 83, 85, 251 n. 6
Land Reclamation by Singapore in and around the Straits of Johor (Malaysia v. Singapore), 85, 251 n. 6
Maritime Delimitation between Barbados and Trinidad & Tobago, 251 n. 6
M.V. Saiga (St. Vincent & the Grenadines v. Guinea), 251 n. 6
MOX Plant Case (Ireland v. The United Kingdom), 59, 90, 92, 251 n. 6
Southern Bluefin Tuna (Australia and New Zealand v. Japan), 251 n. 6
Eritrea v. Yemen not arbitration under, 134
list of arbitrators maintained by UN Secretary-General, 65, 244
qualifications of arbitrators, 257-58
no system of default judgment, 7, 124, 252
Annex VIII
and choice of means of dispute settlement, 246
and non-appearance, 255
Article 1
and Submission No. 11, 85
and Submission No. 12(b), 185
and use of cyanide, 185
and use of dynamite, 185
Article 2
and *Chagos Marine Protected Area Arbitration*, 223, 226
and Submission No. 10, 171-72, 17
and traditional fishing at Scarborough Shoal, 223
and vested rights, 175
Article 5
and Submission No. 10, 171
Article 7
and the Spratly Islands, 156
straight baselines, 156
Article 13
and Article 121(3), 139, 153
and Gaven Reef (South), 213
and Hughes Reef, 213
and Mischief Reef, 213
and Second Thomas Shoal, 213
and Submission No. 4, 41, 143
and Submission No. 6, 41, 143
definition of low-tide elevation, 48, 136, 139-40
and Subi Reef, 213
Article 15
and Article 298, 37
and historic title, 130
and Submission No. 8, 165
Article 21
and Submission No. 13, 43, 194
Article 24
and Submission No. 13, 43, 194
Article 47
and the Philippines, 156
and the Spratly Islands, 156
Article 51
and Submission No. 10, 172, 174
and traditional fishing at Scarborough Shoal, 224
Article 56
and 2012 moratorium on fishing, 214
and IUU, 168
and Submission No. 8, 163-64, 167
and Submission No. 9, 168
and Submission No. 12, 190, 191
and Submission No. 14, 202
Article 58
and fishing by Chinese vessels at Mischief Reef and Second Thomas Shoal, 214
and rights in EEZ of States other than coastal State, 132

and Submission No. 8, 164
and Submission No. 9, 168, 170
Article 60
and Submission No. 12, 189, 190, 191-92
decision on the merits, 216
Viet Nam supports Tribunal's competence to interpret and apply, 9
Article 61
and Submission No. 8, 164
Article 62
and fishing by foreign nationals, 132
and historical fishing, 132
and Submission No. 8, 164
and Submission No. 9, 169
and Submission No. 10, 171, 172, 174
and traditional fishing at Scarborough Shoal, 224
Article 73
and Submission No. 8, 164
Article 74
and Article 298, 37
and Submission No. 8, 165
coastal State's exclusive rights over living and non-living resources, 132
Article 76
and Commission on the Outer Limits of the Continental Shelf, 232
Article 77
and laying of cables and pipelines, 132
and M/V Veritas Voyager, 214
and Submission No. 8, 164, 165, 166, 167
and Submission No. 14, 202
Article 78
and Submission No. 8, 165
Article 79
and Submission No. 8, 164, 165
Article 80
and Submission No. 12, 189, 190
decision on the merits, 216
Viet Nam supports Tribunal's competence to interpret and apply, 9
Article 81
and Submission No. 8, 164
Article 83
and Article 298, 37
and Submission No. 8, 165
Article 94
and Submission No. 13, 43, 194, 196, 198
decision on the merits, 216
Article 121
and jurisdiction, 36
and Spratly Islands, 40
and Submission No. 3, 40, 144-45
and Submission No. 5, 40, 41, 144-45
and Submission No. 7, 41, 144-45
and Submission No. 8, 40, 42, 145, 210
and Submission No. 9, 40, 42, 145, 210
definition of islands, 137, 139-40, 144-45
definition of "rocks", 137, 145
Philippine position on, 145-47
Article 121(3)
and Cuarteron Reef, 12, 155, 213
and expert hydrographer's terms of reference, 116
and Fiery Cross Reef, 12, 155
and Gaven Reef (North), 156, 213
and Johnson Reef, 12, 155, 156, 213
and McKennan Reef, 156, 213
and Scarborough Shoal, 12, 155, 213
and Submission No. 3, 144-60
and Submission No. 4, 139
and Submission No. 5, 144-60
and Submission No. 6, 139
and Submission No. 7, 144-60
and the Spratly Islands, 213
and the Spratly Islands as a whole, 156
and UKHO materials, 120
as a compromise, 154
China's position, 149
travaux préparatoires of, 153-54
Tribunal's interpretation of context of, 153
Tribunal's interpretation of text of, 150-52
Article 123
and Submission No. 11, 180, 183, 187, 188
and Submission No. 12(b), 180, 183, 187, 188
decision on the merits, 214
Article 136
and the common heritage of mankind, 233
Article 137
the Area not subject to sovereignty or sovereign rights, 233
Article 140
mechanism for equitable sharing of benefits from activities in the Area, 233
Article 192
and China's Position Paper, 31
and the CBD, 29, 32
and Submission No. 11, 21, 29, 42, 179, 180, 182-83, 188
and Submission No. 12(b), 21, 29, 179, 180, 182-83, 188
decision on the merits, 215

Article 194
and China's Position Paper, 31
and Submission No. 11, 21, 29, 42, 179, 180, 188
and Submission No. 12(b), 21, 29, 179, 180, 188
and the CBD, 29, 32
decision on the merits, 215
Viet Nam supports Tribunal's competence to interpret and apply, 9
Article 197
and Submission No. 11, 180, 188
and Submission No. 12(b), 180, 188
decision on the merits, 215
Article 204
and Submission No. 11, 183
and Submission No. 12(b), 183
Article 205
and Submission No. 11, 180, 183
and Submission No. 12(b), 180, 183
Article 206
and Submission No. 11, 180, 182, 188
and Submission No. 12(b), 180, 182, 188
decision on the merits, 215
Viet Nam supports Tribunal's competence to interpret and apply, 9
request for Environmental Impact Assessment, 118, 182, 188
Article 246
and marine scientific research, 233
and Okinotorishima, 233
Article 279
and Submission No. 10, 72, 173
and Submission No. 15, 208
decision on the merits, 217
Article 281
and the CBD, 28-30
and the DOC, 23
and other bilateral statements, 26-27
and the TAC, 27-28
choice of means of dispute settlement, 246
decision on, 23-25, 26-27, 28, 29-30
Philippine position on, 27
preconditions to jurisdiction, 22, 23, 25
Article 282
and the CBD, 31-32
and the DOC, 30
decision on, 30-31, 32, 209
Philippine position on, 30, 31
preconditions to jurisdiction, 22, 246
Article 283
China's position on, 32-33
decision on 33, 44, 209
exchange of views required by, 22, 32-34
Philippine position on, 13, 33
Article 286
and Notification and Statement of Claim, 7
submission of dispute to compulsory dispute settlement entailing binding decisions, 246
Article 287
acceptance of arbitration under, 246, 261
China has not made a declaration under, 245
China has not chosen a procedure under, 15, 251
the Philippines has not made a declaration under, 245
the Philippines has not chosen a procedure under, 15, 251
Article 288
and existence of dispute, 15
jurisdiction of court or tribunal, 251
Article 293
and Convention relationship with other norms of international law, 131
and the CBD, 21, 29
Viet Nam supports Tribunal's competence to interpret and apply, 9
Article 294
and China's claim of abuse of legal process, 16-17
Article 296
and Submission No. 14, 205
decision on the merits, 217
Article 297
and China's claim of abuse of legal process, 16
and Scarborough Shoal, 35
and Second Thomas Shoal, 35
and Submission No. 1, 39, 40
and Submission No. 2, 40
and Submission No. 3, 41
and Submission No. 8, 36, 42, 163, 165, 211
and Submission No. 9, 36, 42, 163, 165, 211
and Submission No. 10, 36
and Submission No. 11, 43
and Submission No. 14, 200-01, 203, 205
and the EEZ, 35
limitations to jurisdiction under, 13, 15, 34, 35-36, 39
Notification and Statement of Claim, 7

Philippine position on, 13, 35-36, 38-39
Viet Nam supports Tribunal's competence to interpret and apply, 9
Article 298
and historic bays or titles, 36
and law enforcement activities. 36, 38, 163
and maritime delimitation, 128
and military activities, 36, 38, 211
and Submission No. 1, 39, 40. 126, 127, 128, 129, 130, 131
and Submission No. 2, 39, 40, 126, 127, 128, 129, 130, 131
and Submission No. 3, 41
and Submission No. 5, 41
and Submission No. 7, 41
and Submission No. 8, 40, 42, 164
and Submission No. 9, 40, 42
and Submission No. 10, 40
and Submission No. 11, 43, 179, 182, 211
and Submission No. 12, 40, 43, 179, 182, 191, 211
and Submission No. 13, 40, 43
and Submission No. 14, 40, 44, 200, 203, 204, 212
China's position on, 36
decision on, 39-40
optional exceptions to jurisdiction under, 13, 15, 34, 36-38, 39
Philippine position on, 13, 37-38
Article 299
right of parties to agree upon a procedure, 34
Article 300
and China's claim of abuse of legal process, 16
and Submission No. 10, 171, 172
and Submission No. 14, 201, 202, 203, 205
and Submission No. 15, 208
decision on the merits, 217
Article 305
Taiwan not in the category of entitles that could become parties to the convention, 237
Article 309
prohibits reservations, 15, 132, 133
Article 311
and Convention relationship with other norms of international law, 131
and modification of the Convention's operation, 136
Article 319
and meetings of the States parties to the Convention, 231
as a package, 134-35
as comprehensive legal order for the world's seas and oceans, 6
Chinese text, 129
China's maritime entitlements under, 13
English text, 129
French text, 129
obligations reaffirmed by DOC, 24
Meetings of the States Parties, 65, 182, 229, 231-32, 233-34, 247
Part II
in Amended Statement of Claim, 11, 12
Part V
in Amended Statement of Claim, 11, 12
Part VI
in Amended Statement of Claim, 11, 12
Part XII
obligations under, 180, 182-83
overlap with the CBD, 29
Part XV
and Meetings of the States parties, 231
and Submission No. 8, 166
and the CBD, 29
as compromise, 15
binding on China and the Philippines, 15
flexibility of, 15
not excluded by bilateral statements, 26
not excluded by the DOC, 24
Section 1, 15, 22-34, 34, 40, 41, 42, 43, 44
Section 2, 6, 15, 23, 27, 30, 44
Section 3, 15, 34-40
Preamble, 132
Preparatory Commission for the International Seabed Authority, 71
ratification by China, 6, 126, 247
ratification by the Philippines, 6, 247
reference in bilateral statements, 26
reference in the DOC, 24-25
Russian text, 129
Spanish text, 129
system for dispute settlement as integral part of, 6
See also Commission on the Limits of the Continental Shelf, contiguous zone, continental shelf, default of appearance, exclusive economic zone, non-appearance territorial sea
United Nations Educational, Scientific and Cultural Organization (UNESCO), 61, 72
United Nations Environment Programme

(UNEP), 57
United States
alleged role in the arbitration, 262
alleged support for Duterte administration, 262
and the Jay Treaty, 247-48
Congress, 85
fishing rights of US fishermen in Georges Bank, 133-34
nautical charts as evidence for status of maritime features, 138
protects French claim to Spratly Islands, 128
request to attend hearing on the merits, 117, 237, 262, 263, 264
Sailing Directions, 144, 147
surveys of the South China Sea by, 141
third State in relation to the Convention, 263
votes against the Convention, 263
Uruguay
arbitration with Philip Morris, 82
Use of force
at Scarborough Shoal, 23, 173, 174, 175
PLA threat to use force at Second Thomas Shoal, 199

V

Venezuela
votes against the Convention at UNCLOS III, 263
vertical datum
and meaning of "high tide", 139
and Submission No. 6, 41
decision on the merits, 212
definition, 41 n. 35
vested rights
and acquired rights of German settlers in Poland, 225
and fur seal fishing in the Behring Sea, 225
and the *Chagos Marine Protected Area Arbitration*, 223, 226
and traditional fishing, 173-74, 225
definition, 225
Vienna Convention on the Law of Treaties
and Article 121(3), 152
and *pacta sunt servanda*, 208
and Submissions No. 3, 5, and 7, 152
and Submission No. 15, 208
and the CBD, 21, 29
definition of "State party", 263
definition of "third State", 263
on the interpretation of treaties, 21, 150, 152, 264
provisions for the benefit of third States, 264
Viet Nam
and hearing on jurisdiction and admissibility, 7, 10, 262
and hearing on the merits, 115, 117, 237, 262, 263
fishermen at Scarborough Shoal from, 170, 171, 223, 226
nautical charts as evidence for status of maritime features, 138
no claim that high-tide features are fully-entitled islands, 147
objection to China's "nine-dash line", 9, 126
raises sovereignty claim over Spratly Islands at UNCLOS III, 133
requests copies of documents, 8, 9
reserves the right to intervene in the proceedings, 9
responsibility for damage to coral reefs, 177
sovereignty over maritime features claimed by, 22
submission to Commission on the Limits of the Continental Shelf, 126
supports the Tribunal's competence, 9
whether third party indispensable to proceedings, 22

W

Wang Hanling
criticizes Professor Soons, 259-60
Ward, Selina
appointment as coral reef expert, 119
report submitted by, 120
Western Sahara
Morocco's sovereignty claim over, 230
West York
Chinese name, 269
description, 147, 149, 269
distance from a Chinese baseline, 269
distance from Palawan, 269
incapable of sustaining economic life of their own, 159
incapable of sustaining human habitation, 159
Philippine name, 269
Wolfrum, Rüdiger
academic experience, 69-70
appointed by the Philippines, 8, 56, 254, 257
education, 69
nominated for the list of arbitrators maintained by the UN secretary-General, 258
professional experience, 71-72, 90, 92
publications, 70-71

question on giant clams, sea turtles and reefs, 118
question on Submission No. 1, 48-49
request for "hard facts" on giant clams, 177
signs Declaration on Independence and Impartiality, 8
World Trade Organization (WTO), 87
Worldview family of satellites
and evidence of status of features, 141
WTO *See* World Trade Organization

Y

Yanai, Shunji
appoints arbitrators, 56, 254, 255, 256
China's criticism of, 254-57
election as ITLOS President, 256
election to the ITLOS, 256
professional experience, 256
Yaoundé regional declaration on the law of the sea, 153
Yee, Sienho
in the service of China, 259

Z

Zeitschrift für ausländisches öffentliches Recht und Völkerrecht, 70-71, 76

Printed and bound by CPI Group (UK) Ltd, Croydon, CR0 4YY

13/09/2026

14961105-0001